An Inventory
of the Ancient Monuments in

Brecknock (Brycheiniog)

1 Snow on the Brecon Beacons

Royal Commission
on the Ancient and Historical Monuments of Wales

An Inventory
of the Ancient Monuments in
Brecknock (Brycheiniog)

The Prehistoric and Roman Monuments
Part i: Later Prehistoric Monuments and
Unenclosed Settlements to 1000 A.D.

1997

First published in 1997
by RCAHM (Wales)

Copyright © RCAHM (Wales), 1997

All rights reserved. No part of this publication may be reproduced, stored in a retrieval system, or transmitted, in any form, or by any means, electronic, mechanical, photocopying, recording or otherwise, without the prior permission of the publisher and copyright holder[s].

The author[s] has[ve] asserted the moral right to be identified as the author[s] of this work.

British Library Cataloguing in Publication Data
A catalogue record for this book is available from the British Library

ISBN 1 871184 19 3

Cover: The Saith Maen stone alignment overlooking Craig y Nos in the Upper Tawe valley.

The mapping in this publication is reproduced from Ordnance Survey mapping with the permission of Her Majesty's Stationery Office © Crown copyright. Unauthorised reproduction infringes Crown copyright and may lead to prosecution or civil proceedings.

The copyright of Fig. 32 is held by the National Library of Wales; of Fig. 173 by the National Museum of Wales; of Fig. 11 by Cheltenham Museums; of Fig. 121 by the Geographical Association; that of Figs 7, 8, 9, 16, 21, 30, 34, 43–6, 70, 87 and 100 by the Cambrian Archaeological Association; that of Figs 149, 151–2, 154, 169–70 by the Department of Aerial Photography, Cambridge University and that of Figs 61, 83 and 91 and pl. 2 by the Clwyd-Powys Archaeological Trust. The Commission thanks all for their assistance in providing images and for permission to publish.

Typeset in 10/12pt Times Roman
Typesetting and origination by
Sutton Publishing Limited, Far Thrupp, Stroud, Gloucestershire, GL5 2BU
Printed in Great Britain by WBC Limited, Bridgend

Table of Contents

	Page
List of Figures	vii
Chairman's Preface	xv
Editorial Note	xvi
Report, with List of Monuments selected by the Commissioners	xvii
List of Commissioners and Staff	xxi
Royal Warrant	xxiii
List of Ecclesiastical Parishes with incidence of Monuments	xxvii
List of Civil Parishes with incidence of Monuments	xxx
Abbreviated Titles of References	xxxiv
Presentation of Material	xxxviii

Inventory

Part i: Later Prehistoric Monuments and Unenclosed Settlements to 1000 A.D.

Physical Background and Post-glacial History	1
Cave Archaeology	9
Prehistoric (and later) cave sites (PCS 1–4; OCS 1–3)	11
The Upper Palaeolithic and Mesolithic Periods	17
Upper Palaeolithic and Mesolithic sites and findspots (MS 1–18; RMS 1–3)	19
Neolithic Settlement and Burial	24
Neolithic Court Tombs (CT 1–13; RCT 1–11)	31
Burial and Ritual Structures of the Bronze Age	67
Round Cairns and Barrows of the Bronze Age (RC 1–312)	76
Other Bronze Age Burials and Lost Cairns (BB 1–29; LBB 1–2; LBS 1–10; UCB 1–8; RB 1; RCS 1–8; LC 1–9; Tithe Award and other Placenames)	132
Stone Circles and Stone Settings	142
Stone Circles and Stone Settings: the sites (SC 1–10; RSC 1–8)	147

Standing Stones	162
Standing Stones: the sites (SS 1–41; LSS 1–8; RSS 1–88)	166
Mounds of Burned Stone	184
Burned Mounds (BM 1–22)	186
Later Prehistoric and Protohistoric Settlement	189
Unenclosed Settlements (US 1–113; LS 1–9; D 1)	210
Hillforts (Addendum to Vol 1 (ii)) (HF 65)	276
Early Medieval Landholding, Estates and Ecclesiastical Centres	278
Crannog (CR 1)	281
A Handlist of Early Christian Stones (ECM 1–46; LECM 1–9; RECM 1–3)	284
Later Prehistoric Lithic Finds (SF 1–92)	290
Handlist of Bronze Age Bronze Artefacts (BR 1–35)	296
Index of National Grid References	298
Glossary: General	312
Glossary: Welsh Place-name Elements	313
General Index	314

List of Figures

Fig.	Title	Page
1	Snow on the Brecon Beacons	Frontispiece
2	Ecclesiastical parishes: the numbers on this map correspond to those on pp. xxvii–xxix	xxvi
3	Civil parishes: the numbers on this map correspond to those on pp. xxx–xxxiii	xxx
4	Conventions used on plans	xxxviii
5	Brecknockshire: map of topographical zones showing physical background	2
6	Geology of Brecknockshire	4
7	Plan of Dan yr Ogof, Abercrave (from Mason in *Arch. Camb.* 117 1968)	10
8	Stratigraphy of Dan y Ogof, Abercrave (from Mason in *Arch. Camb.* 117 1968)	12
9	Bronze Age artefacts from Dan yr Ogof: gold bead, dagger, razor and bone objects (from Mason in *Arch.Camb.* 1968)	14
10	Distribution of caves and Mesolithic sites	16
11	Conjectural Reconstruction of Hazleton Long Barrow (by courtesy of Cheltenham Museums)	25
12	Distribution of Neolithic chambered tombs	26
13	Tŷ Illtud (CT 1): plan and section	32
14	Tŷ Illtud (CT 1): plan and section of main chamber	32
15	Tŷ Illtud (CT 1): Henry Longueville Jones's engraving showing entrance in 1867 (from *Arch. Camb.* 22, (1867))	33
16	Tŷ Illtud (CT 1): Rubbings of 'inscriptions' (from *Arch. Camb.* 131 (1981))	33
17	Tŷ Illtud (CT 1): chamber	34
18	Mynydd Troed chambered cairn (CT 2): plan and section	35

19	Tŷ Isaf chambered tomb (CT 3): plan and section	37
20	Pen y wrlod (Talgarth) chambered tomb (CT 4): view showing quarried interior, 1973	38
21	Pen y wrlod (Talgarth) chambered tomb (CT 4): plans and sections (from *Gwernvale*)	39
22	Ffostyll: location showing the sites of two chambered tombs (CT 5–6) and lost cairn site (LBS 10)	40
23	Ffostyll South (CT 5): showing blocked chamber entrance	41
24	Ffostyll South (CT 5): plan and sections	42
25	Ffostyll South (CT 5): details of chambers	42
26	Ffostyll South (CT 5): Vulliamy's plans and sections (*Arch. Camb.* 76 (1921))	43
27	Ffostyll North chambered tomb (CT 6): detail of E chamber: a. section N.–S.; b. plan; c. section W.–E.	44
28	Ffostyll North (CT 6): showing eastern chamber	44
29	Ffostyll North (CT 6): plan and sections	45
30	Ffostyll North: Vulliamy's plan with detail of N chamber (from *Arch. Camb.* 78 (1923))	46
31	Bryn y Groes or Croesllechau (CT 7): engraving from the title page of T. Jones, *Hist. Brecks.* 2 (1), (1809)	47
32	Bryn y Groes or Croesllechau (CT 7): Edward Lhuyd's plan from NLW MS Peniarth	47
33	Bryn y Groes or Croesllechau (CT 7): elements from Lhuyd's plan arranged spatially	48
34	Pipton chambered tomb (CT 8): plan from Savory's excavation (*Arch. Camb.* 100 (1949))	50
35	Pipton chambered tomb (CT 8): plan	51
36	Pipton: plan of chamber (from *Arch. Camb.* 100 (1949))	51
37	Little Lodge chambered tomb (CT 9): plan	52
38	Little Lodge chambered tomb (CT 9): showing orthostats remaining in central area	53
39	Little Lodge chambered tomb (CT 9): detail of central area showing chambers	54
40	Carn Goch cairn (CT 10): view of mound looking to the west	55
41	Carn Goch cairn or chambered tomb (CT 10): plan and section	56
42	Gwernvale chambered tomb (CT 11): view of chamber looking west towards Crickhowell	57

43	Gwernvale chambered tomb (CT 11): pre-excavation location plan showing old road (from *Gwernvale*)	58
44	Gwernvale chambered tomb (CT 11): showing site of excavated cairn in relation to new road (from *Gwernvale*)	58
45	Gwernvale chambered tomb (CT 11): plan showing earliest features (from *Gwernvale*)	58
46	Gwernvale chambered tomb (CT 11): showing blocked and opened tomb entrance (from *Gwernvale*)	59
47	Penywrlod (Llanigon) chambered tomb (CT 12): view of main chamber looking east	61
48	Penywrlod (Llanigon) chambered tomb (CT 12): plan from survey with additional details of excavation 'trenches' taken from *Trans Woolhope Club* (1922)	61
49	Penywrlod (Llanigon) chambered tomb (CT 12): detail of chambers	62
50	Penywrlod (Llanigon) chambered tomb (CT 12): from *Trans Woolhope Club* (1922)	62
51	Clyro Court Farm (Radnorshire) chambered tomb (CT 13): plan	63
52	Clyro Court Farm (Radnorshire) chambered tomb (CT 13): plan of chamber and entrance	63
53	Distribution of Bronze Age cairns	66
54	Distribution of Bronze Age burials	70
55	Distribution of *Carn* place-names and destroyed or lost cairn sites	74
56	Garn Dwad cairn from the NW (RC 51)	83
57	Drygarn Fawr cairn from the W (RC 55)	84
58	Drygarn Fawr cairn East (RC 56) showing outline of original structure under vegetation	85
59	Pen Tŵr barrow (RC 63): plan (from *Arch. Jnl* 30 (1873))	86
60	Cairns on Mynydd y Glôg (among RC 65–73): note the field or enclosure wall to the bottom right (CUAP ARG 31)	87
61	Rhyd Uchaf, near Maen Llia: ringwork (RC 78) (Copyright Clwyd-Powys Archaeological Trust AP 88 2 11)	89
62	Rhyd Uchaf, near Maen Llia (RC 78): plan of ringwork	89
63	Tir y Onnen barrow (RC 107) from the south-west	94
64	Nant Maden structured cairn (RC 111) from the south	95
65	Nant Maden structured cairn (RC 111): plan	96

66	Cwm Cadlan cairn (RC 123): plan	97
67	Cwm Cadlan possible cairn (RC 126) looking north	98
68	Cefn Sychpant showing cairns (RC 123–4) and land boundaries	99
69	Twyn Bryn Glas cairn (RC 127): plan from *B.B.C.S.* 19 (1960)	100
70	Ynys-hir cairn (RC 138): excavation plan (from *Arch. Camb.* 97 (1943))	102
71	Gamrhiw South cairn (RC 171), showing re-use as a shelter and looking at doorway on NE	107
72	Gamrhiw South cairn (RC 171): plan and section	108
73	Upper Neuadd Reservoir: location of cairns (RCs 202–07)	110
74	Upper Neuadd Reservoir: ring cairn (RC 202) to N of island, looking to the south-west	111
75	Upper Neuadd Reservoir: plan of ring cairn to N of island (RC 202)	112
76	Upper Neuadd Reservoir: cairn or hut circle (RC 205) looking south	112
77	Upper Neuadd Reservoir: plan of cairn ring or hut circle (RC 205)	113
78	Upper Neuadd Reservoir: plan of cairn (RC 206)	113
79	Upper Neuadd Reservoir: plan of cairn (RC 207)	113
80	Carn y Bugail (RC 222) showing disturbed central area, looking east towards Carn Felen (RC 223)	115
81	Brecon Beacons, showing location of burial sites in Pen y Fan area including Corn Du (RC 225), Pen y Fan (RC 226): Cribyn (RC 227), Fan y Big (LBS 6) and Upper Neuadd (RCs 202–07)	116
82	Pen y Fan cairn (RC 226): cist under trig point, 1984	118
83	Pen y Fan cairn (RC 229): plan of excavated area (by courtesy of Clwyd-Powys Archaeological Trust)	119
84	Rhiw Trumau cairn showing sheep shelter (RC 274) looking south	124
85	Mynydd Pen y Fal cairn with cist (RC 292): plan	127
86	Mynydd Pen y Fal (RC 292): view over cist	128
87	Twyn y Beddau barrow (RC 311): plan and section (from *Arch. Camb.* 27 (1872))	130
88	Distribution of stone circles, standing stones and stone rows	142
89	Comparison of diameters of stone circles	145

90	Saith Maen (Craig y Nos) stone row (SC 1)	147
91	Nant Tarw stone circles (SC 2), cairn (RC 21) and settlement complex (US 29) (Copyright Clwyd-Powys Archaeological Trust AP 88 MB 184)	148
92	Nant Tarw (SC 2): plan of W. circle	149
93	Nant Tarw (SC 3): plan of E. circle	149
94	Nant Tarw: detailed plan indicating relationship of sites (SC 2, RC 21, US 29)	149
95	Looking south over Cerrig Duon stone circle and Maen Mawr (SC 3 and SS 3)	151
96	Cerrig Duon and Maen Mawr (SC 3 and SS 3): plan from a survey by R. Spicer, with additions	152
97	Trecastle Mountain stone circles and cairns (SC 4): location plan	153
98	Trecastle Mountain stone circles (SC 4): plan	154
99	Ynys-hir: plan of circle (SC 5)	155
100	Ynys-hir stone circle (SC 5), excavation plan (from *Arch. Camb.* 97 1943)	156
101	Saith Maen (Llanwrthwl), stone row (SC 6): plan	157
102	Saith Maen (Llanwrthwl), stone row (SC 6) looking east	157
103	Banc y Celyn stone circle (SC 7): plan after Clwyd-Powys Archaeological Trust, with additions	158
104	Blaen Digedi (Hay Bluff), stone circle (SC 10)	159
105	Blaen Digedi (Hay Bluff), stone circle (SC 10): location plan	160
106	Blaen Digedi (Hay Bluff), stone circle (SC 10): plan	160
107	Troed Rhiw Wen standing stone (SS 1)	167
108	Waen Lleuci (SS 4)	168
109	Waen Lleuci (SS 4) showing stone edgewise	169
110	Waun Lydan (SS 11)	169
111	Maen Llia (SS 12)	170
112	Garreg Fawr (SS 16)	171
113	Maen Richard (SS 17)	172
114	Dol y Felin Dolmaen (SS 20)	173

115	Pencelli standing stone (SS 23)	174
116	The Peterstone (SS 24)	174
117	The Fish Stone (SS 29)	175
118	Gileston (SS 31)	176
119	Llwyn y Fedwen (SS 32)	177
120	Limestone erosion processes showing sink-hole formation	193
121	Limestone and boulder drift (from Thomas, *Geogr. Jnl* 1954)	195
122	Early agricultural clearances and burned mounds	197
123	Distribution of prehistoric stone artefacts	207
124	Panoramic cutaway of the Tawe valley and Cribarth-Haffes-Tawe area	between 210–211
125	Pwll y wythen Fach hut circle in sink hole (US 8 i): section from	214
126	Pwll y wythen Fach hut circle in sink hole (US 8 i)	215
127	The Cwm Haffes-Allt Fach Tawe Fechan area: a. clearances around Twyn Du and Twyn Walter (US 4); b. Cwm Haffes enclosure (US 5); c. Field bank (US 11); d. (US 14), Nant Tawe Fechan showing field banks (US 12); e. Clearance cairns (US 10); f. (US 13); g. (US 7); h. (US 15); i (US 16); j. (US 18); k. (US 19)	218
128	Huts, house-platforms and tracks at Nant y Coetgae (US 20)	219
129	The Upper Cwm Tawe area centring upon Cerrig Duon (SC 3) and Maen Mawr (SS 3) including: platforms at Nant y Coetgae (US 19–20), enclosures at Nant y Wysg (US 26) and a variety of sites in Cwm Tawe (US 33–34)	223
130	Pant Sychpant enclosure (US 36)	227
131	Upper Tawe area rubble walled enclosure in Upper Tawe settlement area (US 37)	228
132	Complex enclosure above the Afon Llia (US 42)	229
133	Lower slopes of Fan Llia, hut platforms (US 43)	230
134	Enclosure at Nant Ganol (US 45)	230
135	Hut platforms above Ystradfellte Reservoir (US 51)	231
136	Enclosure above Nant Garlen Fawr (US 52): plan	231
137	Hut and enclosure between Nant Mawr and Nant Ganol (US 56): plan	232
138	Nant Llywarch, Ton Têg (S.) huts and enclosures (US 58)	233

139	Nant Llywarch, Ton Têg (N.) hut platforms and clearances (US 59)	234
140	Carn Canienydd huts (US 60)	235
141	Walls and enclosures at Dyffryn Nedd (US 68): plan	236
142	Garn Ddu hut group showing sink hole (US 71)	237
143	Mynydd y Garn: clearances, walls and settlements (US 75–77)	240
144	Cefn Esgair Carnau and Waun Tincer: clearances, huts and field walls (US 78–79)	241
145	Pant y Cadair enclosures (US 82)	244
146	Cwm Cadlan and Cefn Sychpant: enclosures, field walls, clearance and ritual cairns (US 83–4: RC 111, 112–16, 117–18, 121–7)	246
147	Craig Cerrig Gleisiad: enclosures and huts (US 86)	247
148	Carn Gafallt clearance cairns and boundaries (US 87)	249
149	Cairns and early boundary on Cefn Cilsanws (US 91) (CUAP ARG 92)	251
150	Cefn Cilsanws cairns, enclosures and boundaries (US 92)	253
151	Cefn Car: hut circles and enclosures (US 95 iv–x) (CUAP CEQ 60)	255
152	Cefn Car: early enclosures (US 95) (CUAP CEQ 83)	256
153	Cefn Car: hut-circles or cairns and clearances (US 95 ii)	257
154	Cefn Car: early wall and enclosures (US 95 iii) (CUAP CEQ 66)	257
155	Cefn Car: wall and enclosures (US 95 iii)	258
156	Cefn Car: enclosures (US 95 iv–v)	258
157	Cefn Car: complex hut and tadpole-shaped enclosure (US 95 vi–vii)	258
158	Cefn Car: looking S.W. into 'tadpole-shaped enclosure' (US 95 vii)	259
159	Cefn Car: huts and enclosure (US 95 viii–x)	260
160	Cefn Car: enclosures and hut (US 95 xii)	260
161	Cwm Moel field system and agricultural clearances (US 96)	260
162	Craig y Llwyni clearances, showing early mineral railway (US 99)	262
163	Cefnpyllauduon cairns and clearances (US 101)	263
164	Cwm Pyrgad settlement features (US 102): plan	264

165	Trefil area: wall or boundary (US 106) running over limestone solution features to Carn Caws with several enclosures	265
166	Blaen Onneu-Waun Llech area clearances and fields (US 106)	266
167	Gilwern Hill clearance cairns (US 109)	268
168	Clearances near Pontneathfechan (LS 1) (from *Gentleman's Magazine* 1801)	270
169	Llyswen parchmarks (LS 7) (CUAP CJJ 77)	272
170	Pipton parchmarks (LS 8) (CUAP CPQ 5)	273
171	Lan Fawr, Llangynidr hillfort (HF 65)	275
172	Brecknockshire during the Early Medieval Period	277
173	Bwlc Crannog: plan, following excavations (by courtesy of the National Museum of Wales)	282
174	Maen Madoc inscribed standing stone (ECM 8)	285

Colour plates (between pp. 168 and 169)

1. Saith Maen, Craig y Nos, stone alignment (SC 1)
2. Waun Fignen Felen peat basin and Mesolithic site (MS 2) (Aerial Photograph courtesy of Clwyd-Powys Archaeological Trust).
3. Standing stone, Battle (SS 25)
4. Standing stone, Carreg Waun Llech (SS 27)
5. Standing stone, Cwrt y Gollen (SS 36)
6. Standing stone, Llangoed Castle (SS 34)
7. Trefil area: wall (US 105) running over limestone solution features to Carn Caws with several enclosures
8. Cefn Sychpant cairn (RC 123)

Chairman's Preface

This publication forms Part i of the Royal Commission's *Inventory of the Prehistoric and Roman remains of the County of Brecknock (Brycheiniog)*. *Part ii, Hill-Forts and Roman remains* was produced in 1986. This volume covers Mesolithic, Neolithic and Bronze Age sites with all undefended and unenclosed settlements of probable pre-Norman date, together with summary finds lists and a handlist of Dark Age inscribed stones. Of particular interest in this volume are plans of the unenclosed settlements, some forming parts of palimpsest landscapes, the survey of which was a new departure for the Royal Commission.

Altogether some 650 sites and monuments are described either in summary or in greater detail. Their whereabouts and descriptions were established from fieldwork, aerial reconnaissance and documentary research. An introductory chapter gives the sites a chronological setting and provides an environmental framework including geology and palynology.

Each part of the volume is divided into two sections: an introduction to the particular monument-type, explaining its probable cultural and chronological contexts, then a list of all relevant sites located during the survey, including monuments now lost or destroyed. The monuments are sectionally listed in National Grid order (as explained in the introductory remarks under *Presentation of Material*).

The inclusion of a monument in the list of those recommended as most worthy of preservation follows the practice adopted in *Brecknock Volume I part ii*.

Corrections to or comments on the contents of this volume are welcome. Any information and/or inquiries should be addressed to the Royal Commission's National Monuments Record, which can be consulted during normal office hours at Plas Crug, Aberystwyth, SY23 INJ.

The contents of the volume, including most of the illustrations, are Crown Copyright. Indication is given where this is not the case. Copies of these and other Royal Commission illustrations and photographs may be purchased on application to the Library and Reader Services section at the above address, or through the Secretary of the Royal Commission.

Finally, it should be noted that the Royal Commission's current Royal Warrant, issued in 1992, revoked the Commissioners' earlier remit to make an inventory and to specify those sites most worthy of preservation. However, since this volume was well advanced and it forms a companion to work already published, it was decided to retain the style and format of Volume I part ii.

J. BEVERLEY SMITH
CHAIRMAN

Editorial Note

The final form of this Inventory is the result of detailed discussion between the Commissioners and their staff. C. S. Briggs compiled and wrote the entire text. Particular mention must be made of certain other staff who contributed to investigation and inventory production. Foremost among those involved in fieldwork was W. E. Griffiths, who, prior to his retirement in 1980, along with C. H. Houlder (retired 1991), devised and executed the original scheme of field reconnaissance for sepulchral and burial sites.

Subsequent survey and investigation were undertaken by C. S. Briggs, D. M. Browne, C. H. Houlder, D. K. Leighton, B. A. Malaws and D. J. Percival. Mr C. H. Houlder began the editorial task.

The maps and figures were drawn by N. Melbourne and C. Green assisted by J. B. Durrant, using figures by B. A. Malaws. Photography was undertaken mainly by I. N. Wright with assistance from F. L. James.

The index was compiled by John Noble.

Report

To the Queen's Most Excellent Majesty

May it please Your Majesty

We, the undersigned Commissioners, appointed to provide for the survey and recording of ancient and historical monuments and constructions connected with, or illustrative of, the contemporary culture, civilisation and conditions of life of the people in Wales and Monmouthshire from the earliest times, humbly submit to Your Majesty the following Report, to accompany the second part of the first volume of the Inventory of Monuments in the County of Brecknock.

2. It is with deep regret that we record the death of our former Commissioners Prof. R. J. C. Atkinson, Mr G.C. Boon, Sir I. Ll. Foster, Prof. W. F. Grimes, Prof. E. M. Jope, Dr J. D. K. Lloyd, Mr D. M. Rees, Prof. D. Prys-Thomas, Prof. D. G. Tucker and Dr R. Wood-Jones.

3. We have also to record the loss by retirement, on expiry of term of office, of our former Chairman Professor Glanmor Williams and Commissioners Michael Ross Apted, John Geraint Jenkins, Prof David Ellis Evans, Arnold Joseph Taylor, and Professor John Gwynn Williams. We desire to record our grateful thanks to these for their excellent service.

4. We have to thank Your Majesty for the appointment of Professor Jenkyn Beverley Smith to be Chairman of this Commission in succession to Professor Glanmor Williams for a period of 5 years from 1990 to 1995, and for a further three years from 1996–1998 under Your Majesty's Royal Sign Manual dated 19 December 1995.

5. We have pleasure in reporting the completion of our enquiries into the Burial Monuments and Related Structures and Settlement Remains up to the year 1000 A.D. in the historic county of Brecknock, which we have retained as the framework of our report in preference to the administrative units which came into being in 1974. We have recorded 644 monuments. Over 1,000 sites were visited.

6. We have prepared a full Inventory of these Monuments which will be issued as a non-Parliamentary publication.

7. We desire to record our special thanks for valuable assistance from the owners and occupants of the land upon which monuments stand: also from Dr M. G. Bell; Miss V. Bellamy; Mr and Mrs G. Bird; Mr K. Brassil; Mr D. Brinn; Mr W. J. Britnell; Mr C. B. Burgess; Mrs A. Caseldine; Dr A. David; Mr M. Davies; Mr P. Dorling; the late Mrs C. Earnshaw; Dr N. Edwards; Miss J. Elsworth; Mr J. Evans; Dr A. M. Gibson; Lt. Col. R. Hayes; Mr J. Jackson; Mr H. Owen-John; Mr P. M. Jones; Mr R. Kelly; Miss F. M. Lynch; Dr K. Mason; Mr C. P. Martin; Mr K. A. Martin; Mr D. Moore; Mr K. Palmer; Dr M. Redknap; Dr S. E. Rees; Dr E. Roese; Prof. Charles Thomas; Mr D. Thompson; Lt. Col. R. Stafford-Tolley; Dr A. H. Ward; Lt. Col. W. Watson; Mr D. R. Wilson; Mrs P. Wiltshire; Mr R. Woods; Dr M. Yates.

8. We desire to express our acknowledgment of the good work of our executive staff. Their names, and indications of their particular contributions, are included in the Inventory volume.

9. We humbly recommend to Your Majesty's notice the following monuments as most worthy of preservation:

Caves

(PCS 1) Dan yr Ogof
(PCS 3) Twll Carw Coch

Mesolithic Sites

(MS 2) Waun Fignen Felen
(MS 14) Bwlc Crannog

Chambered Tombs

(CT 1) Tŷ Illtud
(CT 2) Mynydd Troed
(CT 3) Tŷ Isaf
(CT 4) Pen y Wrlod, Talgarth
(CT 5) Ffostyll South
(CT 6) Ffostyll North
(CT 8) Pipton
(CT 9) Little Lodge
(CT 10) Carn Goch
(CT 12) Penywrlod, Llanigon
(CT 13) Court Farm, Clyro (Radnors)

Round Cairns

(RC 10) Bwlch Bryn Rhudd
(RC 14) Nant y Moch
(RC 21) Godre'r Garn-las
(RC 26) Fan Foel
(RC 27) Twr y Fan Foel
(RC 34) Garn Wen
(RC 35–8) Mynydd Bach, Trecastell
(RC 48) Esgair Garn
(RC 50) Waun Coll
(RC 54) Castell Llysgoden
(RC 55–6) Drygarn Fawr
(RC 60) Esgair Irfon
(RC 61) Carn Paderau
(RC 62) Pen-y-Carngoch
(RC 63) Pen Twr
(RC 65–73) Mynydd y Glog
(RC 74) Nant Cadlan
(RC 78) Rhyd Uchaf/Afon Llia
(RC 79) Afon Llia
(RC 80) Fan Llia
(RC 85) Twyn Garreg-Wen
(RC 90) Coed-y-Garreg
(RC 91) Carnau Gwynion
(RC 92–5) Share y Wlad
(RC 96–7) Carnon Gwynion
(RC 104) Carn Pwll-Mawr
(RC 107) Tir-yr-Onnen
(RC 111) Nant Maden
(RC 120) Cader Fawr
(RC 123–6) Cefn Sychpant
(RC 127) Twyn Bryn Glas
(RC 135) Bedd Illtud
(RC 137) Fan Frynach
(RC 138) Ynys-hir
(RC 140) Twyn Cerrig-Cadarn
(RC 147) Banc y Cwm
(RC 151–3) Tri Chrugiau
(RC 158) Brynceinion
(RC 169–71) Gamrhiw
(RC 127–6) Carngafallt
(RC 194) Nant Cymrun
(RC 196–9) Garth
(RC 201) Cefn Cilnsanws
(RC 202–7) Upper Neuadd Reservoir
(RC 210–12) Cilnsanws Mountain
(RC 219) Twynau-Gwynion
(RC 222) Carn y Bugail
(RC 223) Carn Felen
(RC 225) Corn Du
(RC 226) Pen y Fan
(RC 245) Waun Gunllwch
(RC 253–4) Carn Caws
(RC 264) Chartists' Cave
(RC 266–7) Mynydd Pen-Cyrn
(RC 269–71) Blaen Cwm Uchaf
(RC 274) Pen Trumau
(RC 289) Pentir Hill
(RC 291) Rhiw Cwmstab
(RC 292–3) Mynydd Pen-y-Fal
(RC 294–7) Twr Pen Cyrn
(RC 300) Pen Allt Mawr
(RC 302) Pen Gloch-y-pibwr
(RC 307) Pen Cerrig-Calch
(RC 311) Twyn y Beddau

Stone Circles and Alignments

(SC 1) Saith Maen
(SC 2) Nant Tarw
(SC 3) Cerrig Duon
(SC 4) Trecastle Mountain
(SC 5) Mynydd Epynt
(SC 6) Saith Maen
(SC 7) Banc y Celyn
(SC 8) Pant Serthfa

(SC 9) Dyffren Crawnen
(SC 10) Nant Digedi

Standing Stones

(SS 1) Troed Rhiw Wen
(SS 3) Maen Mawr
(SS 4) Waen Lleuci
(SS 5) Trecastle Mountain
(SS 6) Cwm Irfon
(SS 7) Nant Cerdin
(SS 8) Drum Nant y Gorlan
(SS 9) Carreg Wen Fawr
(SS 12) Maen Llia
(SS 17) Maen Richard
(SS 18) Pen y Gorllwyn
(SS 19) Y Garth
(SS 20) Dolmaen, Dol y Felin
(SS 24) The Peterstone
(SS 25) Battle
(SS 26) Pen-y-bont
(SS 27) Carreg Waun Llech
(SS 29) The Fish Stone
(SS 31) Gileston
(SS 32) Llwyn y Fedwen
(SS 33) Tretower
(SS 34) Llangoed Castle
(SS 36) Cwrt y Gollen
(SS 41) Maen Llwyd

Burned Mounds

(BM 1) Allt Fach
(BM 14) Nant Crew
(BM 15) Cefn Sychpant
(BM 16) Cefn Esgair Carnau
(BM 17) Nant Cadlan
(BM 18) Cefn Esgair Carnau
(BM 21) Cwm Moel
(BM 22) Cefn Moel

Unenclosed Settlements

(US 1) Dorwen
(US 4) Twyn Du – Twyn Walter
(US 5) Cwm Haffes
(US 6–7) Allt Fach
(US 8) Pwll y Wythen Fach
(US 9) Nant Tawe Fechan
(US 12) Cwm Haffes
(US 14) Allt Fach
(US 15, 19) Nant Tawe Fechan
(US 20) Nant y Coetgae
(US 26) Nant y Wysg
(US 29) Nant Tarw
(US 30, 31, 32, 33, 34, 35) Upper Tawe, Cerrig Duon area
(US 36) Pant Sychpant
(US 39–40) Fan Llia
(US 42–3) Afon Llia
(US 51) Ystradfellte Reservoir
(US 58–9) Nant Llywarch
(US 60) Carn Canienydd
(US 63) Taf Fawr
(US 65) Nant Crew
(US 68) Dyffryn Nedd
(US 74) Tir Mawr
(US 75–8) Mynydd y Garn
(US 79–80) Cefn Esgair Carnau
(US 81–2) Pant y Gadair
(US 83) Cwm Cadlan
(US 86) Craig Cerrig Gleisiad
(US 87) Carn Gafallt
(US 90, 92) Cefn Cilnsanws
(US 93) Garn Ddu
(US 95) Nant Car
(US 96) Cwm Moel
(US 102) Nant Pyrgad
(US 103–4) Clo Cadno
(US 105) Llangynidr Common
(US 106) Blaen Onneu
(US 109) Gilwern Hill
(US 112) Cwm Gu

Inscribed Dark Age Stones

(ECM 1, 2) Ystradgynlais Parish Church
(ECM 3, 4) Llywel Parish Church
(ECM 5) Llanwrtyd Parish Church
(ECM 6) Penlan Wen
(ECM 7) Cyfarthfa Castle Museum (Pen y Mynydd)
(ECM 8) Maen Madoc
(ECM 9) Cefn Coed y Cymer Parish Church
(ECM 10–11) Defynnog Parish Church
(ECM 12) Trallong Parish Church
(ECM 13) Brecknock Museum (Treflys)
(ECM 14) Llanlleonfel Parish Churchyard

(ECM 15) Llangammarch Parish Church
(ECM 16–19) Llanafan Fawr Parish Church
(ECM 20–21) Merthyr Tydfil Parish Church
(ECM 22) Pontsticill, Llanddeti
(ECM 23) Llanspyddid Parish Church
(ECM 24) Llanfrynach Parish Church
(ECM 25) Llanfigan, Ty Newydd Farm
(ECM 26–7) Llanhamlach Parish Church
(ECM 28–9) Llandefaelog Fach Church
(ECM 30–31) Llanddew Parish Church
(ECM 32, 33) Brecknock Museum (Llanynis), (Erwhelm)
(ECM 34) Glanusk Park
(ECM 35) Brecknock Museum, 'Victorinus' (Scethrog)
(ECM 36–38) Llangorse Parish Church
(ECM 39) Llanddeti Parish Church
(ECM 40–42) Llanfihangel Cwm Du Parish Church
(ECM 43–4) Llaneleu Parish Church
(ECM 45) Brecknock Museum 'Turpilli Stone', (Glanusk Park)
(ECM 46) Patrishow Parish Church

Dark Age Settlements

(CS 1) Bwlc Crannog

All of which we submit with our humble duty to Your Majesty

(Signed) J. B. SMITH (Chairman)
R. W. Brunskill (Vice Chairman)
R. A. Griffiths
R. M. Haslam
G. B. D. Jones
D. G. Jones
A. Nicol
S. B. Smith
G. J. Wainwright
E. Wiliam
P. R. White (Secretary)

List of Commissioners and Staff

Royal Commission on the Ancient and Historical Monuments of Wales

Chairman
Professor J Beverley Smith M.A., F.R.Hist.S.

Vice Chairman
Professor Ronald W Brunskill O.B.E., Ph.D., F.S.A.

Professor Ralph A Griffiths Ph.D., D.Litt., F.R.Hist.S.
Richard Haslam M.A., F.S.A.
Professor G D Barri Jones D.Phil., F.S.A.
Daniel Gruffydd Jones B.A., F.R.S.A.
Mrs Alexandra Nicol M.A., B.Litt., F.R.Hist.S.
Stuart B Smith M.Sc., F.M.A., F.R.S.A.
Professor Geoffrey J Wainwright M.B.E., Ph.D., F.S.A.
Eurwyn Wiliam Ph.D., F.S.A.

Secretary
Peter Robert White B.A., F.S.A.

During the period of the preparation of this volume (1970–91) the members of the Royal Commission were:

Emeritus Professor William Francis Grimes C.B.E., M.A., D.Litt., F.S.A., F.M.A. 1949–1978
(Chairman 1967–1978)
Herbert Newman Savory M.A., D.Phil., F.S.A. 1970–1983
(Chairman 1978–1983)
Emeritus Professor Richard John Copland Atkinson C.B.E., M.A. 1963–1986
(Chairman 1983–1986)
Emeritus Professor Sir Glanmor Williams C.B.E., M.A., D.Litt., F.B.A., F.S.A., F.R.Hist.S. 1963–1990
(Chairman 1986–1990)
Professor Jenkyn Beverley Smith M.A., F.R.Hist.S. from 1984
(Chairman from 1991)

Michael Ross Apted M.A., Ph.D., F.S.A. 1983–1992
Professor Leslie Alcock M.A., F.R.Hist.S. 1986–1990
George Counsell Boon B.A., F.S.A., F.R.Hist.S., F.R.N.S. 1979–1990
Professor Ronald William Brunskill O.B.E., M.A., Ph.D., F.S.A. 1983 to date
(Vice Chairman from 1994)
Professor David Ellis Evans M.A., D.Phil., F.B.A. 1984–1996
Professor Sir Idris Foster M.A., F.S.A. 1949–1983
Richard Michael Haslam M.A., F.S.A. 1986 to date
John Geraint Jenkins M.A., D.Sc., F.S.A., F.M.A. 1984–1989
Emeritus Professor Edward Martyn Jope M.A., B.Sc., F.B.A. 1963–1985
John Davies Knatchbull Lloyd O.B.E., D.L., J.P., M.A., L.L.D., F.S.A. 1967–1974
David Morgan Rees O.B.E., M.A., F.S.A. 1974–1978
Arnold Joseph Taylor C.B.E., M.A., D.Litt., F.B.A., P.P.S.A., F.R.Hist.S. 1956–1983
Emeritus Professor Dewi Prys Thomas B.Arch., F.R.I.B.A., M.R.T.P.I. 1970–1985
Emeritus Professor David Gordon Tucker Ph.D., D.Sc., C.Eng. 1979–1984
Professor Geoffrey John Wainwright M.B.E., B.A., Ph.D., F.S.A. 1987 to date
Emeritus Professor John Gwynn Williams C.B.E., M.A. 1967–1991
Raymond Bernard Wood-Jones M.A., B.Arch., Ph.D., F.S.A., A.R.I.B.A. 1963–1982

During the preparation of this volume, the following staff have served the Commission: where not otherwise stated, dates in square brackets [] indicate original date of appointment.

Secretary

Dr A. H. A. Hogg, C.B.E., D.Litt., M.A., F.S.A. (1949–1973, died 1989)
Mr P. Smith, Hon. D. Litt. (Wales), B.A., F.S.A. ([1952] 1973–1991)

Principal Investigators

Mr C. H. Houlder, M.A., F.S.A. ([1950] retired 1990)
Mr W. G. Thomas, M.A., F.S.A, ([1954] retired 1988, died 1994)

Investigators and Records Staff

Mr C. S. Briggs, B.A., Ph.D., F.G.S., F.S.A., M.I.F.A. (from 1973)
Mr H. Brooksby, O.B.E., F.S.A. (1963 to 1994)
Mr D. M. Browne, M.A., M.I.F.A., F.R.G.S. (from 1975)
Mrs S. L. Evans (from 1978)
Ms N. P. Figgis, M.A. (1988 to 1993)
Mr N. J. Glanville (from 1982)
Mr M. Griffiths, M.A., D.Phil. (1982 to 1988)
Mr W. E. Griffiths, M.A., F.S.A. (1949 to 1980)
Mr D. B. Hague, A.R.I.B.A., F.S.A. (1948 to 1981, died 1990)
Mr S. R. Hughes, B.A., M.Phil., F.S.A. (from 1973)
Miss R. A. Jones, M.A. (from 1985)
Mr D. K. Leighton, B.Sc., M.I.F.A. (from 1982)
Mr B. A. Malaws, M.I.F.A. ([1977] from 1984)
Mrs H. A. Malaws, B.Lib., M.I.F.A. (from 1977)
Mr C. R. Musson, M.B.E., B.Arch., M.I.F.A. (from 1986)
Mr A. J. Parkinson, M.A., F.S.A. (from 1972 to 1995)
Mr D. J. Percival (from 1984)
Mrs E. T. Richards (1972 to 1978)
Mr D. J. Roberts, N.D.D. (from 1981)
Mrs S. Spink, B.A., A.L.A. (from 1987–1995)
Mr C. J. Spurgeon, B.A., F.S.A. (1968 to 1994)
Mr R. F. Suggett, B.A., B.Litt. (from 1983)

Mr H. J. Thomas, M.A., F.S.A. (1969–95)
Mr G. A. Ward (from 1973)

Illustrating Staff

Mrs L. M. Aiano, B.A. (1974 to 1976)
Mr C. Baker (1970 to 1973)
Mrs J. B. Durrant (from 1979)
Mr J. D. Goodband (1980 to 1983)
Mr C. W. Green (from 1987)
Mr J. W. Johnston (from 1987)
Miss D. C. Long, B.Sc. (1984 to 1987)
Mr B. A. Malaws, M.I.F.A. (1977 to 1984)
Mr M. Parry (from 1984)
Mr D. J. Roberts, N.D.D. (1965 to 1981)
Mr I. Scott-Taylor, S.I.A.D. (1984 to 1988)

Photographic Staff

Mr D. M. S. Evans (1977 to 1979)
Mrs F. L. James (from 1983)
Mr R. G. Nicol (1969 to 1991)
Mr C. J. Parrott (1972 to 1983)
Mr I. N. Wright, F.B.I.I.P. (from 1979)

Administrative and Clerical Staff

Miss B. M. Davies (to 1973)
Mr P. St. J. L. Davies (to 1974)
Miss C. A. Griffiths (from 1970)
Mr D. M. Hughes (from 1978)
Mrs L. M. Jones (from 1980)
Miss S. E. Nicholson (to 1980)
Mrs C. L. Sorensen (1974 to 1978)
Miss D. M. Ward (to 1985)
Mr E. Whatmore (to 1978)
Miss E. M. Williams (1980)

Staff lists since 1991 have been published in the Annual Reports.

Royal Warrant

Elizabeth R.

ELIZABETH THE SECOND, by the Grace of God of the United Kingdom of Great Britain and Northern Ireland and of Our other Realms and Territories QUEEN, Head of the Commonwealth, Defender of the Faith, to

Our Right Trusty and well-beloved:

Jenkyn Beverley Smith

Our Trusty and well-beloved:

Michael Ross Apted
Ronald William Brunskill – **Officer of Our Most Excellent Order of the British Empire**
David Ellis Evans
Ralph Alan Griffiths
Richard Haslam
Daniel Gruffydd Jones
Geraint Dyfed Barri Jones
Stuart Brian Smith
Geoffrey John Wainwright – **Member of Our Most Excellent Order of the British Empire**.

Greeting!

WHEREAS by Warrant under Our Royal Sign Manual bearing date the twenty-eight day of September 1963 it was deemed that the Commissioners appointed to the Royal Commission on the ancient and historical monuments and constructions in Wales, now known as the Royal Commission on Ancient and Historical Monuments of Wales, should make an inventory of all the ancient and historical monuments and constructions connected with, or illustrative of, the contemporary culture, civilisation and conditions of the life of the people of Wales and Monmouthshire from the earliest times and to specify those most worthy of preservation:

AND WHEREAS We have revoked and determined and do by these Presents revoke and determine all the Warrants whereby Commissioners were appointed on the twenty-eighth day of September 1963 and on any subsequent date:

NOW KNOW YE that We reposing great trust and confidence in your knowledge and ability, have authorised and appointed, and do by these Presents authorise and appoint you, the said Jenkyn Beverley Smith (Chairman), Michael Ross Apted, Ronald William Brunskill, David Ellis Evans, Richard Haslam, Ralph Alan Griffiths, Daniel Gruffydd Jones, Geraint Dyfed Barri Jones, Stuart Brian Smith and Geoffrey John Wainwright to be Our Commissioners to provide for the survey and recording of ancient and historical monuments and constructions connected with, or illustrative of, the contemporary culture, civilisation and conditions of the life of the people in Wales and Monmouthshire from the earliest times (including ancient and historical monuments and constructions in, on or under, the sea bed within the United Kingdom territorial sea adjacent to Wales) by compiling, maintaining and curating the National Monuments Record of Wales as the basic national record of the archaeological and historical environment; by identifying, surveying, interpreting and recording all buildings, sites and ancient monuments of archaeological, architectural and historical interest in Wales or within the territorial sea adjacent to Wales, in order both to enhance and update the National Monuments Record of Wales, and also to respond to statutory needs; by providing advice and information relevant to the preservation and conservation of such buildings, sites and ancient monuments of archaeological, architectural and historical interest; by collecting and exchanging data with other record holders and providing an index to data from other sources; by promoting the public use of information available in the National Monuments Record of Wales by all appropriate means; by establishing and maintaining national standards in surveying, recording and curating of records relating to archaeology and historical architecture and providing guidance on these matters to other bodies and by exercising responsibility for the oversight of local Sites and Monuments Records;

AND We do by these Presents will and ordain that Our Commission shall consist of Chairman and not more than 10 other persons, appointed by Us on the advice of Our First Lord of the Treasury in consultation with Our Secretary of State, the terms of appointment of Commissioners and Chairman being determined by Our Secretary of State; and all such Commissioners and Chairman shall hold and vacate and may be removed from office in accordance with their terms of their appointment; a Commissioner other than the Chairman shall not be appointed for a term of more than five years but shall be eligible for re-appointment; and a Commissioner may resign at any time by giving notice in writing to Our Secretary of State; a Vice- Chairman shall be appointed by the Commission from among the Commissioners, and the terms of the appointment shall be determined by the Commission; and if the Secretary of State is satisfied that a Commissioner has been absent from three consecutive meetings of the Commission without the consent of the Commission, or has become bankrupt or made an arrangement with his creditors, or is incapacitated by physical or mental illness, or is otherwise unable or unfit to discharge the function of a Commissioner, Our Secretary of State may remove him from his office:

AND We do further ordain that if a person present at a meeting has any financial interest in any matter which is the subject of consideration at that meeting he shall as soon as practicable after the commencement of the meeting disclose the fact and shall not, without the consent of the other Commissioners present at the meeting, take part in the consideration of or vote on any question with respect to it; this Our Commission may act notwithstanding a vacancy amongst its Commissioners; the validity of any proceedings of this Our Commission shall not. be affected by any defect in the appointment of all or any of the Commissioners; subject as provided by this Our Warrant, the Commission may regulate its own procedure:

AND for the better effecting the purposes of this Our Commission, We do by these Presents give and grant you full power to call on persons with information likely to be needed for the National Monuments Record of Wales; to have access to or call for any books, documents, registers and records as may afford you the fullest information on the subject; to make enquiries about any premises by all other lawful ways and means whatsoever; to publish, by means of an annual report, progress made and activities undertaken. to promote or publish or assist in publishing information; to receive and spend money voted by Our United Kingdom Parliament, subject to any conditions that Our Secretary of State may from time to time impose; and to do all such other things as shall further the attainment of the purposes of this Our Commission (including in appropriate circumstances the grant-aiding of third parties):

AND We do by these Presents will and ordain that all property, rights and liabilities or Our Commission appointed under the 1963 Warrant and subsequent Warrants are hereby transferred to Our Commission appointed under this Warrant; and any agreement, transaction or other thing which has been made, effected or done by or in relation to the Commission appointed under previous Warrants, shall henceforth have effect as if made, effected or done by Our Commission appointed under this Warrant:

AND We do further ordain that anything done or being done (including anything done or being done under any enactment) by or relation to Our Commission appointed under previous Warrants before the date of signing of this Warrant shall, so far as is required for continuing its effect on and after that date, have effect as if done by or in relation to Our Commission appointed under this Warrant; and any reference in any enactment or other document whatsoever to the Commission appointed under previous Warrants shall, unless the contrary intention appears, be construed as a reference to Our ommission appointed under this Warrant:

AND We do further ordain that all monies and property received by this Our Commission, including any money voted by Our United Kingdom Parliament, shall be applied solely towards the promotion of the purposes of Our Commission; and unless so directed by the Secretary of State with the consent of Our Treasury, no payment shall be made by the Commission to the Commissioners except repayment of reasonable and proper out of pocket expenses:

AND We do authorise and empower you to appoint, with the approval of Our Secretary of State, upon such terms as to remuneration, gratuities and otherwise as you with such approval think fit, a Secretary and such other officers on such terms as to remuneration, gratuities and otherwise as you think fit; provide always that such remuneration or other entitlement shall be in accordance with the terms approved by Our Secretary of State:

AND We do by these Presents further ordain that anything authorised or required to be done under this Warrant by Our Commission may be done by any Commissioner or officer of Our Commission who is authorised (generally or specially) for that purpose by the Commission; and every Commissioner and officer of Our Commission shall be indemnified against all costs and expenses and losses for which he may become liable by reason of any act or thing done by him in the proper discharge of his office or duty:

AND We do hereby for Us, Our heirs and Successors, grant and declare that this Our Warrant or the enrolment thereof shall be in all things valid and effectual in law according to the true intent and meaning of the same and shall be taken, construed and adjudged in the most favourable and beneficial sense and for the best advantage of this Our Commission as well as in Our Courts of Record as elsewhere, notwithstanding any non-recital, mis-recital, uncertainty or imperfection in this Our Warrant:

AND We do by these Present will and ordain that this Our Commission shall continue to full force and virtue, and that you, Our said Commissioners, or any five or more of you, may from time to time proceed in the execution thereof, and of every matter and thing therein continued, although the same be not continued from time to time by adjournment:

AND We do further ordain that you, or any five or more of you, shall report periodically on your proceedings under this Our Commission to Our Secretary of State at such times and in such manner as directed by him.

Given at Our Court in Sandringham
the sixth day of April 1992
In the Forty-first Year of Our Reign

By Her Majesty's Command

DAVID HUNT

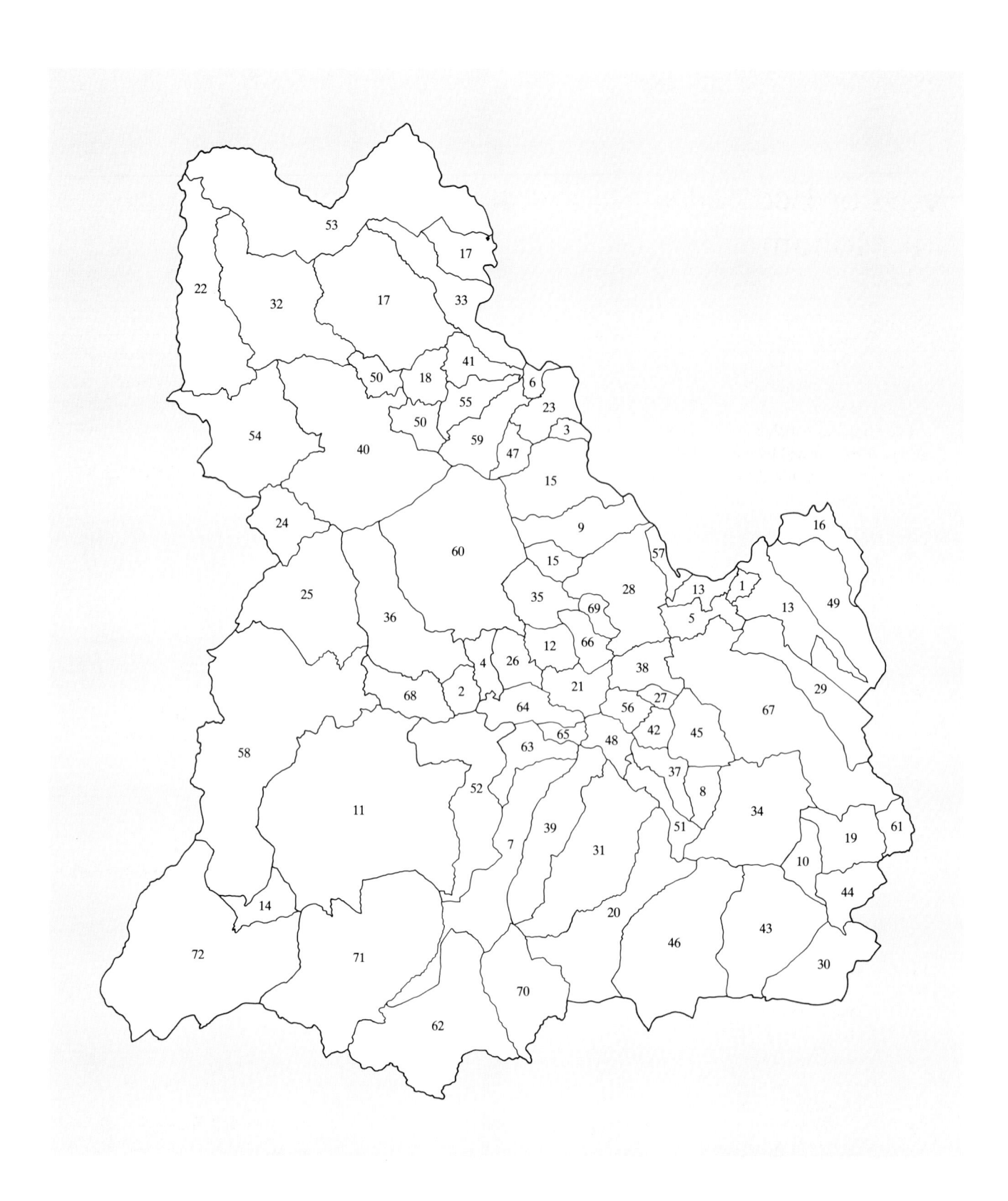

2 Ecclesiastical Parishes: the numbers of this map correspond to those on pp xxvii–xxix.

xxvi

List of Ecclesiastical Parishes, with incidence of Monuments

This list corresponds with the map on the opposite page and indicates the ecclesiastical subdivision of Brecknock into parishes as it stood *c.* 1850, before administrative boundary changes (*cf.* map on p. xxx and list on p. xxxi–xxxiii).

Ecclesiastical parishes are noted at the end of Inventory entries, distinguished by the letter (E) when the monument concerned stands in a different civil parish (C). Spellings of parish names are indicated on the left. These generally correspond with those used upon O.S. maps in 1970. The only departures from this practice (other than cases merely involving hyphens or capitals) are indicated by the addition of map spellings in square brackets. Welsh forms, which follow the recommendations of the Board of Celtic Studies, are given on the right only when these differ from those adopted for use in this Inventory.

Artefacts, rejected standing stones and Early Christian stones have not been included in this concordance.

No.	Parish name used	Correct Welsh form	Monument Nos.
1	Aberllynfi		CT 9
2	Aberysgir [Aberyscir]		RC 144–5
3	Allt-mawr		
4	Battle	Y Batel	RC 230–1; SS 25
5	Bronllys		CT 7
6	Builth	Llanfair-ym-Muallt	
7	Cantref		MS 9–10; RC 85–6, 202–4, 227; LBS 6; BM 14, 16; US 61–6, 71, 78–9
8	Cathedin [Cathedine]		RC 268–71, 280; SS 30
9	Crickadarn	Crucardarn	RC 237, 241–5
10	Crickhowell	Crucywel	MS 15; CT 11; RC 308; SS 37
11	Defynnog [Defynock]		RC 11, 24–5, 33, 76–9, 136–7; SS 12, 14; BM 5–6; US 23–4, 29–35, 38, 85–6
12	Garthbrengi [Garthbrengy]		MS 13
13	Glasbury	Y Clas-ar-Wy	CT 9; RC 290; UCB 6; LS 8
14	Glyntawe		PCS 2; RMS 2; RC 10; US 7, 10, 12–14, 27
15	Gwenddwr		RC 232; SC 7
16	Hay	Y Gelli	RC 310–11
17	Llanafan Fawr		RC 154–5, 157, 161–2 188–9, 246; D1; SS 18–20, 26; BM 19–20
18	Llanafan Fechan		
19	Llanbedr Ystrad Yw [Llanbedr Ystradwy]		RC 307; RSC 8; US 110; RSC 8
20	Llanddeti [Llanddetty]		MS 12; RC 216–24; US 99–100; RCT 4
21	Llan-ddew		
22	Llanddewi Abergwesyn		MS 4; RC 48, 54; SS 9; BM 9–13
23	Llanddewi'r-cwm		

xxvii

No.	Parish name used	Correct Welsh form	Monument Nos.
24	Llanddulas [Llandulas]		
25	Llandeilo'r-fan		MS 3; RC 33–4, 42, 44–5; RCS 2
26	Llandyfaelog Fâch [Llandefaelog Fâch]		
27	Llandefaelog Tre'r-graig		
28	Llandyfalle [Llandefalle]		SS 34
29	Llaneleu [Llanelieu]		MS 16–17; CT 5–6; RC 291; LBS 9–10; LSS 8; RSC 8
30	Llanelli [Llanelly]		US 107, 109; LS 9; 60, 61, 63
31	Llanfigan	Llanfeugan	RC 276; UCB 7; SS 23, 31
32	Llanfihangel Abergwesyn		MS 6; RC 55–8, 160; SS 8; LSS 1; LS 3
33	Llanfihangel Brynpabuan		RC 158; SC 6; SS 21
34	Llanfihangel Cwm Du		RC 269–3, 277–9, 281–9, 300, 302–6; UCB 5; SS 29, 32–3; LSS 4–5; BM 22; US 112–13; LBB 2
35	Llanfihangel Fechan		
36	Llanfihangel Nant Brân		RC 138–41, 142, 150; SC 5; SS 15–17
37	Llanfihangel Tal y llyn		
38	Llanfilo		
39	Llanfrynach		MS 11; RC 203–7; UCB 2–3
40	Llangamarch [Llangammarch]		RC 62, 146, 148–9, 151–3; LS 4
41	Llanganten		RC 163
42	Llangasty Tal y llyn		
43	Llangatwg [Llangattock]		CT 10; RC 264, 266–7, 294–9; SS 27; US 107; UCB 4; LC 7; LS 9
44	Llangenni [Llangenny]		RC 292–3; RB 1; SS 36–40
45	Llan-gors [Llangorse]		MS 14; RC 272; LBS 8; CS 1
46	Llangynidr		PCS 4; OCS 3; RC 247–63, 265, 312; LBS 7; SC 8–9; SS 27–8; US 101–6; HF 65; LC 8
47	Llangynog		
48	Llanhamlach		CT 1; RSC 7; SS 24; LSS 3
49	Llanigon		CT 12; UCB 8; SC 10; RC 310–11
50	Llanllywenfel [Llanlleonfel]		RC 146–7
51	Llansanffraid [Llansantffraed]		CT 1
52	Llansbyddyd [Llanspyddid]		RMS 3; RC 135, 225–6; LBS 3; LBB 1
53	Llanwrthwl		RC 56–7, 59, 157, 164–88, 190–200; RSC 4; SS 9–11, 22; US 87
54	Llanwrtyd		RC 46–7, 49–51; SS 6–7; RSC 3; BM 7–8
55	Llanynys [Llanynis]		
56	Llan y wern [Llanwern]		RCT 2
57	Llys-wen		LSS 6; LS 7
58	Llywel		RC 9, 21–3, 26–32, 37–42, 44–6; SC 2–4; BM 2–6; US 9, 11, 15–20
59	Maesmynys [Maesmynis]		LSS 4
60	Merthyr Cynog		RC 141, 228, 223–6, 238–40; SS 17
61	Patrishow	Patrisio	

No.	Parish name used	Correct Welsh form	Monument Nos.
62	Penderyn		PCS 4; MS 7; RC 64–74, 104, 111–18, 120–34, 208; LBS 2; BM 15, 17–18; US 36, 71, 82–5, 88–9; LS 6
63	St. David Brecon	Aberhonddu	
64	St. John the Evangelist Brecon	Aberhonddu	UCB 1
65	St. Mary Brecon	Aberhonddu	
66	Talach-ddu		
67	Talgarth		MS 17; CT 2–4; RC 274–5, 301, 309; SS 35, 41; US 111; LBS 9; RCT 9
68	Trallwng [Trallong]		RC 143
69	Trawsgoed [Trawscoed]		
70	Vaynor	Y Faenor	RC 201, 209–15; LBS 4–5; BM 21; US 90–8; LS 5; RCS 4
71	Ystradfellte		RC 12–14, 75, 80–4, 87–103, 105–10; SS 13; US 37, 39–60, 67–70, 72–8, 78 (ii–x); RSC 5–6; LS 1
72	Ystradgynlais		PCS 1; OCS 1–2; MS 1–2, 8; RMS 1; RC 1–8, 15–19; SC 1; LBS 1; BM 1; US 1–6, 8, 21–2, 28; LS 2

3 Civil Parishes: the numbers on this map correspond to those on pp xxxi–xxxiii.

List of Civil Parishes, with incidence of Monuments

This list corresponds with the map on p. xxx and indicates the civil subdivision of Brecknock into parishes as it stood at the end of 1970. Some boundaries have undergone changes since the original adoption of the ecclesiastical pattern for secular administrative purposes (*cf.* map on p. xxvi and list on pp. xxvii–ix), and modifications continue to be made.

Civil parishes are noted at the end of the Inventory entries, distinguished by the letter (C) when the monument concerned stands in an ecclesiastical parish of a different name (E). Spellings used are as shown on the left, in general agreeing with those used on the O.S. 1:100,000 Administrative Areas map, 1971. The only departures from this practice (other than cases simply involving hyphens or capitals) are indicated by the addition of the O.S. spelling in square brackets. The Welsh forms, which follow the recommendations of the Board of Celtic Studies, are given on the right only when they differ from those already adopted for use in this Inventory. Artefacts, rejected standing stones and Early Christian stones are not included in this concordance though most rejected sites are.

No.	Parish name used	Correct Welsh form	Monument Nos.
1	Aberllynfi		CT 9
2	Aberysgir [Aberyscir]		RC 144–5
3	Allt-mawr		
4	Battle	Y Batel	RC 229–31; SS 25
5	Bronllys		CT 7
6	Bryn-mawr		
7	Builth	Llanfair-ym-Muallt	
8	Cantref		MS 9–10; US 61–6, 71, 80; RC 85–6, 119, 202–4, 227, 268–71, 280; LBS 6; BM 14, 16; US 61–6, 71, 78–9
9	Cathedin [Cathedine]		RC 268, 280; SS 30
10	Crai [Cray]		US 24–5; RC 11, 23–4, 32; RCS 1; BM 5–6
11	Crickadarn	Crucadarn	RC 237, 241–5
12	Crickhowell	Crucywel	MS 15; CT 11; RC 308; SS 37; RCT 8
13	Fenni-fach	Y Fenni-fach	RC 290
14	Garthbrengi [Garthbrengy]		MS 13
15	Glyn		RC 136–7; US 86
16	Glyn-fach		MS 18; UCB 8
17	Glyntawe		PCS 23; RMS 2; US 7, 10, 12–14, 27; RC 10
18	Gwarafog		RC 146–7
19	Gwenddwr		RC 232; SC 7
20	Hay Rural	Y Gelli	RC 310–11
21	Hay Urban	Y Gelli	
22	Llanafan Fawr		RC 154–7, 161–2; SS 18–20; BM 19; D1

xxxi

No.	Parish name used	Correct Welsh form	Monument Nos.
23	Llanafan Fechan		
24	Llanbedr Ystrad Yw [Llanbedr Ystradwy]		MS 17; RC 307; SS 41; US 110; RSC 8
25	Llanddeti [Llanddetty]		MS 12; RC 216–24; US 99–100; RCT 4
26	Llan-ddew		
27	Llanddewi Abergwesyn		MS 4; RC 48, 54; SS 9; BM 9–13
28	Llanddewi'r-cwm		
29	Llanddulas [Llandulas]		
30	Llandeilo'r-fan		MS 3; RC 33–4, 42, 44–5; RCS 2
31	Llandyfaelog Fâch [Llandefaelog Fâch]		
32	Llandyfalle [Llandefalle]		SS 34
33	Llaneleu [Llanelieu]		MS 16–17; CT 5–6; RC 291; LBS 9–10; RSC 8; LSS 8
34	Llanelli [Llanelly]		US 107, 109; LS 9
35	Llanfigan	Llanfeugan	RC 276; UCB 7; SS 23, 31
36	Llanfihangel Abergwesyn		MS 6; RC 55–8, 60–61, 63, 160; SS 8; LSS 1; US 53
37	Llanfihangel Brynpabuan		RC 158; SC 6; SS 21
38	Llanfihangel Cwm Du		RC 269–73, 277–9, 281–9, 300, 302–6; UCB 5; SS 28, 32–3; LSS 4–5; BM 22; US 112–13; LBB 2
39	Llanfihangel Fechan		
40	Llanfihangel Nant Brân		RC 138–40, 142, 150; SC 5; SS 15–17
41	Llanfihangel Tal-y-llyn		
42	Llanfilo		
43	Llanfrynach		MS 11; RC 203–7; UCB 2–3
44	Llanganten		RC 163
45	Llangasty Tal-y-llyn		
46	Llangatwg [Llangattock]		CT 10; RC 265–7, 294–9; UCB 4; SS 27; US 107; LC 7; LS 9
47	Llangenni [Llangenny]		RC 292–3; RB 1; SS 36–40
48	Llan-gors [Llangorse]		MS 14; RC 272; LBS 8; CS 1
49	Llangynidr		PCS 4; OCS 3; RC 247–63, 265, 312; LC 8; LBS 7; SC 8, 9; SS 27–8; US 101–6; HF 65
50	Llangynog		
51	Llanhamlach		CT 1; RSC 7; SS 24; LSS 3
52	Llanigon		MS 18; CT 12; RC 310–12; UCB 8; SC 10
53	Llanllywenfel [Llanlleonfel]		
54	Llansanffraid [Llansantffraed]		CT 1
55	Llansbyddyd [Llanspyddid]		
56	Llanwrthwl		RC 157, 164–7, 190–200; SS 9–11, 22; US 87
57	Llanwrtyd		RSC 3; SS 7; BM 7–8
58	Llanwrtyd Without		RC 46–7, 49–51; SS 6
59	Llanynys [Llanynis]		
60	Llan y wern [Llanwern]		RCT 2

No.	Parish name used	Correct Welsh form	Monument Nos.
61	Llysdinam		RC 159, 188–9, 246; SS 26; BM 20
62	Llys-wen		LSS 7; LS 7
63	Maescar		SS 14
64	Maesmynys [Maesmynis]		LSS 4
65	Merthyr Cynog		RC 141, 228, 223–6, 238–40; SS 17
66	Modrydd		LBB 1; RMS 3; RC 225–6; LBS 3
67	Patrishow	Patrisio	
68	Penbuallt		RC 146, 148–9, 151–3
69	Penderyn		PCS 3; MS 7; RC 64–74, 104, 111–18, 120–134, 208; LBS 2; BM 15, 17–18; US 36, 71, 82–4, 88–9; LS 6
70	Pen-pont		RC 135
71	Pipton		CT 8; RCS 7; LS 7–8; UCB 6
72	Rhosferig		
73	St. David Within Brecon	Aberhonddu	
74	St. David Without Brecon	Aberhonddu	
75	St. John the Evangelist Brecon	Aberhonddu	UCB 1
76	St. Mary Brecon	Aberhonddu	
77	Senni [Senny]		RC 76–9; SS 12; US 38, 85
78	Talach-ddu		
79	Talgarth		CT 2–4; RC 274–5, 301, 309; SS 35, 41; US 111; LBS 9; RCT 9
80	Traean glas [Traianglas]		RC 9, 21–3, 26–32, 37–42, 44; SC 2, 3, 4; SS 1–5; BM 2–6; US 9, 11, 15–20, 26, 29–35
81	Traean mawr [Traian-mawr]		
82	Trallwng [Trallong]		RC 143
83	Treflys		RC 62; LS 4
84	Tre-goed a Felindre [Tregoyd and Velindre]		RC 290; RCS 8
85	Vaynor	Y Faenor	RC 201, 209–15; LBS 4–5; BM 21; US 90–8; LS 5; RCS 4
86	Ysclydach	Is-clydach	RC 44–5
87	Ystradfellte		MS 8; RC 12–14, 75, 80–4, 87–103, 105–10; RSC 5–6; SS 13; US 37, 39–60, 67–70, 72–8, 78 (ii–x); LS 1
88	Ystradgynlais Higher	Ystradgynlais Uchaf	MS 1; RC 15–19; US 3, 8, 21–2, 28; LS 2
89	Ystradgynlais Lower	Ystradgynlais Isaf	RMS 1; RC 1–8, 15–19; LBS 1; SC 1; RSC 1; BM 1; US 1, 2, 4–6; LS 2

Abbreviated Titles of References

Ant. J.	*Antiquaries Journal*, Society of Antiquaries, London.
A.P.	Aerial photographs, indicating sortie, date, and frame no., refer to the national air cover available from some local and national planning offices. See also C.U.A.P.
Arch. Camb.	*Archaeologia Cambrensis*, Journal of the Cambrian Archaeological Association.
Arch. in Wales	*Archaeology in Wales*, Journal of the Council for British Archaeology, Group 2, (Wales and the Marches).
Arch. Jnl	*The Archaeological Journal*, Journal of the Royal Archaeological Institute.
B.A.R.	*British Archaeological Report* (Oxford).
Barnatt, *Stone Circles*	J. Barnatt, *Stone Circles of Britain: taxonomic and distributional analyses and a catalogue of sites in England, Scotland and Wales*, (Oxford: B.A.R. 215, 1989).
B.B.C.S.	*Bulletin of the Board of Celtic Studies*, University of Wales.
B.L.	British Library, London.
B.M.	British Museum, London.
B.M. (N.H.)	British Museum of Natural History
Brecks Mus.	Brecknocks Museum, Glamorgan Street, Brecon.
B.P.	Before Present (in radiocarbon years)
Britannia	W. Camden, *Britannia*, (ed.)., E. Gibson; 1st edn. (1695); 2nd edn. (1723); (ed.), R. Gough, (London: 1789–1806).
Briggs, *Cardiganshire*	C. S. Briggs, Chapter 2: The Bronze Age, pp.124–218, in J. L. Davies and D. J. Kirby, (eds.), *Cardiganshire County History*, (Cardiff: U.P., 1994).
Briggs, *Problems and Processes,*	C. S. Briggs, 'Some Problems and Processes in later prehistoric Wales and beyond', pp. 59–76 in C. Chevillot and A. Coffyn, (eds.), *L'Age du Bronze Atlantique: ses facies, de L'Ecosse à L'Andalousie et leurs rélations avec le Bronze Continental et la Mediterranée*, (Parc Archéologique de Beynac: Dordogne, 1991).
Burl, *Stone Circles*	H. A. W. Burl, *The Stone Circles of the British Isles*, (London and Yale, 1976).
Cadw	Monuments in Care, Wales.
C. and E.P.W.	J.A. Taylor, (ed.), *Culture and Environment in Prehistoric Wales*, (Oxford: B.A.R. 76, 1980).
Carlisle, *Top. Dict.*	N. Carlisle, *A Topographical Dictionary of Wales*, (London, 1811).
Caseldine, *E.A.*	A. Caseldine, *Environmental Archaeology in Wales*, (Lampeter: St. David's University College, Lampeter, 1990).
C.B.A.	Council for British Archaeology, Bowes Morrell House, 111 Walmgate, York YO1 2UA.
C.I.I.C.	R.A.S. Macalister, *Corpus Inscriptionum Insularum Celticarum*, I, II, (1939, 1949).

Clarke *Corpus*	D. L. Clarke, *Beaker Pottery of Great Britain and Ireland*, (Cambridge, 1970).
C.P.A.T.	Clwyd-Powys Archaeological Trust Ltd., 7a Church Street, Welshpool, Powys.
C.U.A.P.	Cambridge University Collection of Aerial Photographs.
Crawford, *L.B.C.*	O.G.S. Crawford, *The Long Barrows of the Cotswolds*, (Gloucester: Bellows, 1925).
Cult. and Env.	I. Ll. Foster and L. Alcock, (eds.), *Culture and Environment*, (London, 1963).
Daniel, *P.C.T.*	G.E. Daniel, *The Prehistoric Chamber Tombs of England and Wales*, (Cambridge: U.P., 1950).
Darvill, *C.T.*	T. C. Darvill, *The Megalithic Chambered Tombs of the Cotswold-Severn Region*, (Highworth: Vorda, 1982).
Dict. Welsh Biog.	*The Dictionary of Welsh Biography down to 1940*, (London, 1959).
E.C.M.W.	V. E. Nash-Williams, *The Early Christian Monuments of Wales*, (Cardiff, 1950).
Fenton, *Tours*	R. Fenton, *Tours in Wales*, (1804–13), (*Arch. Camb.* supplement, 1917).
Fox, *Life and Death*	C. Fox, *Life and Death in the Bronze Age*, (London, 1959).
G.G.A.T.	Glamorgan-Gwent Archaeological Trust Ltd., Ferryside Warehouse, Bath Lane, Swansea SA1 1RD.
Glanusk	Glanusk edition of *A History of Brecknock*, (Brecknock, 1909, 1911, 1930).
Grimes, *Defence Sites*	*Excavation on Defence Sites: Mainly Neolithic and Bronze Age 1939–45* (London: H.M.S.O., 1960).
Grimes, *Map, L.B.M.*	*Map of South Wales showing the distribution of Long Barrows and Megaliths*, (Ordnance Survey, 1936).
Grimes, *L.C.B.B.M.*	'The Long Cairns of the Breconshire Black Mountains', *Arch. Camb.* 91 (1936), 259–82.
Grimes, *M.M.W.*	W. F. Grimes, 'The Megalithic Monuments of Wales', *Proc. Prehist. Soc.* 2 (1936) 106–39.
Grimes, *Prehist. Wales*	W. F. Grimes, *The Prehistory of Wales*, (Cardiff, 1951).
Grimes, *Stone Circles*	'The Stone Circles and Related Monuments of Wales', 93–152 in *Cult. and Env.*
Grooms, *Giants*	C. Grooms, *The Giants of Wales/Cewri Cymru*, Welsh Studies vol. 10, (Lampeter: Edward Mellen Press), 1993.
Gwernvale	W. J. Britnell and H. N. Savory, *Gwernvale and Pen y wrlod: Two Neolithic Long Cairns in the Black Mountains of Brecknock*, Cambrian Archaeol. Assoc. Monograph no. 2, (Cardiff, 1984).
Hist. Merioneth	E. G. Bowen and C. A. Gresham, *History of Merioneth* (Vol. 1, Dolgelley, 1967).
H.M.S.O.	Her Majesty's Stationery Office, Belfast, Cardiff, Edinburgh and London.
Inv. Angl., Caerns., Glam., Pembs, Rads	R.C.A.M. (Wales), *An Inventory of the Ancient Monuments in Anglesey* (1937); *Caernarvonshire* (3 vols., 1956, 1960, 1964) *Glamorgan* (Vol. 1, 1976); *Pembrokeshire* (1925); *Radnorshire* (1914). All H.M.S.O.
Inv. Br. *I (ii)*	*An Inventory of the Ancient Monuments in Brecknock (Brycheiniog): The Prehistoric and Roman Monuments, Part ii: Hill-forts and Roman Remains*, (H.M.S.O., 1986).
James 1970	D. J. James, *A list of Standing Stones in Brecknockshire*, MS deposited in Brecks. Mus.

James 1978–9	D. J. James, 'The Prehistoric Standing Stones of Breconshire', *Brycheiniog*, 187 (1978–9) pp. 9–30.
Jones, *Hist. Brecks.*	Theophilus Jones, *A History of Brecknock*, (Brecknock, 1805–9); revised and reprinted, Brecknock, 1898.
Jones *Notebook*	*The MS Notebook of Theophilus Jones*, deposited in Brecks. Mus.
Kay MSS	R. Kay, *Field Notebooks*, deposited at R.C.A.M. (Wales).
Kingdom of Brycheiniog	J. Jones-Davies, *A Study of the Kingdom of Brycheiniog at the beginning of the Age of the Saints with special reference to the Llywel Stone*, (Brecon: Brecon and Radnor Express and County Times, 1956). Also published as *The Kingdom of Brycheiniog in the Age of the Saints*.
Land Allotment	H. C. Bowen and P. J. Fowler, (eds.), *Early Land Allotment*, (Oxford: B.A.R. 48, 1978).
Lewis, *Top. Dict.*	S. Lewis, *A Topographical Dictionary of Wales* (2 vols, London, 1833).
Limestone Caves	T. D. Ford, (ed.), *Limestones and Caves of Wales*, (Cambridge, 1989).
Lloyd MSS.	Antiquarian notes and observations of Sir John Lloyd (Abercynrig), in Brecks. Mus.
Longworth, *Collared Urns*	I.H. Longworth, *Collared Urns of the Bronze Age in Great Britain and Ireland*, (Cambridge: University Press), 1984.
Meg. Enq.	T. G. E. Powell *et al. Megalithic Enquiries in the West of Britain*, (Liverpool: U.P., 1969).
Meg. Sites	A. Thom, *Megalithic Sites in Britain*, (Oxford: Clarendon, 1967).
Meg. Rings	A. Thom, A. S. Thom and H. A. W. Burl, *Megalithic Rings*, (Oxford: B.A.R., 1980).
Mesolithic Gazetteer	J. J. Wymer, (ed.), *Gazetteer of Mesolithic sites in England and Wales* and C. J. Bonsall, (ed.), *Gazetteer of Upper Palaeolithic sites in England and Wales*, (London: C.B.A. Res. Rep. no. 22, 1977).
Mins of Evidence	*Report from the Joint Select Committee of the House of Lords and the House of Commons in the Ancient Monuments Consolidation and Amendment (H.L.) and the Ancient Monuments Protection (No. 2) Bill (H.L.), together with the Proceedings of the Committee and Minutes of Evidence*, (London: H.M.S.O., 1912).
N.L.W.	National Library of Wales, Aberystwyth.
N.M.R.	National Monuments Record.
N.M.W.	National Museum of Wales, Cathays, Cardiff.
O.D.	Ordnance Datum.
O.S.	Ordnance Survey.
P. and E. Wales	I. Ll. Foster and G. E. Daniel, (eds.), *Prehistoric and Early Wales*, (London, 1965).
Parochialia	*The Parochialia of Edward Llwyd*, ed. R. H. Morris, *Arch. Camb.* supplements, (Cardiff, 1909–11).
P.M.W.W.	*Prehistoric Man in Wales and the West*, (eds) F. M. Lynch and C. B. Burgess, (Bath: Adams and Dart, 1972).
P.P.S.	*Proceedings of the Prehistoric Society,* London.
Proc. Soc. Antiq. Scot.	*Proceedings of the Society of Antiquaries of Scotland.*
Quaternary Field Guide	*Quaternary Research Association Field Guide to Wales: Gower, Preseli, Fforest Fawr,* D. Q. Bowen and A. Henry, (eds.), (Cambridge: Quaternary Research Association, 1984).
Roese, *Thesis*	*An Investigation into the topographical location and distribution of Neolithic and Bronze Age Monuments in Wales.* H. Eckart Roese, Unpubl. Ph.D. Thesis, University of Wales, (1978).

R.C.A.M.	The Royal Commission on Ancient and Historical Monuments in Wales.
Savory, *Guide*	H. N. Savory, *Guide Catalogue of the Bronze Age Collections, the National Museum of Wales*, (Cardiff: N.M.W., 1980).
Savory, *Prehist Brecks* I, II	H. N. Savory, *Prehist. Brecks.*, I 'Prehistoric Brecknock', *Brycheiniog* 1 (1955), pp. 79–125; II 'Prehistoric Brecknock', *Brycheiniog* 15 (1981), pp. 3–22.
S.A.M.	Scheduled Ancient Monument.
Taf 2	*The Historic Taf Valleys: (vol. 2) In the Brecon Beacons National Park*, (Merthyr: Merthyr Tydfil and District Naturalists' Society, 1982).
Upland Settlement	D. A. Spratt and C. B. Burgess, *Upland Settlement in Britain; the Second Millennium B.C. and after*, (Oxford: B.A.R. 143, 1986).
Welsh Antiquity	*Welsh Antiquity: essays mainly on Prehistoric topics presented to H. N. Savory upon his retirement as keeper of Archaeology*, (ed.) G. C. Boon, (Cardiff, N.M.W, 1976).
Wheeler, *P. and R. Wales*	R. E. M. Wheeler, *Prehistoric and Roman Wales*, (Oxford: U.P., 1925).

Key

The following conventions are employed in this study

Ancient feature

	Slope
	Rubble / Turf
	Rubble / Turf : small scale
	Vertically stone setting
	Section

Map Symbols

•	Clearance Cairn
■	Standing Stone
★	Burial Cairn
▫	Platform
+	Boulder

Natural feature

	Slope
	River
	Stream
	Quarry
380m	Contours

Map Symbols

■	Hut / House foundation
▲	Burnt Mound
○	Hut Circle
∴	Stone Circle
▲	Lime Kiln

Modern feature

	Slope
	Fence / Hedge / Wall / Bank
	Track
	Rubble / Turf : small scale
	Cliff
	Edge of depression or tree stump
	Line of ill-defined earthwork
	Tramway

Map Symbols

——	Enclosure / Wall / Bank
------	Track

4 Conventions used on plans.

Presentation of Material

General Arrangement

Part i of Volume I of the *Inventory of Ancient Monuments in Brycheiniog (Brecknock)* deals with prehistoric funerary and ritual monuments, and with non-defensive settlements of uncertain date, though probably pre-Norman. The pre-Norman section includes a handlist of inscribed Early Christian monuments.

Monuments Included

Some structures cannot be classified satisfactorily by surface investigation, either because of their condition or because they present unusual features. The decision whether or not to include such marginal cases in the Inventory is based only upon subjective judgement as to their likely authenticity; uncertainty is indicated in the discussion of classification and, where appropriate, lost or rejected sites are listed at the ends of sections.

Form of Entries

These provide detailed description, illustrated where possible. This is followed by parish name; where the present civil parish differs from the original ecclesiastical parish, both are named and indicated by (C) and (E) respectively. The last line gives the sheet number of the current 1:10,000 O.S. map; the National Grid reference, to eight figures (wherever possible), of the approximate centre of the monument or group; the date of survey, or of the most recent visit. Information on condition is conveyed in the entries. Where these have been made, observations upon the structural materials used (principally types of stone) are provided, though in general it is presumed these were collected locally.

Surveying and Representation

The conventions employed on the plans presented in this volume are illustrated on fig. 4.

Numbering of Entries

The order of sites within these groups is determined by their O.S. National Grid references. The county is considered to be divided from west to east into a series of vertical strips 10 km wide corresponding to the eastings SN 7, SN 8, SN 9, SO 0, SO 1 and SO 2. Sites within any type group are first separated according to the strip in which they occur. Site no. 1 is then designated as the most southerly of those in the most westerly strip. No. 2 is the next site to the north. Sites are assigned numbers until all within the particular 10 km strip are accounted for. The same process is repeated starting with the most southerly site in the next strip to the east and so on until all sites are numbered. To keep the system simple, no account is taken of the quarter sheet division of 10 km squares used in O.S. 1:10,000 maps. The strictly numerical system is adopted for its simplicity and in the belief that it is at present the most effective ordering system.

Names

Most early structures are anonymous and are indicated on the map merely in descriptive terms. Where a traditional name is known or a specific modern name is well-established, this is provided. In other cases the name of an adjacent farm, village or natural feature is used for convenience of reference, even though its correct application may be to some other object. Unless there is good reason for change, the names used by previous writers are retained. Where confusion has arisen during investigation, an attempt has been made to regularise titles and spellings.

Distribution Maps

The maps accompanying each section are intended primarily to show the distribution of the monuments and finds in relation to relief and drainage. Even one kilometre to two centimetres is insufficiently large a scale to depict the exact location of small sites. The positions of particular monuments, however, are precisely fixed by grid references. Conversely, where the six-figure reference of a monument of a particular type is known, its descriptive entry can be found by use of the Index of Grid References (pp. 298–311); some structures may have escaped record, and information about these would be appreciated (see p. xv).

Parishes

The incidence of monuments within each parish is given on pp. xxvii–xxxiii above. Separate lists are given for civil and ecclesiastical parishes; their boundaries are mapped on p. xxvi and p. xxx. The civil parishes are taken as at the end of 1970 and boundaries of the ecclesiastical parishes are those of $c.$ 1850.

Superimposed Structures of Different Periods

Occasionally structures of widely different date are superimposed or juxtaposed in ways that may be confusing on the ground. In such cases, the structure relevant to the present volume is described in detail, and only summary description provided of other remains. Where appropriate, attempts are made to depict these relationships on text figures (see above under depiction).

Physical Background and Post-Glacial History

Geology of the Country Rock

Three main landforms exist within the county:

1. *Mountains*. These result from late Cenozoic uplift and characteristically rise to over 600 m, the elevation and ruggedness of individual summits being dependent upon the degree to which erosive forces were resisted by the thickness and dip of component strata. Two topographic zones, Fforest Fawr and the Brecon Beacons, and the Black Mountains belong to this category.

2. *Dissected Plateaux*. The general aspect is of rounded uplands dissected by steep, narrow valleys. There has been considerable debate as to how this form originated, whether by sub-aerial erosion, or under marine planation. Recent authorities incline to believe that the plateaux represent marine platforms on which the present drainage pattern developed by extending seawards as the land mass emerged. Sub-aerial erosion has subsequently altered the platforms considerably. Three areas are of this type: the Northern Plateau, part of the High Plateau of Central Wales, the Epynt Plateau, and the Coalfield Fringe.

3. *Valley Lowlands*. The two main zones are the Builth-Llanwrtyd Depression and the Usk-Llynfi Basin.

The strike trends of the rock strata of this landscape were formed long before its final emergence and extensive Caledonian orogenic folding produced the north-east to south-west trend of Mynydd Epynt and the land to the north. South of Epynt, the east–west trend results from later, Hercynian, movements, at the end of the Palaeozoic.

The mountains of *Fforest Fawr* and the *Brecon Beacons* stretching across the south of the county are resistant beds of Old Red Sandstone. They form the northern rim of the South Wales coalfield major syncline with an east–west trend. A string of peaks rises to over 600 m, Pen y Fan being the highest at 886 m. These beds have a long low dip to the south of between 10 and 20 degrees, and the capping deposit, the hard conglomerate of the Plateau Beds, gives the mountains their tableland surface behind a spectacular northern escarpment. Magnificent cirques in this escarpment, and over-deepened valleys, are the major evidence for glacial erosion. The more developed river valleys running south are all narrow and steep-sided. Most level land in these valleys is subject to inundation. A multiplicity of short, steeply-graded streams drain the north escarpment. The Neath and Tawe follow structural lines but others, especially those cutting the Coalfield escarpment to the south, do not relate to the underlying geology and are superimposed.

Like the Beacons, the *Black Mountains* in the east of the county are composed of Old Red Sandstone with strata dipping gently to the south-south-east. The prominent north-west escarpment, less severely dissected than that of the Beacons, rises to over 700 m with a north-east to south-west trend. Some interfluve peaks of the massif attain over 800 m. Pen Cerrig-calch overlooking Crickhowell is an eroded outlier of Carboniferous Limestone capping Old Red Sandstone. Long, steep-sided river valleys running south-south-east dissect the plateau-like surface of the mountains into narrow ridges. Tableland stepping and terracing result from erosion over differentially resistant sandstones, as do valley side ribbing and terracing. The north escarpment shows three major breaks of slope reflecting different degrees of weathering on the capping Brownstones and the lower *Psammosteus* limestones and thin sandstones. The amount of land in this zone available for arable agriculture is extremely limited.

The Ordovician shales, grits and conglomerates of the *Northern Plateau* are considerably folded and the trend of this country coincides with that of the main Tywi anticlinal belt and the smaller Rhiwnant anticline to the north-west. Volcanic rocks outcrop in rugged crags along the Tywi anticline crest north of

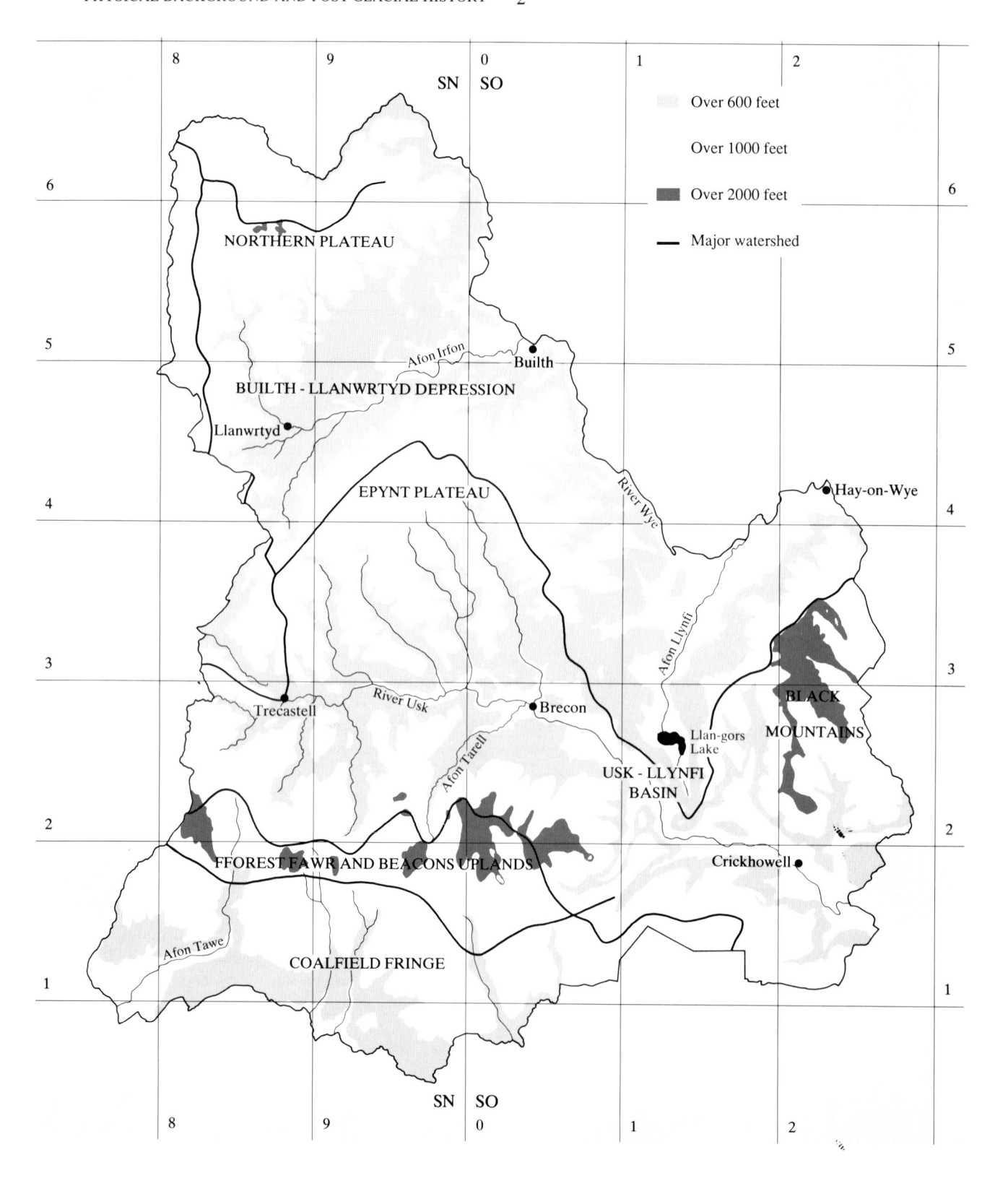

PHYSICAL BACKGROUND AND POST-GLACIAL HISTORY   2

5 Map of topographical zones showing physical background

Llanwrtyd. The highest ground, such as Drygarn Fawr (641 m) and Cerrig-llwyd y Rhestr, is formed by strike ridges of conglomerates. A series of consequent streams dissects the plateau in south-east running, narrow steep-sided valleys. Glaciation has modified the landscape and the Irfon valley has been especially affected by a major ice-flow from a local glacier lying over Pumlumon and Drygarn. Valley side and hilltop form are here again due to differential erosion, the quartz grits and some mudstones being particularly resistant. Relief, elevation and poor-quality soils are among factors making the region generally unsuitable for present day crop production.

The upper surface of the *Epynt Plateau* is formed by eroded Red Marls of the Old Red Sandstone. The trends of the massif crests (up to 474 m above O.D. at Drum-Ddu) conform to the strike of the folded basal Silurian rocks. The underlying structure exerts less influence on the surface appearance of the plateau but the dip of the Silurian Ludlow series accounts for steep slopes on the north-west escarpment. The rounded plateau surface tilts gently south-east and is dissected by several substantial streams flowing in that direction through valleys deepened by glacial erosion. Except towards their mouths, the valleys contain only very small amounts of flattish land.

On the *Coalfield Fringe* along the southern boundary of the county run escarpments of Carboniferous Limestone capped by steep bluffs of resistant Millstone Grit roughly parallel to the north-facing scarp of Fforest Fawr and the Brecon Beacons. A height of over 600 m is reached at Cefn yr Ystrad north of Merthyr Tudful and other parts of the plateau stand between 360 and 550 m above O.D. The general east–west structural trend is broken by the folding and faulting of the Cribarth disturbance (Upper Tawe) and the Neath disturbance. These features determine drainage trends, but elsewhere streams and rivers are superimposed across the underlying trend. Valleys have been over-deepened by glacial action, and ice moulding forms are visible in the Basal Grit south of Fforest Fawr. Rock screes created by frost shattering are also evident. The Carboniferous Limestone areas are distinguished by depressions known as swallow holes, shake-holes or dolines. These and some gorges have been caused by the solution disintegration of underground watercourses, a process in which there may have been partial anthropogenic input (see pp. 000–000). Impressive caves such as those of the upper Tawe valley represent former underground river channels, and modern examples of subterranean rivers include the Mellte near Ystradfellte. Outcropping harder beds and fault lines along the river channels on occasion give rise to spectacular cascades in the south-west of the county.

A narrow belt of the Silurian Wenlock Series extends south-west from Builth along the edge of the Tywi anticline to form the country rock of the *Builth-Llanwrtyd Depression*. This zone is drained by the major subsequent River Irfon running close to the steep north-west scarp of Mynydd Epynt. The landscape between the left bank of the Irfon and the south-west edge of the Northern Plateau is broken, hilly country with rounded summits between about 200 and 300 m above O.D. Several well-developed streams flowing to the Irfon south-east from the Plateau dissect this area, in which the soils are less naturally fertile than in the Old Red Sandstone-based valleys.

Due to good factors of preservation, the *Usk Llynfi Basin*, together with part of the upper Wye valley, is known to have been important for settlement since later prehistoric times. This Basin is formed largely from the relatively easily eroded Old Red Sandstone Red Marls, dipping gently southwards. Glacial erosion has here modified valley profiles and left substantial till deposits and fluvio-glacial landforms, which include melt-water channels, kames and kettle-holes. Llangorse Lake, through which the Llynfi flows, occupies an ice-scoured rock basin, dammed at first by glacial deposits (and subsequently possibly by sediments). These superficial deposits have generally given way to the development of fertile Brown Earth soils.

The Usk flows through a narrow, steep-sided valley between its source in the hilly Carmarthenshire borderlands and Brecon. It drains water from north-westerly streams following the more restricted incised valleys of the Epynt Plateau. To the south, between the Usk and the mountain escarpment, is dissected round-topped hill country lying between about 300 and 400 m above O.D. Although the broad Usk plain is today subject to seasonal flooding between Brecon and Tal-y-bont, it is unclear whether or not these inundations have been accelerated by historic landscape changes of anthropogenic origin. Indeed, the question of dating these changes is underlined by the recent recognition of deserted medieval settlements along this corridor. If the valley bottom was suited to medieval settlement, it is probable that earlier populations had also exploited its fertility (*pace Inv. Br.* I, (ii), p. 6).

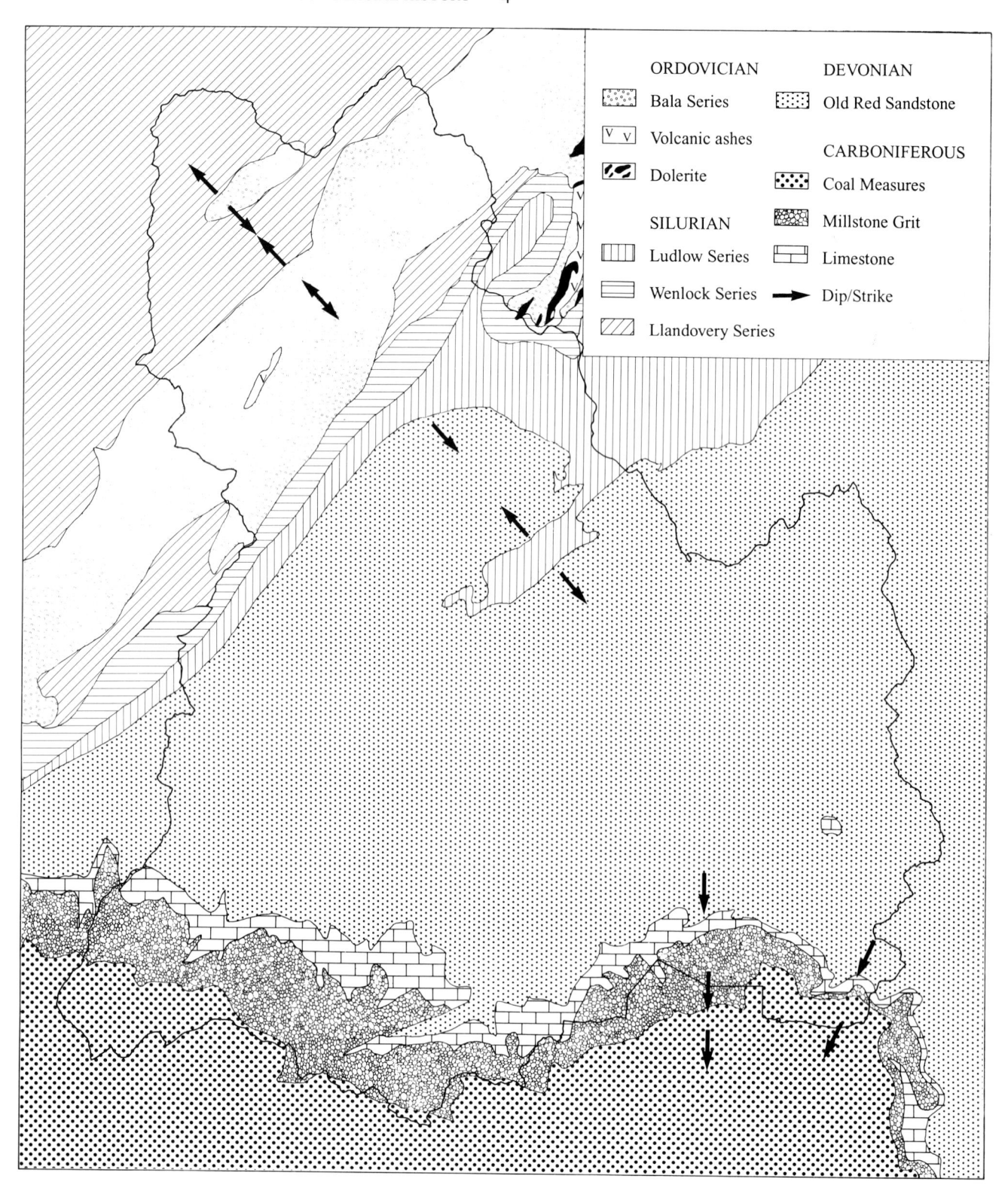

PHYSICAL BACKGROUND AND POST-GLACIAL HISTORY 4

6 Geology of Brecknockshire (adapted from *Brycheiniog* 5 (1959))

The wedge of undulating countryside drained to the north-east by the Llynfi and Dulas rivers has hilltops rising to over 300 m above O.D. but generally gradients present few difficulties for agriculture, particularly as the Wye Valley is approached.

Except at confluences where more gently sloping land is available, the peripheral slopes of the Usk Valley below Llangynidr tend to have a rather steep aspect.

Climatic and Vegetational History

During the Ice Age, the Brecon Beacons formed a local ice-cap,[1] though the region was generally receptive to incoming ice-streams, principally from the west and north, and along the eastern, Marcher side. The western mountain cirque and escarpment landscape, probably of Devensian age, affords outstanding evidence of the last cirque glaciation. A variety of glacial and periglacial features occur, including snow-scree moraine at the foot of Fan Hir and discontinuous morainic features from Llyn-y-Fan Fach on the west, to Llyn-y-Fan Fawr on the south-west. There are also several well-developed debris-cones.[2] In the central Beacons, Craig Cerrig Gleisiad is a cirque containing the only unequivocally dated moraine in South Wales.

During Pleistocene ice movements large erratic blocks of local stone were transported short distances. While initially inhibiting the development of agriculture, these also formed convenient local quarries for fieldwall, road and house building,[3] as well as for the more primitive demands of mineral extraction. Fragments of smaller exotic rocks from much further afield were also recycled into local boulder clays, offering minimal availability of flint and far-travelled metamorphic and igneous rocks suitable for implement making.[4]

No firm evidence is known in Wales for the earliest, the Anglian Glaciation, although its ice carried Welsh erratics into eastern England. The Irish Sea Glaciation is accepted only from fugitive evidence in south-west Dyfed and on the Vale of Glamorgan.[5] Although a Paviland Glaciation is documented, the most important surviving evidence is of Devensian Glaciation, which reached its maximum extent c. 20,000–18,000 B.P. Deglaciation was probably complete in lowland areas by c. 14,500 B.P., but later local montane re-advances are thought to have been likely.

The Late Glacial Environment and Upper Palaeolithic Settlement

In recent years the Brecon Beacons have become an important focal point for late- and post-glacial studies, for example at Craig Cerrig Gleisiad (SN 964 220),[6] Coed Taf (SN 988 108; 990 108; 987 106),[7] Craig y Fro (SN 972 208)[8] and Traeth Mawr (SN 967 257),[9] within the Beacons, and data from other palaeoenvironmental studies in South Wales have led to the suggestion that during the late Upper Palaeolithic (possibly represented in the Gwernvale flint assemblage (MS 15)), local populations may have increasingly exploited this late-glacial environment.[10] The possibility of pollen analytical or charcoal evidence for such early human occupation has been noted at Nant Ffrancon in North Wales,[11] and similarly early environmental interferences have been detected through work at Bwlch Owen (SN 826 619) in the extreme north-west of Brecknockshire.[12] There is, however, need to be mindful of the possibility that some or all of this charcoal may have resulted from natural fires.

Mesolithic

After about 10,000 B.C., events of the earlier Mesolithic took place against a background of climatic warming (the pre-Boreal and Boreal). During this period, woodland vegetation was at first dominated by juniper (*Juniperus*), then by birch (*Betula*) and hazel (*Corylus*). The expansion of oak (*Quercus*) and elm (*Ulmus*) is documented, the former making up considerable stands in the Brecon Beacons by about 9,000 B.C. with elm more frequent at lower levels. By about 6,000 B.C. lime (*Tilia*) and ash (*Fraxinus*) were widespread, particularly at lowland sites.[13] During this period mixed woodlands were probably common to a height of 450 m or even higher.

The effects of human activity upon the later, Boreal-Atlantic forest mantle are detectable from pollen analytical studies, and charcoal recognised during investigations at Nant Helen[14] and Coed Taf[15] has been attributed to the Mesolithic. Indeed, it has been argued that palaeoenvironmental evidence may assist field reconnaissance aimed at locating contemporary settlement sites.[16] One important conclusion drawn from the evidence at Coed Taf was that forest recession and peat inception at the site may have resulted from early human activity.[17] Unfortunately, it is usually difficult to recover pollen spectra from excavated sites in sufficient quantity to be useful in this kind of assessment, and soils accompanying both the Mesolithic flint assemblage from Pant Sychbant (MS 7)[18] (only 1 km S. of Coed Taf), and that from Gwernvale (MS 15) were inadequate for the task.

By way of contrast to these inadequacies, the environmental data forthcoming from Waun Fignen Felen (MS 2 Plate 2)[19] is remarkable in both qualitative and quantitative terms. Here there may have been Mesolithic activity before 8,000 B.P. Regular burning of the vegetation cover, attested by extensive charcoal deposits in basal layers of the peat, suggests human interference over the following two millennia. This activity could have caused mor (acid soil), heather (*Calluna*) heath, and hazel (*Corylus*) copses to develop after much of the birch woodland had been burned off. Continued exploitation is believed to have resulted in altering the fragile ecological balance, bringing about podsolisation and the onset of blanket peat. Similar evidence for Mesolithic activity prior to about 6,000 B.P. was observed at Pen Rhiw-wen (Carmarthenshire; SN 71 38),[20] with the possibility of contemporary discernible interference at Llyn Mire in the Wye Valley (Radnorshire; SN 00 55), 1 km beyond the Brecknockshire county boundary.[21]

Neolithic

Although evidence for pre-Elm Decline agricultural activity is scanty, cereal pollen has been noted from the Nant Helen site,[22] though this does not certainly have agricultural connotations. The presence of ribwort plantain (*Plantago lanceolata* which can appear as a weed of cultivation, but could also be taken as an indicator of pastoralism) at Llyn Mire, during a depression in the Elm (*Ulmus*) curve further strengthens the case for local agricultural clearance in the Wye Valley.[23]

The elm decline itself, at one time considered by palynologists to have been the prime herald of agriculture, is now seen more to have occurred probably through a combination of elm disease and, to a greater extent, from anthropogenic factors.[24] Evidence for vegetation change found around this horizon at Nant Helen was felt to support the argument for anthropogenic environmental changes. Paucity of evidence, probably attributable to inadequate investigation in upland Powys, led Moore to propose the cereal pollen recognised at Llyn Mire as a differential land-use indicator during the Neolithic.[25] However, cereal pollen is recorded on Black Mountain sites in south Powys and east Dyfed,[26] and from a Neolithic context in the upland excavation at Llanelwedd, south Radnorshire.[27]

More generally, the elm decline in South Wales occurs *c.* 5,000 B.P. It is well documented from ten different locations at Waun-Fignen-Felen, where cereal pollen spans the period *c.* 5,500 to 4,950 B.P. A later, second and similar decline occurs at five sites in Waun-Fignen-Felen around 4,600 B.P.[28]

It is generally believed that Neolithic activity was predominantly small-scale, with only short-term clearances, though these had far-reaching effects which in the uplands resulted in blanket peat initiation.[29] Peat initiation was diachronous and its inception seems to be owed to various factors, local and national, at different periods of antiquity.

The overall effects of these and later clearances noted from local pollen diagrams have been chronicled on a grander scale from sediment chemistry, diatoms, palynology and radiocarbon dated cores taken from Llangorse Lake. These showed accelerated lacustrine silting during the period 5,000–2,000 B.P., an acceleration considered to be due to forest clearance.[30]

Brecknockshire is relatively well served by environmental data from excavated Neolithic sites as compared with other parts of Wales. Carbonised plant remains found at Gwernvale megalith (CT 11) included emmer wheat,[31] while Pipton long barrow (CT 8)[32] and Cefn Cilsanws (US 90 (i))[33] provided evidence for the collection of hazelnuts. Cattle, sheep and pig bones were identified at Pen y wrlod (CT 4), Gwernvale and Tŷ Isaf (CT 3), with deer also appearing at the latter two sites.[34]

The Bronze Age

The prelude of Neolithic agricultural practice was followed by a more devastating onslaught from forest clearances reaching into most corners of the countryside in its search for fresh cultivable soils. These clearances are again chronicled at Waun Fignen Felen, where four minima in elm pollen are noted on different sampling cores between *c.* 2,850 B.P. and *c.* 2,650 B.P. Detailed analytical results from this site indicate increased run-off and ground surface humidity, most likely caused by deforestation.[35] So great were these changes that by about 3,000 B.P. there was probably open ground on the south of the Beacons, at least around Coed Taf.[36] Intermittent clearances were initiated in the Black Mountains, on Pen y Gader Fawr (SO 230 285) and at Waun Fach South (SO 217 300) *c.* 3,500 and between *c.* 4,800 and *c.* 2,800 B.P. respectively.[37] A similar story is told at Cefn Ffordd (SN 906 032), where peat was initiated after woodland removal and stock grazing before 3,600 B.P.[38] This site and Llangorse Lake produced particularly early records of rye (*Secale*), a cropping plant previously thought not to have been introduced until the Iron Age or Roman times.[39]

Site-specific investigation like that undertaken at Nant Helen has demonstrated a dramatic increase in prehistoric activity from the peat pollen record, which includes cereal-type pollen. Pollen evidence from soil samples beneath cairns at Nant Helen (RC 16–17) indicates a landscape dominated by either heather or scrub, suggesting great changes by the time of cairn construction.[40] Investigations in 1960 at Nant Maden Cairn (RC 111), showed that after initial Neolithic heathland development, woodland had re-established by the middle Bronze Age,[41] something of a contrast with the results from Chambers' more recent site record at Cefn Ffordd, if indeed the uncalibrated results of the earlier investigation are to be credited.

Besides sightings of rye, which is perhaps better suited to harsher climes than other cereals, wheat and barley have been only occasionally recognised on Early Bronze Age sites in Wales.[42] The only known grain impression, of emmer wheat (*Triticum dicoccum*), appears on the base of the cordoned urn excavated from Fan y Big in 1981 (LBS 6).[43]

The effects of widespread agriculture evidenced from the pollen record, and inferred from the numerous field clearances and some field systems recently mapped in the Welsh Uplands, was to have far-reaching and devastating effects upon the Bronze Age environment. By about 1,200 B.C. blanket peat had begun to grow ubiquitously throughout the uplands and probably also covered some lowland areas. Abandonment of leached, acidic soils brought farming to lower altitudes, possibly creating greater pressure upon the available land. The slow environmental cycle involving major deforestation *c.* 2,200–1,500 B.C., followed by widespread tillage upon most available soils, with subsequent reversion to heathland, was probably caused through poor soil maintenance by routine fertilisation, and the evidence of silting in Llangorse Lake, for example, suggests widespread soil erosion.

Under these conditions, how far it is possible to speak of 'climatic change', and how far it is reasonable to term events 'widespread humanly-induced environmental disaster', remain open questions. However, these events would certainly have direct atmospheric effects; loss of forest trees throughout north-west Europe during the second millennium B.C. would alter transpiration rates; run-off was accelerated, and some soils suffered in consequence; during an unknown timespan under tillage, greater areas of exposed ground would have been subjected to direct sunlight and evaporation. Open ploughland would also have been open to wind and rain, increasing the risk of sheet erosion.

Leached, peaty, heathland soils consume far less nitrogen than do trees. Peatlands have cloud and mist-retaining properties which further prevent insolation. The replacement of much heathland and many tracts of low-lying farmland by forests may have influenced, if not accelerated, climatic change.

The period of climatic deterioration which began in the Early Bronze Age continued through Late Bronze Age and Iron Age times and into the Roman period. Further speculation about the degree of anthropogenic contribution to environmental changes is limited by lack of settlement dating evidence. No Iron Age sites in Brecknockshire have so far yielded environmental evidence,[44] and results from the only Roman site to be examined (Plas y gors)[44] were rather inconclusive.[46]

Pollen diagrams show that clearances and possibly pastoral activity continued in the uplands throughout the Roman period, activities which ceased around 400 A.D. at Waun Fach South.[47] There was peat initiation at Coed Taf around this time,[48] possibly indicating more widespread changes, variously attributed to changed land management practices and climatic deterioration. But in general, environmental information for the Roman and post-Roman period is poor, and Llangorse Crannog (CS 1), from which split oak planks have been studied dendrochronologically, remains the only dated site.[49]

Geology
T. N. George, *South Wales*, I.G.S. Regional Guide, (London, 1970); F. J. North, 'The Geological History of Brecknock', *Brycheiniog* I (1955), pp. 9–77; T. M. Thomas, 'The Geomorphology of Brecknock', *Brycheiniog* V (1959), pp. 55–156; D. Thomas, (ed.), *Wales, a New Study*, (Newton Abbot, 1977); F. V. Emery, *Wales*, (London, 1969); J. G. Evans, S. Limbrey and H. Cleere, (eds.), *The Effects of Man on the Landscape; the Highland*

Zone, (London, 1975); J. A. Taylor, (ed.), *Climate Change with special reference to Wales and its Agriculture*, (Aberystwyth, 1965); *Aspects of Forest Climates*, (Aberystwyth, 1970); *Culture and Environment in Prehistoric Wales*, (Oxford: B.A.R., 1980); I. Simmons and M. Tooley (eds.), *The Environment in British Prehistory*, (London, 1981).

[1] This account owes a great deal to the facility of access to the literature afforded by Caseldine, *E.A.* Where not otherwise attributed, documentation to the outline presented here may be found in that volume. Assistance has also been forthcoming from Prof F. M. Chambers, University of Cheltenham, and Mrs P. Wiltshire, Institute of Archaeology, University of London.

[2] S. Campbell and D. Q. Bowen, *Geological Conservation Review: Quaternary of Wales*, (Nature Conservancy Council, 1989), pp. 103–105; The Cwm Llwch (SO 002 220) and Cwm Crew (SO 008 198) moraines, probably formed during the Loch Lomond Readvance or Stadial (11–10,000 BP), are well illustrated and described by C. Embleton in N. Stephens (ed.), *Natural Landscapes of Britain from the Air*, Cambridge U.P.; (1990); pp. 84–7.

[3] W. S. Symonds, *Records of the Rocks*, p. 246, (1872).

[4] B. B. Clarke, *Proc. Birmingham Nat. Hist. Philos. Soc.* 16 (1936), pp. 155–72.

[5] Campbell and Bowen, *loc. cit.* n. 2.

[6] M. J. C. Walker, *Nature* 287 (1980), pp. 133–5; pp. 91–6 in D. Q. Bowen and A. Henry, (eds.), *Field Guide, Wales: Gower, Preseli and Fforest Fawr*, (Cambridge: Quaternary Research Association, 1984).

[7] F. M. Chambers, *Ecol. Mediterr.* 11 (1985), pp. 73–80; F. M. Chambers, P. Q. Dresser and A. G. Smith, *Nature* 282 (1979), pp. 829–31.

[8] Walker, in *Nature, loc. cit.* n. 6; *New Phytol.* 91 (1982), pp. 147–65; P. D. Moore, *New Phytol.* 69 (1979), pp. 363–75.

[9] M. J. C. Walker, *idem*.

[10] H. S. Green, pp. 70–8, in *Limestone Caves*.

[11] C. J. Burrows, *New Phytol.* 73 (1974), pp. 161–71.

[12] M. Grant, *Stratigraphy and pollen analysis of lake sediments from Bwlch-Owen, Mid-Wales: Evidence of Bølling and Allerød chronostratigraphic equivalents in the Devensian Late-glacial Interstadial*, (Unpubl. B.Sc thesis, Dept. of Biosphere Sciences, King's Coll., London, 1989).

[13] For e.g., Chambers in *Ecol. Mediterr., loc. cit.* n. 7.

[14] Chambers, in P. Dorling and F. M. Chambers, *B.B.C.S.* 37 (1990), pp. 215–46; F. M. Chambers, J. G. A. Lageard and L. Elliott, *Post-glacial history of the Nant Helen opencast site, South Wales: implications for land restoration*, Dept. Occas. Paper No. 15, Dept. of Geography, Univ. of Keele (1988).

[15] F. M. Chambers, *Jnl Ecol.* 71 (1983), pp. 475–87.

[16] Caseldine, *loc. cit.* n. 1, p. 35.

[17] Chambers, in *Jnl Ecol., loc. cit.* n. 15.

[18] Seddon, in T. W. Burke, J. M. Lewis, and B. Seddon, *B.B.C.S.*, 22 (1966), pp. 78–87.

[19] E. W. Cloutman, *Studies of the vegetational history of the Black Mountain range, South Wales*, (Ph.D. thesis, Univ. of Wales, Cardiff, 1983); A. G. Smith and E. W. Cloutman, *Phil. Trans. Roy. Soc. Lond.* 322 (B) (1988), pp. 158–219, (no. 1209).

[20] Cloutman, in Smith and Cloutman, *loc. cit. supra*.

[21] P. D. Moore, *New Phytol.* 80 (1978), pp. 281–302; P. D. Moore and P. J. Beckett, *Nature* 231 (1971), pp. 363–5.

[22] Chambers *et al., loc. cit.* n. 14.

[23] Moore in *New Phytol., loc. cit.* n. 21.

[24] M. Girling, pp. 34–8 in M. Jones, (ed.), *Archaeology and flora of the British Isles*, Oxford Univ. Comm. for Archaeol. Mon. no. 14 and Botanical Soc. of the British Isles Conf. Rep. no. 19 (1988); O. Rackham, *Ancient woodland: its history, vegetation and uses in England*, (London: Arnold, 1980).

[25] Moore in *New Phytol., loc. cit.* n. 21; *Proc. 4th Internat. Palynolog. Conf., Lucknow*, 3 (1981), pp. 279–90.

[26] Cloutman in Smith and Cloutman, *loc. cit.* n. 19.

[27] C. B. Crampton, *B.B.C.S.* 22 (1967), pp. 273–4.

[28] Smith and Cloutman, and Cloutman in *Phil. Trans. Roy. Soc., loc. cit.* n. 19.

[29] Caseldine, *E.A.*, p. 46.

[30] R. Jones, K. Benson-Evans and F. M. Chambers, *Earth Surface Processes and Landforms* 10 (1985), pp. 227–35; R. Jones, K. Benson-Evans, F. M. Chambers, B. Abell Seddon, and Y. C. Tai, *Verh. Internat. Verein, Limnol.* 20 (1985), pp. 642–8; F. M. Chambers in *Ecol. Mediterr., loc. cit.* n. 7.

[31] Moffett and Hillman *in preparation*.

[32] H. A. Hyde in H. N. Savory, *Arch. Camb.* 105 (1956), p. 48.

[33] D. P. Webley, *B.B.C.S.* 18 (1958), pp. 79–88.

[34] Caseldine, *E.A.*, p. 52, table 4.

[35] Smith and Cloutman; Cloutman, *loc. cit.* n. 19.

[36] F. M. Chambers, pp. 110–115 in M. Jones, (ed.), *Archaeology and the Flora of the British Isles*, Oxford. Univ. Comm. for Archaeol. Mon. no. 14 (1988).

[37] M. D. R. Price and P. D. Moore, *Pollen et Spores* 26 (1984), pp. 127–36; P. D. Moore, D. L. Merryfield, and M. D. R. Price, pp. 203–5 in P. D. Moore, (ed.), *European Mires*, (London, 1984).

[38] F. M. Chambers, F. M. Chambers in *Jnl Ecol.* 70 (1982), 445–459.

[39] F. M. Chambers and M. K. Jones, *Antiquity* 58 (1984), pp. 219–24; F. M. Chambers, *6th International Palynological Conference Abstracts*, (Calgary, 1984).

[40] Chambers *et al, loc. cit.* n. 14.

[41] C. B. Crampton and D. P. Webley, *B.B.C.S.* 20 (1964), pp. 440–9.

[42] Caseldine, *E.A.*, p. 65.

[43] C. S. Briggs, W. J. Britnell and A. M. Gibson, *P.P.S.* 56 (1990), pp. 173–9; Fig. 2, p. 175.

[44] Caseldine, *E.A.*, Fig. 2, p. 70.

[45] *Inv. Br.* I, (ii), (MC 3), pp. 153–4.

[46] Crampton and Webley, *loc. cit.* n. 41.

[47] Chambers *et al.*, in *Antiquity, loc. cit.* n. 39.

[48] Chambers, *loc. cit.* n. 15.

[49] C. Groves, *Tree-Ring Analysis of an oak timber from Llangorse Crannog, Powys*, Sheffield (unpubl., 1988).

Cave Archaeology

Introduction

Bearing in mind the number and size of the extensive cave systems now recognised along the east–west Carboniferous Limestone outcrop passing through south Brecknockshire,[1] it is remarkable that so little archaeological evidence has been forthcoming from them. To a lesser degree, this lack of discovery might be because some more sensitive deposits tend to be overlooked in pursuing methods of cave exploration which have not always been compatible with archaeological interests. However, a more reasonable explanation for this absence is probably geological. Palaeolithic occupation debris deposited in caves close to the surface is likely to have been razed by glaciation, or to have been washed away by fluvioglacial processes. Profound effects of earth surface processes are certainly detectable in caves, though preliminary investigations of subterranean sediments in Brecknockshire so far seem to indicate only the broader trends of climatic history.[2]

Limestone solution decay (discussed pp. 192–4) is an agency probably responsible for the collapse of some inhabited caves, thus rendering impossible future assessment of cultural context or stratigraphic succession. Nevertheless, limestone caves and fissures do have a capacity to retain accumulations of relict strata and rock debris over millions of years,[3] so it is probably only a matter of time before greater testimony to troglodytic occupation or more comprehensive environmental evidence emerges in Brecknockshire.

Although cave occupation in Brecknockshire may begin as early as the Mesolithic, doubt has been cast upon the provenance of the flint (RMS 2) said to derive from Ogof Ffynnon Ddu (PCS 2). Since unstratified finds are not reliable dating evidence, this makes radiometric examination of the 1946 skeleton find from the site all the more crucial.

So far, only one location, Ogof yr Esgyrn (PCS 1), offers any real insights into cave archaeology. The finds assemblage from this site clearly indicates Bronze Age occupation, most likely during the Penard Phase (1,050–900 B.C.). But it is yet probably premature to interpret a single rapier as demonstrating unsettled conditions.[4] The premises upon which the Ogof yr Esgyrn ossuary was pronounced Roman are less certain, and although Romano-British ritual and burial cave deposits are known from limestones elsewhere in Britain, it remains possible that this is one of the few collections of Bronze Age bones known from South Wales (see below p. 11).

Whereas some caves are statutorily protected as parts of National Nature Reserves, or as S.S.S.I.s based upon their biological or geological interest, and access is accordingly restricted, few caves are protected for their archaeological potential. In the past, statutory protection has come about only after cave diggers have recovered artefacts or curiosities. From the surveys of such immense cave systems as exist on the South Wales karst, and from the information presented below, an important priority must be to locate sites with scientific potential, both archaeological and environmental, and to restrict their future exploration to systematic interdisciplinary excavation.

[1] P. Chapman, *Caves and Cave Life*, (New Naturalist, 1993, pp. 89–92); P. L. Smart and C. G. Gardener, 'The Mynydd Llangattwg Cave Systems', pp. 124–51. The following chapters in *Limestone Caves* are relevant to this discussion: T. D. Ford, 'The Caves of Nant y Glais, Vaynor', pp. 152–5; T. Waltham and D. G. Everett, 'The Caves of the Mellte and Hepste Valleys area', pp. 155–64; S. Moore, 'The Afon Nedd Fechan Caves', pp. 165–76; P. L. Smart and N. S. J. Christopher, 'Ogof Ffynnon Ddu', pp. 177–9; A. C. Coase, 'Dan yr Ogof', pp. 190–297.

[2] P. A. Bull, 'Cave Sediment Studies in South Wales: towards a reconstruction of a Welsh palaeoclimate by means of the Scanning Electron Microscope', *Studies in Speleology* 3 (1977), pp. 13–24.

[3] This process is illustrated in F. J. North, *The Evolution of the Bristol Channel*, 3rd end., (Cardiff: N.M.W., 1964), p. 32, Fig. 13.

[4] H. S. Green, 'Stone Age Cave Archaeology in South Wales', pp. 70–8, in *Limestone Caves*.

CAVE ARCHAEOLOGY 10

OGOF YR ESGYRN (THE BONE CAVE)
Glyntawe, near Craig-y-nos, S. Wales.
1938-50 Excavations.

The floor from A to K is level and is taken as the datum line.
Numbers give floor levels in feet below datum.

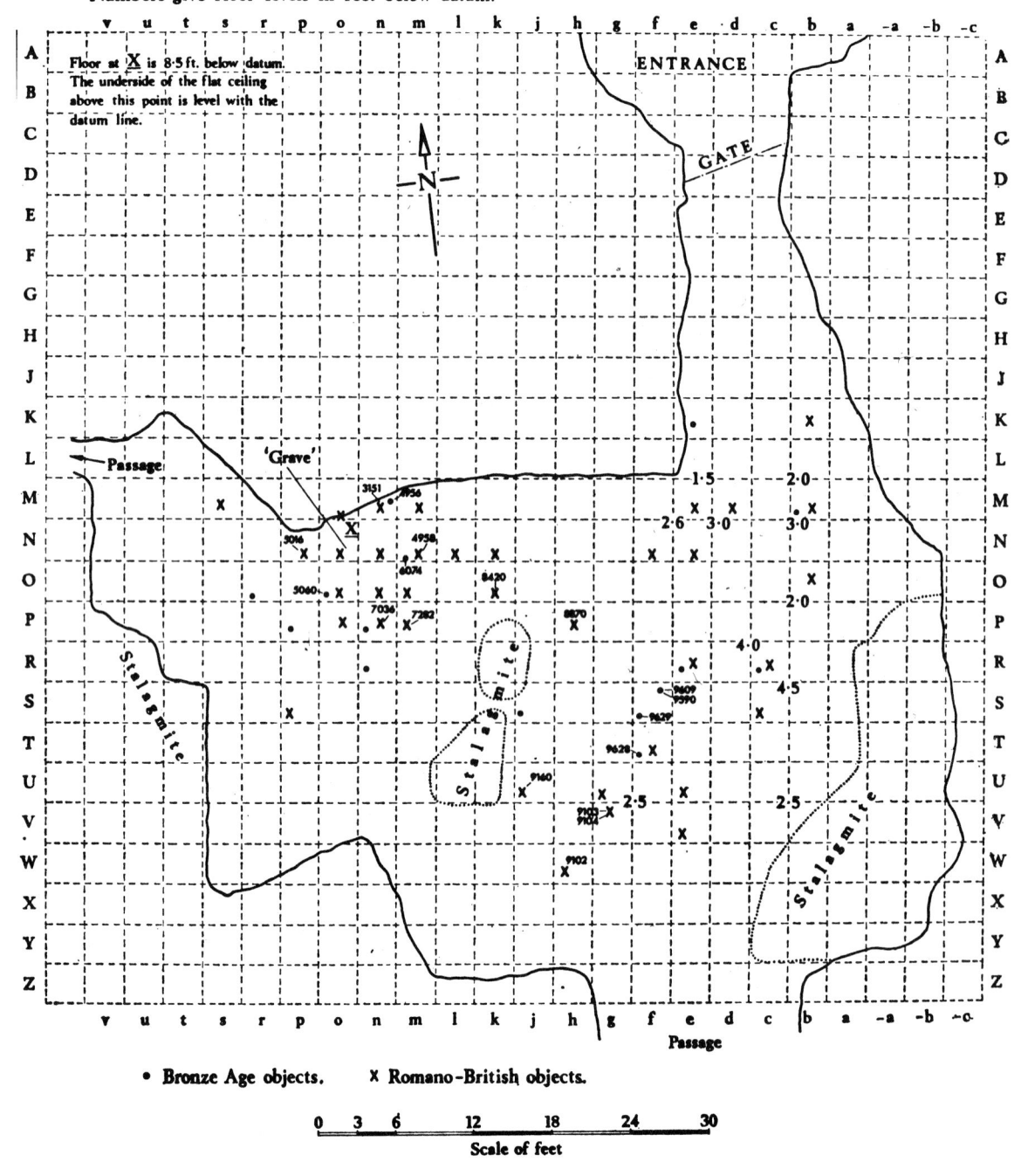

Floor at X is 8·5 ft. below datum.
The underside of the flat ceiling above this point is level with the datum line.

ENTRANCE
GATE
Passage
'Grave'
Stalagmite
Stalagmite
Stalagmite
Passage

• Bronze Age objects.   × Romano-British objects.

0 3 6 12 18 24 30
Scale of feet

7 Dan yr Ogof (Abercrave) cave (PCS 1): plan (from Mason *Arch. Camb.* 117 1968)

Prehistoric (and Later) Cave Sites (PCS 1–4; OCS 1–3)

(PCS 1 Figs 7–9) Ogof yr Esgyrn lies at the source of the Afon Llynfell. It is one of three small caves discovered in 1922, though its archaeological sensitivity was only appreciated in 1923.[1] This cave forms but one small component of a massive system of solution caves lying beneath the Cribarth plateau west of the Upper Tawe, and today best known from its accessible embouchure at the Dan yr Ogof showcave, which gives its name to the system.[2] A variety of finds was made during excavations undertaken between 1923 and 1950,[3] dating *inter alia* from the post-glacial, as indicated by faunal remains, through later prehistoric and Roman times[4] to the historic period.

Several finds deriving from the 1923 excavation were marked upon the earlier plan[5] and although not recognised as such at the time, one was a potsherd of Bronze Age date. A later, more systematic excavation campaign was undertaken between 1938 and 1950 which shed more light upon cave occupation. Unfortunately, coming before the advent of radiocarbon dating, the work leaves unsolved many chronostratigraphic problems.

Habitation and burial were well attested in the chamber; hearths, animal bones and stray-finds representing the former and the skeletal remains of at least forty individuals documenting the latter. All the material of interest was deposited in relatively discrete areas of cave floor, the rest of the site being considered incapable of occupation in antiquity due to the presence of heavy stalagmitic deposit. Removal of part of this floor exposed the skeletal material and some hearths within a sandy pit, occupying one of the few softer parts of the cave floor. It was argued at the time of discovery that since Bronze Age interment practice was exclusively by cremation, these inhumations must have belonged to a later period, and were therefore Roman.[6] Supporting evidence certainly existed in the form of Roman artefacts close to and apparently associated with this ossuary.[7] Matters were, however, complicated by the tight stratigraphical interdigitation of both Roman and earlier material which often made it impossible to perceive any clear distinction between cultural debris of either period. Indeed, so disturbed were the bones and artefact stratification in general, that in retrospect, it now seems equally possible that the bones were deposited in the cave coevally with the Early–Middle Bronze Age bronze rapier,[8] bronze razor, bronze awl, gold bead, bone awl and weaving comb and other minor objects, and Bronze Age pottery sherds (possibly representing as many as six vessels).[9] As it is now clear that both inhumation and cremation burial were practised during the Bronze Age, these bones might now be usefully radiocarbon dated.

[1] R. H. D'Elboux, *Arch. Camb.* 79 (1924), pp. 113–24.

[2] A. C. Coase, 'Dan yr Ogof', pp. 190–207, in *Limestone Caves*; A. C. Coase and D. M. Judson, *Trans. British Cave Res. Assoc.* 4, 1–2, (1977), pp. 245–344; *Dan-yr-Ogof Caves: Swansea Valley Caves*, souvenir guide, E. J. Mason (ed.), (Dan yr Ogof: Swansea, *c.* 1960); *Dan yr Ogof Showcaves*, Souvenir Colour Guide, (Clydach: W. Walters, Son and Co., Ltd. (Printers) and the Proprietors, Dan yr Ogof Showcave, Abercrave, u.d. [1990]).

[3] E. J. Mason, *Arch. Camb.* 117 (1968), pp. 18–71; E. J. Mason, *Trans. Cave Res. Gp G.B.* 13, 1, (1971), pp. 57–62; *S. Wales Caving Club Newsl.* 89 (June 1978), pp. 3–7.

[4] *Inv. Br.* I, (ii), p. 182.

[5] Mason *loc. cit.* 1968.

[6] D'Elboux, *loc. cit.* n. 1, Fig. 4; this interpretation is followed by K. Brannigan and M. J. Dearne in *Romano-British Cavemen: Cave use in Roman Britain*, Oxbow Monograph, no. 19, (Oxford, 1992), pp. 35, 65.

[7] Mason in *Arch. Camb., loc. cit.* n. 3, p. 22; *cf. Inv. Br.* I, (ii), p. 182.

[8] C. B. Burgess and S. Gerloff, *The Dirks and Rapiers of Great Britain and Ireland*, Praehistorische Bronzefünde, Abt. IV, Bd 7, (München: C. Beck's Verl., 1981); p. 98, no. 876, p. 105; p. 115, no. 29, metal analysis, p. 120.

[9] In 1992 the cave proprietors commissioned the imaginative reconstruction of an 'Iron Age Farm' on the site (Anon., *The Great Dan yr Ogof Day Out: Souvenir Brochure*, (1992), pp. 22–3). Whilst this fulfils a basic educational purpose, its cultural context appears to be unrelated to finds made locally (which are admittedly few), and the style of structure it portrays is more reminiscent of lowland, rather than of upland settlement building traditions.

Ystradgynlais (E), Ystradgynlais Higher (C)
SN 81 N.W. (8276 1601)　　　　　　　　　11 x 93

(PCS 2) Ogof Ffynnon Ddu,[1] one of the most complex caves in Britain and the first cave to merit recognition as a National Nature Reserve in 1976,[2] is entered through at least a dozen entrances lying between about 340 m and 520 m above O.D.[3] It was opened by members of the South Wales Caving Club in 1946.[4] Entering from a dry side-passage, they discovered a small chamber containing a skeleton, a photograph of which was sent to the National Museum of Wales. The skeleton was in a recumbent position on its right side on a small rock platform at the foot of a rock fall. Both legs were bent at the hip joint, the right being much

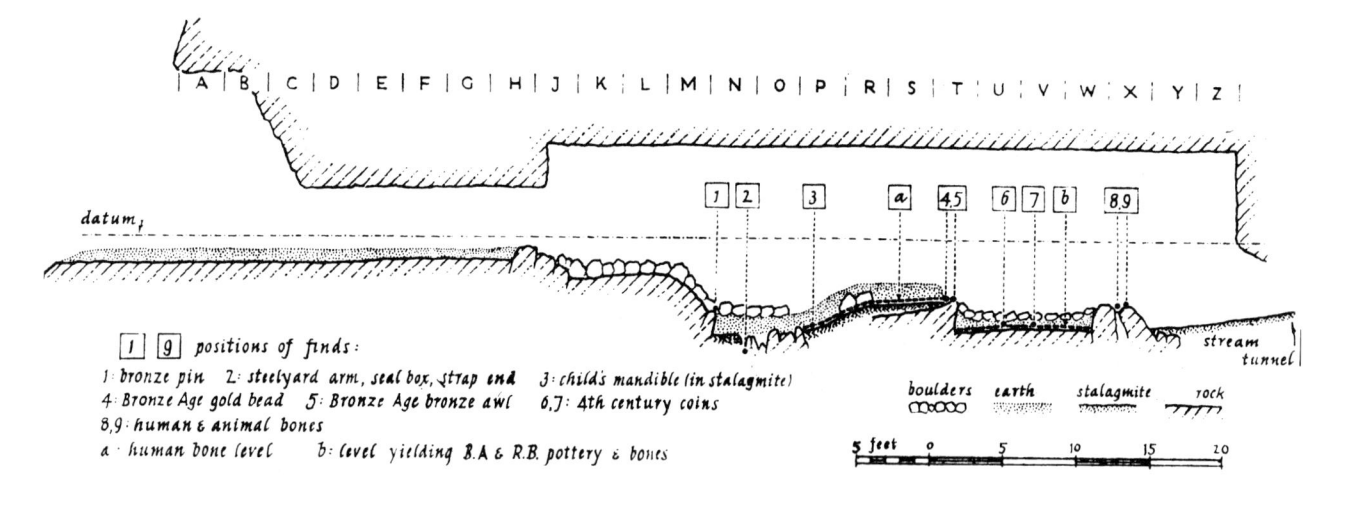

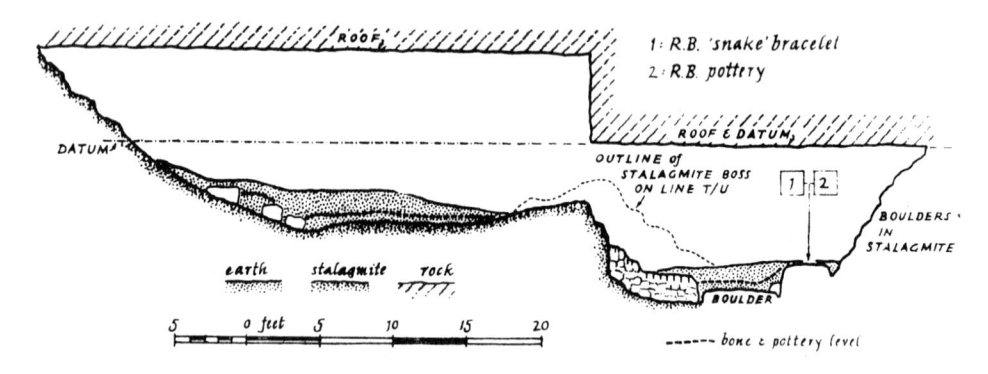

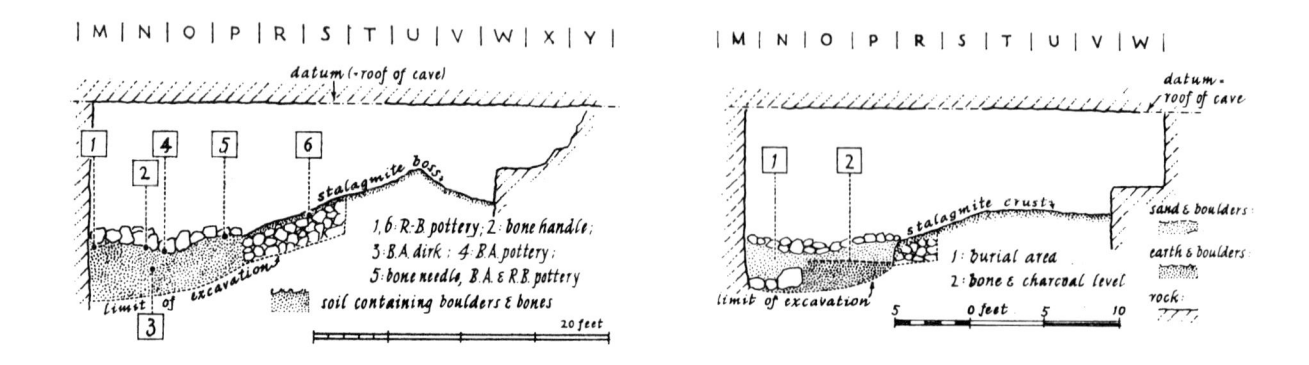

8 Dan yr Ogof (Abercrave) stratigraphy (from Mason *Arch. Camb.* 117 (1968))

bent at the knee and the left slightly extended. At the time of discovery opinion inclined to the view that the bones (which are now lost), belonged to an accidental death of recent, historic origin. However, a re-appraisal of their deposition circumstances suggests the skeleton might better fit a deliberate burial, probably within a prehistoric context.[5] Later excavation through an ancient collapse within the cave brought to light a horse skeleton, for which a Mesolithic date has been advanced, largely because it is presumed that the animal was undomesticated.[6]

Uncertainty surrounds the context of a Mesolithic

flint core (RMS 1)[7] allegedly found in this cave close to a 'fine large flint flake knife', with secondary working at each end and all along one long side and probably of 'Beaker' date.[8] Neither find was either stratified or in any way connected with the skeleton. Indeed, it has been suggested that the flints fell through a crevice from the groundsoil above.[9]

[1] R. J. Haycock, *Nature in Wales*, N.S.2 (1983), pp. 34–9.
[2] P. Chapman, *loc. cit.* p. 92.
[3] 'Ogof Ffynnon Ddu – A Topographical Survey', unpubl. typescript, 23 August 1980.
[4] E. J. Mason, 'Report on Human Skeleton discovered on 4th August 1946 in Ogof Ffynnon Ddu at Rhongyr Uchaf, Swansea Valley', *Trans. Cardiff Nat. Soc.* 79 (1945–8) [1950], pp. 60–61; *Caves and Caving in Britain*, (London: R. Hale, 1977).
[5] M. Davies, *S. Wales Caving Club Newsl.* 92 (1980), pp. 19–20.
[6] M. Davies, *idem.*
[7] Savory, 'Prehistoric Brecknocks', II, pp. 6, 16; this find is now in the National Museum of Wales (Acc. No. 70.36H/1); O.S. Card SN 81 NE 12.
[8] Savory, *loc. cit.* p. 6.
[9] *ibid*. p. 16.

Glyntawe
SN 81 N.W./N.E. Top entrance (8635 1589); lower entrance (8476 1514)   Not entered

(PCS 3) Twll Carw Coch lies 'somewhere upon Cadair Fawr' (N.W. of Penderyn).[1] Excavations designed to locate a cave entrance were sunk some 25 ft [7.62 m]. From an elliptical hole 15 ft [4.57 m] by 10 ft [3.05 m], human and animal bones were recovered. Among these were two human skulls, the younger of which was claimed to be about 600 years old. An uncorroborated radiocarbon date of around 2,000 B.C. was obtained for the second skull.[2] Animal bones ('six refuse bagfuls') included red deer, *bos* sp., dog and pig. The older skull is believed lost; the animal bones were given to schoolchildren and the younger skull remains in private possession.

[1] J. C. Jones (Y Dyn Bodlon), 'Twll Carw Coch', *S. Wales Caving Club Newsl.* 99 (1985), p. 21; J. C. Jones, pers. comm.; originally drawn to the Commission's attention by M. Davies, Swansea; corroborated *in personam* by Mr J. C. Jones.
[2] At the Cardiff University Radiocarbon Laboratory.

Penderyn
SN 91 S.E. (983 126)   Not visited

(PCS 4) Chartist's Cave or Ogof Fawr lies 540 m above O.D. At the turn of the nineteenth century it was known as Stabl Fawr, because at that time horses and other animals sought shelter in it.[1] During an excavation there in 1970 by members of the Severn Valley Caving Club under the direction of R. G. Lewis, human and animal bones, a clay pipe, coal, and a flat perforated stone were recovered. It is possible the latter was of considerable antiquity. Information on the human bones presented at an inquest (by Dr Bernard Knight), suggested them to be relatively recent (50–100 years old). They were thought to have belonged to at least three individuals.[2] One thigh bone had been mutilated, leaving open the possibility that the victims in the burial group may have been secreted in this place after one or more local disturbance.[3] The animal bones are lost and it is not known where the human ones were deposited.[4]

[1] T. Jones, *Hist. Brecks.*, II, ii (1809), p. 517.
[2] R. G. Jones, 'Chartist Cave, Brecon', *The Red Dragon* [*Jnl Cambr. Cav. Counc.*] 7 (1976), pp. 1–4.
[3] Typescript letter from Dr H. N. Savory (N.M.W.) to P. M. Jones of Tredegar, 10th September 1974.
[4] Further unpublished information was provided by M. Davies, Swansea.

Llangynidr
SO 11 N.W. (1273 1519)   91

Omitted Cave Sites (OCS 1–3)

These are sites at one time thought to have been inhabited, or which are considered ancient in antiquarian or folkloristic tradition.

(OCS 1) Overlooking Craig y Nos on Craig y Rhiwarth, 320 m above O.D., is a cave known as Eglwys Caradog. This is a subterranean chamber 12 ft [*c.* 4 m] by 6 ft by 6 ft [2 m] first mentioned early in the nineteenth century as the place where 'Gunless', Prince of Glewissig was believed to have died in the arms of his son Cathwg or Cadecus.[1] Jones, the County Historian, described it as the saint's summer residence only. Changing traditions related it to the dwelling place of St. Gunleus.[2]

[1] Nicholson, *Cambrian Traveller's Guide*, (1815), p. 965; T. Jones, *Hist. Brecks.*, II, ii, p. 653, erroneously placed the site in Glyntawe and called it 'Eglwys Cradoc'.
[2] R. L. Davies, *Essay on the History of the Swansea Valley*, (1881).

Ystradgynlais (E), Ystradgynlais Hr (C)
SN 81 N.E. (8449 1580) (Not entered)   22 iii 88

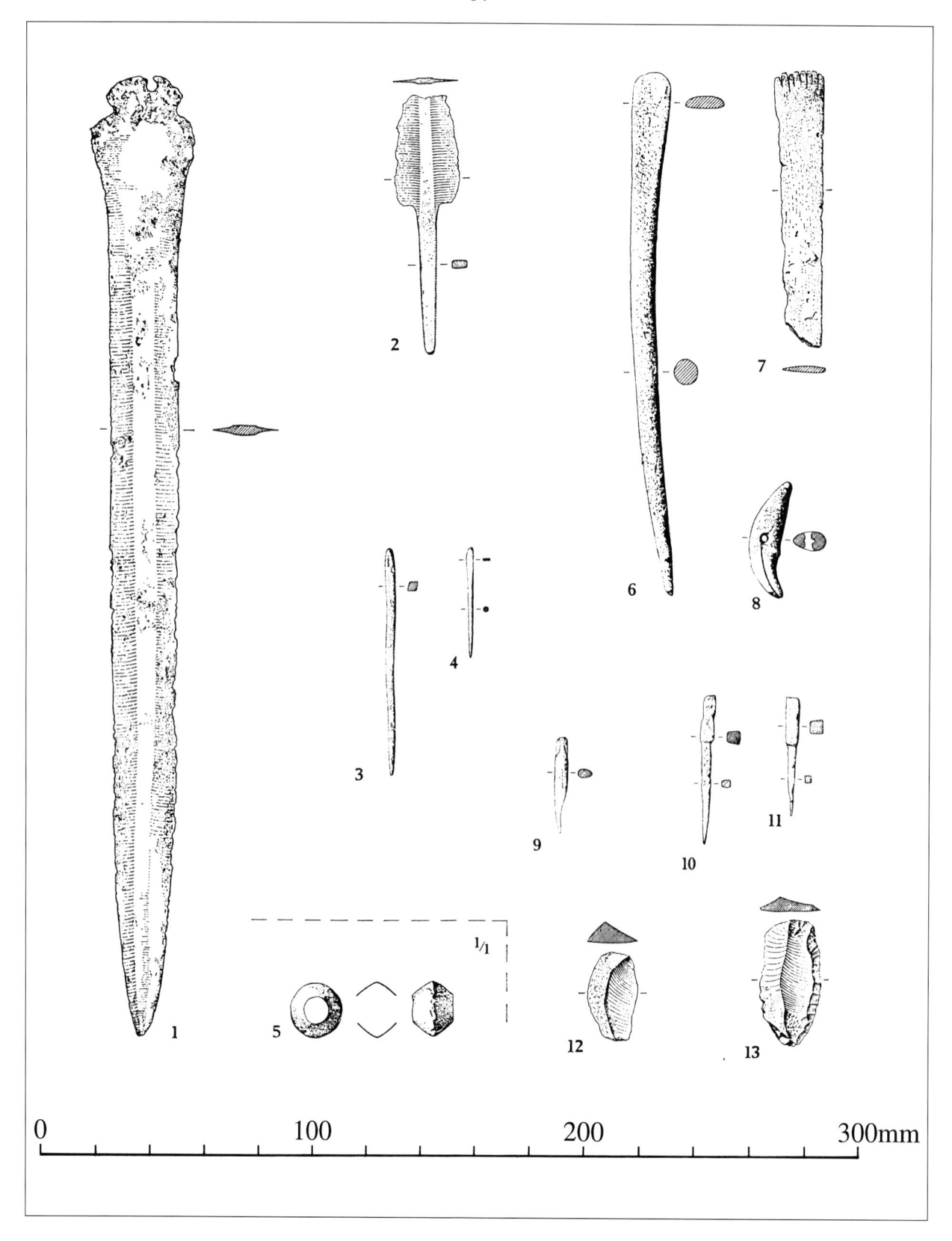

9 Dan yr Ogof (Abercrave) cave (PCS 1): Bronze Age artefacts: gold bead, rapier, razor and bone objects (*Arch Camb*. (1968))

(OCS 2) Powell's or Penwyllt Cave, is a long tunnel alongside the A4067 from Abercrave to Penwyllt village. An excavation undertaken here in 1926[1] produced evidence of brown bear, horse and red deer.[2]

[1] M. Davies, 'Powell's Cave, Penwyllt: identification of bones from the excavations of 1926', *S. Wales Caving Club* (forthcoming).
[2] *cf.* G. T. Jefferson, 'Cave Biology in South Wales', pp. 56–69 in *Limestone Caves,* who records this as an invertebrate site (p. 64), where it is suggested cave bear was discovered.

Ystradgynlais (E), Ystradgynlais Hr (C)
SN 81 N.W. (8498 1533)

(OCS 3) The cave entrance to Eglwys Faen is situated about 460 m above O.D. It is but one of several caves believed to form part of a much larger underground system (among the most extensive in Britain).[1] The cave lies beneath the Craig y Ciliau nature reserve and was first noted by Theophilus Jones.[2]

It is unclear whether or not the cave planned by John Ellwood in 1818 at Darren Ciliau,[3] also belonged to this cave formation, though it lay in the same general area. There seems to exist no evidence that Upper Palaeolithic bone tools were found in it associated with antler, as was at one time suggested.[4]

An excavation at Eglwys Faen in 1971 conducted under the direction of M. Davies for the Nature Conservancy Council was undertaken with the object of investigating its potential for preserved early cave stratigraphy and because of a local tradition that the site was known to the Chartists. No finds were made.[5]

[1] O.S. Card SO 21 NW 37; P. L. Smart and C. G. Gardener, 'The Mynydd Llangattwg Cave Systems', pp. 124–51 in *Limestone Caves*; *cf.* Chapman, *loc. cit.* p. 89.
[2] T. Jones, *Hist. Brecks.*, II, ii (1809), p. 493.
[3] Plan of a Cave at Darren-y-kille, Pitt-Rivers Museum, Oxford.
[4] J. B. Campbell, *Upper Palaeolithic Sites in Britain*, vol. 2, (Oxford, 1977), p. 122.
[5] Information from M. Davies, Swansea.

Llangynidr/Llangatwg
SO 11 N.E. (1926 1566) Eglwys Faen
SO 21 N.W. (2051 1530) Ogof Darren Ciliau

Not visited

10 Distribution of Caves and Mesolithic sites

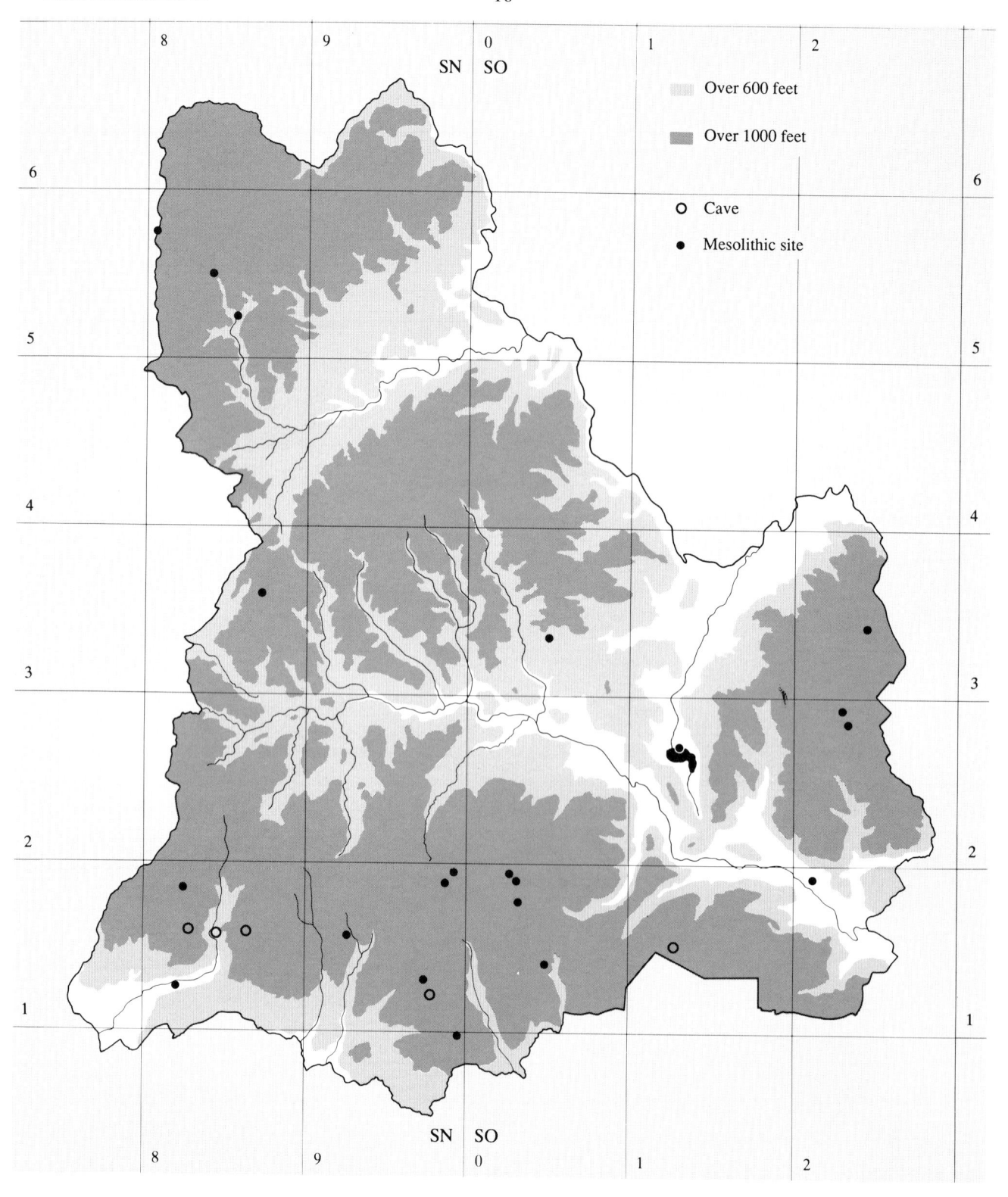

The Upper Palaeolithic and Mesolithic Periods

Introduction

Although 18 Mesolithic sites and findspots are listed, only four assemblages (Waun Fignen Felen (MS 1), Pant Sychpant (MS 7), Bwlc (MS 14), and Gwernvale (MS 15)) have been excavated, and only three of these were dug during the *floruit* of radiocarbon dating. Of the findspot locations listed, several are quite vague, one at least may be inaccurate, and most, if not all, reflect either random or opportunist collection from adventitiously exposed ground. Few were found through systematic fieldwork.

A brief account of the environmental conditions obtaining during post-glacial times has already been outlined (pp. 5–6). The most notable indications of a hunger-gatherer or herder-collector presence prior to the Neolithic are indicated by interferences in the pollen record. Shallow layers of charcoal, or sporadic charcoal fragments found interspersed among forest tree pollen, testify that inroads were being made into the Holocene forest. Some clearances may have been intended to create new settlement areas, whilst others, attested by more widespread burning, are thought to have been used as a management tool in animal and plant control since the Upper Palaeolithic. It is acknowledged that not all clearances were anthropogenic, and only long-term interdisciplinary investigation will help clarify the degree to which some were caused by spontaneous combustion or by lightning. However, so marked and so widespread are pre-Neolithic clearances that it has been proposed pollen analytical evidence might be used to trace sites which have so far remained elusive in archaeological reconnaissance.

The recent suggestion of an Upper Palaeolithic presence in the Usk Valley, within a region recovering from the dramatic effects of the ultimate glaciation, is so far based upon only one diagnostic flint artefact and a handful of less certainly Palaeolithic flints from Gwernvale (MS 15),[1] combined with a reconsideration of the implications of recent pollen analytical investigations. As already noted (p. 5), during this early period, vegetational interference is rare, so, attractive though the suggestion is, until more evidence is forthcoming the idea must be treated with caution.

The possibility that Palaeolithic or Mesolithic cave sites or shelters await discovery amongst the extensive cave systems of the east–west Carboniferous Limestone outcrop passing through Brecknockshire has been noted (p. 9 above), and in this respect lack of a properly authenticated context for the flint core found in Ogof Ffynnon Ddu (RMS 2; PCS 2) is the more frustrating. When considering the potential location of Upper Palaeolithic open settlement sites it is also important to recall Britnell's reminder that more findspots like Gwernvale could be forthcoming from future reconnaissance in similar valley locations.[2] Contemporary and subsequent periglacial conditions, which included permafrost and solifluction, may however have militated against site recognition or even survival.[3]

Although in the main, Mesolithic tool assemblages may only be ascribed to approximate phases, Mesolithic artefact assemblages in Wales are now known to date from at least 9,200 B.P.[4] The most useful dates from the South Wales uplands come from Waun Fignen Felen (MS 2), where radiocarbon determinations are complemented by pollen analytical studies to demonstrate the inroads being made into mixed woodlands during the first six or seven millennia following deglaciation.[5] Preliminary publication of the microliths ascribes them to both Early and Late Mesolithic horizons,[6] thus spanning most of the Holocene until the establishment of farming cultures in the fourth millennium. Without greater detail of the finds, ascription to cultural milieux is, however, difficult, and speculation as to whether these lithic assemblages represent seasonal activity, or derive from the more permanent stations of hunting groups, is not possible.

Jacobi suggested seasonal movement from coastal areas to the South Wales uplands during the later Mesolithic, basing the proposal upon evidence of lithic assemblages at Ogmore-on-Sea (Glamorgan), with complementary upland finds from Craig y Llyn (Glamorgan) and Pant Sychpant (MS 7).[7] Healey and Green elaborated upon the idea, propounding 'bi-polar exploitation' at Gwernvale, activity in which ungulates or bovids would have been herded,[8] perhaps pursued into the headwater valleys of the Usk and Wye.

Jacobi's thesis rests upon the belief that the flint exploited for toolmaking inland must derive from coastal pebble occurrences, which would therefore need to have been carried considerable distances.[9] However, pebble flint is not an uncommon component of the drift in some parts of South Wales, where suitable material is known from extensive deposits, for example, around the Llanfihangel Crucorney moraine, Gwent. Although in common with later stone-using culture groups, Mesolithic populations are likely to have been more dependent upon local materials than has hitherto been considered probable,[10] such dependence in no way negates the possibility or likelihood of contemporary seasonal movement involving either plant or animal exploitation. Indeed, if Mesolithic groups were as mobile as is suggested by the theories of seasonal behaviour so far found acceptable, early communities would have been familiar with such minor occurrences of utilisable lithic material as might easily be overlooked in present-day geological reconnaissance.

[1] E. Healey and H. S. Green, pp. 113–32, in *Gwernvale*, p. 118; the finds are also discussed, and one illustrated by H. S. Green, pp. 70–8, in *Limestone Caves*, Fig. 6.9.

[2] W. J. Britnell, *Gwernvale*, p. 136.

[3] For example, A. E. U. David, 'Late Glacial Archaeological Residues from Wales: A selection', pp. 141–159 in N. Barton, A. J. Roberts and D. A. Roe (eds.), *The Late Glacial in north-west Europe: human adaptation and environmental change at the end of the Pleistocene*, C.B.A. Res. Rep. no. 77, (London: 1991).

[4] A. E. U. David, *The Palaeolithic and Mesolithic Settlement of Wales*, Unpubl. Ph.D. thesis, University of Lancaster.

[5] A. G. Smith and E. W. Cloutman, *Phil. Trans Roy. Soc. Lond.* i, 322 (B) (1988), pp. 158–219 (no. 1209).

[6] P. J. Berridge, *Arch. in Wales* 19 (1979), p. 11; 20 (1980), p. 19; 21 (1981), pp. 20–1.

[7] R. M. Jacobi, pp. 131–206, in *C. and E.P.W.*, pp. 194–5, Fig. 4.33, p. 197.

[8] Healey and Green, *loc. cit.* n. 1.

[9] Jacobi, *loc. cit.* n. 7.

[10] C. S. Briggs, pp. 185–90, in M. Hart and G. de G. Sieveking, (eds.), *Proc. Fourth International Congress on Flint*, Brighton, 1983, (Cambridge: U.P., 1986); see also note requesting information on natural occurrence of flint in Wales, C. S. Briggs, *Arch. in Wales* 24 (1984), pp. 10–11.

Upper Palaeolithic and Mesolithic Sites and Findspots (MS 1–18; RMS 1–3)

This section includes information about locations from which assemblages have been recovered suggestive of temporary or permanent settlement, as well as accounts of stray finds believed to be diagnostically pre-Neolithic.

(MS 1) A Mesolithic chert implement was found in 1968 2 ft (0.6 m) below the surface between two houses at 2 Garth View, Abercrave.

Savory, *Prehist. Brecks.*, II, p. 6; the finder, Mr I. Williams, presented it to the Brecon Museum.

Ystradgynlais (E), Ystradgynlais Hr (C)
SN 81 S.W. (8199 1263)

(MS 2 Plate 2) Waun Fignen Felen is a large boggy peat basin some 1 km in diameter lying on the limestone plateau about 490 m above O.D. In 1979 at several locations around and within it, scatters of Mesolithic flint artefact and waste were observed to be eroding from the peat around a bog, the northern part of which was a post-glacial lake. Excavations and fieldwalking were undertaken subsequently in 1980–82. Random finds have been noted since.

Two main sites were excavated. The first produced a dozen microliths, but these presented no valid stratification as they had been sorted naturally within a waterlain deposit. The second site produced a scatter of 51 flints, including 3 microliths, a scraper and a notched blade. These were associated with a sand mound, a pit and a stone setting, but upon retrospection it was found difficult to be certain whether or not this had been a man-made settlement feature on the one hand, or represented micro-landforms of glacial or post-glacial origin, on the other.

Further discoveries of artefacts included 10 microliths, an abraded elongated pebble associated with a wide scatter of 55 flints, and a tanged and barbed arrowhead (presumably of the Bronze Age).

Of the 40 microliths recovered, 29 (including the 12 from site 1), are scalene triangles which are considered typical of Late Mesolithic industries. The remaining 10 comprise 6 (including 2 obliquely blunted blades from the second site) which were felt more diagnostically to be Early Mesolithic in form.

One test pit excavated a short distance from the lake edge produced a small flint-working floor, upon which the presence of burned flints might have indicated a fireplace. A further test pit, close to the former lake edge, revealed a small flint-working floor which included two obliquely blunted blades and a small perforated shale disc comparable to those from Nab Head, Freshwater East and Star Carr. Environmental sampling established the presence of a post-glacial lake or reed-bed within the area later covered by bog. Charcoal layers detected in bog stratigraphy hinted at specific episodes of human activity during its growth.

This account is drawn from the following sources: *Clwyd-Powys Archaeological Trust: Review of Projects*, 1979; P. J. Berridge, *Arch. in Wales* 19 (1979), p. 11; 20 (1980), p. 19; 21 (1981), pp. 20–1; P. Dorling, *Arch. in Wales* 31 (1991), p. 14; A. G. Smith and E. W. Cloutman, pp. 83–90, in *Quaternary Field Guide*; *Phil. Trans Roy. Soc. Lond.* i, 322 (B) (1988), pp. 158–219 (no. 1209).

Whilst this volume was going through the press, a full account of the industries and palaeoecology of the site appeared in *P.P.S.* 61 (1995), pp. 81–116, by R. N. E. Barton, P. J. Berridge, M. J. C. Walker and R. E. Bevins.

Ystradgynlais (E), Ystradgynlais Lr (C)
SN 81 N.W. (824 184)   vii 88

(MS 3) A Mesolithic flint blade was found on Bwlch y Groes, Mynydd Epynt, 450 m above O.D.

Savory, *op. cit. supra* MS 1 p. 6; O.S. Card SN 83 NE 11; presented to Brecknock Museum by Mr Brychan Davies.

Llandeilo'r Fan
SN 83 N.E. (871 360)

(MS 4) A collection of flints, mostly spalls and fragments, the only distinctive forms being a crude thumb-scraper and three cores, were found at Nant-y-Stalwen, 350 m above O.D. Their presence may signify a Mesolithic or later settlement site.

W. F. Grimes, *Prehist. Wales*, p. 161, no. 244 (N.M.W. Cardiff, 1951); bequeathed to the National Museum of Wales by Evan Jones (N.M.W. Acc. no. 33.72.3); O.S. Card SN 85 NW 4.

Llanddewi Abergwesyn
SN 85 N.W. (805 575)

(MS 5) A perforated pebble macehead, believed to be of Mesolithic type, was found at Abergwesyn.

D. J. Davies, *Brycheiniog* 15 (1971), p. 10; O.S. Card SN 85 NW 5.

Llanfihangel Abergwesyn
SN 85 N.W. (840 550)

(MS 6) On Pentwyn farm, in a field known as Dol y Maen (now Cae Dol Maen Isaf) 260–275 m above O.D., on the valley floor of the River Irfon, a 'flint manufactory' was found in 1923.[1] It produced waste chips and flakes, faceted cores, scrapers and arrowheads. The only distinctive piece is a core and fragmentary small leaf-shaped point.[2] This may have been a Mesolithic or Neolithic settlement site, though there remains a possibility that much or most of the flint-knapping was undertaken to make strike-a-lights during the historic period in a house which formerly stood on the field.

[1] O.S. Card SN 85 SE 4; E. Jones, *Arch. Camb.* 78 (1923), p. 155.
[2] Grimes, *Prehist. Wales*, p. 161.

Llanfihangel Abergwesyn
SN 85 S.E. (85 52)

(MS 7) After preparations for planting by the Forestry Commission to the W. of a cairn on Pant Sychpant (RC 74), 330 m above O.D., an excavation was undertaken to recover lithic material, indications of which had been thrown up by the plough.[1] A great density of flints was found a few metres W. of the cairn. This was a rescue operation in which plough furrows were searched and a network of small squares was excavated. Although the topography of the site, a knoll, would have been suited to a settlement, the exploration produced no structures, but there was a good scatter of several cores, over 1,000 waste flakes, some pottery sherds and concentrations of some worked pieces in two main locations. Products, fashioned from several different varieties of poor-quality flint, were found beneath a peat layer which soil analysis confidently regarded as post-Neolithic.[2] The collection included 18 microliths, an assemblage which comprised seven backed blades (including a scalene triangle), six points and three rods. There were also thirty round scrapers, six arrowheads (three leaf-shaped, three barbed and tanged), a plano-convex knife and a javelin point, which suggest overall cultural affinities ranging from the Mesolithic to Bronze Age.

At the time, attention was drawn[3] to what were considered 'Sauveterrian affinities' of the Mesolithic material, but in view of its lack of stratigraphic context it is difficult to offer a more culturally diagnostic interpretation.

[1] O.S. Card SN 91 NE; T. W. Burke, *B.B.C.S.* 19 (1961), pp. 165–6; 22 (1966), pp. 78–87.
[2] B. Seddon, pp. 84–6, in Burke, *loc. cit.* n. 1.
[3] J. M. Lewis, *loc. cit.* n. 1, pp. 83–4; the finds were presented to the N.M.W.

Penderyn
SN 90 N.E. (994 098)

(MS 8) A microlith, flakes of flint and dark grey chert (some fire-cracked) were found in a freshly-cut forestry fire-break 'about 500 yds. E. of Maen Madoc Ystradfellte'. The area covered by the grid-reference and the direction indicated is not afforested and lies about 390 m above O.D. However, it seems probable that the site would have lain to the N. of the reference provided, the closest likely point being SN 921 157. Had it been as far E. as suggested, the site would have had to be much further N., around SN 924 160.

H. N. Savory, *in. lit.* 22 xii 1975; N.M.W. acc. no. 72.15N.

Ystradfellte
SN 91 N.W. (925 157)

(MS 9) During maintenance work in the Beacons Reservoir at a height of about 396 m above O.D., a petit tranchet derivative arrowhead of heavily calcined flint was found by Mr K. Palmer of Llanfihangel Crucorney (Gwent), in 1986.

C. S. Briggs, *Arch. in Wales* 26 (1986), pp. 60–1; p. 61, no. 10; the find is in private possession.

Cantref
SN 91 N.E. (9865 1889)

(MS 10) Numerous flints and one chert artefact were collected by several fieldworkers in 1976[1] from four or more areas of erosion temporarily exposed by drought conditions at the Upper Neuadd Reservoir between 450 and 460 m above O.D. Finds included waste flakes, arrowheads (some probably post-Mesolithic), blades, cores, knives, two or more microliths, long spalls and scrapers.[2]

(MS 10 i) Close to the point where the Blaen Taf Fechan enters the reservoir was a site producing considerable waste and one diagnostically late Mesolithic microlith.[3]

(MS 10 ii) To the S.E. of the island, and within about 40 m of one of the cairns in the reservoir (RC 205), was an exposure yielding one oblique arrowhead and chisel arrowhead fragment, numerous waste flakes and another late Mesolithic microlith.

(MS 10 iii) Only one artefact was recovered from this site, close to the E. shoreline. It was described as a double-ended scraper.

(MS 10 iv) The third major concentration of finds was along a traverse about 100 m long below the S.E. shoreline. This produced several scrapers, spalls and numerous flakes, but no diagnostically Mesolithic material. There was a polished flint fragment, possibly broken from an axe, though whether Mesolithic or Neolithic is uncertain.

Some of the finds were dispersed soon after recovery. Few are available for study. However, a number were temporarily loaned to the National Museum. As no further discoveries were made in an intensive search while surveying the nearby cairns during the drought of 1989, it can be assumed that the earlier collecting was quite exhaustive.

[1] The Commission is particularly grateful to Mr and Mrs G. Bird of Aberdare, who first drew attention to this discovery. Staff at the National Museum of Wales should also be thanked for help in making available further information (including preliminary lists of unpublished finds, together with grid references) in advance of more definitive publication.

[2] Information from Mrs Bird and N.M.W. staff; see also: A. Robertson, 'Prehistory', pp. 143–160, in Merthyr Teachers' Centre Group (eds.), *Merthyr Tydfil: A Valley Community*, (Cowbridge, 1981), p. 147; *Taf* 2, Fig. 51, p. 88.

[3] Identifications of the assemblage are by Dr H. S. Green and Ms Yolanda Stanton, N.M.W.

Cantref
SO 01 N.W. (MS 10 i) (0265 1938); (MS 10 ii) (0292 1910); (MS 10 iii) (0300 1915); (MS 10 iv) (between 0305 1905 and 0305 1892)   ix 89

(MS 11) Flint flakes were discovered after deep ploughing on forestry land in the valley to S. of the Upper Neuadd Reservoir by Mr B. O'Hanlon in 1974. The flakes are miniscule and derived from a grey podsol horizon beneath the peat. There was also modern pottery and coal ash in the vicinity which may have been associated with a workers' shanty.

Arch. in Wales 14 (1974), p. 7.

Llanfrynach
SO 01 N.W. (0315 1780)   ii 75

(MS 12) A chipping site is reported by H. N. Savory which was discovered by T. W. Burke during the 1960s. It produced a scalene microlith and a core, in an area between Ty'n Coed and the Trawsnant, Blaencar.

Savory, *Prehist. Brecks.*, II, p. 5.

Llanddeti
SO 01 S.E. (048 141)

(MS 13) Blades and scrapers are recorded from Dan yr Eglwys 280 m above O.D.

Mesolithic Gazetteer, p. 18; these are in the D. P. Webley Collection.

Garthbrengi
SO 03 S.W. (049 335)

(MS 14) During excavations at Ynys Bwlc (pp 281–3) a number of Mesolithic flints have been discovered.

Information from Dr M. Redknap, N.M.W.

Llan-gors
SO 12 N.W. (1289 2690)   19 ix 91

(MS 15) A large assemblage of lithic artefactual debris and finished tools was found during excavation of the Neolithic chambered tomb at Gwernvale (CT 11). This included finds considered to represent Upper Palaeolithic cultures as well as diagnostically Mesolithic material.

A close examination of the flint cores suggested them to be 'highly specialised blade cores . . . characteristic of Mesolithic industries'. Core rejuvenation flakes of similar cultural or functional affinities were also recognised.[1]

Seven backed burned flint tools, mainly of indiscernible type, were believed to be of late Palaeolithic origin.[2] Only one, of chalcedonic chert, was capable of more diagnostic classification, though flakes, blades and spalls were considered of possibly the same age.[3]

From pre-cairn soil levels at the E. end of the cairn, and in contexts suggesting the contamination of some Neolithic features, 56 microliths and microlith fragments were recovered. Of these, 23 were broad-backed and characteristic of early Mesolithic industries, 25 were either scalene micro-triangles or were rod-like backed blades characteristic of the later Mesolithic, and the remaining 11 fragments were unclassifiable.

There were 10 microburins, mainly from pre-cairn contexts; 5 poorly stratified notched blades; 23 burins, mostly from pre-cairn unstratified or Neolithic pit contexts; and 10 truncated blades (which need not have been exclusively Mesolithic).[4]

Gwernvale has been claimed the first late Upper Palaeolithic open site to be found in Wales (c. 10,000–8,000 B.C.), and upon the evidence of these few artefacts, an economic model for contemporary pastoral and hunting practices involving bipolar settlement patterns has been advanced.[5]

Analysis of the microlithic component from the site suggests the presence of both early (c. 8,000–6,500 B.C.) and later Mesolithic (c. 6,500–3,500 B.C.) at Gwernvale, and the site was forwarded as a temporary camp for the exploitation of ungulates. Unfortunately there was only one radiocarbon date (of c. 4945 b.c.) for pre-cairn activity, and this was not considered relevant to Mesolithic exploitation.[6]

Perhaps the most important conclusion was Britnell's, pertinently drawing attention to the random nature of discovery through excavation of a feature of later date, and the possibility or likelihood that numerous other comparable lithic assemblages may have survived in similar topographical locations elsewhere in this, if not in other, mid- or South Wales valleys.[7]

[1] E. Healey and H. S. Green, pp. 113–32 in *Gwernvale*, p. 118; the finds are also discussed, and one is illustrated by H. S. Green in *Limestone Caves*, Fig. 6.9.
[2] Healey and Green, *loc. cit.* n. 1, p. 120.
[3] *idem*, p. 121.
[4] *idem*, pp. 122–3.
[5] *idem*, p. 129; W. J. Britnell, *Gwernvale*, p. 136.
[6] Healey and Green, *idem*, p. 130; Britnell, *loc. cit.* n. 5.
[7] Britnell, *idem*.

Crickhowell
SO 21 N.W. (211 192)

(MS 16) A tranchet axe sharpening flake, blades and scrapers, an axe and microlith were found between Pen y Gader Fawr and Waun Fach at a height of about 760 m above O.D. in the Black Mountains on sandy grit where the peat cover was exposed.

Mesolithic Gazetteer, p. 18; now in the David Reeves Collection.

Llaneleu
SO 22 N.W. (228 293)

(MS 17) About 300 m S.E. of the summit of Y Gader, some 760 m above O.D.,[1] an implement described as 'adze of Wiltshire chert' was found under peat containing birch and oak. This may be a Neolithic implement, as has been suggested,[2] but seems more likely a Mesolithic flake axe, the findspot of which is remarkably close to the preceding.

[1] O.S. Card SO 22 NW 1.
[2] Wheeler, *P. and R. Wales*, pp. 58–9; Grimes, *Prehist. Wales*, p. 148; no petrographic evidence for this identification has been presented.

Talgarth/Llaneleu (E), Llanbedr Ystrad Wy/Llaneleu
SO 22 N.W. (230 287)

(MS 18) A Mesolithic graver was found by C. J. Dunn at Glynfach, Gospel Pass, in the Black Mountains.

Mesolithic Gazetteer, p. 18; now in N.M.W. ex-C. J. Dunn.

Llanigan (E), Glyn fach (C)
SO 23 S.W. (243 342)

Rejected Mesolithic Finds

(RMS 1) A punch-struck blade from the (presumed) Bronze Age cairn of Garn Goch (RC 16) was described as 'possibly of Mesolithic date'. However, its mode of removal from the parent core was not felt to warrant such a date on the basis of a single flake, since struck flakes might also be produced by percussion.

H. S. Green, in P. Dorling and F. M. Chambers, *B.B.C.S.* 37 (1990), pp. 215–246.

Ystradgynlais (E), Ystradgynlais Lr (C)
SN 81 S.W. (8178 1077)

(RMS 2) A large Mesolithic core of grey flint is recorded[1] from Ogof Ffynnon Ddu (PCS 2). Although Savory believed it had probably fallen in through a fissure, doubt has now been cast upon the context of the find.[2]

[1] Savory, *Prehist. Brecks.*, II, pp. 6, 16; this is now in the N.M.W. (Acc. No. 70.36H/1); O.S. Card SN 81 NE 12.
[2] by M. Davies, Swansea, *in lit.* 22nd July 1991.

Glyntawe
SN 81 N.E. (835 189)   Not visited

(RMS 3) Worked flake, possibly a petit-tranchet derivative arrowhead, found on the path below Corn Du (RC 225). This is not certainly Mesolithic.

K. Palmer, *Arch. in Wales* 18 (1978), p. 31, no. 7.

Llansbyddyd (E), Modrydd (C)
SO 02 S.W. (000 205)

Neolithic Settlement and Burial

Neolithic Settlement Sites

Although much Neolithic settlement debris is known from chambered tomb excavations in south Powys, only two sites have so far produced habitation structures. Excavations close to and actually within a stone clearance cairn on Cefn Cilnsanws (US 90) revealed 46 stake-holes in a roughly rectangular plan. Finds included flint and chert artefacts (including flint arrowheads), hazel-nut shells and sherds of at least three Neolithic pottery vessels. Internal divisions were recognised within the feature and fragments of ash (*Fraxinus*) charcoal could have been utilised as withies within this flimsy wooden structure.[1]

A second Neolithic wooden structure lay beneath the megalithic tomb at Gwernvale[2] (Fig. 46) which, it is assumed, though there is no certainty, was also domestic in origin. Its general horizon was radiocarbon dated to *c*. 3,100 B.C., though this single date came from a pit outside the house structure and was not certainly associated with it. Evidence for occupation comprised flintwork and lithic waste, quern fragments, potsherds and charred organic remains, including cereal grains. The pattern of post-holes and footing trenches indicates either the presence of a substantial rectilinear timber building, or possibly of two structures, the later one associated with the cairn's funereal role. Its excavator thought the latter interpretation more likely. The Gwernvale 'house' was compared to similar examples in Ireland, at Ballyglass and Ballynagilly, and closer to hand at Llandegai, Fussell's Lodge and Wayland's Smithy.

Fragments of a round-bottomed bowl, thought to be Neolithic, were found within what may have been a pit, sealed beneath the later rampart, during excavation of the Iron Age hillfort in Gwernyfed Park.[3] These sherds, with several others from beneath a clearance cairn (US 90 i) (of which there are many), and long barrows, of which there are few, help emphasise the importance of examining land surfaces sealed beneath upstanding earthwork monuments. The discovery of a small decomposed Neolithic potsherd about 2.5 cm across in the mouth of a rock shelter on plateau land in the Onllwyn area may signal the presence of other contemporary settlements on this part of Pant Sychpant.[4]

Lithic implements of the period occur throughout the county. These include axes of igneous and volcanic rocks and of flint, together with numerous flint and some chert tools and unworked flakes (Map Fig. 12). The distribution of these artefacts indicates the presence of early farming communities in diverse topographical locations during the Neolithic.

However, the clearest evidence for widespread adoption of farming practices in Brecknockshire at this period comes from pollen analytical work upon both peat profiles and through cuttings excavated into chambered tombs and other sites. Palynological and pedological studies at some sites have shed considerable light upon the environments in which the monuments were constructed (see p. 6 for discussion).

History of Tomb Study and Excavation

Whereas Tŷ Illtud (CT 1) may have been described by John Aubrey (see below, p. 31), the earliest certain field accounts of Brecknockshire megalithic tombs come from Edward Lhuyd's manuscripts. Apart from an account of the same tomb copied from Lhuyd into Stowe MS 1023–4, the most valuable contemporary survey record is that of Bryn y groes (CT 7), which survives from an original fieldwork notebook. Only Tŷ Illtud was mentioned by Lhuyd in his contribution to Bishop Edmund Gibson's first re-

11 Conjectural Reconstruction of Hazleton Long Barrow (by courtesy of Cheltenham Museums)

editing of Camden's *Britannia*, and not until the later eighteenth century, when early tourists explored the Usk Valley, did Gwernvale first enter the topographical literature.

Investigations at Gwernvale, both antiquarian and recent, provided remarkable records, which were milestones in Welsh megalith studies. Straddling the main tourist route into mid-Wales, the site was noted by Pennant,[5] the Rev. Evan Evans,[6] Colt Hoare[7] and George Manby.[8] It was later noticed in the *County History* and by the Rev. Henry Thomas Payne.

The excavation campaign of 1804 can be reconstructed to a greater degree from MS sources. This early 'dig' resulted from a meeting between Sir Richard Colt Hoare and *inter alia* Theophilus Jones and Henry Thomas Payne, at Llanbedr in late May 1804. Detail taken from the four surviving accounts showed the site to have possessed drystone walling between the orthostats, and it brought to light charcoal and bones. Gwernvale seems to have been the first long barrow excavation by Colt Hoare, and it remains the best documented megalith excavation in Wales before *c*. 1850.[9] Interestingly, the excavators did not entirely concur upon the resolution of the question they had originally posed: was the site sepulchral or altaral? How far it may still properly be claimed that 'in digging Gwernvale, Colt Hoare was to implant the seed from which grew scientific excavation in Wales'[10] remains an open question.

Gwernvale apart, no long barrows of the Black Mountain group appear to have been excavated during the nineteenth century, though it should be noted that artefacts were collected in the mid-century discovery of Carn Goch (CT 10), and it is possible that one of the Ffostyll sites yielded a Beaker burial (LB 9) during stone-quarrying.

Between the two World Wars excavations were undertaken at Tŷ Isaf (CT 3), Ffostyll (CT 5 and CT 6), Pipton (CT 8), Little Lodge (CT 9) and Penywrlod Llanigon (CT 12). The quality of record surviving from some of these explorations was not always adequate by the standards of the day. During the past 50 years major excavations were undertaken at Mynydd Troed (CT 2), Pipton (CT 8), Pen y wrlod Talgarth (CT 4) and Gwernvale (CT 11).

NEOLITHIC SITES AND MEGALITHIC TOMBS

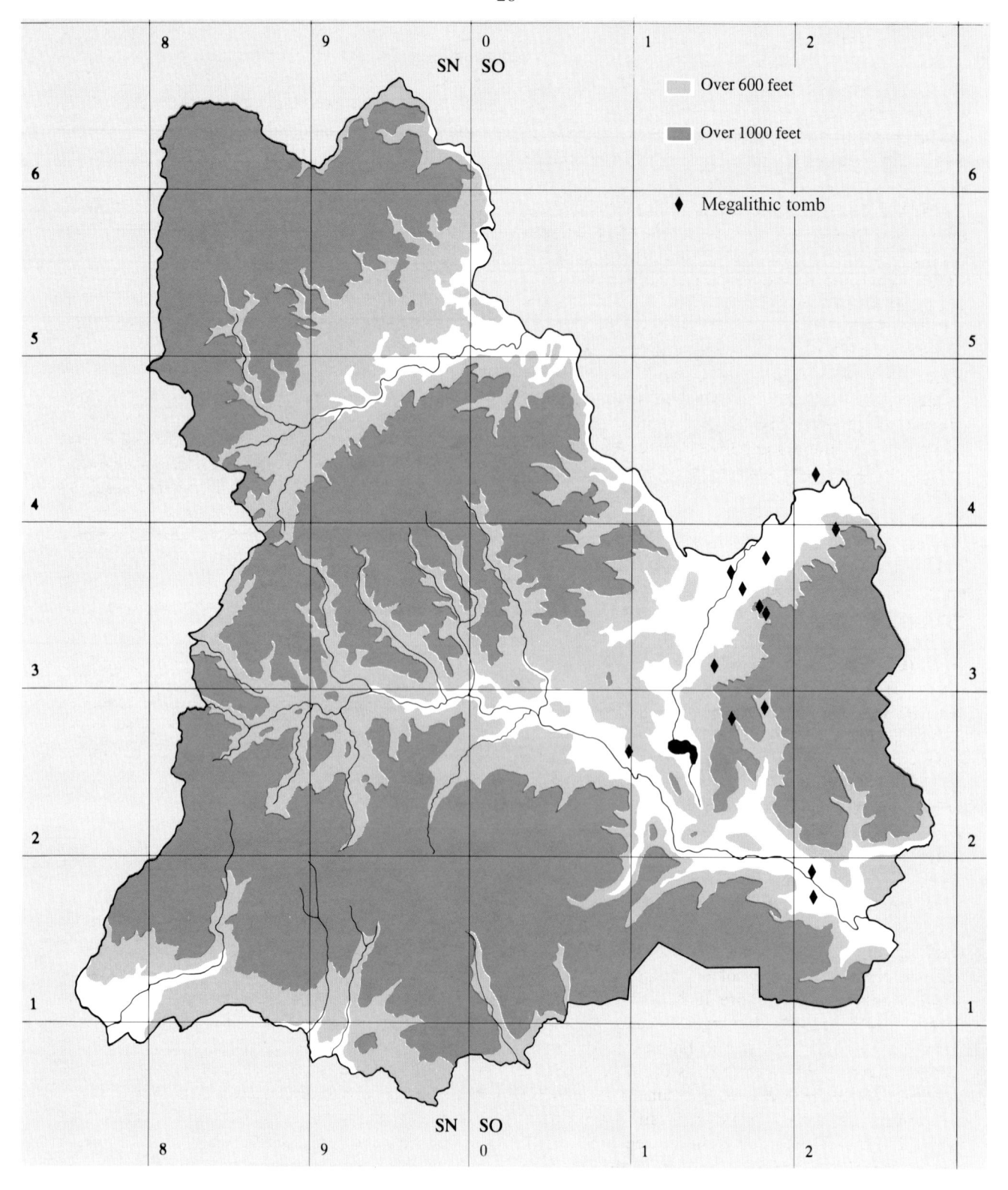

12 Distribution of Neolithic chambered tombs

Distribution

The Brecknockshire tombs form a relatively compact and isolated group,[11] with virtually all the sites lying on the north-western slopes of the Black Mountains, within a 10-mile radius of Tŷ Isaf. Whilst not strictly speaking relevant to this account, the three cairns of the Herefordshire Golden Valley are integral to the group. And though it is difficult to ascribe a definite Neolithic origin to the Newchurch site (SO 2052 4910), a more certain Radnorshire tomb is now known at Clyro Court Farm (CT 13), which lies only 15 km N.E. from Tŷ Isaf.

How far this present distribution represents a true original settlement density, or alternatively is more a reflection of environmental factors, is difficult to determine. However, the locations and condition of surviving monuments are best considered through environmental history, an appreciation of continuing agricultural practice, and in the light of the lithology of their architectural components.

A majority of the tombs in this group occupied valley bottoms or river terraces, but some are sited upon land which is topographically undistinguished: Pen y wrlod Talgarth (CT 4), the Ffostylls (CT 5 and 6), Bryn y groes (CT 7), Little Lodge (CT 9), Carn Goch (CT 10), Gwernvale (CT 11) and Court Farm Clyro (CT 13). The position of Mynydd Troed (CT 2) is montane, whilst Tŷ Illtud (CT 1), Tŷ Isaf (CT 3), Pipton (CT 8) and Penywrlod Llanigon (CT 12) occupy more prominent or plateau positions. In detail there is wide diversity of location, which would seem to indicate that no particular position was favoured. This contrasts with Cotswold tombs further east, which have been more definitely noted to lie along the upper limits of modern agriculture.[12]

All the Brecknock tombs lie upon the Old Red Sandstone (or, in the case of Gwernvale and Carn Goch, on alluvial sands and gravels).[13] The Devonian bedrock presents a variety of lithology ranging from durable compacted to more fissile varieties. It is generally well bedded, cleaving into large flagstones, smaller flags and thin, fissile laminates variously coloured dark brown through hues of red and yellow and green.[14] The effects upon monument survival of tomb-building with the more fissile stones are probably greater than has hitherto been imagined. Tomb survival rates are likely to relate to the degree to which easily cleaved rocks suffer long-term exposure. Covered in earth, or an overburden of fragmented fieldstone, chambers remain well protected from the elements. Once exposed, some slabs easily disintegrate. Whilst exposed between 1973 and 1992, the stonework of the Pen y wrlod Talgarth tomb (CT 4) deteriorated considerably, resulting in the need for much remedial work. Combined natural and human destructive agents could thus account for the disappearance of an unknown number of similar sites.

Webley studied ten Black Mountain tombs in relation to soils,[15] deriving soil samples from fields or exposures close to the tombs and carrying out a mechanical analysis of their matrices. Three main soil groups emerged from the analyses. Eight were of glacial drift, six were of silty sands, and two comprised quantities of both sand and silt. As might have been expected, the sandy soil is believed to result from the breakdown of the local country rock. These results convinced the analyst that the clay layer earlier noted beneath Pipton (CT 8) and Tŷ Isaf (CT 3) cairns was in both cases an artificial feature.[16] The higher fractions of sand in samples from Ty Illtud and Little Lodge were explained in terms of their topographies.[17] It was noted that Neolithic tombs did not appear to occupy any clay soils. Reaching more general conclusions about the nature of vegetation and climate upon the basis of such an analysis is probably to press the evidence beyond its useful limits.[18] Suggestions that the Neolithic tomb-builders found the area covered in stunted heathy scrub or sessile oak forest[19] must therefore be treated with circumspection and should be compared with the more detailed evidence for vegetational change presented above (p. 6).

Severn-Cotswold Tombs

The term 'Cotswold-Severn' was first coined by Daniel in 1937.[20] It was meant to encompass those chambered tombs lying in central southern and parts of western England, together with south-east Wales. Although analysis of Cotswold-Severn tomb morphology has a long history with diverse opinion as to origins and development, there is general agreement upon grouping into three main tomb sub-types: those with simple box-like terminal chambers; sites possessing transepted terminal chambers (or transepted gallery graves); and tombs in which multiple chambers, occasionally transepted, were entered from the side of the mound (laterally chambered graves). Whether or not these form an evolutionary or devolutionary sequence from the more simple to the complex or vice versa still remains an open question.[21] Origins for the more complex trapezoid cairns have been sought in Brittany (where similar transepted chambers are known) with proposed migrant entry through the Severn estuary and subsequent spread into South Wales, on the one hand, and the Cotswolds, on the other. This theory foundered with the advent of radiocarbon dating, which demonstrated it was unsustainable.

The Typology of the Black Mountains Group of Cotswold-Severn Tombs

In local terms, it is generally considered that the Black Mountains Group comprises tombs with greater structural diversity than that of the South Wales Coastal Group.[22] The task of relating this local group to the wider family of south-west British tombs is hampered by the fragmentary nature of the surviving, planned sites, and the limitation of early investigators' accounts. Partial, upstanding remains, like those which existed at Gwernvale prior to its excavation in 1977, may not be reliable indicators upon which to base judgements on what lies beneath. Similarly, it should be argued that if some cairns had been built in several phases, later features may mask re-structuring unlikely to be detected without detailed excavation.

The most complex of the Black Mountains tombs are Tŷ Isaf (CT 3), Pen y wrlod Talgarth (CT 4), Pipton (CT 8) and Gwernvale. All have blind entrances and one or more lateral chambers, three of which appear transepted, Pen y wrlod Talgarth being the exception. Apart from the uncertainty of type for the main chamber at Pen y wrlod Talgarth, and of the fourth chamber on the west end of Gwernvale, all four tombs appear to exhibit traits derived from both transepted and laterally-chambered traditions. The reconstructed layout of Croesllechau (CT 7; Fig. 33) might also be taken to indicate a tomb with lateral chambers (north and south), as well as with a simple eastern terminal chamber and a possibly transepted passage on the west. All five sites may reasonably be classified as hybrids to the general classification.[23] These laterally-chambered tombs are considered more characteristic of Brecknock and Gloucestershire.[24]

Although in plan the rotunda at Tŷ Isaf has every appearance of having been an earlier and independent site,[25] its excavator believed the entire long barrow belonged to a single original architectural plan.[26] Ffostyll South (CT 5) possesses a rectangular chamber set terminally in a long cairn and one or more simple chambers are recorded from Mynydd Troed (CT 2). Ffostyll North (CT 6), Little Lodge (CT 9) and Penywrlod Llanigon (CT 12). Carn Goch (CT 10) also appears to surround a fairly simple chamber, but there must remain some question as to whether or not this might be a rare example of a large Bronze Age cist in which bones had been unusually saved from acidic conditions by the presence of such a large capstone.

Corcoran suggested that both single chamber elements at Penywrlod Llanigon and Mynydd Troed may have comprised individual elements in the development of multi-period sites.[27] Absence of detailed excavation evidence from Ffostyll South makes it difficult to assess the value of Corcoran's suggestion that its central chamber may also have been built in a multi-period mound.

Artefacts from the Black Mountains Group

The artefacts recovered from excavations are described in each entry, and summary accounts of both artefacts and bones are presented by Britnell.[28] Prehistoric artefacts are recorded from Tŷ Isaf (CT 3), Pen y wrlod Talgarth (CT 4), the Ffostylls (CT 5 and 6), Pipton (CT 8), Gwernvale (CT 11) and Penywrlod Llanigon (CT 12). Human bones, now lost, were disinterred from Carn Goch (CT 10), and Vulliamy eviscerated both human and animal bones from Little Lodge (CT 9), also now partly lost.

Tŷ Isaf (CT 3) and Ffostyll South (CT 5) produced two or three sherds of undiagnostic dark-brown, burnished Neolithic pottery, the former described by Lynch as 'clinker-like'.[29] Several sites produced what have been assumed to be secondary burials (p. 133; BB 22–4, 28). Most of the excavated sites yielded some flint flakes as well as lithic material (pp. 290–5; SF 17, 20, 23, 88).

Most of the finds seem to indicate domestic occupation close to, or even upon, some tomb sites. The only finds which hint at non-domestic activity are the bead, bone pin and stone disc from Tŷ Isaf, and a small bone music pipe from Pen y wrlod Talgarth (CT 4).

Funerary Practice

One current theory of Neolithic burial suggests that bones were circulated as part of a funerary practice based upon social controls over fertility and vitality, or even over the natural environment. Thomas[30] believes that removal of bones from chambers was part of the normal use of laterally-chambered mounds. The theory was felt to be supported by the evidence of lateral chambers which are found basically devoid of large bone deposits. The examples of Tŷ Isaf (CT 3) Chamber 4, Pipton (CT 8) Chamber 1, and Gwernvale (CT 11) Chamber 3 were considered pertinent to this argument. However, in common with the other two sites, Gwernvale Chamber 3, thought by the excavator to have been entered and sealed on numerous occasions,[31] could have been robbed of bones at almost any time and might equally have lost them through natural or human agencies. In fact, a serious objection to this argument is the likely disappearance of bone through poor soil conditions. Records of bone scraps from several tombs cited by Thomas might be all that survived after natural attrition. These could equally be used in support of more negative argument. Organic deposits in lateral chambers, by their very locations on the edge of a monument, are more likely to suffer water percolation damage than are bones sealed beneath capped, more centrally-situated chambers, where overburden positively acts as interment protection. It might be argued that bones are unlikely to survive unless so protected.

Analysis of finds from some laterally-chambered sites shows that bones were piled against the side walls of Chamber 2 at Pen y wrlod Talgarth (CT 4), with skulls against the north wall,[32] the latter feature also being noted at Tŷ Isaf (CT 3). The positioning of disarticulated skeletal material well into the chambers at Tŷ Isaf could demonstrate the difficulty of moving entire bodies between chambers.[33]

At Pen y wrlod Talgarth, there is evidence of blocked chamber entrances, even though the outer cairn wall is thought to have been visible throughout the functional life of the tomb. Entry could thus be gained only by removing revetment wall stone courses.[34] It has long been accepted that chambers were covered in cairn mass[35] and one of the most important outstanding questions has to be: at what point was a tomb finally sealed? Or was it necessary to re-locate or on occasion even re-excavate chambers for renewed interment?

Associated with this problem is that of extra-revetment material, since piled outer stonework was for long considered to have been deliberately placed. At Gwernvale it was felt that extra-revetment was built against revetment walls coevally with sealing the tomb purposely to produce 'the "instant" . . . archaic form '. . . – a tomb which had clearly ceased to be used for formal mortuary activities'.[36]

It is felt possible that forecourt deposits such as hearths and pits (cf. Pen y wrlod, CT 4) may be indications of feasting in celebration of the dead, and it has been suggested that such feasting coincided with removal or deposition of bones.[37] Recent interpretations of Neolithic tombs tend to emphasise their roles in social or political structuring within contemporary culture groups.[38]

Chronology of the Black Mountains Group

Despite the shortcomings of radiocarbon dating bones (which might represent long interment periods), the earliest radiocarbon dates from those more recently-excavated tombs place laterally-chambered monuments in the later fourth millennium B.C., that is, fairly early in the Cotswold-Severn tradition. Among these are Gwernvale (CAR-113) 3020 +/– 80 b.c. and Pen y wrlod (HAR-674) 3020 +/– ?80 b.c. as well as seven dates from Hazleton North.[39]

Neolithic Economy

It is only possible to speculate that a tomb-building society was supported by a mixed farming economy, since the excavated evidence is so meagre. It has been suggested[40] that the complementary rather than exclusive nature of the distribution of Mesolithic material and megalithic tombs in Wales generally may imply either severe competition between late hunter-gatherer groups and alien incoming agriculturalists, or alternatively an indigenous development from one economic system to another. However, this suggestion may be of limited value, since in recent years Mesolithic artefacts have been recognised at more low-lying valley sites, including excavated contexts both at Gwernvale and Bwlc Crannog. Owing to poor survival rates in bone assemblages on locally acidic soils, it is likely that the most useful future progress in economic studies of tomb-using will result from pollen analytical study.

[1] D. P. Webley, 'A "Cairn Cemetery" and Secondary Neolithic Dwelling on Cefn Cilnsanws, Vaynor (Brecks.)', *B.B.C.S*, 18 (1958), pp. 79–88; for an up-to-date discussion of Neolithic houses, see T. Darvill and J. Thomas (eds), *Neolithic Houses in North-West Europe and Beyond*, Neolithic Studies Group Seminar Papers (1), (Oxford: Oxbow, 1996).

[2] Britnell, *Gwernvale*, pp. 51–5, 138–42.

[3] H. N. Savory, *Brycheiniog* 4 (1958), pp. 66–7; *Inv. Br.* I (ii), HF58, pp. 111–12.

[4] D. P. Webley, *B.B.C.S.*, 16 (1956), pp. 298–299; the site is located at about SN 999 091 (O.S. Card SN 90 NE 1).

[5] Annotated version of H. P. Wyndham, *A Gentleman's Tour through Monmouthshire and Wales*, 1774, N.L.W. MS 25898, fo. 198a.

[6] N.L.W. MS 20498, fo. 44.

[7] Cardiff Public Libraries MS 4.302, fo. 5; 3.127 3/6, fo. 11.

[8] G. M. Manby, *An Historic and Picturesque Guide from Clifton through the Counties of Monmouth, Glamorgan and Brecknock*, (Bristol, 1802), p. 207.

[9] C. S. Briggs in *Gwernvale*, pp. 45–8; for Payne's description of the site before excavation see N.L.W. MS 4378, p. 169, (1787); his account of the excavation is in Payne MSS., Brecks. Mus.

[10] *Gwernvale*, p. 47.

[11] *idem.*, p. 3.

[12] A. Marshall, 'Neolithic and Bronze Age settlement in the northern Cotswolds', *Trans Bristol Glouc. Archaeol. Soc.* 103 (1985), pp. 23–54; J. Thomas, *Man* 23 (1988), p. 545.

[13] D. P. Webley, 'The Neolithic colonisation of the Breconshire Black Mountains', *B.B.C.S.*, 18 (1959), pp. 290–4; p. 291.

[14] J. R. L. Allen, 'The Devonian Rocks of Wales and the Welsh Borderland', pp. 47–84, in T. R. Owen (ed.), *The Upper Palaeozoic and Post-Palaeozoic Rocks of Wales*, (Cardiff: U.P., 1974).

[15] Webley, *op. cit.*, n. 13, p. 291; the sample includes Arthur's Stone, Herefords.

[16] *idem.*, p. 293; see tables p. 292.

[17] *idem.*

[18] *cf.* Webley, *loc. cit.* n. 13, pp. 293–4.

[19] *idem.*

[20] G. E. Daniel, 'The chambered long barrow at Parc Le Breos Cwm', *P.P.S.*, 3 (1937), pp. 71–86.

[21] J. X. W. P. Corcoran, pp. 13–106, in *Meg. Enq.* 'The Severn-Cotswold Group: 1. Distribution, Morphology, and Artifacts', p. 14; *Gwernvale*, p. 4.

[22] Corcoran in *Meg. Enq.*, p. 22.

[23] see *Meg. Enq.*, p. 23 for Pipton and Tŷ Isaf; *cf. Gwernvale*, p. 4.

[24] H. N. Savory, 'The personality of the Southern Marches of Wales in the Neolithic and Early Bronze Age', pp. 25–52 in *Cult. and Env.*; pp. 30–1; Fig. 7.

[25] *Meg. Enq.*, pp. 63–5.

[26] Grimes, *M.M.W.*

[27] *Meg. Enq.*, pp. 43–4.

[28] *Gwernvale*, pp. 5–6.

[29] F. M. Lynch, 'The Contents of Excavated Tombs in North Wales', pp. 149–174, in *Meg. Enq.*, p. 171.

[30] J. Thomas, *loc. cit.* n. 12, pp. 545–6.

[31] Britnell in *Gwernvale*, p. 80.

[32] *idem.*, p. 19.

[33] Thomas, *loc. cit.* n. 12, p. 543.

[34] Britnell in *Gwernvale*, p. 32.

[35] *cf. idem.*, p. 143.

[36] Britnell, *idem.*, p. 150.

[37] Thomas, *loc. cit.* n. 12, p. 550.

[38] For example, Darvill (*C.T.* pp. 81, ff.) suggests the tombs to have been 'information processing nodes' within a segmentary hierarchy of social groups. Notions such as this owe much to Renfrew's ideas of 1976 'Megaliths, Territories and Population', pp. 198–220, in S. de Laet, (ed.), *Acculturation and continuity in Atlantic Europe*, (Bruges: de Tempel, 1976).

[39] W. J. Britnell, 'Radiocarbon dates from the Gwernvale chambered tomb, Crickhowell, Powys', *Antiquity* 54 (1980), p. 147; *Gwernvale*.

[40] *Gwernvale*, p. 3.

Neolithic Court Tombs (CT1–13; RCT 1–11)

(CT 1) Tŷ Illtud (Figs. 13–17)

John Aubrey, who had strong Brecknockshire connections,[1] may have been referring to Tŷ Illtud, now the only surviving cairn in the parish of Llansantffraid, when he described:[2]

> The Carn at Cravannesh in the parish of Llansandfred in the Countie of Brecknock; sc. a heape of stanes alyd in order, as [long] high as the wall of the Inner-Temple garden, and as long as the garden. [³] There is an Englin, (I) a versicle in Welch concerning it, which is printed in the Welch Grammar of J. David Rhees M.D. [⁴] There is no [illeg.] mentioned of anyones name: but, that under this Carn is hid great treasure. The Doctor caused it to be digged; and there rose such a horrid tempest of thunder & lightening, that the workmen would work no longer; and they sayd they sawe strange apparitions; but they found a Cake of Gold, which [ ] was of a considerable value. This was about 1612. From Sr Tho: Williams Baronet, Chymist to K. Charles II.[⁵]

This is the earliest known reference to a megalithic tomb in Brecknockshire, and if it was Tŷ Illtud, it seems reasonable to suppose that the extensive cairn originally covered a greater part of the hill-top than does the remaining site, and that its disappearance could have been due to seventeenth-century quarrying.

The surviving site lies S. of a low sandstone exposure on the prominent S.W. corner of a broad ridge 320 m above O.D. overlooking the floodplain of the Afon Usk.[6] At the end of the seventeenth century the site was certainly noted by Edward Lhuyd[7] who described a chamber of three uprights and one capstone, with graffiti on both sidestones. Lhuyd also described a former circular structure around the monument (RSC 7).[8]

The form of the cairn (Fig. 13). The oval mound, 23.0 m N.–S. by 15.5 m wide, falls steeply to the W. and S. The more level central area is about 17.0 m long by 7.0 m wide within sloping sides giving a height of 1.5 m on the lower (W.) side and 1.0 m on the upper. The surviving features fall into two parts. The S. end is a platform about 7.0 m by 5.5 m, and the N. appears as an uneven surface resulting from cairn robbing, lower than the other end and c. 9.0 by 6.0 m.

Internal features (Figs. 14, 17). The chamber, 1.0 m by slightly under 2.0 m internally, faces N., standing about 2 m E. of the monument's central axis. Of its four main components the eastern side stone (A) is 1.5 m long, 0.35 m thick and over 0.5 m high, split along part of its length from the N. end. The western side stone (B) is 2.1 m long, more than 0.35 m thick, standing 0.65 m above the floor. The southern end stone (C) is 1.0 m long, 0.1 m thick, standing 0.5 m high; the capstone is of irregular shape, 2.0 m by 1.75 m in plan, varying in thickness from 0.1 to 0.35 m and declining to the N. at 15 degrees, supported only by the two side stones. The internal chamber height is now only half Lhuyd's recorded 4 ft (1.2 m), which suggests later infilling.

N. of the chamber are five further stones, three roughly aligned across its end. One on the W. is a square-shaped column (D) of about 0.5 m side, 0.95 m high. Stone E is 0.5 m long, 0.1 m thick and 0.4 m high. Stone F is at least 0.5 m long, 0.2 m thick and exposed to a height of 0.5 m. Beyond the chamber, E. of, but aligned on the main axis of the monument, is an upright slab (G), 1.8 m long, 0.75 m high and 0.4 m thick. An opposing upright slab (H), traced by probing, seems to be just under 1 m long. There are two stones lying loose on the mound, 5.0 m and 6.8 m S.E. of the chamber, measuring respectively 0.85 m by 0.65 m by 0.2 m thick and 1.05 m by 0.85 m by 0.3 m thick.

Both Grimes[9] and Longueville Jones[10] (Fig. 15) showed the fifth upright, probably defining the W. side of another chamber, about 3.45 m E.–W. by 2.75 m N.–S. Longueville Jones also showed two small stones between D and H. Both showed some dry walling on either side of stone E. A forecourt to the main tomb structure might be suggested without any demonstrable portal structure.

The graffiti (Fig. 16). Five stones bear inscriptions and symbols. Stone D is said to bear the date 1510 just above ground level, and stone G the date mcccxii. Of the two chamber side slabs, stone A carries at least eight crosses and a series of ill-formed initials, but stone B bears more than sixty symbols, the majority being crosses either plain, enclosed in lozenges, doubled or crossleted. Stone C depicts only what may be a five-stringed lyre. More graffiti probably survive below present ground level.

Grinsell reviewed the interpretation of these graffiti through three centuries.[11] He favoured the view that the chamber was at one time used as a hermit's cell. Opinion since Lhuyd tends to favour a medieval date, the chief dissenters being Breuil[7] and Crawford,[8] who argued an origin at least prehistoric if not actually contemporary with the tomb. However, such an early dating seems unlikely since the graffiti do have close parallels in mason's marks, and it seems most probable that these were incised in the chamber during exploitation of the flagstone exposure immediately N. of the cairn.

Interpretation. Whereas the plan suggests the possibility that this was built as a simple terminal chamber tomb, the former existence of a further chamber complicates this thesis, making it difficult to classify the site more precisely without excavation.

[1] A. Powell, *John Aubrey and His Friends*, (London: Eyre Spottiswoode, 1948); M. Hunter, *John Aubrey and the Realm of Learning*, (London: Duckworth, 1975).

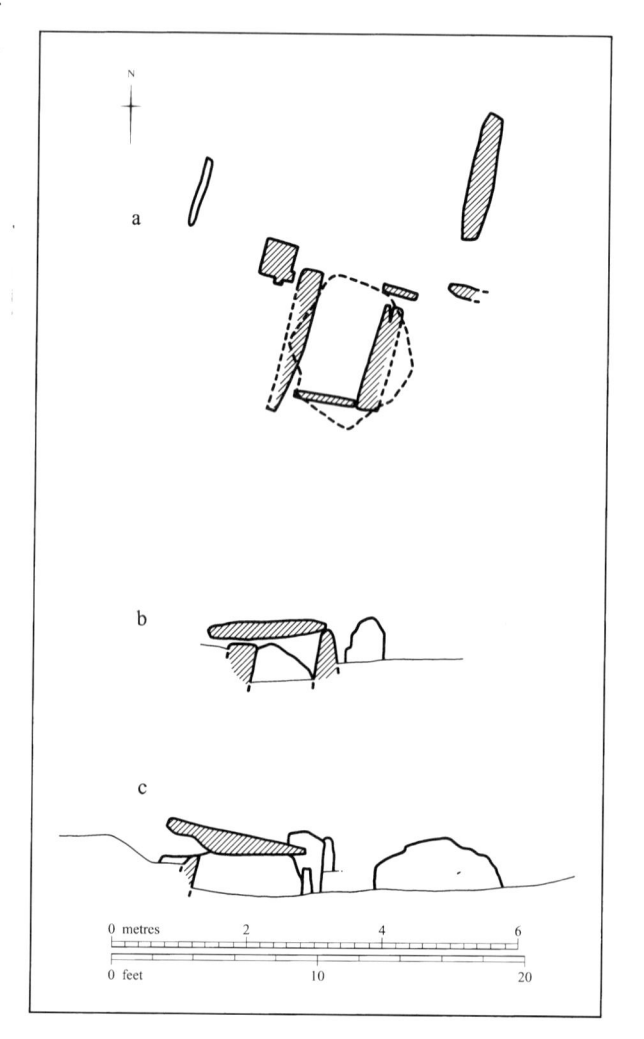

13 Tŷ Illtud (CT 1): plan and section

14 Tŷ Illtud (CT 1): plan and section of main chamber

15   Tŷ Illtud (CT 1): Henry Longueville Jones's engraving showing entrance in 1867 (from *Arch. Camb.* 22, (1867))

16   Tŷ Illtud (CT 1): Rubbings of 'inscriptions' (from *Arch. Camb.* 131 (1981))

17 Tŷ Illtud (CT 1): chamber

[2] MS *Monumenta Britannica* fo. 67/[49] Bodleian Library MS; the Commission records its thanks to the late Professor R. J. C. Atkinson for originally loaning copies of this MS for study purposes. See also transcription with slight variation in J. Fowles and R. Legg (eds.), *John Aubrey's Monumenta Britannica: First edition*, (Sherborne: Dorset Publishing Co., 1980), pp. 832–3. A less accurate transcription is given by Stukeley in his MS *Devizes Museum Commonplace Book* (of c. 1720), fo. 19 (Wiltshire Archaeological Society).

[3] It is difficult to know what he meant by the 'garden'. At the time of his note, the Temple (Inner and Middle) possessed a garden about 200 yds wide which originally might have been longer than this measurement (plan, p. 144, *RCAHM England*, vol. iv, *London (The City)*, H.M.S.O., 1929). It is now virtually impossible to determine the original wall height, though 10–ft [3.5–4.0 m] would seem to have been around the norm for a contemporary garden enclosure.

[4] For Sion Dafydd Rhys (1534–1609?), see *Dict. Welsh Biog*.

[5] The identity of this Thomas Williams is at present unclear.

[6] O.S. Card SO 02 NE 6 (superseded version).

[7] *Britannia* (ed. Gibson, 1695), col. 594; Lhuyd's original account is Brit. Lib. Stowe MS 1023, fol. 162.

[8] Jones, *Hist. Brecks*. II, ii, p. 578; H. Longueville Jones, *Arch. Camb*. 22 (1867), pp. 347–55.

[9] Grimes, *M.M.W.*, p. 280, Fig. 20; cf. Crawford, *L.B.C.*, pp. 63–5.

[10] Longueville Jones, *op. cit*. n. 8.

[11] L. V. Grinsell, *Arch. Camb*. 131 (1981), pp. 131–9.

[12] H. Breuil, *P.P.S. East Anglia* 7 (1934), p. 290.

[13] O. G. S. Crawford, *P.P.S.* 21 (1955), p. 156, n.

S.A.M. B 11

Llanhamlach/Llansanffraid
SO 02 N.E. (0984 2638)   24 ix 91

(CT 2) Mynydd Troed (Fig. 18)

This mound overlooks the basin centred upon Llangorse Lake, just over 350 m above O.D. on the S.-facing slope ascending the col between Mynydd Troed to the N.E. (609 m) and Mynydd Llangorse to the S. (506 m).

The site was discovered by O. G. S. Crawford in 1921,[1] when only two uprights were visible. Grimes made a sketch plan in 1926, showing possibly three orthostats and three exposed stone faces within a mound showing considerable disturbance.[2]

In 1966 sections were cut from opposite sides of the mound to provide information on the original ground surface and superincumbent deposits for soil and pollen study.[3]

The form of the cairn (Fig. 18). The barrow's long axis is aligned 20 degrees E. of true N. and at about 30 degrees E. of the maximum slope of the ground, which here rises at about 7 degrees. The mound is 26.3 m by 15.0 m wide, and 1.4 m high from the hillslope, which falls just over 0.3 m along the cairn's length. The shape of the mound is roughly quadrangular with a rounded tail to the S., though with a more square northern perimeter. To the N. the site merges into the irregular surface of a natural, level platform. There are now three hollows on the mound, the possible sites of former chambers.

Cairn construction. A perimeter wall built upon unprepared ground was located in the excavation. It still stood up to 22 courses (and 0.43 m) high by 11 m across. This had collapsed in the W. cut but, protected by a 'canted pile of slabs', was extant on the E.. The only other feature revealed was a vertically placed slab 0.6 m long, 1.1 m within the line of the western wall.

Internal features. The exposed chamber occupies the most northerly hollow and comprises three upstanding stones,[4] the western one 1.15 m long and 0.3 m wide, leaning S.E. at 24 degrees from the vertical, and the northern one 0.7 m long and 0.15 m thick, leaning S. at 23 degrees. The remaining stone is 0.75 m long by about 0.12 m thick, leaning to the S. at 26 degrees. None of the hollows is more than 0.3 m deep, nor is any stone of greater visible height. The tips of two further stones, possibly orthostatic, about 0.4 m long and 0.1 to 0.15 m thick, and aligned roughly E.–W., appear near the centre line of the cairn, to the W. of the central hollow. At least five more stones were shown to be visible at the surface, four being proposed as possible capstones.

Excavation yielded some cherty flint flakes and three types of Neolithic pottery very similar to that from Tŷ Isaf from the buried surface. Both surviving and excavated features suggest a denuded long barrow contained by a revetment wall, the remains of one certain chamber, and hints of the presence of two others. The status of 'extra-revetment material' is discussed elsewhere (p. 29).

Interpretation. Possession of a single eastern chamber might suggest that this was a terminal-chambered tomb.

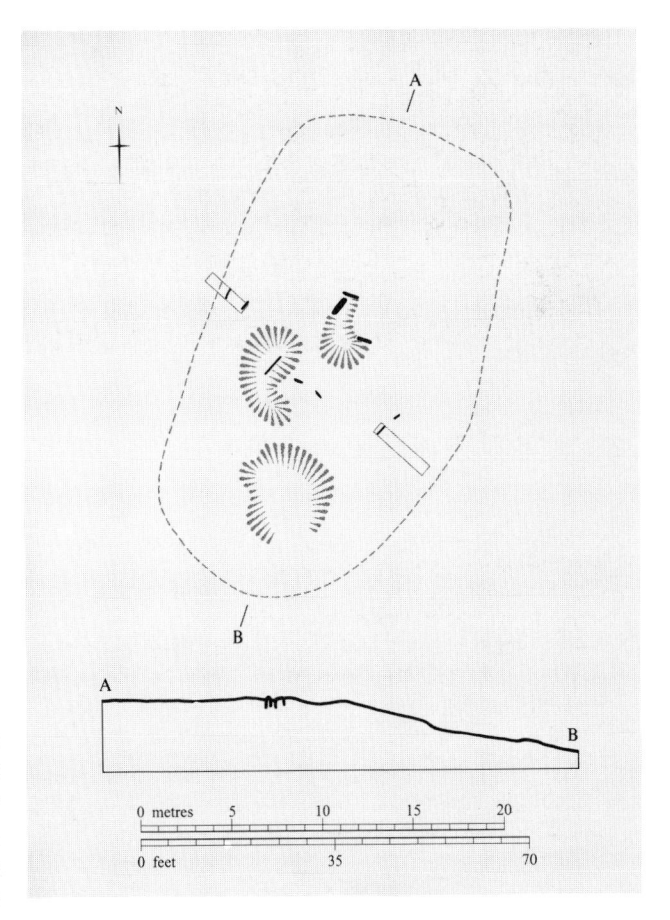

18 Mynydd Troed chambered cairn (CT 2): plan and section

However, as there appear to be indications of other chambers, more exhaustive excavation is required before the precise morphology of the site can be ascertained.

[1] O.S. Card SO 12 NE 2; Crawford, *L.B.C.*, p. 63.
[2] Plan by W. F. Grimes among Grimes MSS at N.M.R.; see n. 4.
[3] C. B. Crampton and D. P. Webley, *B.B.C.S.*, 22 (1966), pp. 71–7.
[4] Depicted by Grimes, *L.C.B.B.M.*, p. 279, Fig. 19 and on plan *loc. cit.* n. 2.

S.A.M. B 13

Talgarth
SO 12 N.E. (1615 2843) 7 xi 73

(CT 3) Tŷ Isaf (Fig. 19)

The mound at Tŷ Isaf lies about 265 m above O.D. at the lower end of the ridge descending from Castell Dinas, between the Afon Rhiangoll and a small tributary joining it from the N.W. It was discovered by O. G. S. Crawford in 1921, when two chambers were visible, with indications of others.[1] The chambers were totally excavated in 1938 by W. F. Grimes for the Brecknock Society.[2] Before excavation the mound was of pointed-oval shape, 32.9 m long, 15.25 m wide and up to 1.8 m high, orientated slightly E. of N.. The extent of structures revealed was 30.2 m, the greatest width probably being at least 17 m, reducing to 13.5 m at about two-thirds of the original length, with a maximum height of 1.5 m. After excavation the mound was carefully restored to its previous dimensions and, although these still remain the same, one capstone has disappeared and the site and its environs are vulnerable to erosion from farm animals and agricultural machinery.

The form of the cairn. The overall structure comprised:
(1) A wedge-shaped cairn with double drystone walls (with extra-revetment) extending far beyond the superficial limits of the mound, its northern and wider end having incurved horns ending on:
(2) The false portal, in the form of an H. Behind this were:
(3) A pair of chambers (I–II) symmetrically placed back to back at right-angles to the main axis, entered independently from the sides of the cairn. A short distance S. was
(4) A double walled rotunda linked with the cairn revetment walls on the E. side, and enclosing
(5) A large transepted gallery (III), its main axis lying roughly N.W.–S.E., and entered from the S.E. Immediately outside the rotunda at the S. end was
(6) Another much-ruined chamber (IV), placed upon, though at right-angles to, the main axis. It opened originally to the E.

Cairn construction. Levelling was suspected on the E. side with the use of marker stones during a preparation stage. Around the principal structures (of which chamber III and its rotunda were thought to have been built before chambers I and II), the body of the cairn consisted of loosely packed sandstone blocks and slabs. Large flat slabs were pitched with a buttressing effect for revetment walling. In upper levels these were laid horizontally. Cairn mass was retained by a double line of revetment, the inner being more coarsely built and sinuous than the outer, which was more truly aligned and consisted of carefully laid, thin slabs. This attained a maximum height of 0.43 m with 15 courses.

On the W. side the revetments appeared independent of other structures, spaced only 0.5 m apart at their eroded S. end but 1.3 m apart at the entrance to chamber I and round the N.W. horn, where the inner line broke before reaching the portal. On the E. side both revetments were virtually destroyed in the N.E. quarter of the cairn. It is possible that no inner wall ever existed there. Towards the S. both lines were a continuation of those forming the rotunda encircling chamber III at a spacing of up to 2.0 m. The inner walling here remained to a maximum height of 0.56 m, enclosing an oval area of about 10.4 m by 7.3 m, and showing contemporaneity with the inner cairn revetment in the smooth merging of foundation courses. The outer rotunda circuit was of good thin slabs reaching a maximum height of about 1.7 m, well reinforced by slabs pitched against it within the cairn body.

Though its false portal was probably set in the original ground surface at about the same time as the chamber uprights, the inturned walling of the funnel-shaped forecourt sides was laid upon a deposit which deepened to almost 1 m at the portal. The first construction phase would therefore seem to have progressed from S. to N., ending at the forecourt.

The chambers. The positioning of the four chambers respected the cairn's axial symmetry, though the axis of Chamber III lay askew to the main orientation. Old Red Sandstone uprights formed principal elements of their compartments. Inner passages were supplemented with dry walling where necessary, even corbelled inwards to lessen the gaps to be spanned with coverstones. The outer passages through the double revetments were lined only with laid slab walling. Chamber I on the W. was rectangular, about 3.3 m deep by 1.2 m, its orthostats ranging in height from 0.86 to 0.96 m. A small inner compartment was paved with slabs and the passage to the outside had the form of an ante-chamber defined by two pairs of slabs set transversely. Chamber II on the E. was also rectangular, some 2.7 m deep by 1.5 m, three of its four side orthostats leaning inward, but the N.E. entrance pillar supporting one remaining capstone at a height similar to that of Chamber I. The passage to the inner revetment was narrow at about 0.7 m. Chamber III, entered from the S.E. of the rotunda by a passage that widened from 0.7 m to 1.5 m, led over a low sill into a central chamber 2.1 m deep by 1.5 m. The S.W. and N.E. transepts, both entered through small openings formed on one side by leaning conglomerate pillars, measured about 3.3 m by 1.2 m and 1.7 m by 1.2 m respectively. The plan of Chamber IV at the extreme S. end of the cairn was incomplete, but it must have been at least 2.7 m long E.–W. by 1.2 m. The survival of some cairn material to the S. suggested that access here was from the E.

Use of the cairn. The burial chambers seem to have been used as ossuaries over an indeterminate period which involved the practice of collecting bones from decomposed corpses. Chamber I contained bone groups from at least 17 individuals, mainly at the side walls and even pushed into crevices. At primary levels were leaf-shaped arrowheads, a complete stone axe, a bone pin and plain pottery. In Chamber II, by contrast, were the remains of only one person with parts of at least six bowls, but there had been two final burials in the passage. Chamber III contained the grouped remains of at least nine individuals, including two more finally laid out in the passage. Artefacts were confined to plain potsherds. Chamber IV, though possibly original in the layout of the Neolithic tomb, contained only cremated bone and the flat base of a Bronze Age cinerary urn. Chamber I had also been re-used. This was demonstrated by a few Beaker fragments at an upper level.

Completion of the cairn and its forecourt with a neatly laid outer revetment was seen by the excavator as a comparatively late event in the construction sequence, with a formal shaping of the whole tomb involving the addition of extra-revetment material for stability. As a solution to the problem of re-entry to chambers thus closed at ground level, Grimes suggested access from above, into the unroofed part of the passages between the two lines of walling.[3] The poorly preserved state of the S. end of the cairn may well result from less substantial construction there, owing to the attachment of less importance to that end.

Interpretation. The plan of the monument does not fit comfortably with any of the three tomb types. Its

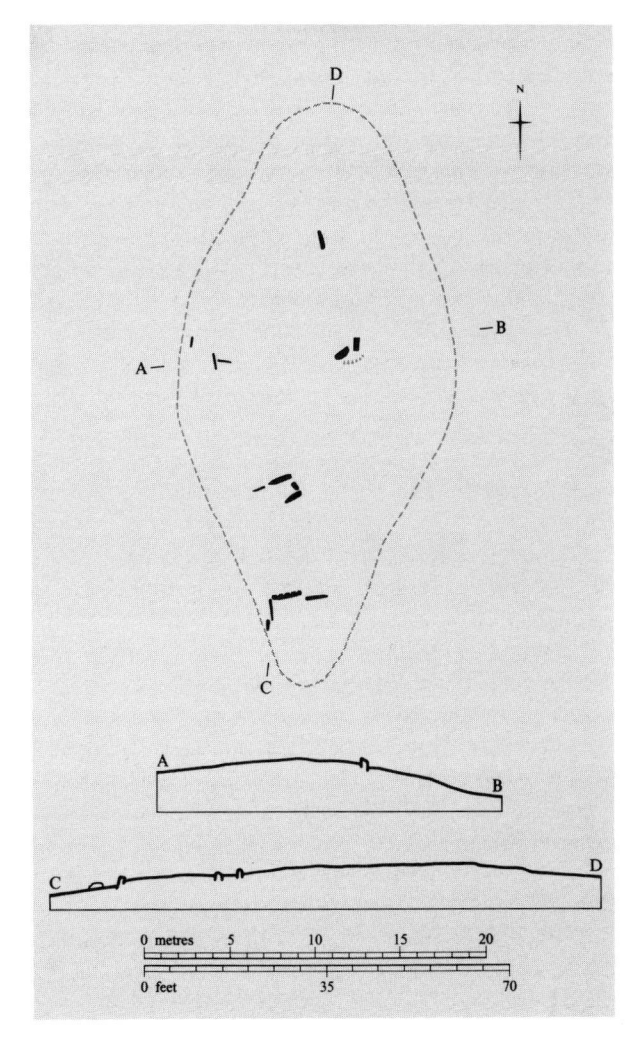

19 Tŷ Isaf chambered tomb (CT 3): plan and section

rotunda, a particularly unusual feature, might reasonably be interpreted as having formed an earlier focus for the trapezoid long cairn. The presence of such a feature has drawn some to suggest that it was a multi-period site, built in stages,[4] an interpretation not favoured by the excavator.

[1] O.S. Card SO 12 NE 3; Crawford, *L.B.C.*, p. 65.
[2] W. F. Grimes, *P.P.S.*, 5 (1939), pp. 119–42, from which this account has been mainly compiled.
[3] W. F. Grimes, *Defence Sites*, p. 94.
[4] For example, Corcoran, *Meg. Enq.*, pp. 84–6.

S.A.M. B 6

Talgarth
SO 12 N.E. (1819 2906)   21 vii 76

(CT 4) Pen y wrlod, Talgarth (Figs. 20–21)

Situated 400 m S.W. of Penywrlod Farm, 260 m above O.D., near the crest of a ridge ascending from the valley system of the Afon Llynfi and at the edge of a widening tract of cultivable land, this is the largest and most substantial long cairn of the Black Mountains group. In spite of its prominent position and size it eluded recognition until 1972, partly disguised by tree cover. Its existence was only appreciated after removal of stone for use as agricultural hard-core had exposed and wrecked some internal structures. Excavation in September 1972[1] had the limited objectives of examining and recording disturbed areas prior to moth-balling the site for access at an unknown future date.

The form of the cairn (Fig. 21). In its natural condition before excavation the grass-grown mound was 60 m long N.W.–S.E., its maximum width near the broader, S.E. end was 25 m and its maximum height 3 m. The quarry had been driven in near the E. corner, passing over and destroying one side-chamber and exposing another on the N.E. side, thereby revealing some of the main elements of a false portal and of a main chamber beyond the axis of the mound.

During excavation the cairn's original outline was defined by exposure of revetment walls at the N.E. corner of the narrow end, around the greater part of the S.E. horn of a forecourt, and adjacent to the entrances of three side-chambers in the N.E. side. The main structure was 52.0 m long, by an estimated width of from 22.5 m across the broader, S.E. end, to 11 m at the other, and its orientation was 33 degrees W. of N. The forecourt horns curved in to a depth of about 6 m, ending at the remains of a false portal deduced to have been formed by two parallel slabs 1.5 m apart, between which a low transverse threshold would have carried a blocking of drystone walling, the whole H-shaped arrangement being capped by a large slab now displaced to the N.E.

Cairn construction. Cairn mass comprised weathered or split sandstone blocks and slabs, with an outer casing of small stones and earth. Stability of the interior during construction had been ensured by a strong cross-wall at one point, possibly one of a series. Outward thrust was borne by two lines of revetment up to 1.5 m apart. The inner one was solidly built to a greater height than the outer, which in turn was of 'thin, cleft sandstone plaques', surviving to 0.3 m high in six or seven courses. The original height of the outer cairn line was felt unlikely to have risen more than 0.5 m, in contrast to the 1.5 m achieved upon the

20 Pen y wrlod (Talgarth) chambered tomb (CT 4): view showing quarried interior, 1973

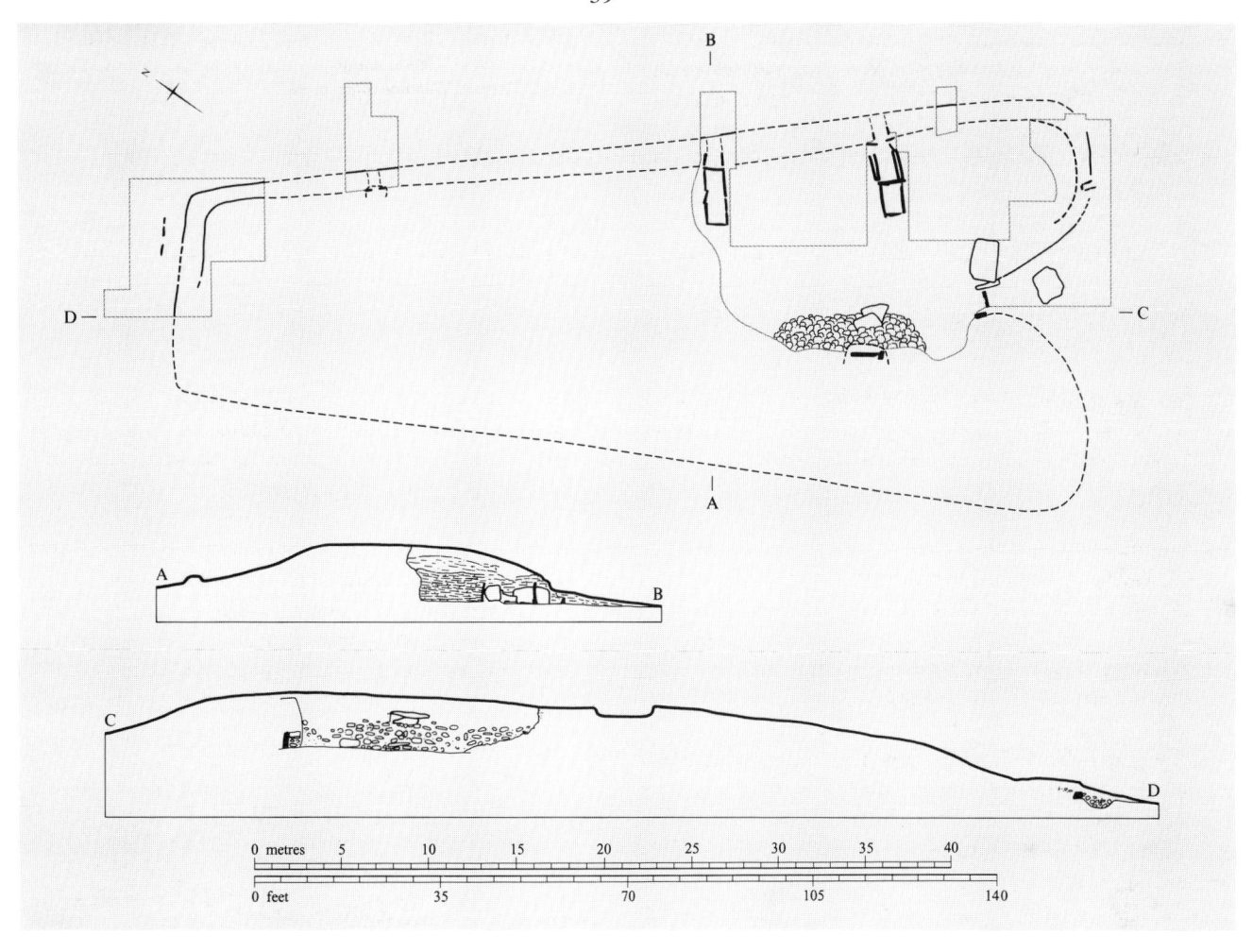

21 Pen y wrlod (Talgarth) chambered tomb (CT 4): plans and sections (from *Gwernvale*)

forecourt flank leading to the portal. Some extra-revetment material was present, notably at the N.W. end, where a slab-filled trench provided foundation for what may have been buttressing.

The chambers. Of the unexcavated main chamber, the only one so far detected on the S.W., and presumably entered from that side, only two orthostats were visible. Between these was a supposedly deliberate filling of earth and sandstone chips almost to the under surface of the partly exposed capstone. Stability of the uprights here had been ensured by an inner cairn of large, inward tilted thrust-blocks. Of the three lateral chambers on the N.E. side, Chamber NE I had been almost totally destroyed. It had consisted of orthostatic slabs forming two separate compartments placed end to end, 2.0 m by 1.2 m and 1.6 m by 1.0 m, the outer one entered from a short passage between the revetment walls, through a gap of 0.5 m between small portal slabs. Chamber NE II had lost its coverstones and its remaining side slabs had fallen inwards, but its original form was clear as a single chamber 2.85 m long by 1.0 m wide and up to 1.3 m high, sealed by a structural slab from a formal but false entrance passage between the revetment walls. Chamber NE III was not explored much beyond its entrance passage between the revetment walls. It had a functional entrance 0.3 m wide between portal slabs (similar to those of Chamber NE I) beneath the edge of a coverstone 1.2 m broad.

Use of the cairn. Though no undamaged chamber has been fully explored, and the main chamber in particular may contain essential functional evidence, variation may already be seen in the use of the side-chambers. No substantial human remains had survived in Chamber NE I, but those in the inner compartment could represent a dedicatory deposit, as also may some in Chamber NE II. The latter had contained a considerable quantity of disarticulated human bones, the long bones piled against the foot of the side walls. In Chamber NE III disarticulated remains forming only part of the potential ossuary deposit were recovered from the chamber's outer end, with a flint knife, part of a possible bone flute and a variety of animal bones. From beneath the extra-revetment material opposite the entrance here came several fragments of Abingdon ware.

Tomb type. The excavator felt the site had been planned and erected in a single phase. Though full assessment requires further excavation, it is clearly related to the laterally-chambered class with dummy forecourt. Whether or not its portal originally sheltered a terminal chamber is at present unclear.

[1] O.S. Card SO 21 NW 2; this account has been compiled from *Gwernvale*, pp. 11–39; *Antiquity* 47 (1973), pp. 187–92; and W. J. Britnell, *Penywrlod Long Cairn Talgarth, Powys; Survey and Recommendations*, Clwyd-Powys Archaeological Trust: unpubl. rep. (Welshpool, 1992).
[2] *Radiocarbon* 19 (1977), p. 417.

S.A.M. B 175

Talgarth
SO 13 S.E. (1505 3156)   1985

(CT 5–6) Ffostyll (Figs. 22–30)

The two chambered long barrows at Ffostyll lie upon an extensive tract of good arable land gently falling to the S. at 310 m above O.D., overlooking the valleys of the Afons Wye and Llynfi to the N. and W. These were first mentioned in the early nineteenth century by the Rev. Thomas Price (*Carnhuanauc*).[1] A nearby round barrow (LBS 10) has completely disappeared. It is quite unclear which of these mounds was in 1832 'full of cistvaens of some size – one of which' . . . had recently been . . . 'broken up for the sake of the stones' and which was then still sufficiently well-preserved to give the impression of a passage . . . '10 feet [*c.* 3 m] long, 5 feet [1.5 m] wide and 8 feet [2.5 m] deep formed of great stones one at each end and two on each side and covered with corresponding stones'.[2]

As is suggested below, a Beaker burial discovered in the early nineteenth century in the parish of Talgarth (LBS 9 pp. 135–6) may have derived from one of these Ffostyll mounds.

Although attempts were made by O. G. S. Crawford to prevent it,[3] both long barrows were subjected to rather undisciplined exploratory digging in the 1920s by C. E. Vulliamy assisted by A. F. Gwynne, prior to their Statutory Protection as Ancient Monuments.[4]

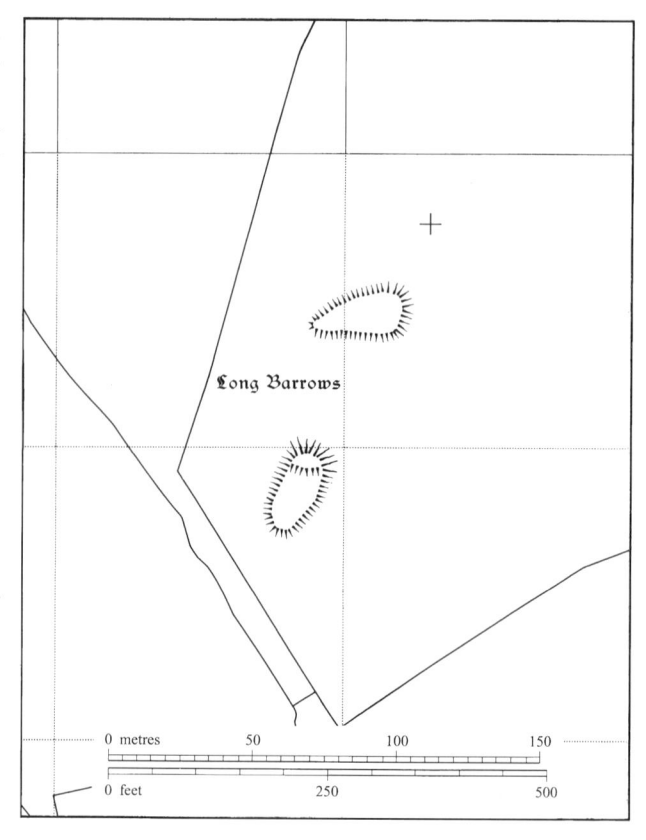

22 Ffostyll: location showing the sites of two chambered tombs (CT 5–6) and lost cairn site (LBS 10)

(CT 5) Ffostyll South (Figs. 23–26)

The present form of the southern barrow is roughly sub-rectangular in plan with rounded corners, 36 m long (N.N.E.–S.S.W.) by 23 m broad (Fig. 24). It tapers in slightly from the N. end, the shape having been largely determined by ploughing. Towards the N. end the mound stands about 2 m above field level, and at the S. end two-thirds of the barrow area forms a plateau about 0.5 m high.[5]

Within the remaining stony mound at the N. end is a series of seven upright slabs of local, finely laminated, irregularly-weathered sandstone representing a former chamber (Figs 23, 25). Two on the E. and four on the W. are separated by 1.6 m, and are joined at the N. end by a vertical blocking stone 1.2 m high by 0.23 m thick. Because of weathering only one stone survives on the W. 1.3 m above the present floor of the chamber and on the E. the stones are 0.9 m high. There is a broken line of talus to the N. of the chamber, among which appear the margins of smaller orthostats of unknown structural significance. One or two flat stones, up to 1.0 m across and 0.2 m thick, lie scattered around the mound, but none is identifiable as a former capstone. The mound has suffered considerably from robbing and agricultural usage. This is particularly seen in the flattening and extension of its southern end by about 2 m since its excavation in the 1920s.

Excavation. Three brief seasons' digging were conducted at the southern barrow by Vulliamy, 1921–3.[6] The farmer believed that the mound had formerly been higher, and that quantities of human bones had come to light during quarrying for road-making around 1875.

The burial chamber was cleared the first year. Internally it was about 3.3 m long by 1.2 m wide. The E. side of the chamber had collapsed inwards, revealing individual slabs up to 2.0 m high, 1.3 m wide and 0.2 m thick. A large covering slab, at least. 2.4 m by 2.1 m, had been displaced to the S.W., and an additional stone found in the chamber may also have covered part of it. Finds from chamber filling included bones at two levels. Associated with charcoal not far below the surface were burnt bones, fragmented and small, possibly of goat, pig, ox and other domestic animals. Some 0.3 m to 0.45 m lower, apparently on the original floor of the chamber and throughout its full length, was a large quantity of human bones with fewer animal bones of a similar fauna, though including cat. These lay in confusion and few appeared anatomically related. The majority were split and broken, many tightly wedged between stones. There was no pottery, and only three flint fragments were noted.

The body of the mound outside the N. end of the chamber yielded further burials in 1922, including a cremated child of six, some adult bones, and the tibia of a 7-month-old foetus; also animal bones, fragments of rough pottery and 17 pieces of calcined flint and chert. Finally, in 1923, nothing was found in a large, deep pit sunk by the E. side of the chamber, but the site of the 1922 discoveries again yielded a cremated child's skeleton, unburnt adult bones, and fragments of flint. There was also

23   Ffostyll South (CT 5): showing blocked chamber entrance

24 Ffostyll South (CT 5): plan and sections

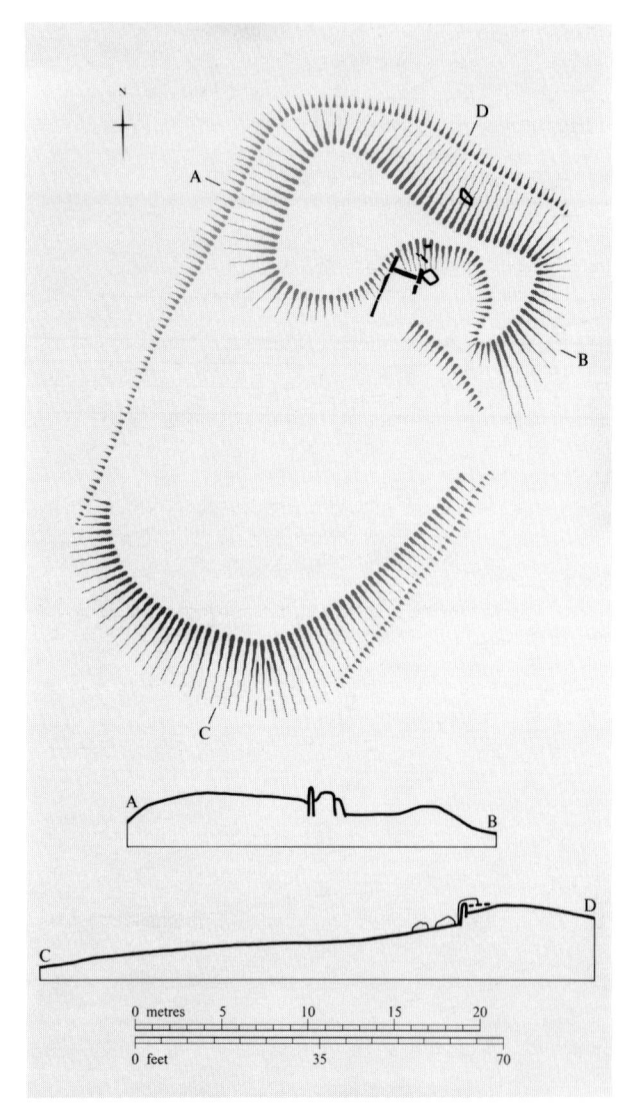

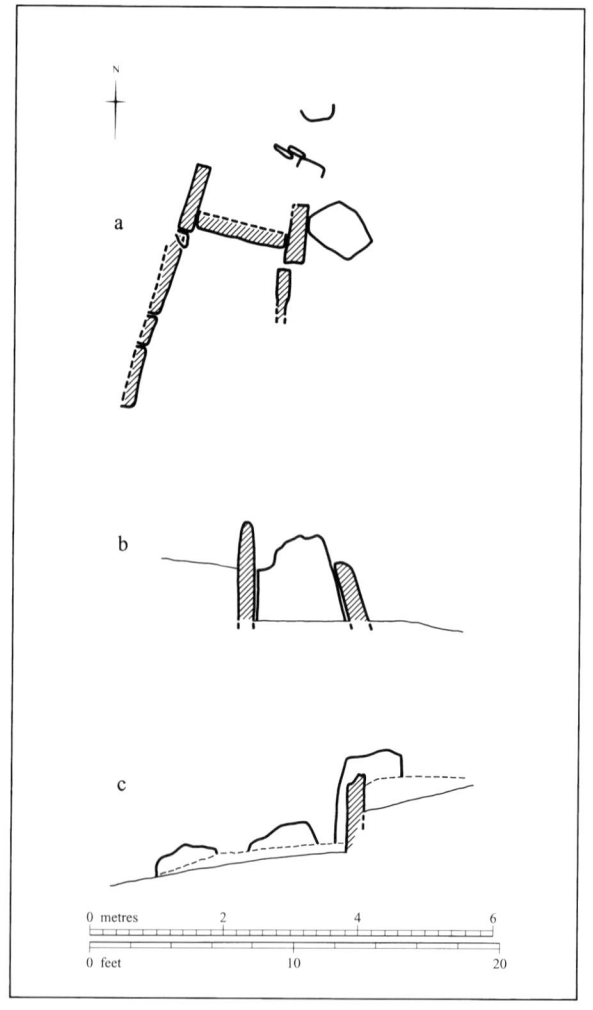

25 Ffostyll South (CT 5) details of chamber

a sherd of coarse blackish pottery (later interpreted as of a round-bottomed bowl of Neolithic A type).[7]

The human remains from the chamber consisted of some 600 fragments of bones and teeth[8] representing nine or more individuals of both sexes and various ages. Although they were principally inhumed, there were fragments from cremations of a youth and a very young child. Pelvic, vertebral and hand or foot bones were notably absent. Sir Arthur Keith commented that one skull with a cephalic index of 70 had a cranium 22 mm narrower than any Neolithic specimen previously recorded from Wales. This was thought to have belonged to an adult male of about 40 years and about 5 ft 4 ins [1.625 m] tall.

Tomb type. It is difficult to match some features of the current survey with the pre-excavation plan. However, the tomb clearly had at least one chamber. Although it has been suggested that the site may be a variant upon the terminal-chamber class,[9] due to the method of excavation and the large amount of material already removed from the monument, the site may originally have been terminally transepted.

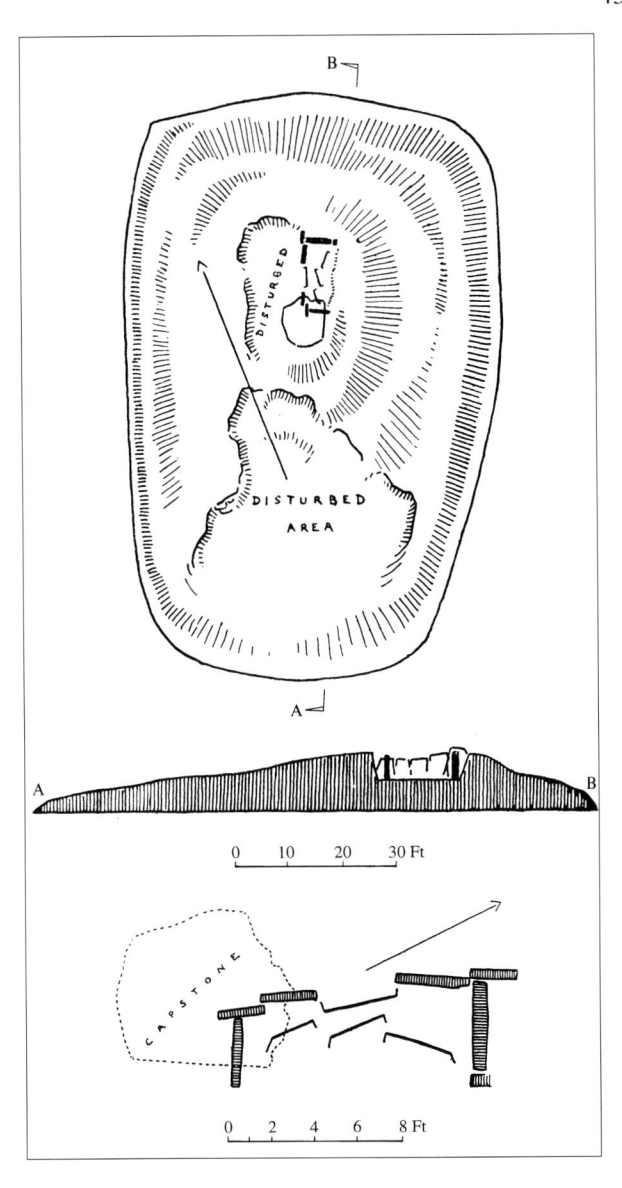

[1] T. Price, *Hanes Cymru*, (1842), p. 32.
[2] *idem*.
[3] MS letter O. G. S. Crawford to W. J. Hemp, 29 viii 21, in the Inspectorate of Ancient Monuments archive, Cardiff.
[4] MS letter of W. J. Hemp to E. E. Morgan, 28 ix 21; source *idem*.
[5] O. S. Card 13 SE 1.
[6] Vulliamy, *Arch. Camb.* 76, (1921), pp. 300–5; *Man* 86 (Oct. 1922), pp. 150–2; *Arch. Camb.* 78 (1923), p. 320; these accounts are popularly summarised in Vulliamy's, *Our Prehistoric Forerunners*, (London, 1925), pp. 161–2; see also Crawford, *L.B.C.*, pp. 56–9.
[7] Grimes, *L.C.B.B.M.*, p. 279; but 'indeterminate Western Neolithic' to Daniel, *P.C.T.*, p. 127; pottery from the 1922 and 1923 seasons equates with fragments now at N.M.W. (reg. no. 788.34.2 & 1 respectively).
[8] Most of the bones deposited with Sir Arthur Keith at the Royal College of Surgeons were lost in the war, but some surviving at B.M. (N.H.) include a mandible (reg. no. RCS 4.901); others may have survived at N.M.W. but could not be located in 1977 (*in. lit.* H. S. Green to C. S. Briggs, 28 iv 77).
[9] Daniel, *P.C.T.*, pp. 79, 158, 213; *Meg. Enq.*, pp. 45–6; see also p. 274.

S.A.M. B 2

Llaneleu
SO 13 S.E. (1789 3489)   12 vi 75

26 Ffostyll South (CT 5): Vulliamy's plan and sections (*Arch. Camb.* 76 (1921))

(CT 6) Ffostyll North (Figs 27–30)

This barrow is rather larger than the other.[1] It seems most likely the one described by Rev. T. Price as being '45 yards [41 m] long, 20 yards [18 m] wide and about 2 yards [1.8 m] high'.[2] This compares with current dimensions of 41.5 m long by 22.0 m at widest for an oval-shaped mound which remains roughly the same height (Fig. 29). Its S. flank has been eroded into a straight scarp by ploughing, giving the western tip a pointed form. The mound's surface has been greatly disturbed by early excavation and through invasion by uncontrolled livestock. Within the western end is an oval hollow about 3.0 m in diameter. The broader, eastern end has the only extant chamber, without capstone. The central area is roughly level, 15 m long by 9 m wide, on which lie two large slabs, the most northerly being trapezoid, 2.7 m long by 2.3 m wide by 0.25 m thick, the other 2.3 m long by 0.9 m wide and 0.12 m thick. To the S.E. are a further four slabs,

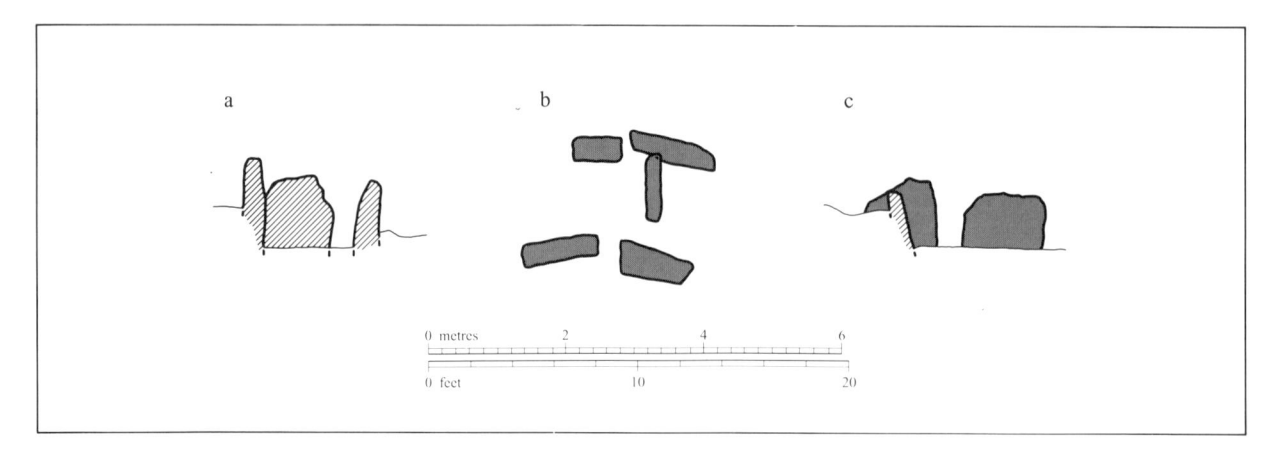

27 Ffostyll North chambered tomb (CT 6): detail of E chamber: a. section N.–S.; b. plan; c. section W.–E.

28 Ffostyll North (CT 6): showing eastern chamber

one of which is 2.6 m long and 0.9 m wide by 0.27 m thick.

The principal chamber in the E. end of the barrow consists of five upright stones, with no surviving capstone. The central stone, blocking the space between the eastern pair of side stones, leans to the E., and both stones of the N. side of the chamber lean outward. All are from 0.8–1.0 m high from the present surface and from 0.7–1.3 m wide, by 0.25–0.5 m thick.

According to Vulliamy, prior to his excavation the main burial chamber had been rifled and the broad end of the mound flattened.[3]

Excavation. The surviving eastern chamber had already been despoiled by 1922 when a new western chamber was discovered, and a covered cist (Fig. 30) was found in the middle of the N. side of the mound.[4]

This covered cist was of local sandstone, 1.3 by

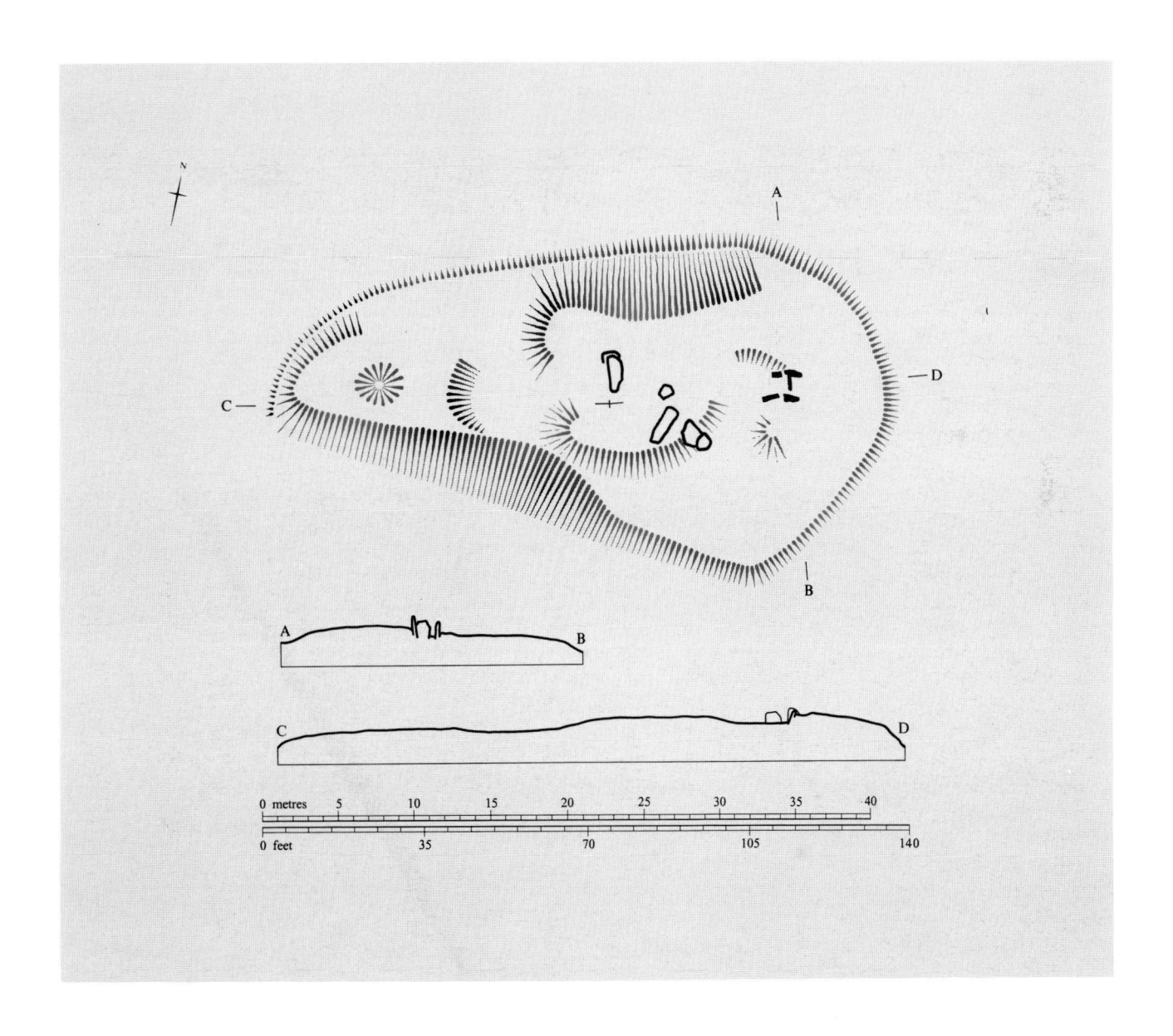

29 Ffostyll North (CT 6): plan and sections

0.9 m by 1.1 m high, and was capped by a smooth-bellied stone 2.6 m long and 0.3–0.6 m thick. Vulliamy's photograph[5] of the exploratory entrance into this site shows that the digging method was badger-like.

Three of the slabs now lying in the N. central area (Fig. 29) (two of them over 2 m long by 0.12–0.2 m thick) probably derive from this cist but the largest one does not adequately match, in size or position, the capstone depicted in the excavation report. S.E. of these a group of four slabs may have belonged to the same cist or to the eastern chamber. The longest, 3.5 m by 1.0 m by 0.27 m, could have been a principal supporter of the latter, but the other three are at most 1.0–1.7 m long by not more than 0.2 m thick.

The chamber contained human remains, together with horse, dog, ox and pig bones, within the lowest part of undisturbed deposits. These were scattered and broken, some in correct anatomical relation to each other. Some flint waste flakes were noted, and 'pottery of a finer paste and more compact texture than that from the S. barrow'. Among the six or seven individuals represented in the cist were two children between 6 and 11 years old. Sir Arthur Keith had drawn attention to the vertebra of a rheumatoid female and the mandible of a hefty male, and there were various hand and foot bones.

The western chamber comprised two widely-spaced massive side-slabs attaining 1.05 m in height above the level where the bones of four individuals were found with animal bones and one flint flake. There is now a slight hollow adjacent to the site of this excavated chamber.

Interpretation. Vulliamy's opinion that the mound had been enlarged to a long shape from an original round cairn has generally been ignored, though it is unclear as to quite why the claim was made in the first place. Corcoran suggests that it was originally trapezoid in plan, and that its present form results from multi-period construction. Also, the possibility is mooted that the N. and E. chambers may have originally occupied smaller, individual cairns.[6] Unfortunately the excavation record is so poor as to defy reasonable re-interpretation. It is possible that the eastern chamber was the principal funerary element, but there is no certainty as to the relative status of the other chambers.

[1] O.S. Card SO SE 1.
[2] CT 5 n. 1.
[3] C. E. Vulliamy, *Arch. Camb.* 78 (1923), pp. 320–4.
[4] C. E. Vulliamy, *Our Prehistoric Forerunners*, (London, 1925), p. 161.
[5] *idem.* opp. p. 160.
[6] *Meg. Enq.*, pp. 43, 274.

S.A.M. B 2

Llaneleu
SO 13 S.E. (1791 3495)   15 × 91

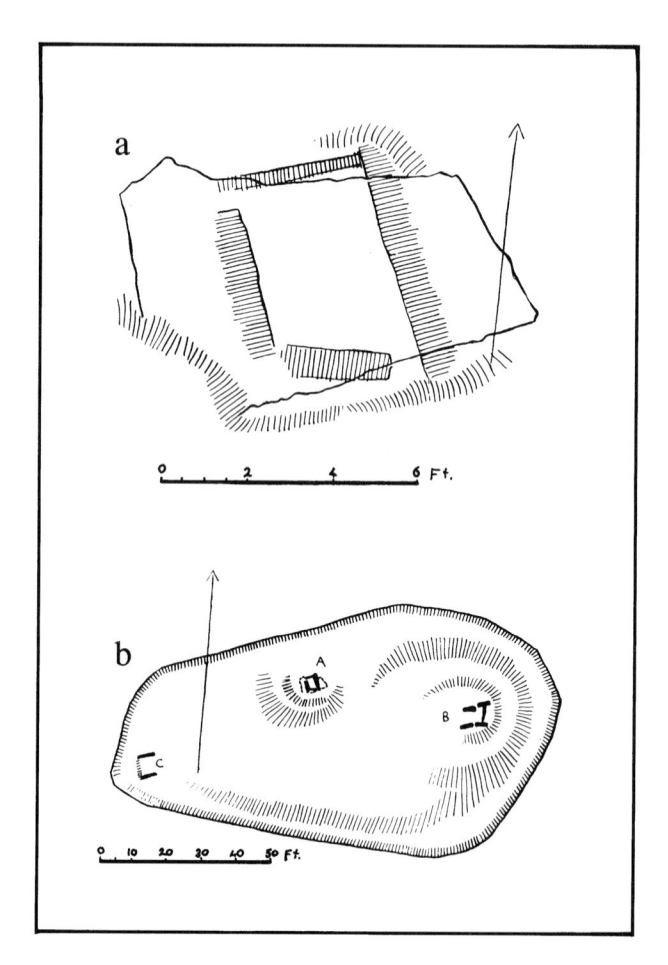

30 Ffostyll North: Vulliamy's plan with detail of N chamber (from *Arch. Camb.* 78 (1923))

(CT 7) Bryn y Groes or Croesllechau (Figs. 31–3)

About 500 m S.W. of Pontithel, about 120 m above O.D., close to the site of the former farm Bryn y Groes, stood a chambered tomb which has entirely disappeared. Interpretation of the site is almost entirely dependent upon Edward Lhuyd's description of c. 1700.[1]

Under the heading 'Yn Glos y Lhecheu in Brynlhysk par: Brecon', Lhuyd[2] described five features by means of annotated sketches:

1) depicts a megalithic chamber with its coverstone in place, stating 'This Crom' was formerly supported by 5 stones but at present by 2. Some small stones are interpos'd between ye rest it mount southward 5 ft. & a half long & 3 foot & a half broad and ft. thick ye concave is abt a yd. high'.
2) shows two stones entitled 'abt 2 yd long dist. from ye Crom' abt 2 yd & a halfe'.
3) seems to represent a long slab either in plan or standing on edge: 'This is ye farthest from ye Crom. this is sidewise abt 15 yd dist. from ye Crom, westward abt 10 ft. long & 3 broad'.
4) shows three stones in plan, apparently upright in the ground, forming three sides of a box-like structure: 'This is a Kistvaen dist. from ye Cromlech about 6 yd northw''. The individual stones were: 'A foot & a half high, 5 ft. long'; '3 ft. & a half long, & above 2 ft. high'; '3 ft. & a half long & 2 high'.
5) is the plan of three sides of a long chamber; 'This is abt 12 ft. Long & 4 broad, dist. from ye Crom about 13 yd westward'. The end stone was '6 ft. long', fully covering the thickness of the side slabs, with an added note 'ye rest a ft. high'. One side was apparently composed of four contiguous stones, beside which is a note '4 ft L & i broad'. The other side shows two separate stones noted as '6 ft L' and 'abt 6 L'.

31 Bryn y Groes or Croesllechau (CT 7): engraving from the title page of T. Jones, *Hist. Brecks* 2 (i), (1809)

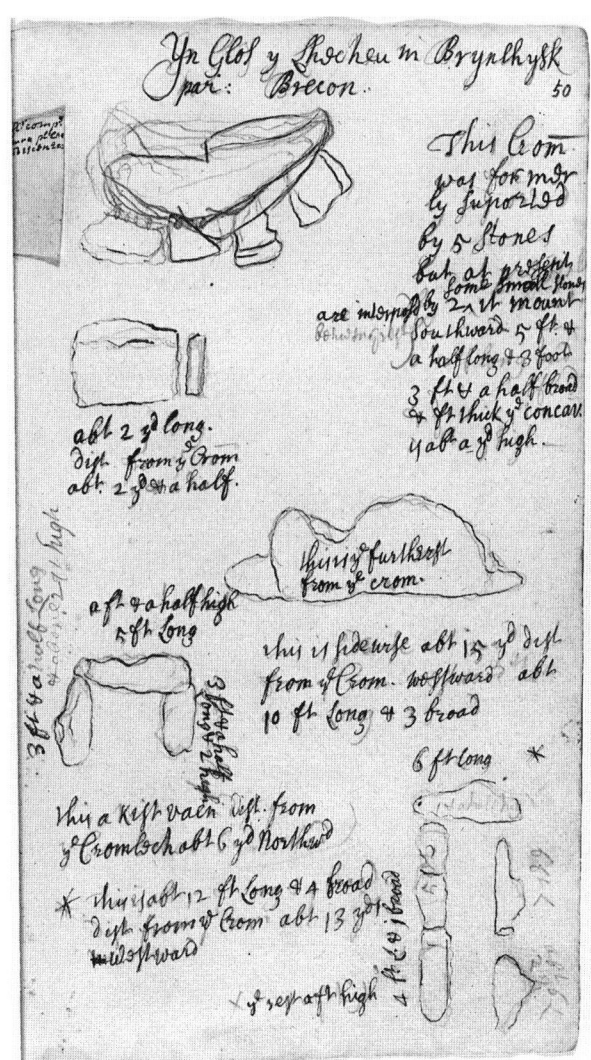

32 Bryn y Groes or Croesllechau (CT 7): Edward Lhuyd's plan from NLW MS Peniarth (by permission of the National Library of Wales)

Despite ignorance of their individual orientations these features may be variously interpreted as:

(1) a megalithic chamber of uncertain size at the eastern end of the group;
(2) an attendant element adjacent to the chamber, possibly a false portal, though its relative attitude is not known;
(3) from its dimensions and general location this was conceivably the capstone of the long chamber (5);
(4) clearly depicts a small side chamber of three walls with no capstone; and
(5) describes a major second chamber at the W. end of the group.

This monument survived in whole or in part at least until the first decade of the nineteenth century, when it was noted by Colt Hoare[3] and Fenton.[4] They also located it in the field *Clos y Ilechau*, then on Bryn y Groes farm. Theophilus Jones,[5] using in an engraving a sketch by Colt Hoare, was the first to refer to the field name Croeslechau (*sic*). Although the unpublished 1814 O.S. map[6] shows and names Bryn y Groes farm, and the printed 1832 1-inch map[7] depicts a cromlech symbol immediately adjacent on the S. and named Croesllechau in Antiquity type, the farm had been abandoned before the tithe assessment of 1839 and by then the names of both farm and field were no longer in use.[8] The site is now lost[9] and its location has been deduced using only these earlier written sources.

On the basis of Lhuyd's sketch (presented here as a theoretical composite, Fig. 33), the chambers were accommodated on a site about 20 m by 10 m.

The site has been examined for traces of the structure, but whereas part of the monument's spine may yet be located by excavation from beneath a hedge, most of the area occupied by this tomb appears to have been taken into arable during or before the early nineteenth century. Consequently, at present, not a trace remains visible.

[1] O.S. Card SO 13 NE 6.
[2] E. Lhuyd, field notebook (N.L.W. Peniarth MS 251 [formerly Hengwrt MS 397], fo. 50 opp. p. 38); printed in *Parochialia*, II, p. 32.

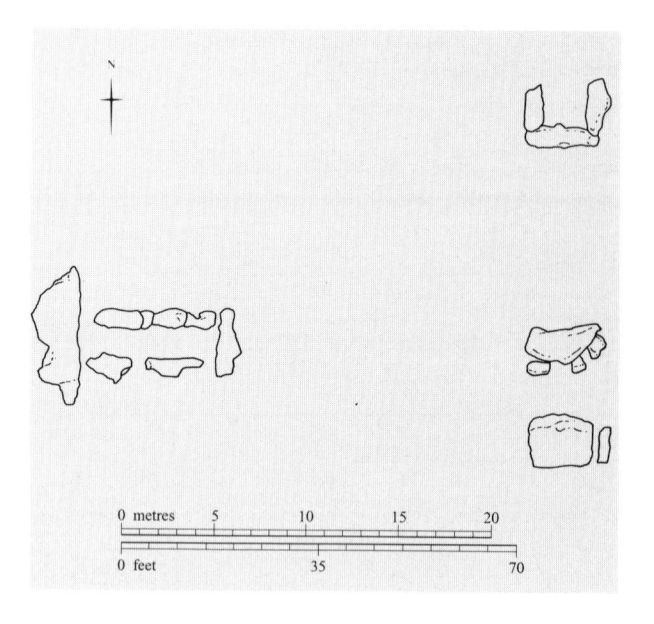

33 Bryn y Groes or Croesllechau (CT 7): elements from Lhuyd's plan arranged spatially

[3] *Tour in 1802* by Sir Richard Colt Hoare, Cardiff Public Library MS 4.302.1/6, fo. 108/277.
[4] Fenton, *Tours*, p. 22; mention by the Rev. T. Rees in *A Topographical and Historical Description of South Wales*, (London: Sherwood, Neely and Jones, 1815), p. 138, is probably derivative of T. Jones' *Hist. Brecks.* account.
[5] Jones, *Hist. Brecks*. II, i (1809), p. 338 and title page (both parts I and II). This erroneous variation of the field name has been retained in recent listings, but to resolve difficulties, the farm name is used here.
[6] O.S. 2-inch MS survey, sheet 195.
[7] O.S. 1-inch survey, sheet 58, David and Charles reprint.
[8] Map and schedule for Bron-llys parish in N.L.W. The Bryn y Groes holding is listed under Baradwys (*sic*), and the field immediately S. of the former farm site is tantalisingly unnamed.
[9] Crawford, *L.B.C.*, pp. 53–4; *Meg. Enq.*, p. 275; Daniel, *P.C.T.* p. 214; the O.S. suggestion (Card SO 13 NE 6) that some stones at SO 1695 3547 may be the sole remnants of the monument, apparently following Crawford's siting of Bryn y Groes farm at about SO 1685 3560, should be disregarded.

Bronllys
SO 13 N.E. (1672 3626)   23 v 74

(CT 8) Pipton (Figs. 34–6)

The chambered long cairn about 1 km S.W. of Pipton stands about 150 m above O.D., looking down the N.E. end of a ridge dividing the Afon Wye from its tributary the Afon Llynfi.[1] The site was first published in 1925, and was excavated in 1949 by Savory for the Brecknock Society and the National Museum of Wales.[2] Before excavation the tree-grown mound (Fig. 35) was about 37 m long, the N.E. end about 22 m broad and the height varying from 1 m to 2.2 m. A pair of upright stones protruded from the surface, set transversely in the centre of the broad end. After its restoration to the original form the mound appears slightly broader at about 25 m, still bearing several tree stumps.

The form of the cairn. During excavation enough of the outermost of the two main lines of revetment of the cairn was identified to deduce that it was wedge-shaped, 32 m long on an axis aligned at about 31 degrees E. of N. The greatest width was 16 m near the N.E. end, which contained a forecourt funnelled in from smoothly rounded terminals to a false portal 2.5 m wide at a depth of about 5.5 m. The S.E. side was straight but the N.W. side slightly concave, converging to give an estimated width of about 10 m at the S.W. end. The body of the cairn reached a maximum height of nearly 2 m above a prepared ground surface, the tallest feature being one of the two portal stones at 2.4 m. Within the cairn only two chambers were identified, Chamber I centred only 5.5 m from the portal and entered from the N.W. side, Chamber II being apparently a closed cist on the same side. An internal revetment wall, comparable to the rotunda feature at Ty Isaf (CT 3), curved across the cairn to the S.W. of each of the chambers. Two canted slabs in the S. part of the cairn may have had a ritual purpose if they were not simply functional buttresses.

The construction of the cairn (Fig. 34). Excavation revealed a levelled surface sunk into the crest of a ridge, stripped to subsoil where charcoal and sandstone chips accumulated during the building process, with a single 'featureless scrap of neolithic pottery'. Several horizontal and vertical slabs on this surface were seen by Savory as marker stones for the laying out process. None of the upright stones were deeply bedded, rather relying for stability on wedging and filling with dry walling. The stony core of the cairn around the chambers consisted mainly of sandstone blocks and flags, with some thin micaceous flags and water-rolled blocks and pebbles, for the most part piled loosely, but tightly wedged in a few places.

The inner cairn revetment was more coarsely and less consistently built than the outer revetment, evidently built for strength rather than appearance up to 1.5 m away from the outer, even virtually converging with it in two places, and in another resolving into a triple line. The more northerly rotunda wall was similarly coarse, as was the innermost of the double line around Chamber II, where the outer one was of a quality comparable to that of the outer walling of the sides of the cairn. The best preserved of the outer revetment consisted of up to 24 courses of split slabs in a height of about 0.75 m, possibly exceeded only in the forecourt, where it reached 0.9 m. This finer type of laid walling was used also to fill spaces between megalithic uprights in the chambers and between the portal slabs.

Extra-revetment material, consisting mainly of small slabs and chips lying quite loosely, and in places holding slabs vertically against the revetment, was accepted by Savory as a deliberate element of the finished monument. This added material was seen to extend outwards to about 3.6 m outside the entrance of Chamber I, where its heavier composition gave it a more significant blocking function, as also in the forecourt, where there was no reason to doubt deliberate filling to the height of the flanking walls. As a final act of closure at the end of its use 'it was plain that the stony core of the cairn had been covered by an envelope of pinkish clayey earth with small stones, which descended in a continuous slope over the extra-revetment material on the W. side of the cairn, and took the place of the revetment and extra-revetment at the southern tip of the cairn'.

The chambers. The main T-shaped structure of Chamber I was entered first through an outer passage between the cairn revetments lined only with laid walling and roofed probably with 'false vaulting', then through a narrow inner passage taking a zig-zag course between portals roofed at a height of about 1.4 m over a distance of some 4 m to the main gallery. This was entered through the N. side of its W. end over a sill of small upright slabs, and consisted of three compartments, 4 m long overall by up to 1 m, expanding at its E. end into two unequal transepts. One capstone measuring 2.0 m by 1.5 m remained over the W. end of the main gallery, resting with maximum headroom of 1.3 m on a transverse divider and the upright slab 2.7 m long forming most of the S. side.

The N. transept, of two unequal compartments divided by a septal slab and measuring 3.5 m by 1.0 m overall, was brought to a similar height by corbelling added to its upright slabs, but no capstones remained. The S. transept measured about 1.0 m by 0.8 m, its single capstone split and fallen from a height of over a metre achieved with walling added to the small upright slabs of its walls. All other capstones of the chamber and main passage had been removed.

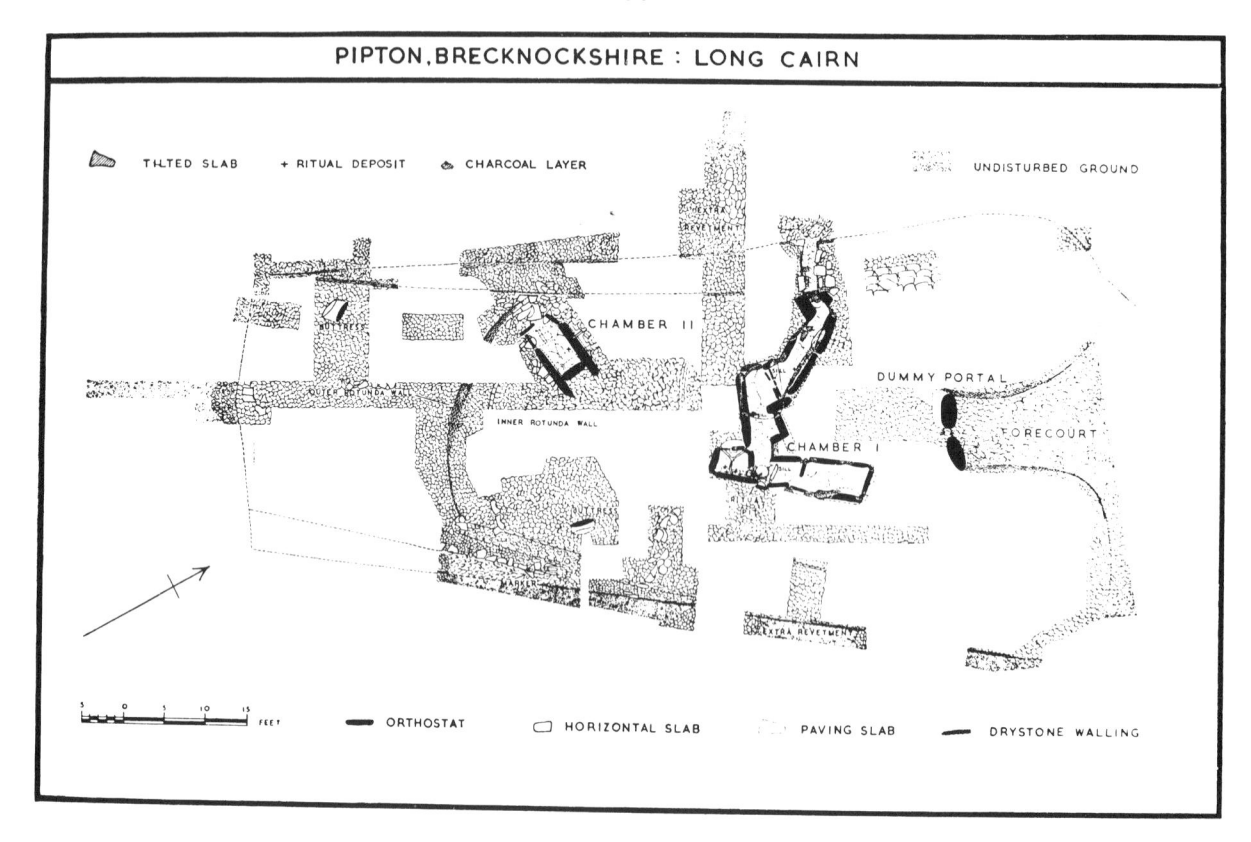

34 Pipton chambered tomb (CT 8): plan from Savory's excavation (*Arch. Camb.* 100 (1949))

Chamber II (Fig. 36), also on the N.W. side and measuring internally 1.95 m by 1.0 m, was formed of a pair of slabs about 2.2 m long held apart by a heavy back slab, but the outer end, just within the conjunction of the outer rotunda wall and the inner cairn revetment, was of smaller slabs. There was no formal entrance through the side of the cairn, so that access must have been from above, though there seemed once to have been a large coverstone supported on the inner orthostats and on supplementary corbelling.

Use of the cairn. A layer of sterile sandy earth, onto which the robbing of capstones had caused the collapse of corbelling and other roofing material, covered the floor of Chamber 1 and its passage, mostly 0.3 m to 0.6 m deep but deeper at the passage portal. At the junction of the transepts in the E. end was a ritual pit showing signs of fire which extended to the N. transept and beneath the sill-stone of the S. transept. Of a ritual character also were deposits of bone, comprising an incomplete assemblage of human material beneath floor slabs in the S. transept, as well as various human and animal bones and a flint flake in the passage complex, protected by structural features. Savory interpreted the sterile earth deposit as 'a deliberate filling of the chamber in antiquity, before any burials had taken place, or after the complete removal of any burials that once existed', and further suggested that 'chamber I might be a dummy built for ritual purposes rather than for the practical purposes of disposal of the dead'.

In Chamber II a deposit of small human bones beneath the paving was probably dedicatory, as in Chamber I, whereas the seven groups of bones heaped

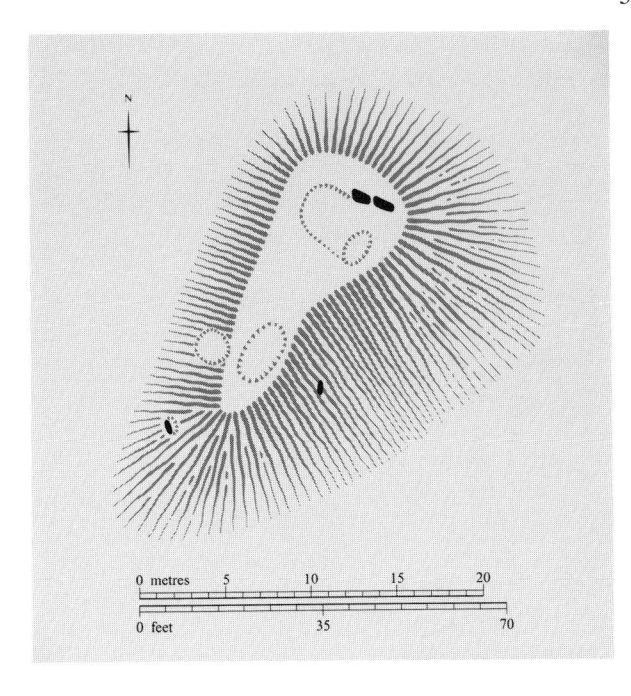

35 Pipton chambered tomb (CT 8): plan

against the side walls and in the centre, and covered with a layer of brown earth probably inserted deliberately, represented use of this chamber as a secondary resting place for remains that had decomposed elsewhere, possibly in Chamber I, though there was no evidence there of such use.

Interpretation. Although the tomb was entered through one or possibly two entrances on the W. side, and the forecourt was certainly blocked, because the building sequence is unclear, and owing to the difficulty of knowing whether or not erection was single or multi-period, the site is difficult to classify. Historical erosive factors may have been responsible for obscuring interpretations of the sealed deposits, which appear to represent a minimal period of burial.

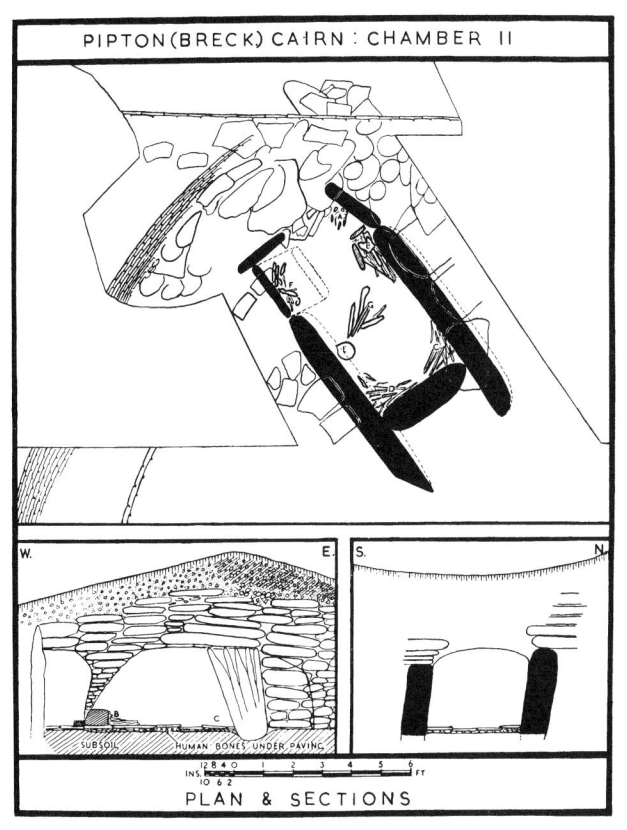

36 Pipton: plan of chamber (from *Arch. Camb.* 100 (1949))

[1] O.S. SO 13 NE 2; Grimes, *L.C.B.B.M.*, pp. 266–70, 274; fieldnotes and sketch in Grimes MSS, N.M.R. Daniel, *P.C.T.*, p. 214.
[2] Crawford, *L.B.C.*, pp. 62–3, quoting notification by C. E. Vulliamy, but discovery attributed by Savory to A. F. Gwynne.
[3] Excavation report by H. N. Savory, *Arch. Camb.* 100 (1949), pp. 7–48, from which this account has been mainly compiled.

S.A.M. B 29

Glasbury (E), Pipton (C)
SO 13 N.E. (1604 3727)   15 vii 76

(CT 9) Little Lodge (Figs. 37–39)

The long barrow 320 m W. of Little Lodge Farm occupies gently-sloping ground above the steep northern side of a tributary valley of the River Wye, about 130 m above O.D.[1] The site was first described and is still best known from excavations by C. E. Vulliamy undertaken in 1929[2] when a major chamber complex was identified just S. of the mound's centre, with a contiguous pair of small chambers in the S. end.

The present form of the mound (Fig. 37) is a broad

robbed, and survives to a maximum height of only 1.8 m, the remnant surface covered in earth and stones, some of which, measuring up to 0.5 by 0.3 m, may derived from destroyed chambers.

The main chamber complex, 19 m from the S. end of the mound, was dominated by a large transverse slab, to the N.E. of which six upright slabs and some dry-laid walling defined the outline. Only three of these are now detectable, the most prominent standing transversely 2.8 m long, 0.45 m thick and 0.9 m high. On the evidence of Vulliamy's plan, there was a main chamber of uncertain size with at least one transeptal chamber about 1.5 m square and at least 1 m high. The chamber contained many unburnt human bones, apparently without artefacts. Besides charcoal flecks the funerary deposit included bones of a red deer,[4] an ovid and a small bovid. The human bones represented five adult males, an old woman, and two (or possibly three) children. Recent re-examination of some of the bones[5] shows they represent one youth and four adults, mostly male. Among the items in this bone collection is 'a very heavily worn upper right M1 [molar] of a red deer'.

The two southern chambers, now in disarray, when excavated lay contiguous with one common side. Though planned, they were not described in detail by Vulliamy. The larger was wedge-shaped, its S.E. corner badly disrupted by tree roots. It measures 2.0 m N.–S. by 1.4 m and consists of five stones, the tallest on the N. side being 0.9 m high. The smaller chamber to the W. formerly measured about 1.3 m by 0.8 m but has lost its N. and W. slabs, which may be among those now seen on edge outside the S. slab and in the middle of the larger chamber (which appear to have been added). Three slabs just breaking the surface W. of this complex, and another adjacent on the S., are of unclear function. The only find here was an untrimmed flint flake.

Interpretation. Both chambers uncovered by Vulliamy might well have been of side-transepted entry, though the mound is so badly disturbed that in its present form it defies more precise classification.

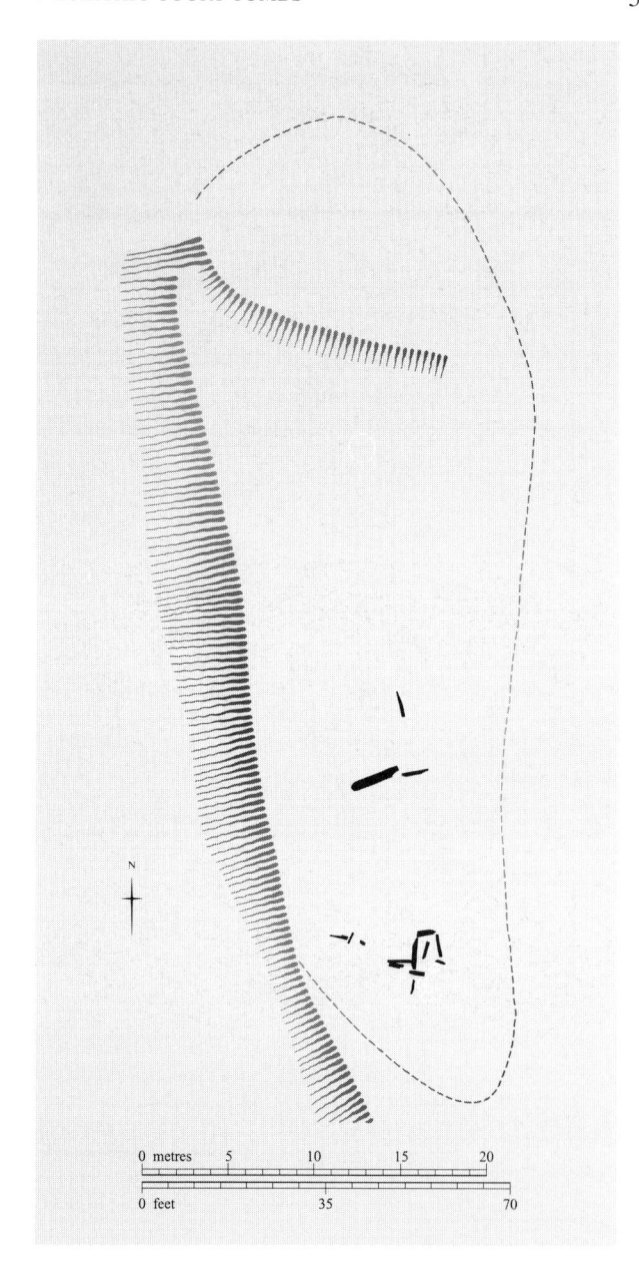

37 Little Lodge chambered tomb (CT 9): plan

platform 55.5 m long on a N.–S. axis, its outline emphasised by cultivation at the ends and on the concave E. side.[3] The W. side is straighter, partly protected by a hedge and with a more definite scarp that seems to continue as a natural feature to the S. The maximum width of 22 m is now seen at about 17 m from the rounded N. end. The site is extensively

[1] O.S. Card SO 13 NE 3.
[2] *Man* 20 (1920), pp. 34–6; Grimes, *L.C.B.B.M.*, p. 282; Daniel, *P.C.T.*, p. 160; *Meg. Enq.*, p. 274.
[3] The plan published by Darvill, *C.T.* (p. 99, Fig. 18), is

38 Little Lodge chambered tomb (CT 9): showing orthostats remaining in central area

completely at variance with the surviving stones, and seems to result from a misinterpretation of Vulliamy's miniscule published plan.

[4] Only one deer molar was noticed among the bones re-examined in 1975 (see n. 5 below). This was identified by Andrew Currant. No ovid or bovid bones appear to survive at the Royal College of Surgeons.

[5] Report on material housed at Royal College of Surgeons, London, in lit. Rosemary Powers of B.M. (N.H.) to C. S. Briggs, in 1975. These were originally presented to the College in 1934 by C. E. Vulliamy through Stuart Piggott. These were re-catalogued in 1955 and are now registered RCS 4.901–4.9015. It is probable that some of the original specimens were not present for this later report.

S.A.M. B 67

Aberllynfi
SO 13 N.E. (1822 3806)

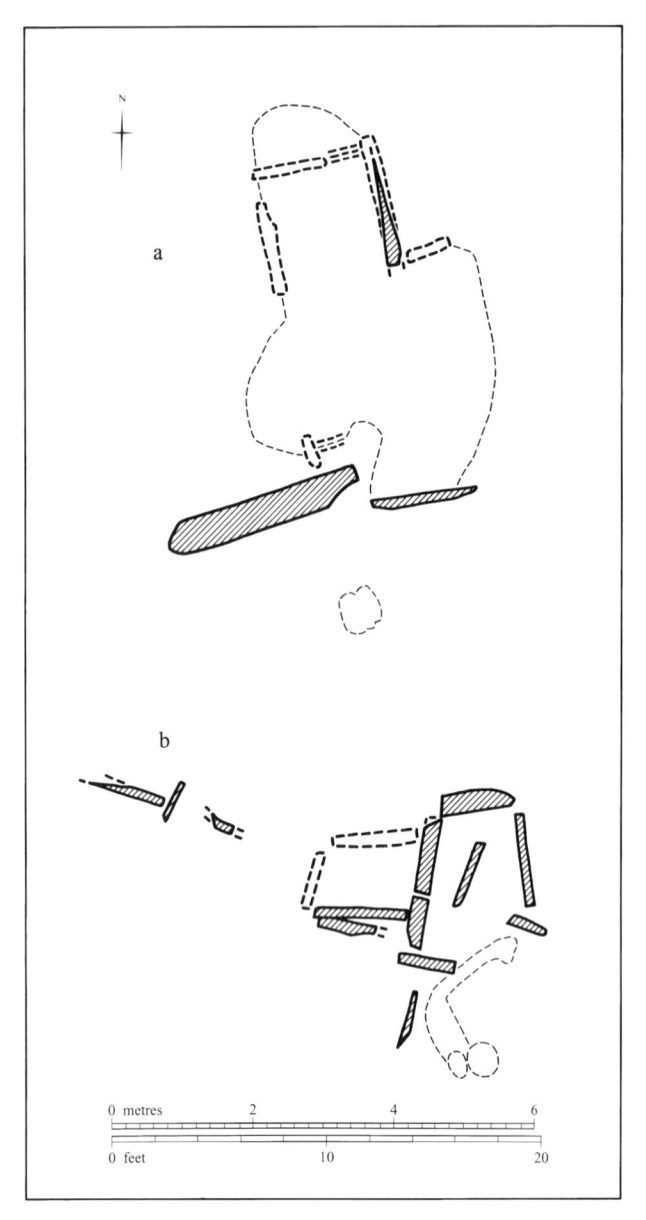

39   Little Lodge chambered tomb (CT 9): detail of central area showing chambers

(CT 10) Carn Goch (Figs. 40–1)

Carn Goch is a large tumulus of earth and stones occupying level, low-lying ground some 85 m above O.D. in a recreation ground-cum-public park on the edge of Llangattock village.[1]

It was discovered by accident in 1847 by workmen engaged in clearing away a large heap of stones in Llangattock Park, then a seat of the Duke of Beaufort.[2] According to the contemporary account,[3] the mound housed a 'cist or cromlech . . . of four rude uprights under a covering stone', inside which '. . . a quantity of human bones were discovered, some of which soon crumbled to dust; but the bone of the arm and also the upper part of the jaw, part of the skull, and a row of teeth were quite perfect, all of which were carefully collected and preserved'.

40 Carn Goch cairn (CT 10): view of mound looking to the west

The interior was 2.6 m long, about 1.22 m wide and 0.7 m high, and contained 'a considerable quantity of fresh looking charcoal . . . mixed with the bones, which apparently belonged to a man of forty or fifty years of age'.

The present diameter of the tumulus is 17.4 m, and its height is 1.4 m. Trees grow on it, there are many signs of modern disturbance, and it is not possible to obtain all the details of the chamber, of which the large slab about 1.5 m square and 20 cm thick now seen lying flat on the surface towards the E. side is possibly a capstone, with two stones just visible beneath its N.E. edge. Opinion has been divided between those who felt this was probably a round barrow[4] and those convinced that it was of greater antiquity than the Bronze Age,[5] even going so far as to claim a faint tail could be discerned.[6] This would elongate the barrow to about 24.4 m by 15 to 18 m wide. Only excavation will determine more precisely.[7]

The bones are now lost, and the fate of the six coins washed out of the cairn in the winter following the first discovery 'sent by his Grace to Lord Northampton' is not known. With one exception the coins were of Constantinian.

[1] O.S. Card SO 21 NW 6.
[2] Anon., *The Gentleman's Magazine* (1847), pt. 2, p. 526.
[3] Anon., *Arch. Camb.*, 9 (1854), p. 148.
[4] Daniel, *P.C.T.*, p. 215.
[5] Crawford, *L.B.C.*, p. 53.
[6] Grimes, *L.C.B.B.M.*, p. 282; also field notes of 21st May 1926 in Grimes MSS, N.M.R.
[7] *Meg. Enq.*, p. 275.

S.A.M. B 28

Llangatwg
SO 21 N.W. (2123 1771)   14 v 85

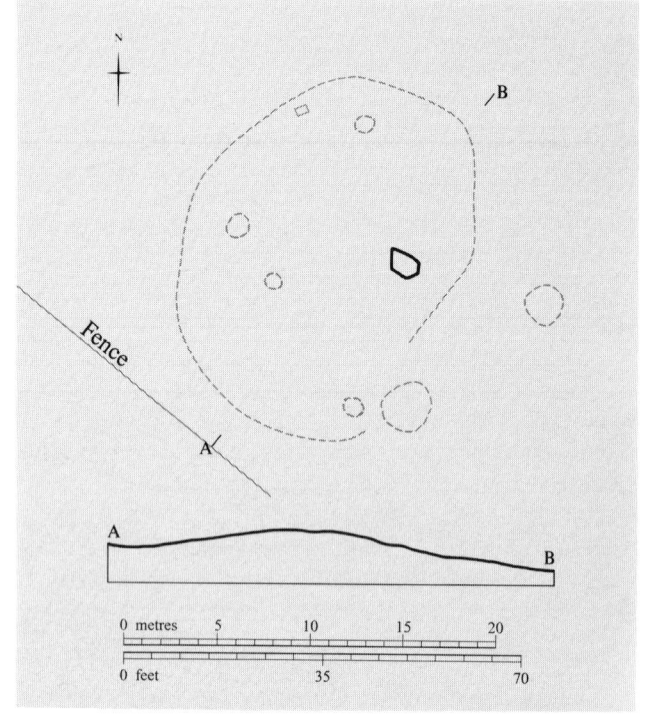

41   Carn Goch cairn or chambered tomb (CT 10): plan and section

(CT 11) Gwernvale (Figs 42–6)

The Gwernvale chambered long cairn is sited on an alluvial terrace about 76 m above O.D., 5 m above the flood plain on the N. side of the Usk valley 0.5 km W. of Crickhowell.[1] Only the most prominent stones of one chamber survive, exposed in the levelled verge on the N. side of the A40 trunk road, of which the realignment was the occasion for a major excavation by W. J. Britnell in 1977–8 (Fig. 43).[2] Exposed to the elements since excavation, the stones are now weathering and de-laminating. Several of the concrete markers meant to facilitate interpretation of the site have been dislodged, probably through road accidents.

Before excavation and through two centuries of antiquarian observation (discussed above p. 26),[3] the one visible chamber was enclosed in a small field passed on its N. side by the former road, but there was no conclusive evidence of a mound, nor had any further stone structures been suspected. Apparently the monument at one time served as a land boundary.[4]

From contemporary accounts, in the eighteenth century the remains appeared as 'a huge tablet of unhewn rock, mounted upon five supporters . . . inclining to the S., and open in the front to the N.; it was placed on a high mound . . . and formerly there seem to have been stones placed edgewise also round what is now almost a semi-circle'.[5] During the excavation they 'found nothing but small bits of Charcoal and several small Bones. There was a piece of dry wall regularly built between two of the upright stones.'[6] The chamber was 'nearly 7 ft 4 ins [2.2 m] long, 4 ft 6 ins [1.4 m] deep and only 2 ft 6 ins [0.75 m] high. The incumbent stone measured 10 ft [3.1 m] in length, 7 ft 8 ins [2.3 m] in breadth and 1 ft 6 ins [0.45 m] in thickness.'[7]

Poole was keen to apportion blame to Colt Hoare and his circle for ransacking the monument.[8] The surviving chamber was planned by Grimes during the 1920s.[9]

Pre-cairn activity. Evidence for Mesolithic activity is noted elsewhere (pp. 17–18), and Neolithic occupation beneath the E. end of the cairn is discussed above (p. 24). It remains possible that the timber post-hole structure (Fig. 46) was connected with mortuary practices rather than with domestic occupation.

The form of the cairn. The original cairn within its outer revetment was just over 45 m long, narrowing

42 Gwernvale chambered tomb (CT 11): view of chamber looking west towards Crickhowell

from its greatest width of just under 17 m near the E. end to only about 6.5 m at the eroded W. end. Though only one side of the forecourt survived, its funnel shape could be deduced as penetrating to a depth of about 5 m between two fairly straight lengths of revetment angled in from a broadly curved E. end and reducing in width from 6 m to the 2 m length of a blocking slab at the base of a false portal. The height of the completed cairn can be deduced, from extant features of the chambers, to have decreased from at least 2.5 m at the false portal of the forecourt, through 2 m over Chamber 1 and 1.5 m over Chambers 2 and 3 at mid-length, to perhaps as little as a final 0.5 m at the W. end.

The construction of the cairn. The excavators have proposed a sequence of building phases, beginning with erection of the chambers and their main passages, stabilised with heavy material, within a predetermined plan, then built up as successive lines of inner and outer revetment. The body of the cairn and the inner walling were of weathered sandstone slabs and boulders, the outer walling being of generally smaller (apparently) quarried stone. The outer revetment was originally continuous across the entrance to the chambers, the material between it and the inner revetment being stabilised into cross-walling where necessary to form extensions of the true chamber passages, to be opened and closed again after access for burial.

The chambers. The four chambers were sited in neat relationship to the cairn axis, the most westerly having been virtually obliterated. The other three were lined with upright slabs or pillars of which only a few had survived to their full height, with neat filling of dry walling in the intervening spaces. They were entered by way of supposedly slab-roofed passages with similar walling, which increased in height from low lintels at the inner revetment.

Chamber 1 (the former 'cromlech'), measuring 3.0 m by 1.6 m internally, was the highest, with headroom of some 1.7 m. It occupied the central part of the cairn 9 m from the forecourt and was formed polygonally by six uprights. The approach was by a curving passage from a point 3 m further to the W. on the S. side of the cairn.

Chambers 2 and 3 were sited virtually back to back, about 2 m apart and set transversely to their short

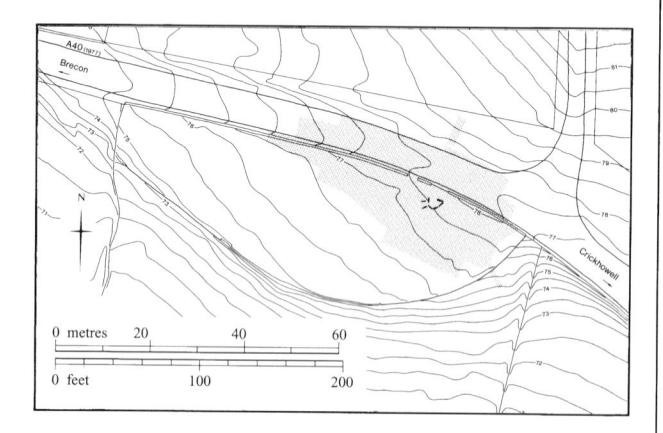

43 Gwernvale chambered tomb (CT 11): pre-excavation location plan showing old road (from *Gwernvale*)

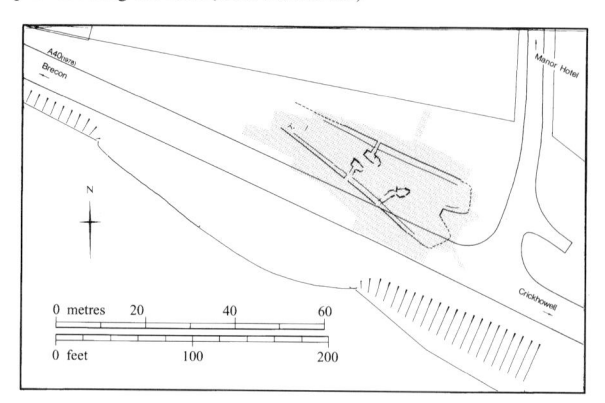

44 Gwernvale chambered tomb (CT 11): showing site of excavated cairn in relation to new road (from *Gwernvale*)

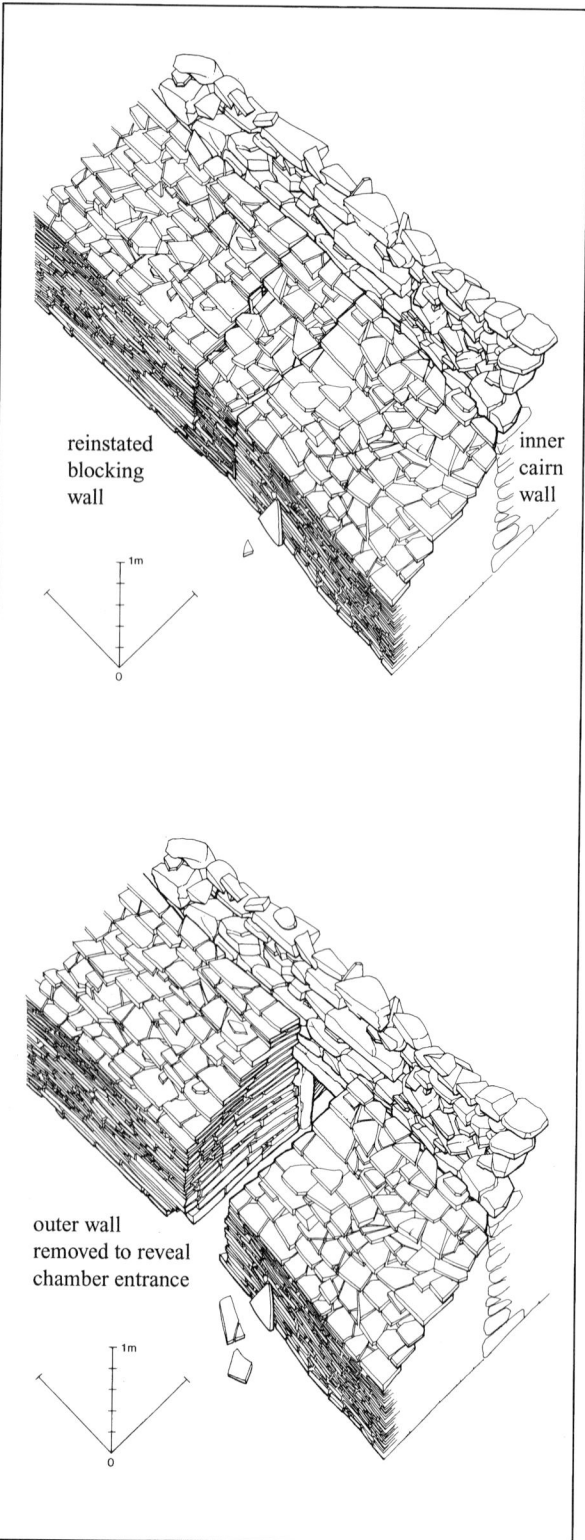

45 Gwernvale chambered tomb (CT 11): plan showing earliest features (from *Gwernvale*)

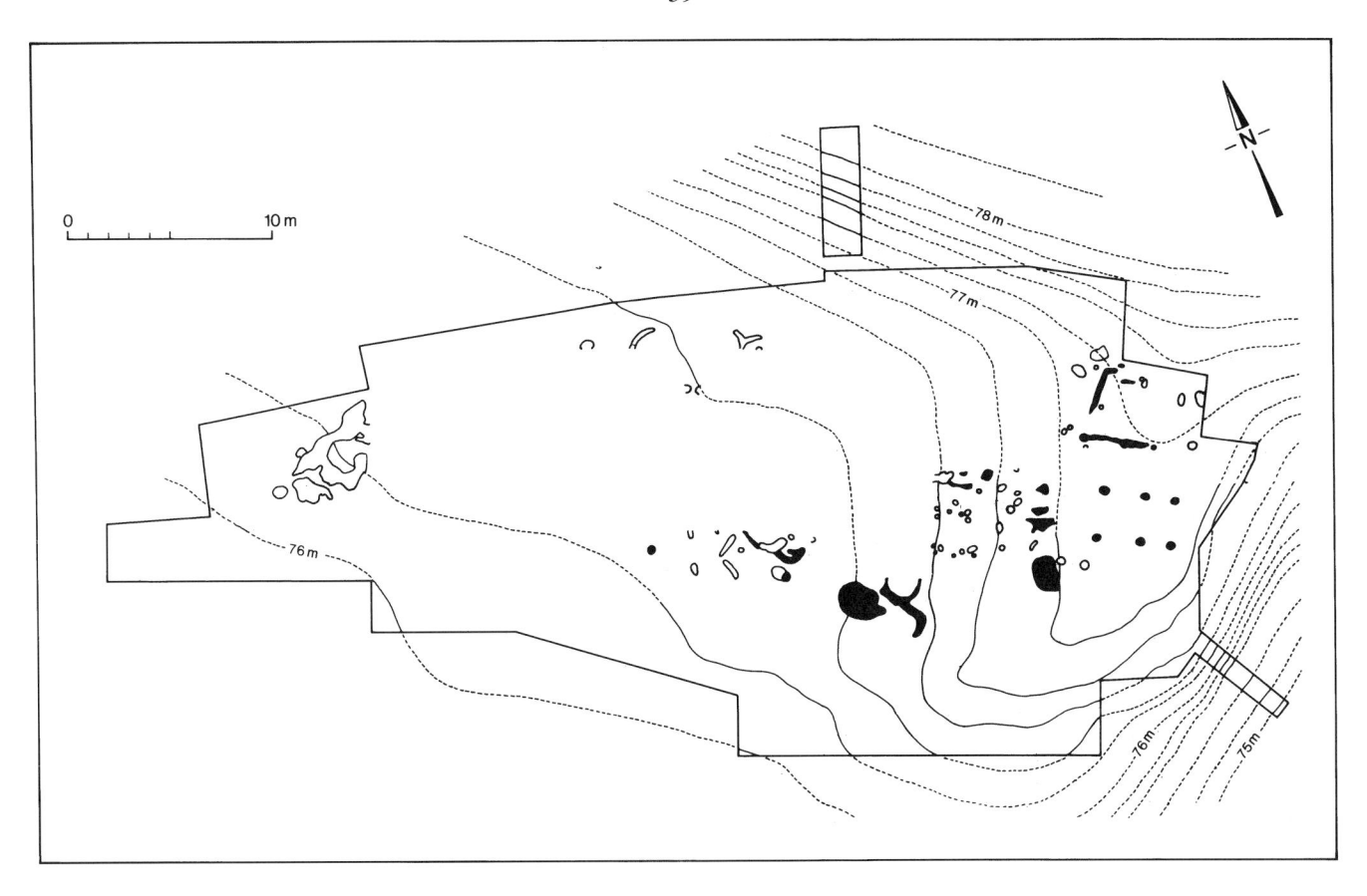

46 Gwernvale chambered tomb (CT 11): showing blocked and opened tomb entrance (from *Gwernvale*)

passages from the S. and N. sides respectively, measuring 2.7 m by 1.2 m and 4.0 m by 1.4 m, and both having an internal height of at least 1.3 m.

The former existence of Chamber 4, entered from the S. side, was deduced from residual features close to the eroded W. end of the cairn that could only be explained through similarity to elements of the other chambers. A short concave stretch of walling in the centre of the cairn just to the E., and similar in type to the inner revetment, could have formed the limit of this chamber, but it also seemed to mark a change in the cairn material to a mass of slabs similar to those used in the outer revetment.

Use of the cairn. Intermittent opening and closing of Chambers 1–3, presumably for successive occasions of burial and possibly extending over a period of some 600 years, may be deduced from the disturbance of the deliberate blocking material of their passages. Final external blocking of access to the chambers, possibly at the same time as of the forecourt, 'was effected partly by raking down unstable stretches of the cairn walling and partly by the importation of new quantities of stone, with the apparent intention of masking all the external features of the cairn'.

Finds. Very little human skeletal material was found. In Chamber 1, which had already been thoroughly disturbed, were fragments of at least two individuals, and of only one in Chamber 2, which suggested to their excavator deliberate emptying just before final closure. Chamber 2 was also the only reliable source of contemporary pottery, comprising fragments of six bowls belonging to the general tradition of undecorated Abingdon ware. By contrast the pottery associated with the final blocking process included decorated Peterborough tradition vessels. The only other certain Neolithic finds were an arrowhead fragment and a flint core, though a number of stray-finds were probably also of Neolithic date.

Interpretation. The Gwernvale tomb is a lateral-chambered example with a dummy forecourt. The excavator felt that some effort had been made to create an archaic form – a tomb which had clearly ceased to be used for formal mortuary activities – may have been a primary objective'. On the basis of radiocarbon dating[10] Britnell proposes that the cairn, begun around the end of the fourth millennium, had remained in use for up to about 600 years.

[1] O.S. Card SO 21 NW 2; Crawford, *L.B.C.*, pp. 59–60; Grimes, *L.C.B.B.M.*, p. 271; Daniel, *P.C.T.*, p. 214; *Meg. Enq.*, p. 274.
[2] *Gwernvale*, pp. 41–154; *Antiquity* 53 (1979), pp. 132–4.
[3] The history of the site is reviewed by C. S. Briggs in *Gwernvale*, pp. 45–8 and *supra* p. 25.
[4] Jones, *Hist. Brecks.*, II, ii (1809), p. 667, fn.
[5] *idem.* pp. 434–5.
[6] Fenton, *Tours*, pp. 25–6.
[7] Payne Llanbedr MS, (1806), fo. 42.
[8] Poole, *Hist. Brecks.*, p. 2. 'It is to be regretted that those savans had not the wit to dig the ample space beneath the capstone without removing it.'
[9] Grimes, *loc. cit.* n. 1; see field plan in Grimes MSS, N.M.R.
[10] In *Antiquity* 54 (1980), p. 147.

S.A.M. B 16

Crickhowell
SO 21 N.W. (2110 1920)   15 x 85

(CT 12) Penywrlod, Llanigon (Figs 47–50)

Facing N.W. on a slope, about 450 m E. of Pen y wrlod, about 260 m above O.D. on the edge of farmland probably enclosed during the late eighteenth century,[1] are the denuded remains of a chambered long cairn consisting mainly of small sandstone slabs up to about 1.5 m high (Fig. 48).[2] The pear-shaped mound is 18.2 m long (oriented 70 degrees E. of N.), and 9.5 m wide near the broader (E.) end, reducing to 7.5 m near the W. end. The site was made more accessible in 1991 by felling trees.

The ground immediately adjacent and above the site is disturbed by minor stone quarrying. Several large tabular slabs protrude from the surface, and similar stones were used in chamber construction. The site has been closely confined by recent boundary features on three sides, obviously absorbing much cairn material and affecting its present form. It is possible that reference to the site as a Druidical Altar in 1898 might infer the survival of a capstone until that date.[3]

Excavation.[4] (Fig. 50) The site's condition has been dramatically affected by excavation. During digging campaigns in 1920 and 1921 the Woolhope Club sank a central trench 14 ft [4.3 m] along the mound axis and cleared out the main chamber. Exploration from the western apex revealed the elements of the smaller, western chamber. Trial holes were also made in other parts of the mound which included a trench from the N.W. towards the main chamber, in vain search of a retaining wall, surrounding upright stones or a ditch. It seems likely that considerable damage was done on the N.E. side of the chamber, and that stones were dislodged by an unknown interloper.[5] So, although representative of sites considered original by the excavators, the current positions of all visible stones almost certainly result from resetting during the excavation.

The mound was found to lie upon a 'natural soil' which sloped from S. to N., the stone debris on the N. tailing out much further than on the S. Its mass consisted almost entirely of large flat stones placed in horizontal layers from the ground upwards, the interstices filled with smaller stones. There was practically no soil except at the surface. It was not possible to determine the origin of a charcoal deposit several inches thick lying to the S.E. of the cist.

The main chamber (Figs. 47, 49). What now appears as a roughly rectangular chamber, about 2.0 m long by 1.0 m, was originally about 2 ft 6 ins wide [0.7 m], by 5 ft 6 ins [1.7 m] long by 5 ft [1.5 m] high. No stone now protrudes higher than 0.9 m. The end stones leaned westward and the side stones leaned northward, probably under the weight of a capstone. 'A supporting wall of thin slabs' about 0.6 m high had been built against the outer faces of the eastern end stone and the southern side stone; the western end stone 'rested on the original level of the site, and was embedded to a depth of 5 to 6 inches [0.15 m] in the clay bed'. The stones are 0.16–0.30 m thick. The

47 Penywrlod (Llanigon) chambered tomb (CT 12): view of main chamber looking east

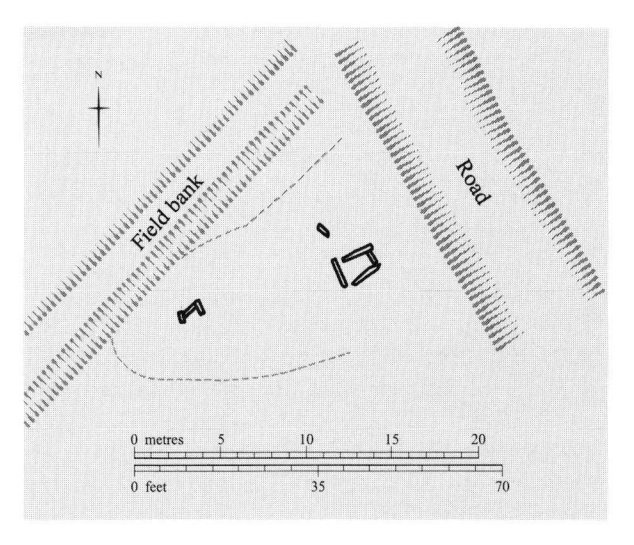

48 Penywrlod (Llanigon) chambered tomb (CT 12): plan from survey with additional details of excavation 'trenches' taken from *Trans Woolhope Club* (1922)

chamber had been filled to a depth of about 1.2 m with stones and black earth containing bones. There were traces of fire, not certainly ancient. No burned material was found except two bones. At the base of the chamber were more bones and two black coarse potsherds from a vessel about 6 inches [0.15 m] in basal diameter. The chamber was floored with rough paving slabs.

The western chamber (Fig. 49) on the N. side of the axis of the mound comprised two parallel slabs 4 ft [1.2 m] apart, but now only 0.95 m apart, forming the E. and W. ends of a cist. There was only one remaining side stone, broken, fallen in from the N., whilst a slab resting on the eastern end stone and sloping away to the E. was probably a displaced capstone. The S.E. angle of the chamber contained a small pocket surrounded and covered by stones. Within this, in a confined space, small charcoal fragments were interdigitated with small stones.

Another upright stone similar in size to the eastern end stone of the western chamber stood parallel to it 1.0 m further E., but the excavators discounted its possible structural significance, as also they dismissed the smaller upright slabs on the N. side of the mound near the larger chamber, whilst a slab lying flat at the southern edge was found not to be the coverstone of a cist.

The finds from the excavation,[6] which were not obtained in consistently controlled conditions, belong to at least three distinct periods. The coarse sherds and the bones from the lowest level in the chamber are presumably from primary inhumation. But sherds of unprovenanced coarse, reddish pottery[7] are conceivably from a later burial phase. Unfortunately twenty-seven teeth, several flint flakes and a scraper were also taken from disturbed earth. In the circumstances it is impossible to distinguish any grouping in the twenty or so individuals represented,[8] including children of various ages as well as adult men and women.

The excavation spoil also yielded dozens of small blue glass beads, and tubes of vitreous paste, divided externally into rounded segments, probably of Romano-British date,[9] together with an unstratified Roman small brass coin of Crispus (A.D. 317–326)

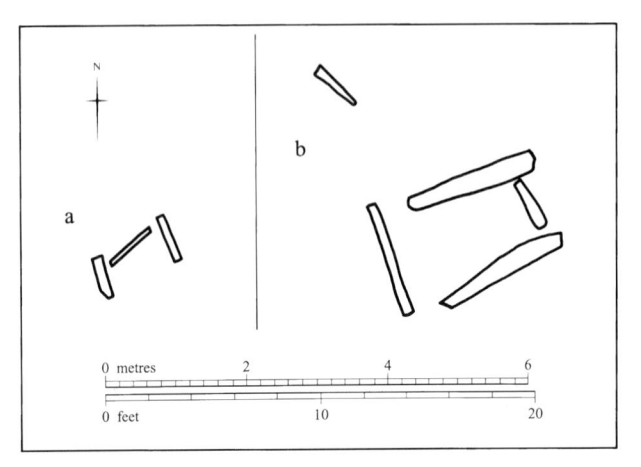

49 Penywrlod (Llanigon) chambered tomb (CT 12): detail of chambers

picked up near the N.W. corner of the main chamber. These may have been planted to confuse the excavators.

On the available evidence, the site seems to represent a variety of terminal-chamber tomb. But much may have been lost through erosion and the excavation record is poor. Drawing attention to its unusual pear-shape, Corcoran suggested a two-stage building for the site, forwarding the idea that the more eastern chamber may originally have been built in a circular cairn.[10] However, it is doubtful if there is yet sufficient evidence to support such a multi-period theory.

[1] Agricultural improvements are noted 'at Penyrworlood, near Hay' by Arthur Young in his tour of 1776 (*Tours in England and Wales: Selected from the Annals of Agriculture*), London School of Economics and Political Science Reprints, no. 14, (London: 1932), pp. 18–19).

[2] O.S. Card SO 23 NW 1.

[3] W. E. T. Morgan, *Trans. Woolhope Club* (1898), p. 40.

[4] The circumstances of this excavation are of interest to the integrity of the finds, some of which might have been planted as a joke. According to a letter from O. G. S. Crawford to W. J. Hemp (29 viii 21; copy in R.C.A.M. archive), 'Mr Vulliamy is strongly suspected by Mr Morgan of being the author of surreptitious fossicking in the Long Barrow at Penywrlod (Llanigon) . . . I saw the result. Two of the four uprights enclosing the "chamber" at the E. end have been thrown down. The chamber itself has been filled with debris.' Crawford provided a sketch plan of the disturbed area.

[5] W. E. T. Morgan and G. Marshall, interim report, *Arch. Camb.* 76 (1921), pp. 296–9; final report (from which descriptive passages quoted here are taken), *Trans. Woolhope Club* (1922), pp. 30–40, with plan, and reports on bones by Sir Arthur Keith and also on beads by H. C. Beck.

[6] Those preserved in The National Museum of Wales are listed in Grimes, *Prehist. Wales*, p. 153, nos. 172–3; C. E. Vulliamy, *Man*, (Jan. 1922), pp. 11–13.

[7] Described by Grimes (*M.M.W.*, p. 117) as 'poor but undoubted beaker'.

[8] As reported by Sir Arthur Keith, loc. cit. n. 5.

[9] H. C. Beck and J. F. S. Stone, *Archaeologia* 85 (1936), p. 211.

[10] In *Meg. Enq.*, p. 43 and Fig. 10, p. 44.

S.A.M. B 12

Llanigon
SO 23 N.W. (2248 3986)   8 xi 73

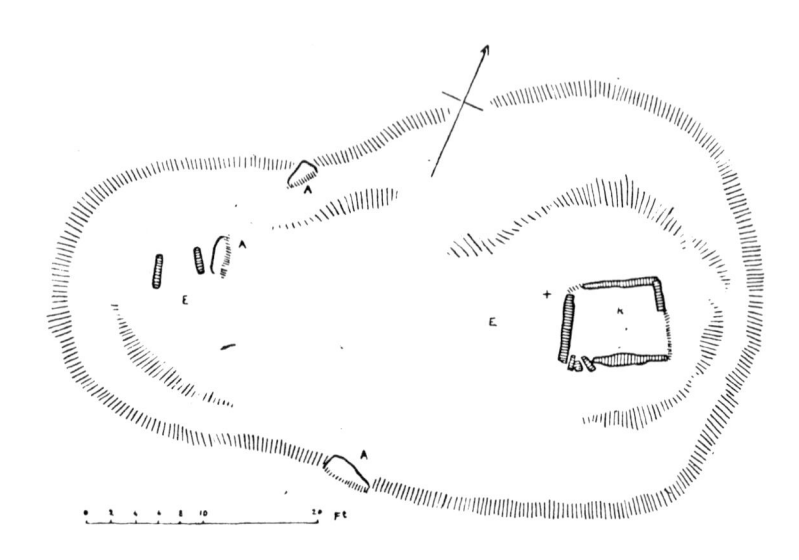

50 Penywrlod (Llanigon) chambered tomb (CT 12): from *Man* (Jan. 1922)

(CT 13) Court Farm, Clyro (Radnorshire) (Figs. 51–2)

The vestigial remains of a megalithic tomb were recognised at Clyro Court in 1973 by W. E. Griffiths,[1] lying in hummocky pasture on a river terrace about 10 m above the River Wye some 60 m above O.D.

History. Curiously, the site has been a well-known landmark for several centuries, the name Carnaf [=Carnau, or the Cairns] being the title given by the monks of Abbey Cwmhir to lands they administered in this locality at Clyro.[2]

The site. The tomb remains lie among several other low, enigmatic earthworks surviving in the surrounding field which appear to be early domestic boundary or garden divisions probably of medieval origin. The N.W. end of the megalith, which seems to have been re-shaped by built or dumped stone, may at some time have been incorporated into these, possibly as the base of a summer house or dove cote.

The mound. A recognisable mound survives about 32 m long (N.E.–S.W.) with a maximum breadth of 16.5 m about a third of the distance from the N.E. end. It stands up to 1.1 m high about 8 m from the S.W. end. Along the scarp edge the site has been modified by creation of a slight but straight bank, now low, but which at some time presumably formed an effective boundary.

Chambers. The remains of one, possibly two chambers survive within a slight hollow towards the S.W. end of the earthwork. These comprise four large slabs of a local sedimentary rock up to 1.6 m long, 0.1–2 m thick and standing up to 0.5 m high. They are paired in two groups. All are tangentially aligned, the more southerly pair set almost at right-angles, as if the two sides comprise half a robbed chamber. The rear of the south-western slab is exposed to show packing stones helping to maintain its upright position.

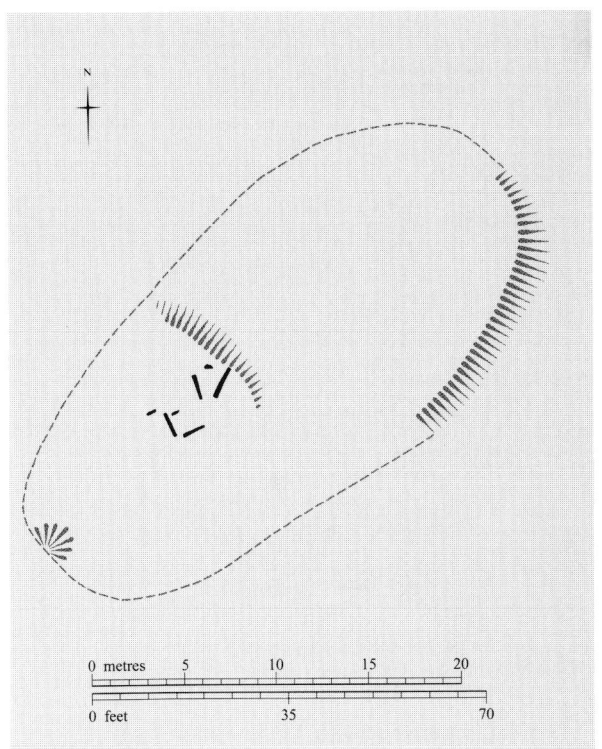

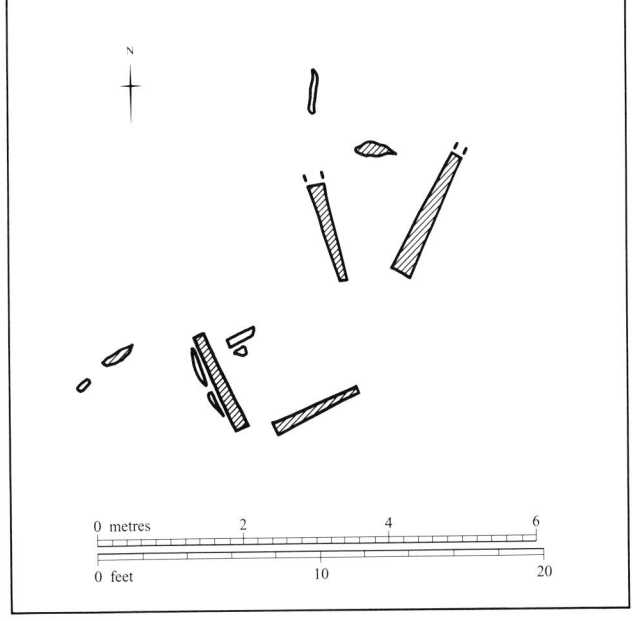

51 Clyro Court Farm (Radnorshire) chambered tomb (CT 13): plan

52 Clyro Court Farm (Radnorshire) chambered tomb (CT 13): plan of chamber and entrance

The other pair are not so readily identified as part of a structure, the south-western slab lying approximately N.–S., its partner converging to narrow their distance apart from a gap about 1.5 m wide on the S. to about 0.5 m on the N.. A small, flat, outlying slab along the same alignment as the W. stone in a northward direction may be original and could hint at the existence of a longer, transepted gallery. The structural relationship of several other, smaller upright stones is unclear.

The area is one which has produced a considerable number of flints attesting to prehistoric activity from the Mesolithic to the Bronze Age.[3]

[1] O.S. Card SO 24 SW 18; C. H. Houlder, *Arch. in Wales* 13 (1973), p. 63.
[2] R.C.A.M., *Inv. Rads*, no. 120, Clyro Court Farm, p. 35.
[3] *Trans Radnors. Soc.* 30 (1960), pp. 57–61; 31 (1961), pp. 47–52; barbed and tanged arrowhead Brecknock Museum, R.302.3.

Clyro
SO 24 S.W. (212 431)   ii 91

Rejected Sites (RCT 1–11)

The following entries relate to sites which have been at some time considered to be Neolithic tombs or long barrows, but for which, upon re-consideration, it is now felt a different interpretation is more appropriate.

(RCT 1) Pen y Garn Goch (SN 8848 5029), see RC 62

(RCT 2) King's Stone

Theophilus Jones first noted a cromlech here in 1809.[1] Its authenticity was first disputed in 1853,[2] and later in 1921 by Crawford.[3] The feature comprises a large slab, the supposed capstone of a cromlech, about 3.7 m by 2.7 m by 0.8 m thick, which protrudes fairly steeply from the edge of a rough knoll in a naturally detached part of the local rock formation.

[1] Jones, *Hist. Brecks.* II, ii (1809), p. 561.
[2] *Arch. Camb.* 8 (1853), pp. 139, 309, 316.
[3] Crawford, *L.B.C.*, pp. 185–6.

Llan-y-wern
SO 03 S.E. (0877 3037)   15 x 86

(RCT 3) Llaneglwys

An E.–W. oriented earthen long mound 65–70 ft [20–22 m] long by 35 ft [10.5 m] wide and 4–5 ft [1.2–1.5 m] high was at one time noted on the northern slope of the Rhiwiau Brook valley.[1] No feature resembling a long barrow could be located at this spot.[2]

[1] D. P. Webley, *B.B.C.S,.* 17 (1956–8), p. 55.
[2] O.S. Card SO 03 NE 3.

Crickadarn
SO 03 N.E. (072 395)   10 x 74

(RCT 4) Tump Wood

Around 1930 Sir Cyril Fox[1] noted a disturbed cairn of large stones and boulders, about 29 m long and aligned N.–S., lying in the hollow of a re-entrant, which obscured its true width. No associated megalithic stones were described. There is an accumulation of stones at this spot but this is unlikely to be Neolithic.

[1] O.S. Card SO 12 SW 16; C. Fox, N.M.W., MS notebook III, p. 91; N.M.W. Record O.S. 6-inch XXXIV.

Llanddeti
SO 12 S.W. (1130 2140)   25 xi 75

(RCT 5) Cwrt y Prior

In 1909 the Rev. Daniel Lewis mentioned 'the remains of a cromlech' here, but in his time 'there was only one stone of considerable dimensions remaining'.[1] Although some large stones can be traced in fields in this area, none can be definitely associated with a burial chamber.

[1] R.C.A.H.M., *Minutes of Evidence*, I (1912), p. 50, para. 1476; Roese *Thesis* no. 252.

Llan-gors
SO 12 N.E. (150 282)   26 viii 86

(RCT 6) Cwm Fforest

A structure first noted on the edge in the bank of the Afon Rhiangoll at this site in 1924,[1] was long considered to be a chambered tomb.[2] Re-examination reveals this to be a ruined corn-drying kiln. Its rectangular kiln chamber and the low, slab-roofed flue passage facing into the river gorge below, demonstrate the need for its re-interpretation.[3]

[1] O.S. Card SO 12 NE 4; Crawford, *L.B.C.*, pp. 54–5.
[2] Grimes, *M.M.W.*, p. 139; Daniel, *P.C.T.*, p. 214; Savory, *Prehist. Breck.* I, p. 88; Corcoran, *Meg. Enq.*, p. 275.
[3] As was hinted at by Roese's remark (*Thesis*, no. 255), that the construction was 'non-tomb-like'.

S.A.M. B 7

Talgarth
SO 12 N.E. (1833 2944)   15 xi 73

(RCT 7) Rhos Fach or Fawr

An oval, irregularly mounded area here, about 22.6 m long, 10.4 m wide and only 0.4 m high, was at one time interpreted as a wrecked long cairn with 'definite evidence of a passageway leading from the edge of the mound towards the centre'.[1] However, the remains are too slight for this interpretation, and are probably not prehistoric.

[1] O.S. Card SO 13 SE 13; C. B. Crampton and D. P. Webley, *B.B.C.S.,* 22 (1966–8), pp. 72–3.

Llaneleu
SO 13 S.E. (1833 3365)   24 iii 75

(RCT 8) Glanyrafon

In 1886 Edwin Poole referred to 'a small but perfect cromlech' on the estate here, 'evidently . . . overlooked by the antiquary, as Dr Nicholas is the only writer on the subject who we find notices it'.[1] No further detail was given by Nicholas.[2] This 'cromlech' was an eighteenth- or nineteenth-century estate feature in the grounds of the present Glanyrafon House until its one surviving component, a standing stone, was excavated without significant discovery prior to building development in 1993.[3]

[1] O.S. SO 21 NW 4; Poole, *Hist. Brecks.*, p. 2.
[2] T. Nicholas, *Annals and Antiquities of the Counties and County Families of Wales*, (London, 1872), (unpag.).
[3] N.A. Page, *Arch. in Wales* 33 (1993), p. 45.

Crickhowell
SO 21 N.W. (219 180)   26 vi 74

(RCT 9) Maes Coch or Blaen Digedi Fawr (see SC 10)

Near Maes Coch there is a mound and at Blaen Digedi Fawr there is a stone circle. Confusion between these by several investigators believing one to have been a megalithic tomb seems to be the result of a misprinted grid reference. The Commission records a mound considered to be natural at SO 2357 3797. First located in 1956 by Webley at SO 239 378,[1] and described as 'in a ruinous condition' in 1971,[2] the mound alluded to would appear to be located at SO 239 373 (the site of an old quarry and a 'stone').[3]

[1] O.S. Card SO 23 NW 31; D. P. Webley, *B.B.C.S* 17 (1956–58), p. 55.
[2] Savory, *Prehist. Breck.* I, p. 8.
[3] Correspondence between C. H. Houlder and D. P. Webley, January 1974, in N.M.R.

Talgarth
SO 23 N.W. (2357 3797 and 239 373)

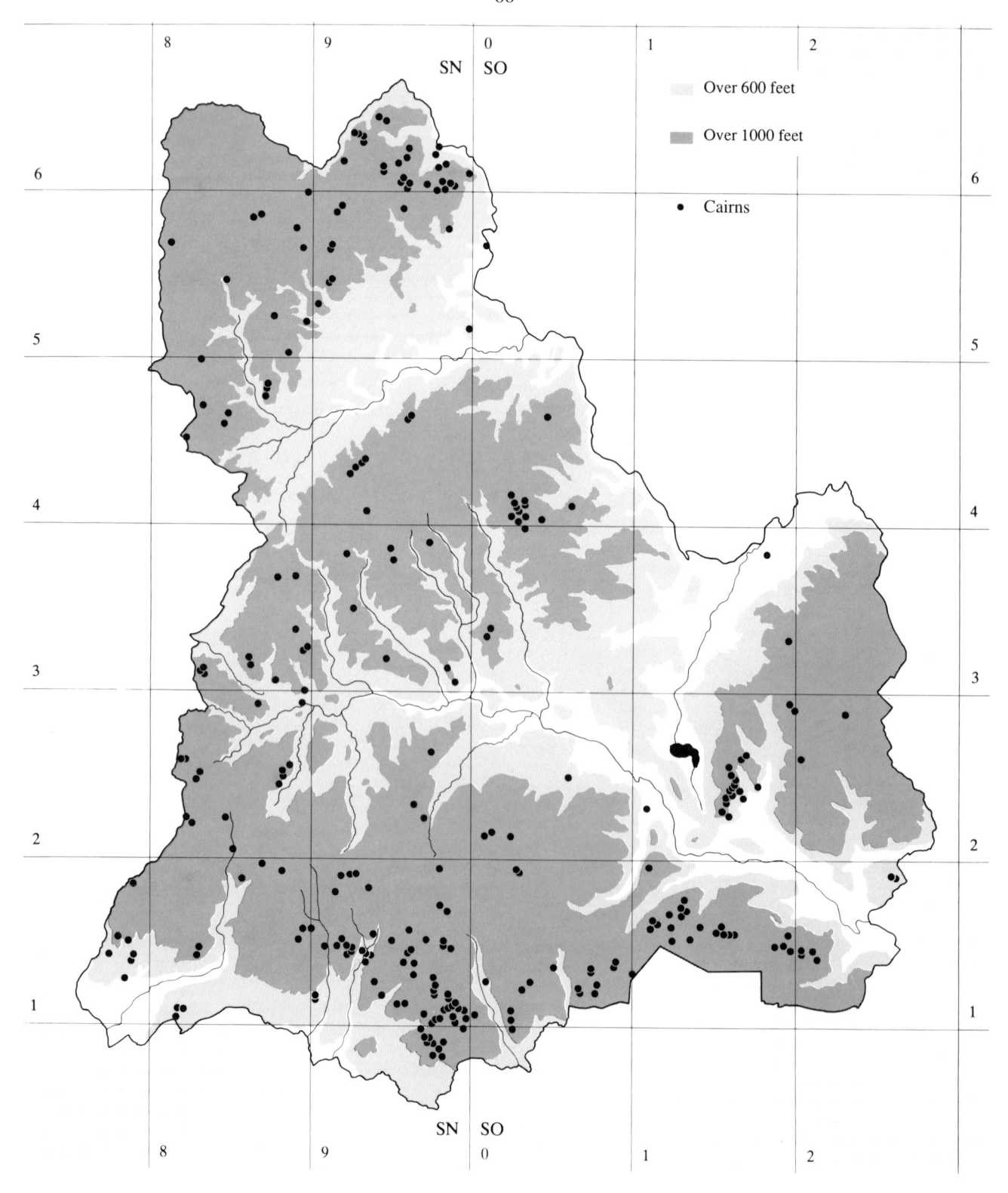

53 Distribution of Bronze Age cairns

Burial and Ritual Structures of the Bronze Age

Round Cairns

Introduction

The origins of circular burial sites lie chronologically within later Neolithic traditions[1] deriving in part from insular passage graves (*c.* 4,000–2,000 B.C.) which originated on the continent. Circular, stone-structured cairns of the types described here were probably constructed as early as *c.* 2,000 and may have continued in use until *c.* 1,000 B.C.[2] Unfortunately, even after careful excavation, it is not always easy to distinguish between the functions of ritual and burial within cairns, and there is not universal agreement upon the uses to which particular structural components were originally put, if indeed recognisable components are now in evidence.

The sites presented in this section are those considered most likely to have fulfilled a burial or ritual function. However, it is acknowledged that the origin of some stone mounds may have been entirely agricultural. It is similarly possible that excavation of individual mounds listed among the field clearance features might also produce burial sites.

Cairns were used as boundary markers during the Dark Ages,[3] a practice which probably continued for estate and community purposes until the present century.

History of Discovery

Although the earliest recorded cairn excavation in South Wales is by Sir Joseph Banks, excavation as an antiquarian tool only came to Wales through the work of Sir Richard Colt Hoare and his circle at Gwernvale megalith in 1804 (see p. 26). Around that time, and probably following that event, Archdeacon Henry Thomas Payne seems to have embarked upon a local two-year digging campaign. So Gwernvale's excavation appears to have been a major catalyst to cairn excavation in this part of Wales.

Payne dug on the hills above (and south of) Llangattock in May 1806. His personal account explains that he was:

'accompanied by my friend, Sir William Ouseley, Mr Bird, and some other Gentlemen with labourers, I endeavoured by opening these heaps, to ascertain the object of their erection – but had the mortification to find that we were too late in our enquiries. One of them had been completely hollowed out in the middle to the surface of the ground and now presents a mere empty bason . . . The other had been considerably demolished by some workmen, who had employed the stone in erecting a Watchhouse for the Duke of Beaufort's game keeper, during the growing season. We however proceed to an examination of this last . . . and in the centre of the Heap, discovered a cist 3 ft long by 3 ft wide and 2 deep, formed of 4 strong stones, pitched edgewise in the ground, back 3 deep with others of the same kind and covered over with a heavy tablet. The soil at the bottom had been excavated to a depth of at least 4 ft and the hollow filled in with very small washed pebbles, such as are usually found by the sides of rivers. We removed them all, till the native yellow clay appeared, which we dug out to a considerable depth when it became very wet. We then desisted, as conceiving it useless to proceed further, particularly as the clay exhibited no appearance of having been previously disturbed . . . [with] no deposit . . . I should have observed that the incumbent table was cracked through, though it was not disturbed. From the [shape] and size of the cist, it would seem to have been intended for the preservation of an urn, . . . the stones in the bottom . . . for drainage'.[4]

These sites, difficult to re-identify, might be equated specifically with RC 264 and RC 299, though they could be either RCs 266 or 267 or RCs 294–299.

On Mynydd Llangynidr, where, according to Theophilus Jones and Nicholas Carlisle there were three or four cairns,[5] Payne and his associates excavated Trevil Glas Cairn, a cairn of great size.[6] This, too, proved to be empty, but may be equated with RC 264. On another occasion, having spent two days' laborious exertions above and to the N. of Crickhowell, Payne wrote, 'we attacked two large Carnau upon the Breanog Mountain in the height above the British Encampment of Crug Howell, but found no marks whatever, either of cremation or interment'.[7] These sites may lie upon Cerrig Calch (RCs 306–7).

Further east, Payne and the same Mr Bird had 'previously opened some other Carnau, upon the Mountain which separated Llanthony from the Coed Grono, in every one of which was discovered stone cists, containing bones, sand and bits of charcoal, but no other remains'.[8] Some of these are certainly in Monmouthshire, but one may have been Carn Disgwylfa (RC 309), which is today heavily cratered.

A final, notable discovery of this period was the Llanelieu [Llaneleu] flint dagger burial, also mentioned by Payne, though also noted by the antiquary Richard Fenton, and published by the county historian, Theophilus Jones (LBS 9).

Nicholas Carlisle, in his *Topographical Dictionary*, appears to have introduced the story of a 'Twm Bach' who had come from North Wales to dig for treasure in 'a Carn' in the hamlet of Glyn Collwyn (UCB 7), but who in exhuming 'a large Cist' had instead found 'various antiquities . . . [of which] . . . none . . . were preserved, as the finder sold them to an itinerant Jew'.[9]

Whereas records survive of occasional antiquarian visits to cairns during the nineteenth century, few are reliable excavation records. William Rees's work on Mynydd Bach Trecastell (RC 35–8), though quite illuminating for its day, leaves the most important questions unanswered: exactly which cairns were dug? Records of the urn find near Abercar (LBS 4) made in 1866 are equally disappointing.

Not until T. C. Cantrill systematically combed the limestone pavements around Ystradfellte and the Cribarth, and searched other parts of the uplands during the late 1890s, was a more scientific interest taken in prehistoric sites. Cantrill was engaged in producing geological memoirs by the Geological Survey, and therefore had an ideal opportunity to examine rarely visited landscapes.[10] In the context of cairn studies, his most important contribution was through the excavation of sites upon Fan Foel (RC 26), near Carnon Gwynion (RC 91) and Share y Wlad (RC 92–5), together with contemporary site descriptions (RC 96–7, RC 123; LBS 1). Cantrill's importance lies in his careful sifting and collecting of fragmented flint, potsherds and other contents held in the old ground surfaces, and in the detail and system of his descriptive accounts. His work was scarcely approached in quality by the efforts of the Woolhope Club at Twyn y Beddau in the 1870s which seem to have occasioned Kilvert such mirth (RC 311; Fig. 87).

By Cantrill's time many cairns had already been marked upon large-scale O.S. maps during trigonometrical reconnaissance going back almost a century, so it is possible that had the Ordnance Survey's records survived (they were destroyed in Southampton by enemy action in World War II), these might have provided insights into the antiquarian activities of individuals whose personal contributions have since been overlooked.

Cantrill's work was followed by a handful of investigations of varying quality. Vulliamy's contribution to round cairn digging (LBS 10) was as unremarkable as that upon long barrows (p. 25). Sir John Conway Lloyd's dig on Mynydd Epynt (RC 151–3) and that of Rev. V. E. Davies (RC 302) upon Pen Gloch-y-Pibwr added both negative and positive sightings of cairn and cist interiors to the more adventitious finds of Beaker graves on Pant y Waun (LBS 2) and Dol-y-gaer (LBS 5).

G. C. Dunning's excavation at Ynys-hir (RC 138; Fig. 70), undertaken in advance of the military requisition of Mynydd Epynt, ranks as one of the most important and well-conducted investigations the county has ever seen, and it is unfortunate that radiometric dating and pollen analysis were not available at that time.

Excavation in this part of Wales were dominated after 1950 by the interdisciplinary work of C. B. Crampton and D. P. Webley and of their associate, T. W. Burke. Their most notable contribution was at Twyn Bryn Glas (RC 127; Fig. 69), but important re-appraisals and site descriptions were undertaken of the cairn which produced a sandstone disc on Cefn Sychpant (RC 125) and the bronze knife-dagger from Cefn Cilsanws (RC 201, 211 or 212). Considerable interest also attaches to excavation around a cairn (RC 74) in Nant Cadlan which produced an interesting flint assemblage, ranging in date from Mesolithic (MS 7) to Bronze Age. Employment of soil and pollen analytical techniques at this site rendered the work particularly valuable. Similar scientific investigation undertaken in conjunction with the excavation at Nant Maden, a classic kerb cairn (RC 111; Figs 64–5), help mark this as one of the most important investigations of the post-war period.

In recent years the Clwyd-Powys Archaeological Trust has recorded and excavated cairns and burials.

Emergency recording of two urns from the path at Fan-y-Big (LBS 6) followed the careful research work of Crew at Corn Du (RC 225). In 1991–2, it was necessary to excavate the cairn capping the highest peak in South Wales, at Pen y Fan (RC 226), owing to the damaging threat of visitor erosion. Due to similar pressures, a re-examination of Corn Du followed in 1993. The exploration of various sites on Mynydd y Drum (RC 16–17; US 28) in advance of opencast coal extraction produced limited evidence for Bronze Age burial activity.

Although a greatly enhanced record of cairns was collected during a government employment scheme administered by the Trust in the early 1980s from which record forms have provided the Commission with otherwise inaccessible information (Ordnance Survey Antiquities Division Staff apart), it is to H. Eckart Roese and Peter M. Jones that most credit is due for field observation and discovery during the 1970s and 1980s.

Eckart Roese's doctoral dissertation[11] was partly based upon comprehensive cairn site lists and descriptions taken at first hand from field observation and archival investigation. This included up to one hundred references to Brecknockshire round cairns. Through regular contributions to *Archaeology in Wales*, Peter Jones has augmented the numerical and locational information on cairns.

Density and Population

Some 311 cairns are listed in this section, together with 10 lost burial sites (LBS 1–10), 10 burials unclassifiable due to lack of up-to-date information (UCB 1–8), several unproven cropmark or lost sites (LC 1–9) and eight sites rejected as not demonstrably Bronze Age (RCS 1–8). One site (RBB 1) is shown not to lie in Brecknockshire. The total of approximately 350 burial cairns or burial sites compares with 164 from Caernarfonshire,[12] 320 in Cardiganshire,[13] 383 (400 separate monuments) in Glamorgan,[14] and 113 from Merioneth.[15] These figures have to be seen against regionally differential destruction rates, and considered alongside varying pedological and geological conditions. Because aerial photography has not been particularly helpful in charting barrow distributions upon valley ploughland in Wales, it is difficult to relate these figures to numerical estimates of original Bronze Age populations. Questions of demography become even more problematical when it is shown that cairns and barrows may merely have acted as the focal point to numerous otherwise unmarked burials (see p. 73).

Cairn Form and Dimensions

Among the Brecknockshire cairns are structures ranging from about 2.5 m in diameter to stone spreads of 25 or 30 m in diameter, or even, more rarely, up to 50 m in diameter; some perhaps representing lost or robbed cairns. Few stand above 1 m in height, though Twyn y Beddau (RC 311; Fig. 87) attained 2.8 m (comparable to the 12 ft given by Theophilus Jones in 1809), and others (RC 44, 47, 222–3 and 302) are likely to have approached that height.

The shapes of the Brecknockshire cairns are conventionally circular, though in some cases recent destruction has brought about shapelessness. Two cairns (RC 186 and 188) are unusual in having square 'platforms' on their perimeters. The only known parallel to this is at Abercamddwr, Trefeurig, Ceredigion.[16]

Most cairns encountered, however, were without recognisable structure, and were therefore incapable of further definition. Structured cairns are now generally divided into two main types for convenience of description. Those having a peristalithic ring revetting or enclosing the cairn mass are kerb cairns. Monuments having an internal area completely free of stone, though encompassed by some sort of overall stone enclosure, are ring cairns. The term 'platform cairn' has not been employed.

Kerb Cairns

The most common structural element recognisable in cairns is kerbing. These encircling uprights may be seen alternatively as necessary revetments to cairn mass,[17] or as architectural features designed to give cairns a more mystical and aesthetic quality, which notionally relates their builders to the surrounding landscape.[18] From precise mensuration of the peristaliths in stone circles and structured cairns, further theorists advance an astronomical explanation for their layout (pp. 143, 145–6).

The origin and ancestry of the term kerb cairn has recently been reviewed.[19] Following its introduction in

BRONZE AGE BURIAL AND RITUAL STRUCTURES

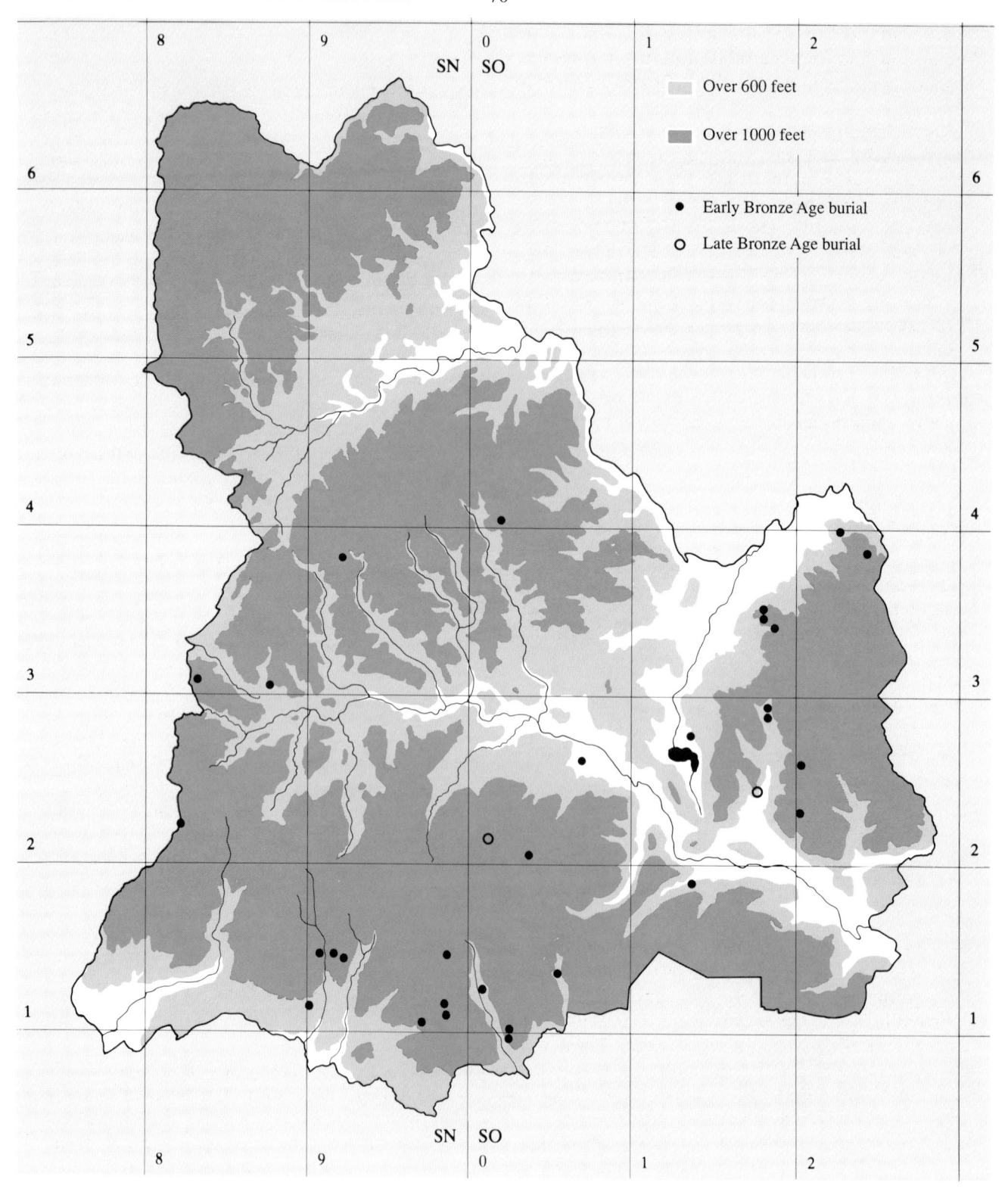

54 Distribution of Bronze Age burials

a paper of 1972 by Lynch,[20] its definition has been simplified and kerb cairn is now the term most commonly adopted for peristalithic Bronze Age burial sites.

Only about 10 per cent of the total cairn sample from Brecknocks have produced any evidence suggestive of structural revetment. Kerbing, or hinted kerbstones were seen at: RC 16, 20, 53–6, 68, 77, 85, 91, 104, 107, 111, 151, 186, 190, 198, 217, 219, 222, 225–6, 232, 249, 270, 281, 283–4, 287, 292, 308 and 311. One cairn on the Cribarth (RC 19) appears to be revetted by drystone walling. The rarity of recognisable orthostats could be dependent upon local lithological factors, particularly the availability of large, durable stone slabs or boulders. Absence of larger orthostats could equally result from stone robbing during the historic period.

Ring Cairns

The problem of what constitutes, or is acceptable as, a ring cairn, is a vexed one, largely because of the difficulty in distinguishing between annular structures which may have been huts, on the one hand, and those which were used as ritual and burial sites, on the other.[21] Matters are further complicated because circles of small stones may often be all that survive after stone robbing and clearance of the cairn's central area in recent historic times. The first of these difficulties is encountered in perceptions of Cantrill's 'hut circle' on Carnon Gwynion (RC 97), here listed as a ring cairn, though with no absolute certainty as to its original function.

Nineteen possible or certain ring cairns are recorded from the county (RC 5, 10, 14, 50, 78, 79, 96–7, 99, 164, 182, 202, 205–6, 209, 235–7 and 238, together with (possibly) RC 49). Whereas most ring cairns described here are of stone, two in Ystradfellte are complex earthworks, more like the classic barrow types found upon chalk downland. These are the triple concentric earthwork near Rhyd Uchaf (RC 78; Figs. 61, 62) and the simpler example near Tir yr Onnen, the former situated close to some early settlement features (US 45–6), the latter lying within the palimpsest landscape of Mynydd y Garn (US 75–8). A similar monument was illustrated by Sir George Clark at Pen Twr in 1873 (RC 63; Fig. 59).

Barrows

Only a small proportion of the recorded burial sites from Brecknockshire seem to have been of earth. However, since excavation has shown some cairns, like Twyn Bryn Glas (RC 127; Fig. 69), Ynys-hir (RC 138; Fig. 70) and Nant Maden (RC 111; Fig. 64–5), to have comprised layers of earth, and as some 'barrows' like Twyn y Beddau (RC 311; Fig. 87) included layers of stone, typological division is obviously to some degree arbitrary. Indeed, some, many or even most of the cairns may at one time have possessed cappings of earth which have either leached away naturally, or have been subjected to soil scavenging.

At one time a number of upstanding valley bottom sites were considered to have survived since the Bronze Age,[22] but a clearer understanding shows some, at least, to be field clearances of recent construction (see pp. 204–5 for discussion).[23]

Topographical Distribution (Fig. 54)

It has been conclusively demonstrated by Roese that the distribution of cairns in south Powys owes most to factors of survival, and that any absence from the record of burial sites from the valley floors must be due to human and natural erosion factors.[24] Most recorded cairns occur in situations now designated as Common Land, or lie within areas employed as sheepwalks, or for rough grazing of cattle or ponies. Factors both natural and human, more generally affecting the survival of cairns in the uplands, are discussed in detail elsewhere (pp. 191–4).

Discovery and the Excavation of burials

Although some thirty-seven possible instances of Bronze Age burial are known from the county, these account for only a small number (perhaps 5 to 10 per cent) of the known burial monuments. Since most cairns are believed to have been intended as places for the dead, want of investigation therefore means that few have produced any real evidence of burial. Many cairns have obviously been robbed and, furthermore, certain of the antiquarian (and some recent) finds derive from sites destroyed with scant record. The grave groups from Abercar, Vaynor (LBS 4), Cwm Car, Dol y gaer (LBS 5), Waun Ddu, Llangynidr (LBS 7) and Tŷ Du, Llanelieu (LBS 9), fall within this category. Unfortunately, the total of recorded burials producing artefacts through scientific excavation comprises less than one per cent of known cairns.

Excavation has produced cremations and their gravegoods from a variety of structures. At Ynys-hir (RC 138; Fig. 70), a cairn sited close to the stone circle (SC 5; Fig. 100), though with no demonstrable stratigraphic connection, the mound type falls loosely within the definition of kerb cairn, even though in this case it was earth-capped. From it came a pygmy cup protected by a pit within a gap (thought to have been an entrance) in its original kerb. Other important finds included a fragment of cloth and a lignite bead. The cairn type represented at Twyn Bryn Glas (RC 127; Fig. 69), though boat-shaped, is loosely comparable. This produced similar finds; a pygmy cup in a primary position, with fragments of Beaker underlying parts of the cairn. From Nant Maden (RC 111; Fig. 64–5), only 1 km to the west of Twyn Bryn Glas, a variety of pottery traditions was recognised. The fragments lay both within and beneath the boulder-revetted cairn mass.

The continuity of sanctity of long barrows throughout the early Bronze Age in lowland Brecknockshire is attested by discoveries of cremations with urn in several megalithic tombs.

Bronze Age ceramic traditions in southern Powys include a variety of pottery types. Beaker pottery is known from 11 locations: two Neolithic chambered cairns, Tŷ Isaf (CT 3) and Penywrlod, Llanigon (CT 12); from the round cairns Coed-y-garreg and Plas y gors, Ystradfellte (RC 90–91), Twyn Bryn Glas (RC 127) and Pen Gloch y Pibwr, Cwm du (RC 302); and from lost cists or cairns in Cwm Car, Dol y gaer (LBS 5) and Tŷ Du (or Ffostyll) (LBS 9) and in unknown circumstances at Pant y Waun (LBS 2). Clarke also claimed to have recognised Beaker among the sherds from Nant Maden (RC 111). Classic Beaker groupings are represented by three of these: Tŷ du/Ffostyll (LBS 9), Plas-y-gors (RC 91) and Cwm Car (LBS 5). The pressure-flaked flint daggers accompanying the former two burials are among only five known from Wales. Barbed and tanged flint arrowheads, such as the one from Cwm Car, though commonly encountered as stray-finds in the Beacons, are rarer as discoveries from local burials.

Fragments of Enlarged Food Vessel were excavated from the eastern chamber of the Penywrlod (Llanigon) long barrow (CT 12); Food Vessel came from the northern lateral chamber of the Ffostyll N. long cairn (CT 5), and was found in a primary position at Nant Maden (RC 111).

Among the more evolved early Bronze Age pottery traditions are examples of Overhanging Rim Urn from Twyn Bryn Glas, Penderyn (RC 127), Nant Maden (RC 111) (where these accompanied secondary cremations), and Waun Ddu, Llangynidr (LBS 8).

Cinerary Urn was the sole burial at Abercar and Waun Ddu, and was also represented in the Tŷ Isaf long barrow (CT 3). Cordoned Urns are known from Abercar (with a pygmy cup; LBS 4), and paired, from Fan y Big (LBS 6). An urn of uncertain tradition (a base) was excavated from Tŷ Isaf (CT 3), but the unknown variety (probably Roman) recorded as having come from Llangenny (RB 1) was actually an Abergavenny find.

Pygmy cups have survived well in Mid- and South Wales, seven having been found in Brecknockshire: Twyn Bryn Glas (RC 127), within a primary interment at the Ffostyll round barrow, where one accompanied a triangular worked flake (LBS 10); at Abercar, where it was deposited with an urn (LBS 4); in the excavated Ynys-hir cairn, accompanying a flint knife, anthracite and pottery beads and fragments of woven material; at Pen Allt Mawr (RC 300) and at Varlen (RC 41) and possibly 'from a cairn on Trecastle Mountain' (one of RC 34–7).

It is possible that later Bronze Age traditions are represented among the sherds from Ogof yr Esgyrn (PCS 1), but it remains unclear whether or not the single sherd derived from a 'Deverel-Rimbury globular urn', found along with a charcoal deposit in a pipe trench near Merthyr Cynog, represented burial or settlement.[25]

Mode of Burial

Where the burial practice has been ascertained, most examples appear to have been cremated. Whether or not protected in cists or unprotected in pits, bone rarely survives the acidic soil conditions which follow prolonged land abandonment. In this sense it is lamentable that the inhumation from Brecon Boys' Grammar School (UCB 1) could not be properly investigated or dated, but it is equally important to reconsider the possibility that the Ogof yr Esgyrn

(PCS 1) inhumations might have been Bronze Age skeletons surviving precisely because they were interred within a preserving environment. So because of poor bone survival rates in mid-Wales, the apparently greater percentages of recorded cremation burial need not be truly representative of original burial traditions, which probably included many more inhumations, both unprotected and protected.

As no full survey or analysis of burial traditions exists for Wales as a whole, it is difficult to reach conclusions about the genesis of specific burial traits. Although it has been suggested that culture contact may have brought extended inhumation burial from Ireland to South Wales,[26] it now seems more likely that local inhumation traditions relate to eastern, English counterparts. However, the likelihood that multiple Beaker burials were a characteristic of Mid- and South Wales is emphasised by the number of Beaker arrowheads recovered at Gwernvale (CT 11), as well as by the widespread distribution of comparable stray finds. Other important contemporary cultural indications include associations of copper, or of copper-bronze artefacts with these burials, such as the Cefn Cilnsanws find, a discovery made all the more tantalising by continuing speculation as to precisely which cairn it derived from (RC 201, 211 or 212). Such difficulties of provenance would obviously inhibit future re-investigation aimed at establishing its cultural associations through pottery or lithic tradition. Even greater problems bedevil the re-location of the Llanelieu flint dagger barrow (LBS 9). The more certain association of a copper or bronze awl with Cordoned Urns in a pit at Fan y Big (LBS 6) is noteworthy.

Cairn Siting

As has been noted above, the survival of cairns can only partially reflect the original distribution of the monuments. Roese has argued convincingly from nationwide analysis of over two thousand cairns that there seems to have been no general preference for their sitings.[27] As a general rule elsewhere in Wales burial monuments are being shown by aerial photography to be more common in valley locations than upon the hills.[28] It is therefore likely that valley bottom settlement was originally much denser than would be ascertainable from surveys of upstanding field monuments.[29]

Notions of deliberate cairn emplacement variously on 'false crest', upon hilltops (to take advantage of the view), or elsewhere in exposed situations remote at the present day may therefore have limited value when extrapolated into the possible. Indeed, some cairns were probably intentionally placed upon stony upland ridges in order to avoid invasion of the better agricultural soils which pollen analytical work suggests were being tilled at the time of their erection. As many sites appear to have been lost from the river valleys (for e.g. LS 8), carefully siting burial monuments would appear to have held limited importance for the cairn builders, and it may never be known whether or not deliberate siting was intended.

Structural Details

Recently, it has been shown that the appearance of cairns differs markedly from the monument design intended by their builders. Both human and natural erosional forces (treated elsewhere, pp. 191–98) have conspired to effect this.[31] Many sites have changed dramatically through loss of cairn mass. Some cairns, like Corn Du and Pen y Fan (RC 225–6) are fast disappearing, or like Fan y Big (LBS 6) have been completely lost through the attraction of cairns to hill walkers as quarries for casting stones. Next to kerbstones, the most obvious recognisable structural elements are those of cists. Accounts of investigations by Payne and others mentioned above illustrate why there is such strong belief in central encistment even at the present day. The existence of this belief easily explains why there are so many central robbing craters among the cairns examined in this survey.

Some cairns like Pen y Fan (RC 226) possessed more than one cist. Several are attested in other, excavated, examples, although one or more may have been off-centre. Some cists or pits have been shown to lie outside the general cairn area, demonstrating cairns and barrows to have been nuclear to long-term cemeteries.[32]

Among the sites examined, 20 almost certainly held cists (RC 35–6, 46, 53–4, 60, 65, 81, 90–91, 119, 225–6, 268, 291–2, 300, 302, and 310–11), though indications of centrally-placed orthostats or similar signs indicate the probability of their existence at a further 8, viz: RC 8, 97, 206, 219, 232, 252, 282 and 286.

Interestingly, whereas cists are to be anticipated on

BRONZE AGE BURIAL AND RITUAL STRUCTURES

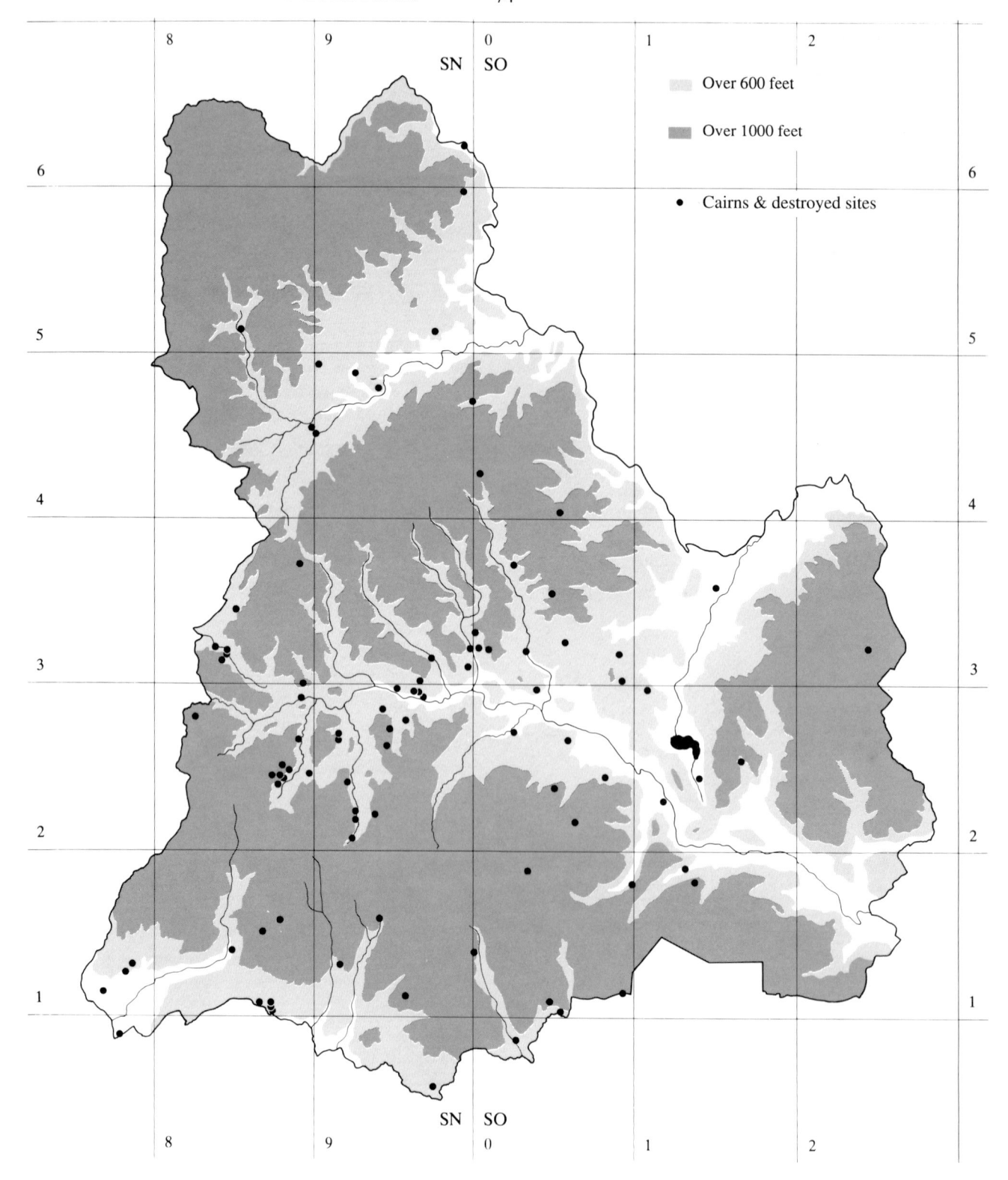

55 Distribution of *Carn* place-names and destroyed or lost cairn sites

stone-built burial sites or elsewhere where suitable slab-stones are available, small unmarked pits acted as alternative receptacles for burned or inhumed bone. Where cists are not now obvious upon the surface, only excavation may detect them or burial pits.

Sometimes, the objective of the stone thief is unclear. It may have been the construction of a track, road, building or field wall. In some cases evidence for cairn dismemberment remains on the premises in the form of 'sheep-shelters' (of which Gamrhiw is a good example: RC 171; Figs. 71–2), folds or 'hafod' constructions, of which there are 20–30. Many sites were modified and retained as effective parish (and other) boundaries, and in recent times the erection of picturesque beacons (like Drygarn Fawr, RC 55–6), either as way-markers or as decorative landscape features, is noteworthy.

[1] I. Kinnes, *Round Barrows and Ring Ditches in the British Neolithic*, (London: Brit. Mus. Occas. Paper, 1979).

[2] C. B. Burgess, *The Age of Stonehenge*, (1981), *passim*; Savory, *Guide*, pp. 18–33.

[3] W. Davies, *An Early Welsh Microcosm: The Llandaff Charters*, (London: Roy. Hist. Soc., 1978), p. 30.

[4] Brecks. Mus. Llanbedr MS I (1806), fol. 154; *cf.* Carlisle, *Top. Dict.*, s.v. Llangattwg.

[5] T. Jones, *Hist. Brecks.*, II, ii (1809), p. 516; Carlisle, *Top. Dict.*, s.v. Llangynidr.

[6] N.L.W. MS 4278, fol. 186.

[7] N.L.W. MS. 15257 D, fol. 19; Llanbedr MS I (1806), fols. 43, 180.

[8] Llanbedr MS *idem.*; Mr Bird could have been John Bird, clerk to the Marquess of Bute, whose business may well have taken him into this area (*The Diaries of John Bird of Cardiff: Clerk to the first Marquess of Bute*, ed. H. M. Thomas, (Cardiff: South Wales Record Society and Glamorgan Archive Service, 1987)).

[9] Carlisle, *Top. Dict.*, s.v. Llanfigan.

[10] H. E. Roese, *Arch. Camb.* 128 (1979), pp. 147–55.

[11] H. E. Roese, *Thesis*.

[12] *Inv. Caerns.* III, lvi–lix; field reconnaisance over the past three–four decades may well have vastly increased this number.

[13] Briggs, *Cardiganshire*, pp. 132–45, 157–9.

[14] W. E. Griffiths, *Inv. Glam.*, I (i), pp. 42–9.

[15] *Hist. Merioneth.*, pp. 72–108.

[16] E. C. Marshall and K. Murphy, *Arch. Camb.* 140 (1991), pp. 28–76, (Aber Camddwr).

[17] C. S. Briggs, *Landscape History* 8 (1986), pp. 5–12.

[18] F. M. Lynch, pp. 124–7, in J. G. Evans, S. Limbrey and H. Cleere, (eds.), *The effect of man on the landscape: the Highland zone*, (London: C.B.A. Res. Rep. no. 7, 1976).

[19] Briggs, *op. cit.* n. 17.

[20] F. M. Lynch, *Scot. Archaeol. Forum* 4 (1972), pp. 61–80.

[21] These interpretational difficulties are well illustrated with respect to the excavation at Cefn Bryn, Gower, *P.P.S.*, 54 (1988), pp. 163–72.

[22] D. P. Webley, *B.B.C.S.*, 17, (1956–8), pp. 54–5.

[23] J. Parkhouse, *Glamorgan-Gwent Arch. Trust Ann. Rep.* (1981), p. 32.

[24] H. E. Roese, *B.B.C.S.* 29 (1981), pp. 575–87.

[25] H. N. Savory, *Arch. Camb.* 107 (1958), Fig. 5; *Prehist. Brecks.* II, p. 18; *Antiquity* (1971), p. 257, Figs. 2, 4.

[26] H. N. Savory, pp. 117–139 in *P.M.W.W.*

[27] Roese, *loc. cit.* n. 24.

[28] *idem.* pp. 578–9.

[29] *idem.* p. 581.

[30] *pace* Roese, *idem.* p. 585; *pace* Lynch *loc. cit.* n. 18.

[31] J. B. Stevenson, (pp. 104–8) in J. G. Evans and S. Limbrey, (eds.), *op. cit.* n. 18.

[32] D. G. Benson *et al.*, *Ceredigion* 9 (1982), pp. 281–92; P. Crew, *B.B.C.S.* 33 (1985), pp. 290–325; W. Warrilow, G. Owen and W. J. Britnell, *P.P.S.* 52 (1986), pp. 53–88.

Round Cairns and Barrows of the Bronze Age (RC 1–312)

(RC 1) On Llwyncwmstabl 3 km N.E. of Ystradowen, on the nose of a ridge and close to its highest point 310 m above O.D., is a small round cairn. It measures 7 m in diameter, and 0.3 m high, and consists of mixed grade rubble.

Ystradgynlais (E), Ystradgynlais Lr (C)
SN 71 N.E. (7790 1519)   8 vii 84

(RC 2) Between Gwys Fawr and Afon Twrch on moorland, 420 m above O.D., S. of Llyn y Fan and Gareg Las, Cantrill encountered two cairns, lying 240 m apart. Roese was unable to locate them. There is, however, an undisturbed cairn lying among shake-holes on a shelf overlooking the upper reaches of the Afon Twrch. It consists of a turf-covered, stony mound 8 m across N.W.–S.E. by 6.5 m, and 1 m high, the edge being particularly well defined on the E. side.

  T. C. Cantrill, *Arch. Camb.* 53 (1898), pp. 248–64; Roese, *Thesis*, no. 220.

Ystradgynlais (E), Ystradgynlais Lr (C)
SN 71 N.E. (7882 1835)   24 ix 88

(RC 3) On the S. end of Llwyncwmstabl, S. of Dorwen, on a S.W.-facing slope, 260 m above O.D., lies a cairn 6 m in diameter and 0.3 m high. It is composed of loose rubble, with a shallow central depression.

Ystradgynlais (E), Ystradgynlais Lr (C)
SN 71 S.E. (773 141)   8 viii 84

(RC 4–5) On the N.-facing slope at the E. end of Nant Gwys, upon Cae Garn (T.A. 1238), 198 m above O.D., two cairns are situated upon a ridge of the outcropping rock.
  (RC 4) At the W.S.W. end is a circular cairn 9.1 m in diameter and 0.9 m high.
  (RC 5) 7.5 m to the E.N.E. is a ruined site, possibly originally a ring cairn 8.2 m in external diameter. Though largely destroyed on the N., the stone ring is 2.5 m wide and 0.5 m high.

Ystradgynlais (E), Ystradgynlais Lr (C)
SN 71 S.E. (RC 4–5) (7833 1267)   8 iv 69

(RC 6) To the S.E. of Cwm Fforch Wen, 240 m above O.D. is a small, turf-covered mound some 4 m in diameter and about 0.4 m high, topped with loose stones.

Ystradgynlais (E), Ystradgynlais Lr (C)
SN 71 S.E. (7873 1379)   19 v 88

(RC 7) On the nose at the extreme S. of the Llorfa ridge, 330 m above O.D., lies a robbed cairn of earth and stones, 9 m in diameter and 0.25 m high with a central depression.

Ystradgynlais (E), Ystradgynlais Lr (C)
SN 71 S.E. (785 149)   7 viii 84

(RC 8) Due E. of Cwm Fforch Wen on the crest of a ridge 260 m above O.D. is a disturbed cairn 7 m N.E.–S.W. by 6 m, and 0.3 m high. There is a slab 1.6 m long, 0.2 m thick and 0.3 m high aligned N.W.–S.E. embedded in its S.W. edge, possibly all that remains of a cist.

Ystradgynlais (E), Ystradgynlais Lr (C)
SN 71 S.E. (7886 1400)   19 v 88

(RC 9) On the S.E.-facing slope of the southern tip of Cefn Cul, about 360 m above O.D., is a flat-bottomed circular hollow 9.2 m in diameter, the side 0.3 m high internally, probably the remains of a robbed cairn. Vestiges of an outer bank 0.2 m high remain around the W. side. In the centre is a recumbent pointed stone 1.1 m by 1.7 m by 0.3 m.

Llywel (E), Traean-glas (C)
SN 81 N.E. (8558 1871)   5 vi 85

There are a number of cairns lying upon the Dan yr Ogof plateau N. of Cribarth. These are considered most likely to be clearance cairns, and are described elsewhere (US 3–4).

(RC 10) In Bwlch Bryn Rhudd, 396 m above O.D., on level ground in the saddle at the head of the valley, are the remains of a possible ring cairn 7 m in internal diameter, still surrounded on the N., S. and W. by a low ring of boulders, 1.2 to 2.1 m wide and 0.3 m high.

Glyntawe
SN 81 N.E. (8684 1958)   27 vi 85

(RC 11) On the summit of Fan Gihirych 722 m above O.D. is a structureless cairn of small grade stones 11.0 m in diameter N.–S., 9.0 m transversely, and 0.9 m in height. There is a small modern heap of stone dumped on top.

Defynnog (E), Crai (C)
SN 81 N.E. (8805 1915)   15 vi 85

(RC 12) On a limestone ridge about 440 m above O.D., N.E. of Sand Hill, is a cairn of loose stones about 4 or 5 m across and 0.2 m high, lying in a slight natural hollow flanked on two sides by incipient shake-holes, into which the site is falling.

Ystradfellte
SN 81 N.E. (8949 1573)   25 x 88

(RC 13) On the N. of Pant Mawr to the E. of Sand Hill, 445 m above O.D., is a circular cairn 9.5 m in diameter and 0.7 m high. It is of Carboniferous Limestone and Old Red Sandstone rubble, and is capped by a modern pyramidal cairn 1 m high.

Ystradfellte
SN 81 N.E. (8909 1507)   18 v 87

(RC 14) On limestone pavement at 410 m above O.D. to the S. of Nant y Moch valley lies a ring cairn. It is 19.2 m in N.–S. diameter externally, 17.7 m in diameter E.–W., the ring varying between 2.1 m and 4.3 m in width and 0.3 m high.

Ystradfellte
SN 81 N.E. (8987 1571)   15 v 87

(RC 15) On the S. of Mynydd y Drum and N. of Bryn Llechwen, about 275 m above O.D., is a denuded circular cairn 15.5 m in diameter, up to 0.3 m high, particularly on the crest of the outer perimeter, with a circular central depression, 2.1 m in diameter. This might have been the site of a burial cist. The O.S. suggest this probably represents a mutilated ring cairn, but the site is so robbed as to make it impossible to determine the original form.

O.S. Card SN 81 SW 5.

Ystradgynlais (E), Ystradgynlais Lr (C)
SN 81 S.W. (8152 1035)   5 viii 83

(RC 16–17) On Mynydd y Drum in an area which has produced fugitive evidence for early settlement (see (US 28)), are two cairns lying about 280 m above O.D. Both were excavated by the Clwyd-Powys Archaeological Trust in 1983 and 1987 in advance of their total destruction through opencast coal extraction.[1]

(RC 16) Garn Goch, about 265 m above O.D., was found prior to its excavation, to be a robbed cairn 17.4 m in diameter (N.E.–S.W.), and 0.25 m high above the early ground surface. The interior had recently been damaged by hole digging and an irregular excavation on the N.E. perimeter had partially exposed an embedded stone slab oriented N.N.E.–S.S.W. measuring 1.0 m by 0.4 m by 0.2 m. Later interference was very extensive, so great in fact, that features of recent date were to a degree intermixed with the earliest occupation. Excavation suggested an original diameter of about 15 m; the lower layers, which included stones up to 0.75 m in diameter, were of both angular rounded stones, the upper part was of stones 0.15–0.2 m across, more uniform in size and appearance.

The cairn lay upon stony bedrock, largely bereft of soil or vegetation. Cairn-building had been preceded by several irregular scoops excavated into the bedrock. Charcoal from one of these produced a date of a.d. 980 +/- 70 (CAR-1172). From another scoop came oak, birch, rowan (or hawthorn) charcoal yielding a date of a.d. 510 +/- 60 (CAR-1173).

The original cairn mass was encircled by an almost continuous length of walling (about 17 long by up to 0.3 m high). It comprised sub-angular to angular sandstone blocks and slabs, some as large as *c.* 0.6 by 0.35 and 0.3 m high. The wall's average width was about 1 m wide (though it varied from 0.8 to 1.5 m).

Both inner and outer wall faces were recognisable. The inner face was generally built of larger stones, the outer, more of slabs. Infilling was of smaller rubble. It was found difficult to determine how far this was originally intended as a partial revetment to the cairn mass, and how far its present form was owed to later denudation.

No clear indications of a Bronze Age burial were recorded from the centre of the cairn. However, a flint scatter from the N.W. sector of the excavated area indicated prehistoric activity. Rim sherds representing two pottery vessels were also located from outside the cairn. Some were undecorated and too fragmentary to assist useful identification; others were considered to have belonged to the Deverel-Rimbury tradition.[3] It is possible that the radiocarbon dates broadly reflect either grave robbing at a particularly early date, or indicate a more recent introduction of peat to the cairn in an area where there are other indications that peat-digging was an important post-medieval activity.

(RC 17) The second site, which had also been disturbed, though not so extensively as the first, was a ring cairn 15.5–16 m in diameter. Its ring varied in width from 3 m on the N.W. to 4 m on the E. The inner edge of the ring was defined by larger stones enclosing a central area 8.75 m in diameter. Its outer edge was ill-defined and ragged in appearance and the structure appeared to have been built by laying down a series of concentric circles, possibly starting from the central area. The cairn matrix comprised both sandstones as well as grits and shales, comparable in size to those found on the other site. There appeared to be no pre-cairn surface; the stones were laid directly onto soil, and these had then partially sunk lower, into boulder clay. The site produced a burnt flint scraper from the soil surface, and a flint flake from the pre-peat soil outside the ring on its N.W.

There were three features within the central area; a circular, bowl-shaped scoop, a stake-hole and a shallow scoop, all devoid either of finds or of sufficient charcoal for radiocarbon dating. The central buried soil surface also produced a flint knife and scraper with two flakes, one of flint, the other of chert.

Using pollen taken from beneath these sites, and comparative data from a nearby mire, it was argued that the cairns were probably erected in a heathland environment already substantially disforested through earlier human activity.[4]

[1] P. Dorling and F. M. Chambers, *B.B.C.S.*, 37 (1990), pp. 215–46.
[2] O.S. Card SN 81 SW 4.
[3] A. M. Gibson, p. 229, in Dorling and Chambers, *op. cit.* n. 1.
[4] Chambers, *idem.* p. 244; F. M. Chambers,'*Studies on the Initiation, Growth-rate and Humification of 'Blanket Peats' in South Wales*, (Dept. Geog. Occas. paper No. 9, University of Keele, 1988).

Ystradgynlais (E), Ystradgynlais Lr (C)
SN 81 S.W. (RC 16) (8178 1077); (RC 17) (8188 1073)
5 viii 83

(RC 18–19) Two limestone and sandstone boulder cairns are sited about 200 m apart on the S.-facing summit of the limestone ridge Cribarth.

(RC 18) The S.W. cairn, 423 m above O.D., is 13.7 m in diameter and 0.9–1.2 m high. Its mass has partially collapsed downslope, and its top is interfered with by a small modern shelter.[1]

(RC 19) The N.E. cairn, about 400 m above O.D., is 19.8 m in diameter, and 1.8 m high on the N. and E., though elsewhere its height increases up to about 3 m due to sloping ground. The S. perimeter is reveted by drystone walling for about 5.5 m.[2]

[1] O.S. Card SN 81 SW 2; T. C. Cantrill, *loc. cit.* RC 2; Roese, *Thesis*, no. 37.
[2] O.S. Card SN 81 SW 1; Cantrill, *loc. cit.*; Roese, *Thesis*, no. 39.

Ystradgynlais (E), Ystradgynlais Hr (C)
SN 81 S.W. (RC 18) (8290 1443);
(RC 19) (8290 1443)
10 vi 69

(RC 20) 100 m due W. of the Nant Tarw circles (SC 2), about 350 m above O.D., is a small cairn 8–10 m in diameter. On its W. side two stone slabs are set on edge, one 0.4 m high. On the surface N.W. of the mound is a large recumbent boulder 1.7 m long by 1.4 m wide and 0.6 m thick.

Llywel (E), Traean-glas (C)
SN 82 N.W. (8178 2585)
90

(RC 21) Towards the N. end of Godre'r Garn-las on the W. side of Nant Tarw about 410 m above O.D. and 90 m due N. of the E. stone circle (SC 2), is a cairn-like feature. It comprises a layer of stones some 0.3 m high, and 16 by 11 m. The arc-shaped W. side is perhaps all that remains to define the cairn. At the E. extremity the stones form a detached heap 5.5 m long N.–S. by 3 m wide, with traces of large fallen slabs, especially along the E. edge.

The site has clearly been denuded since the turn of the century, when it was described[1] as 'represented by a fairly defined ring of small stones, about 16 yards

[14.63 m] across, more in the form of an ellipse than a circle, and five or six erect stones (averaging 2 feet [0.61 m] by 1 foot 6 inches [0.45 m] by 1 foot [0.3 m] on the circumference of a circle, not quite coinciding with the eastern side of the ellipse, there are several boulders scattered about, which seem to have been displaced. The cairn could never have been of any great size, it has every appearance of having been disturbed, and it is possible that the elliptical ring was formed in the disturbance.'

¹ Ll. Morgan, *Trans. Swansea Sci. Soc.* (1907–8), p. 151.

Llywel (E), Traean-glas (C)
SN 82 N.W. (8198 2586)   7 viii 89

(RC 22) 300 m S. of Tyle Mawr, to the N. of the main road, 355 m above O.D. stands a mound of earth and stones, possibly a burial cairn. It is 11 m long E.–W by 8.5 m wide, 1.2 m high and with a defined top 4.9 by 4 m.

Llywel (E), Traean-glas (C)
SN 82 N.E. (8654 2920)   2 iv 80

(RC 23) A cairn was marked near Twyn y Garn 335 m above O.D. on O.S. 1-inch and 2-inch maps before afforestation. This could not be located through extensive searching and it must be considered destroyed.

Roese, *Thesis*, no. 55.

Defynnog (E), Crai (C)
SN 82 N.E. (8808 2506)   13 iv 78

(RC 24) 500 m W. by S. from Berth Ivan, 315 m above O.D., is a heap of large Old Red Sandstone boulders 4.5 m by 3 m in diameter, 0.9 m high.

Defynnog (E), Crai (C)
SN 82 N.E. (8852 2553)   4 vii 68

(RC 25) 600 m E. by S. of Penfai, 230 m above O.D. is a turf-covered stony mound 6.1 m E.–W. by 5.7 m N.–S. in diameter and 0.3 m high, possibly a barrow. Two loose boulders lying on the surface appear recently deposited, and probably derive from field clearance.

Noted from A.P.s, O.S. 75/384, 1377–8.

Llywel (E), Traean-mawr
SN 82 N.E. (8934 2918)   1 vii 91

(RC 26) On the northern, highest point of Fan Foel, 760 m above O.D., is an almost circular grass-grown mound of Old Red Sandstone, 16 m in overall diameter, 0.9 m high, on the N. and E., and almost imperceptible on the W. There is a level central depression about 9.1 m in diameter, and 0.3 m lower than the surrounding rim, probably the result of excavation. This is now surmounted by a small modern cairn 1 m high.

It is possible that this is the disturbed cairn from which in 1898 T. C. Cantrill took 'flint flakes and a string of burnt clay beads'.

T. C. Cantrill, *op. cit.* RC 2; *Jnl Roy. Anthrop. Inst.* 27 (1898), pp. 3–4; W. F. Grimes, 'The T. C. Cantrill Collection', *B.B.C.S.*, 6 (1931–3), p. 93; Roese, *Thesis*, no. 198; Roese in *Arch. Camb.*, 18 (1978–9); p. 150; p. 75 n. 10 *supra* and *Brycheiniog*, pp. 31–2, Fig. 5.

Llywel (E), Traean-glas (C)
SN 82 S.W. (8213 2234)   21 iii 73

(RC 27) On the tip of a promontory of the N.E.-facing escarpment of Twr y Fan Foel, 760 m above O.D., is a small turf-covered cairn 11 m in diameter and 1.2 m high.

Llywel (E), Traean-glas (C)
SN 82 S.W. (8243 2206)   23 iv 80

(RC 28–9) There are two cairns on Garn Las.

(RC 28) On a ridge 455 m above O.D. is a cairn 18 m in diameter and 0.9 m high, its N. part much disturbed with the remains of two sheep shelters at the centre and to the S.E. of centre.

(RC 29) Lying on a natural shelf below the ridge, is another cairn 8 m in diameter and 0.5 m high, with a central depression 0.3 m deep.

Llywel (E), Traean-glas (C)
SN 82 S.W. (RC 28) (8278 2476); (RC 29) (8287 2499)
        23 iv 80

(RC 30) On the S.-facing slope of Moel Feity above Blaen Tawe, 550 m above O.D., is a stone-built cairn of Old Red Sandstone, 7.9 m in diameter and 0.5 m high. There is a slight elongation of cairn material to the S.E.

Llywel (E), Traean-glas (C)
SN 82 S.W. (8453 2235)   21 iii 73

(RC 31) On the S. end of the Maen Mawr interfluve, 370 m above O.D., lies an oval grass-grown mound of large grade Old Red Sandstone. It is 9.8 m long

N.W.–S.E. by 7.6 m wide, and stands 0.9 m to 1.2 m in height (allowing for the fall in ground). There is a central trench N.W. to S.E., 4.3 m long, 1.4 m wide and 0.9 m deep; towards its S.E. end, at 2.4 m from the cairn edge, are two stone uprights, each 0.6 m high and 0.3 m apart.

Llywel (E), Traean-glas (C)
SN 82 S.E. (8514 2046)   2 iv 80

(RC 32) To the N.E. of the farm at Post-Dy, about 325 m above O.D., on the edge of a plantation partly obscured by trees, lies a circular cairn at least 18.3 m in diameter, and about 0.9 m high. At the centre is a shallow robber crater.

Defynnog (E), Crai (C)
SN 82 S.E. (8812 2486)   2 iv 80

(RC 33) On a broad ridge at the N. end of Mynydd Bwlch y Groes, at a height of 439 m above O.D., lies a cairn marked on the O.S. maps as Garn Wen. In 1974 it stood 20 m in diameter, and 1.5 m high. After continued military manoeuvres, it is now c. 1 m high, though scarcely recognisable, having had a post 0.3 m in diameter and 0.45 m high inserted centrally, and a trench 0.6 m wide by 4 m long (E.–W.) dug roughly through the middle. Turf has been stripped off, showing a stony surface beneath.

S.A.M. B107

Llandeilo'r fan
SN 83 N.E. (8772 3677)   3 iii 74 and 8 xi 91

(RC 34) Lying in a slight saddle between Garn Wen and Bryn y Garn, 433 m above O.D., is a circular, partly peat- and grass-grown cairn 30 m in diameter E.–W. by 29 m, rising 2.4 m above the bog on the S. It is now distinguishable by distinctive yellow vegetation and has been trenched on the E., and most extensively on the N., where there is a filled-in trench 4 m long by 0.5 m wide. There are signs of other trenches and digging beyond the limits of the mound. The central area (12 m N.–S. by 10 m E.–W.) is raised slightly, 1.8 m high, with a circular central depression 6 m in diameter and 0.7 m deep.

S.A.M. B108

Llandeilo'r fan
SN 83 N.E. (8885 3687)   3 iii 74 and 22 viii 89

(RC 35–8) During the nineteenth century there were said (by William Rees) to have been a number of cairns about 320 m above O.D. on Mynydd Bach Trecastell.[1] The largest, about 90 ft [c. 27.5 m] in diameter, was excavated in 1824 by John Holford, who found two cinerary urns. Another cairn opened at the same time contained an undecorated biconical pygmy cup, now lost.[2] In 1849 Francis Green, together with Rees, found a tumulus on the edge of the marsh of Waun Ddu (SN 83 S.W.). The proximity of these finds to two stone circles is noteworthy (SC 4), and one round cairn on Mynydd Bach Trecastell is now a S.A.M.

Three, possibly four, cairns can now be identified on Trecastell Mountain.

(RC 35; SC 4 iv) Lying about 120 m S. by E. from the stone circles (SC 4) and almost in line with them, there is a turf-covered mound of Old Red Sandstone on a low eminence, up to 0.8 m high and 11.6 m in diameter, with a central hollow. This is considered by both Roese and the O.S. to be the tumulus excavated by Holford.[3]

(RC 36) The second cairn is also turf-covered and lies just below some linear quarry workings. It is c. 9.0 m in diameter and up to 0.9 m high with a hollow in the centre, through which upright, edge-set stones are exposed, probably the remains of a cist.

(RC 37) A third cairn is situated on the ground falling S.E. below the rampart of the Roman Camp. It is 4.3 m in diameter, and 0.45 m high with a central rectangular hollow 1.5 m by 0.9 m, against the S.W. side of which is a slab on edge, whilst two or three other half-buried stones are loose nearby, possibly from a rifled cist.

(RC 38) On the mountain summit is a circular grass-grown mound about 10.7 m in diameter and 1.0 m high, damaged by ploughing on the N.E. It is surmounted by an O.S. trig. point.

[1] W. Rees, *Arch. Camb.* 7 (1854), pp. 127, 132–3. A search among the Rees papers at Cardiff Public Library has not brought to light any documentation of John Holford's excavation.
[2] W. O. Stanley and A. Way, *Arch. Camb.* 23 (1868), p. 262; H. N. Savory, in *B.B.C.S.*, 18 (1958–60), p. 112, no. 17.
[3] Roese, *Thesis*, no. 44; O.S. Card SN 83 SW 5.

Llywel (E), Traean-glas (C)
SN 83 S.W. (RC 35) (8314 3098); (RC 36) (8305 3118); (RC 37) (8305 3101); (RC 38) (8462 3002)
                                      30 iii 77

(RC 39–40) There are two cairns on Blaen Clydach-Bach.

(RC 39) About 370 m above O.D. are the remains of a cairn 17 m in diameter, now of irregular appearance, reaching a height of 0.5 m. It has been dug into from the E. side, probably to obtain stone for the construction of the nearby track and fieldbank.[1]

(RC 40) Nearby is a similar damaged cairn, though with more loose stone visible, on the crest of a N.E.-facing slope 376 m above O.D.[2]

[1] O.S. Card SN 83 SE 11.
[2] O.S. Card SN 83 SE 10.

Llywel (E), Traean-glas (C)
SN 83 S.E. (RC 39) (8600 3185); (RC 40) (8604 3170)

(RC 41) In 1925 a Bronze Age pygmy cup was found during an undocumented excavation in a barrow at Varlen, near Llywel.[1] The excavated barrow has been equated[2] with a small turf-covered cairn, noted from O.S. aerial photographs,[3] which is situated on arable land above the steep scarp of a S.-facing hill slope 335 m above O.D. It is 8.0 m in diameter and up to 0.5 m high on the S. side with a central excavation pit 2.5 m in diameter and 0.5 m deep in which the stone content of the mound is exposed. Excavated material has been dumped on the S.W. periphery of the mound creating an artificial elongated N.E.–S.W. axis of 9.5 m.

[1] G. E. Evans, *Trans. Carms. Antiq. Soc.* 21 (1929), p. 60; H. N. Savory, *Prehist. Brecks.* I, pp. 100–1, Fig. 4.2.
[2] O.S. Cards SN 83 SE 8 and 5.
[3] A.P.s, O.S. 75/384/1359.

Llywel (E), Traean-glas (C)
SN 83 S.E. (8764 3060)   29 iv 81

(RC 42) S. of Llyn Nant Llys, 392 m above O.D., on a gentle S.E.-facing slope is a turf-covered cairn of small fieldstone, 13.5 m in diameter and 0.8 m high. Its centre has been mutilated and it is of irregular appearance.

O.S. Card SN 83 SE 9.

Llandeilo'r fan
SN 83 S.E. (8885 3364)   18 ii 77

(RC 43) N.E. of Penfai, about 290 m above O.D., is a grass-grown cairn platform 11.0 m in diameter and 0.5 m high. Two large stones standing proud of its centre appear to have been dumped there in recent field clearance.

O.S. Card SN 83 SE 12.

Llywel (E), Traean-glas (C)
SN 83 S.E. (8942 3005)   2 iv 73

(RC 44–5) To the E. of Nant y Ddalfa, on the line of the old parish boundary, about 330 and 345 m above O.D., are two mounds marked on the O.S. 6-inch map (1964 Revision).

(RC 44) The first is a shapeless grass-grown mound about 15.9 m in diameter N.W.–S.E. by 13.7 m wide. In general it is only 0.3 m high, though on the N.E. and S.E. with upcast, it attains 0.6 m and is possibly a denuded cairn.

(RC 45) The second, a similar site, though apparently undisturbed and measuring 11.7 m N. to S. by 12.3 m E. to W. and standing 0.4 m high. The nearby fieldbank appears to deviate in order to avoid this monument, suggesting that it is of some antiquity.

O.S. Card SN 83 SE 6.

Llandeilo'r fan (E and C)/Llywel (E), Ysclydach (C)
SN 83 S.E. (RC 44) (8941 3251); (RC 45) (8949 3256)
                                                         20 iii 74

(RC 46) Close to the county boundary on the E. side of Cynant Fach towards the W. end of Esgair Dafydd, about 425 m above O.D., are the mutilated remains of a round stony cairn. At the time of investigation it was approached along a forestry firebreak, surrounded on three sides by conifers and on the E. by a fence. The site lies on the crest of a ridge overlooking the steep valley to the N.W. and the cairn measures approximately 10.5 m in diameter and 0.5 m high. There is a central large stone oriented N.E.–S.W. 1.4 m long by 0.25 m wide, apparently the side slab of a ruined cist. About a metre to the N.W. from this, lying loose on the cairn material, is another stone, 1.2 m long by 0.5 m wide and 0.2 m thick. It would appear to have become recently dislodged. In 1972 two small circular sheep shelters had been built into the cairn on the N. and disturbance seems to have continued since.

O.S. Card SN 84 NW 12.

Llanwrtyd (E), Llanwrtyd Without (C)
SN 84 N.W. (8215 4515)
                                                7 xi 77 and 28 xi 91

(RC 47) Near the summit of Cnapau Hafod Llewelyn, 487 m above O.D., is a circular platform cairn 11.3 m in diameter and between 0.3 and 0.6 m high. Its centre is overlain by a modern cairn. Visits by the O.S. since its original discovery by R.C.A.M. have failed to locate the cairn,[1] and it may now be under afforested ground, though a site resembling this description may be observed on aerial photographs.[2]

[1] O.S. Card SN 84 NW 8.
[2] A.P.s, R.A.F. 106G/UK 1471/3095–6.

Llanwrtyd (E), Llanwrtyd Without (C)
SN 84 N.W. (8321 4708)   30 i 69

(RC 48) On the W. end of Esgair Garn 465 m above O.D. on the crest of a moorland spur is a circular stone-built cairn, which includes blocks of quartz. It is 15.9 m in diameter and 0.9 m high at the centre, where a modern cairn adds 0.6 m of height.

O.S. Card SN 84 NW 3.

Llanddewi Abergwesyn
SN 84 N.W. (8308 4983)   18 x 72

(RC 49) On the S. aspect of Garn Wen 512 m above O.D. on level ground is a large circular stone-built cairn, 16.1 m in diameter and 2.5 m high, the uppermost 0.9 m being a modern pile forming a circular shelter for the O.S. trig. point. It is encircled at the base on the N. and W. only by a ditch 1.8 to 2.8 m wide and up to 0.5 m deep.

O.S. Card SN 84 NW 4; A.P.s, R.A.F. 3916/0114–5; 7 xi 60.

Llanwrtyd (E), Llanwrtyd Without (C)
SN 84 N.W. (8451 4597)   30 i 69

(RC 50) On the E. part of Waun Coll 472 m above O.D. on a spur is a partly grass-grown circular bank of stones, 16.8 m in diameter, about 2.5 m wide and 0.6 m high. The bank surrounds an inner, much disturbed mass of stones reaching a maximum height of 1.5 m, where a modern cairn surmounts the original. On the N.W. a gap in the bank, 5.5 m wide, may be an original entrance, though alternatively it could be due to robbing.

O.S. Card SN 84 NW 5.

Llanwrtyd (E), Llanwrtyd Without (C)
SN 84 N.W. (8475 4660)   30 i 69

(RC 51–3; Fig. 56) There are three cairns on Garn Dwad, a ridge running N.N.E.–S.S.W. from E. of Llanwrtyd.

(RC 51) 380 m above O.D. is a boat-shaped setting of at least 18 large boulders, externally 4.6 m in length N.W.–S.E., 1.2 m wide at the 'stern' and 2.6 m 'amidships'. The boulders vary in size from 0.25 m by 0.18 m in height to 0.74 m long by 0.61 m wide by 0.61 m high. All appear loose rather than earthfast.

(RC 52) 395 m above O.D. is a circular stone-built cairn 10.1 m in diameter and 0.45 m high. It has an inverted saucer profile, with a slightly grass-grown rim 1.5 m wide. Slightly W. of centre, excavation has disclosed a rough cist about 0.45 m square and 0.3 m deep.

(RC 53) 410 m above O.D. is a small circular platform cairn 5.8 m in diameter and 0.45 m high. To the W. of centre are several slabs aligned N.–S. along an axis 1.8 m long, which may indicate an inner setting.

O.S. Card SN 84 NE 4; Garn Dwad noted from O.S. 1-inch map, 1840; sites not visible on A.P.s, F44 58/3916 0101–2.

Llanwrtyd (E), Llanwrtyd Without (C)
SN 84 N.E. (RC 51) (8706 4775); (RC 52) (8712 4809); (RC 53) (8715 4820)   i 85

(RC 54) On Castell Llysgoden, 490 m above O.D., is a circular platform of stones 13.7 m in diameter and 0.3 m high with indications of a perimeter made of larger kerbstones. The central area, about 4.0 m across, is slightly higher than the rest and contains a partly buried slab on edge and two other slabs that appear to have been displaced from a cist. On the S. the central area is obscured by a modern cairn 1.5 m high, constructed of stones scraped up from the surface of the platform. A tiny pile of stones 4.6 m from the S.W. edge of the cairn is probably a modern sheep burial.

O.S. Card SN 85 NW 1.

Llanddewi Abergwesyn
SN 85 N.W. (8119 5688)   15 ix 72

On Drum Nant y Gorlan (SN 85 N.W.) there is a mound which may be associated with the standing stone (described under SS 8).

(RC 55–6) There are cairns on either end of Drygarn Fawr on land belonging to the National Trust. Both are surmounted by modern cairns which take the form of beehive towers.[1] It is unclear exactly when these were built, but they may have been erected as markers during the present century.

(RC 55; Fig. 57) The more westerly, on the summit of the ridge and 645 m above O.D., is stone-built and 9.8

56 Garn Dwad cairn from the NW (RC 51)

m (N.–S.) by 8.8 m (E.–W.) in diameter. The remains of a kerb of blocks set end to end may be traced around its perimeter. Some blocks are up to 1.3 m long. Although the interior only attains a height of 0.6 m, the modern drystone cairn, which is of solid masonry, stands 5.8 m in diameter and 3.7 m high, surmounted by a small cap of white quartz stones and a concrete boundary pillar.[2]

(RC 56; Fig. 58) The more easterly, 630 m above O.D., is similar to the former, though stonier and more ruined, especially on the E. and S.E. This one is also kerbed, though this is not so easily traceable. There is an outer ring which represents the original cairn. This measures 12.2 m (E.–W.) by 13.2 m (N.–S.). What may be an inner kerbstone ring, is traceable about 1.3 m outside the modern cairn. This includes stones up to 1.9 m long which are best seen on the S., W. and N. The E. side is covered with loose stones. The modern cairn which surmounts it centrally is slightly smaller than the W. example, 5.6 m in diameter and 2.7 m high. It is similarly capped by white quartz and has a concrete boundary pillar inset halfway down the E. side.[3]

[1] O.S. Card SN 85 NE 5; W. E. Griffiths, *Arch. in Wales* 12 (1972), p. 5.
[2] O.S. Card SN 85 NE 2.

Llanwrthwl/Llanfihangel Abergwesyn
SN 85 N.E. (RC 55) (8628 5841); (RC 56) (8675 5857)
26 xi 91

57 Drygarn Fawr Cairn (West RC 55)

(RC 57) On the ridge Carnau, 537 m above O.D., are the stony remains of a circular cairn 8.8 m in diameter. Its centre is occupied by a crude modern stone-walled shelter about 1.8 m high.

O.S. SN 85 NE 3.

Llanfihangel Abergwesyn
SN 85 N.E. (8897 5775)   29 ix 72

(RC 58) On the N.–S. ridge Esgair Fraith, 470 m above O.D., slightly to the E. of its crest, is a stone-built cairn about 8.5 m in diameter, overgrown at the edges. It appears to have no kerb, and seems little disturbed.

O.S. SN 85 NE 4.

Llanfihangel Abergwesyn
SN 85 N.E. (8939 5657)   3 x 72

(RC 59) To the W. of Careg y Fedw, 505 m above O.D., is a stone-built circular cairn 10.7 m in diameter, of volcanic breccia boulders. It is 0.9 m in height, but is surmounted by a small stone shelter 2.1 m across, adding 0.6 m to the cairn's height.

O.S. SN 85 NE 1.

Llanwrthwl
SN 85 N.E. (8970 5790)   29 ix 72

58 Drygarn Fawr Cairn (East RC 56) showing outline of original structure under vegetation

(RC 60) On Esgair Irfon, 425 m above O.D., is a circular grass-grown mound, which probing revealed to be stony. It is 4.6 m in diameter and 0.3 m high. At the centre is a rectangular cist, each side formed of a single edge-set slab, though lacking capstone. Internally it is 0.76 m long N.–S. by 0.45 m wide by 0.43 m deep. The slabs are up to 0.18 m thick.

O.S. SN 85 SW 1.

Llanfihangel Abergwesyn
SN 85 S.W. (8464 5463)　　　　　　　　　26 iii 74

(RC 61) On the crest of the N.E.–S.W. ridge Banc Paderau, 440 m above O.D., is a grass-grown mound (Carn Paderau) 15.5 m in diameter and 1.2 m high.

S.A.M.; O.S. Card SN 85 SE 3; marked as a mound on O.S. field drawings (1819–20) [investigation by Mrs R. Bidgood of Abergwesyn]; 25-inch 1888:X.1.

Llanfihangel Abergwesyn
SN 85 S.E. (8757 5248)　　　　　　　　　22 iii 72

(RC 62) To the W. of Carcwm at Pen y Carn-goch, 487 m above O.D. in a clearing within the forestry plantation are three conjoined cairns forming one long boulder cairn. This has been disturbed in recent years for sheep shelters.[1]

The site was at one time considered by W. F. Grimes[2] to have been a chambered cairn of the Severn-Cotswold Group, a view with which Savory originally concurred.[3] However, Daniel later pointed out that the site showed no evidence of a chamber,[4] and having revisited the site in 1960, Grimes altered his opinion, suggesting that what might otherwise have been the only mountain-top long cairn in the county, was instead three small cairns.[5]

[1] S.A.M., Cadw site visit 29 x 86; O.S. Card SN 85 SE 2.
[2] Grimes, *M.M.W.*, p. 139, no. 44.
[3] Savory, *Prehist. Brecks.* I, p. 86.
[4] Daniel, *P.C.T.*, (1950), p. 215.
[5] *in. lit.* to O.S.; 9 v 60.

Llangammarch (E), Treflys (C)
SN 85 S.E. (8848 5029)   6 i 83

(RC 63; Fig. 59) On Pen Twr above the E.–W. ridge Cefn Gardys, 370 m above O.D., is a circular enclosure, probably a ring cairn, 16.0 m in internal diameter, surrounded by a bank of grass-grown earth and small stones 3.1–3.9 m wide at the base and 0.3–0.8 m high.[1] The interior level rises in the form of a shallow dome slightly above that of the ground outside, but this elevation may be a natural feature. There is a short length (6.5 m) of counterscarp bank 2.1 m wide and 0.3 m high, visible externally on the W. side. Within the N.W. quadrant is a level terrace, 6.5–7.0 m wide externally. The site has no ditch, entrance or internal features. The bank is being eroded by sheep. It was first described by G. T. Clark in 1873. Clark placed it above 'Cwm Cowydd' and pointed out that it lay close to an old ridge-way, formerly an extremely important drovers' road.[2] He also believed it to have been a dwelling site, and indeed, its true function will only be ascertained by excavation.

[1] O.S. Card SN 85 5; visible on A.P.s, R.A.F. F22/58/3618/0176–7; 21 vi 60.
[2] G. T. Clark, *Arch. Jnl* 30 (1873), pp. 264–266, (Plan, lower).

Llanfihangel Abergwesyn
SN 85 S.E. (8960 5213)   27 vi 91

(RC 64) To the S.E. of Wern Las, 200 m above O.D., within enclosed land on the wide dry valley base is a platform raised about 0.6 m above field level. It is amorphous, and its content of limestone and conglomerate. A possibly pentagonal outline was

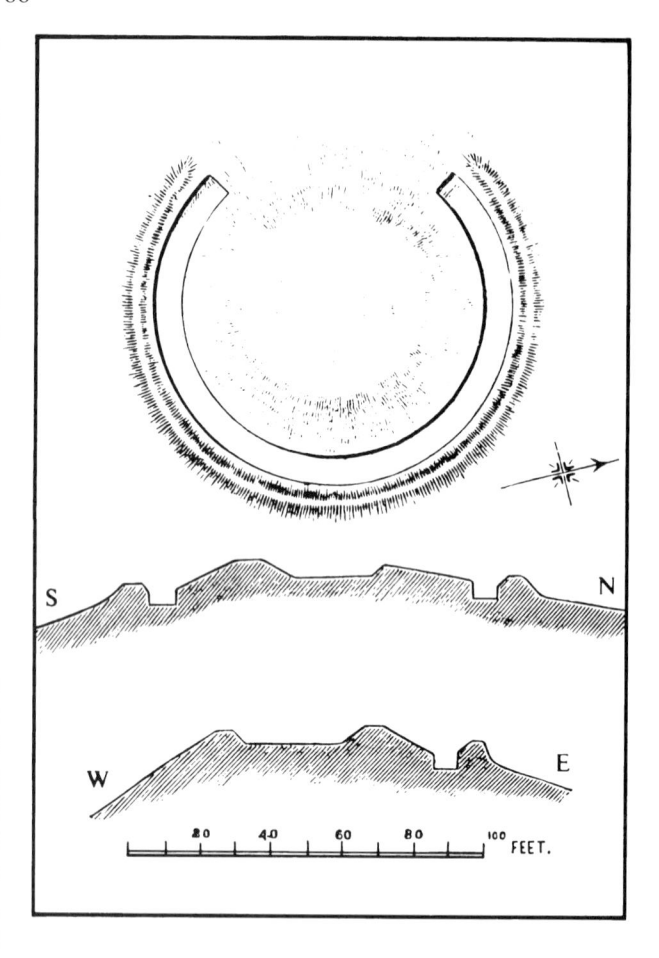

59 Pen Twr barrow (RC 63) plan (from *Arch. Jnl* 30 (1873))

traced, rather than a circle or an oval. Its maximum length E.–W. is 14.6 m and its breadth 12.5 m, the E. side being 8.5 m long; the N., 12.2 m; the W., 6.7 m and the S.E., 7.3 m. The platform is surrounded by a massive bank or revetment of small stones some 3.4 m thick, edged on the outside by a row of large boulders which are best preserved along the N. side. The central area, within this 'wall', is slightly dished, and at the approximate centre is a stone-lined hollow about 1.5 m square. The site may possibly be a prehistoric cairn.

Penderyn
SN 90 N.E. (9681 0981)   13 x 76

(RC 65–73; Fig. 60) On Mynydd y Glog, a mountainous ridge of denuding limestone pavement, there are nine cairns of varying sizes, mainly built of massive limestone boulders. Without excavation it is

60 Cairns on Mynydd y Glog (among RC 65–73): note the field or enclosure wall to the bottom right (CUAP ARG 31)

difficult to categorise these cairns definitively either as of sepulchral or field clearance origin; it was in all likelihood a combination of both.

(RC 65) The first is on the summit of the ridge, 380 m above O.D. It comprises a large conical cairn of Millstone Grit and Old Red Sandstone boulders 15.5 m in diameter and 1.8 m high. Its centre is badly disturbed by a robber crater. According to Lady Fox the cairn originally possessed four built cists,[1] but this seems unlikely, and the features she recorded were probably robbing hollows.[2]

(RC 66) To the S.E. of the above, on level ground, 370 m above O.D. the cairn is also conical in shape and of similar material. It stands 15.2 m in diameter and 2.1 m high, and again is centrally robbed, with a crater 4.6 m in diameter and 1.5 m deep.

(RC 67) To the S.W. is a partly overgrown cairn 0.6 m in height, its circumference not ascertained, as the perimeter is very overgrown.[3]

(RC 68) 365 m above O.D. on the crest of a slope falling to the E. is a stone-built cairn 15.2 m in diameter and 1.2 m high. The remains of a kerb are traceable, but the site is being destroyed by shelter building.[4]

(RC 69) 370 m above O.D. is a cairn 14.6 m in diameter, about 2.8 m high on the W. and with a small robber crater at its centre. Its centre is hollowed, with evidence of crude chambering, one on the S.W. edge and the other on the S.E. edge. Both appear to have been recently disturbed. To the S.W. is a small heap of stone 0.5 m high which may have been a burial cairn.[5]

(RC 70) 365 m above O.D. is a cairn 8.5 m in diameter and 0.9 m high, hollowed in the centre with a modern shelter.[6]

(RC 71) 370 m above O.D. is a cairn 5.8 m in diameter and 0.6 m high, slightly disturbed at the centre.

(RC 72) 350 m above O.D. on a slope of south-easterly aspect is a cairn 11 m in diameter and 0.9 m high with a crater-like disturbance to the W. of centre.[7]

(RC 73) 388 m above O.D. on the summit ridge of Mynydd y Glog is a stone-built cairn 12.2 m in diameter and 1.5 m high. It is much disturbed by shelter building, which Roese has documented to be a continuous and destructive activity.[8]

[1] O.S. Card SN 90 NE 3a.
[2] H. N. Savory, *P.M.W.W.*, p. 133.
[3] O.S. Card SN 90 NE 3c.
[4] O.S. Card SN 90 NE 4.
[5] O.S. Card SN 90 NE 5.
[6] O.S. Card SN 90 NE 7.
[7] O.S. Card SN 90 NE 6.
[8] O.S. Card SN 90 NE 8; Roese, *Thesis*, no. 95.

General References: N.M.W. Record O.S. 6-inch Map, (A. Fox, 1936); Savory, *op. cit.* n. 2; the sites are also visible on C.U.A.P. nos. ARG 31–3.

Penderyn
SN 90 N.E. (RC 65) (9742 0899); (RC 66) (9749 0884); (RC 67) (9735 0890); (RC 68) (9759 0827); (RC 69) (9766 0871); (RC 70) (9790 0853); (RC 71) (9710 0909); (RC 72) (9812 0818); (RC 73) (9818 0886)   6 x 69

(RC 74) On the S. side of Nant Cadlan at the base of ground falling N.W. into the Sychpant valley, about 325 m above O.D., is a circular cairn, 16.2 m in diameter, 1.2 m in height on the uphill side and 2.1 m on the downhill side. There is a large central crater. Excavation near this site produced a large and important flint assemblage ranging from Mesolithic to Bronze Age in date (see MS 7).

T. W. Burke, *B.B.C.S.*, 22 (1966–8), pp. 78–87; p. 78; Roese, *Thesis*, no. 101.

Penderyn
SN 90 N.E. (9947 0979)   5 v 75

(RC 75) Near Plas y Gors on the crest of a ridge about 405 m above O.D., close to a fence, is a mound of large stones and boulders 7 m in diameter and 0.6 m high. It is damaged by an excavation trench cut from the S.

Ystradfellte
SN 91 N.W. (9184 1507)   1 v 85

(RC 76) On a gently-sloping shelf just below the crest of Fan Nedd, 630 m above O.D., is a small overgrown circular mound, 8.2 m in diameter and 0.6 m high. Probing within the mound suggested that it was not stone-built. There is a shallow depression at its centre. This is either an eroded turf stack, clearance, or sepulchral cairn.

Defynnog (E), Senni (C)
SN 91 N.W. (9140 1790)   21 ii 84

(RC 77) On the N. end of Fan Nedd, 550 m above O.D., on the edge of a level shelf in ground falling to the E. is a slight mound with visible stones, which could be kerbstones. The feature is circular, about 4.9 m in diameter and 0.45 m high. Though possibly natural, it seems more likely to be a cairn.

O.S. Card SN 91 NW 18.

Defynnog (E), Senni (C)
SN 91 N.W. (9182 1887)   18 xii 84

(RC 78; Figs 61–2) 400 m W.N.W. from Rhyd Uchaf, 440 m above O.D. on a shelf on the W. side of the N.W. col at the N. end of Afon Llia is an overgrown double ringwork or cairn, possibly related to the Maen Llia (SS 12; Fig. 111).

The site comprises an inner ring-bank separated by a ditch from an outer bank with traces of an outer ditch, and, on the S. and S.E., there are traces of a third bank. The monument is roughly circular but is slightly elongated in an E.–W. direction, on which axis also there are signs, on the E., of an entrance through the rings. The gap in the inner ring is evident; the outer ring appears to be continuous but is much flattened at the site of the 'entrance', and there is a corresponding gap in the lower ditch. A modern drainage ditch with its accompanying bank has obliterated the outermost part of the site on the W. and S.W. and there is nothing in the central space except a small central grass-grown hole, which looks modern.

The dimensions of the inner bank are 9.2–10.1 m in diameter, 2.5–3.1 m wide, 0.6 m high above the

61 Rhyd Uchaf, near Maen Llia: ringwork (RC 78) (Copyright Clwyd-Powys Archaeological Trust AP 88 2 11)

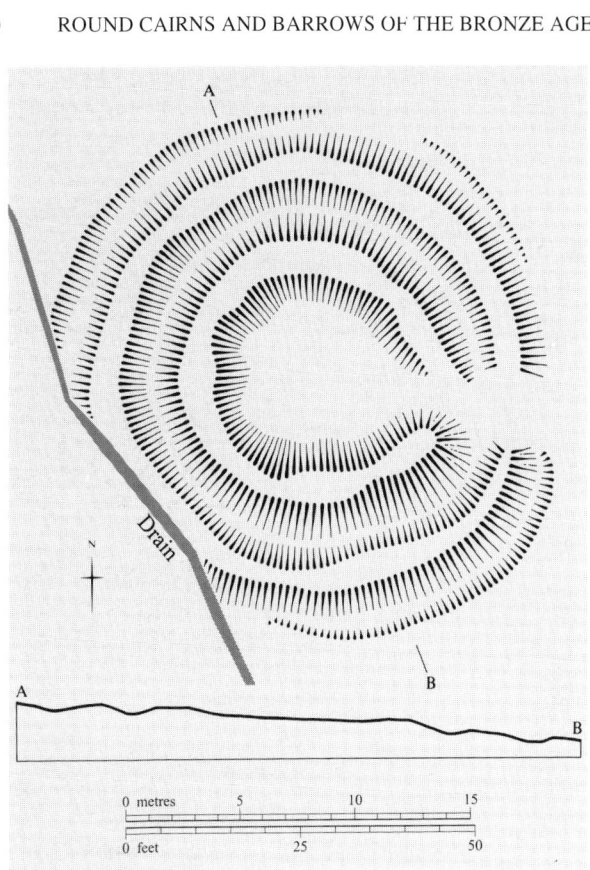

62 Rhyd Uchaf, near Maen Llia (RC 78): plan of ringwork

ditches, but only 0.3 m above the central space. The outer bank is 16.5–17.4 m in diameter, 2.5–3.1 m in width, 0.6 m high above the ditches, and the outer ditch is 0.3 m high above the surrounding ground. The outermost bank is 2.5–2.9 m in width and the overall dimensions of the site, 25.6 m N.W.–S.W. by 18.5 m. No stones are visible, though it is possible that there may have been a central upright here, like the Maen Llia.

cf., Inv. Caerns. III, no. 162; first noted by W. E. Griffiths, *Arch. in Wales* 9, (1969), p. 8.

Defynnog (E), Senni (C)
SN 91 N.W. (9233 1896)   15 viii 88

(RC 79) On the eastern side of Afon Llia, opposite the above site, 425 m above O.D., is a site with the appearance of a grass-grown ring cairn, with only a few stones protruding through the vegetation, and comprising the rim of a robbed cairn of ordinary form. However, its proximity to RC 78, also of ring-bank form, lends credence to the idea that this also might have been a monument of ring-cairn type. In external diameter it is 10.1 m, the rim-bank is 1.8–2.5 m wide, and 0.3 m high above the central area, but with an external height of 0.6 m on the N. An 'entrance' 3 m wide on the N.-E. is probably the gap through which the stones of the cairn were carted away. There is a small central depression, which is probably modern.

References as RC 78.

Defynnog (E), Senni (C)
SN 91 N.W. (9264 1896)   15 viii 88

(RC 80) On the S. end of the summit ridge of Fan Llia, 614 m above O.D., is a wrecked flat-topped circular cairn of Old Red Sandstone slabs up to 0.25 m across, grass-grown at the edge. It is 8.5 m in diameter and up to 0.8 m high. Some of the stones have been piled on the N.W. edge to form a modern cairn 0.9 m high, and the cairn centre is disturbed by digging.

Ystradfellte
SN 91 N.W. (9353 1816)   15 iii 84

(RC 81) On the interfluve between Nant y Wydd and the Afon Dringarth, 345 m above O.D., is an oval, almost circular grass-grown mound of earth and stones. It is 14 m in diameter E.–W. and 12.8 m N.–S. with an ill-defined rim 0.45 m high and a broad, dished centre about 10 m in diameter. At its centre an edge-set slab 0.61 m N.–S. by 0.1 m thick protrudes on the E. side of a square hollow, possibly all that remains of a cist. The site is almost certainly a cairn base.

Visible on A.P., R.A.F. 4107-CPE/UK/2487; 10 iii 48.

Ystradfellte
SN 91 N.W. (9385 1540)   24 iv 74

(RC 82) At Pen Father Uchaf on a broad shelf overlooking the Dringarth valley, 435 m above O.D., is a cairn 8.2 m in diameter and 0.3 m high, consisting of medium grade stones and some rubble. On the E. side, cairn mass has slipped into a more recent shake-hole, distorting the shape of the mound.

Ystradfellte
SN 91 N.W. (9496 1401)   31 i 85

(RC 83) On Waun Dywarch overlooking Nant Mawr, 440 m above O.D., is a small cairn about 4 m in diameter and 0.6 m high, of small boulders consolidated with turf.

Ystradfellte
SN 91 N.E. (9602 1564)   31 i 85

(RC 84) At the N. end of Waun Tincer in a slight hollow on a S.E.-facing slope 410 m above O.D. is a round mound of mixed grade rubble. It is 8.8 m in diameter and 0.4 m high. The cairn appears to be undisturbed.

Detected upon A.P.s, R.A.F. F22 583618, 0016–17.

Ystradfellte
SN 91 N.E. (9713 1508)   5 iii 85

(RC 85) On Twyn Garreg Wen, 475 m above O.D., is a slightly oval flat-topped cairn lying on ground sloping gently to the S.E. It is 8 m E.–W. by 7.1 m N.–S. in diameter and 0.25 m high. The cairn is of mixed grade stones slightly overgrown. It has been superficially disturbed and the rim is slightly raised. On the E. and N. perimeter a number of upright, leaning slabs protrude which are possibly part of a kerb. Two are adjacent and lean inwardly on the E. Each is exposed for a distance of 0.7 m where they appear 0.5 m and 0.6 m thick.

References as RC 84.

Cantref
SN 91 N.E. (9845 1679)   13 ii 85

(RC 86) On the W. slope of Pant Brwynog at a site marked Garn Wen on some O.S. 6-inch maps, and about 490 m above O.D., are stones testifying to the former presence of one, possibly two cairns. On the E. is a roughly circular patch, level with the ground, 2.4 m in diameter. To the W. of this patch 9.1 m at the crest of a slight fall to the W. is a similar patch, the easternmost of four or five further patches, which all appear modern. Only the former more E. of these two appears genuine, and the whole seems best interpreted as the destruction and scattering of a single larger cairn.

Cantref
SN 91 N.E. (9800 1712)   13 ii 85

(RC 87–9) About 300 m S. by E. from the farm Gors Wen, some 295 m above O.D., are three cairns now on the edge of or within dense forest.

(RC 87) A site marked by a lot of scattered stone 7.7 m in diameter and 0.4 m high. This may be the site from which flints and charcoal were taken in 1903 by T. C. Cantrill.[1]

(RC 88) A similar destroyed site, 8.0 m in diameter by 0.2 m high.

(RC 89) Within the forest is a low mound of Millstone Grit, limestone and some sandstone blocks up to 0.25 m across. A trench 0.9 m wide and about the same in depth cuts the site N.W.–S.E. This is probably where P. Murray-Threipland excavated in 1936.[2] The ascertainable size of the mound is 7.5 m in diameter and 0.5 m high.

[1] Now in N.M.W.; see W. F. Grimes, *B.B.C.S.* 6 (1931–3), p. 93.
[2] Correspondence between Sir C. Fox and O.S. [O.S. Card SN 91 SW 3]; Roese, *Thesis*, no. 60.

Ystradfellte
SN 91 S.W. (RC 87) (9013 1151); (RC 88) (9014 1160); (RC 89) (9016 1161)   6 x 70

(RC 90) To the W. of the holding at Coed y Garreg, 350 m above O.D., on the slope of a ridge dropping towards the upper reaches of the River Neath, is a large shrub-covered conical earthen mound.[1] It measures 23.0 m N.–S. by 22.0 m E.–W., rises to a height of 2.1 m and has a slightly hollowed top. Faint traces of a ditch are to be seen on the N. and W.

The site was excavated by K. Holloway in 1965,[2] when fragments of a long-necked Beaker, flint flakes and fragmentary burnt and unburnt human and animal remains were recovered from a previously disturbed cist.[3]

[1] O.S. Card SN 91 SW 6.
[2] *Arch. in Wales* 5 (1965), p. 6.
[3] Savory, *Prehist. Brecks.* I, pp. 12–13, 15–16; Fig. 4.2; Savory, *Guide*, p. 140, no. 382; the flint is illustrated by Roese, *Brycheiniog* 18 (1978–9), pp. 31–46; Fig. 2, p. 33.

Ystradfellte
SN 91 S.W. (9075 1466)   6 xi 72

(RC 91) To the S. of Carnon Gwynion, 395 m above O.D., on the summit of the limestone plateau is a limestone cairn 8.2 m in diameter and 0.6 m high, six furlongs S.W. of Plas y Gors farm.[1] The central part is stony and stands up to 1.1 m high, probably the result of a central excavation which has been refilled.

The site was excavated by T. C. Cantrill in 1897 and yielded Beaker sherds, together with a flint dagger and other flints including a plano-convex knife, two blades and two scrapers.[2]

These finds were recovered from around or below stone structures, one of which, about 1.0 m S. of the centre, comprised three stone blocks, and had probably served as a cist. The dagger was found unassociated with any apparent structure, about 1.8 m from the centre. 'A few feet' to the N.E. of the centre was a cremation accompanied by fragments of the Beaker,[3] or Enlarged Food Vessel,[4] as it has since been interpreted. Some fifty flint flakes were also found within the mound.[5]

A later, unpublished account[6] suggested that about nineteen blocks of sandstone were set 3 ft (*c.* 1 m) apart, forming a kerb around the edge of the mound. These had remained invisible until the turf was removed.

[1] O.S. Card SN 91 SW 6.
[2] T. C. Cantrill, *op. cit.* RC 2.
[3] W. E. Griffiths, *P.P.S.* 23 (1957), p. 77; Clarke, *Corpus*, no. 912.
[4] Wheeler, *P. and R. Wales*, p. 132; Savory, *Brycheiniog* 1 (1955), p. 9; H. N. Savory and D. P. Webley, *B.B.C.S.*, 17 (1956–8), p. 232.
[5] Cantrill, *op. cit.*

[6] A verbal account from Mr Thomas Jones of Mellte Castle, Ystradfellte to Dr Eckart Roese, explaining how he had taken part in Cantrill's excavation; E. Roese, *Arch. Camb.* 128 (1979), pp. 147–55; p. 149.

Ystradfellte
SN 91 S.W. (9156 1466)   16 vi 70

(RC 92–5) On Share y Wlad (SN 92 14), about 385 m above O.D., are several cairns, some of which were opened by T. C. Cantrill late in 1897.

Cantrill wrote: 'Two small cairns were visible in the quarried northern part of the spur of limestone, forming the eastern part of Share y Wlad. As Mr. Thomas Jones of Mellte Castle in 1897 found an unusual tooth (incisor?) of some animal in one of them, they may require excavation.'[1]

Roese[2] notes that the location actually given on Cantrill's sketch map[3] is at approximately SN 919 145, though his description better fits SN 921 146.

Their excavator continued: 'Two inconspicuous round cairns in the S.E. corner of Share y Wlad. These fall within Breconshire 44 NE. They stand in a line ranging N. 25 deg. E. and S. 25 deg. W. and are about 20 yds. apart [SN 922 144]. These I opened in November and December 1897 with the following results:–

(a) The N.-E. cairn [SN 9220 1440; see RC 95 below for present condition], which measured 27 ft. in diameter and rose about 2+ ft. above the surrounding surface of natural limestone, *i.e.* grey oolite, consisted of small blocks of limestone, with occasional pieces of red sandstone from the local drift, with a little soil, between them. The surface of the carn was covered with thin soil and turf. In the centre of the thickness of the carn was found to be only about 15 ins. and I concluded that since the carn was built, the surface of the surrounding unprotected limestone had been lowered some 12 ins. to 15 ins. by the solvent action of the rain. From the S. wide trench was opened northward to the centre, when it was enlarged to a circle, and the loose stones were removed down to the underlying limestone. The surrounding fringe of the mound was left intact. The only object found was a single flint flake, at the centre, among the lowest of the blocks, fragments and soil that formed the carn. No pottery was seen, no bones or ashes and no charcoal, and there was no sign of cremation. Opened 11th November 1897 in the presence of a stepson of Mr. D. Powell of Nant y Croen.

(b) The S.W. carn [SN 9219 1437; see RC 94 below], similar in character, measured 19 ft. in diameter and about 2 ft. in height. The material of the mount (pieces of limestone with a few red sandstone) rested on 3–6 ins. of sandy drift overlying the limestone. A trench was carried northward from the S. edge and enlarged around the centre, the fringe being left unexplored. The following objects were found on the floor:–
(i) A scraper, about 3 ft. from the S. edge.
(ii) A broken flake about 5 ft., from the S. edge.

(iii) A fragment of charcoal (of the size of a pea), about 6 ft. from the S. edge.

(iv) A spall of flint, about 7 ft. from the S. edge.

No objects occurred in the centre of the floor, and again no pottery, bones, ashes or evidence of cremation in situ were found. Opened 4th December 1897 in the presence of Thomas Jones from Mellte Castle, Ystradfellte, and my cousin Mr. A. Wheeler Haines, of Birmingham.'

(RC 92) A partly grass-grown, oval cairn of limestone with some red sandstone boulders, 8.4 m long N.–S. by 7 m wide and 0.6 m high.

(RC 93) On a limestone plateau there is a circular cairn of limestone and red sandstone boulders. It is 6–7 m in diameter and 0.45 m high.

(RC 94) 390 m above O.D. on the same limestone plateau as the above (RC 93), is a circular cairn of similar material, 6.1 m in diameter, 0.45 m high with a slight central hollow. This equates with Cantrill's cairn (b), excavated in 1897.

(RC 95) At the same height and close to RC 94, is a circular limestone boulder cairn 7.9 m in diameter and 0.6 m high. There is a central hollow 3 m long and 1.8 m wide. This seems most likely Cantrill's excavated cairn (a).

[1] H. E. Roese, 'Archaeological Discoveries by T. C. Cantrill', *Arch. Camb.* 128 (1979), pp. 147–55; p. 149; *idem.* 'Some Unpublished Objects from Excavated Neolithic and Bronze Age Sites in Breconshire', *Brycheiniog* 18, (1978–9), pp. 31–46; Fig. 4, p. 33; Cantrill MSS, N.M.W. and Brit. Geol. Surv. MS field notebook no. 1; the cairns are visible on A.P., CPE UK/2079, 2110.

[2] Roese, *Thesis*, no. 233 (RC 93), and nos. 63–4 (RC 94–5).

[3] N.M.W. Cantrill MSS, published in Roese, *Arch. Camb. loc. cit.* n. 1, Fig. 1, p. 151.

Ystradfellte
SN 91 S.W. (RC 92) (9207 1437); (RC 93) (9217 1458); (RC 94) (9219 1437); (RC 95) (9220 1440)

13 iv 78

(RC 96–7) To the N.-E. of Carnon Gwynion, about 360 m above O.D., lie two cairn- or barrow-like features.

(RC 96) On a broad shelf falling to the E., is a faint, circular grass-grown bank, 2.1 m wide, 10.4 m in external diameter, surrounding a barrow area of about 5.0 m diameter. The bank of earth, with some stones, rises only 0.45 m above the bottom of the ditch.

(RC 97) The second site is almost hengiform, 12 m in overall diameter, with a ditch up to 0.6 m deep surrounding an area about 9 m in diameter. The outer earthen bank 0.2 m high is broken on the E. by what appears to be a causewayed entrance flanked by a fallen stone, possibly a portal. Two small stones (of Old Red Sandstone) protrude 0.1 m above the turf roughly in the centre of the monument.

This site equates with detailed description of a 'Hut-circle' noted by T. C. Cantrill in 1897 which lay '730 yds. [*c.* 670 m] due west of Nant-y-Croen Farmhouse' (see LS 2).

O.S. Card SN 91 SW 13; Cantrill MSS., N.M.W., fo. 18, no. 44; Brit. Geol. Surv. Cantrill MS field notebook, 1:21.

Ystradfellte
SN 91 S.W. (RC 96) (9239 1447); (RC 97) (9240 1445)

13 x 76

(RC 98) Upon Gwaen Hepste, about 335 m above O.D., is a cairn of limestone and gritstone boulders, named Carn yr Arian on the second edition O.S. 6-inch map. It is about 18 m in diameter, and up to 1.7 m high, with a hollow centre 1.6 m deep with traces of kerbing. The depth to which the central excavation has been sunk suggests that the structure may lie upon a natural, infilled shake-hole. According to the Ordnance Survey the site was excavated by Lady Aileen Fox in 1936.

O.S. Card SN 91 SW 2; Roese, *Thesis*, no. 68.

Ystradfellte
SN 91 S.W. (9390 1252)

16 vi 70

(RC 99) To the S.E. of Cwm Nant on the valley bottom, 250 m above O.D., is a grass-grown ring-bank of red sandstone boulders 25.3 m in overall diameter, 13.7 m in diameter between the crests of the banks. The bank is about 8.5 m in width at the base and 1.2 m wide upon the crest, standing 1 m high, thus falling more sharply on the inside than on the outside. The interior is crater-like, and at the same level as the ground outside.

The ditch, 3 m wide and 1 m deep running E.–W. along the S. side at a few metres from the site, is probably unconnected with it.

D. P. Webley, 'An unrecorded chambered long-cairn in Brecknockshire', *B.B.C.S.* 17 (1956), p. 54, no. 5; O.S. Card SN 91 SW 9.

Ystradfellte
SN 91 S.W. (9325 1387)

9 iv 73

(RC 100–2) Close to Pen y Gorof, 270 m above O.D. on the valley floor of the Afon Mellte are three sandstone cairns of glacial or river boulders.

(RC 100) The more northerly is oval-shaped about 9.2 m in long diameter (N.–S.) and 3.7 m wide by 1 m high.

(RC 101) The southerly site occupies a natural stony knoll, and measures 9.1 m in diameter by 0.75 m high.

(RC 102) A further cairn of uneven boulders lies 325 m above O.D.

All lie in a cultivated area and recent field clearance has added to the cairn mass in each case.

Roese, *Thesis*, nos. 70 and 234; D. P. Webley, *loc. cit.* under RC 99, nos. 3–4; O.S. Card SN 91 SW 8.

Ystradfellte
SN 91 S.W. (RC 100) (9332 1432); (RC 101) (9333 1425); (RC 102) (9338 1413)   14 ix 91

(RC 103) To the W. of Tir Duweunydd, on Gwaunydd Hepste, 310 m above O.D., is a turf-covered mound 4.0 m in diameter and 0.3 m high.

Roese, *Thesis*, no. 235.

Ystradfellte
SN 91 S.W. (9435 1169)   20 ii 59

(RC 104) To the N. of Carn Pwll Mawr lying on a broad shelf at 350 m above O.D. is a slightly oval cairn of mixed grade stone and small boulders, 6.5 m E.–W. by 6.2 m N.–S. and 0.3 m high. The presence of larger perimeter boulders, particularly on the S., the largest of 1.0 m long and 0.4 m wide, suggests the possibility that there was formerly a kerb. Additional material may have been added at the E. side, after the original construction date.

Penderyn
SN 91 S.E. (9533 1120)   16 ix 91

(RC 105) On the S.E. of Mynydd y Garn is a cairn 10 m N.–S. and 8.7 m wide and 0.6 m high, of loose rubble consolidated by vegetation around the edges.

O.S. Card SN 91 SE 31.

Ystradfellte
SN 91 S.E. (9569 1372)   16 viii 83

(RC 106) To the S. of Glog Las, about 410 m above O.D., lies a cairn 6 m in diameter and 0.3 m high, of loose rubble and unsorted mixed grade stones consolidated by vegetation at the perimeter.

O.S. Card SN 91 SE 36.

Ystradfellte
SN 91 S.E. (9597 1436)   16 viii 83

(RC 107; Fig. 63) To the N.-E. of Tir yr Onnen on a slight natural eminence 150 m N.W. of the River Hepste, 320 m above O.D., is a hengiform monument. It comprises an outer bank of earth and stone, 2.0 m wide, 12.5 m N.–S. by 11 m, standing about 0.3 m above the height of the interior and 0.6 m above that of the internal ditch. The central platform is at roughly the same height as the surrounding ground, and is 5.7 m in diameter with a maximum height of 0.4 m above the ditch. The platform is slightly depressed at the centre and there is a small earthfast boulder about 0.6 m by 0.5 m, projecting 0.1 m on the lip in the S.W. quadrant. A distinct break in the bank in the E. is flanked on the S. by a low stone slab, suggestive of an original entrance. This is accompanied by a slight ovalising of the central platform, possibly to be interpreted as a causeway. There is another break on the N. side where the bank reduces to ground level in a regular manner, but this seems unlikely to represent an entrance as there is no accompanying causeway.

O.S. Card SN 91 SE 13; A.P.s, R.A.F. F21/58/3618/0097–8.

Ystradfellte
SN 91 S.E. (9633 1296)   viii 85

(RC 108) Within the field system upon Mynydd y Garn (US 78–81), about 380 m above O.D. on the S.W.-facing slope of a small, dry valley, is a cairn 6 m (E.–W.) by 5 m standing up to 0.3 m high and composed of mixed grade consolidated rubble, mainly sandstone, though with some larger limestone blocks.

Ystradfellte
SN 91 S.E. (9615 1384)   26 iv 84

(RC 109) Between Mynydd y Garn and Hepste Fechan, closer to the latter and associated with clearance and enclosure features (US 78), about 378 m above O.D., is a cairn comprising a scatter of sandstone 10 m in diameter and 0.8 m high.

O.S. Card SN 91 SE 35; Roese, *Thesis*, no. 237.

Ystradfellte
SN 91 S.E. (9639 1366)   xii 85

(RC 110) On the E. of Glog Las, about 420 m above O.D., is a cairn of erratic Old Red Sandstone boulders

63   Tir yr Onnen barrow (RC 107) from the south-west

6.5 m in diameter and 0.6 m high, lying on a limestone knoll. There are signs of slight central disturbance.

Roese, *Thesis*, no. 76.

Ystradfellte
SN 91 S.E. (9605 1439)   10 ix 69

(RC 111; Fig. 64–65) At Nant Maden, about 335 m above O.D., is a massive, largely overgrown, stony mound,[1] some 24.7 m in overall diameter and 1.8 m high. To a greater degree, its present condition is probably owed to changes made during excavations undertaken in the 1960s. The mound is encompassed by a conglomerate boulder peristalith some 19.0 m in diameter. Set central to the mound, probably after the excavation, is an upright conglomerate slab, roughly square, but embedded on one corner, 1.6 m wide across the diagonal, by 0.2 m thick and 1.35 m high above ground-level.

In the cairn's present state the original positions of all the boulders are difficult to ascertain with complete confidence. As the structure now appears, a quickset hedge growing from a bank comprising mainly small stones, appears to lie outside and S. of the continuous line of some 15 peristalithic boulders. Evidence of excavation cuttings can be seen at either end of this line, the boulders disappearing into cairn mass on the W., and

64 Nant Maden cairn (RC 111) from the south

being partly overlain by a baulk on the S.E., with the twelfth stone (from W.) protruding through it. A segment of up to c. 5.0 m radius is now exposed on the inside of this kerb. It is now unclear as to whether or not the build-up of material upon the outer stony bank is owed to this excavation, to earlier disturbances during historic times, or to cairn material which overspilled soon after the structure had been completed.

More enigmatic disturbance appears on the W. side, where the remains of an excavation trench seem to have been cut by stone quarrying for about 2 m into the mound. Adjacent to this and to the N. lies a semicircle of boulders, the structural significance or permanence of which is unclear.

The cairn was excavated by D. P. Webley in 1960 and later,[2] when the boulder kerb is believed to have been exposed. This was found to enclose a D-shaped central structure built over rubble, yielding fragments of either a 'B1' Beaker or Food Vessel. Within this central structure, the upright slab was found to mark the site of an empty rectangular pit, 1. 5 m long by 0.75 m wide and 1.2 m deep. Elsewhere in the cairn were found four disturbed cremation burials with sherds of Overhanging-Rim Urns.[3] A pollen diagram drawn from the sampling of the vertical section of the mound,[4] led to the suggestion that the cairn had been established upon heathland, and that forest regeneration had resulted in an oak maximum in this area during the

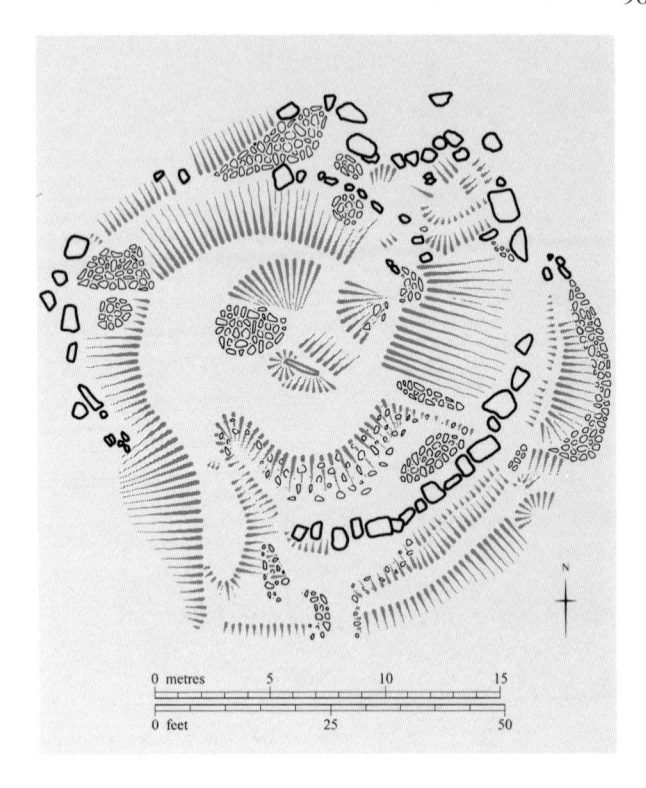

65 Nant Maden structured cairn (RC 111): plan

Bronze Age. Unfortunately, because the investigation was not complemented by radiometric dating, it remains of limited value. The cairn profile and description accompanying this study[5] is the only one which survives from the excavation campaign.

[1] O.S. SN 91 SE 6; Roese, *Thesis*, no. 8.
[2] D. P. Webley, *P.P.S.* 26 (1960), p. 349; 27 (1961), p. 351; Savory, *Prehist. Brecks.* II, 15; a site description, plan and view, drawn during the excavation, were made by R. E. Kay, see MS Notes Ser. III, Vol. xi, fols. 952–954 [26 vi 60] (N.M.R. Kay MSS).
[3] The precise type of ceramic must remain undiagnostic since interim reports suggest that 'food vessel sherds' were found in the investigation and no Overhanging-Rim Urn from this site is listed by Longworth, *Collared Urns, passim*; the excavation notes are now in the possession of Miss F. M. Lynch, who kindly made available a xerographic copy of the excavator's site plan.
[4] C. B. Crampton and D. P. Webley, 'Preliminary Studies of the Historic Succession of Plants and Soils on Selected Archaeological Sites in South Wales', *B.B.C.S.*, 20 (1964), pp. 400–499; Fig. 3, p. 444.
[5] *idem.*, barrow section Fig. 4, excavated section description, Table 1, opp. p. 448.

Penderyn
SN 91 S.E. (9709 1059)   23 ix 87

(RC 112–16) At the W. end of Cefn Sychpant and almost due S. of Blaen Cadlan Uchaf between 355 and 365 m above O.D. is a scattered group of cairns which, though noted as burial monuments, are probably related to the nearby clearance cairns noted elsewhere (US 84).

(RC 112) A cairn 7 m in diameter and 0.3 m high, of medium grade stones, largely consolidated by vegetation, with a slight depression at its centre.

(RC 113) A scatter of stones and small boulders some 6–7 m in diameter, apparently indicative of a former cairn.

(RC 114) A small turf-covered stony mound, 6 m in diameter with a height of 0.3 m, having a central depression.

(RC 115) A round cairn 8 m by 7 m, and 0.3 m high, the longer axis lying N.–S. It is surmounted by a recent cairn and consists of mixed grade rubble.

(RC 116) 380 m above O.D. is a cairn of limestone and Old Red Sandstone, 14.6–15.3 m in diameter, standing up to 1.5 m high from the S. owing to the fall of ground in that direction, and 0.6 m high from the N., with traces of a boulder kerb. There is central disturbance and a stone-built sheep shelter 2 m square and up to 1 m high has been built into the southern quarter.

O.S. Card SN 91 SE 9 (RC 116); Roese, *Thesis*, no. 83.

Penderyn
SN 91 S.E. (RC 112) (9750 1015); (RC 113) (9766 1025); (RC 114) (9775 1023); (RC 115) (9779 1025); (RC 116) (9795 1032)
                                                          9 iv 84

(RC 117–18) To the N.N.E. of Blaen Cadlan Uchaf, on an undulating limestone plateau, about 425 m above O.D., there are two cairns and a cairnfield, most likely connected with field clearance (US 83).

(RC 117) Lying between two shake-holes is a patch of stones, comprising mixed grade rubble and small boulders, probably representing the remains of a ruined cairn. It is now 7.5 m in diameter and 0.3 m high.

(RC 118) 117 m in the direction 147° Mag. from the above is another cairn of similar materials, 6.1 m by 7.1 m (E.–W.) in diameter, 0.3 m high with a depression on the W. probably caused by the disappearance of limestone in solution.

Penderyn
SN 91 S.E. (RC 117) (9772 1199); (RC 118) (9779 1191)
                                                          29 xi 82

(RC 119) On the limestone plateau 400 m above O.D. N.W. of Cader Fawr is a cairn 8.2 m (N.–S.) by 7 m and 0.5 m high. Slightly S. of its centre are two thin leaning stone slabs 0.9 m in overall length, aligned N.–S., possibly from a destroyed cist.

Cantref
SN 91 S.E. (9757 1271)   16 ix 91

(RC 120) On the summit of Cader Fawr, 405 m above O.D., are the remains of a cairn 9.5 m in diameter and up to 1 m high, with considerable central disturbance. Some incorporated boulders are up to 1 m long and 0.7 by 0.4 m wide.

   O.S. Card SN 91 SE 8; Roese, *Thesis*, no. 85.

Penderyn
SN 91 S.E. (9773 1221)   16 ix 91

Cefn Sychpant is a low E.–W. ridge of Millstone Grit about 3 km long and up to 0.5 km wide forming the natural division between Cwm Cadlan on the N. and Mynydd Y Glog to the S. It is lightly covered in glacial till and the heather and grass vegetation is badly scarred by overgrazing. An important aspect of the surface topography is the survival of several boulder trains which have probably been enhanced by early agricultural clearances.

(RC 121–2) On the S.E. slope of a N.-E.–S.W. spur of Cefn Sychpant, below the southerly crest, and just N. of Nant Cadlan are two round cairns.

(RC 121) The first, 380 m above O.D., is a badly disturbed cairn of mixed grade rubble 15–16 m in diameter and 1.2–1.5 m high. There is a central crater 5 m in diameter and small circular drystone shelters on the N. and S.E. edge of the cairn and on the E. edge of the crater. The edge of the cairn has been reveted by short lengths of wall or kerbing.[1]

(RC 122) To the south, about 365 m above O.D., is a disturbed cairn about 14.5 m in diameter and 0.9–1.2 m high.[2]

   [1] Roese, *Thesis*, no. 97.
   [2] Roese, *Thesis*, no. 98; O.S. Card SN 91 SE 40.

Penderyn
SN 91 S.E. (RC 121) (9889 1026); (RC 122) (9895 1014)   17 ix 91

(RC 123–6) Running roughly N.N.E.–S.S.W. along Cefn Sychpant are a number of cairns and cairn-like features. Most appear to be the direct result of agricultural land clearances, and are listed as field clearance cairns (US 83). Only those which appear to have been intended for burial are listed here (see also RC 112–16).

(RC 123; Pl. 8, Figs 66, 68) On the N.W. end of Cefn Sychpant, 395 m above O.D., is an annular oval bank[1] of mixed grade rubble and boulders without an entrance. It measures 20.7 m internally, E.–W. by 18.3 m, and is 2.5 to 4.3 m wide and 0.7 m high. There is a shake-hole on the S.W. the edge of which appears to have been respected by the cairn-builders, though this conclusion may be illusory. A small recumbent boulder (0.8 by 0.8 m and 0.4 m high) is set near the centre, possibly part of a former cist or at least indicating a putative site for a pit burial, and stones are piled (possibly recently) on the S.W.[2] There seems little way of knowing how likely this had been intended as a ring cairn, on the one hand, or if, on the other hand, it was a large free-standing burial monument comparable to its immediate neighbour (RC 124). Few large boulders survive, attesting to the existence of a peristalith. Systematic robbing of the central area for its limestone content could be expected

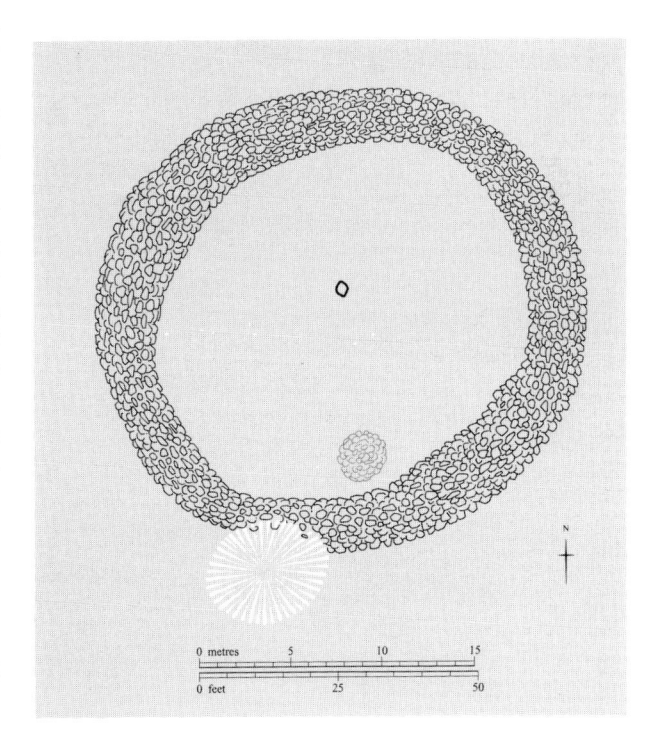

66 Cwm Cadlan cairn (RC 123): plan

at a site so close to the road. The monument has been affected slightly on the S. and S.E. by the erection of a grave (presumably for sheep).

[1] O.S. Card SN 91 SE 24; A.P.s, R.A.F. CPE/UK 2079/1093–4; 19 x 47.
[2] Roese, *Thesis*, no. 241. Probably following Cantrill (MSS N.M.W.; see p. 189) Roese notes this site to have been in an area of goose corralling.

Penderyn
SN 91 S.E. (9833 1088)   17 ix 91

(RC 124; Fig. 68) About 200 m E. by N. from RC 123, 395 m above O.D., are the remains of a cairn 18.6 m in diameter and up to 1.8 m high. It is very mutilated.

O.S. Card SN 91 SE 4; Roese, *Thesis*, no. 100.

Penderyn
SN 91 S.E. (9855 1095)   25 vi 69

(RC 125) Along the same ridge (Cefn Sychpant),[1] as RC 124, 395 m above O.D., lies a grass-grown stony bank about 0.3 m high, 1.2 m wide, and with an external diameter of about 10.5–11.5 m. There is slight evidence for an inner kerb; one particular edge-set stone on the S. side is 0.6 by 0.2 m and 0.3 m high. Immediately within the ring, the ground is covered with a wide stony apron, leaving a central grass-grown patch. The grass may be fortuitous, and the interior may be a stony platform. This badly robbed cairn has

67 Cwm Cadlan possible cairn (RC 126) looking north

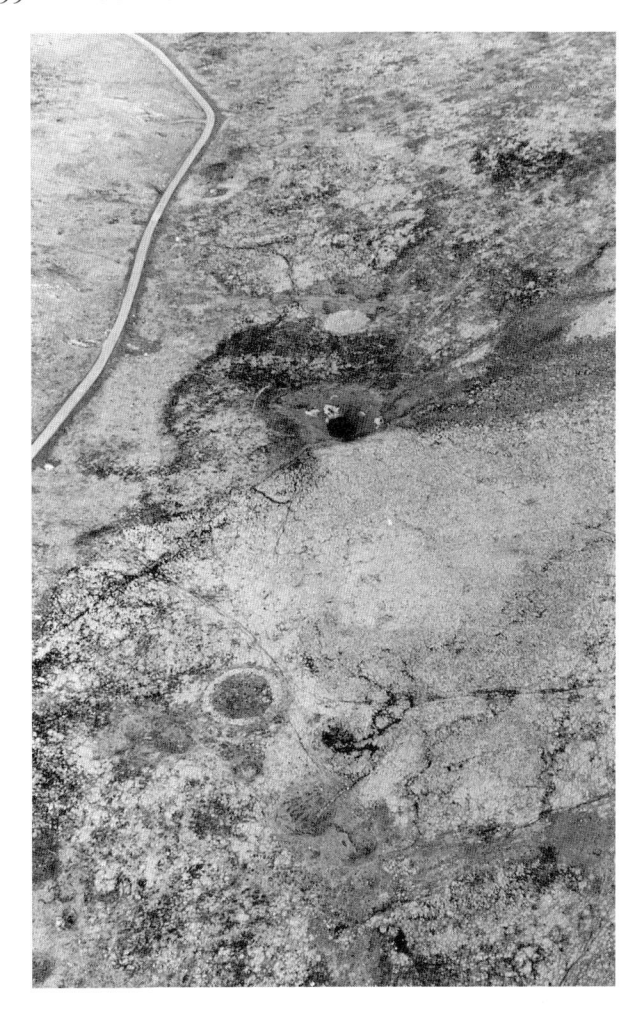

68 Cefn Sychpant showing cairns (of RC 123–4).

suffered constant visitor disturbance, probably creating an illusion as to its true original form.[2] In 1953 D. P. Webley[3] noted here a 'wrecked central cist' containing a sandstone disc 4 cm in diameter and 1 cm thick.

[1] O.S. Card SN 91 SE 4.
[2] Roese, *Thesis*, no. 96.
[3] D. P. Webley, 'A Neolithic Sandstone Disc from Cwm Cadlan', *B.B.C.S.*, 15 (1954), p. 303.

Penderyn
SN 91 S.E. (9864 1101)   17 ix 91

(RC 127; Fig. 69) On Twyn Bryn Glas, though not exactly upon its summit,[1] 440 m above O.D. is a cairn of sandstone and Millstone Grit[2] boulders 10.1 m in diameter and 0.9 m high with the suggestion of a spaced or discontinuous kerb formed of upright boulders of a larger size than the remaining stones of the cairn. There is a little mound of small stones and earth alongside the cairn.

The site was excavated by D. P. Webley in 1958,[3] when three periods of construction were recognised:

(i) A central boat-shaped cist of stones, 3.2 m long by 2.8 m broad, surrounded by a ring of built stones, 6.2 m in internal diameter and 0.55–0.75 m in width. The cist was empty, but under the ring was found a fragment of Beaker pottery, whilst from the old ground surface between the cist and the ring (as also from the

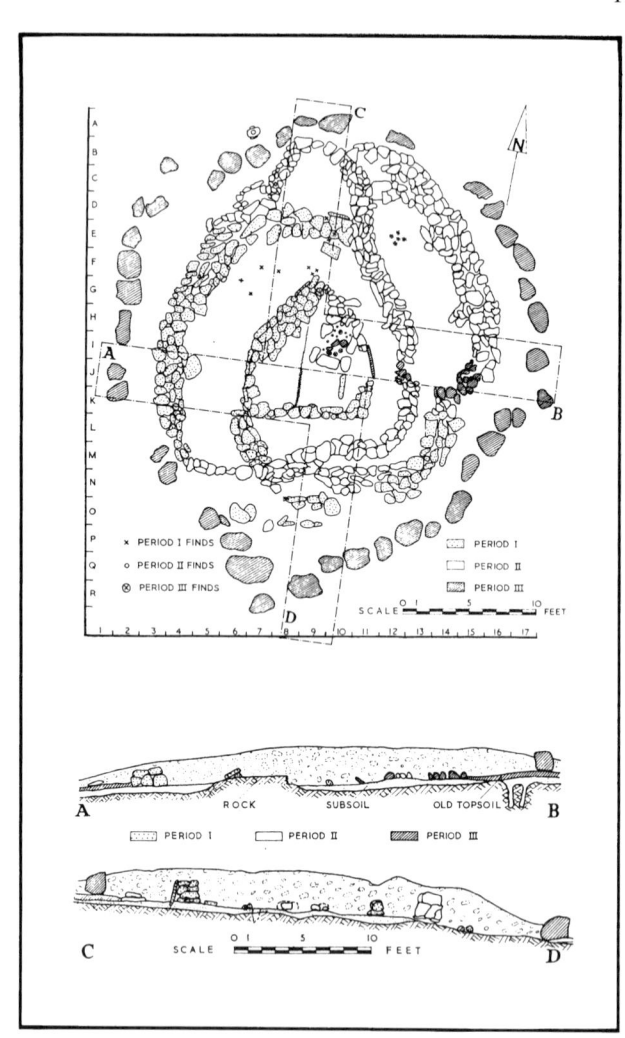

69 Twyn Bryn Glas cairn (RC 127): plan from *B.B.C.S.* 19 (1960)

make-up of the structures of periods (ii) and (iii)) came a scatter of sherds of an Overhanging-Rim Urn.

(ii) A larger boat-shaped structure of stones, originally 7.3 m long by 5.2 m broad, and re-built on the E. to incorporate a crescentic façade, forming a more nearly circular wall with a central rectangular cist containing a smashed Handled A Beaker found overlying a quantity of burnt animal bones.

(iii) A ring of large boulders, 10.4 m in diameter, forming the kerb of the cairn as still visible. The period (ii) cist was cleared out and a small new cist built in it, containing a pygmy cup and a small heap of cremated bone.

Although it has been suggested that this site is a typical Welsh ring cairn,[4] ring cairns are not normally completely filled with stone. This cairn is encompassed by boulders in the manner of a kerb cairn (pp. 69–70 *supra*). In its present state there is little to indicate the existence of the structural features known from excavation.

[1] O.S. Card SN 91 SE 5; A.P.s, R.A.F. F22/58/3618/0010–11; 21 vi 60.
[2] Roese, *Thesis*, no. 99.
[3] D. P. Webley, *B.B.C.S.* 19 (1960); Savory, *Prehist. Brecks.* II, pp. 13–14.
[4] F. M. Lynch, *Scot. Archaeol. Forum* 4 (1972), p. 63.

Penderyn
SN 91 S.E. (9850 1166)   15 ii 89

(RC 128) Beyond the N. end of Cefn Esgair Carnau, 385 m above O.D. on a S.-facing slope, is a much disturbed round cairn 8.8 m N.E.–S.W. by 8 m, rising to 0.25 m.

Penderyn
SN 91 S.E. (9814 1459)   26 iv 84

(RC 129) To the N. of Cefn Esgair, 395 m above O.D., among a number of amorphous cairns, is a cairn 27.5 m E.–W. by 14 m, some 0.5 m high and of unconsolidated rubble. The mound is in two parts; to the S. a piece measuring 12 m N.–S. comprises small and medium grade stones; the N. part consists of larger stones and small boulders. The two areas are separated by a strip about 1.6 m wide, of consolidated material. Unformed coursing is recognisable on the N. There is a shallow depression about 2 m wide and 0.3 m deep to the W. of the site.

O.S. Card SN 91 SE 41.

Penderyn
SN 91 S.E. (9815 1464)   20 i 83

(RC 130) On the W. slope of Pant y Waun, about 395 m above O.D., lying on a narrow shelf, the ground beyond falling away down the valley to the S., is a cairn 7.0 m N.–S. by 5 m and 0.6 m high, with a shallow central depression. It is consolidated and of small and medium grade stones.

Penderyn
SN 91 S.E. (9820 1482)   20 i 82

(RC 131) On the N.-facing nose of a ridge overlooking the Taf Fawr valley is a round cairn 7 m in diameter and 0.3 m high. It consists of mixed grade stones consolidated with peat and grass and appears undisturbed.

Penderyn
SN 91 S.E. (9916 1092)   7 iii 84

(RC 132) On the E. end of Cefn Sychpant, to the S. of Coed Taf Fawr is a recumbent stone 1.1 m long and up to 0.5 m wide, surrounded W.-N.-E. by a low penannular bank of 7.5 m diameter E.-W., up to 1.2 m wide and 0.3 m high. The stone is oriented N.-S. Although the stones within the bank resemble a kerb, they seem not earthfast.

O.S. Card SN 91 SE 37.

Penderyn
SN 91 S.E. (9944 1088)   22 ix 82

(RC 133) Further to the E. on the same ridge as the above is a partly grass-grown cairn of small and medium grade stones, 12.5 m in diameter with a raised rim up to 2 m wide. It appears to be a robbed cairn.

O.S. Card SN 91 SE 38.

Penderyn
SN 91 S.E. (9959 1081)   23 ix 82

(RC 134) About 420 m S. by E. of RC 132, overlooking Nant Cadlan is a round cairn of mixed grade stones and small boulders, 13.2 m N.W.-S.E. by 12.3 m transversely and 1.0 m high. The centre has been mutilated and a modern sheep shelter 1.1 m high superimposed upon it. Large flat stone slabs incorporated into this shelter may derive from the cist.

O.S. Card SN 91 SE 39.

Penderyn
SN 91 S.E. (9965 1040)   23 ix 82

(RC 135) Bedd Illtud lies on the crest of the broad ridge of Mynydd Illtud, 340 m above O.D.[1] This feature may be either a robbed cairn, or a ring cairn, 14 m in diameter, the outer irregular bank now 3 m wide. At the centre is a circular hollow 2.4 m in diameter, containing a large recumbent boulder, 1.52 m long by 0.5 m wide by 0.43 m deep. Some 2.4 m to the N. of this is another partly buried boulder of which the visible portion measures 1.16 m by 0.4 m.

These may be the remains of a cist of megalithic proportions.

The mound seems to have changed little since Theophilus Jones first described it,[2] as comprising 'two large stones placed at a distance of about six feet, with a small tumulus between them'.[3] It is illustrated in Lord Glanusk's edition of the County History.[4]

[1] O.S. Card SN 92 NE 4.
[2] Jones, *Hist. Brecks.* II, ii (1809), pp. 682–3.
[3] Roese, *Thesis*, no. 93.
[4] Glanusk, IV (1930), p. 24.

Llansbyddyd (E), Pen-pont (C)
SN 92 N.E. (9739 2639)   15 ii 90

(RC 136) On the E. side of Fan Frynach, 370 m above O.D., is an oval stone mound 8.5 m long E.-W. by 6.1 m wide N.-S., probably originally circular in plan. The large boulders of a circle are traceable outside it and the internal diameter of the circle is 11.6 m. Five or six boulders survive, lying at internals of about 3 m on the W., N. and E. Other large boulders lying scattered to the E. may have come from the destroyed S. side. The only boulder which appears to be undisturbed is on the N.W. and is a large rough slab on edge, 1.37 m long by 0.38 m wide by 0.61 m high. Some of the others, up to 1.45 m long, may be fallen uprights. The site might have been either a kerb cairn, or merely a field clearance cairn or destroyed farm site.

Defynnog (E), Glyn (C)
SN 92 S.E. (9696 2237)   22 viii 74

(RC 137) On the N. end of the crest of a mountain spur on Fan Frynach, 580 m above O.D., are the denuded remains of a circular cairn, 18.9 m in diameter, 0.45 m high from the S.W., 0.9 m high from the N.E. owing to the slope of the ground in that direction. A modern cairn occupies the centre of the site, bringing up the height to 1.2 m.

O.S. Card SN 92 SE 1; Roese, *Thesis*, no. 77.

Defynnog (E), Glyn (C)
SN 92 S.E. (9631 2320)   22 viii 74

Pont Ar Daf (see LBS 3)

(RC 138; Fig. 70) At Ynys-hir, on the S.W. spur of Mynydd Epynt 395 m above O.D., and S.W. of the

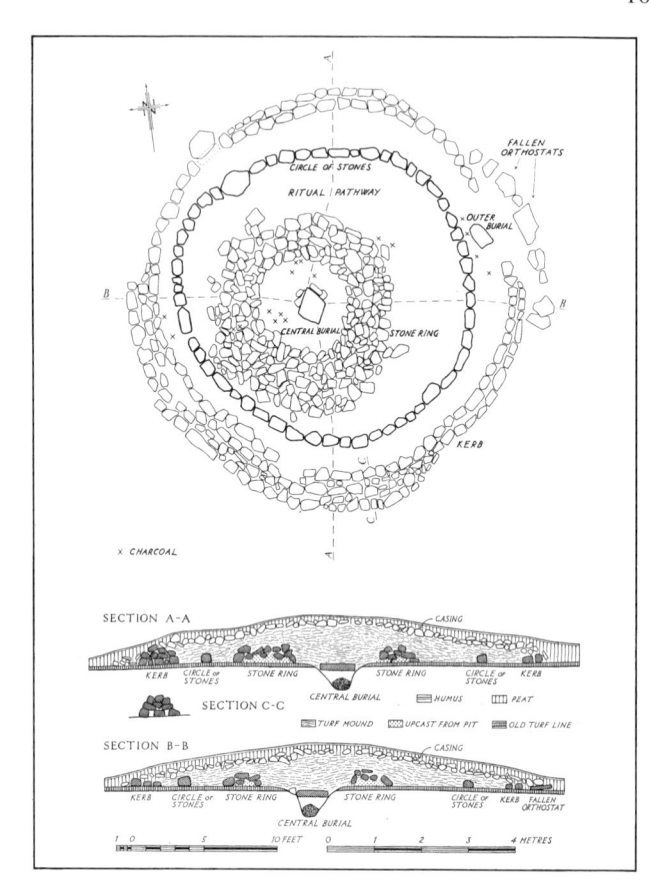

70 Ynyshir cairn (RC 138): excavation plan (from *Arch. Camb.* 97 (1943))

stone circle (SC 5), is a mound comprising both stone and turf which was excavated in 1940.[1]

Around the perimeter of a mound 9.8 m in diameter was a kerb, mainly of double-laid rounded stones up to 0.4 m in length by 0.3 m wide. This outer kerb may conveniently be divided into five unequal sections. Around the northern part is a double line of stones; the N.E. section is at first of single stones, then there is a gap of about 1.5 m, on the outer side of which there appears a sort of outer protecting skirt, perhaps an indication of blocking after infilling the interior. The S.W. section is again of double coursing, then the S. and S.E. two-fifths are roughly twice as wide, up to four courses of stone. Finally, the N.W. section is of single stones.

Within the 'entrance' gap formed by the stone 'apron' on the N.E., was found a burial beneath a rectangular slab about 0.5 m by 0.3 m and 0.1 m thick. The pit was about 0.3 m in diameter and was beehive-shaped, 0.45 m deep. It contained charcoal, burned bones, fragments of a pygmy cup, a flint flake, beads and small pieces of woven material.

Moving towards the centre of the cairn, there was next a single-course stone ring, roughly concentric with the outer kerb or wall, which enclosed a heap of stones in the form of a mini ring cairn, 4.0 m in diameter, 1.5 m wide and 0.3 m high. Although circular,

this was set eccentrically to the other two ring features, so that its central burial lay about 1.6 m E. of the projected centre of the cairn structure. This central feature was about 0.9 m square and 0.9 m deep below the old ground surface. It was covered by slabs of Old Red Sandstone 0.9 m by 0.8 m. Beneath this stone covering were pieces of charcoal and burnt bone.

The mound was of turf, with some stone in the outer layers.

The site is still a flat grass-grown mound 9.5 m in diameter and 0.9 m high. There is now insufficient evidence to indicate that it was once a ring cairn.[2] Lying within the impact zone of an artillery range, it is hardly surprising that there are some small depressions upon the cairn mass caused by the explosion of shells. The finds are at the National Museum of Wales.[3]

[1] G. C. Dunning, *Arch. Camb.* 95 (1940), pp. 169–94, espec. pp. 179–91.
[2] O.S. Card SN 93 NW 2, citing F. M. Lynch, *Scot. Archaeol. Forum* 4 (1972), p. 78.
[3] Savory, *Guide* (1980), pp. 25, 28, 29, 71, 155, 157, illus. 199 and 219.

Llanfihangel Nant Bran
SN 93 N.W. (9207 3825)   23 viii 89

(RC 139) On the broad high ridge which separates the valleys of the Bran and the Cilieni, 420 m above O.D., is a barrow marked Y Crug in Antiquity type on the O.S. Map.[1] It is circular, 17 m in diameter, 0.9 m high, with a flat summit 7.6 m in diameter and covered in vegetation.[2]

[1] Six-inch sheet 1964 revision.
[2] O.S. Card SN 93 NW 4; S.A.M.

S.A.M. B 106

Llanfihangel Nant Bran
SN 93 N.W. (9497 3788)   21 iv 76

(RC 140) About 1 km N. by W. of cairn RC 139, about 410 m above O.D., is another grass-grown barrow, marked in Antiquity type Twyn Cerrig-Cadarn.[1] This is 22 m in diameter, 1.7 m high and appears undisturbed. There is a small concrete pillar set upright in its centre.[2] It is encircled by 23 large modern-set protecting stones. On the N. side is a small excavation some 2 m by 1 m by 0.3 m deep. There is a further hole on the W. of a similar size.

[1] Six-inch sheet SN 93 N.W. 1964 revision; A.P.s, R.A.F. 58/3916/0197–8; 7 xi 60.
[2] O.S. Card SN 93 NW 3; S.A.M.

Llanfihangel Nant Bran
SN 93 N.W. (9480 3856)   23 viii 89

(RC 141) On Cefn Merthyr Cynog, topping a low swell in the wide ridge top, about 400 m above O.D., is a robbed cairn 7 m in diameter and no more than 0.3 m high.

R. E. Kay, *in. lit.*, 12 iii 71.

Merthyr Cynog
SN 93 N.E. (972 389)
On artillery range; not visited.

(RC 142) On the interfluve separating the River Brân from the River Cilieni, atop a rounded hill 413 m above O.D., on a circular grass-grown mound, 16.5 m in diameter and 1 m high, is a cairn. The centre displays considerable disturbance.

O.S. Card SN 93 SW 1; visible on A.P., R.A.F. F42 58/3916; 7 xi 60; marked in Antiquity type on O.S. 6-inch map 1964 revision.

S.A.M. B104
Llanfihangel Nant Bran
SN 93 S.W. (9252 3475)   21 iii 73

(RC 143) On the crest of the broad ridge 800 m N. of Gwern y Figyn Uchaf is a slight circular mound 7.3 m in diameter and 0.3 m high, possibly the base of a cairn from which the centre has been removed either in antiquity or through quarrying, or possibly damaged immediately post-War by military activity. The former seems the most likely.

Trallong
SN 93 S.W. (9454 3195)   28 viii 89

(RC 144) Roughly equidistant between Cusop, Cil Rhudd and Tor y Ffynnon, 300 m above O.D., is a cairn 8.5 m in diameter and 0.7 m high on a terrace overlooking the River Usk.

O.S. Card SN 93 SW 5.

Aberysgir
SN 93 S.E. (9888 3057)   8 iv 74

(RC 145) About 250 m E. by N. of Llwyn Llwyd, the Tithe Award Map indicates a field known as Carn y Geifr. At 310 m above O.D., on the crest of an undulating N.–S. ridge, overlooking a steep fall to the W. is a group of tumbled boulders occupying a small shelf or hollow, forming an oval area with sunken centre, 6.1 m long N.–S. by 4.6 m. The original shape of the site is no longer ascertainable. Possibly an early cairn.

Tithe Award, Aberyscir ph, field no. 296, N.L.W.

Aberysgir
SN 93 S.W. (9838 3140)   8 iv 74

(RC 146–7) Overlooking and S.W. of Banc y Cwm on the military range are two earthfast barrows or cairns on a slight plateau about 470 m above O.D. Both are encroached upon by peat to a depth of about 0.4 m.

(RC 146) The first, which lies astride the parish boundary of Penbuallt with Gwarafog, is flat-topped, 26 m in diameter and 1.8 m high with a slight central concavity. There is track damage to both W. and N.N.W. sides.

O.S. Card SN 94 NE 2.

Llangammarch/Llanllywenfel (E), Penbuallt/Gwarafog (C)

(RC 147) It is not easy to ascertain the shape of the second, which is rush-covered, 16 m in diameter and with a slightly higher profile than the previous, 1.5 m high. Former War Department concrete posts are affixed upon the E. side. The site is badly damaged by tracks on the N.

O.S. Card SN 94 NE 3; A.P.s, O.S. 72/330, 845–6; 22 viii 72 (both sites).

Llanllywenfel (E), Gwarafog (C)
SN 94 N.E. (RC 149) (9612 4642); (RC 150) (9604 4635)   28 viii 89

(RC 148–9) There are two cairns on the ridge running N.-E. from Ffynnon Dafydd Bevan.
(RC 148) The more southerly, 460 m above O.D., is a circular, grass-grown cairn 20.7 m in diameter and 1.7 m high with an inverted bowl profile with a sharply defined edge. A strip some 2.5 m long by 0.3 m wide and 0.15 m deep has been taken out of the top. On the N.W. side a segment 2 m wide and up to 0.3 m deep has also been cut, showing a peat and podsol horizon lying over clay, and there is a hole 2.5 m in diameter and 2 m deep on the S. side.[1]
(RC 149) On the summit of Mynydd Epynt, 475 m above O.D., is a similar site 18 m in diameter and 1.4 m high, crowned centrally by an O.S. trig. point. There

appears to be no recent disturbance, though the site has probably been crossed by old tracks on the S.W.[2]

[1] O.S. Card SN 94 SW 3.
[2] O.S. Card SN 94 SW 4.

S.A.M. B100

Llangammarch (E), Penbuallt (C)
SN 94 S.W. (RC 148) (9248 4307); (RC 149) (9274 4336) 22 viii 89

(RC 150) Between the artillery range and Crug Du, about 425 m above O.D. and close to the source of a stream draining W. into the Nant Brân, is a cairn marked in Antiquity type as Garn Wen. This has not been visited owing to military activities.

O.S. 6-inch map 1964 revision.

S.A.M. B103

Llanfihangel Nant Brân
SN 94 S.W. (9341 4076)

(RC 151–3) Lying on the ridge N.E. of RCs 149–50, 464 m above O.D., are three cairns marked in Antiquity type on the O.S. 6-inch map[1] as Tri Chrugiau. One was excavated prior to 1934 by Colonel Sir John Lloyd, when a few kerb stones were found but no burial located.[2] The mounds were already suffering erosion, having been 'cut on one side by the ancient road which runs along the ridge'.[3] The newspaper account probably conflates a longer report, since it offers detail of his digging party's excavating one mound only (cutting trenches both N.–S. and E.–W. across it), whereas the field evidence seems to indicate that all three were trenched. The most pertinent observation now to be distilled from Lloyd's account, is that beneath the one mound, he found a layer of ash and black soil. Finding no central burial or burials, he concluded that the mounds had been erected as waymarkers on the drovers' route across Mynydd Epynt.

(RC 151) The S.W. barrow is circular, 21.6 m in diameter and 1.5 m high. There are traces of one robber trench, W.–E. towards the centre. Lying flat on the S. side are large peristalithic stones (probably a gritstone), over 0.6 m in diameter, and another about 0.3 m in diameter lying flat on the S. side. The track on the W. side cuts some 2–3 m into the site, leaving a section about 0.5 m deep.

(RC 152) The central site is now oval, 22.3 m long, N.E.–S.W. by 17.1 m wide, and 1.8 m high, also having a robber trench at its centre. This is tracked from W.–E. and truncated by the road. There is rig and furrow ploughing immediately to the W.

(RC 153) The N.-E. site is circular, though slightly truncated on the N.W. by the track, 18.9 m in diameter and 1.5 m high. There is here also a central robber trench. Rig and furrow abuts onto the W. side of this cairn, but this one is undamaged by the road, which passes 15 m away. This is also trenched (presumably before Sir John Lloyd's day).

[1] O.S. 6-inch 1964 ed.; O.S. Card SN 94 SW 1.
[2] G. C. Dunning, *Arch. Camb.* 97 (1943), p. 170.
[3] *Western Mail*, 22nd September, 1934, 'Ancient Mounds of Epynt Hills'.

S.A.M. B101

Llangammarch (E), Penbuallt (C)
SN 94 S.W. (RC 151) (9314 4365); (RC 152) (9321 4373); (RC 153) (SN 9328 4380) 22 viii 89

(RC 154–5) There are two cairns on the S. slope of Darren, below the crest of a ridge, 490 m above O.D.

(RC 154) The first,[1] lying immediately below the crest of the ridge, comprises a spread of small boulders and fieldstone, 10.5 m in diameter N.E.–S.W. by 9.5 m, the height decreasing from 0.5 m to 0.3 m with the hill.

(RC 155) About 120 m to the S.W. is the base of a ruined oval cairn, some 12 m in diameter and 0.3 m high. It is overlain on the N.E. side by a low spread of stones and boulders, again about 12 m across and 0.5 m in depth, thrown out during the wrecking of the cairn.[2]

[1] O.S. Card SN 95 NW 4.
[2] O.S. Card SN 95 NW 8.

Llanafan Fawr
SN 95 N.W. (RC 154) (9113 5655); (RC 155) (9120 5663) 5 x 72 (RC 155 only)

(RC 156–7) On Pen y Gorllwyn, on the moorland ridge to the N. of sites RC 154–5, are two further cairns.

(RC 156) The more southwesterly,[1] some 595 m above O.D., is 13.4 m in diameter and 0.75 m high, having on the E. a modern sheep shelter with walls 1.2 m high and in the centre, a modern cairn or beacon 2.6 m high. There is an associated fallen standing stone (SS 18) 36.6 m to its S.W.

(RC 157) On the very summit of the ridge 612 m above O.D., is a circular stone-built cairn,[2] 14 m in diameter and 1.2 m high. There is an O.S. trig. point near its S.W. margin and a concrete boundary post in the centre.

[1] O.S. Card SN 95 NW 2.
[2] O.S. Card SN 95 NW 3.

Llanafan Fawr (RC 156); Llanafan Fawr/Llanwrthwl (RC 157)
SN 95 N.W. (RC 156) (9160 5883); (RC 157) (9180 5905)   29 ix 72

(RC 158) To the N.E. of Brynceinion, on a level shelf, 420 m above O.D. on the S. side of a mountain spur, is a cairn of mixed grade rubble marked Carn Pantmaenllwyd in Antiquity type upon the O.S. 6-inch map. It is circular, 18.3 m in diameter, and 0.9 m high at the centre, with an ill-defined rim. Some 3.8 m from the S.W. edge, large boulders have been pulled aside to reveal a hole about 0.9 m across. There is extensive disturbance within the S.E. quadrant, where the old ground surface is exposed, except along the perimeter.

O.S. 6-inch map 1964 revision; O.S. Card SN 95 NE 1.

Llanfihangel Brynpabuan
SN 95 N.E. (9567 5895)   5 x 72

(RC 159) On Cefn Tŷ Mawr, 295 m above O.D., is a cairn consisting of a robbed stony platform, largely grass-grown, having a faintly raised rim with irregular inner edge. It is approximately circular, 19.5–20.4 m in diameter and 0.5 m high. The S.E. edge tends to run straight and has an outer length of walling, 12.2 m long and 0.9 m wide, some 0.9–1.2 m outside the main bank. On the W. is a gap 7.5 m wide, possibly original since the jambs seem to be faced with boulders. However, this leads to a much robbed area, and may itself be a modern feature. A trench has been dug on the S.E. and stony soil has been thrown up on the outside of that to form a bank.

Marked in Antiquity type on O.S. 6-inch map 1964 revision; O.S. Card SN 95 NE 10.

S.A.M. B97

Llanafan Fawr (E), Llysdinam (C)
SN 95 N.E. (9852 5773)   11 ix 70

(RC 160) On Garn Wen, 445 m above O.D., is a circular cairn, 10.4 m in diameter, 1.2 m high on the upper side of the hill and 1.8 m on the S.E. owing to the fall of ground. There is a central crater 4 m wide, excavated almost to ground level, containing an O.S. trig. point. Three small modern cairns are strung out along the ridge to the S.W.

Marked in Antiquity type on O.S. 15-inch 1888 VII:15; 6-inch 1964 revision; O.S. Card SN 95 SW 7; C.U.A.P. AQD 58.

Llanfihangel Abergwesyn
SN 95 S.W. (9033 5320)   18 x 72

(RC 161–2) On the broad mountain ridge E. of Llethyr Melyn, 455 m above O.D., are two cairns.[1]
(RC 161) The more southwesterly[2] is the base of a circular cairn 13.1 m in diameter, though only a few cms high. It consists of a stony platform with a slightly raised area 5.2 m in diameter, a little E. of centre.
(RC 162) To the E. of the main site is a small modern cairn about 0.75 m high and further N.E.,[3] lies a robbed circular cairn 6.4 m in diameter and 0.3 m high.

[1] Both are marked in Antiquity type on O.S. 25-inch 1888; VII:15, and 6-inch map 1964 revision.
[2] O.S. Card SN 95 SW 6.
[3] O.S. Card SN 95 SW 5.

Llanafan Fawr
SN 95 S.W. (RC 161) (9110 5457); (RC 162) (9117 5463)   3 x 72

(RC 163) In a roadside field on the W. of Tower Hill, to the S.E. of Gwaun Nelly, 170 m above O.D., is a round barrow 14 m in diameter and 0.9 m high. It is flat topped with central disturbance, but has been badly reduced in height through ploughing.

O.S. Card SN 95 SE 2; A.P.s, R.A.F. F44 58/3916/ 0135–6; 7 xi 60; N.M.W. Rec. 6-inch XI N.E.

Llanganten
SN 95 S.E. (9978 5176)   Not visited

(RC 164) On Garn Lwyd, 395 m above O.D., on a narrow shelf above ground falling N. into the Elan Valley is a site resembling a ring cairn. It consists of loose stones 9.1–9.8 m in internal diameter with a bank 3.1–4 m wide and up to 0.6 m high. There is no apparent entrance, though a slight break appears on the E. On the N. and N.W. there is a tendency for the bank of stones to form a terrace owing to the difference in level within and without the ring.

O.S. SN 96 SW 6; marked in Antiquity type on O.S. 6-inch map 1964 revision.

Llanwrthwl
SN 96 S.W. (9195 6182)   16 x 72

(RC 165) To the N.-E. of Tŷ n'y Pant, 420 m above O.D., is a circular cairn of earth and stones, 12.8 m in diameter and 0.9 m high. There is a central circular hollow with the detached cist capstone lying on its E. lip. This is 1.68 m long by 0.84 m wide and 0.23 m thick.

O.S. Card SN 96 SW 13.

Llanwrthwl
SN 96 S.W. (9285 6336)   8 v 78

(RC 166) About 300 m N. by E. of Tŷ n'y Pant, about 410 m above O.D., is a grass and heather-grown circular cairn, 6.1 m in diameter and 0.45 m high. It appears to have been disturbed in the N. half.

O.S. SN 96 SW 11.

Llanwrthwl
SN 96 S.W. (9303 6332)   8 v 78

(RC 167) About 250 m E. by S. of the above cairn, and about 425 m above O.D., sheltered to the S. by Crugiau Bach, is a grass-grown cairn 7 m in diameter and 0.45 m high.

O.S. Card SN 96 SW 12.

Llanwrthwl
SN 96 S.W. (9314 6307)   8 v 78

(RC 168) About 150 m N. by E. of RC 170, about 420 m above O.D., is a mutilated, partly turf-covered round cairn 7 m in diameter and 0.5 m high. It has been damaged centrally by a crater 2.5 m in diameter and 0.3 m deep.

O.S. Card SN 96 SW 14.

SN 96 S.W. (9317 6320)   8 v 78

(RC 169–71) Three cairns are situated in the area between and upon the summit ridge of Gamrhiw and Carnau on the W. There is a pair to the N. at about 590 m above O.D., and a single one on the S. lying about 595 m above O.D. These are probably the 'cairns on an eminence . . . called Gemrhiw', known in 1833.[1]

(RC 169) The more easterly of the N. pair is a boulder cairn, approximately circular but varies from 14.9 m to 16.7 m in diameter, owing to its ruinous state, and is up to 1.8 m high.

(RC 170) Its western neighbour lies 17.4 m away, is also approximately circular, but with N. and S. edges ill-defined because of tumble, about 15.2 m in diameter. The cairn is about 1.5 m high but rises to 2.4 m on the N. owing to a fall of ground on that side. Like the more E. site, this one is much disturbed, most of its centre being occupied by a large crater containing rough stone shelters.[2]

(RC 171; Fig. 71–72) To the S., on the W. end of the main summit ridge of Gamrhiw at 595 m above O.D. is an oval boulder cairn 20.4 m long N.–S. by 16.6 m wide and 2 m high. The centre is completely wrecked and now contains a carefully-built upstanding drystone building of recent date. This building is an almost perfect oval externally, though internally it is roughly rectangular with rounded corners, measuring 3 m long N.–S. by 2 m wide. The walls are up to 2.1 m high and average 0.9 m thick; the N.E. and N.W. corners are carefully buttressed by walls that merge into the cairn material. On the N.E. corner of the building is a lintelled doorway 1.4 m high and 0.45 m wide.[3]

[1] Lewis, *Top. Dict.* vol. 2 (1833, unpag.), *s.v.* Llanwrthwl.
[2] O.S. Card SN 96 SW 5 for RC 170–1; all three are marked in Antiquity type on O.S. 6-inch map 1964 revision. They are not discernible on A.P.s, R.A.F. 541/34/4143–4; 19 v 48.
[3] O.S. Card SN 96 SW 4.

Llanwrthwl
SN 96 S.W. (RC 169) (9439 6142); (RC 170)
(9437 6141); (RC 171) (9441 6122)   16 xi 76

(RC 172–6) On the S. plateau edge of Carn Gafallt (part of Llanwrthwl Commons), 410 m above O.D., there are three structureless cairns, two of which appear to comprise separate conjoined cairns; so there may originally have been five.[1] In her translation of the *Mabinogion*, Lady Charlotte Guest identified this site[2] as the Carn Cabal mentioned in the ninth-century *Historia Britonum* where King Arthur's dog's footprint was impressed in a stone lying upon a stone heap.[3]

(RC 172–3) The most westerly comprises a stony mass 16.5 m long E.–W. by 9.5 m wide, originally two conjoined circular cairns, each about 8.2 m in diameter

71 Gamrhiw South cairn (RC 171), showing re-use as a shelter and looking at doorway on NE

E.–W., perhaps slightly more, about 9.1 m in diameter N.–S. The W. cairn is 1.2 m high, the E., slightly higher at about 1.5 m. There are signs of disturbance, particularly in the E. site.

(RC 174) The central site is a ruined circular boulder cairn, 11.9 m in diameter and 1.5 m high. This, again, is centrally cratered by disturbance. Close to the N., cairnstones have been laid to form a shelter or fold 5.5 m long E.–W., by 3.1 m wide.

(RC 175–6) The E. site is a mass of tumbled stone 18.3 m long E.–W., with a maximum width of 11 m and 1.5 m high. This is also probably two conjoined circular cairns, each about 9.1 m in diameter and both centrally disturbed, together with a tiny modern cairn.

[1] O.S. Card SN 96 SW 2; visible on A.P.s, R.A.F. CPE/UK/25311/4342–3; 24 iii 48.

[2] C. Guest, *The Mabinogion from the Llyfr Coch of Hergest and other ancient Welsh Manuscripts, with an English Translation and Notes*, (3 vols, London, 1849), vol. II (1840), pp. 359–60. The Commission is indebted to Dr O. Padel of Truro for this reference.

[3] Nennius, *Historia Britonum*, (London: English Historical Society, 1838), p. 60.

Llanwrthwl
SN 96 S.W. (RC 172–3) (9422 6442); (RC 174) (9431 6440); (RC 175–6) (9434 6437)   16 i 91

(RC 177–84) On the ridge between Rhos y Saith Maen and Drum Ddu are six large and two small cairns,

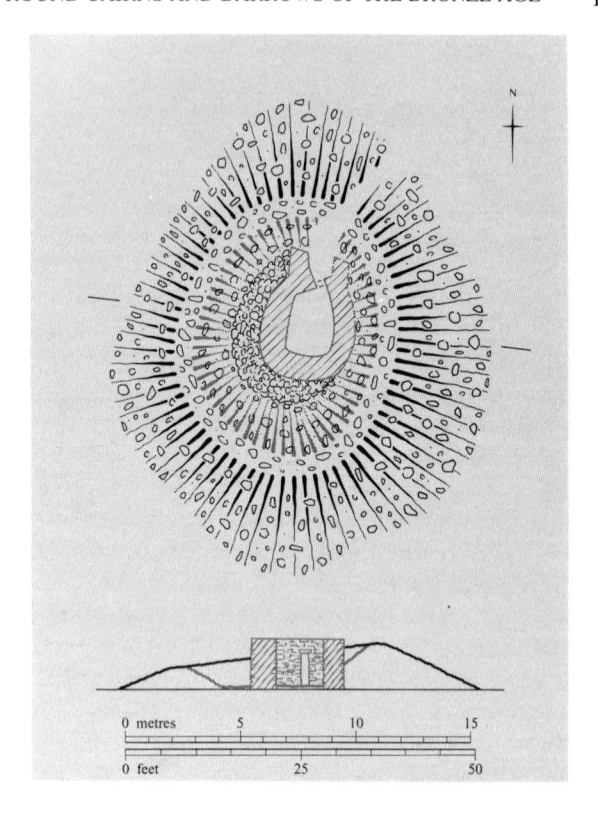

72 Gamrhiw South cairn (RC 171): plan and section

collectively known as Carnau Cefn y Ffordd,[1] lying about 405 m above O.D.

RCs 177–9 lie on ground falling to the N., especially RC 179, which is at the edge of ground falling N.E. into the Nant Cymrum at the source of which it lies. There is some doubt as to the authenticity of RCs 180 and 182 (the smaller cairns), which are included owing to the overall grouping of the sites.[2]

(RC 177) A stone cairn 7.3 m in diameter and 0.7 m high.

(RC 178) A cairn 2.7 m in diameter and 0.3 m high.

(RC 179) A much disturbed, now low, stone cairn 17.4 m in diameter and 0.7 m high.

(RC 180) Practically adjoining RC 182 on the N. is a collapsed sheep-fold measuring, internally, 6.5 m by 4.4 m and standing 0.5 m high at greatest. A later circular sheep shelter, 2 m across, open to the N., has been erected over the S. corner and cuts into the perimeter of the cairn.

(RC 181) The base of a stone cairn 3.4 m in diameter.

(RC 182) A ring cairn or hut, 10.7 m in external diameter. The bank is 1.8 m wide on the W., 2.5 m on the S. and 3 m on the N., averaging 0.5 m high. Internally it is 7 m E.–W. by 4.5 m N.–S. and within the hut is a raised platform across the W. side, 2.2 m deep and 0.2 m high. An entrance at the N.E. is flanked by boulders.

(RC 183) A slightly disturbed low stone cairn 19.2 m in diameter and 0.7 m high. A small modern shelter is built upon its N.E.

(RC 184) A round boulder and stone cairn, 7 m in diameter and 0.3 m high. Its surface is much disturbed and remains of a sheep shelter are built over the centre. The perimeter is defined by a ring of earthfast boulders.

An associated standing stone at SN 9545 6061 is listed separately (see LSS 2).

[1] Although the name appears in Antiquity type on the O.S. 6-inch 1964 revision, it is not confirmed as in vernacular use; O.S. Card SN 96 SE 6.

[2] Seven only are mentioned in *Arch. in Wales* 12 (1972), p. 10.

Llanwrthwl
SN 96 S.E. (RC 177) (9561 6068); (RC 178) (9567 6064); (RC 179–80) (9570 6044); (RC 181) (9571 6060); (RC 182) (9572 6052); (RC 183) (9578 6053); (RC 184) (9548 6057)   19 vi 70

(RC 185–7) On the W. of the ridge plateau stretching from Gamrhiw to Ffosfaehog are three cairns, spaced 400–500 m apart and aligned roughly N.N.E.–S.S.W.[1]

(RC 185) The most southerly, a much disturbed cairn, stands 350 m above O.D., lying 650 m due N. of the track Rhiw Saeson. It is of boulders, 12.5–13.4 m in diameter and 0.9 m high.[2]

(RC 186) The second site, 535 m above O.D., is a boulder cairn, slightly oval, 14.9 m long N.–S. by 13.1 m wide and 1 m high, much disturbed centrally. Lying contiguous to it on the N.E. is a small rectangular annexe, 6.7 m long E.–W. by 5.2 m wide. On the N. of the cairn is a modern sheep shelter 2 m across and 1 m high.[3]

(RC 187) The most northerly lies 470 m above O.D. on the edge of the ridge overlooking the Wye Valley to the E. This site is a cairn base only, 8.5 m in diameter and 0.5 m high, 0.7 m on the S.E. owing to the slight fall of the ground in that direction. There is a small modern sheep shelter to the N.W., 1 m high.[4]

[1] All are marked in Antiquity type on the O.S. 6-inch map 1964 revision. None visible upon A.P.s, R.A.F. 541/34/346–7; 19 v 48.

[2] O.S. Card SN 96 SE 7.
[3] O.S. Card SN 96 SE 8.
[4] O.S. Card SN 96 SE 9.

Llanwrthwl
SN 96 S.E. (RC 185) (9532 6171); (RC 186)
(9586 6204); (RC 187) (9599 6256)   19 vi 70

(RC 188) On the brow of the ridge known as Drum Ddu lying astride the parish boundaries of Llanfihangel Brynpabuan and Llysdinam, 535 m above O.D., is a boulder cairn known as Carn y Geifr. It is 15.9 m long N.–S. by 13.1 m wide and 0.9 m high, attaining a height of 1.5 m on the N. owing to the fall of ground in that direction. On the W. side of the cairn is a projecting platform of partly-turfed stones, extending 5.5 m from the perimeter, 4 m wide and 0.1 m high.

The centre is much disturbed and a rectangular sheepfold 4 m square, 1 m high, entrance to the S. has been erected upon it.

O.S. Card SN 96 SE 11; marked in Antiquity type upon O.S. 6-inch 1964 revision.

S.A.M. B95

Llanafan Fawr/Llanwrthwl (E), Llysdinam/
Llanwrthwl (C) SN 96 S.E. (9712 6043)   11 ix 70

(RC 189) On Llethyr Waun Lwyd, 455 m above O.D., on a broad, almost level shelf is a much-disturbed circular cairn 12.8 m in diameter and 0.5 m high. It is surmounted by two small modern cairns.

O.S. Card SN 96 SE 5; marked in Antiquity type on O.S. 1888: 25-inch, 6-inch 1964 revision.

Llanafan Fawr (E), Llysdinam (C)
SN 96 S.E. (9784 6007)   13 vii 77

(RC 190–3) On the W. end of the hill known as Trembyd, on the N. side of Bancystradwen, are four cairns. All lie on the crest-line of the ridge, looking over a sharp fall to the N. Cairn 194 lies 445 m above O.D. on the end of a spur overlooking the old track (Rhiw Llanwrthwl). The others are 460 m above O.D. on a higher shelf to the E.

(RC 190) A saucer-shaped circular cairn 13.1 m in diameter and 0.75 m high at centre. There is evidence of a boulder kerb. There is some slight disturbance at the centre, otherwise the condition of the site is good.

(RC 191) A circular cairn 4.9 m in diameter and 0.3 m high.

(RC 192) A scattered cairn 4.3 m in diameter and 0.45 m high.

(RC 193) A circular cairn 10.4 m in diameter and 0.6 m high. It is much disturbed centrally and to the N.W., by the erection of a sheep shelter, which has increased wall height to about 0.9 m.

O.S. Card SN 96 SE 10; not visible on A.P.s, R.A.F. 106G/UK1470/3464–5; 4 v 46.

S.A.M. B94

Llanwrthwl
SN 96 S.E. (RC 190) (9796 6147); (RC 191) (9813 6150); (RC 192) (9816 6153); (RC 193) (9823 6157)
     16 xi 76

(RC 194) On cultivated land between the Nant Cymrun and Crynfryn at a height of 225 m above O.D. stands a cairn 11.3 m in diameter and 0.6 m high, one of two which formerly occupied the field, the other now having completely disappeared. At the centre of the cairn is a robbed cist 1.37 m long internally by 0.61 m wide, the sides (the top edges of which are flush with the surface of the cairn) formed by single slabs (that on the N. a modern insertion), 0.45 m deep and up to 0.25 m thick. To the S.W. of the cist lies the shifted capstone, a slab 1.57 m long by 0.96 m wide by 0.3 m thick.

O.S. Card SN 96 SE 21; *Trans. Radnors Soc.* 47 (1977), p. 11.

Llanwrthwl
SN 96 S.E. (9767 6226)   8 v 78

(RC 195) On the E. slope of Cae Garu, E. of Cwm Betws, 190 m above O.D., on ground falling away gently N. on the brink of a steep fall to the River Wye, is a cairn 14.5 m in diameter and 0.9 m high. There is much central disturbance, as if the monument had been trenched E.–W. There is an element of doubt as to its authenticity, and this may have been a much ruined building or a clearance cairn.

O.S. Card SN 96 SE 19; *Trans. Radnors Soc.* 47 (1977), p. 11.

Llanwrthwl
SN 96 S.E. (9788 6268)   8 v 78

(RC 196–9) On Garth, a moorland plateau, sloping gently to the E., are three cairns aligned roughly N.W.–S.E., together with a fourth, more southerly burial mound, close to Ffynnon Mary.

(RC 196) Carn Wen, 460 m above O.D., on land falling gently to the E., is a circular cairn, 23.8 m in diameter and 0.8 m high. It has been much disturbed so that two modern cairns surmount the N.W., and a double-compartmented sheep shelter lies on the S.E. On the N.E., E. and possibly also S.E. edges of the cairn are tongue-like projecting platforms or stone aprons, 3.1–4.6 m in length and breadth. Their true nature or significance is not clear, though they seem to be original features.[1]

(RC 197) Near Ffynnon Mary and 425 m above O.D., is a partly grass-grown cairn, 2.7 m in diameter and 0.3 m high.[2]

(RC 198) There is a cairn lying in a hollow about 430 m above O.D. It is circular and forms a stony grass-grown platform about 0.3 m high, having traces of digging at its centre, but showing traces of what may have been a kerb of large boulders, 8.2 m in diameter.[3]

(RC 199) There is an oval, partly grass-grown, stony mound, 13.1 m long N.–S. by 10.7 m wide lying 430 m above O.D. It comprises an arc of boulders up to 0.3 m high around the circumference, but these seem more likely modern than an original kerb, since the stones are not earthfast. There is a modern central cairn.[4]

[1] O.S. Card SN 96 SE 10; marked Garn Wen in Antiquity type upon O.S. 6-inch map 1964 revision.
[2] O.S. Card SN 96 SE 22.
[3] O.S. Card SN 96 SE 4.
[4] O.S. Card SN 96 SE 3.

Llanwrthwl
SN 96 S.E. (RC 196) (9810 6047); (RC 197) (9822 6016); (RC 198) (9855 6033); (RC 199) (9873 6030)   11 ix 70

(RC 200) To the N. of Penlan Wood and on the land of Rhos-y-Beddau to its W., some 320 m above O.D., is a cairn on the crest of a broad grassy spur. It is oval 14 m long E.–W. by 11.3 m wide and 0.75 m high. An infilled trench, 1.5 m long, has been cut across it from N.–S. near the W. end. A bank, extending S. for 12 m from its S.W. edge, is the remains of an old field bank, the line of which can be seen to be continued further S. by a row of trees. There is a field clearance mound piled against its W. side. The W. end of the mound terminates abruptly where it is incorporated into the field bank, but it was probably originally circular.

O.S. Card SN 96 SE 24.

Llanwrthwl
SN 96 S.E. (9975 6110)   13 vii 77

(RC 201) Towards the S. end of Cefn Cilsanws, 340 m above O.D., is a cairn[1] of limestone boulders 13.7 m in diameter and 0.9 m high. It lies to the S. of, though may be considered part of a more extensive, dispersed cairn group, mostly felt to result from field clearance (US 90). This one appears to be damaged by a trench driven through from N. to S., the stones having been piled on either side, especially on the W., where they form a small rectangular shelter.[2] This is possibly the cairn which in 1908 produced a riveted dagger and some human remains.[3]

[1] O.S. Card SO 00 NW 1 and 4.
[2] Mentioned by D. P. Webley, *B.B.C.S.*, 17 (1957), pp. 195–6; S. Gerloff, *The Early Bronze Age Daggers in Great Britain*, Prähistorische Bronzefünde Abt. VI.2, (München, [C. H. Beck'sche Verlagsbuchhandlung], 1975), p. 66, no. 94, erroneously places the site in Cefn Coed y Cymmer, but otherwise follows Webley.
[3] D. B. Evans, *et al.*, (eds.), *The Story of Merthyr Tydfil*, (Cardiff, 1932), p. 34.

Vaynor
SO 00 N.W. (0250 0981)   15 vi 70

(RC 202–7; Figs. 73–79) Within and immediately to the N. of the Upper Neuadd Reservoir at a height of about 460 m above O.D., are six circular structures, included in the cairn section for convenience, though

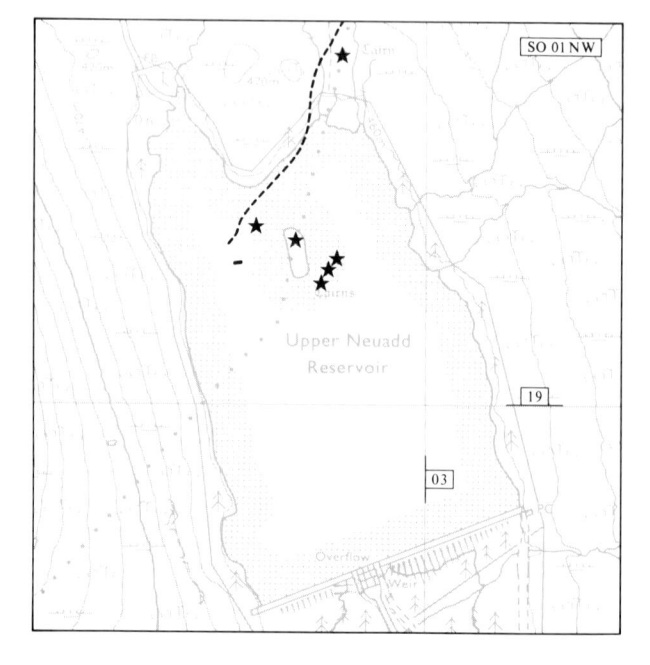

73 Upper Neuadd Reservoir: location of cairns (RCs 202–07)

74 Upper Neuadd Reservoir: ring cairn (RC 202) to N. of island, looking to the south-west

not all are certainly cairns. Four could be ring cairns or even early huts. Under normal circumstances, only one site (RC 204) is accessible. The others are either submerged or isolated upon the island. Without excavation it is not possible to ascertain their functions. So badly eroded are three of the sites, that even excavation may not elucidate their origins. The island itself appears to comprise a relatively shallow collection of boulders and stones up to about 1 m in depth, now entirely overlain by a pine plantation 70–100 years old. Prior to planting, this may have had the appearance of a massive clearance or sepulchral cairn, a possibility borne out by the fact that the island is marked upon the O.S. 25-inch plan as a cairn.[1] It is noteworthy that both flint-working sites and arrowheads of Bronze Age type have also been discovered within the reservoir (MS 10).[2]

(RC 202) About halfway between the N. shore and the island, though to its W., is a peat-covered oval feature resembling a ring cairn, 6.5 m long externally (N.–S.) by 5.2 m wide, its scattered boulder ring, 0.6–1.0 m wide still lying within a peaty matrix, and the stones protruding from the peat to a maximum of about 0.2 m. Many of its component stones appear to be earthfast, though this was not found easy to determine in every case (Figs. 74–5).

(RC 203) On the extreme N.W. tip of the island, is a small amorphous cairn about 3.5 m in diameter and up

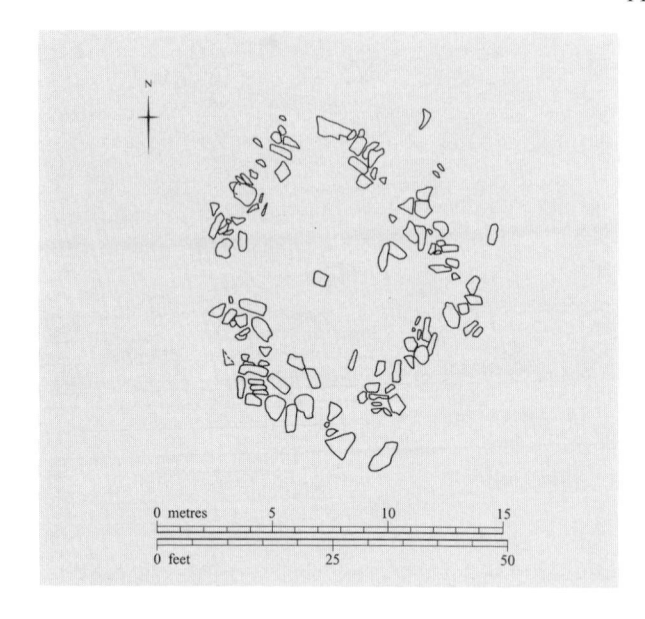

75 Upper Neuadd Reservoir: plan of ring cairn to N of island (RC 202)

to 0.3 m high. The stones, up to 1 m long, appear to have been carefully laid.

(RC 204) To the N.E. of the reservoir, 470 m above O.D., is an oval cairn 6.1 m long from N.W. to S.E. by 5.2 m wide in diameter and 0.45 m high, standing on a slight knoll in marshy ground, recently 'improved' by the addition of further cairn material. The stones are small, many of them rounded. These appear to have been gathered up either from the stream or from land clearances which may not have been of any great antiquity.

Lying to the S.W. of the island are three juxtaposed circular structures.[3] All lie on ground sloping towards the lake-bed.

(RC 205) The northwestern circle (Figs. 76–7) is about 10 m (N.–S.) by 9 m (E.–W.) in external diameter. It comprises a bank of both rounded boulders and more sharp, angular pieces with some of paving stone quality heaped about 0.3 m high, around a fairly empty central area about 4.5 m in

76 Upper Neuadd Reservoir: cairn or hut circle (RC 205) looking south

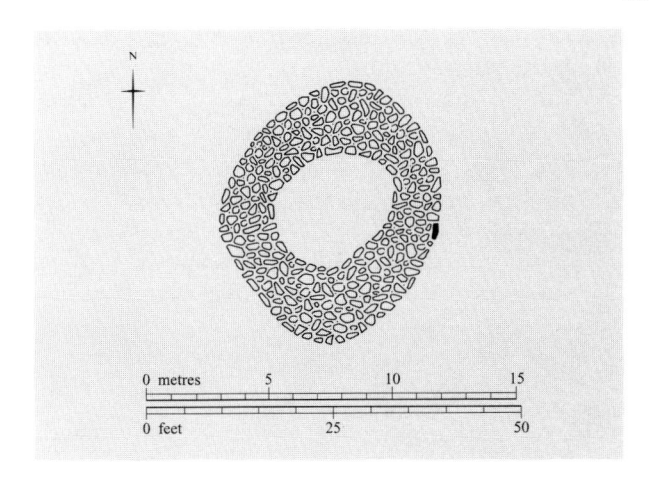

77 Upper Neuadd Reservoir: plan of cairn ring or hut circle (RC 205)

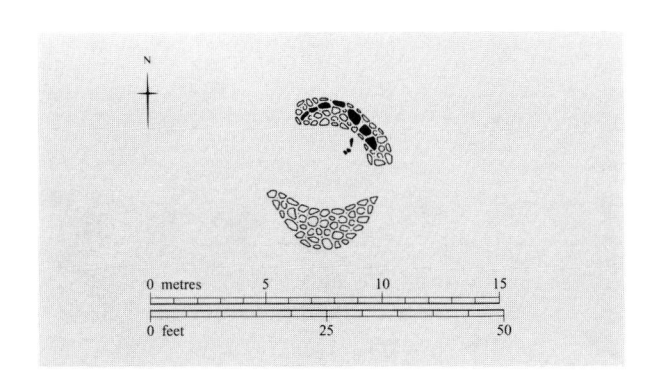

78 Upper Neuadd Reservoir: plan of cairn (RC 206)

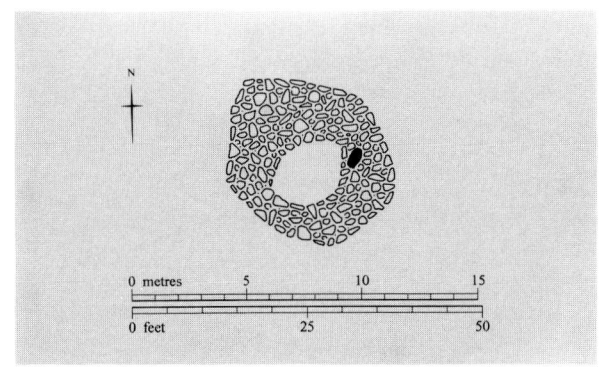

79 Upper Neuadd Reservoir: plan of cairn (RC 207)

diameter. Little soil survives in this area, though some may be preserved beneath silt within the flatter, central area.

(RC 206; Fig. 78) Some 9 m from the S. of the outer bank of RC 208 lies the perimeter of a much smaller structure. This is c. 6 m in diameter N.–S. by 5 m E.–W. and appears to have been centred upon a circular orthostatic structure forming a circumferential arc of about 3 m. Orthostats may survive on the S. side, but these lie in stony debris up to 0.3 m deep. Within the central space there are two earthfast stones placed slightly off-centre on the E. These may mark the site of a cist or stone-lined pit.

(RC 207; Fig. 79) Separated by only 5 m or so from RC 205 and to its E. lies another feature of roughly the same dimensions as RC 206. This is 6 m N.–S. by 7 m E.–W. and comprises an unbroken annular bank of mainly angular stones up to 1 m long and standing up to 0.4 m high.

[1] For example, O.S. Second Edition 25-inch plan (BR xxxix 3, 1905).
[2] *Taf*, 2, Fig. 51, p. 88; personal communication from Mr and Mrs G. Bird of Tir Henydd, Aberdare.
[3] R. Miller, *Folklife* 5 (1967), pp. 107–110; Miller observed these submerged sites, suggesting that they were early 'shiels'.

Cantref (RC 202); Cantref/Llanfrynach (RC 203–4); Llanfrynach (RC 205–7)

SO 01 N.W. (RC 202) (0278 1924); (RC 203) (0281 1923); (RC 204) (0288 1948); (RC 206) (0289 1914); (RC 206) (0289 1916); (RC 207) (0290 1918)

2 ix 89

SO 01 N.E. (for RC 312 see addenda)

(RC 208) On the E. end of Cefn Sychpant, 365 m above O.D., lies a circular cairn, 12.2 m in diameter and 0.3 m high with a pronounced outer stone bank some 2.4 m wide, giving rise to the suggestion that this may be a ring cairn.

Roese, *Thesis*, no. 243.

Penderyn
SO 01 S.W. (0012 1055)   24 vi 74

(RC 209) Lying W. of Daren Fach on the N.-facing hillslope, 425 m above O.D., S. of Coedcae'r Ychain is a swathe of stones 4.6 m wide, 0.6 m high and about 18.3 m in diameter. The feature is symmetrically placed on a grass-grown stony knoll about 0.9 m high, of inverted-saucer profile. Although closely resembling a ring cairn, some reserve is held as to its antiquity.

O.S. Card SO 01 SW 3; Roese, *Thesis*, no. 248.

Vaynor
SO 01 S.W. (0241 1081) 15 ii 80

(RC 210–12) On the limestone summit of Cilnsanws Mountain, 460 m above O.D., are three cairns. All are circular and grass-grown, and from one, (RC 211, 214 or 201 above), it is believed a bronze knife dagger was recovered in 1908 (see RC 201).

(RC 210) A cairn 0.3–0.6 m high and 5.8 m in diameter with a slight excavation at the summit.[1]

(RC 211) The limestone exposure is surmounted by traces of a cairn of limestone, about 11.0 m in diameter by 1.2 m high, hollowed out at the centre to form a modern shelter adding a further 0.6 m to the cairn's profile.[2]

(RC 212) An apparently undisturbed cairn 11.0 m in diameter and 0.6 m high on the W. and 0.9 m high on the E.[3]

[1] Roese, *Thesis*, no. 111.
[2] Roese, *Thesis*, no. 249; D. P. Webley, *B.B.C.S.*, 17 (1954), pp. 54–5.
[3] Roese, *Thesis*, no. 114.

Vaynor
SO 01 S.W. (RC 210) (0240 1027); (RC 211) (0243 1028); (RC 212) (0246 1027) 9 xi 78

for cairns at Coedcae'r Gwartheg, see US 91

(RC 213) To the S.E. of Garn Ddu, on a S.-facing slope, 400 m above O.D., is a robbed-out cairn comprising a roughly circular bank of consolidated mixed grade stone, and measuring 6.5 m in overall diameter, and 0.4 m high. The centre is occupied by loose rubble 2 m in diameter and 0.2 m high. A scatter of unconsolidated stony material can be traced to the S.

Vaynor
SO 01 S.W. (0310 1211) 12 viii 82

(RC 214–15) Garn Ddu is first mentioned by Theophilus Jones in 1809[1] and the site was mapped in 1835.[1] Two main cairns can now be traced 425 m above O.D.

(RC 214) An oval cairn 18.3 m in diameter (N.–S.) by 16.8 m (E.–W.) and 1 m high. There is a central robber crater about 6 m in diameter.[3]

(RC 215) Lying 45.7 m to S.E. of RC 214 are traces of three juxtaposed small stone piles, probably representing the remains of a much larger monument. From N. to S. these are: (i) 5 m by 2.5 m in diameter by 0.15 m high; (ii) 5 m by 2.5 m in diameter by 0.15 m high; and (iii) 2 m by 1.5 m in diameter by 0.15 m high.

[1] Jones, *Hist. Brecks*. II, ii (1809), p. 624 'Y Garn Ddu'.
[2] O.S. First Edition one-inch map, 1835.
[3] O.S. Card SO 01 SW 17.

Vaynor
SO 01 S.W. (RC 214) (0358 1259); (RC 215) (0388 1230) 12 viii 82

(RC 216–17) East of Pontsticill Junction on the first hillside terrace of Cefn yr Ystrad are two cairns, about 440 m above O.D.

(RC 216) One is represented only by a thin scatter of loose limestone field stones about 14.6 m in diameter and 0.6 m which have probably been robbed to build a neighbouring wall.

(RC 217) The other site is an overgrown mound 6.1 m in diameter and 0.5 m high showing signs of a kerb.

Roese, *Thesis*, nos. 123 (RC 217) and 124 (RC 216).

Llanddeti
SO 01 S.W. (RC 216) (0662 1208); (RC 217) (1665 1196) 9 iv 80

(RC 218) To the W. of Waun y Gwair, 565 m above O.D., stood a limestone cairn 4.6 m in diameter and 0.6 m high. At some time during the late 1970s this was wrecked and converted into a shelter 2.4 m internally by 4.9 m externally, with walls some 1.4 m high and an entrance 0.9 m wide.

O.S. Card SO 01 SE 6; Roese, *Thesis*, no. 128.

SO 01 S.E. (0162 1198) 6 iii 69 and 16 iv 80

(RC 219) Some 300 m E. by N. of RC 218, and 565 m above O.D. on a steep scarp at the S.W. end of Twynau Gwynion is a much ruined, partly overgrown cairn 0.9 m high. It is composed of limestone and gritstone boulders. Originally 6.1 m in diameter and circular, the cairn mass has been enlarged to the N.E. by an apron of boulders thrown out of the central hollow. This hollow is circular, 2.4 m in diameter, and appears to be surrounded, below the level of the original cairn surface, by a circle of large blocks laid end to end. There is a central flat stone 1.05 m long by 0.45 m wide and 0.15 m thick, probably the capstone of a cist.

<small>O.S. Card SO 01 SE 10.</small>

Llanddeti
SO 01 S.E. (0769 1228)　　　　　　　　　　16 iv 80

(RC 220–1) Between Buarth y Caerau and Cefn yr Ystrad, 470 m above O.D., are two cairns.

(RC 220) The smaller is a peat-covered circular cairn 4 m in diameter and up to 0.4 m high, only 2 m from the stream in Cwm Criban. A much larger cairn of loose rubble, 11 m in diameter and 0.8 m high (RC 221), lies nearby. There is a central robber crater 4.6 m in diameter and excavated stones are piled on the S. Two other cairns shown near here at SO 0706 1327 and SO 0718 1334 by Webley in 1957[1] have not been located.[2]

<small>[1] D. P. Webley, *Arch. Camb.* 106 (1957), p. 120, map.
[2] O.S. Card SO 01 SE 2; Roese, *Thesis*, no. 127.</small>

Llanddeti
SO 01 S.E. (RC 220) (0734 1328); (RC 221)
(0735 1331)　　　　　　　　　　　　　　　6 iii 69

(RC 222–3) On the summit of Cefn yr Ystrad are two cairns about 610 m above O.D.

(RC 222; Fig. 80) Carn y Bugail[1] is now basin-

80   Carn y Bugail (RC 222) showing disturbed central area, looking east towards Carn Felen (RC 223)

shaped, 18.9 m in diameter and 2.1 m high. It is composed of limestone and gritstone boulders. The former appear to form a kerb on the N.E., though these may be part of the outcropping rock. The centre and E. side of the cairn are much disturbed and two small modern cairns cap the larger, older, base.

Some 30 m N., a gritstone boulder 1 m long by 0.3 m wide by 0.3 m thick lies upon broken limestone fragments. This may also have comprised part of the prehistoric burial complex.

(RC 223) Garn Felen[2] comprises largely limestone boulders, extending to 15.9 m in diameter and 2.1 m high (2.8 m on the N.E. where there is a fall of ground). It also has a large robber crater 1.2 m deep.

[1] O.S. Card SO 01 SE 9; Roese, *Thesis*, n. 132, cites J. Bailey, *Arch. Camb.* 8 (1853), pp. 307–38; p. 317 (but intending p. 318) as the source for information that Edward Lhuyd had opened these cairns. Bailey was in fact referring to Carn Bugail, Gelligaer, Glamorgan, (*Glam. Inv.* I, i, p. 70, no. 156).
[2] O.S. Card SO 01 SE 9; Roese, *Thesis*, no. 132.

Llanddeti
SO 01 S.E. (RC 222) (0880 1361); (RC 223) (0884 1370)   3 vii 85

(RC 224) To the N. of Cefnpyllauduon, 550 m above O.D., on the crest of a limestone ridge is a circular basin-shaped cairn of limestone boulders 12.8 m in diameter and 1.8 m high. The slight central depression may be an original feature or an attempt to rob the site.

Llanddeti
SO 01 S.E. (SO 0993 1311)   16 iv 80

(RC 225) On Corn Du, 873 m above O.D., is a modern marker cairn which varies in size and height from year to year, but normally attains about 0.75 m. It overlies a more level, sub-circular cairn of up to 12 m in diameter standing about 0.25 m above the outcropping rock, from which it is separated by soft black eroding peat.

Excavation in 1978 demonstrated the remains of a complex cist beneath it, which consisted of a double set of flat, angular, edge-set stones.[1] The cist measured 1.3 m by 0.8 m and was 0.5 m deep internally. The N.E. slab was missing and it is unclear whether or not there had been a coverstone. It had been robbed, probably during the late nineteenth century, but the site was still surrounded by a large number of close-set orthostatic slabs forming a rough circle of 2 m diameter, pointed slightly at the N.E.

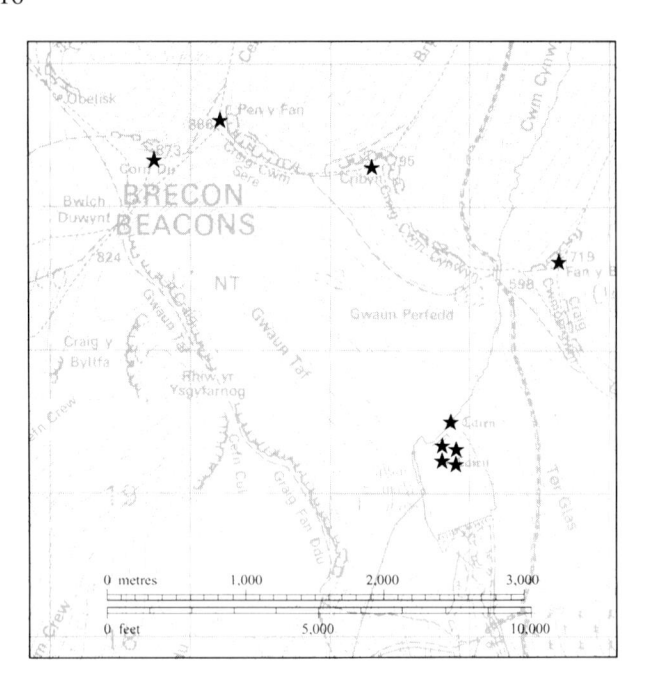

81 Brecon Beacons, showing location of burial sites in Pen y Fan area including: Corn Du (RC 225), Pen y Fan (RC 226): Cribyn (RC 227), Fan y Big (LBS 6) and Upper Neuadd (RCs 202–07)

The cist lay upon layers of foundation slabs directly upon sphagnum peat.[2] Of these four or five layers, the uppermost included the cist base. Orthostats of the cairn's inner stone box were closely set around this base, flagstones resting upon a lower layer of stone. The outer stone setting, up to four slabs thick, rested upon the lower foundation layers and was supported on the inner box slabs. The outermost slabs were variously supported, some inward leaning examples rested on the old ground surface with the other squarish blocks at their foot; others appeared to have been driven into the peat whilst large slabs had been set into a shallow slot cut into the old ground surface.

These outermost slabs were further supported by a layer of re-deposited peat, now up to 0.5 m thick, which in turn was found to be sealed by a capping of large overlapping sandstone flagstones three to four layers thick.

Visitor pressure continued and re-survey in 1990[3] demonstrated further considerable deterioration in its condition. By summer 1991, kerbstones had been removed, exposing a large portion of the northeastern arc of the cairn. From this exposed cairn mass, stone had been quarried to erect a walkers' cairn over the central cist.[4] An excavation by the Clwyd-Powys Archaeological Trust was undertaken in 1992.

[1] P.M. Jones, *Arch. in Wales* 12 (1972), p. 11; P. Crew, *Arch. in Wales* 18 (1978), p. 31; O.S. Card SO 02 SW 13; A.P.s, R.A.F. CPE/UK 1471/6458-9.
[2] A. G. Smith and C. A. Morgan, *Environmental History of the Corn Du site, Powys*, unpubl. report.
[3] A. M. Gibson, *A Survey of Pen y Fan and Corn Du*, unpublished typescript and plan undertaken by Clwyd-Powys Archaeological Trust for the National Trust, August 1990.
[4] Personal communication from Dr A. M. Gibson, to whom the Commission is indebted for useful discussion of this site, and see note 8 (RC 226), below.

Llansbyddyd (E), Modrydd (C)
SO 02 S.W. (0075 2133)   21 ii 89

(RC 226; Figs. 81–82) On the summit of Pen y Fan (the highest point in South Wales), 885 m above O.D., is a much denuded cairn surmounted by the O.S. trig. point pillar. The name Cadyr Arthur given it by the Woolhope Club in 1882[1] does not seem to have been in vernacular use on maps.[2] It is one of three, possibly four, burial cairns, known to have been built along this prominent ridge. Besides Cribyn and Corn Du, these would have included Fan y Big (LBS 6).

In 1974 and 1975[3] it measured up to 14 m in diameter and stood 0.9 m high. The original surface of the mound appears to have been earth-covered, and few structural features were visible as early as 1970, although the tip of a kerb may then have been in evidence.[4] By 1978, through visitor erosion of cairn mass, the O.S. pillar could be seen to surmount a roughly central cist measuring some 1.5 m (E.–W.) by 0.75 m.[5] In March 1983 continuing erosion brought to light a further cist lying about 2 m S.W. of the main cist. It comprised two orthostats, floor slabs and possibly even a capstone (though very much damaged).[6] By August of that year only one orthostat (that on the N.) remained, balanced over the broken floor slab, the two halves of which were roughly equal in size, and with the presumed S. orthostat (of similar size) lying loose a little to the W. Peat was visible through the interstice in the cist floor. Further peat was evidence elsewhere, stratified in such a way as to suggest that it pre-dated the cairn (*cf.* RC 226).

By July 1984 peat could be seen underlying the site, and that summer P. M. Jones attempted to safeguard the fabric of the satellite cist structure by protecting it beneath stone taken from a new beacon built by climbers immediately alongside the cairn. Although a short-term deterrent to would-be cairn-builders and vandals, this proved ineffective in the long term.

Of the cairn originally recorded by Griffiths in 1974, only about one half remained by January 1989. The two orthostats which had defined the southerly satellite cist lay upon bare bedrock, and peat could be seen to underlie most of the cairn mass. In section, stone slabs were shown to lie closely packed, apparently much as those seen in the excavation at Corn Du. Several large orthostatic slabs encircled the remaining part of the cairn, though these became difficult to distinguish owing to the severity of erosion.

The cairn was planned in detail by A. M. Gibson of the Clwyd-Powys Archaeological Trust for the National Trust in May 1990 (Fig. 83).[7] During excavations which followed this, in summer 1991, it was demonstrated that a turf mound had originally been built around the central stone cist. This mound had been capped in stone. Scraps of Bronze Age pottery, wooden artefacts and a hoard of Bronze Age bronzes were recovered.

The cairn was shown to have been built upon a peaty soil. A most unusual survival here, under damp, anaerobic conditions, was the comprehensive range of contemporary prehistoric plant remains (starmoss, bilberry and cotton grass) which survived to emerge from the excavated ground in original green condition. Further environmental analysis of these plants, and of the underlying stratified peat, is anticipated.[8]

[1] *Trans. Woolhope Club* (1882), p. 199.
[2] For example, *Reprint of the first edition of the one-inch Ordnance Survey of England and Wales*, (Newton Abbot: David and Charles, 1971).
[3] W. E. Griffiths, R.C.A.M. files; Roese, *Thesis*, no. 105.
[4] Photos by R. Adams (formerly of Brecon Beacons National Park Mountain Centre), 29 iv 70 (copied as R.C.A.M. nos. 860080-83).
[5] P. M. Jones, *Arch. in Wales* 18 (1978), p. 31.
[6] Communication to R.C.A.M. by P. M. Jones, 15th March 1983.
[7] A. M. Gibson, *A Survey of Pen y Fan and Corn Du*, unpublished typescript and plan undertaken by Clwyd-Powys Archaeological Trust for the National Trust, August 1990.
[8] Personal communication from Dr A. M. Gibson, to whom the Commission is grateful for useful discussion of the excavation results prior to their definitive publication. See also A.M. Gibson, 'The Brecon Beacons: Pen y Fan and Corn Dû', *Current Archaeol.* 133 (1993), pp. 35–7, and 'Excavation and Palaeoenvironmental Investigations on Pen y Fan and Corn Dû, Brecon Beacons, Powys', *forthcoming*.

Llansbyddyd (E), Modrydd (C)
SO 02 S.W. (0121 2158)   21 ii 89

82 Pen y Fan cairn (RC 226): cist under trig point, 1984

(RC 227) On Cribyn, 795 m above O.D., is an almost level circular stony area in which long thin stone slabs are set, suggestive of a cairn base.

Roese, *Thesis*, no. 110.

Cantref
SO 02 S.W. (0237 2132)   21 ii 89

(RC 228) On the S.E. of Cefn Clawdd, 395 m above O.D. on open plateau moorland is a grass-grown stony

119 ROUND CAIRNS AND BARROWS OF THE BRONZE AGE

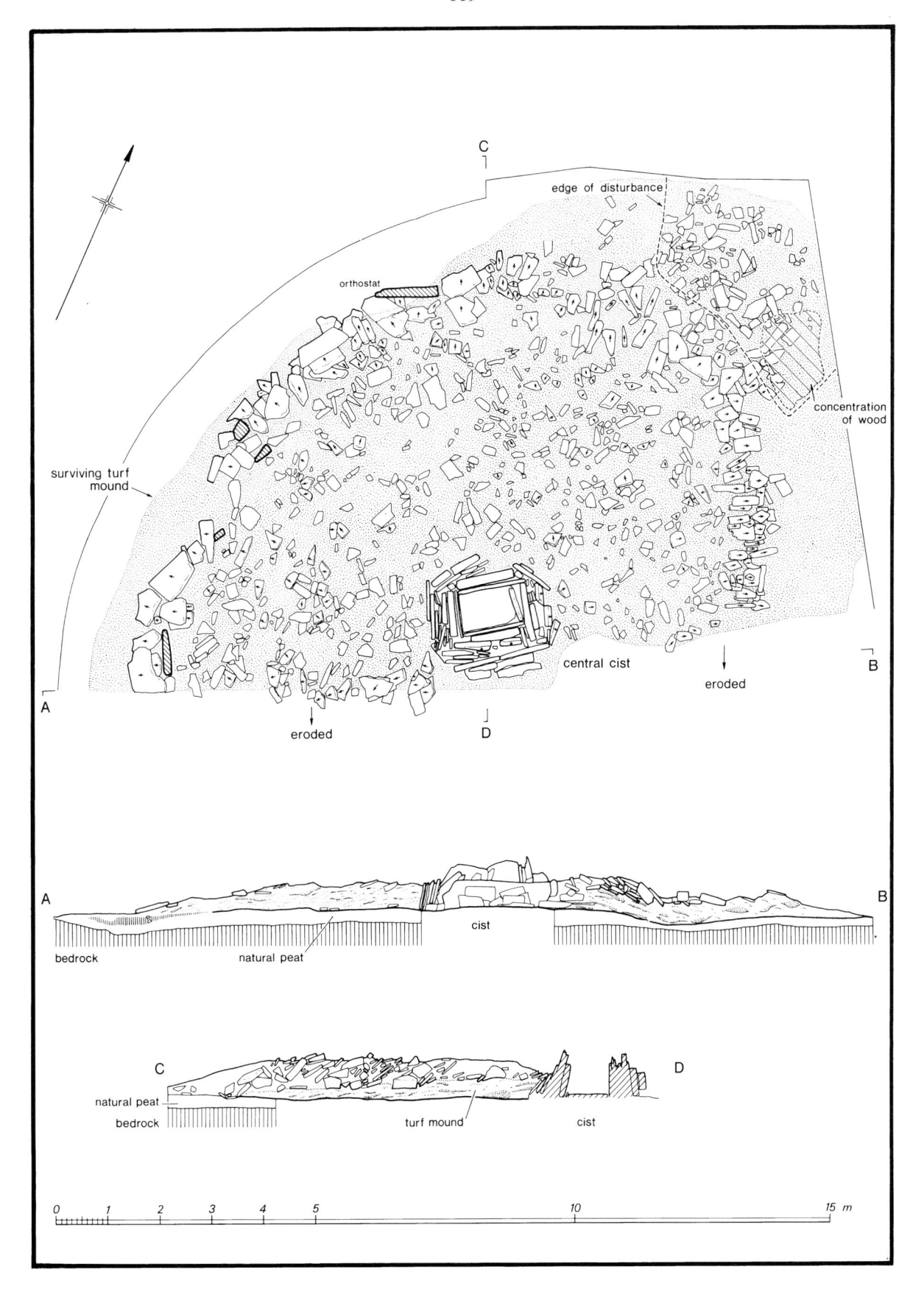

83 Pen y Fan Cairn (RC 229): plan of excavated area (by courtesy of Clwyd-Powys Archaeological Trust)

area, approximately circular, possibly the base of a wrecked and robbed cairn.

Merthyr Cynog
SO 03 N.W. (0315 3988)   13 xi 78

(RC 229–30; Fig. 83) About 700 m N. by E. from Battle Fach, 332 m above O.D., are the vestigial remains of two cairns, extensively robbed and traceable only as crescentic mounds 8 m long, 5 m wide and up to 1 m high.

   O.S. Card SO 03 SW 5.

Battle
SO 03 S.W. (0084 3328 and 0086 3331)   Not visited

(RC 231) About 500 m E. by N. of RC 29–30, some 375 m above O.D., is an approximately circular mound of earth and stones 5.5–6.1 m in diameter and 0.6 m high. Other, less regular cairns in the vicinity have not been investigated.

Battle
SO 03 S.W. (0106 3376)   26 iv 76

(RC 232) Twyn y Big, 380 m above O.D., is a small cairn lying on level ground at the southern limit of Banc y Celyn heathland. It forms an irregular mound about 10 m N.–S. by 13 m and stands 0.6 m high in places. On the E. side one kerb slab remains. This measures 0.9 m long, 0.4 m high and 0.2 m thick. A similar slab is set slightly W. of centre and may have belonged to an otherwise destroyed cist.

   O.S. Card SO 04 NW 4; *Arch. in Wales* 8 (1968), p. 6.

Gwenddwr
SO 04 N.W. (0463 4648)   17 v 68

(RC 233) About 300 m S.W. of Twyn y Post (RCs 256–8), about 415 m above O.D., is a flat-topped cairn 5.5 m in diameter and 0.4 m high.

   O.S. Card SO 04 SW 14.

Merthyr Cynog
SO 04 S.W. (0255 4057)   Not visited

(RC 234–6) At Twyn y Post, 420 m above O.D., on the crest of a moorland tract, are the remains of three cairns.

  (RC 234) A mutilated flat-topped round cairn 11 m in diameter and 0.4 m high. The N.W. side has been roughly cleared but is still traceable.

  (RC 235) Some 15 m to the S.S.E. are the remains of a small ring cairn, 8 m in diameter, with a surviving bank of earth 2.5 m wide and up to 0.4 m high surviving on the W. This bank tapers off to the E. and is destroyed in the N.E. quadrant.

  (RC 236) A grass-grown ring cairn 12 m in external diameter, the bank 2.6–3.2 m wide at the base, 0.6–1.5 m across the top and 0.3 m high externally, though up to 0.6 m internally as it has an inner ditch encircling the central dome which is 5.1–5.5 m in diameter at the base, 3.6–4.2 m in diameter on top and 0.3 m high. W. of the centre is a small robber hollow 1.2–1.5 m across. On the S.E. the bank appears to be broken by an entrance about 1.1 m wide.

   O.S. Card SO 04 SW 5; A.P.s, R.A.F. F41/58/3916/0083–4; 7 xi 60.

Merthyr Cynog
SO 04 S.W. (RC 234) (SO 0280 4090); (RC 235) (0281 4089); (RC 236) (0282 4087)   13 xi 72

(RC 237) S.W. of Twyn y Post and on the W. side of Cefn Clawdd, 410 m above O.D., is a small circular patch of stones 2.4 m in diameter. It has a sunken centre – possibly through robbing, or possibly the site of a former post or pillar.

Crickadarn
SO 04 S.W. (0289 4077)   13 xi 78

(RC 238) About 600 m S. of Twyn y Post is an area of stones enclosed by a low circular bank about 50 m in diameter, possibly the site of a cairn. The bank encircles the rounded summit of a small spur between two valleys. It comprises a swathe of stones some 5 m wide, though in the N.E. quadrant it seems to have inner and outer stony banks with a rubble infill. In some places there remains transverse walling. This may have been either strengthening features or building walls. This wall has been mutilated on the S., where the perimeter is marked by only a few scattered stones. There is a narrow entrance in the E. and on the S. this the walling appears too narrow and turns sharply outwards, possibly through destruction rather than the result of original design. No evidence of habitation could be found in the stony interior.

   O.S. Card SO 04 SW 5; A.P.s, R.A.F. 106G/UK/1471/4148–9; 4 v 46.

Merthyr Cynog
SO 04 S.W. (0296 4026)   Not visited

(RC 239) About 400 m S. of Pen y Lan, 385 m above O.D., alongside the track running N.–S., is a small grass-grown mound 4.6 m long E.–W. by 4 m wide and 0.45 m high. Whereas this may have been a cairn in antiquity, it might equally have carried a more recent boundary post.

Merthyr Cynog
SO 04 S.W. (0247 4164)   8 xi 72

(RC 240) About 300 m S. of RC 242 and 37 m W. of the old N.–S. track, 395 m above O.D., is a circular low grass-grown stony mound 7–7.6 m in diameter and 0.3 m high. This seems to be the mutilated remains of a cairn. A boulder 0.7 m long by 0.7 m wide and 0.2 m thick stands 1.5 m S. of centre and may have been part of a cist.

O.S. Card SO 04 SW 9.

Merthyr Cynog
SO 04 S.W. (0264 4128)   8 xi 72

(RC 241) On the W. part of Cefn Clawdd, 420 m above O.D., is a grass- and reed-grown stony cairn, probably originally circular about 10.7 m in diameter and 0.3 m high.

O.S. Card SO 04 SW 2.

Crickadarn
SO 04 S.W. (0321 4053)   8 xi 72

(RC 242) On the N.W. part of Cefn Clawdd, about 350 m above O.D., is a cairn 5.4 m in diameter and up to 0.4 m high.

O.S. Card SO 04 SW 11.

Crickadarn
SO 04 S.W. (0321 4122)   Not visited

(RC 243) Some 120 m S. of the above is a stone-built cairn 9.5 m E.–W. by 8.7 m N.–S. and 0.6 m high. It may have had a peripheral bank of small stones but the irregularity of its profile makes it difficult to be certain.

O.S. Card SO 04 SW 12.

Crickadarn
SO 04 S.W. (0322 4110)   Not visited

(RC 244) About 90 m N.W. of the small tarn on the S. of Cefn Clawdd is a cairn 18 m in diameter and up to 1.2 m high. Its centre is occupied by a large mutilation crater 9.1 m in diameter.

R. E. Kay, *in. lit.* 26 ii 71; O.S. Card SO 04 SW 10.

Crickadarn
SO 04 S.W. (0432 4032)   8 xi 72

(RC 245) On Waun Gunllwch, about 380 m above O.D., on the S.E.-facing slope of a gently-founded hill, is a bank of stones 0.6 m high and 15 m in overall diameter, broken on the W. by a slight gap. The enclosed area is dished and seems to be basically free of stone. This is either an amorphous, denuded cairn, or a ring cairn. As the area has been well cleared during medieval times, the former seems the more likely explanation.

O.S. Card SO 04 SE 5; A.P., R.C.A.M. 87 MB 252; C. B. Crampton, *Arch. Camb.* 116 (1967), pp. 57–60.

Crickadarn
SO 04 S.W. (0615 4113)   Not visited

(RC 246) About 25 m N. of Ystrad, 155 m above O.D., on a low spur overlooking the River Wye, is a circular stony mound 12 m in diameter and 0.75 m high.

O.S. Card SO 05 NW 6; marked in Antiquity type on O.S. 6-inch map 1964.

Llanafan Fawr (E), Llysdinam (C)
SO 05 N.W. (0085 5676)   28 x 76

(RC 247) About 470 m above O.D. on the S.W. of Twyn y Llyn is a cairn on the E.-facing side of a natural hump, above two small streams. It is 8.5 m in diameter and about 0.3 m high, built of sandstone boulders on a limestone country rock.

Roese, *Thesis*, no. 251.

Llangynidr
SO 11 N.W. (1103 1585)   7 vi 89

(RC 248) On the N.W.-facing scarp of Mynydd Llangynidr at a height of 495 m above O.D. is a cairn 13 m (N.–S.) by 11 m and about 0.4 m high. It is composed of consolidated stones with some loose rubble, some larger stones situated centrally and a possible kerbstone on the S. perimeter. The site has

Llangynidr
SO 11 N.W. (1127 1234) 22 iv 87

(RC 249) On the rocky escarpment of Clo Cadno, 505 m above O.D., are the denuded remains of a cairn 18.5 m in diameter and 1 m high. It is possible that a fugitive wall or kerb may be distinguished within the bounding scarp of the mound.

O.S. Card SO 11 NW 15.

Llangynidr
SO 11 N.W. (1159 1619) 6 v 87

(RC 250) On Blaen Cwm Cleister overlooking the col which separates it from Clo Cadno at more than 515 m above O.D. is a small collection of Millstone Grit and limestone boulders some 3 m in diameter about 0.3 m high, which may at one time have been a more substantial cairn.

O.S. Card SO 11 NW 34; P.A.R. Site Visit Form.

Llangynidr
SO 11 N.W. (1225 1590) 7 vi 89

(RC 251) On Garn Fawr, 550 m above O.D., is a large, much disturbed cairn of limestone and Millstone Grit boulders 20.1 m in diameter and up to 2.4 m high. There is a large central robber crater 8.8 m in diameter and 1.5 m deep.

O.S. Card SO 11 NW 5; Roese, *Thesis*, no. 140, citing T. Jones (presumably Glanusk) 1911 without page number.

Llangynidr
SO 11 N.W. (1233 1511) 7 vi 89

(RC 252) N.E. of Pant Serthfa, 495 m above O.D., on a high point near the edge of a rocky bluff is a grassed-over cairn 7 m in diameter and 0.6 m high. There is a square central depression about 1.2 m each way, on the E. the upper edge of a slab 0.81 m is visible and on the S. the top of a smaller slab 0.35 m long, possibly indicating the position of a cist.

O.S. Card SO 11 NW 14.

Llangynidr
SO 11 N.W. (1219 1668) 15 vi 77

(RC 253) Some 200 m N. of Carn Caws, 50 m above O.D., is a Millstone Grit and limestone small boulder cairn of saucer-shape 16.5 m in diameter and 0.9 m high in the centre.

O.S. Card SO 11 NW 7; Roese, *Thesis*, no. 141.

Llangynidr
SO 11 N.W. (1296 1699) 21 v 73

(RC 254) Carn Caws (the Cheese Cairn) lies 515 m above O.D. on a limestone summit. It is of limestone and Millstone Grit, circular, 17.1 m high and 1.8 m high, in a ruinous condition, and has been converted to a sheep shelter 6.1 m long by 3.4 m wide by 1.5 m deep. This is entered through a opening in the S.E. side of the monument. There appear to be satellites of consolidated boulders up to 3 m in diameter to the N. and S., and the monument may be connected to the wall (US 105) which traverses the hill, approaching from the N., and continuing to its S.

O.S. Card SO 11 NW 6; Roese, *Thesis*, no. 142, citing Jones, *Hist. Brecks.* 1911, III, p. 188.

Llangynidr
SO 11 N.W. (1297 1678) viii 90

(RC 255) Above Nant Calisfor, 520 m above O.D., was a cairn of Millstone Grit and some limestone, with a slightly dished centre formerly 6.4 m in diameter and 0.6 m high. The site is now occupied by two modern cairns and a sheep shelter.

O.S. Card SO 11 NW 8; Roese, *Thesis*, no. 143.

Llangynidr
SO 11 N.W. (1340 1520) 19 iii 90

(RC 256) About 200 m E. of Carn Caws, 505 m above O.D., is a diminutive low circular grass-grown mound 4 m in diameter and 0.4 m high.

O.S. Card SN 11 NW 13.

Llangynidr
SO 11 N.W. (1312 1682) 15 vi 90

been cut on the S.E. edge by a short trench 1.5 m long, 0.75 m wide and 0.4 m deep and the central interior of the mound has been disturbed by the digging of a shallow L-shaped trench. Loose stone deriving from this hole is to be seen nearby.

(RC 257) At Carreg Wen Fawr y Rugos, on a natural terrace about 420 m above O.D., is a cairn 11.5 m in diameter, 0.6 m high externally and 0.3 m internally. It is consolidated by vegetation. Although its saucer-like shape is considered most likely to reflect ground disturbance, it remains possible that this may have been a ring cairn.

O.S. Card SN 11 NW 32; P.A.R. site visit form 19 i 81.

SO 11 N.W. (1306 1750)   22 vi 87

(RC 258–62) On the W. of Cefn Onneu, 525–35 m above O.D., is a series of small cairns marked 'Piles of Stones' on the O.S. 6-inch map (1964). It is difficult to distinguish between ancient cairns and stone heaps of more recent origin. Some may have been associated with clearance and settlement, rather than with burial. This entry should therefore be read in conjunction with entries on nearby settlement (US 106).

(RC 258) A circular mound of stones 4.3 m in diameter and 0.45 m high.[1]

(RC 259) A circular cairn 10.1 m in diameter and 1 m high, the centre having been dug out for a rough sheep shelter.

(RC 260) On the edge of a scree patch is a circular pile of boulders 8.2 m in diameter and 1.4 m high. A circular structure is built centrally 3.4 m in internal diameter. Although this may have been a grouse butt, the large amount of loose stone might suggest something more in the nature of a tower.[2]

(RC 261) An oval-shaped mound 4 m by 1.8 m and 0.45 m in diameter. To the W. of this and 265 is a small rectangular hollow or pit, separated by a space of about 1.2 m.

(RC 262) A ruined oblong pile of stones 3.1 m by 1.8 m and 0.45 m high.[3]

[1] O.S. Card SN 11 NE M4; Roese, *Thesis*, no. 253.
[2] O.S. Card SO 11 NE M5.
[3] O.S. Card SO 11 NE M6.

Llangynidr
SO 11 N.E. (RC 258) (1526 1563); (RC 259) (1538 1583); (RC 260) (1541 1566); (RC 261) (1568 1560 approx.); (RC 262) (1579 1560)   19 iii 73

(RC 263) On the S.-facing aspect of Twyn Disgwylfa on moorland at 410 m above O.D. is a cairn 14 m in diameter and 0.4 m high, composed of mixed grade stones with some loose material. There is a large slab 1 m by 0.8 m W. of centre, possibly though not certainly part of a cist. Some stone blocks embedded in the W. and S. of the cairn may be remains of a kerb.

The mound is extensively damaged, especially on the N.W. segment, probably due to the construction of a wall, now apparently in the S.W. segment.

Llangynidr
SO 11 N.E. (1623 1772)   30 iv 87

(RC 264) On the N. edge of the limestone escarpment above Chwar Mawr, 465 m above O.D., is a ruined circular cairn of limestone blocks with some Millstone Grit. This is possibly one of those explored by H. T. Payne in the early 1800s.[1] It is 11.9 m in diameter, 0.6 m high on the S. and 1.2 m on the N., owing to the fall of ground. The interior has been disturbed to form a saucer-like depression in which a modern cairn has been built with an additional height of 2.1 m.[2]

[1] Lewis, *Top. Dict. q.v.* Llangynider [sic]: 'A large natural cavern Stable Vawr, on the great Stable, above which is a large heap of stones, evidently a beacon, as no deposits were found beneath it, is still visible.'
[2] O.S. Card SO 11 NE 7; Roese, *Thesis*, no. 181.

Llangatwg
SO 11 N.E. (1946 1540)   19 v 75

(RC 265) About 350 m S. of Tŷ Aderyn (an old limekiln), and 525 m above O.D., is a conical-shaped cairn of Millstone Grit with some limestone, 10.5 m in diameter, 2 m high, with an infilled trench on the eastern side.

Roese, *Thesis*, no. 139, citing Glanusk, III, (1911), p. 188.

Llangynidr
SO 11 S.W. (1289 1431)   Not visited

According to S. Lewis's *Topographical Dictionary* of 1833, there were two cairns opened in this locality by Archdeacon Payne. See pp. 67–8 for discussion.

(RC 266) On the N.W. end of Mynydd Pen Cyrn, 505 m above O.D., is a ruined cairn of limestone and Millstone Grit. It is 1 m high and about 13.7 m in diameter, although disturbance has been so extensive as to make it difficult to distinguish a perimeter. It has been robbed and there are shelters built within the cairn, 1.5 m inside, on the N.E. and S.W.

O.S. Card SO 11 SE 2; Roese, *Thesis*, no. 173.

Llangatwg
SO 11 S.E. (1872 1477)   25 ix 91

(RC 267) The cairn which lies to the W. of the summit of Mynydd Pen Cyrn 520 m above O.D., measures 10.7 m in diameter and stands 1.2 m high. There is a central crater about 3.0 m across.

O.S. Card SO 11 SE 1; O.S. 6-inch map 1903; Roese, *Thesis*, no. 180.

Llangatwg
SO 11 S.E. (1968 1453)   25 ix 91

(RC 268) About midway between Cwm Shenkin and Blaen Cam Uchaf, 455 m above O.D., is a cairn 6.7 m in diameter and 0.45 m high. At the approximate centre is the edge of a buried upright slab 10.4 m long and 0.15 m wide, and a little to the S. of this, lying loose at the surface, is a large slab 1.09 m long by 0.71 m wide and 0.13 m thick. This is probably the remains of a destroyed cist.

P. M. Jones, *Arch. in Wales* 15 (1975), p. 26.

Cathedine
SO 12 N.E. (1579 2550)   22 xi 75

(RC 269–71) On the N. end of Cefn Moel, about 0.5 km W.S.W. of Blaen Cwm Uchaf, 415 m above O.D., are three round cairns of Old Red Sandstone:[1]

(RC 269) A low turf-covered mound[2] 14.6 m in diameter and 1.2 m high. The centre occupied by a robber crater 3.7 m in diameter with a small modern cairn 0.6 m high on its N. lip.

(RC 270) This, the largest,[3] is a low turf-covered dome-shaped mound 14 m in diameter 0.9 m high and is surmounted by a modern cairn 0.6 m high and 2 m in diameter. There are traces of a kerb, particularly on the W.

(RC 271) A low dome-shaped mound[4] 7.6 m in diameter and 0.6 m high.

[1] O.S. Card SO 12 NE 6; marked 'Cairns' in Antiquity type on O.S. 6-inch map (1964)
[2] Roese, *Thesis*, no. 160.
[3] Roese, *Thesis*, no. 162.
[4] Roese, *Thesis*, no. 161.

Llanfihangel Cwm Du
SO 12 N.E. (RC 269) (1594 2501); (RC 270) (1595 2500); (RC 271) (1595 2502)   16 iv 73

(RC 272) On the S.E. slope of Mynydd Llangorse, about 0.5 km W.S.W. of Cil Haul, 420 m above O.D., is a grass-grown mutilated round cairn of Old Red Sandstone 23 m in diameter and 1.8 m high, surmounted by a modern cairn 2 m in diameter and 0.8 m high.

O.S. Card SO 12 NE 5; marked in Gothic script on O.S. 6-inch map (1964); Roese, *Thesis*, no. 165.

Llanfihangel Cwm Du/Llan-gors
SO 12 N.E. (1658 2612)   16 iv 73

(RC 273) About 350 m W.S.W. from Cil Haul, 410 m above O.D. on a terrace 15 m below the ridge top is a small Old Red Sandstone, badly disturbed, flat mound about 7 m in diameter, 0.6 m high.

Roese, *Thesis*, no. 166.

Llanfihangel Cwmdu
SO 12 N.E. (1678 2622)   Not visited

(RC 274; Fig. 84) To the N. of Rhiw Trumau on the W. slope of Pen Trumau, on the W. edge of a wide shelf above a W.-facing steep slope, 575 m above O.D., is a large stone cairn 20 m in diameter and up to 1.8 m high. It is mutilated centrally and on the E. side a deteriorating sheep shelter 1.1 m high has been built from the cairn fabric.

84 Rhiw Trumau cairn showing sheep shelter (RC 274) looking south

O.S. Card SO 12 NE 10; Roese, *Thesis*, no. 183.

S.A.M. B129a

Talgarth
SO 12 N.E. (1963 2924)   15 x 91

(RC 275) About 250 m S.S.E. of RC 274, 590 m above O.D., is a disturbed oval boulder cairn 15.9 m long N.–S. by 13.7 m wide and 0.9 m high. A small rough sheep shelter has been built on it near the N. edge.

Immediately due N. of the site are the remains of a hut circle, 4 m in diameter, overall. This consists of a stony grass-grown bank 0.8 m wide by 0.2 m high.

O.S. Card SO 12 NW 10; Roese, *Thesis*, no. 182.

Talgarth
SO 12 N.E. (1986 2911)   15 ix 91

(RC 276) About 300 m S.S.W. of Coity Bach, 152 m above O.D., is a large tree and grass-grown circular mound of stones, 35 m in diameter 0.6 m high on the E. and 0.3 m high on the W. Its central area comprises a cairn feature which appears almost superimposed upon the lower one, and this measures 21.3 m N.–S by 15.2 m E.–W., the additional height bringing the mound to 1.5 m high.

Llanfigan
SO 12 S.W. (1076 2304)   30 iv 80

(RC 277) On the open heathland of Cefn Moel to the N.E. of Bwlch, 363 m above O.D. and next to the track forming the Rural District Boundary, is a cairn marked on the O.S. 6-inch map.[1] Of Old Red Sandstone,[2] it is 19 m in diameter and 1.2 m high but is disturbed by a central depression 0.9 m deep and 3.5 m in diameter. A modern cairn has been built on the N.W. quadrant 1.5 m high and 1.5 m in diameter.

[1] O.S. 6-inch 1964; O.S. Card SO 12 SE 14; A.P., R.A.F. 106G/UK 1652; 11 vii 46.
[2] Roese, *Thesis*, no. 147.

S.A.M. B124

Llanfihangel Cwm Du
SO 12 S.E. (1546 2291)   16 iv 75

(RC 278) On Cefn Moel, about 385 m above O.D., is an irregularly shaped cairn 6.1 m in diameter and 0.9 m high, of which the material may derive from a hollow on the N. some 5.5 m in diameter. The cairn may be of recent origin.

O.S. Card SO 12 SE 28; P. M. Jones, *Arch. in Wales* 16 (1976), p. 17.

Llanfihangel Cwm Du
SO 12 S.E. (1570 2270)   9 iii 77

(RC 279) To the E. of the same track and 0.5 km almost due N. on Cefn Moel, about 355 m above O.D., is a grass- and bracken-covered circular mound[1] 8.2 m in diameter and 0.45 m high. It is dished centrally, probably through disturbance, and some stones are visible throughout the mound.

[1] O.S. Card SO 12 SE 50.

Llanfihangel Cwm Du
SO 12 S.E. (1561 2342)   15 xi 76

(RC 280) To the W. of the same track on Cefn Moel, at 355 m above O.D., is a grass-grown circular cairn[1] of Old Red Sandstone, 14.3 m in diameter up to 1.8 m in height on the N. and N.W., though elsewhere mainly only 0.6–0.9 m high. According to E. Whittle[2] there is a second cairn to the N.E. about 14 m in diameter and 0.9 m high.

[1] O.S. Card SO 12 SE 13; marked 'Tumulus' in Antiquity type on O.S. 6-inch map (1964); not visible on A.P., R.A.F. 106G/UK 1652; 11 vii 46.
[2] Cadw warden Ancient Monuments Record Form (ANC/0568), 17 vi 1988.

S.A.M. B125a

Cathedine
SO 12 S.E. (1561 2371)   16 iv 73

(RC 281) About 100 m due E. from the track on Cefn Moel, 370 m above O.D., is a low circular grass- and bracken-covered mound 5.2 m in diameter and 0.3 m high. There is a slight central hollow and large half-buried perimeter boulders.

Llanfihangel Cwm Du
SO 12 S.E. (1591 2398)   9 iii 77

(RC 282) To the E. of the N.–S. track on Cefn Moel, 380 m above O.D. and close to a spring marked on the O.S. 6-inch map (1964), is a grass-grown stony cairn 8.2 m in diameter and 0.3–0.6 m high. There is a slight central disturbance 1.2 m across, possibly on the site of a cist, and a large, half-buried slab on the S.E. side could well be the dislodged capstone 0.9 m long and 0.18 m thick.

O.S. Card SO 12 SE 34; P. M. Jones, *Arch. in Wales* 16 (1976), p. 46.

Llanfihangel Cwm Du
SO 12 S.E. (1593 2422)   9 iii 77

(RC 283) About 100 m to the E. of the N.–S. track on Cefn Moel, 390 m above O.D., is a circular grass-grown stony cairn 8.2 m in diameter and 0.3–0.6 m in height. There are slight central disturbances which include a small crater about 1.2 m across, possibly the original site of the cist. To its S.E. a large half-buried slab, 0.9 m long and 0.18 m thick, could well be the dislodged capstone, although there are no signs of side stones.

At 6.7 m beyond the E. cairn perimeter there is an arc of five large stones on edge, 3.7 m long N.–S. of uncertain significance. This looks like the surviving portion of the kerb of an earlier cairn, robbed to build the present one.

There are two nearby standing stones: (i) at SO 1601 2433, is a stone 0.71 m high and 0.71 m N.–S. by 0.38 m E.–W. at the base. This is in a dubious relationship with the cairn. (ii) A similar stone lies at SO 1579 2540.

P. M. Jones, *Arch. in Wales* 16 (1976), p. 18; Roese, *Thesis*, no. 159.

Llanfihangel Cwm Du
SO 12 S.E. (1597 2430)   9 iii 77

(RC 284–5) Above Pen yr Heol, 305 m above O.D., are two sites.[1]

(RC 284) A half-circle like a cairn, the W. and N. sides level with the natural surface and not traceable, 8.5 m in diameter and 1 m high on the E. and S., where also massive kerb slabs can be seen at intervals. 8.2 m W.N.W. is a partly-buried slab on edge 1.04 m long by 0.28 m wide by 0.3 m high, which might be a fallen outlier.

(RC 285) There is a further cairn in the middle of the shelf 5.5 m in diameter and 0.45 m high with large stones visible centrally.

[1] One of these is possibly the site at SO 167 238 noted by P. M. Jones in *Arch. in Wales* 17 (1977), p. 12.

Llanfihangel Cwm Du
SO 12 S.E. (RC 284) (1658 2387); (RC 285) (1654 2388)   9 iii 77

(RC 286) On the N. part of Cefn Moel, 395 m above O.D., are traces of a grass-grown stony mound about 6.1 m in diameter, merging into the natural surface on the N., though it stands 0.9 m high on the S. At the centre is a rectangular sunk chamber with neatly built drystone walls at least 1.2 m N.–S., though the S. wall is not visible. The walls are at least 0.45 m deep but the chamber is choked with fallen stone. This appears to be a well-chamber, though may be a cist.

O.S. Card SO 12 SE 33; P. M. Jones, *Arch. in Wales* 16 (1976), p. 18, no. 10.

Llanfihangel Cwm Du
SO 12 S.E. (1610 2441)   9 iii 77

(RC 287) About 0.5 km N. of Cefn Moel, about 380 m above O.D., is a bracken-covered mound 7.6 m in diameter and 0.45 m high with one or two stones visible along the perimeter. It is slightly dished in the centre.

O.S. Card SO 12 SE 57.

Llanfihangel Cwm Du
SO 12 S.E. (1621 2475)   9 iii 77

(RC 288) About 200 m N. of RCs 284–5, 360 m above O.D., is a cairn 7 m in diameter 0.75 m high with some disturbance on the W. side.

O.S. Card SO 12 SE 48.

Llanfihangel Cwm Du
SO 12 S.E. (1643 2406)   9 iii 77

(RC 289 [possibly UCB 5]) There is a stone-built cairn on Pentir Hill 320 m above O.D., 11.6 m in diameter and 0.9 m high. It has a central robber crater 4.9 m long W.–E. by 2.7 m wide.[1] Around 1912 or 13 a sword was found in a heap of stones near the top of this hill, above Wern Farm (SO 177 247). This is probably the site of that discovery.[2]

[1] O.S. Card SO 12 SE 10.
[2] E. Davies, *Arch. Camb.* 75 (1920), p. 282; Grimes, *Prehist. Wales*, p. 184 (illustration of sword).

Llanfihangel Cwm Du
SO 12 S.E. (1758 2440)   6 iv 76

(RC 290) The top of the hill to the E. of Glasbury Church is capped by a circular grass-grown barrow about 22 m N.W.–S.E. by 18.3 m by 1.2 m high on the N. and E. and 2.4 m high on W. and S. where the ground falls away.[1] C. E. Vulliamy is reputed to have excavated here during the 1930s but without result.[2]

[1] O.S. Card SO 13 NE 10.
[2] H. N. Savory, *B.B.C.S.*, 15 (1952–4), pp. 3–6.

Fenni-fach (E), Tregoyd and Felindre (C)
SO 13 N.E. (1808 3832)   24 iii 75

(RC 291) On Rhiw Cwmstab 420 m above O.D. is a cairn marked Tumulus in Antiquity type on the O.S. 6-inch map (1964). It is about 6 m in diameter and 0.45 m high. The S. and E. sides of a stone cist have been exposed by robbing. The E. side stone is 0.76 m long and 0.06 m thick. The S. side consists of two similar slabs, or one broken piece, 0.43 m in total length.

O.S. Card SO 13 SE 6; Roese, *Thesis*, no. 184.

Llaneleu
SO 13 S.E. (1945 3315)   24 iii 75

(RC 292; Fig. 85–86) On the W. end of Mynydd Pen y Fal, about 400 m above O.D., is a low overgrown stone mound 10.5 m in diameter and 0.3–0.5 m high which encloses a cist. The cist, 1.3 m long and 0.7 m wide, comprises four stones but is not complete. It is aligned roughly 45° W. of N. and one side slab leans inward from the E., whilst the W. slab is broken or has been removed. The remaining side slab is 0.47 m deep. The cairn has an outlying limb on the N.E. side about 3 m long and 2.5 m wide. Protruding orthostats on the S. may represent original kerbstones.

O.S. Card SO 21 NE 13; discovered by S. Probert, formerly of 41 Union Road, Abergavenny.

Llangenni
SO 21 N.E. (2587 1896)   26 ix 91

(RC 293) About 100 m E. of the above, on a local summit, is a bilberry-covered mound about 7 m in diameter and 0.6 m high, lying to the S. of the E.–W. path and close to a junction. There is a hollow 1.2 m across by 0.4 m deep.

O.S. Card SO 21 NE; discovered by S. Probert.

Llangenni
SO 21 N.E. (2600 1895)   26 xi 91

(RC 294–7) On Twr Pen Cyrn, 525–539 m above O.D., is a group of four grit and limestone cairns.
(RC 294) A small modern heap of stones 5.2 m in diameter and 0.9 m high, with a central hollow, which probably overlies an ancient cairn.[1]
(RC 295) A large cairn between 14 and 17 m in diameter and 2 m high, the centre hollowed out to form a crater 5.3 m N.–S. by 7.2 m in diameter and about 1.0 m deep. On the S.W. rim of this is a small modern cairn 0.9 m high. Contiguous with this cairn are the remains of a circular mortared structure 5.3 m in external and 3.0 m in internal diameter. An O.S. trig. point is mounted centrally to this.[2]
(RC 296) A patch of loose stones 4 m E.–W. by 3 m and 0.3 m high, which may have been a cairn.
(RC 297) A cairn centrally disturbed, 16–18 m in diameter and up to 2.4 m high.[3]

[1] Roese, *Thesis*, no. 256.
[2] Roese, *Thesis*, no. 185.
[3] O.S. Card SO 21 SW 5; Roese, *Thesis*, no. 186.

Llangatwg
SO 21 S.W. (RC 294) (2027 1445); (RC 295) (2030 1447); (RC 296) (2031 1441); (RC 297) (2032 1445)
                                          25 ix 91

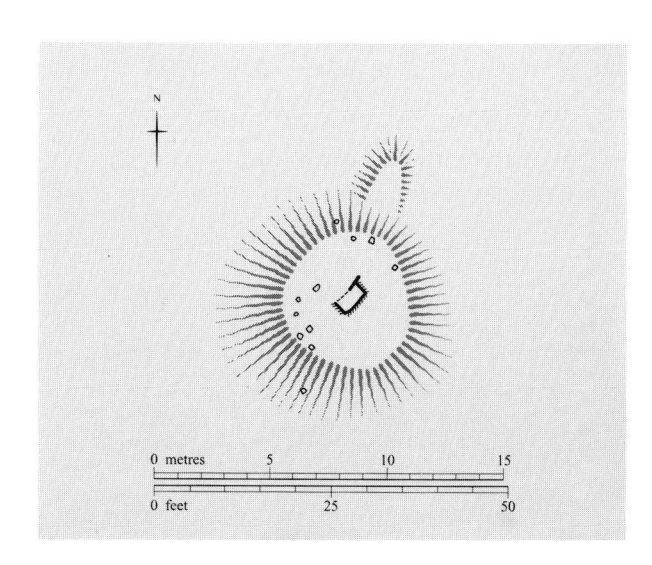

85 Mynydd Pen y Fal cairn with cist (RC 292): plan

86 Mynydd Pen y Fal (RC 292): view over cist

(RC 298) On the N.E. edge of the Mynydd Cyrn plateau is a mutilated cairn 12.5 m in diameter and 1.3 m deep with a sheep shelter on the E.

O.S. Card SO 21 NW 4; Roese, *Thesis*, no. 191.

Llangatwg
SO 21 S.W. (2101 1452)   17 vi 70

(RC 299) On the S. corner of the eastern promontory of Mynydd Pen Cyrn is a mutilated cairn 12 m in diameter and 1 m high. The central robbing forms an oval chamber 5.2 m long N.W.–S.E. by about 3.1 m wide, the entrance 1.5 m wide on the S.E., probably a sheep-shelter.

O.S. Card SO 21 NW 1; Roese, *Thesis*, no. 190; Kay MSS; probably opened by H. T. Payne in 1806 (Jones, *Hist. Brecks.* II, ii (1809), p. 487); Llangattock Parish Scrapbook, *Brycheiniog* 7 (1961), p. 120.

Llangatwg
SO 21 S.W. (2130 1403)   17 vi 70

(RC 300) On the N. end of Pen Allt Mawr, and on the W. side of Pentwynglas, 455 m above O.D., stands a mutilated cairn of Old Red Sandstone slabs 12.5 m in diameter and 1 m high.[1] An excavation conducted by R. G. Sandeman late in 1936 brought to light a centrally-placed primary cist containing a debased pygmy cup.² Unpublished notes among W. F. Grimes's papers³ suggest that before the dig this cairn was covered in humus above a gravelly soil. The cairn itself lay upon a subsoil containing charcoal and the pygmy cup was found at the base of the cist, within or upon clay containing charcoal and bones. Signs of E.–W. trenching are still visible, and despite the excavator's claims that he had back-filled the work, much of the centre appears mutilated.

¹ O.S. Card SO 22 NW 3; Roese, *Thesis*, no. 189.
² Savory, *Prehist. Brecks*. I, pp. 100–01; Pl. VII, 2 (pygmy cup); *Guide*, p. 155.
³ In the N.M.R.

Llanfihangel Cwm Du
SO 22 N.W. (2026 2607)   28 iv 75

(RC 301) On Pen y Gader Fawr, 800 m above O.D., is a sandstone cairn 17 m in diameter, 1.8 m high. Around the S. side are slight remains of a bank reducing to a berm on the S.E. This berm is only a maximum of 0.3 m high and cannot be identified where the cairn lies against a steep natural scarp falling to the N. and N.W.

O.S. Card SO 22 NW 8; Roese, *Thesis*, no. 195.

Talgarth
SO 22 N.W. (2294 2877)   13 vi 73

(RC 302) On the end of a spur of the Black Mountains and upon the very top of Pen Gloch y Pibwr, 655 m above O.D., is a large ruined circular cairn of limestone slabs and boulders, 16.5 m in diameter. There is much central disturbance and cratering, with a series of neatly-built modern cairns, the largest of which is 2.1 m high.¹

This is believed to be the site where on 2nd July 1924, the Rector of Llanfihangel Cwm-Du, Rev. V. E. Davies and two companions took shelter. They removed stones to a depth of 0.75 m to disclose a ruined cist, from which they obtained a piece of pottery. Returning the following day with Major Conway Lloyd and Mr E. E. Morgan of Brecon, they raised a fallen slab and recovered further sherds which were given to the Brecknockshire Society, who in turn deposited them at the N.M.W. where the vessel was restored.² It is a handled 'A' Beaker.³

¹ O.S. Card SO 22 SW 2; not visible on A.P.s, R.A.F. 106G/UK/1652/3089–90; 11 vii 46.
² V. E. Davies, *Arch. Camb*. 79 (1924), p. 410; C. Fox, *Arch. Camb*. 80 (1925), pp. 11 ff.
³ Wheeler, *P. and R. Wales*, p. 117, Fig. 36, 15, p. 126; Grimes, *Guide*, p. 202, no. 599; Fig. 73, no. 6; *B.B.C.S.*, 16 (1955), p. 234, E1; Savory, *Prehist. Brecks*. (I), p. 98, Pl. vii, 1; *P.P.S.* (1957), pp. 62–3, Fig. 2.1.

Llanfihangel Cwm Du
SO 22 S.W. (2019 2319)   7 vi 73

(RC 303) On the N.W. edge of Pen Gloch y Pibwr is a small partly-turfed round cairn, centrally mutilated and 8.8 m by 0.6 m.

O.S. Card SO 22 SW 10.

Llanfihangel Cwm Du
SO 22 N.W. (2028 2331)   Not visited

(RC 304) Between Pen Gloch y Pibwr and Pen Allt Mawr, 685 m above O.D., is a large ruined boulder cairn about 16.2 m in diameter and 0.75 m high on the E. and S., though 1.8 m high on the N. and W. The central area is much disturbed and formed into small modern cairns and craters.

O.S. Card SO 22 SW 8; Roese, *Thesis*, no. 188.

Llanfihangel Cwm Du
SO 22 S.W. (2062 2386)   7 vi 73

(RC 305) On the end of the ridge Pen Allt Mawr, 719 m above O.D., are traces of what may have been a circular cairn 12.5 m in diameter and 0.5 m high. Besides an O.S. trig. point a drystone shelter has been built upon it.

O.S. Card SO 22 SW 9.

Llanfihangel Cwm Du
SO 22 S.W. (2069 2433)   14 VI 75

(RC 306) On the rounded summit of Pen Cerrig Calch, 698 m above O.D., is a cairn of limestone boulders 14.6 m in diameter and 1.2 m high. The centre is occupied by a large robber crater, 7.3 m in diameter, now occupied by a walkers' large drystone windbreak.

O.S. Card SO 22 SW 7.

Llanfihangel Cwm Du
SO 22 S.W. (2166 2241)   7 vi 73

(RC 307) Immediately below the summit of Pen Cerrig Calch, 685 m above O.D., is a round cairn 16.5 m in diameter. It stands 1.1 m high from the hill on the N. side and 2.5 m on the downhill, S. side. The centre is occupied by a robber crater 3.4 m wide and 1.2 m deep, showing the cairn to be uniformly built of large limestone blocks.

O.S. Card SO 22 SW 6.

Llanbedr Ystrad yw
SO 22 S.W. (2175 2223)   7 vi 73

(RC 308) At the bottom of the narrow valley, Cwm Banw, 270 m above O.D. and close to a stream, is a roughly dome-shaped mound of stones 9.1 m in diameter and 1 m high. There are traces of a kerb of slabs on the edge.

Crickhowell
SO 22 S.W. (2278 2316)   27 xi 76

(RC 309) Carn Disgwylfa is of Old Red Sandstone and lies at a height of 530 m above O.D. overlooking the Grwyne Fawr. It is grass- and bilberry-grown, 9.8 m in diameter and 0.75 m high, the entire centre badly cratered up to about 4 m in diameter.

O.S. Card 22 SE 16; Roese, *Thesis*, no. 203.

Talgarth
SO 22 S.E. (2596 2344)   21 v 75

(RC 310) On the summit of Pen y Beacon, 676 m above O.D. and on the very edge of the Black Mountains escarpment, there are traces of a wrecked cairn of indeterminate dimensions (though the O.S. provides measurements of 10.5 m N.–S. by 12.1 m E.–W.). Its only diagnostic feature is a rectangular stone cist, the stone sides now flush with the turf. The S. stone is 0.91 m long by 0.1 m thick, the E. end stone 0.66 m by 0.1 m thick.

O.S. Card SO 23 NW 9; Roese, *Thesis*, no. 201.

Hay (E), Hay Rural (C)/Llanigon
SO 23 N.W. (2442 3676)   22 iv 74

(RC 311; Fig. 87) Twyn y Beddau is an earthen barrow lying on the plateau land of Hay Bluff, 390 m above O.D., a ridge forming the natural extension of Pen y Beacon first mentioned by Theophilus Jones at the turn of the nineteenth century.[1] It is a turf-covered conical mound 22.9 m in diameter and 1.8 m high and with a slightly dished centre. At the base of the mound on the N.W. are two partly-buried upright slabs, probably fallen from the mound. Further to the N.W., on the opposite side of the road, shallow hollows in the turf are probably fortuitous, and may be what the O.S. and O. G. S. Crawford (see below) took to be cists.[2]

The site was opened in 1871 by the Woolhope Club,[3] an excavation made notorious by the planting of a forged Saxon coin, an act bemusedly recorded by contemporary diarist Kilvert.[4]

The original excavation report suggests it to have been a two-period site.[5] The first mound was of turf capped by stone. A central stone cist (A) was placed high in the mound and covered with a slab some 1.19 m by 0.43 m. This contained a human skull. When later enlarged, the mound was piled with earth and a second capping of stones, charcoal intervening between work of the two periods suggesting that the

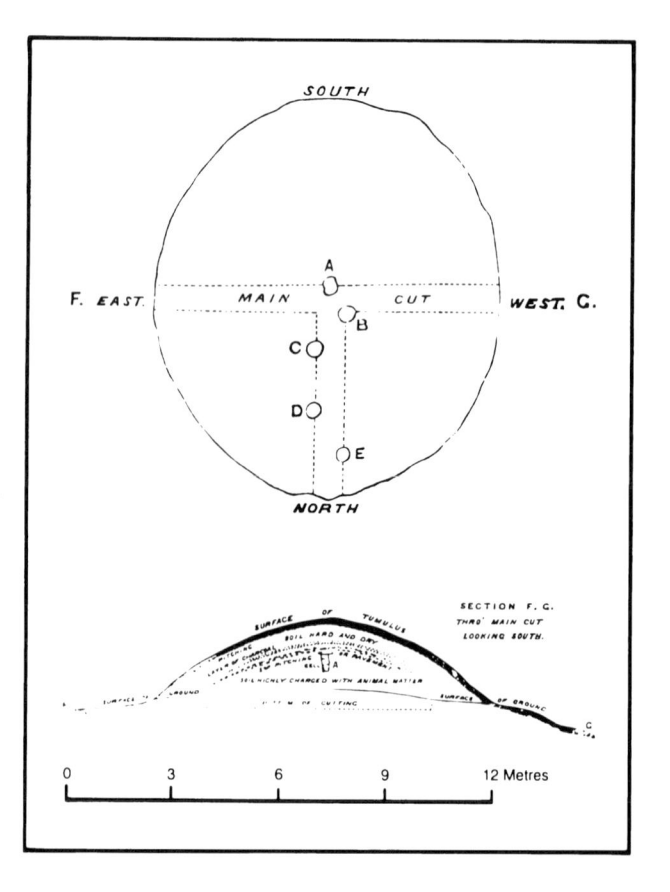

87 Twyn y Beddau barrow (RC 311): plan and section (from *Arch. Camb.* 27 (1872))

first stage in enlargement had been a ritual burning. Four further stone cists were located, though it is unclear to which period these belonged. The second cist (B) was capped by a slab measuring 1.22 m by 0.99 m. Cists (C) and (D) contained cremation burials and cist (E) a large quantity of human teeth. The mound also yielded numbers of flint flakes, including a lanceolate blade with secondary working;[6] and in the stone capping of the secondary mound, a slate whetstone.

Details of features ancillary to the mound are contained in several of the earlier accounts. One states that on the S.W. side were three small upright stones.[7] Others mention two, or perhaps three, stone cists about 32 m to the N.W.[8] These were endorsed by O. G. S. Crawford in 1921; his notes in the O.S. records mention two upright stones on the S.W. and two cists some 50 m W. of the mound, one 1.2 m and the other 1.8 m long.[9]

[1] Jones *Hist. Brecks.* II, ii (1809), pp. 401–402; Lewis, *Top. Dict.*; marked on 1st ed. O.S. 1-inch, (1832).
[2] O.S. Card SO 23 NW 3; Roese, *Thesis*, no. 202.
[3] J. Cam, *Trans. Woolhope Club* (1871), pp. 1–2; (1898), p. 37.
[4] F. Kilvert, *Diary*, 26th and 29th May and 2nd June 1871.
[5] E. J. Thomas, *Arch. Camb.* 27 (1872), pp. 1–4; E. Poole, *Hist. Brecks.* (1886), p. 215; Glanusk, III (1911), pp. 107, 108–109.
[6] J. Evans, *Ancient Stone Implements*, (2nd ed., 1897), p. 328.
[7] For e.g. Poole *op. cit.*, n. 5.
[8] T. Jones, *loc. cit.* n. 1 states 'On the N.W. side, about 35 yards distant, had been 3 graves, one of which had been defaced, the others were lined with slabs at the sides.'
[9] O. G. S. Crawford on O.S. record map; 12 iii 21.

Hay (E), Hay Rural (C)/Llanigon
SO 23 N.W. (2416 3860)   5 iii 93

Addenda

(RC 312) On the edge of the gently undulating plateau of Gwaun Dan y Daren, overlooking Gwaun Nant Ddu about 70 m E. of a spring head at a height of 495 m above O.D., is a collection exclusively of sandstone fieldstone and boulders about 5 m (E.–W.) by 10 m (N.–S.) which appears to be a robbed-out cairn. There are two large well-bedded edge-set slabs on the S. which may represent the site of a cist.

Llangynidr
SO 01 N.E. (0875 1537) (unconfirmed)   29 iii 93

Other Bronze Age Burials and Lost Cairns

Correlation of Bronze Age Burials BB 1–29 (pp. 132–3)

Cairns Containing Later Bronze Age Deposits LBB 1–2 (p. 133)

Lost Burials and Burial Sites LBS 1–10 (pp. 134–6)

Unclassified Burials UCB 1–8 (pp. 136–7)

Rejected Bronze Age Burial RB 1 (p. 137)

Rejected Bronze Age Cairn Sites RCS 1–8 (pp. 137–8)

Unproven Cairn Sites LC 1–9 (pp. 138–9)

Tithe Award Sites and Placenames (unnumbered) (pp. 139–141)

Numbered correlation of Bronze Age burials in Brecknockshire (BB 1–29)

This lists only the major artefacts recovered from burial sites. Where burials can be associated with field monuments, the monument number is given. Further bibliographical information is provided only when it has not been found possible to re-locate the site.

(BB 1) Fan Foel, Glas (RC 26)
A string of clay beads and flint flakes.
Llywel (E), Traean-glas (C), SN 82 N.W. (8213 2234)

(BB 2) Trecastle Mountain (RC 35)
Plain biconical pygmy cup.
Llywel (E), Traean-glas (C), SN 83 S.W. (8315 3098)

(BB 3) Varlen, nr Llywel (RC 41)
Pygmy cup.
Llywel (E), Traean-glas (C), SN 83 S.E. (8764 3060)

(BB 4) Gorswen, (near) Ystradfellte (RC 87)
Fragments of flint and charcoal.
Ystradfellte, SN 91 S.W. (9013 1151)

(BB 5) Coed y Garreg, Ystradfellte (RC 90)
Fragments of Beaker, flint flakes, bones of adult human and dog.
Ystradfellte, SN 91 S.W. (9075 1466)

(BB 6) Plas y Gors, Ystradfellte (RC 91)
Flint dagger, plano-convex knife, flint blades, scrapers and fragments of flint with Beaker or Food Vessel.
Ystradfellte, SN 91 S.W. (9156 1466)

(BB 7) Share y Wlad, Ystradfellte (RC 95)
Flints and charcoal.
Ystradfellte, SN 91 S.W. (9220 1440)

(BB 8) Nant Maden, Penderyn (RC 111)
Beaker, Food Vessel and possibly Overhanging-Rim Urn.
Penderyn, SN 91 S.E. (9709 1059)

(BB 9) Cefn Sychpant, Penderyn (Cairn N. of) (RC 125)
Stone disc from excavation.
Penderyn, SN 91 S.E. (9864 1101)

(BB 10) Twyn Bryn Glas (RC 127)
Beaker, pygmy cup, flint flake.
Penderyn, SN 91 S.E. (9850 1166)

(BB 11) Pant y Waun, nr Cantref Reservoir, Nant Ddu (LBS 2)

Beaker fragments and possibly a spindlewhorl.
Penderyn, SN 91 S.E. (9865 1459)

(BB 12) Ynys-hir, Mynydd Epynt (RC 138)
Pygmy cup, flint knife and flint flakes, anthracite bead, clay bead, woven material.
Llanfihangel Nant Bran, SN 93 N.W. (9207 3825)

(BB 13) Cefn Cilnsanws, Vaynor (RC 201)
Bronze knife-dagger with human remains.
Vaynor, SO 00 S.W. (0250 0981)

(BB 14) Cefn Cilnsanws, Vaynor, mounds (US 90 i)
Flint flakes and charcoal.
Vaynor, SO 01 N.W. (0248 0995)

(BB 15) Abercar, Cwmtaff, Vaynor (LBS 4)
Pygmy cup and urn, cremated bone.
Vaynor, SO 01 S.W. (008 125)

(BB 16) Cwm Car, Dolygaer, Merthyr Tydfil (LBS 5)
Beaker with burnt bones, tanged and barbed arrowhead.
Vaynor, SO 01 S.E. (054 135 approx.)

(BB 17) Fan y Big burial site (LBS 6)
Two urns and bronze awl.
Llanspyddyd (E), Modrydd (C), SO 02 S.W. (0371 2057)

(BB 18) Maesderwen, Llanfrynach (UCB 3)
?Bronze daggers or knives, urns and accessory vessels.
Llanfrynach, SO 02 S.E. (065 262)

(BB 19) Cornelau Uchaf, Upper Chapel
Deverel Rimbury sherd. ?burial. Text *supra* p. 72.
Merthyr Cynog, SO 04 S.W. (018 405)

(BB 20) Waun Ddu, Llangynidr (LBS 7)
Overhanging-Rim Urn with cremation.
Llangynidr, SO 11 N.W. (136 189)

(BB 21) Llangorse Vicarage (LBS 8)
Three flint arrowheads from destroyed tumulus.
Llan-gors, SO 12 N.W. (135 277)

(BB 22) Tŷ Isaf Neolithic long barrow (CT 3)
Urn fragments, bone pin, bone handle plate from secondary burial.
Talgarth, SO 12 N.E. (1819 2906)

(BB 23) Ffostyll N., Llanelieu, Neolithic long barrow (CT 5)
?Food vessel in secondary burial.
Llanelieu, SO 13 S.E. (1792 3495)

(BB 24) Ffostyll, Llanelieu, round barrow (LBS 10)
Pygmy cup, bone, charcoal, flints.
Llanelieu, SO 13 S.E. (1795 3501)

(BB 25) Tŷ Du, Llanelieu (possibly Ffostyll) (LBS 9)
Beaker accompanied by flint dagger.
Llanelieu, SO 13 S.E. (179 349)

(BB 26) Pen Allt Mawr, Llanfihangel Cwm Du (RC 300)
Pygmy cup with cremation.
Llanfihangel Cwm Du, SO 22 N.W. (2026 2607)

(BB 27) Pen Gloch y Pibwr, Cwm Du (RC 302)
Handled Beaker.
Llanfihangel Cwm Du, SO 22 S.W. (2019 2319)

(BB 28) Penywrlod, Llanigon (CT 12)
Beaker fragments, bone, charcoal, ?Enlarged Food Vessel.
Llanigon, SO 23 N.W. (22148 39186)

(BB 29) Twyn y Beddau, Hay (RC 311).
Cremation, flint flakes, slate whetstone.
Hay (E), Hay Rural (C)/Llanigon, SO 23 N.W. (2416 3860)

Cairns containing Later Bronze Age Deposits (LBB 1–2)

(LBB 1) Pen y Fan. Bronze hoard deposited in cairn (RC 226)
Llanspyddid (E), Modrydd (C), SO 02 S.W. (0121 2158)

(LBB 2) Pentir, Cwm Du. Sword. Tenuous association with cairn (RC 289)
Llanfihangel Cwm Du, SO 12 S.E. (1758 2440)

Lost Burials and Burial Sites (LBS 1–10)

This section includes sites for which evidence of a Bronze Age origin is either certain or strong, because artefacts have survived, or because the circumstances of site association or the quality of contemporary observation makes such a dating likely. All are sites for which evidence of location is imperfect, or where disinterred burials have come from apparently unmarked graves.

(LBS 1) On the W. side of the Afon Giedd, 275 m W.S.W. of Pwll y Cig, Cantrill recorded a demolished 'Kistfaen'. The area in which the site was located is now extremely remote, the ground tundra-like in its virtual lack of vegetation. Although some groups of small stones are to be found here, nothing resembling a cist could be located.

T. C. Cantrill, *Arch. Camb.* 53 (1898), pp. 248–264; Roese, *Thesis*, no. 221; R.C.A.M. site visit, 2 v 86.

Ystradgynlais (E), Ystradgynlais Lr, SN 81 N.W. (8110 1838)

(LBS 2) Close to, and W. of the track crossing Pant y Waun a fragment of Beaker pottery and a spindle whorl were discovered in 1930. The original newspaper account provides much information on the supposed Mediterranean origins of Beaker invaders but explains nothing of the find circumstances. The site has not been located, and is presumed destroyed.

W. F. Grimes, *Prehist. Wales*, p. 203; Clarke, *Beaker Pottery* (1970), pp. 440, 525; *Western Mail*, 1st August 1939.

Penderyn, SN 91 S.E. (9865 1459)

(LBS 3) The flattened remains of a cairn were exposed by visitor erosion on the path leading from Pont ar Daf to Corn Du in 1989, at a height of 570 m above O.D. It appeared to comprise eight edge-set stones about 2 m in diameter. Removal of surface stone and peat brought to light a large central slab, some 3 m in diameter, which was defined externally by a substantial bedding trench. The bedding trench contained packing stones and flecks of charcoal. It was 0.45 m wide and 0.3 m deep. There were close-set post-impressions 0.15–0.2 m in diameter in the ditch bottom. Flint flakes occurred both beneath the stone slab and in the ditch.[1]

A radiocarbon date of 3150+/- 50 BP (UB-3216) was obtained for the timber circle.[2] Although of the Bronze Age (*c.* 1900–1750 B.C.), the site's function is unclear; it could have been either for burial or a settlement feature.

[1] A. M. Gibson, *Arch. in Wales* 29 (1989), p. 42; 30 (1990), p. 41.

Llansbyddyd (E), Modrydd (C), SN 92 S.E. (9955 2005)

(LBS 4) A Bronze Age burial was disinterred in 1859 on land immediately in front of Abercar farmhouse close to the stream and now submerged beneath the Cwm Taf Reservoir, 274 m above O.D. The spot was believed to have been formerly covered by a mound. From 10 ins (0.3 m) below ground surface a large cinerary urn was found inverted over crushed bones and a pygmy cup containing charcoal.

The farmhouse area was partially exposed during the drought of 1989, but a thorough investigation of the area brought to light no further clues as to the site of this discovery. The find was of a cremation interred within a cinerary urn and pygmy cup.

Glanusk, III (1911), p. 60; Longworth, *Corpus*, p. 329, no. 2163, Pl. 83d; C. Wilkins, *Arch. Camb.* (1886), pp. 93–4.

Vaynor, SO 01 S.W. (008 125)   ix 89

(LBS 5) In March 1900, a Beaker, said to have contained burnt bones, and a barbed and tanged arrowhead were disinterred from a cist at Cwm Car, Dolygaer.[1] Although much of the pot was distributed among souvenir hunters, John Storrie managed to collect together sufficient pieces to be able to reconstruct it.[2] The cist, from which the lid was lifted, was 2 ft 2 ins (0.65 m) long by 1 ft 7 ins (0.46 m) wide by 1 ft (0.3 m) deep.[3] The Beaker appears to have contained burnt bones and birch charcoal and coal fragments were also found.

The site of the find, 'by the side of the footpath leading to Cwm Car Farm', can now only be guessed at. The Beaker is of the long-necked variety.

[1] *Arch. Camb.* 57 (1902), pp. 25–28; 91 (1936), p. 107; *Archaeologia* 76 (1926–7), pp. 91, 97, Fig. 22; Abercromby, I, p. 27.

[2] Clarke, *Corpus* II, p. 523, no. 1853.
[3] *Western Mail*, 22nd May 1900.

Vaynor, SO 01 S.E. (054 135 approx.)

(LBS 6) In 1981 two cordoned urns and a bronze implement were recovered from the remains of a cremation burial lying on the site of the path passing Fan y Big, 655 m above O.D.[1] The base of one of the urns was marked with the impression of a grain of emmer wheat, *Triticum dicoccum*. There was evidence suggesting the presence of one individual, possibly a 20-year-old male. It is generally believed that a cairn originally occupied the site of this discovery, and it is said to have been visible post-World War II. Its disappearance is owed to walkers, who over the years have thrown its component stones over the cliff.[2]

[1] C. S. Briggs, W. J. Britnell and A. M. Gibson, *P.P.S.* 56 (1990), pp. 173–178.
[2] Information from Mr and Mrs G. Bird of Aberdare.

Cantref, SO 02 S.W. (0371 2057)

(LBS 7) Cremated bones were found encisted with a fragmentary urn beneath a cairn in a meadow N.E. of Waun Ddu, in 1909.[1] The urn is in the Overhanging-Rim Urn tradition[2] and is now in the N.M.W.[3]

[1] *Arch. Camb.* 74 (1919), pp. 95–100; N.M.W. *Ann. Rep.* 1813–14, p. 24.
[2] Longworth, *Corpus*, p. 329, no. 2166, Pl. 212C.
[3] Grimes, *Prehist. Wales* 206, no. 620, Fig. 76, 6.

Llangynidr, SO 11 N.W. (136 189)

(LBS 8) Three flint arrowheads were recovered from a destroyed tumulus behind Llangorse Vicarage.

Llan-gors, SO 12 N.W. (135 277)

Mins of Evidence (1912), no. 1466.

(LBS 9) According to Richard Fenton, at some time prior to 1804, the farmer at Porthamal 'opened a Tumulus near Talgarth, and found an Urn and a Flint Spearhead, an exact drawing of which [was with] Mr. Theo. Jones'.[1] Jones published his illustration[2] adding that the burial had been found by Mr William Davies 'within a Carn' in the parish of Llanelieu. He also drew attention to a further cairn upon the same landowner's holding. Further locational details were lacking, until in 1871 it was claimed that the finds came from a 'broomy field on Ty-ddu, adjoining the Black Mountain'.[3]

The relocation of this burial cairn might best be considered in the light of contemporary and later antiquarian sources.[4]

Although research is needed to establish contemporary tenurial relationships between the lands of Tŷ Ddu, Porthamal and Ffostyll, it would seem strange that not one but two mounds should have entirely disappeared without further notice from an area which otherwise retains continuity of antiquarian tradition about both Croesllechau from the 1690s (CT 7) and the Ffostyll group (CT 5 and 6) from the 1840s.

Whereas there are no obvious early burial sites within a couple of miles of Porthamal upon the MS draft O.S. map of 1814,[5] both Croesllechau and Ffostyll (as 'Tumulus') are marked in Antiquity type upon the printed first edition O.S. map of 1832.[6] Since Ty Ddu lies adjacent to Ffostyll, it seems reasonable to equate the surviving Ffostyll mounds with the site of the original Beaker burial discovery of *c.* 1800. The likelihood that early Bronze Age interments might have been made in these barrows in supported by an urn fragment among finds from the site donated to the National Museum by C. E. Vulliamy from his 1921 excavations,[7] and is further strengthened by his report of an early Bronze Age cremation which came to light during the destruction of a small and otherwise unnoticed cairn in the field adjoining the long barrows (see overleaf, LBS 10).

Although it has been suggested that the Beaker grave group was accompanied by later artefacts,[8] these probably result from contamination by unrelated antiquarian collector's pieces. The importance of this discovery lies in the association of a classic Bell Beaker[9] with a flint dagger,[10] forming a grave group which might have been deposited around the turn of the second millennium B.C.[11]

[1] Fenton, p. 23; colour wash drawing in Theophilus Jones sketchbook, Brecks. Mus. MS. A104/1/2/(2); see also drawing in H. T. Payne, N.L.W. MS 184A, fos. 160, 276.
[2] T. Jones, *Hist. Brecks.* II, i (1809), p. 369.
[3] *Arch. Camb.* 26 (1871), pp. 327–30.
[4] Lewis, *Top. Dict. s.v.* Llanelieu, gives its provenance as the Porthaml Estate.
[5] O.S. 2-inch MS survey, Brit. Lib. (Brecknocks, Sheet 195).
[6] First edition map (1832), O.S. 1-inch, David and Charles reprint.
[7] Grimes, *Guide*, p. 153, no. 175; see account of CT 5.
[8] Roman coins were reputed to have been found here during the original excavation (*Arch. Camb.* (1863), pp. 377–378; (1871),

pp. 327–30; their presence at the site is disputed and rejected *Inv. Br.* I (ii), p. 185, no. xii.

[9] Clarke, *Corpus*, p. 523, no. 1834.

[10] Grimes, *P. P. S. E. Anglia* 6 (1931), pp. 352, 354; H. S. Green et al., *Proc. Prehist. Soc.* 48 (1982), pp. 492–501.

[11] R. J. Harrison, *The Beaker Folk*, (London, 1980).

Llaneleu, SO 13 S.E. [Ffostyll] (179 349)

(LBS 10) In 1921 C. E. Vulliamy excavated a pygmy cup, charred bone, charcoal and flints (including a triangular worked flake) from a round cairn in a field adjacent to the long barrows (CT 5 and 6).[1]

The site was later flattened[2] and is no longer recognisable.[3]

[1] *Western Mail*, 29th November 1921; *Trans. Woolhope Club* (1925), pp. l–li.
[2] *Arch. Camb.* 83 (1928), pp. 192–4.
[3] R.C.A.M. site visit.

Llaneleu, SO 13 N.E. (1795 3501)   12 vi 75

Burials of unknown status, possibly Bronze Age: Unclassified Burials (UCB 1–8)

Sites are listed in this category where a record of burial exists, but in which the antiquarian account is unclear or ambiguous as to its age or status.

(UCB 1) In 1961, an irregular, pentagonal cist containing the bones of at least one adult were discovered during bulldozing in connecting with the building of playing fields for the Boys' Grammar School. It is possible that artefacts were also disinterred, but such were the circumstances of finding, that nothing is recorded.

Savory, *Prehist. Brecks.* II, pp. 11–12, Pls. 1B–E.

St. John the Evangelist Brecon, SO 02 N.E. (052 296)

(UCB 2) In 1808 an 'immense heap of stones' was cleared from a field called Cae Gwin on Tŷ Yn y Llwyn, in Llanfrynach. At its base

'was found a Cistfaen or stone coffin, formed of four stones set edgewise, eighteen inches high, with a fifth on top of them, but as usual without any inscription, and (which is rather singular) human bones, particularly fragments of the skull and the lower part of the tibia, terminating with the Malleolus were found not only within the inclosure, but also in a more perfect state, and in greater quantity upon the cover or lid. The side stones of this ancient and rude sepulchre were of that kind used for foot pavements, called flags; they were six feet in length, three feet across at the top, and two feet six at the bottom, where the stone placed across has been so far drived in by the superincumbent weight . . . to reduce the length of the enclosed space to four feet five; the bottom of pure earth, which evidently never had been dug up or removed, and the covering stone, still more rude and shapeless than the sides, was of a blueish rock or river stone, in general of about half a foot in thickness.'[1]

The site of the discovery has not been re-located.[2]

[1] Jones, *Hist. Brecks.* II, ii (1809), pp. 599–600.
[2] O.S. Card SO 02 SE 1; R.C.A.M. visit, ii 76.

Llanfrynach, SO 02 S.E. (059 249) (approx.)

(UCB 3) About 400 yards North from the hypocaust [at Maesderwen[1]] were found some human bones, with signes of fire upon them, intermixt with Earth, in a rude Stone Coffin 19 inches by 13, and covered with Stones, also Fragments of an urn, 3 inches diameter and 2 and a half high, made of coarse earth. Some broken pieces of round brick pipes for conveying water to the Bath, were taken up at the fourth angle thereof.

There were likewise found the head of an Iron Lance or Dart 4 and a half inches long; and a Spear 1 and a quarter inches in the broadest part.

It is possible to interpret this burial in a number of ways. First, so close to a villa site, it could have been Roman. Had the accompanying urn been of a finer ceramic, this explanation would have seemed the most plausible. However, the small urn could have been a pygmy cup, and the 'round brick pipes' seem more likely to represent large fragments of urn, rather than broken drainage pipes (which are unlikely discoveries in this particular topographical location anyway). Given that in contemporary rural parlance iron was a term encompassing almost any metal, it is possible to argue that this find actually represented a Bronze Age burial accompanied by one or more bronze daggers. Finally, it remains possible (though less likely) that the burial might have been of post-Roman, Anglo-Saxon, Viking or even medieval origin, although it would be difficult to explain a context for such a find in this area.

[1] *Inv. Br.* I (ii), pp. 179–82.

[2] Extract of letter to Thomas Jones from Charles Hay, 23rd October 1784 on the subject of the Breconshire Hypocaust: Society of Antiquaries' Minutes, vol. xx, fos. 7–8, and accompanying autograph letter (now lost). The Commission is indebted to Mr J. Hopkins, formerly Librarian, for providing a xerographic copy of the surviving MS.

Llanfrynach, SO 02 N.E. (069 262) approx.

(UCB 4) According to the Rev. Geo. Howell, 'In the parish of Llangattock, Breconshire, a mound or cairn was opened many years ago, and the remains of a human being were found, with a sword and dagger by his side.'

Jnl Brit. Archaeol. Assoc. 3 (1848), p. 60; R.C.A.M. *Mins of Evidence* (1912), nos. 1467–8; J. Evans, *Ancient Bronze Implements*, (1881), pp. 273–4; C. B. Burgess, *Welsh Antiquity* (1976), p. 87.

Llangatwg, [SO 11]

(UCB 5) Pen Tir, Cwm Du (RC 289)
Sword. Possibly in association with cairn.

Llanfihangel Cwm Du, SO 12 S.E. (1758 2440)

(UCB 6) A burial mound was cut through by the construction of the railway near Tredustan Court. It is reputed to have contained human bones and bronze implements.

M. Owen, *The Story of Breconshire*, (1911), p. 27.

Glasbury (E), Pipton (C), SO 13 S.W. (142 326)

(UCB 7) Glyn Collwn, Llanfigan. 'Various antiquities . . . none preserved . . . in a cairn in this chapelry.'

Lewis, *Top. Dict.*, s.v. Glyn-Collwyn.

Llanfigan, SO 22

(UCB 8) Caetwmpyn, Maesgoch, Llanigon. Ploughed mound, 'Rude earthen pipkin'.

Jones, *Hist. Brecks.* II, i (1809), p. 400.

Llanigon (E), Llanigon/Glyn-fach (C), SO 23 N.W. (234 379)

Rejected Bronze Age burials (RB 1)

(RB 1) An account of 1909 by Edward Anwyl[1] suggests that before 1876 one urn containing burned bones within another vessel was found 'on the grounds of Mr. George Moore, about 300 yards from the Grwyne River Upper Paper Mills,' Llangenny. The account probably refers to a Roman find and derives from the Catalogue of the Museum exhibited at Abergavenny in 1876. However, this site was on Hereford Road, Abergavenny.[2]

[1] *Arch. Camb.* 64 (1909), p. 276.
[2] *Arch. Camb.* 31 (1876), p. 348.

(Llangenni)
[SO 21 N.W. (24 17)] Abergavenny (Monmouthshire)

Rejected sites at one time thought to have been Bronze Age cairns (RCS 1–8)

(RCS 1) Erw'r Garn. Probably a natural mound.
Defynnog (E), Crai (C) SN 82 S.E. (8961 2470).

(RCS 2) Cwm y Meirch (N. of). Platforms and upcast from industrial operation.
Llandeilo'r Fan, SN 83 S.W. (8202 3246)

(RCS 3) In Fan Nedd is a turf-covered mound 8.2 m in diameter and 0.6 m high; probably an eroded peat stack.
Ystradfellte, SN 91 S.W. (9140 1790)

(RCS 4) On the edge of the river terrace overlooking the Afon Taf at Darren Fawr, about 235 m above O.D., was a cairn about 3.0 m high and 10.0 m in diameter, at one time thought to have been Bronze Age.[1] When excavated in 1979, it was found to be a recent field clearance cairn.[2]

[1] D. P. Webley, *B.B.C.S.* 17 (1956–8), p. 54, no. 1.
[2] J. Parkhouse, *Glamorgan-Gwent Arch. Trust Ann. Rep.* (1981), p. 32.

Vaynor, SO 00 N.W. (0190 0984)

(RCS 5–6) There were formerly two mounds close to Y Dderw farm, only one of which (RCS 6) now survives.

(RCS 5) Excavations upon the mound closest to the house,[1] occasioned by a road-widening scheme in 1976,[2] proved negative, and the site is now considered to have been a garden viewing platform.[3]

(RCS 6) A further cairn, some 25.6 m in diameter, was reported to the E. of the house.[4] This is also probably a garden viewing platform.[5]

[1] O.S. Card SO 13 NW 5; H. N. Savory, *B.B.C.S.* 15 (1952–4), pp. 305–7.
[2] R. Cain, *Arch. in Wales* 16 (1976), p. 17.
[3] C. S. Briggs, pp. 138–159, in A. E. Brown, (ed.), *Garden Archaeology*, (London: C.B.A. Res. Rep. 78, 1991), p. 149, Fig. 12.10.
[4] O.S. Card SO 13 NW 10; N.M.W. Record 6-inch map BR XXIII; C. J. and M. J. Dunn, *Arch. in Wales* 13 (1973), p. 14.
[5] Briggs, *loc. cit.* n. 3.

Llys-wen, SO 13 N.W. (RCS 5) (1386 3748) [destroyed]; (RCS 6) (1425 3768)

(RCS 7) At Pipton on level meadow between the Wye and the Llynfi is a circular grass- and tree-grown mound, 17.1 m in diameter and 1.5 m high.[1] Although traditionally considered to have been Bronze Age,[2] its proximity to the manorial centre of Pipton makes it more likely this was a medieval viewing platform.[3]

[1] Illustrated in *Trans. Woolhope Club* (1933), Pl. IV, opp. p. 41.
[2] Savory, *op. cit.* n. 1, (RCS 5–6) above, p. 306.
[3] Briggs, *op. cit.* n. 2, (RCS 5–6) above, p. 148.

S.A.M. B 79.

Pipton, SO 13 N.E. (SO 1679 3811)

(RCS 8) A mound some 20 ft (6.1 m) in diameter and 15 ins (0.38 m) high observed between Old Gwernyfed and Velindre in 1973,[1] could either have been natural[2] or may have been the site of a viewing platform.[3]

[1] O.S. Card SO 13 NE 25; W. R. Pye, 'The Oil Pipeline Survey, Brecon to Wolverhampton Seisdon 1973', *Arch. in Wales* 13 (1973), pp. 12–13.
[2] R.C.A.M. site visit 20 xi 78.
[3] Briggs, *loc. cit.* (RCS 5–6) n. 3, p. 151.

Glasbury (E), Tre-goed and Felindre (C), SO 13 N.E. (1784 3630)

Unproven cropmarks and lost cairns not certainly used for burial (LC 1–9)

(LC 1) Circular cropmark about 50 m in diameter. A.P.s, R.A.F. F22/58/1452/0021–2, A4105. SN 81 N.E. (8784 1576)

(LC 2) Twyn y Garn (nr), marked on O.S. 1-inch and 2-inch maps before afforestation. SN 82 N.E. (8808 2506)

(LC 3) Near Penfai, 2 cairns cleared away in agricultural operations. SN 82 N.E. (8919 2915 and 8933 2999)

(LC 4) Cae Carne Uchaf T.A. 270 former cairn or cairns cleared into heap by agricultural operations. SN 82 S.E. (8792 2447)

(LC 5) At Garn Ddu (Penderyn) (SN 9577 1122) there was formerly a cairn,[1] not now visible[2] on aerial photographs and untraceable on the ground.[3]

[1] T. Jones, *Hist. Brecks.* II, ii (1809), *q.v.* Vaynor, p. 624; O.S. 1-inch 1840.
[2] A.P.s, R.A.F. F21/58/3618/0100–12; 1 vi 60.
[3] R.C.A.M., 10 ix 73; Roese, *Thesis*, no. 228.

Penderyn SN 91 S.E. (9577 1122)

(LC 6) On Fan Bwlch Chwyth, a cairn is recorded which was ploughed up in 1956. Nothing now remains of it (2 iv 80).

H. N. Savory, *B.B.C.S.* 16 (1955), p. 210; Roese, *Thesis*, no. 232.

SN 92 S.W. (9210 2412)

(LC 7) According to two independent fieldworkers, on the N. side of Mynydd Pen Cyrn, 495 m above O.D., stood a limestone cairn 10 m in diameter and 0.9 m high in poor condition. Prolonged searching in this area produced no signs of a cairn. The site indicated by the grid reference lies within a sphagnum peat bog.

Roese, *Thesis*, no. 179; Kay MSS.

Llangatwg SO 11 S.E. (1922 1485)   25 ix 91

(LC 8) On Blaen Onneu, 450 m above O.D., a mutilated cairn 6.25 m in diameter is recorded. This could not be located (30 iv 80).

O.S. Card SO 11 NW 21; P.A.R. Site Visit Form, 18 xii 80.

Llangynidr SO 11 N.W. (1470 1593)

Tithe award and other placenames

SN 70 N.E.	Cae Garn TA 2347, 67 m above O.D. SN 7783 0887			Cae Caerau TA 1310, 274 m above O.D. SN 8423 3152
SN 71 S.E.	Cae y Domen TA 2109, 160 m above O.D. SN 7680 1150			Cae Garn TA 1326, 243 m above O.D. SN 8450 3200
	Cae Garn y Bath TA 1830, 191 m above O.D. SN 7820 1273			Carrau (presumably for Carnau). TA 1328, 213 m above O.D SN 8450 3210
	Cae Garn TA 1304, 190 m above O.D. SN 7860 1320		SN 83 S.E.	Cae Dan y Domen, Caer Garn TA 800, 243 m above O.D SN 8512 3455
SN 81 S.W.	Cae Garn T 246, 200 m above O.D. SN 8482 1403		SN 84 N.E.	Cae Garn Uchaf TA 440, 250 m above O.D. SN 8993 4535
SN 81 S.E.	Garn Llwyd Fawr TA 1885, 225 m above O.D. SN 8655 1078		SN 85 S.E.	Cae Garn Lwyd TA 4, 290 m above O.D. SN 8540 5140
	Garn TA 1849, 235 m above O.D. SN 8727 1063		SN 90 N.E.	Cae Garn Ucha TA 463, 210 m above O.D. SN 9740 0580
	Garnllwyd TA 1856, 230 m above O.D. SN 8730 1040			Cae Carn TA 20, 23, 320 m above O.D. SN 9419 1592
	Ton Carne TA 1855, 230 m above O.D. SN 8730 1040		SN 91 S.W.	Cae'r Garn TA 475, 310 m above O.D. SN 9157 1315
SN 82 N.W.	Faint ring A.P. A 4105, 420 m above O.D. SN 8255 2815		SN 91 S.E.	Garn Ddu O.S. (1840) 380 m above O.D. SN 9577 1122
	Cae'r Carnau TA 486, 350 m above O.D. SN 8902 2680		SN 92 N.W.	Cae Carreg Fawr TA 1219, 240 m above O.D. SN 9155 2683
SN 82 S.E.	Cae Garn Bach TA 217, 370 m above O.D. SN 8778 2410			Graeg y Carney TA 1220, 240 m above O.D. SN 9153 2700
	Cae Carne Isaf TA 271, 360 m above O.D. SN 8799 2438			Garn Fawr TA 496, 497, 506, 240 m above O.D. SN 9460 2640
	Cae Carne Uchaf TA 270, 420 m above O.D. SN 8792 2447			Cae Maen Gwyn Maen TA 710, 360 m above O.D. SN 9475 2740
	Cae Carn Gerrig TA 292, 300 m above O.D. SN 8839 2489			Cae Garreg Wen TA 914, 265 m above O.D. SN 9435 2860
	Erw'r Garn 420 m above O.D. SN 8966 2470		SN 92 N.E.	Cae Tumpin TA 155, 260 m above O.D. SN 9575 2795
SN 83 N.E.	Y Garn TA 346, 360 m above O.D. SN 8907 3733			Cae Garn TA 526, 210 m above O.D. SN 952 298
SN 83 S.W.	Ynys Garnwen TA 1355, 200 m above O.D. SN 8383 3235			

	Cae Domen TA 369, 245 m above O.D. SN 9646 2960	SO 01 N.E.	Cae Garn TA 832, 213 m above O.D. SO 0985 1807
	Garnog Isaf TA 474, 180 m above O.D. SN 9680 2930	SO 01 S.W.	Cae Garn TA 1408, 310 m above O.D. SO 0008 1395
	Garnog Uchaf TA 475, 210 m above O.D. SN 9670 2950	SO 01 S.W.	Cae Garn Ddu TA 519, 335 m above O.D. SO 0476 1093
SN 92 S.W.	Erw Garn TA 360, 280 m above O.D. SN 9242 2077	SO 01 S.E.	Cae Garn TA 602, 310 m above O.D. SO 0544 1037
	Erw Garn TA 284, 280 m above O.D. SN 9260 2218	SO 01 S.E.	Carn yr Helyg (O.S.), 482 m above O.D. SO 0930 1140
	Ard Dan y Domen TA 291, 260 m above O.D. SN 9262 2230	SO 02 N.W.	Cae Garn TA 194, 170 m above O.D. SO 0250 2725
	Cae Garn TA 730, 320 m above O.D. SN 9386 2225		Cae Carn TA 342–3, 205 m above O.D. SO 039 298
SN 93 S.E.	Caernau TA 383, 280 m above O.D. SN 966 302	SO 02 N.E.	Pen y Garn and Bryn y Garn TA 414, 250 m above O.D. SO 0585 2680
	Cae Garn TA 58, 200 m above O.D. SN 9737 3170	SO 02 S.E.	Coed y Garn Hen TA 360, 305 m above O.D. SO 0505 2390
	Cae Garn TA 69, and mark on AP 6434, 230 m above O.D.		Gista Wen (O.S.), 565 m above O.D. SO 0635 2180 (near)
	Erw y Garn TA 34, 200 m above O.D. SN 9990 3227		Cae Garn TA 214, 230 m above O.D. SO 0815 2453
SN 94 N.W.	Cae Garn TA 423, 215 m above O.D. SN 9003 4515	SO 03 N.W.	Cae Garn TA 741, 260 m above O.D. SO 0250 3730
	Dol y Garn TA 198, 220 m above O.D. SN 9020 4930		Cae Pengarn TA 648, 320 m above O.D. SO 0484 3556
	Cae Dan y Domen TA 346, 200 m above O.D. SN 9256 4875	SO 03 S.W.	Maes y Garn Wen TA 175, 230 m above O.D. SO 0035 3230
	Cae'r Dommen TA 687, 190 m above O.D. SN 9404 4785		Cae Carne TA 238, 290 m above O.D. SO 0010 3320
SN 94 N.E.	Cae Twmpin TA 477, 200 m above O.D. SN 9995 4710		Waun Glas Cairn TA 274, 195 m above O.D. SO 0320 3210
SN 95 N.E.	Carnau TA 267, 290 m above O.D. SN 9930 5972		Cae and Coed Garn TA 126–131, 270 m above O.D. SO 0090 3220
SN 95 S.E.	Cae Twmpin TA 106, 200 m above O.D. SN 9753 5130	SO 03 S.E.	Cae Carnau TA 372, 230 m above O.D. SO 0565 3265
SN 96 S.E.	Dol Garn TA 893, 160 m above O.D. SN 9947 6263		Maes y Garn (O.S.), 260 m above O.D. SO 0924 3035
SO 00 N.W.	Carn Gwilym Goch (O.S.), 255 m above O.D. SO 0260 0860		Garn Galed (O.S.), 215 m above O.D. SO 0909 3200
SO 00 N.W.	Cae Carnau TA 327, 250 m above O.D. SO 0336 0883		

SO 04 S.W. Cae Maes Garn TA 1936, 320 m above O.D. SO 0037 4272

SO 04 S.E. Maes y Garn TA 482, 380 m above O.D. SO 0530 4035

SO 11 N.W. Pen y Garn (O.S.), 220 m above O.D. SO 1374 1820
Maes y Beddau (O.S.), 205 m above O.D. SO 1318 1900

SO 12 N.W. Cae Tumpin TA 248, 251 m above O.D. SO 1080 2982

SO 12 N.E. Cae Garn TA 9, 10, 290 m above O.D. SO 1656 2552

SO 12 S.W. Cae Garn TA 540, 120 m above O.D. SO 1180 2310
Worlod y Garn TA 203, 165 m above O.D. SO 140 244

SO 13 N.E. Twmp (O.S.), 120 m above O.D. SO 1502 3597

SO 21 S.E. Carn y Gorfydd (O.S.), 430 m above O.D. SO 272 111
Garn Ddyrys (O.S.), 460 m above O.D. SO 260 118

SO 23 S.W. Carnau (O.S.), 410 m above O.D. SO 2445 3225

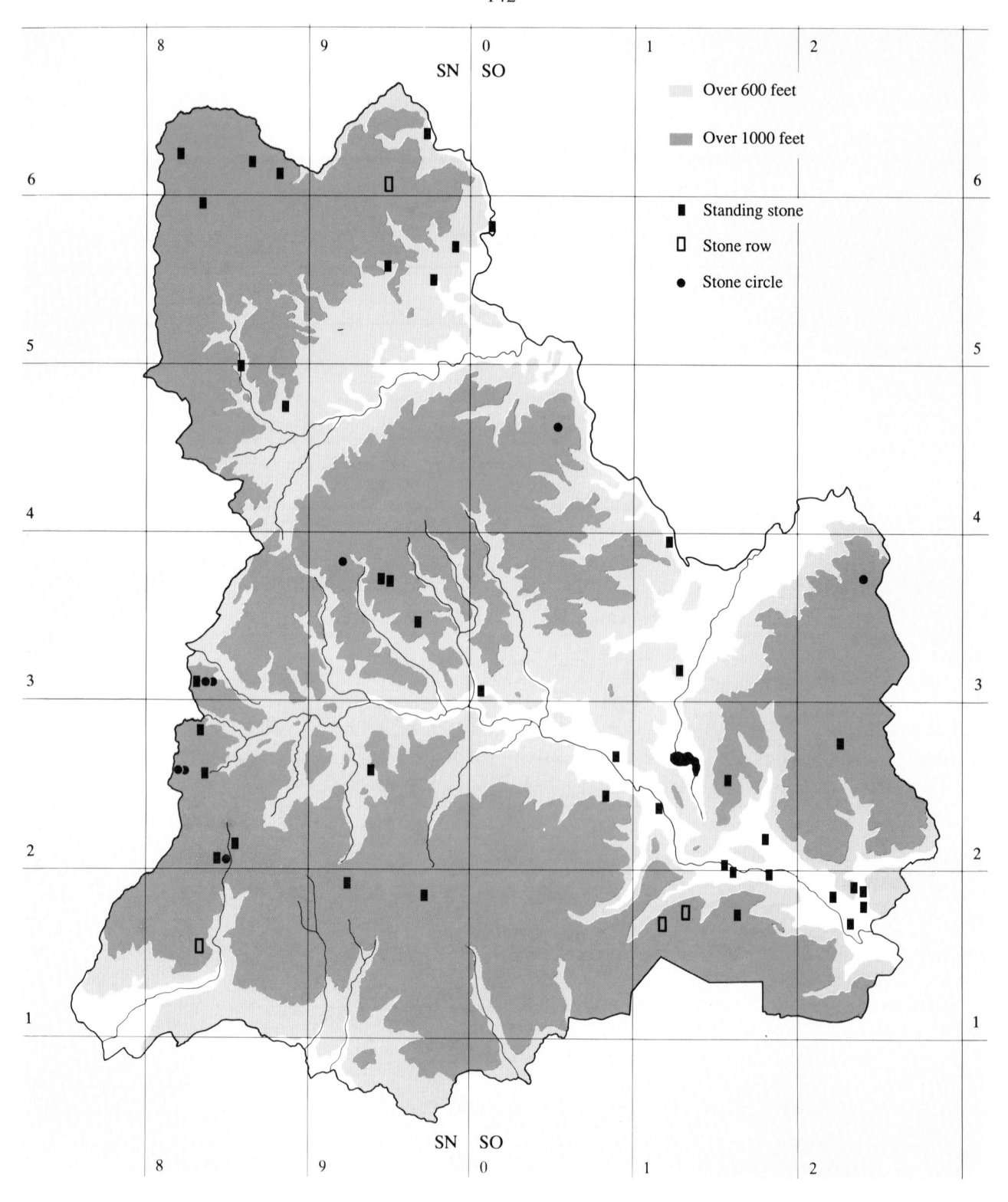

88 Distribution of stone circles, standing stones and stone rows

Stone Circles and Stone Settings

Introduction

A stone circle may be described as a group of stone uprights enclosing an area basically devoid of other structures.[1] More than a handful survive in Brecknockshire, giving the county a greater surviving density of stone circles than any other in South Wales.[2] They are closely related to kerb cairns,[3] and, cairn mass apart, the two monument forms occur in similar topographical settings. Each type appears to be metrically and culturally complementary, if not, in some cases, so similar as to be almost indistinguishable one from another.[4]

Some occur in pairs or groups; others are associated with cairns, single standing stones or stone rows. They are found in later Neolithic and early Bronze Age contexts, from c. 2500 to c. 1200 B.C. Many were clearly intended for burial.[5] In their study a potential ritual function has been stressed in past work,[6] though currently it is considered the monuments played more a 'communal' or 'public' role in prehistoric society.[7] Over the years, following careful measurement of many stone uprights, ancient astronomical activities have also been considered possible.[8]

The general distribution of stone circles is basically complementary to those of timber, which were built on the relatively stone-free lowlands.[9] Nevertheless, many stone circles probably owe their present forms more to factors of survival and preservation than is generally appreciated. Some may represent only the skeletons of intended, unfinished or robbed monuments.[10]

Early Accounts

At the turn of the nineteenth century, Theophilus Jones mentioned three sites, two of which may still be equated with existing circles. Jones's first circle group lay:–

> Upon the hill called the Gader, or the chair, being part of that range of hills, usually called the Black mountains, are stone circles, evidently Druidical . . . The circles are placed, so as to form, if a line were drawn from each, and from them to a large stone, an irregular triangle, they are of small loose stones, the whole about twenty yards in circumference, at the apex is a large stone, about seven feet high; at the distance of eight hundred paces from this stone, in a direct line along the north side of this triangle, one of those circles occurs to which a small stone is attached, on the south side are two others of the same kind, a larger and a smaller, but at the distance of four hundred paces only from the great stone.[11]

Whilst Theophilus Jones did not consider the Maen Llia to have been a 'Druidical monument', in the parish of Defynnog there were at least two. One was:–

> at the extreme north western end [of the parish], near the junction with Llywel and Ystradgynlais; [and] consisted of seven large stones placed at small distances from each other, and ranged in the same order as the Pleiades or seven stars; they were called Meini'r peder Gawres, or the memorial stones of the four heroines; there is not the most distant tradition to whom they relate, and, vae mihi! a few years back they were converted with others by some civilized Goth into part of a wall of a sheep fold.[12]

Although never converted into an animal pen as here suggested, this clearly refers to the Saith Maen stone row (SC 1). Jones continues:

> The other [Druidical Monument] . . . on the hill near the road from Glyntawe to Trecastle, Cerig Duon or the black stones and the pass near them Bwlch y cerig duon; the stones are fixed in the ground and form a circle, on the N. side is a stone much larger than the rest, and at a distance of a few yards from the ring; it perfectly resembles the Hustler's in Cornwall, except from them the huge stone is missing . . .[13]

This was indubitably Cerrig Duon (SC 3) and the Maen Mawr (SS 3).

Samuel Lewis's *Topographical Dictionary* repeats something of both accounts, albeit in a rather garbled form, this time going further and leaving an impression that by the mid-1830s both monuments had disappeared.[14]

As there are few monuments on Mynydd Epynt, Ynys-hir (SC 5) is probable the site where Jones recorded this circle, ring cairn and a single cairn:–

> On the Epynt Hills, at a place called Pen y Pebyll, or the summit of tents (I believe within the parish of Merthyr) are two circles similar to the Senor circles, described by Borlase . . .; the largest is about fifty paces in diameter, the loose surrounding agger of stones about 7 or 8 feet in thickness, with an entrance on the east; the smaller about 14 paces in diameter, and near it a carn or raised heap of stones.[15]

Curiously, although two stone circles survive on the Epynt, at Banc y Celyn and Ynys-hir, neither is in the parish of Merthyr Cynog. However, on balance the quotation seems to suit Ynys-hir better than either Banc y Celyn, in Gwenddwr (SC 7) to the north, or Nant Tarw in Llywel (SC 2) well to the south, a site which also partially fits this description.

On current evidence, it seems unlikely a circle ever stood near the megalithic tomb of Tŷ Illtud, as was suggested in the eighteenth and nineteenth centuries (RSC 7).

The Topographical Settings of the Circles

Whereas most surviving stone circles are preserved in remote places,[16] the degree of remoteness has to be seen against land-use history. Of the six surviving circles or circle groups in Breconshire, three, possibly four (SC 2, SC 3, SC 4, and SC 7), later became associated with major sheep drovers' routes which passed by them. The most westerly of these routes skirted Nant Tarw (SC 2) crossing over the Breconshire side of the county boundary from Carmarthenshire, where another circle is preserved at Bannau Sir Gaer (SN 8085 2439).[17] It is therefore possible that these monuments were respected in historic times as visible route markers in the more treacherous montane terrain. In the northern part of the county, Dunning believed that Ynyshir marked the medieval sheep droving route over Mynydd Epynt,[18] and it is not inconceivable that the survival of a circle structure on Banc y Celyn was similarly related to local sheep movements.

In their present forms, the Maen Mawr standing stone (SS 3) and circle at Cerrig Duon (SC 3) have also long served as markers upon a roughly N.–S. route through the Upper Tawe Valley, into its watershed to the Usk at Trecastle. Evidence of the road, rutted by wheeled vehicles, remains in the form of steep, incised, intersecting tracks passing over the adjacent moorland, visible from aerial photographs. 'Stone piles' marked upon the nineteenth-century O.S. 25-inch plans appear to have defined its more northern path[19] possibly before the construction of the Brecon Forest Tramroad.[20]

The status of the circles upon Trecastle Mountain is less clear, and the absence of descriptions prior to 1854[21] is strange, since the adjacent route was well travelled until abandoned around 1800 when a new Turnpike was driven along the valley bottom. The scars of tile quarrying within an area immediately to their W.,[22] the ground now occupied by Roman practice camps on what is now Common Land, made the Bronze Age sites extremely vulnerable to destruction through stone-drawing in the historic period.

Another site remarkable for its survival, particularly when demands for freestone are taken into account, is the circle now almost imperceptible upon Hay Bluff (SC 10), as marks of quarrying (or mining) have eaten into the cliffs abutting onto the plateau upon which it stands.[23]

Both antiquarian and field studies help shed light upon the earlier, more original, state of the monuments. Sadly, upstanding monuments now survive mainly in areas exclusive of agriculture, so it is unlikely that present numbers of stone circles in Brecknockshire properly reflect their original distribution. Stone circles are unlikely to have survived in the lowlands, though, as already hinted, circular cropmarks may mark the sites of typologically related timber rings.

Current discussion of stone circles tends to be dominated by present day concepts of landscape beauty,[24] and remoteness.[25] However, it is important to view both concepts against factors of human and natural erosion. Furthermore, it should be appreciated that today's landscape aesthetics owe their origins to the recent, eighteenth-century, concept of picturesque beauty. As it is clear that the uplands were well settled at several different periods in the past and the circles therefore occupied landscapes populated under successive vegetational changes, today's visual aesthetics must have a limited use in evaluating their topographical locations.

Palaeoenvironmental Evidence from the Neighbourhood of Circles

Although some of the sites listed here are barely visible above molinia cover, it is clear that this was not the original vegetation. The Bronze Age environment was very different from that in which the upstanding monuments survive (see pp. 6–7), and although no palaeoecological work has been undertaken from the immediate vicinities of any Brecknockshire sites, some appreciation of this may be had from the pollen analytical work undertaken in a mire close to the early Bronze Age complex at Cefn Gwernffrwd, Carmarthenshire about 10 km to the N.W. of the Brecknockshire county boundary.[26] This investigation[27] suggested that the site was originally set in a wooded environment affected by agriculture since Neolithic times.[28] Farming is considered directly responsible for the environmental deterioration, initiating local blanket peat growth which eventually began to invade and cover these sites.[29]

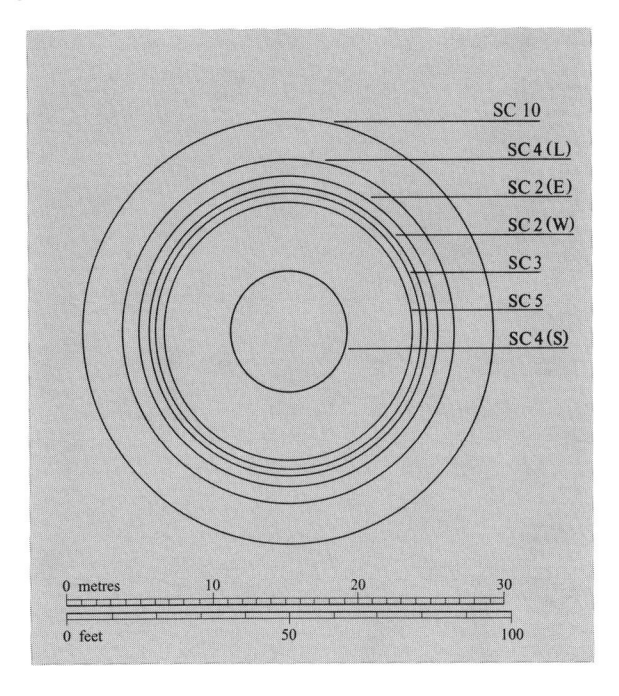

89 Comparison of diameters of stone circles

The Size of the Monuments (Fig. 89)

The most significant factor believed to separate stone circles proper from kerbs of cairns is size. It has been noted that free-standing circles were thought to have been the larger monument, cairns with kerbs the smaller.[30] The astro-archaeological studies of A. and A. S. Thom ignored size differential, calling virtually all circular stone structures stone circles.[31] Burl rectified these terminological inexactitudes when editing the Thoms' corpus of useful surveys, carefully observing the presence or absence of cairn material in the mound, and noting 'much evidence of the merging of customs in the combination, . . . of cairn and free-standing circle'.[32] In Wales the average size of circles is 18.2 m,[33] as against 5–20 m diameter for kerb cairns in Caernarvonshire and 10.24 m for mid-Wales.[34]

As there is considerable overlap in size of kerbs and circles, both among the larger and the smaller sites, a proportion, possibly even the greater number, of stone circles could originally have been built as kerbed cairns which either remained unfinished, or were later denuded.

Burial

Only a handful of Welsh circles has been excavated. The one excavated Brecknockshire site is Ynys-hir (SC 5).[35] Unfortunately, without advantage of protective cairn mass, the recognition of burials is rare upon shallow soils, or from sites where the covering material has been removed, since acidic soils tend to completely dissolve bone (both inhumed and cremated) as well as the more durable gravegoods. As might have been expected, there was no detectable indication of burial in the Ynys-hir circle, though the adjacent cairn (RC 138; Fig. 70) provided ample evidence of interment.[36]

Conclusion

It is impossible to speak with absolute confidence of either the original uses or forms of the Brecknockshire stone circles. All seem to have suffered both natural and human erosion and might be partial remains of monument structures which were originally more complex. From analogous sites outside Wales, burial and associated ritual is the most likely activity.

Detailed examination of the Brecknockshire sites has not proved an astronomical significance and further useful data illuminating their uses must await future excavation.

[1] Burl, *Stone Circles*, *passim*.
[2] W. F. Grimes, *Stone Circles*, *passim*.
[3] F. M. Lynch, *Scot. Archaeol. Forum* 4 (1972), pp. 61–80.
[4] C. S. Briggs, *Landscape History* 8 (1986), pp. 5–13.
[5] J. Barnatt and S. Pierpoint, *Scot. Archaeol. Rev.* 2 (1983), pp. 101–15.
[6] For example Burl, *loc. cit.* n. 1; Grimes, *loc. cit.* n. 2.
[7] J. Barnatt, *Stone Circles of Britain: Taxonomic and distributional analyses and a catalogue of sites in England, Scotland and Wales*, (Oxford: B.A.R. 215, 1989), espec. pp. 211–226.
[8] A. Thom, *Megalithic Lunar Observatories*, (Oxford, 1967).
[9] A. Gibson, 'Sarn y Bryn Caled', *P.P.S.* 59 (1993).
[10] D. K. Leighton, *P.P.S.* 50 (1984), pp. 319–50; Briggs, *loc. cit.* n. 4; Briggs, pp. 139–40.
[11] Jones, *Hist. Brecks.* II, ii (1809), p. 338; a similar statement, almost certainly derivative of this account, appears in T. Rees, *A Topographical and Historical Description of South Wales*, (London: Sherwood, Neely and Jones, 1815), p. 138.
[12] Jones, *ibid.* II, ii, p. 684.
[13] *idem.*
[14] S. Lewis, *Top. Dict.*, *q.v.* Devynock.
[15] Jones, *loc. cit.*, addendum.
[16] See n. 6.
[17] Recently discovered by P. M. Jones, *Arch. in Wales* 17 (1977), p. 17; O.S. Card SN 82 SW 8. It has not been found possible to re-locate another circle on the Brecknockshire side of the boundary said to lie at SN 8223 2312 (*Arch. in Wales* 19 (1979), p. 9; O.S. Card SN 82 SW 7).

[18] G. C. Dunning, *Arch. Camb.* 97 (1943), pp. 169–94.
[19] O.S. 25-inch 1889, sheet XXXII: plan 9.
[20] S. R. Hughes, *The Brecon Forest Tramroad*, (R.C.A.M., 1991).
[21] W. Rees, *Arch. Camb.* 8 (1854), pp. 125–35.
[22] C.U.A.P. A.P.s, BAK 74–80; AQR 40; AWY 78–85; AZR 99; VDR 51; QJ 15–24; QN 63–75; QJ 15–23. See also *Inv. Br.* I (ii), RMC 1 and 2, Fig. 177.
[23] R.C.A.M. A.P. 87-MB-217.
[24] The most influential paper in this respect has been F. M. Lynch, pp. 124–7, in J. G. Evans, S. Limbrey and H. Cleere, (eds.), *The effect of man on the landscape; the Highland Zone*, C.B.A. Res. Rep. No. 7, (London, 1975). See above (p. 69) for further discussion.
[25] Burl, *loc. cit.* n. 1.
[26] C. S. Briggs, *Arch. Camb.* 124 (1974), pp. 162–164; J. G. Morgan and C. L. N. Ruggles, 'Indications at the Cefn Gwernffrwd site', *Arch. Camb.* 125 (1976), pp. 162–5.
[27] F. M. Chambers, *New Phyt.* 92 (1982), pp. 607–15; *P.P.S.* 49 (1983), pp. 303–16.
[28] *idem.*; *cf.* Lynch, *loc. cit.* n. 24, p. 125, where it is suggested that circles were being erected in a treeless environment at the Brenig, Denbighshire.
[29] Chambers, *loc. cit.* n. 23, (1983), p. 315.
[30] Discussed in Briggs, *loc. cit.* n. 4; it is puzzling that in such a comprehensive work as Roese's, no comparisons are drawn between the sizes of cairns and circles; *vide* E. C. Roese, *B.B.C.S.* 19 (1980), pp. 164–70; *B.B.C.S.* 29 (1981), pp. 575–87.
[31] A. Thom, *loc. cit.* n. 8.
[32] *Meg. Rings*, p. 371 and *passim*.
[33] Burl, *Stone Circles*, p. 372.
[34] These figures are taken from Leighton, *loc. cit.* n. 10, pp. 322, 332–48.
[35] Dunning, *loc. cit.* n. 18.
[36] *idem.*

Stone Circles and Stone Settings: the sites (SC 1–10; RSC 1–8)

(SC 1; Fig. 90) At Saith Maen, (plate 1) 700 m W. of Craig y Nos is a stone row, comprising seven uprights (or stones formerly upright). In the general area of the site, the locally thin peat cover is rapidly eroding under climatic, touristic and grazing pressures, to reveal a leached grey-white silica-rich clay and gravel subsoil into which the stones are set. All the stones are surrounded by erosion hollows, and corresponding socket holes up to about 0.25 m deep mark the line of the fallen recumbent stones. With one exception ((v) below, which is a rounded boulder of Old Red Sandstone), all are of Carboniferous silicious grit. The slab-shaped stones are aligned with their flat planes bearing along an axis of 025° (true). They are evenly spaced at intervals of 1.2 to 1.5 m. From S. to N. the stones are:

(i)   Leaning to E., 0.6 m by 0.7 m by 0.3 m.
(ii)   Leaning to W., 0.7 m by 0.9 m by 0.2 m.
(iii)   Upright, 0.9 m by 0.8 m by 0.3 m.
(iv)   Recumbent, 2.9 m by 1.1 m by 0.4 m.
(v)   Upright, 1.1 m by 0.8 m by 0.3 m.
(vi)   Recumbent, 2.2 m by 0.7 m by 0.2 m.
(vii)   Upright, 1.7 m by 0.9 m by 0.2 m.

About 20 m S. of the alignment, there is a pile of gritstone standing about 0.25 m above the bared ground surface. This might be interpreted as the former site of a weathered down Millstone Grit orthostat. Immediately N. of the alignment (though not dead on line) is a large shake-hole.

Although Theophilus Jones claimed the stones had been incorporated into a sheepfold, there is today no evidence to support this suggestion.

Cantrill MSS, Brit. Geol. Surv. Notebook I, p. 25; James, *Standing Stones* (1970), Plan Fig. 3c, Photos Pl. 5a–c; Ll. Morgan, *Proc. Swansea Sci. Soc.* (1907–8), pp. 159–60; Grimes, *M.M.W.*, no. 20; Jones, *Hist. Brecks.* II, ii (1809), p. 684; Savory, *Prehist. Brecks.* (I), p. 108; Thom, *Vistas in Astronomy* 7 (1966), Fig. 33; *Megalithic Sites*, (1967), table 12.1.

S.A.M. B 72
Ystradgynlais (E), Ystradgynlais Lr (C)
SN 81 N.W. (8331 1539)   26 ii 91

(SC 2; Figs. 91–92) On the W. side of Nant Tarw, on a flat part of the interfluve between the Afon Tarw and a more westerly, unnamed stream, is a complex of sites including two circles (SC 2 i and ii),[1] a robbed cairn (SC 2 iii),[2] a stone setting (SC 2 iv), a monolith (SC 2 v) and a small embanked enclosure (SC 2 vi),[3] lying alongside and within a slight hollow astride an old drovers' route over the Carmarthenshire Fans. From its

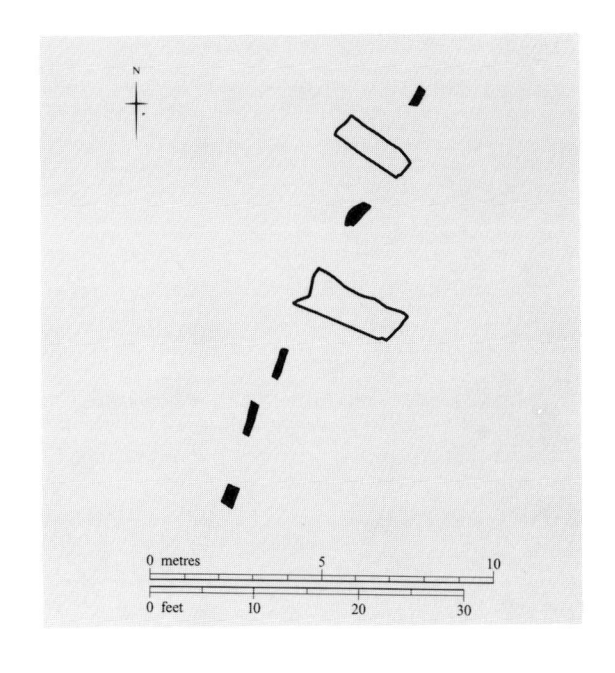

90 Saith Maen (Craig y Nos) stone row (SC 1)

STONE CIRCLES AND STONE SETTINGS: THE SITES

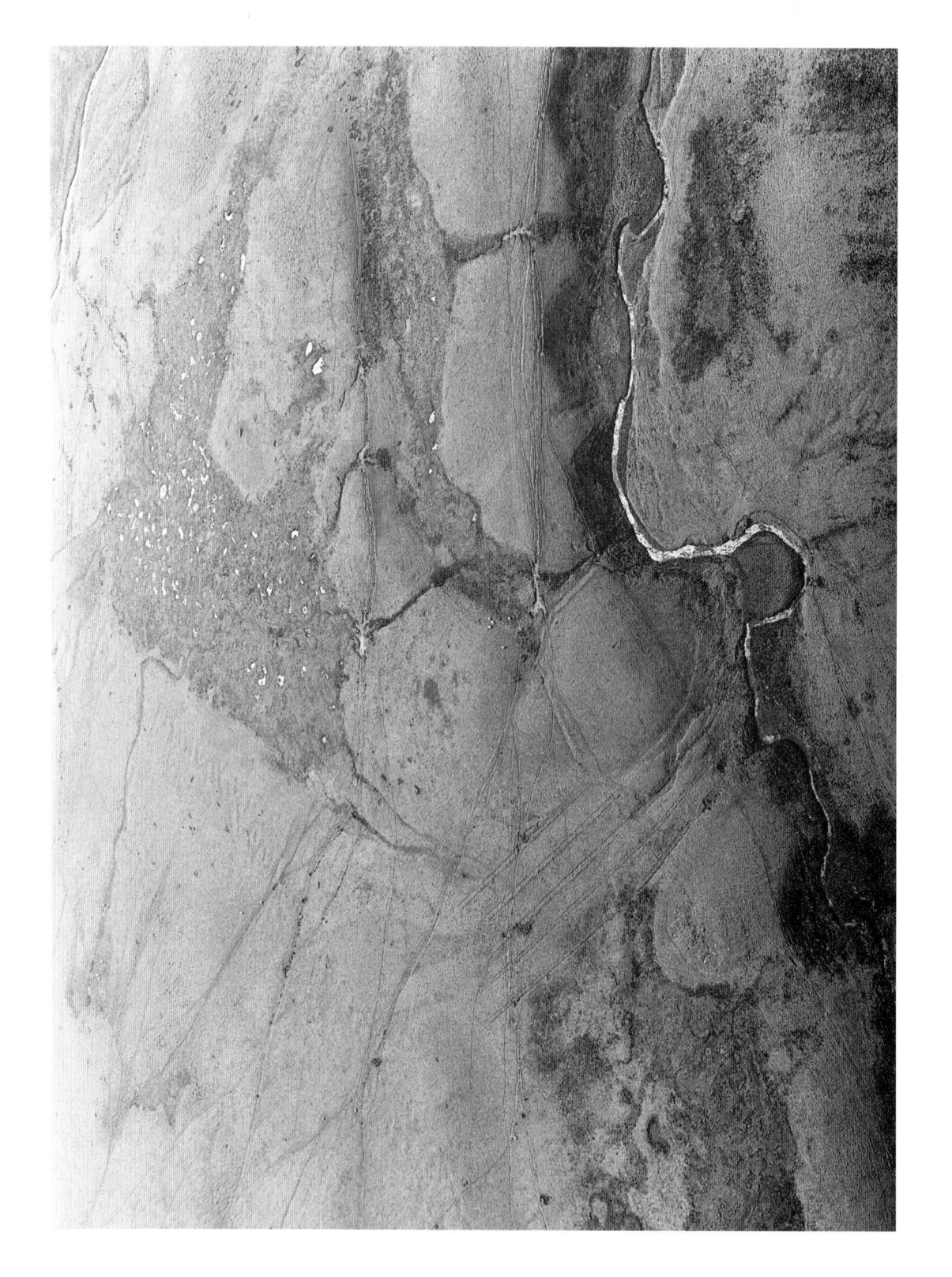

91 Nant Tarw stone circles (SC 2), cairn (RC 21) and settlement complex (US 29) (Copyright Clwyd-Powys Archaeological Trust AP 88 MB 184)

STONE CIRCLES AND STONE SETTINGS: THE SITES

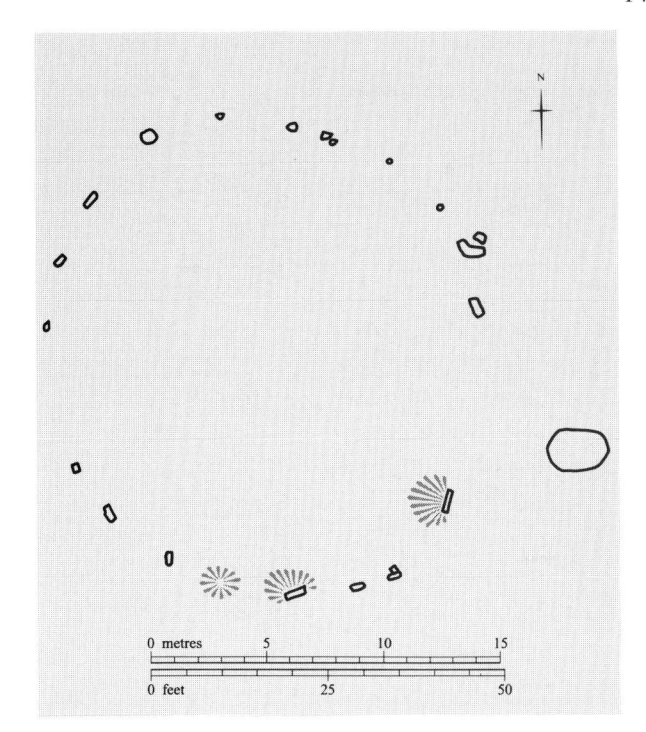

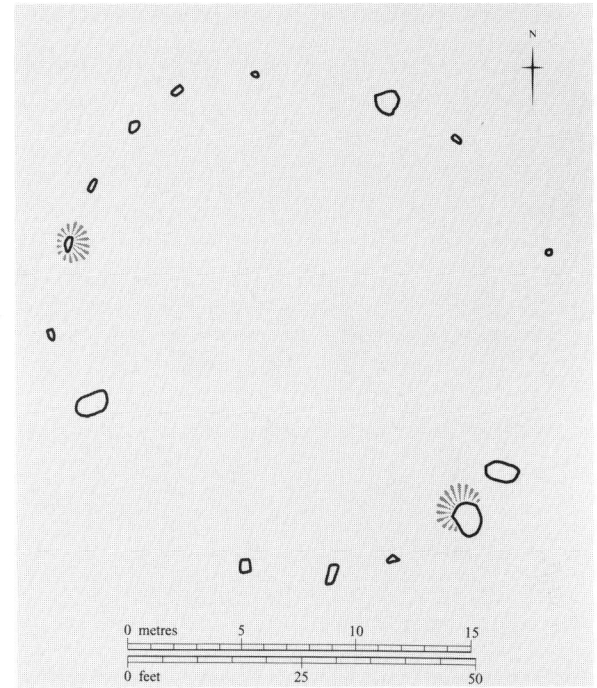

92 Nant Tarw (SC 2i): plan of W. circle

93 Nant Tarw (SC 2ii): plan of E. circle

situation upon a knoll to the N., the enclosure overlooks both circles and the cairn, which lie about 350 m above O.D. The circles are 110 m apart, the more westerly slightly higher than the other. Surrounding the general area occupied by these sites, on the W. and S. is a series of low parallel ridges, which at first sight appear to be rig and furrow ploughing.[4] However, upon closer inspection these seem better interpreted as post-glacial erosion features. Many river and stream meander cores in the area are occupied by undatable settlement features such as hut platforms and small enclosures. During field survey, flecks of charcoal were observed beneath an overburden of ploughsoil in the profile of the eroding river bluff to the N. of the sites (at SN 8189 2598). These could indicate prehistoric or later woodland clearances in the area.

(SC 2 i) The western circle is 19.2 m in diameter (N.–S.) and 20.1 m (E.–W.) and comprises 15 surviving stones (plus a post-hole on the S.). They vary in height from 15 m to 1 m (on the E.), and are regularly spaced except on the S., W., E., and N.W., where gaps imply lost stones. Uprights include a variety of stone varying from boulder to slab-like.

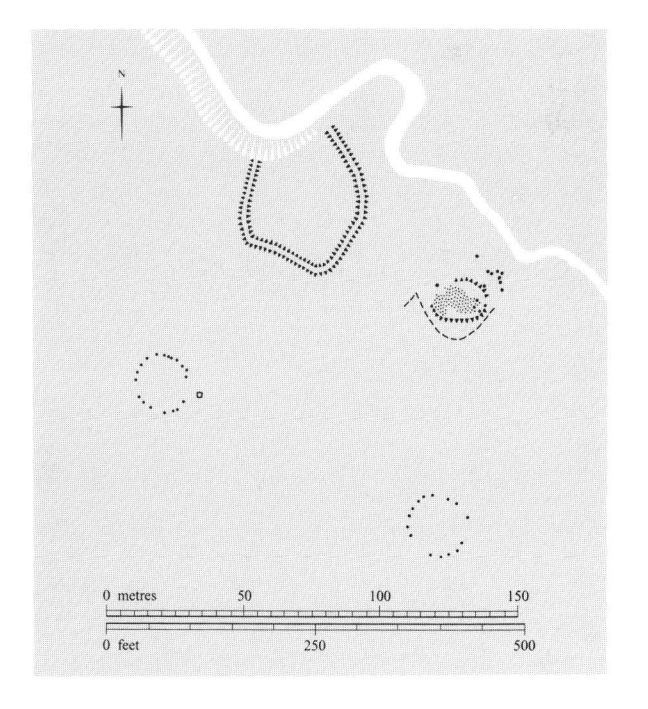

94 Nant Tarw: detailed plan indicating relationship of sites (SC 2, RC 21, US 29)

Four of the boulders are almost completely buried. Two pairs of stones on the N. are more closely spaced than elsewhere, and Grimes has suggested that this juxtaposition may have been deliberate.[5]

Some 3 m to the E. of this circle is a massive recumbent slab, perhaps a fallen standing stone, about 2.5 m long, 1.5 m wide by 0.6 m thick. It lies just to the N. of the axial line between the circle centres. Morgan attached significance to the width of the gap on this side of the circle, suggesting that the stones defining it were set back within the true circumference in order to emphasise the relationship between circle and outlier.[6]

(SC 2 ii) The eastern circle comprises twelve stones upon an incomplete circumference, there being a gap of 3 m on the E. Eight are fallen, five are partly buried. The diameter is 18.5 m (N.–S.) by 22 m (E.-W.). The tallest stone is 1.25 m in height; the smallest, only 5 cm above the ground. Some fallen stones must have been taller than this; on the E. is one that must have been almost 1.5 m high.

(SC 2 iii) The cairn is described elsewhere (RC 21).

(SC 2 iv) Apparently associated with the circles are four outlying monoliths or embedded erratic boulders. One stone, which has toppled northwards, lies 115 m W. from the centre of the eastern circle and measures some 3 m long and 0.75 m thick. Its base is stone-packed. Two further stones stand behind it, 0.43 m and 0.28 m high respectively. Grimes was drawn to compare the relationship of the spacing of this setting with that of the Maen Mawr at Cerrig Duon (SC 3 below).[7]

(SC 2 v) A further boulder about 1.25 m high, 0.9 m wide and 0.35 m thick, lies embedded in W. river bank about 85 m S.S.E. from the centre of the cairn (RC 21). Out of sight from the circle complex, its relationship to the other monuments is unclear. It may have been naturally deposited in this position.

(SC 2 vi) The pentagonal enclosure is described elsewhere (US 29).

[1] For general references, see: O.S. Card SN 82 NW 5; Burl, *Stone Circles*, p. 369; James, *Surveys*, 1970; Grimes, *Map L.B.M.*, 1936, no. 18; *Stone Circles*, p. 137; H. N. Savory, *Prehist. Brecks.* (I), p. 108; A. Thom, *Meg. Sites*, Fig. 6.23; *Meg. Rings*, pp. 394–5 (plan); Barnatt, *Stone Circles*, pp. 388–9, nos. 13:36–7.

[2] First noted by W. Ll. Morgan in *Trans. Swansea Sci. Soc.* (1907–8), pp. 150–5.

[3] Discovered by Commission staff during field survey in January 1989.

[4] A.P.s, R.C.A.M. 88 MB 183–5.

[5] Grimes, *Stone Circles*, p. 137.

[6] loc. cit. n. 2.
[7] loc. cit. n. 5.

S.A.M. B 70

Llywel (E), Traean-glas (C)
SN 82 N.W. (SC 2 i) (8187 2583); (SC 2 ii) (8197 2578); (SC 2 iii) (8199 2589); (SC 2 iv) (8177 2585); (SC 2 v) (8208 2505); (SC 2 vi) (8193 2593)   viii 89

(SC 3; Figs. 95–6) Cerrig Duon stone circle and its well-known associated standing stone the Maen Mawr, lie 380 m above O.D. and dominate the skyline of a low plateau on the pass approaching the source of the River Tawe. Though well visited[1] and frequently described, the site is usually considered in complete isolation from its environs:[2] only Grimes mentioned the existence of early trackways and steeply-incised streambeds.[3] Recent fieldwork and close aerial photography show the complex to lie within a landscape bisected and heavily rutted by old tracks and also surrounded by numerous early settlement features. Hut platforms and clearance cairns are scattered along the hillslope to the W. and it is possible that the circle complex is itself located within a relict field, bounded by a low bank (US 33 iii) just to its S. However, in the absence of pollen analytical studies and excavation, land-use history is conjectural. Although it is possible that the settlement sites were contemporary with the circle, these may equally have been medieval or later. At earliest, the tracks are probably post-Roman, but they are felt most likely to result from medieval or later long-distance sheep droving,[4] or from activity in relatively recent times when packhorses and carts carried lime from the limestone area to the S. onto the western and northern part of the Fforest Fawr. The site includes a circle (SC 3 i), standing stone (SC 3 ii), and avenue (SC 3 iii).

(SC 3 i; Figs. 95, 96) The circle comprises 20 stones, of which one is fallen and another scarcely visible, the others rising to no more than about 0.6 m in height. They are mostly slab-like, roughly rectangular at base, and of Pennant Sandstone. Although fairly evenly spaced, there are obvious gaps where stones are missing, so spacing is between 1.3 m and 5.5 m between uprights, which lie upon a circle with a diameter of 18.5 m N.–S. and 17.5 m E.–W. The stones appear to be set in a low bank on the S.W., but this is almost certainly upcast from a small excavation which appears to have been made there. Indeed, there is no sign of a bank elsewhere around the monument. On the S. side there is what appears to be an empty

95 Looking south over Cerrig Duon stone circle and Maen Mawr (SC 3 and SS 3)

stone hole, and this might accord with a count of 21 stones in both 1907[5] and 1936.[6]

(SC 3 ii) The standing stone Maen Mawr (SS 3) lies some 10 m N. of the circle in a slight animal- and weather-eroded hollow, is 1.9 m in height above the ground, and measures 1.2 m wide on the E. to 1.4 m on the W. and is 0.9 m thick. It is oriented due N.–S. and is packed with stones.

About 3 m beyond the monolith are two small upright stones, and 9.5 m W. of this is a similar small stone. These define the S. end of an avenue some 23 m long and about 9 m wide leading northwards from the circle. The stones protrude above the grass only slightly; some may even be naturally set. Immediately beyond the avenue the ground falls away into one of the abandoned road hollows.

(SC 3 iii) Lying to the N.E. of the circle, some 14.3 m from it at the nearest point, is a near-parallel avenue of low, upright stones. The two stone rows diverge northwards, separated by just over 6 m at the S. end, and by 6.4 m after 9.42 m where the more eastern appears to terminate. In its surviving state the stones in both rows are more closely set towards the S. than towards the N. but, as Grimes cogently observes, this may be an accidental result of stones having disappeared.[7] Sixteen stones now survive on the W. side, which is now 45 m long. Only eleven stones remain on the eastern side, which is 24.7 m long.

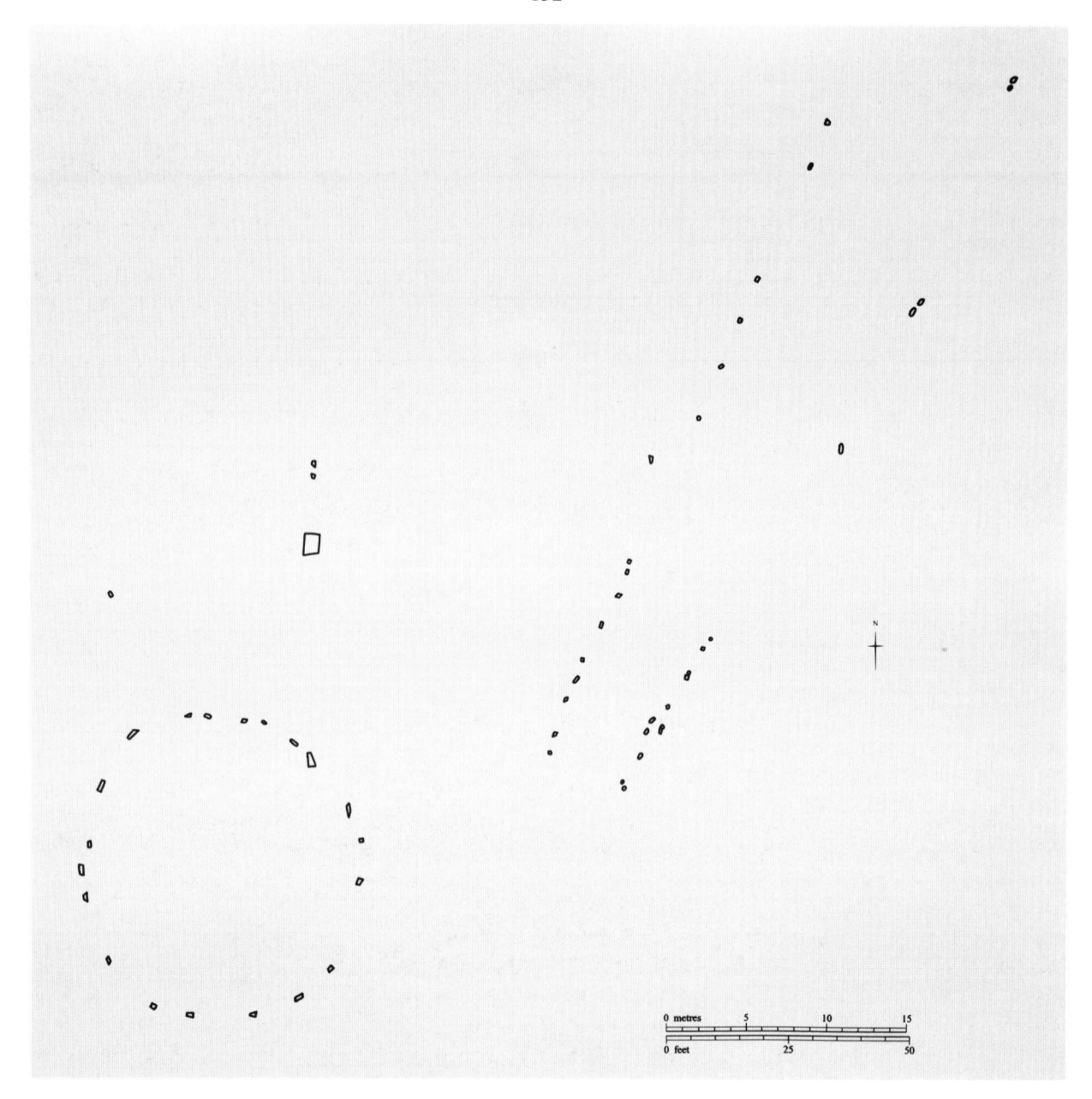

96 Cerrig Duon and Maen Mawr (SC 3 and SS 3): plan from a survey by R. Spicer, with additions

Some stones have clearly fallen, and some must remain buried. In Llewellyn Morgan's day only nine were visible in the W. avenue which was then only about 43 m long, and although the number of stones he recorded on the E. side was eleven, the same number as survives, the avenue was then apparently much longer, at 33.5 m in length.[8] Some stones have probably therefore disappeared or may well be buried in the turf, since they are mostly very low, rarely exceeding 15 cm in height. In the main, their axes appear to be aligned along the avenue.

[1] O.S. Card SN 82 SE 2; the account given by Theophilus Jones (in *Hist. Brecks.* II, ii, p. 684 in 1809) is the earliest known at

present. Notes in Rees' *South Wales*, (1815), p. 187 and in Samuel Lewis's *Top. Dict., s.v.,* 'Brecknockshire' and 'Devynock', of 1833, are almost certainly derivative.

[2] For example, Grimes, *Map L.B.M.,* pp. 17, 25, no. 19; Grimes, *M.M.W.,* pp. 108–9, Fig. 2; *Stone Circles,* pp. 138–9; Burl, *Stone Circles,* p. 369; *Literary Guide to South Wales,* (1913), p. 50; Kay MSS notebook X, ser. III, pp. 926–8; Savory, *Prehist. Brecks.,* (I), p. 106; Spicer MSS; A. Thom, *Vistas in Astronomy* 7, 1 (1966), pp. 1–57, Fig. 34; *Meg. Sites,* table 12.1; *Meg. Rings* pp. 392–3 (plan); Barnatt, *Stone Circles,* p. 377, no. 13:9.

[3] Grimes, *Stone Circles,* p. 138.

[4] *Ibid.*

[5] W. Ll. Morgan, *Proc. Swansea Sci. Soc.* (1907–8), p. 155 (plan).

[6] Grimes, *M.M.W.,* pp. 108–109, Fig. 2; *Map L.B.M.* p. 17.

[7] Grimes, *Stone Circles,* p. 148.

[8] Morgan, *loc. cit.* n. 5.

S.A.M. B 71

Llywel (E), Traean-glas (C)
SN 82 S.E. (SC 3 i) (8512 2062); (SC 3 ii) (8511 2060); (SC 3 iii) (8514 2064)　　　　　　　　　　　　　　i 89

(SC 4; Figs. 97–98) On Trecastle Mountain, on an undulating plateau sloping gently towards the N. at 370 m above O.D. are the remains of two circles (SC 4 i and ii), a cairn (SC 4 iii), three scattered groups of stone (SC 4 iv) and a recumbent standing stone (SC 4 v). The stone alignments and monolith are not certainly anthropogenic in origin. Lying about 400 m E. of Y Pigwn Roman practice camps, the circles may at one time have acted as waymarkers on the open moorland beside the course of the former coach road (based upon the Roman route) from Brecon to Llandovery. Curiously they are not depicted upon the earliest editions of the Ordnance Maps[1] and William Rees, the celebrated Swansea scholar-printer, said the group had been found in 1849 by John Rhys Jones.[2] Circles (SC 4 i–ii) and (SC 4 iii) were not planned until the turn of the century.[3] Several later fieldworkers also surveyed the sites,[4] variously ascribing their functions to ritual,[5] and more commonly in recent years, to astronomical uses.[6] It is still possibly to detect an E.–W. track actually passing through the site, immediately N. of, and slightly truncating, the more southerly circle.[7]

The whole complex lies within a curvilinear enclosure comprising a substantial bank and ditch, the southern length of which runs roughly E.–W., and its E. boundary runs N.–S., about 50 m E. of the recumbent stone. This E.–W. bank continues in a westerly direction to the Roman fort, where its overall alignment coincides almost precisely with that of the

N. bank of the interior fort, although the two do not appear to join. The bank's dating is unclear, but it seems unlikely to have been Roman and presumably marks the boundaries of a medieval agricultural or pastoral enclosure.

Not only is the area around the Roman fort heavily mined by quarrying, but minor quarries pock-mark this entire area. The activity of stone-drawing from the common was probably responsible for helping denude all upstanding stone-filled monuments of such cairn material as might have been notionally reveted by the surviving orthostats which make up the circles. As the area was also in military use for some time after the Second World War, it is possible that some of these pock-marks and tracks may derive from that activity.

(SC 4 i) About midway between the two upstanding circles are three stones, which if plotted out would lie upon a circumference of about 10.6 m in diameter. They comprise a block 0.64 m by 0.58 m by 0.4 m high; a fallen pillar 0.5 m by 0.23 m by 0.91 m high (when upright) and a block 0.86 m by 0.55 m by 0.48 m high. Its location suggests that this could be the fugitive remnant of a feature seen more complete during the 1930s by Grimes.[8]

(SC 4 ii) Of the surviving circles, the smaller, more westerly is 7.9 m in diameter and consists of four

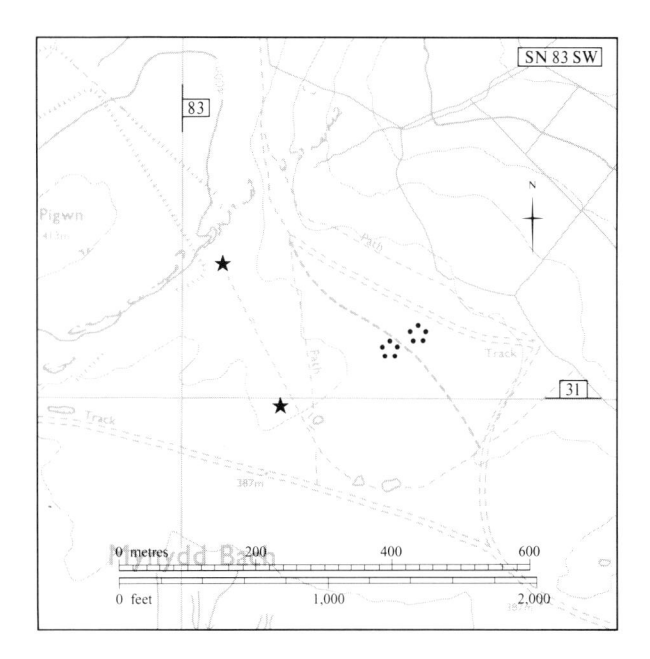

97 Trecastle Mountain stone circles and cairns (SC 4): location plan

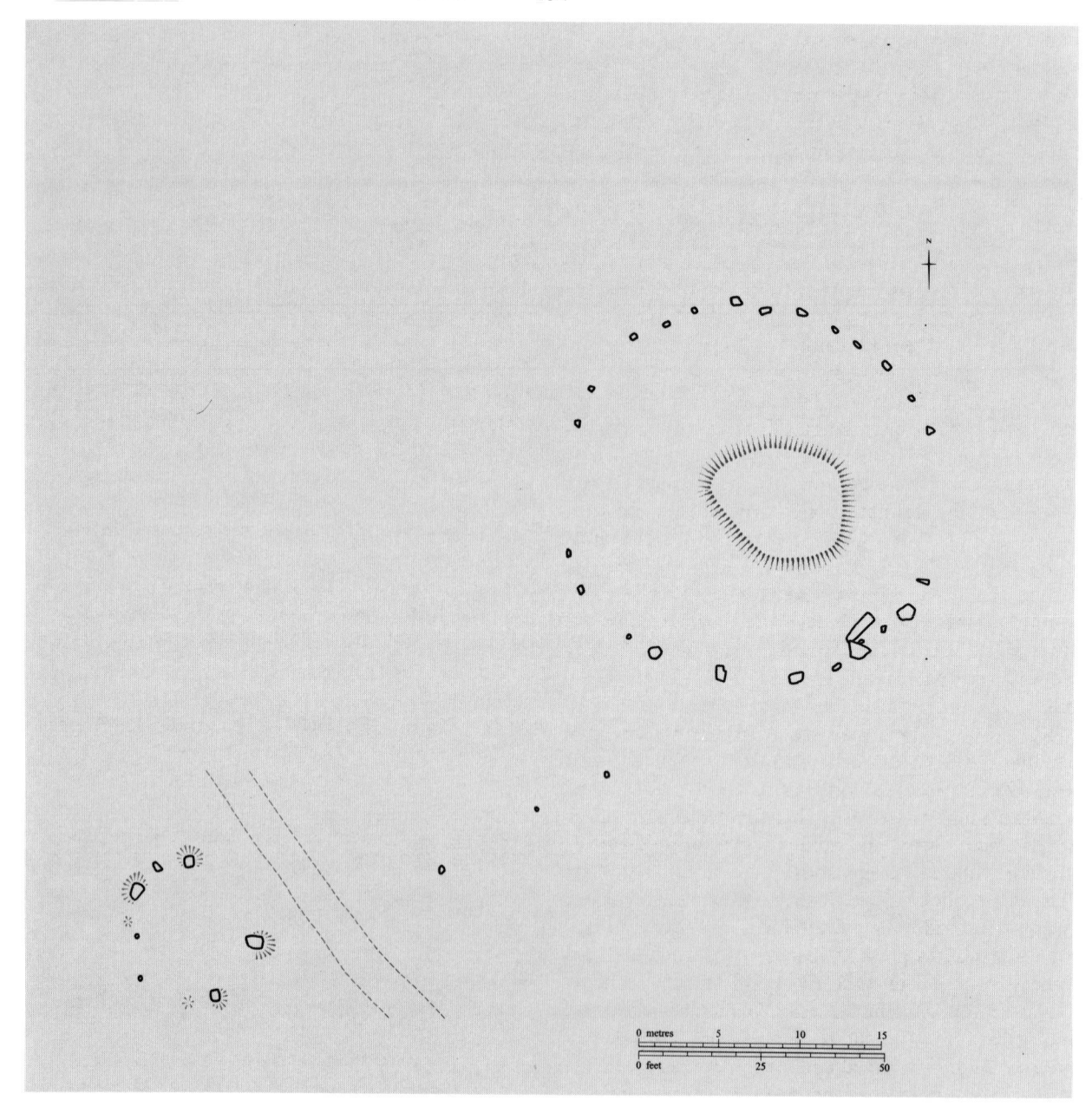

98 Trecastle Mountain stone circles (SC 4 i–iii): plan

irregularly spaced massive slabs now leaning outwards. Each is about 0.6 m wide and stands 0.9 m high. The ground around the orthostats is very badly eroded by sheep, to form deep hollows which have collected water.

(SC 4 iii) The second and larger, northeastern circle, is 23.1 in diameter N.E.–S.W. by 22 m and consists of twenty-one uprights from 0.1 to 0.5 m high, with at least five stone-holes, with a regular spacing at intervals of about 2.6 m. Some stones are well weathered, or even frost-shattered into angular stumps, whereas others are more boulder-like in form. Between two orthostats rather larger than the rest on the S.E., the Old Red Sandstone is exposed over an area about 3 m long and 1 m wide (along the cairn perimeter). On the S.W. is a gap of 5.5 m between stones which it has been suggested[9] may have been an entrance. There is a slight irregular mound about 6–7 m in diameter lying towards the northern part of the site, which may be all that remains of a former cairn infill, or alternatively may represent the capping of a near-central burial.

(SC 4 iv) A stone-built cairn, see (RC 35).

(SC 4 v) Depending upon the number included in the grouping, there are four or five groups of outlying uprights, none of which is certainly associated with the circles, and indeed, some or all may even be natural. Running between the two circles and aligned N.–S. along their E. perimeters are three stones. To the immediate W. of the S.W. circle are two more, and beyond, to the S. of it, two further pairs of apparently unrelated stones. Roughly at right angles to this grouping, and about 40 m from it, is a further alignment of four stones. It has been suggested[10] that at one time, at least some of these stones may have formed part of a field boundary.

(SC 4 vi) At 385 m above O.D. is a recumbent standing stone with a pointed end, lying to the E., some 125 m from the northeastern circle and 143 m from the southwestern. If the stone ever had any significance within this monument group, it would probably have projected above ground about 1.5 m high, at an oblique angle. However, the stone appears to have formed part of an outcropping band of sandstone, and its presence here may be adventitious. It measures 1.16 m wide by 0.74 m thick and the original stump, now much weathered and rounded, is at least 1 m thick. About 10 m due S. of this there is another stone (not marked upon the plan), also with an almost vertical bedding plane, and about 1 m in length. It appears to form part of the same rock exposure.

[1] MS O.S. Maps, Brit. Lib. (1818); A.P.s, C.U.A.P. QJ 15, 17; A.P., R.C.A.M., 88 MB 69–72.

[2] The site is first noted by W. Rees, *Arch. Camb.* 8 (1854), pp. 125–34.

[3] W. Ll. Morgan, *Proc. Swansea Sci. Soc.* (1907–8), pp. 146–9 (plan).

[4] Grimes, *Map L.B.M.*; *Stone Circles*, pp. 135–6.

[5] Burl, *Stone Circles*, pp. 260–262, 369 (plan).

[6] Thom, *Meg. Sites*, table.

[7] An unsigned MS of 30th July 1933, which includes sketch plans of two circles and notes about them written upon Castle of Brecon Hotel notepaper, probably in the hand of W. F. Grimes,

suggests there were at that time many more outlying stones than later survived. The writer felt that a handful of stones may at one time have belonged to an outer circle. It is difficult to correlate the second circle described in this MS with the present known sitings. It had eight peristaliths, was some 95 feet (about 29 m) in diameter, also had a slightly raised centre, and apparently lay roughly equidistant between the known, larger, N.E. circle, and the N.W. corner of Y Pigwn Roman camp (Lloyd MSS).

[8] See O.S. Card SN 83 SW 6 and Grimes *loc. cit.*, n. 4 above.

[9] W. E Griffiths in R.C.A.M. files.

[10] By the O.S.; see O.S. Card SN 83 SW 6.

S.A.M. B 69 (SC 4 i–iii only)

Llywel (E), Traean-glas (C)
SN 83 S.W. (SC 4 i) (8319 3118); (SC 4 ii) (8331 3106); (SC 4 iii) (8335 3109); (SC 4 iv) (8314 3098); (SC 4 v) various positions: see plan Fig. 55; (SC 4 vi) (8339 3107)   21 ii 90

(SC 5; Figs. 99–100) Upon the central part of Mynydd Epynt on a slight saddle at Ynys-hir about 400 m above O.D. are a stone circle and cairn (RC 138), both excavated in 1940[1] prior to the take-over of this tract as a military training area. Theophilus Jones may have alluded to this site around 1800, albeit rather vaguely (see quotation above, p. 144).[2] If Jones's account is to be credited, a larger circle had already disappeared when Col. Llewellyn Morgan first planned the site around the turn of the century.[3] It was probably a ring cairn.

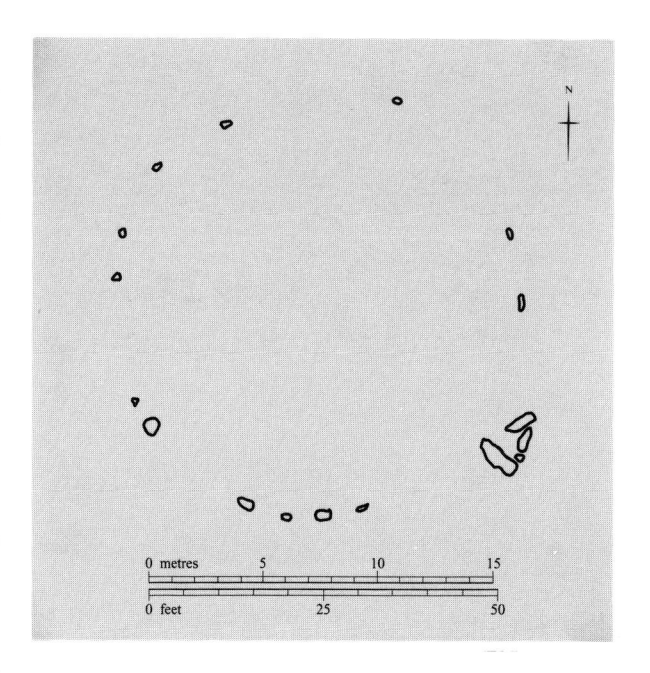

99 Ynys-hir: plan of circle (SC 5)

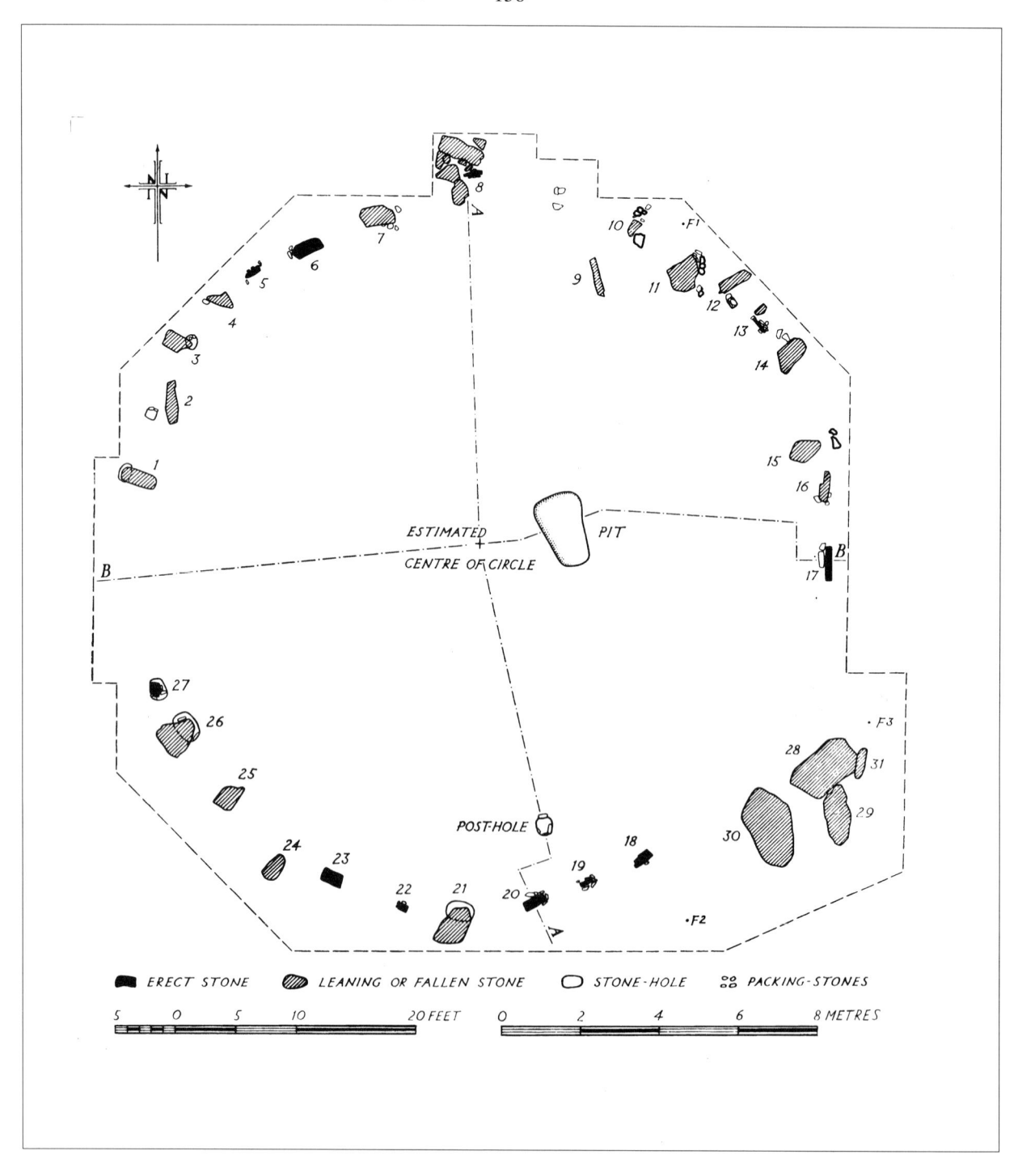

100 Ynys-hir stone circle (SC 5), excavation plan (from *Arch. Camb.* 97 (1943))

The surviving monument[4] is a circle of small uprights with an average diameter of *c.* 17 m. It originally consisted of twenty-seven stones, of which twelve protruded above the ground at the time of excavation. Only eleven are now visible.

Three glacial erratics incorporated into the S.E. side were probably left there because they were too heavy to move. About 1.5 m inside the perimeter was a post-hole and near the circle centre, a pit about 0.4 m deep, probably resulting from recent fossicking.

Dunning numbered the stones 1–31 on his plan. Of these, the erratics already noted (nos. 28–31) remain visible on the S.E. Two stones have been thrown off the site well to the N.E. Stones nos. 9–15 are not visible, and though it is possible that no. 13 has fallen, and might lie flat with others beneath the turf, all might now be lost. Stones nos. 1, 2, 6, 7, 8, 16 and 17 are visible, but it is unclear how many missing stones are buried, or whether or not they are completely lost. An attempt was made to probe, but this proved inconclusive because it was impossible to distinguish between smaller stones and larger, perimeter stones.

[1] G. C. Dunning, *Arch. Camb.* 97 (1943), pp. 169–94.
[2] Jones, *Hist. Brecks.* II, ii, (1809), addenda.
[3] W. Ll. Morgan, *Ann. Rep. Swansea Sci. Soc.* (1910–11), pp. 117–19 (plan); Burl, *Stone Circles*, p. 369.
[4] Grimes, *Stone Circles*, p. 134; O.S. Card SN 93 NW 1; *Meg. Rings*, pp. 396–7. It is unclear whether or not this study is based upon a new survey, or relies upon Dunning's; Barnatt, *Stone Circles*, p. 393, no. 13:50.

S.A.M. B 68

Llanfihangel Nant Brân
SN 93 N.W. (9211 3826)   22 viii 89

(SC 6; Fig. 101–02) Saith Maen is a single row of stones standing about 395 m above O.D., overlooking the headwaters of the Afon Chwefru to the S. This is probably the site recorded by Theophilus Jones in 1809:

> On the road from Llandovery and Llangammarch to Rhayader are seen stones placed irregularly in the ground, which have given a common partly in this parish and partly in Llanafan, the name of Rhos saith maen, or seven stone common; whether they are sepulchral, military or druidical remains is not known.[1]

This is a monument of eight stones, not seven as implied by the name. The row is 7.5 m long, along an E.–W. bearing (096 degrees Mag. [1991]), comprising small stones, six appearing to lie on the line, the remaining two slightly off it. From W. to E.

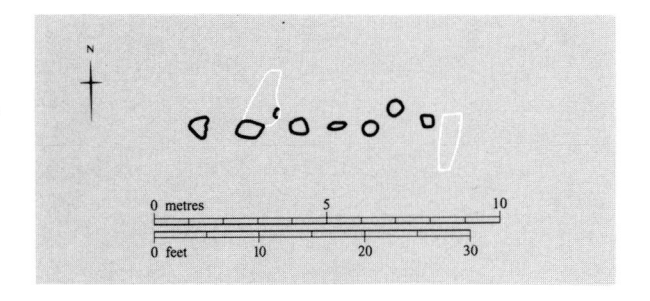

101 Saith Maen (Llanwrthwl), stone row (SC 6): plan

102 Saith Maen (Llanwrthwl), stone row (SC 6) looking east

nos. 2 and 4 are the largest; 2, 0.61 m wide and 0.51 m high; 4, 0.38 m wide and 0.46 m high. An uncontrolled excavation was undertaken at the site in 1972, and the trench has been left open to the E.[2] The site appears to have changed little since planned by Grimes in 1934.[3]

[1] Jones, *Hist. Brecks.* II, i (1809), p. 235; the statement is repeated by Lewis, *Top. Dict., s.v.* Llanwrthwl.

[2] James, 1970, plan Fig. 3a, Photo Pl. 1; 1978-9, p. 21, 11/1.
[3] Plans in Grimes MSS, N.M.R.

S.A.M. B 65

Llanfihangel Brynpabuan
SN 96 S.W. (9492 6030)   ii 91

(SC 7; Fig. 103) In open moorland on a slight E.–W. spur of Banc y Celyn, about 1 km W.N.W. of Blaen Firnant, at a height of 454.5 m above O.D., lies a circle of 24 stones, some 18.5 m E.–W. by 15 m N.–S. Of this number, some nineteen lie roughly upon the circle diameter. Of the remaining 5, 3 stones are lying flat, two of them outside the circle, a large one (2 m by 1.3 m) over 2 m to the N.W., a smaller one less than half this size S. by E. of the diameter. The third flat stone (2.2 m by 1.2 m) is now placed within a sort of entrance formed by the emplacement of the outstanding two uprights which lie at right angle to the circle's diameter. The southern half of this entrance area is slightly raised and masked by the addition or retention of extraneous earth or stones covering an area around 2.5 m across, which might indicate the former existence of mound material generally, or at that particular spot.

Although nine of the stones no longer protrude above the vegetation, virtually all are marked by slightly raised tussocks of vegetation. There is a well-eroded hollow, possibly formed by sheep, around the entire base of the largest upright, which lies on the W. and measures about 1.3 m long by 0.2 m thick by 0.62 m high. A nearby cairn is noted elsewhere.

This site, discovered by the late Mrs Carole Earnshaw of nearby Tir Parker, was drawn to the Commission's attention by Mr Mark Walters in July 1993 and surveyed by Mr Nigel Jones, both of the Clwyd-Powys Archaeological Trust, to all of whom the Commission is indebted for assistance and information.[1] Additional observations were subsequently made by Commission staff.

[1] See N. Jones in *Arch. in Wales* 33 (1993), p. 45.

S.A.M. 206

Gwenddwr
SO 04 N.W./N.E. (0500 4635)   18 xi 93

(SC 8) On a local summit N. of Pant Serthfa, some 485 m above O.D., lies a stone row consisting of four uprights spaced out 6.3 m and aligned almost due N.–S. and varying in height from 0.4 to 0.8 m.

The most northerly stone is a recumbent limestone slab, 1.3 m square and 0.45 m thick; to the S. the next stone, partly turf-covered, is also of limestone, 1.5 m N.–S. by 0.5 m high and 0.25 m thick. The remaining two are gently-tapered round-topped sandstone monoliths. These are 0.55 m square by 0.75 m high and leaning to the S.W., and 0.45 m square and 0.8 m high, fallen to the S.

O.S. Card SO 11 NW 16.

Llangynidr
SN 11 N.W. (1186 1673)   11 xii 91

(SC 9) On the N.-facing slope of Dyffren Crawnen on a slight plateau close to lime-workings 385 m above O.D. is a S.W.–N.E. 6 m long alignment known as Carreg Wen Fawr y Rugos. It comprises five closely-spaced upright stones ranging between 0.5 m and 1 m high. They are surrounded by shallow peat and some appear to be loose in their sockets. The S.W. end seems to terminate in a fallen stone about 2.9 m long, 0.8 m wide. It is aligned N.W.–S.E. and tapers to a point at the S.E. end. About 44 m to the N.E. of the

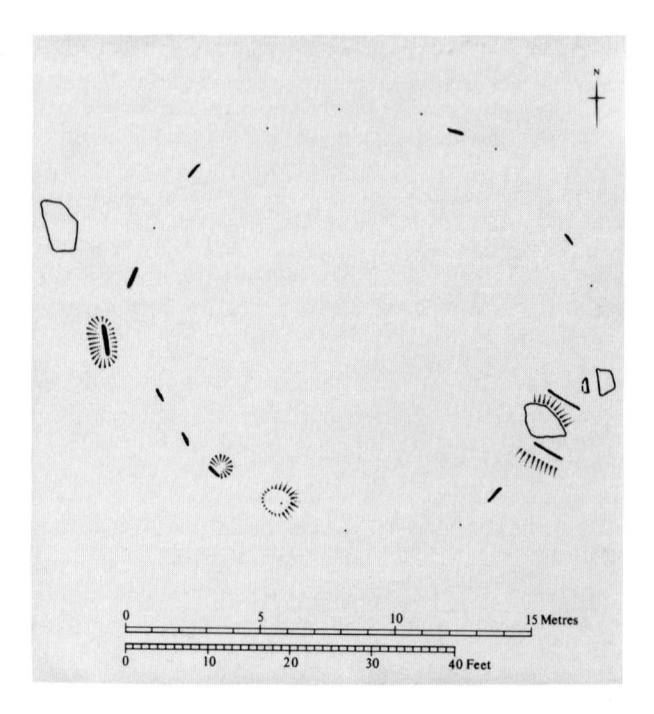

103 Banc y Celyn stone circle (SC 7): plan after Clwyd-Powys Archaeological Trust, with additions

104 Blaen Digedi (Hay Bluff), stone circle (SC 10)

row and roughly on the same bearing, is an outlier also set loosely in the peat.

O.S. Card SO 11 NW 33.

Llangynidr
SO 11 N.W. (1325 1758)   22 v 87

(SC 10; Figs. 104–06) Beside the road traversing Hay Bluff on the plateau below Pen y Beacon, overlooking the Digedi Brook Valley at 470 m above O.D., is a circle (also known as Blaenau) only one stone of which is now clearly visible.[1] A car park has been located adjacent to the site, which is separated and partly protected from vehicle erosion by large stones deposited between car park and circle. These new stones initially confuse interpretation of the more fugitive, older features. Changes in site use have resulted from hardcore dumping alongside the car park margin in the recent past. Pitting on the site may possibly be due to the use of metal detectors. Extensive quarrying scars the hillside immediately below the site (on the W.), so the survival of any nearby stone features, loose or ground-set, is quite remarkable.

Antiquaries appear to have been aware that something ancient existed upon this site, and the surviving large upright might be one of those stones referred to by Edward Poole in the nineteenth century. A site styled 'The Ancient King' in local folklore seems to fit the location.[2] During the 1950s, appreciating the stone grouping and more obvious upright to have been man-made, D. P. Webley first recorded a site (at Maes Coch) as a denuded long

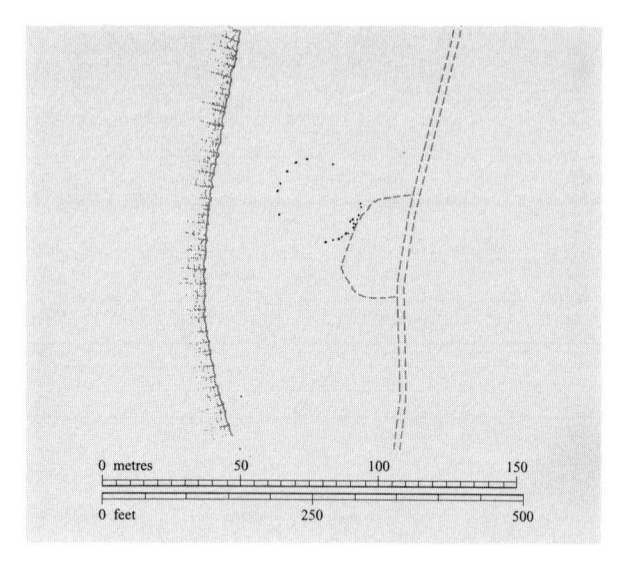

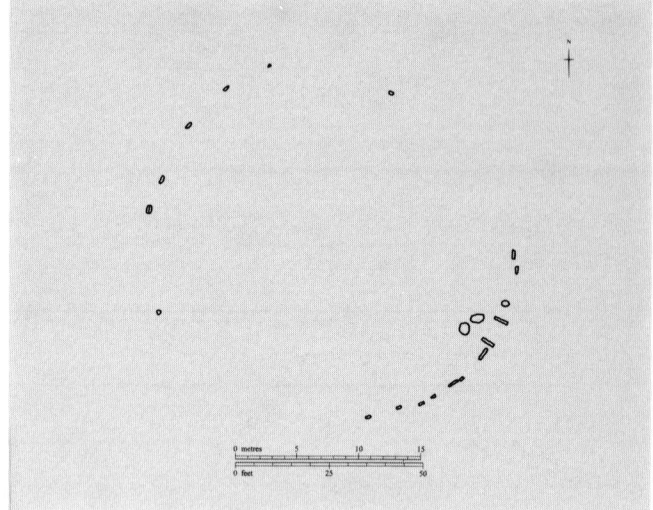

105 Blaen Digedi (Hay Bluff), stone circle (SC 10): location plan

106 Blaen Digedi (Hay Bluff), stone circle (SC 10): plan

barrow.³ Only a later independent record made by D. G. Benson in 1970 properly demonstrated the existence of the circle.⁴

Of seventeen recognisable stones (Fig. 106), the circle is between 29.5 and 30 m in diameter, the slab-like stones set tangentially, excepting two taller examples on the S.E. which lie radially. The latter appear as an unusual, entrance-like feature, somewhat like that on the circle at Banc y Celyn, where its significance is also unclear. Rock is exposed internally, immediately behind the more southerly of these radials, and just over 1 m to the N. there appears to be a fallen, amorphously-shaped upright. Orthostats survive mainly in the S.E. and N.W. sectors, the closest spacing being less than a metre on the S.E. The nearby car park neatly avoids this ancient feature.⁵

¹ O.S. Card SO 23 NW 9; A.P., R.C.A.M. 87 MB 217.
² E. Poole, *Hist. Brecks.* (1886), pp. 215–16.
³ D. P. Webley, 'An unrecorded chambered long-cairn in Breconshire', *B.B.C.S.* 17 (1956–8), pp. 54–5.
⁴ D. G. Benson, survey *in. lit.* to R.C.A.M.; C. H. Houlder, *Arch. in Wales* 13 (1973), p. 62.
⁵ *Pace* Barnatt, *Stone Circles*, p. 389, no. 13:39.5.

S.A.M. B 167 (descheduled)

Llanigon
SO 23 N.W. (2395 3735)   iii 91

Lost or Rejected Stone Circles and Stone Rows (RSC 1–8)

(RSC 1) In an area full of many industrial remains, of opencasts and derelict buildings, at a height of about 274 m above O.D. at Dorwen on the E. side of Cwmtwrch adjacent to a spring draining into a nearby bog, lies a roughly circular feature comprising about thirty small stones protruding above the peat. These are set in a rough circle around a monolith, slightly N. of centre and some 1.21 m high. Most stones are of Millstone Grit, though some are Old Red Sandstone. Although in plan there are arcs suggestive of a stone circle, it seems unlikely that this is a prehistoric ritual monument, and the present form of the stones may be largely fortuitous.

This account is based on a survey and report of 5 June 1985, undertaken by Mr M. Davies and Mr J.

Rowlands, to whom the Commission is indebted for this information.

Ystradgynlais/Ystradgynlais Isaf

SN 71 S.E. (773 142)

(RSC 2) Saith Maen Penwyllt (see also RSS 22) 81 N.E. (8608 1458)

(RSC 3) A stone circle in fair state of preservation was reported 'beyond the church of Llanwrtyd' (D. E. Owen, *Trans. Radnors. Soc.* 18 (1948), p. 7). but in spite of extensive local inquiries, this has not been re-located. It is possible that afforestation now covers the place where the Rev. D. E. Owen saw this feature prior to 1922 (the date of his death; O.S. Card SN 84 NE 13, 29 vii 80).

Llanwrtyd
SN 84 N.E. (8636 4779)

(RSC 4) In Bwlch y Ddau Faen, 525 m above O.D., are set four low partly-buried upright stone slabs which seem to lie on a circle 29.3 m in diameter. The circle is only conjectural, however, since its entire southern half is missing; not all the stones can be made to fit, indeed any three would always lie on its diameter whilst the fourth remained outside or inside. The largest stone lies on the N.N.E. and comprises a slab 1 m wide by 0.18 m thick and 0.9 m high. Those to its W. are smaller, being 0.43 m, 0.6 m and 0.4 m in height respectively E.–W. It remains possible that these stones mark a cattle route through the mountains.

O.S. Card SN 85 NE 9.

Llanwrthwl
SN 85 N.E. (8942 5830)   29 ix 72

(RSC 5) At Blaen Nedd Uchaf is a circle of 51 stones thought to be prehistoric. (L. A. Wilson *in. lit.* to R.C.A.M., 25 x 82). This appears to be entirely natural.

Ystradfellte
SN 91 N.W. (9082 1535)

(RSC 6) On the northern end of Ton Teg, 455 m above O.D., are two upright stones marked on the O.S. maps as Bedd Llywarch. Lying 3.28 m apart, the more easterly leans to the S.W. and is 0.18 m by 0.15 m and 0.64 m high. The other stone is 0.15 m by 0.10 m and 0.31 m high. It is kept upright by small packing stones. They are so small as to have been almost invisible from any distance and are reputed to mark the grave of a farmer whose life had been spent wrangling with a neighbour over the limits of their respective lands. He was buried here, on the spot where he asserted the boundary to be, so that he could watch over it in death as in life. Rather than a prehistoric stone row, this site is a local traditional landmark.

O.S. 6-inch 1964. O.S. Card SN 91 2.

Ystradfellte
SN 91 N.E. (9626 1604)   24 iv 74

(RSC 7) In the antiquarian literature, associated with the megalithic tomb Ty Illtud (CT 1) is the notion of a stone circle which, according to H. T. Payne, had been 'recently carted away', possibly in the 1780s.[1] It is unclear precisely what originally occupied this site,[2] and the circle alluded to may have been the revetting slabs of the megalithic tomb.

[1] N.L.W., MS 4278, fol. 353.
[2] E. Gibson, *Britannia*, (1st ed.) (1695), col. 594.

Llanhamlach
SO 02 N.E. (09 26)

(RSC 8) According to Theophilus Jones (see p. 143 above), at the turn of the nineteenth century there were stone circles on Gader (which presumably means Gader Fawr).

This area has been searched thoroughly, but no circles are now in evidence.

O.S. Card SO 22 NW 2.

Llanbedr Ystrad Yw/Llaneleu
SO 22 N.W. (22 28)

Standing Stones

Introduction

Forty-nine stones known to the Commission for which claims of antiquity have at some time been made are listed below. These include eight examples which are now lost. This overall total usefully compares with the 48 presented in a recent study of standing stones in the county,[1] the differences in the particular sites included emphasising difficulties of ascribing antiquity to unexcavated upright stones. Although a further seventy-five sites are listed, these are rejected on the grounds either that they appear to be natural, or are recently placed. This latter list also includes fieldnames and nineteenth-century parish boundary markers.

As a group, standing stones are among the most enigmatic monuments to classify with any certainty, since it is rarely possible to distinguish with confidence between natural stones (some of which were left upright in the boulder clay by retreating ice), and stones intentionally placed in similar positions by man. Clearer distinction as to function or date among humanly set uprights is equally problematical because, whereas some were certainly erected in antiquity with a ritual, burial, or other, unknown, intention, many are known to have acted as waymarkers or boundary stones in recent, historic times. Only excavation can assist clarification of these problems and even then, the outcome may remain unclear.

Only one Brecknockshire standing stone – Maen Madoc – has been excavated.[2] As a Dark Age inscribed stone this does not offer a particularly good starting point for a discussion of earlier stones. The three most salient facts about it are: first, excavation did not establish the original date of its erection with any degree of certainty; second, the stone's historic siting was probably intended to mark the way through an upland pass along a Roman route; and, third, the stone may have been re-erected at least twice during historic times within the same basic locality, and though the penultimate re-erection was almost certainly in the nineteenth century, there is no written record of this. Rehearsal of these conclusions is felt pertinent despite the stone's inscription, since the difficulties of investigating this stone underline more general problems in interpretation.

Through presentation of site case histories, an effort is made below to evaluate the original status of both included and omitted monuments. Where known, antiquarian record is provided in order to document lost sites and to better appreciate developing attitudes to those stones which have survived.

Standing Stones: Early Accounts

The first accounts of Brecknockshire standing stones come from correspondents of Edward Lhuyd. One was situated in Cwm Irfon (SS 6). Another is possibly SS 34, near Llangoed in the Wye Valley. Later, eighteenth-century sources for stones include Emmanuel Bowen's *Map of South Wales* (Maen Llia SS 12) and John Strange's various tours, in which Cwm Irfon sites were again noted.

Theophilus Jones later mentioned these in his *County History* (albeit in a different form), whilst adding several more: Dol y Felin Dolmaen (SS 20), the Gileston Farm stone (SS 31), a stone near Llandefalle (possibly RSS 10), the Cwrt y Gollen stone (SS 36) and Maen Llwyd on Pen y Gader Fawr (SS 41). Fuller detail is given of these and others by Archdeacon Henry Thomas Payne. Payne's reference to the Waun Llech (SS 27) is of particular interest due to a combination of two factors, both probably adventitious: its status as a parish boundary stone and its location within early field clearances, cairns and walls.

Meini Hirion ('tall columnar stones') are noted by Payne from beneath the valley peat at Dan y Graig. These appear not to have survived and may have been early field boundaries (LS 9) rather than lost ritual alignments.

Around the same period in antiquarian history, two upright stones were located near Llangenny. One 'rough unhewn' example was 8 ft 7 ins long by 1 ft 7 ins wide 'with a rude inscription, rather deeply scratched on the surface, with some pointed instrument, than the work of a chisel and ... [was] in the midst of rubbish, under a hedge'. It is unclear as to which site this alludes. The other stone could be seen 'from the High Road leading from Abergavenny to Crickhowell, standing in a meadow on the Right hand nr. Cwrt y Gollen' (SS 36).

Although both Carlisle's and Lewis's *Topographical Dictionaries* are to a greater degree derivative from contemporary County Histories, Carlisle additionally noted an otherwise unknown, now lost stone, from Maesmynys (LSS 4). Hill sketches for the first Ordnance Survey maps undertaken between 1818 and 1821 depicted stones on Drum Nant y Gorlan (SS 8) and Pen Maen Wern (SS 10).

Prehistoric Standing Stones

Excavation has demonstrated the prehistoric origins of a few standing stones, though (Maen Madoc apart) none has been scientifically examined in the county. Elsewhere in Wales, at the Devil's Quoit, Stackpole, Pembrokeshire, for example, a stone comparable in size to those at Llwyn y Fedwen, Penmyarth and Cwrt y Gollen (2–3 m high) was found to be central to successive Bronze Age ritual and habitation features, its base surrounded by a heel-shaped floor of edge-set upright stones.[3] Excavations at other sites in Dyfed suggest the existence of two basic standing stone types. The first type comprises large examples which appear to have been central to some form of ritual or perhaps burial activities. Examples of these include Kilpaison Burrows, Rhoscrowther, Rhos y Clegryn, St. Nicholas, and the Longstone, St. Ishmaels as well as the Devil's Quoit.[4] A second, smaller variety, seem to occur most frequently in relation to other burial and ritual monuments. They are often found in multiples and protrude only slightly above the soil. Excavation shows some at least to have been erected to mark the sites of burial pits. Examples of this type are known, for example, at Aber Camddwr, Ceredigion.[5] Stones of this sort seem to have existed at Twyn y Beddau (RC 311), with precisely the same function, and it is likely that small stones noted close to a number of cairns and circles in Brecknockshire served the same purpose.

Besides demonstrating ritual or sepulchral functions for early standing stones, a number of other interpretations have been advanced. These range from waymarkers on ancient trackways to cattle rubbing posts.[6] Some uses are attested within living memory at some local sites; like the Maen Madoc, a number have clearly been placed in prominent places to assist safe movement over the moorlands. In this regard, the age of the Maen Mawr, Cerrig Duon (SS 3), and the question of its contemporaneity with the stone circle (SC 3) are points worthy of further investigation. In a comprehensive discussion of their potential uses, Williams has suggested that some Dark Age orthostats may have borne lost painted inscriptions or patterns.[7] All things considered, it is not possible at present to be certain that any Brecknockshire standing stones were actually erected during later prehistoric times.

Historic Uses

Upright Stones as Monastic Boundaries

In 1979 D. J. James advanced the possibility that a prehistoric standing stone alignment had existed in the vicinity of Bwlch,[8] and in subsequent discussion by G. J. Morgan,[9] attention was pertinently drawn to a MS documenting the tithe claims of Brecon monks over local rectorial rights of Llanfihangel Cwm Du in 1234.[10] The transcript explicitly alludes to 'a stone' which stood near the junction (*furcus*) of a 'great road (or) way', (*via magna*).

The question of relocating this medieval boundary stone becomes more crucial when it is appreciated that three, perhaps four, upright stones are now known, or have been known, in the area, which might have a bearing on this documented territorial boundary. Taking the text at its most literal, and assuming that 'near the fork or junction' means close to it, Morgan proposed the Llygadwy stone (RSS 44; RECM 3) as the lost monastic marker. It lies within the bounds of the historic titheland, to the N. of the Llangynidr junction. However, Morgan made several observations which cast doubt upon the antiquity of this stone's siting,[11] though curiously this, together with a similar stone at Heol Ddu, was, nevertheless, considered likely to be prehistoric.

Neither Theophilus Jones nor G. J. Morgan considered the possibility that in 1234 the *via magna* (which Jones first equated with the 'Brecon road') may not actually refer to the present road from Pont y Bryn Hurt to Bwlch, but instead to the earlier, abandoned route through the Usk Valley, which crossed the Usk at Coed yr Ynys (Llangynidr) and met one of three or four different junctions immediately south of Bwlch. A re-examination of historic changes in these routes might well accommodate the Llwyn y Fedwen stone (SS 32) within a 'fork' adjacent to that road, though still within the described titheland bounds. This upright seems more reasonably to correlate with the *lapide* of the 1234 deed, since, unlike the alternative examples advanced by Morgan, Llwyn y Fedwen has been a stone of note to topographical writers since the eighteenth century. But even this identification leaves the almost insoluble problem posed by Jones's statement that the stone had already been 'thrown down' when he wrote in 1809,[12] since Payne had spoken of it as being upstanding in the 1780s.[13]

Theophilus Jones understood the tithe apportionment to include all land encompassed by the Ewyn Brook on the north (from its junction with the Rhiangoll), 'up to Bwlch, south by east to the Usk, including the narrow slang between Miarth and Usk, and then following the course of Rhiangoll upwards till it receives the rivulet of Ewyn'. This being the case, the presence of two further standing stones just within the southern boundary of the tithelands (SS 28 and 29), and another one 600 m due north of the Rhiangoll-Ewyn junction (SS 33) (a junction which could have formerly occupied a site much closer to the stone SS 32, is noteworthy.

This cursory investigation of early landholding strongly hints at a medieval boundary function for the Llwyn y Fedwen stone and suggests the possibility that other local uprights might similarly have had territorial functions to define the monastic lands around Tretower. There is no proof that any of these markers were erected by the monks, yet neither is there certainty of their existence before medieval times.

Parish Boundaries

Standing stones and cairns may remain the only tangible records of early ecclesiastical parish boundaries. In a perambulation of the bounds of Llangattock parish of around 1780, H. T. Payne noted the deliberate digging of crosses, the erection of cairns and, in one case, the preservation of an earlier standing stone to accentuate territorial reference points. The stone in question was Waun Llech (SS 27) which took

> its name from its situation in a stony soil. It is rude and of considerable size, much resembling those Druidical Monuments called Meini Hirion. It is more commonly known among the natives by the Name of Maen Garchast, or Maen Ymerchert, the first word signifying excellence, a great action, or exploit; the latter alluding, as some have imagined, to ancient Battle, found near the spot . . . there are likewise other traditional accounts relating to it.[14]

Payne himself believed Waun Llech to have been of recent, historic erection, symbolising the spot of some boundary limitation dispute between the adjoining parishes. Given the position of an ancient boulder wall following this parish boundary some distance to its south (US 106 iii–iv), caution is obviously due in dating these apparently associated moorland features.

Clear evidence for the importance of diverse larger stones as parish boundary markers is detailed in a colourful nineteenth-century perambulation of Bettws Penpont in 1884. In it, children were exhorted to remember 'some old stones marking the boundary, and a very antient oak'.[15]

Other Historic Uses

The presence of large stones on medieval or Renaissance estates like Gileston (SS 31) and Peterstone (SS 24) suggests the possibility that they may have been nuclear to an important contemporary symbolic or social function. This would perhaps be comparable to the stone lying in the centre of Llanbadarn Fawr, Ceredigion, which until this century remained a focal point for the reading of notices by an individual nominated as the lord of the manor's crier.[16]

The Sitings of the Stones

Great interest has attached to analysing the positions of standing stones, particularly in view of popular media interests in 'earth magic' and 'ley-lines'.[17] The study has been put on a more scientific footing through analyses such as that of Bird in Cardiganshire, who felt the stones marked early routes through mountain passes;[18] Wilson, who demonstrated that the stones of Anglesey seemed to occupy random positions and were of any lithology that came to hand;[19] and more pertinently, Roese, whose analysis of the larger Brecknockshire stones (those over 1.6 m high and 1.2 m wide) demonstrated that the entire sample lay in the proximity of water courses – on floodplains, valley footslopes, or in passes. Apparently, the longer sides of those stones with rectangular sections were always aligned at right angles to the water courses.[20] Whilst it is difficult to find any rational explanation for these remarkable data or to accept such features as entirely deliberate, the definition of a water course seems in this case sufficiently vague to encompass a very broad spectrum of topographical settings.

Topographical site analysis is currently limited by the parameters already discussed. Historical records of lost sites are presented below. These suggest that the surviving sample is so partial, and definitions of what actually constitutes a standing stone still so uncertain, that locational analysis is of limited value.

[1] James, (1978–9), pp. 9–30.

[2] C. Fox, *Arch. Camb.* 97 (1942), pp. 210–16.

[3] D. G. Benson, J. G. Evans and G. H. Williams, *P.P.S.* 56 (1990), pp. 179–246.

[4] G. H. Williams, *Standing Stones in S. W. Wales*, (Oxford: B.A.R. 188, 1988). This work contains much valuable information for discussion, but omits the dimensions of most stones in the gazetteer.

[5] E. C. Marshall and K. Murphy, 'The Excavation of two Bronze Age Cairns with Associated Standing Stones in Dyfed: Parc Maen and Aber Camddwr II', *Arch. Camb.* 140 (1991), pp. 28–75.

[6] Summarised by Williams, *op. cit.* n. 4, pp. 14–15.

[7] *ibid.*

[8] *loc. cit.* n.1.

[9] G. J. Morgan, *Brycheiniog* 20 (1982–3), pp. 41–7.

[10] The Latin deed is transcribed and translated in Jones, *Hist. Brecks.* II, ii (1809), p. 501.

[11] Morgan, *op. cit.* n. 9, pp. 43–5.

[12] See n. 10.

[13] Payne NLW MSS 4278C fo. 207. Llwynfedwen.

[14] *idem.* fo. 33 Waun Llech.

[15] Poole, *Hist. Brecks.*, pp. 261–2; account taken from *The Brecon County Times* describing the event of Tuesday, May 20th 1884. The degree to which meer-stones and cairns formed integral components of parish boundaries is illustrated in the account of bound-beating in early nineteenth-century Merthyr (presumably Vaynor Parish), C. Wilkins, *The History of Merthyr Tydfil*, (Merthyr: Express Office, 1867), p. 137.

[16] The stones are mentioned by T. O. Morgan in *Aberystwyth Guide* (2nd ed., 1851), p. 79.

[17] For example, C. Barber and J. G. Williams, *The Ancient Stones of Wales*, (Abergavenny: Blorenge Books, 1989). Sadly, the interpretations of standing stone distributions and function here are quite without reasonable foundation; furthermore those details listing positions and histories of monuments are extremely inaccurate, thereby rendering the survey of limited value for serious research.

[18] A. J. Bird, *Ceredigion* 11 (1972), pp. 40–5.

[19] J. W. Wilson, *B.B.C.S.* 30 (1983), pp. 363–89.

[20] H. E. Roese, *B.B.C.S.* 28 (1978), pp. 129–35, espec. pp. 133–4; see also H. E. Roese, *B.B.C.S.* 28 (1980), pp. 645–55.

Standing Stones; the sites (SS 1–41)

This list is divided into three sections: the first includes surviving stones believed to be ancient (SS 1–41); the second, of lost sites, comprises lost or destroyed stones which may have been of some antiquity (LSS 1–8), or which were noted by antiquaries; and the third group comprises boundary stones, field names and others, some of which are probably natural, or which are known to have been erected in recent historic times (RSS 1–87).

(SS 1; Fig. 107) There is a massive erect boulder some 343 m above O.D., 230 m S. by E. of Troed Rhiw Wen. The monolith, of Old Red Sandstone, is rectangular in plan, 1.3 m long from E. to W. by 0.94 m wide, rising to a flat head at a height of 1.67 m. The base is surrounded by a platform of stones forming a cairn 3 m in diameter, probably from field clearance.

A similar stone is recumbent at the W. end of the terrace, possibly having been at one time erect. This is 0.81 m wide, 0.4 m thick and 1.7 m long.

O.S. Card SN 82 NW; James 1970, Pl. 34a–b; 1978–9, p. 27, no. 11/40; Roese, *Thesis*, no. 42.

Llywel (E), Traean-glas (C)
SN 82 N.W. (8360 2567)   9 iv 76

(SS 2) About 150 m W. of the Dwr Llwydan at a height of 335 m above O.D., about 500 m S.W. of Gwern Wyddog is a large lozenge-shaped limestone conglomerate monolith. It is 1.2 m by 1.4 m thick at the base and stands 2.3 m high.

O.S. Card SN 82 NW 4; James 1970, Pl. 23a–b; 1978–9, p. 26, no. 11/27.

Llywel (E), Traean-glas (C)
SN 82 N.W. (8333 2835)   4 vii 68

(SS 3) Maen Mawr (described under Cerrig Duon SC 3ii).
SN 82 S.E. (8512 2062)

(SS 4; figs. 108–09) On the W. slope of Waen Lleuci, 450 m above O.D., standing upon a platform 10 m in diameter, is an upright of badly weathered Old Red Sandstone, 1.95 m in height, 1.55 m in width, and at present 0.25 m thick.

O.S. Card SN 82 SE 4; Probably the stone illustrated in Llew Morgan's photograph in *Cerddi'r Mynydd Du*, W. Griffiths, (ed.), (Brecon: *Brecon and Radnor Express*, 1913), opp. p. 50; James 1970, Pl. 24a–b; 1978–9, p. 26, no. 11/28; Kay MSS Notebook X, iii, 928 (RCAM); Roese, *Thesis*, no. 51; Savory, *Prehist. Brecks.*, II, p. 32.

Llywel (E), Traean-glas (C)
SN 82 S.E. (8546 2150)   18 i 89

(SS 5) There is a recumbent stone on Trecastle Mountain SN 83 S.E. (8339 3107) (see SC 4).

(SS 6) In Cwm Irfon, 243 m above O.D. incorporated into a hedgebank is an upright monolith of shaly rock, rhomboidal in plan, 1.2 m along the N. hedge side, 1.2 m along the S. side and joined by sides of 1 m through the hedge. It stands 1.35 m above the top of the bank, though its total height above field level is 2.0–2.1 m. There is another smaller upright in the bank 2.3 m to the N.W. This is 0.7 by 0.7 m in plan and stands 0.7 m above the top of the bank.

It is possible that the former is that 'large rude stone by Nant y Walch but unaccountable only sd to be set up in ye time of ye giants', referred to by Edward Lhuyd.[1] There is a further, eighteenth-century reference by the traveller John Strange, to 'two very large stones . . . in . . . [the] vale of Ithon [Irfon] . . . [seen on his] road from Brecknock by Llanvihangle Abergwassin into Cardiganshire . . . [which are] eight or nine feet high and about four feet wide, of an irregular form, standing nearly a furlong distant from each other in some low grounds, a mile South East of Llanworthid [Llanwrtyd] wells'.[2] It is understandable how later, an anonymous correspondent to the Cambrian Archaeological Association lamented that,

107 Troed Rhiw Wen standing stone (SS 1)

although several stones had formerly stood in this parish, most were prostrate by 1854.[3]

[1] *Parochialia* III, (1911), p. 50 (from Bod. Lib. (ex-Ashmolean) MS 1820a, fol. 135).
[2] J. Strange, 'An account of some remains of Roman and other antiquities in and near the county of Brecknock in south Wales', *Archaeologia* 1 (1787), pp. 292–304; 4 (1804), pp. 1–26.
[3] Article signed 'K', *Arch. Camb.* 5 (1854), pp. 64–5; Grooms, *Giants*, p. 99.

Llanwrtyd (E), Llanwrtyd Without (C)
SN 84 N.E. (8585 4984)   27 vi 91

(SS 7) On the S. side of the main Builth–Llandovery road opposite the Cambrian Factory at Llanwrtyd above Nant Cerdin about 230 m above O.D. stands a large rectangular monolith. It measures 0.96 m by 0.76 m at the base and stands 2.41 m high with a rounded head. Two or three round hollows in the face of the stone are probably of natural origin. It is difficult to ascertain how much of the stone thrown around the base was for packing, and how much derives from field clearance, but there nevertheless appears a slight circular basal mound about 5.5 m in diameter.

108   Waen Lleuci (SS 4)

O.S. Card SN 84 NE 1; depicted on O.S. 6-inch maps since 1904; James, 1978–9, p. 24, no. 11/15; Lloyd MSS; M. Owen, *The Story of Breconshire*, (1911), p. 27; 'K' *loc. cit.* (SS 6 above), p. 65.

S.A.M. B 132

Llanwrtyd
SN 84 N.E. (8849 4744)   14 xi 72

(SS 8) On Drum Nant y Gorlan, 550 m above O.D., is a fallen monolith of white quartz, roughly rectangular in section 0.8 m by 0.8 m and 2.7 m in length. It appears to have fallen to the S.W. and its base on the E. remains partly buried. It tops a ridge on a S.W.-projecting moorland spur. From cartographic study it has been proposed[1] that a cairn originally stood nearby. However, the earliest available source shows a quartz block here[2] and the first published O.S. map depicts an enigmatic uninscribed circle.[3]

Lying on the S.E. edge of the same spur, some 24 m to the S.S.W. of the stone, is an oval, turf-covered mound. Its diameter is 13.8 m (N.E.–S.W.) by 9.5 m by up to 1 m high. Stone projecting from beneath it on the S.E., might indicate the existence of a kerb if the site is man-made.

Plate 1. Saith Maen, Craig y Nos, stone alignment (SC 1)

Plate 2. Waun Fignen Felen peat Basin and Mesolithic Site (MS 2) (Aerial Photograph courtesy of Clwyd-Powys Archaeological Trust)

Plate 4. Standing stone, Carreg Waum-Llech (SS 27)

Plate 3. Standing stone, Battle (SS 25)

Plate 6. Llangoed Castle (SS 34)

Plate 5. Cwrt y Gollen (SS 36)

Plate 7. Trefil Area: wall (US 105) running over limestone solution features to Carn Caws with several enclosures

Plate 8. Cefn Sychpant Cairn (RC 123)

109 Waen Lleuci (SS 4) showing stone edgewise

110 Waun Lydan (SS 11)

[1] O.S. Card SN 85 NW 3; W. E. Griffiths, *Arch. in Wales* 12 (1972), p. 10.
[2] O.S. 2-inch MS drawing 310 W (1820–21).
[3] O.S. First edn. 1-inch (1835).

Llanfihangel Abergwesyn
SN 85 N.W. (8343 5960)   10 xii 91

(SS 9) Carreg Wen Fawr, 526 m above O.D., is a recumbent and partly buried block of quartz crowning the summit of a hill. It is 1.4 m long, 1.14 m wide and 0.5 m thick and has probably fallen to the N. Two small quartz slabs, partly buried under the N. end, may be packing stones or broken pieces from the main stone. Only 1 m to the E. is another recumbent quartz pillar 1.37 m long by 0.55 m wide and 0.25 m thick, probably also fallen, so there may originally have been two uprights.

O.S. Card SN 86 SW 3.

Llanwrthwl/Llanddewi Abergwesyn
SN 86 S.W. (8210 6247)   2 vi 76

(SS 10) On the summit of Pen Maen Wern, 544 m above O.D., is a quartz standing stone 1.6 m high, 1.4 m. long (E.–W.) by 0.8 m thick at the base. It leans slightly to the S. and sheep have exposed packing stones around the base.

O.S. 2-inch MS drawing 310 E (1820–21).

Llanwrthwl
SN 86 S.E. (8644 6201)   19 ix 91

(SS 11; Fig. 110) On the N. part of Waun Lydan, 500 m above O.D. on a local summit, is a standing stone 1.5 m high and 1.1 m (N.–S.) by 0.8 m at the base. It is of quartz-veined rock with sandstone packing stones visible around the base where eroded from above the peat by sheep.

O.S. 2-inch MS drawing 310 E (1820–21).

Llanwrthwl
SN 86 S.E. (8813 6136)   92

Maen Madoc
SN 91 N.W. (9183 1577). See ECM 8.

111 Maen Llia (SS 12)

(SS 12; Fig. 111) In the upper reaches and close to the source of the Afon Llia stands Maen Llia, 430 m above O.D. at the head of the pass between Fan Llia and Fan Nedd. It is of sandstone conglomerate trapezoidally shaped 3.61 m high, 2.75 m in breadth and 0.76 m thick and is bedded in the centre of an oval depression 6.1 m N.–S. by 5.2 m and 0.6 m deep.[1]

Faint traces of inscriptions in the lower right-hand quarter of the stone's W. face, first noticed by Macalister in 1922, were elaborated upon in 1945 with the suggested reading ROVEVI / S....SOVI in Roman characters and VASSO (G?) in Ogam.[2]

[1] (General references): O.S. Card SN 91 NW 3; E. Bowen, *A New and Accurate Map of South Wales*, (1792), 'Blaen Llia, a stone for direction'; James 1970, Pls. 7a–b; 1978–9, p. 23, no. 11/7; Jones, *Hist. Breck.* II, ii, (1809), p. 685; *ibid.* (Glanusk edn.) IV (1930), p. 118; W.E. Griffiths, *Arch. in Wales* 9 (1969), p. 8; Kay MSS fol. 799; Roese, *Thesis*, no. 97; Payne MS notebook, fol. 68.
[2] Macalister, *C.I.I.C.* I, pp. 329–330; Nash-Williams omitted the inscription from *E.C.M.W.*, (1950) for want of certain evidence.

Defynnog (E), Senni (C)
SN 91 N.W. (9242 1918)   15 vi 81

(SS 13) On the W. bank of a small stream in the upper reaches of the Afon y Waun, about 600 m above O.D., is a large quadrangular stone 2.6 m long, 1.8 m wide at its widest, 1.1 m at its narrowest and 0.7 m deep.

O.S. Card SN 91 NE 8.

Ystradfellte
SN 91 N.E. (9722 1848)   Not visited

(SS 14) Lying 305 m above O.D. to the N.E. of Cefn Brynich, Tyle Bychan near the edge of a field on the road from Maescar to Defynnog is a standing stone 0.69 m wide by 0.28 m thick and 1.45 m high. It thins to a blunt point and at a height of 1.16 m contracts to 0.48 m in width to form a shoulder on the E. side of the stone.

O.S. Card SN 92 NW 5; D. P. Webley, *B.B.C.S.* 16 (1954–6), p. 299.

Defynnog (E), Maescar (C)
SN 92 N.W. (9387 2595)   2 vi 75

(SS 15) In a broad saddle E.S.E. of Garreg Fawr (see below, SS 16), about 415 m above O.D., is a pillar of conglomerate sandstone which has fallen to the S. When upright it would have been pointed at the S. end. It measures 4 m in length, 1.5 m wide (E.–W.) and 0.8 m thick. Its upper surface is naturally grooved.

Llanfihangel Nant Brân
SN 93 N.W. (9498 3720)   8 xi 91

(SS 16; Fig. 112) Lying in the centre of a water-filled hollow (6.5 m across by 0.4 m deep), below a local summit, 429 m above O.D., is a large recumbent, conglomerate sandstone monolith, known as Garreg Fawr which appears to have fallen to the N. Lying alongside on the W. are two large fragments probably detached in recent times. The recumbent stone measures 3.76 m (N.–S.), 1.4 m high and 1.8 m across. The larger, adjacent fragment, is 2.4 m long, 1.15 m high and 1 m wide. If re-assembled, the stone would be 2.5 m wide (E.–W.).

Llanfihangel Nant Brân
SN 93 N.W. (9450 3729)   8 xi 91

112 Garreg Fawr (SS 16)

(SS 17; Fig. 113) Maen Richard stands 420 m above O.D. on the parish boundary between Llanfihangel Nant Brân and Merthyr Cynog. It occupies a circular hollow and appears to be of a volcanic agglomerate 1.52 m high, and 0.81 m by 0.45 m at the base. There is a bench mark incised on its N. face.

O.S. Card SN 93 SE 2; James 1971, Pls. 14a–b; 1978–9, p. 25, no. 11/26; Lloyd MSS.

Llanfihangel Nant Brân/Merthyr Cynog
SN 93 S.E. (9675 3468)   8 xi 72

(SS 18) On Pen y Gorllwyn, 585 m above O.D. and 37 m from the stone-built cairn (RC 156), is a recumbent monolith with a blunted end, of rectangular section 0.9 m by 0.75 m and 3.53 m long. It has fallen to the W. and has a basal hollow with packing stones on the E. end 1.2 m across.

Llanafan Fawr
SN 95 N.W. (9160 5878)   29 ix 72

(SS 19) At Y Garth, 290 m above O.D., is a volcanic monolith about 1.83 m high and 1.35 m by 0.61 m at the base. In line to the W. lie the tips of two further pieces of it, detached at some time in antiquity and now lying beneath the grass. The first is 1.8 m from the monolith and measures 0.86 m by 0.74 m by 0.3 m high. The second lies 2.1 m further on and measures 0.69 m by 0.5 m by 0.13 m high. The original stone would have stood about 2.8–3.0 m high overall.

O.S. Card SN 95 NW 7; James 1971, Pls. 20a–b; 1978–9, p. 25, no. 11/23.

S.A.M. B 90

Llanafan Fawr
SN 95 N.W. (9486 5584)   18 x 72

(SS 20; Fig. 114) At Llanafan Fawr, 185 m above O.D., Dol y Felin Dolmaen is a stone 2.16 m high, of quadrilateral section 1.27 m (N. face) by 1.3 m (E. face) by 0.61 m (S. face) by 1.52 m (W. face). It leans slightly and rises to a blunt point. This traditionally marks the site of St. Afan's murder in the sixth century. According to one source there was formerly an incised cross in a circle on one face.

O.S. Card SN 95 NE 5; Jones, *Hist. Brecks.* II, i (1809), p. 239; Glanusk, (1911), p. 226; *Arch. Camb.* 66 (1911), p. 127; James 1971, Pls. 21a–b; 1978–9, p. 25, no. 11/24.

S.A.M. B 91

Llanafan Fawr
SN 95 N.E. (9766 5503)   14 xi 72

(SS 21) At Tre-Felin, 190 m above O.D., is an upright conglomerate or breccia stone 4.9 m in diameter and 0.6 m high. It is rectangular at the base 1.52 m by 0.96 m.

O.S. Card SN 95 NE 9; James 1971, Pls. 21a–b; 1978–9, p. 25, no. 11/25.

Llanfihangel Brynpabuan
SN 95 N.E. (9900 5698)   14 xi 72

(SS 22) Beside the S. door of Llanwrthwl Church, 180 m above O.D., is a standing stone 1.83 m high, 1.27 m by 1.16 m by 0.74 m at the base.

O.S. Card SN 96 SE 1; James 1971, Pls. 30a–b; 1978–9, p. 27, no. 11/36.

Llanwrthwl
SN 96 S.E. (9757 6372)   8 v 78

113 Maen Richard (SS 17)

(SS 23 Fig. 115) At Pencelli in a hedge 230 m W. of Llanfigan Church, about 205 m above O.D., is a pointed sandstone monolith of rectangular section 1.83 m high by 0.71 m by 0.53 m thick. There are two circular cup-marks 5.7 cm in diameter and 2.5 cm deep on the S.E. face, near the E. edge and close to the top of the stone, but these are probably natural.

James 1978–9, p. 28, no. 11/44, gives different measurements.

Llanfigan
SO 02 S.E. (0836 2447)   6 v 74

(SS 24; Fig. 116) A monolith known as Peterstone lies by the roadside at Llanhamlach 135 m above O.D. It is an upright pillar of rectangular section 1.45 m high with a sloping top and appears to have been partly worked; all faces except the N.W. have been partly smoothed and the E. and S. edges are worked to a bevel 0.1 m wide.

O.S. Card SO 02 NE 7; marked on O.S. 25-inch 1887 as Maen Hir; James 1978–9, p. 28, no. 11/16, suggests it may have been Roman or Early Christian but offers no reason.

Llanhamlach
SO 02 N.E. (0894 2675)   6 v 74

(SS 25; Pl. 3) On farmland at Battle, 168 m above O.D., is a blunt-pointed sandstone monolith about 1 m square at the base. It leans slightly to the E. and stands 3.96 m high

114 Dol y Felin Dolmaen (SS 20)

swelling to 1.22 m at the broadest, giving the impression of being top-heavy and sits at the S. end of a stony mound 10 m long N.–S. and 0.9 m high – possibly originally a cairn. The nearby tumulus (at SO 0060 3075, 190 m above O.D.) mentioned by James, is the spoil-heap from an old quarry. Another mound-like feature in the field incorporating fieldstones is probably modern.

O.S. Card SO 03 SW 3; James 1971, Pls. 33a–b; 1978–9, p. 27, no. 11/39; Lewis, *Top. Dict.*, *s.v.* Battle; O.S. 25-inch plan 1887.

S.A.M. B 138

Battle
SO 03 S.W. (0063 3063)   26 iv 76

(SS 26) On farmland S. of Pen-y-Bont at Newbridge 152 m above O.D. is a fine-grained hard, grey stone 1.75 m high from the bottom of the hollow in which it stands, 0.2 m deep by 3.5 m broad. It is 1.2 m E.–W. at the base, by 0.75, and leans to N. about 25°. Its base (1.14 m by 0.76 m) is roughly rectangular and the S. face is featureless. The stone is otherwise irregular in form, with a flat head. Packing stones are visible around the base. It was found when a hedge was removed shortly after the turn of the century.

O.S. Card SO 05 NW 2; *Arch. Camb.* 66 (1911), p. 121; James 1970, Pls. 29a–b.

Llanafan Fawr (E), Llysdinam (C)
SO 05 N.W. (0131 5804)   29 x 91

STANDING STONES: THE SITES 174

115 Pencelli standing stone (SS 23)

116 The Peterstone (SS 24)

(SS 27) Carreg Waun Llech (plate 4) is a large weathered limestone block standing 387 m above O.D. in a marshy hollow on a limestone plateau. It is 2.62 m high, a maximum of 1.27 m broad and 0.4 m thick. Features resembling cup-marks appear on the E. and W. faces, but these are almost certainly due to natural erosion. It leans about 10° to the east but has a general orientation N.E.–S.W.

This stone has probably been a boundary marker between Llangatwg and Llangynidr since medieval times (see p. 164).

O.S. Card SO 11 NE 1; first noted on E. Bowen's map (1729) as 'Croes Sion Kusmon a heap of stones'; James 1970, Pls. 9a–b; 1978–9, p. 23, no. 11/9; Payne MS, N.L.W. MS 4278C fo. 33; Roese, *Thesis*, no. 164.

Llangatwg/Llangynidr
SO 11 N.E. (1638 1738)   19 v 75

(SS 28) At Coed yr Ynys, on the N. side of a hedge on Aberyail Farm, 50 m E. of the Brecon to Newport Canal, 107 m above O.D., is a red sandstone upright 0.9 m high, 0.40 m broad (E.–W.) and 0.35 m thick. It has a pointed top in the N.E. corner. This may have been used as a medieval boundary marker (see above p. 164).

James 1978–9, p. 26, no. 11/23.

Llangynidr
SO 11 N.E. (1586 1995)   30 x 91

(SS 29; Fig. 117) The Fish Stone in Penmyarth Park 91 m above O.D. stands 4.27 m high, 1.22 m broad and 0.41 m thick. The stone's name derives from its profile, like that of an upstanding fish. It is of Old Red Sandstone. This may have been used as a medieval boundary marker (see above p. 164).

O.S. Card SO 11 NE 2; Jones, *Hist. Brecks.* II, ii (1809), p. 502; James 1978–9, p. 24, no. 11/19; *Arch. Camb.* 8 (1853), p. 323; Jones, *Hist. Brecks.* III, (1911), p. 172; Roese, *Thesis*, no. 174;

117   The Fish Stone (SS 29)

according to *The Ancient Stones of Wales*, C. Barber and J. G. Williams, (eds.), (Abergavenny, 1989), p. 165, the stone is 'shown on a plan of a lease dated March, 1825, from William Augustus Gott to Thomas Johnson'. No source is given.

S.A.M. B 133

Llanfihangel Cwm Du
SO 11 N.E. (1828 1985)   26 xi 75

(SS 30) About midway between Cwm Shenkin and Blaen y Cwm Uchaf 425 m above O.D. is a roughly flat-topped stone 0.74 m high, 0.71 m long N.–S. and 0.53 m wide.

P. M. Jones, *Arch. in Wales* 15 (1975), p. 26.

Cathedin
SO 12 N.E. (1579 2540)   22 xi 76

(SS 31; Fig. 118) At Gileston Farm 122 m above O.D. is a large weathered exfoliating erratic boulder 2.97 m high, 2.44 m broad and 1.37 m thick.[1] It is supposed to have given name to Sir Giles Pierrepont's house.[2]

[1] O.S. Card SO 12 SW 9; James 1970, Pls. 11a–b; 1978–9, p. 24, no. 11/12; Roese, *Thesis*, no. 138.
[2] Jones, *Hist. Brecks.* II, ii (1809), p. 593.

S.A.M. B 140

Llanfigan
SO 12 S.W. (1168 2375)   4 xi 75

(SS 32; Fig. 119) At Llwyn y Fedwen 107 m above O.D. is a standing stone of erratic limestone, 4.27 m high 1.42 m broad and 1.01 m thick. Although not apparently erected upon 'a slight mound' (*pace* an O.S. Antiquity Report of 1938), it is sited on a small natural knoll about 60 m long and 4 m high, possibly part of an early river terrace enhanced by ploughing. It leans slightly towards the N. and is among the tallest in Wales. Heaps of small stones seen in 1938 and still present in 1985 probably result from recent field clearance. This is probably the stone used as a marker for tithelands by Brecon monks in the thirteenth century (see above, p. 164).

O.S. Card SO 12 SE 4; O.S. MS Antiquity Report GEL/1, 25 iii 38, (N.M.R.); James 1970, Pls. 17a–b; 1978–9, no. 11/18; Jones, *Hist. Brecks.* II, ii (1809), p. 501; N.L.W. MS 4278, fol. 207 (Payne) 'Mein hir 12 ft high from the ground'; J. Bailey, *Arch. Camb.* 8 (1853), p. 309; Roese, *Thesis*, no. 146; Savory, *Prehist. Brecks I*, (1955), p. 108.

S.A.M. B 112

Llanfihangel Cwm Du
SO 12 S.E. (1562 2038)   1985

for stones at SO 1597 2430 and SO 1601 2433 see RC 283.

(SS 33) About 100 m from the main road leading N.W. from Tretower 135 m above O.D. is a pillar-like standing stone of Old Red Sandstone, standing in a hedgebank. It is 2.25 m high, 1.15 m wide (N.–S.) by 0.85 m (E.–W.) and weathered at the top.

O.S. Card SO 12 SE 6; O.S. MS Antiquity Report GEL/2, 26 iii 38; James 1970, Pl. 12; Roese, *Thesis*, no. 175.

Llanfihangel Cwm Du
SO 12 S.E. (1804 2192)   26 ix 91

(SS 34) About 0.5 km S. of Llangoed Castle (plate 6) is a stone 95 m above O.D. and about 100 m W. of the River Wye.[1] It stands 2.34 m high and is rectangular in section, rising to a sharp point. It is of sandy or gritty

118 Gileston (SS 31)

rock and 0.79 m wide by 0.55 m thick, 2.34 m high, 0.84 m broad and 0.56 m thick. It leans slightly to the W. This is possibly the site referred to by E. Lhuyd during the 1690s.[2]

[1] O.S. Card SO 13 NW 3; James 1978–9, p. 24, no. 11/17.
[2] N.L.W. Peniarth MS 251, fol. 6, 'Y mân pîg a high stone near Llan Gôd' *Parochialia* II, p. 29; see also Jones, *Hist. Brecks.* II, ii (1809), p. 308; Savory, *Prehist. Brecks.* II, (marked on map only).

S.A.M. B 86

Llandefalle
SO 13 N.W. (1229 3958)   13 iii 73

(SS 35) About 200 m S.W. of Burrow Wood, 240 m above O.D., on a ridge, is a large recumbent slab, partly buried, which may have stood upright with its long axis N.–S. but now lying to the W. It is about 3.35 m long, 2.15 m wide and 0.38 m thick.

Talgarth
SO 13 S.W. (1278 3191)   12 xii 73

(SS 36) At the entrance to Cwrt y Gollen Army Training School (plate 5), 67 m above O.D., is a red sandstone monolith 4.15 m high, 1.05 m broad (N.–S.) by 0.7 m, fenced in and set into a bed of ornamental

119 Llwyn y Fedwen (SS 32)

cobbles. There is a crescent-shaped notch 1 m from top of E. edge.

O.S. Card SO 21 NW 11; James 1978–9, p. 23, no. 11/6; A.P., R.A.F. AO/62/145/4; Jones, *Hist. Brecks.* II, ii (1809), p. 470; Jones MS sketchbook (Brecknocks Museum), illus. fol. 33; N.L.W., MS 4278, fol. 160 (H. T. Payne) sketch with dimensions, *ibid.*, fol. 79; *Arch. Camb.* 31 (1876), p. 593; Carlisle, *Top. Dict.*, s.v. Llangeney; Lewis, *Top. Dict.*, s.v. Llangeney; Roese, *Thesis*, no. 197.

S.A.M. B 113

Llangenni
SO 21 N.W. (2125 1686)   29 x 91

(SS 37) Below and to the S.S.W. of Coed Cefn 128 m above O.D. is a large, upright sandstone slab 1.98 m high with a bluntly pointed head, roughly rectangular in section, 1.65 m long by 0.65 m thick. The N.E. face (bearing 299°) is badly fissured vertically and prior to 1921 was inscribed '1844', but this has now weathered away. Traces of an oval surrounding mound which in 1962 measured about 15 m long by 9 m wide, the longer axis aligned N.N.W., are no longer visible. It is impossible to know if the position it now occupies in an angle of the parish boundary is owed to a prehistoric or a medieval origin.

O.S. Card SO 21 NW 4; James 1970, Pls. 18a–b; 1978–9, p. 25, no. 11/20; Roese, *Thesis*, no. 257.

Crickhowell/Llangenni
SO 21 N.W. (2218 1846)   18 v 77

(SS 38–9) In Llangenny, 800 m behind the church on a steeply wooded slope at a height of 143 m above O.D., are two standing stones.
  (SS 38) One is 1.88 m high, 1.98 m broad and 0.53 m thick.
  (SS 39) The other, some 40 m distant S.W., is 0.84 m high, 0.64 m broad and 0.51 m thick.

James 1978–9, p. 28, no. 11/47–8.

Llangenni
SO 21 N.W. (SS 38) (2396 1784);
(SS 39) (2398 1781)   18 v 77

(SS 40) The Druid's Altar stone is of limestone and stands on the W. bank above the Grwyne Fawr, 88 m above O.D. It is 1.22 m high, 0.61 m broad and 0.3 m thick.

James 1978–9, p. 25, no. 11/22.

Llangenni
SO 21 N.E. (2405 1787)   18 v 77

(SS 41) Maen Llwyd on Pen y Gader Fawr,[1] 573 m above O.D., is a standing stone 2.18 m high, 0.94 m broad and 0.3 m thick.[2] It is one of the highest in the county,[3] occupies part of a field boundary and may have been erected for this purpose.[4]

[1] Jones, *Hist. Brecks.* II, ii (1809), p. 338.
[2] O.S. Card SO 22 NW 4.
[3] James 1978–9, p. 23, no. 11/10.
[4] Roese, *Thesis*, no. 194.

Talgarth (E), Llanbedr Ystrad Yw (C)
SO 22 N.W. (2260 2762)   13 vi 73

Standing Stones: Lost, Omitted and Rejected Sites

Lost Stones (LSS 1–8)

(LSS 1) A standing stone is marked on O.S. 1-inch first edition 1835 on Lan Fawr but cannot now be found.

Llanfihangel Abergwesyn, SN 85 S.E. (888 547)
Not found

(LSS 2) On Carnau Cefn y Ffordd about 400 m above O.D. is a cairn group (RC 177–80) near which is an associated standing stone.[1] It is said to lie about 43 m. N. of cairn (RC 177) but its siting has not yet been independently confirmed.[2]

[1] James 1970, Pl. 38.
[2] O.S. Card SN 96 SE 6.

Llanwrthwl
SN 96 S.E. (9545 6061)

(LSS 3) It is recorded by Lhuyd that a 'Maen Illtud' had formerly stood close to the tomb of Ty Illtud (about 137 m above O.D.), but that this was taken away.

Gibson, *Britannia*, (1695), (1st edn.) col. 594; Carlisle, *Top. Dict.*, s.v. Llan aml llech (sic); James 1978–9, p. 29, no. 11/32; G. F. Dawson, *The Brecknockshire Churches*, (1909).

Llanhamlach, SO 02 N.E. (097 262) approx.

(LSS 4) According to the Rev. Charles Price:

There formerly stood about a quarter mile W. from the church [Maesmynis], a stone set on end, about 7½ feet high, and on a small eminence, close by a large wood, called Gilfach Dedwydd, or the Blissful Retreat. This stone was of a kind not to be found in the neighbourhood, and was, doubtless, conveyed from far: some suppose it to be composed of small white pebbles and a certain cement (probably the millstone or puddingstone). It appears to have been a Druid Altar, and many droll stories are told concerning it. It was blasted to pieces by gunpowder, about 10 years ago by the owner of the land.

It seems likely that this was an erratic stone, with a lithology either of a coarse Aberystwyth Grit, brought from the W., or of a Old Red Sandstone, brought from some distance to the S.

N. Carlisle, *Top. Dict.*, s.v. Llanynis.

Maesmynys
SO 04 N.W. (022 497) approx.

(LSS 5–6) To the S.E. of Maes Clytha Wood is a cairn (RC 282) and an alignment of six contiguous stones deeply sunk into the ground in a straight line. These appear to be associated with two others:
(LSS 5) vertical and 1.25 m high and
(LSS 6) 1 m square, and lying to the E. of the track.

O.S. Card SO 12 SE 30; P. M. Jones, *Arch. in Wales* 16 (1976), p. 18, no. 13.

Llanfihangel Cwm Du
SO 12 S.E. (LSS 5) (159 243); (LSS 6) (159 244)
9 iii 77

(LSS 7) In Llangoed Wood there were two standing stones,[1] now lost. Sir John Lloyd photographed a stone, now also unlocated, at Llyswen, 116 m above O.D. and it is possible that this should be equated with one of those in Llangoed Wood, though if the wood was formerly more widespread in extent it is possible one of them may have been the surviving stone SS 34.

[1] *Trans. Woolhope Club* (1933), p. 41, and Pls. II and III; James 1978–9, p. 29, no. 11/50, gives location at SO 122 388.
[2] Lloyd MSS.

Llys-wen
SN 13 N.W. (1212 3897)   Not found

(LSS 8) According to D. J. James, 'Sir John Lloyd's report shows a photograph of a "track" stone at the cross roads 400 m S.E. of the long cairns [Ffostyll CT 5–6], now removed. Some older maps show "Stone Circles" at this approximate location.' This stone has not been re-located and no early O.S. maps are known showing stone circles in this locality.

Lloyd MSS; James 1978–9, p. 29, 11/54.
James 1978–9, p. 27, no. 11/42.

Llaneleu
SO 13 S.E. (1820 3475)   Not found

Rejected Stones (RSS 1–87)

These are divided between Boundary Stones, RSS 1–19; Natural Boulders, RSS 20–42; Memorial or Inscribed Stones (other than Early Christian), RSS 43–5; Others, RSS 46–74 and indicative Field Names, RSS 75–87.

Boundary Stones

(RSS 1) SN 81 S.E. (8852 1326). Maen Gweddiau. Boundary stone.

(RSS 2) SN 83 S.E. (8860 3310). 'Stone' on O.S. map. Boundary stone, now replaced by one inscribed 'W.D.'

(RSS 3) SN 83 S.E. (8922 3242). 'Boulder' on O.S. map. An erratic used as a boundary stone.

O.S. Card SN 83 SE M10.

(RSS 4) SN 92 N.E. (9638 2538) On Mynydd Illtud, 320 m above O.D., is a recumbent partly-buried monolith 1.85 m long, 0.43 m thick and 0.74 m wide. It lies at the point where the boundaries of Maescar and Glyn cross a stream.

O.S. Card SN 92 NE 23; James 1978–9, p. 27, no. 11/42.

(RSS 5) SN 92 N.E. (9640 2599). 315 m above O.D. to the S. of the road following the crest of Mynydd Illtud is a recumbent block of weathered sandstone 2.44 m long, 2.15 m wide and 0.76 m thick. It lies close to the junction of the parishes of Maescar, Penpont and Glyn.

(RSS 6) SN 92 N.E. (9762 2650). On Mynydd Illtud, 340 m above O.D., is a stone leaning slightly to the E. to the S. of the old track over the crest of the hill. It is 0.86 m high, 0.69 m broad and 0.48 m thick with a blunt head. It lies about 100 m W. of the Modrydd –Maescar parish boundary.

See Maen Richard (SS 17) SN 93 S.E. (9675 3468)

(RSS 7) SN 94 S.W. (9129 4044 and (132 4122). 'Boulder' and 'Boulders' marked on O.S. 6-inch (3rd edn. 1964). On the boundary between Llandeilo'r Fan and Llanfihangel Nant Bran.

(RSS 8) SN 96 S.W. (9333 6259, 9326 6243 and 9319 6246). Three moorland boulders. (Kay MSS)

(RSS 9) SO 03 S.W. (0173 3017). About 300 m S.E. of Cradoc Station, 168 m above O.D. on the foot of an embankment of the former Brecon to Sennybridge railway line is a stone of Millstone Grit 2 m high, 1.25 m wide and 0.4 m thick. The letters B.M. 10 cm high, appear on its N. face. It is unclear what this stood for, but it seems most likely to have been a boundary stone. On the E. face is scratched D.J., inscribed vertically. On the N.E. angle are five quarry wedge marks at heights of 0.2 m, 0.71 m, 1.11 m, 1.32 m and 1.6 m above ground. The wedges were driven in from the N. and each is 8–10 cm long by 10–13 cm wide at the edge of the stone, tapering to 5–8 cm wide at the end of the wedge; 2.5–4 cm deep at the edge of the stone, tapering to nil at the end of the wedge. The wedge marks are angled slightly upwards from the horizontal.

The site appears as B.S. on the map[1] and marks the boundary between the parishes of Fennifach and St. John the Evangelist. A further 17 similarly inscribed stones delimit the boundary between Battle and Llandefaelog Fach S. from Bedd y Forwyn, though these are smaller in size. One, now lying on the ground (at SO 0147 3465) is inscribed 'B.M. 1828'. Another, perhaps more typical example is at SO 0120 3384 and stands 0.58 m high, 0.35 m wide and 0.19 m thick. The inscription on its W. face uses the same form of letters as that on the Cradoc stone, although those on the latter are larger.

It is noteworthy how the parish boundary diverges to take in an odd-shaped piece of land at the apex of which this stone lies.

O.S. 25-inch map 1905; noted in *Arch. Camb.* 27 (1872), p. 384; James 1978–9, p. 23, no. 11/8.

S.A.M. B 189.

(RSS 10) Boundary stones on Llandefalle Hill
Boundary stones are marked at the following locations on the O.S. 6-inch and later maps:

(a) SO 03 N.E. (SO 0697 3738), 365 m above O.D. (lost);

(b–c) SO 0754 3696 and 0766 3695, both 365 m above O.D. (both lost);

(d) SO 0707 3703, at 360 m above O.D.; two stones, one broken, having been replaced by the other. The complete one has a rounded head, is 0.74 m high by 0.35 m wide and 0.18 m thick with the following inscription: A.M.L. / LORD / Ashburnha [m] / 1815.

(e) SO 0709 3752, 385 m above O.D. Similar to above.

(f) SO 0850 3895, 370 m above O.D. Two further stones as above.

(g) SO 0862 3845, 360 m above O.D. Another boundary stone 0.69 m high by 0.4 m wide and 0.09 m thick inscribed on S. face CANTRESELIFF / SIR / J. Bailey Bar. / M.P. / 1847.

Note: Theophilus Jones notes a stone 'of about four feet high . . . on the E. side of the E.–W. running lane Pen Heol Einion . . . near a gate leading to Crickadarn . . . which some have supposed to be sepulchral', but which Jones himself felt to have been a boundary marking the extremity of Einion's property (*Hist. Brecks.* II, i (1809), p. 317). The most reasonable siting for this stone would seem to lie among the above boundary locations, particularly (f) or (g), which lie adjacent to a moorland track traversing north to Crickadarn.

(RSS 11) SO 0900 3840 at 350 m above O.D. (lost). Llandefalle   13 iii 73

(RSS 12) SO 04 S.W. (0028 4029) 'Stone'. 315 m above O.D. in hedgebank inscribed DYFFRYN HONNDY / UPPER LOWER / DIVISION.
                                                                                   9 xi 78

(RSS 13) SO 04 S.W. (0280 4103). 410 m above O.D. Boundary stone just W. of track, in a hollow 2.7 m across is a shapeless fallen monolith 1.27 m long by 0.74 m wide and 0.48 m deep.   8 xi 72

(RSS 14) SO 04 S.E. (0806 4342 and 0809 4348). Stones and Stone 260 m above O.D. are recumbent, shattered and partly-buried monoliths of local shaly rock. Three only are marked on the map but there are others. Possibly natural or boundary stones.
                                                                                   25 x 76

(RSS 15) SO 12 S.E. (1579 2020). On the S. bank of the River Usk is a boundary stone of undressed Old Red Sandstone 1.5 m high, 1.6 m broad and 0.25 m thick inscribed E.M.J./W.C.W./1882.

James 1970, Pls. 28a–b; 1978–9, p. 26.

(RSS 16) SO 12 S.E. (1590 2309). Three isolated upright stones probably marking the course of an old track: (i) 0.99 m long, 0.35 m wide and 0.45 m high with a bluntly-pointed head; (ii) 40.5 m from this latter is another monolith leaning to the N.E.; (iii) at SO 1594 2304 is a smaller sandstone boulder 0.35 m by 0.25 m and 0.53 m high.

O.S. Card SO 12 SE 27; P. M. Jones, *Arch. in Wales* 16 (1976), p. 17, no. 2.

(RSS 17) SO 13 N.W. (1000 3887). 340 m above O.D., 300 m N. of Perthi-Duon (Llandefalle) is a boundary stone 0.94 m high and 0.5 m by 0.3 m in section at base, inscribed M or W and another indecipherable scratch on the E. face.

(RSS 18) SO 21 S.W. (2382 1133). Carreg Maen Taro. Boundary stone.

(RSS 19) SO 21 S.W. (2423 1253). Careg Gywir. Boundary stone.

Natural Boulders

(RSS 20) SN 81 N.W. (8488 1709). Tafarn y Garreg Inn. A natural boulder or mounting block.

cf. James 1978–9, p. 29, no. 11/53.

(RSS 21) SN 81 N.E. (8535 1962). Cefn Cul. Natural boulder.

(RSS 22) SN 81 S.E. (8608 1458), Saith Maen, Penwyllt. Natural boulder. See also RSC 1.

cf. Grimes, 1931–3, p. 88; James 1978–9, p. 22, no. 11/31, referring to Jones, *Hist. Brecks.*, (1809), (no page ref.).

(RSS 23) SN 82 N.W. (8407 2732). Cwm Gors (due N. of), near Bryn Tywarch. Natural boulder.

(RSS 24) SN 82 N.W. (8425 2611). Blaenau Isaf. Natural boulder.

(RSS 25) SN 82 S.W. (8599 2456). Ffynnon y Gwyddau, 398 m above O.D. is a leaning stone 0.6 m high, 50 m from the nearby cross roads. Possibly natural.

James 1978–9, p. 29, no. 11/55; *cf.* O.S. Card SN 82 SE 20; *cf.* also the 'badly-leaning' stone Sir John Lloyd photographed at Cray. It was said to be about 1 m high (James 1978–9, p. 29, no. 11/51; Lloyd MSS).

(RSS 26) SN 82 S.W. (SN 8744 2337). Near Gochgarreg, is a recent erection.

(RSS 27) SN 84 N.E. (856 498). Reputed standing stone in forestry near Cwm Irfon, above Cwm Irfon Bridge.

(RSS 28) SN 85 S.E. (8692 5425). Large recumbent conglomerate boulder. Natural.

(RSS 29) SN 93 N.E. (9645 3864). 'Stone' marked on O.S. map (3rd edn. 6-inch 1964). Several natural boulders, possibly former hedge line.

(RSS 30) SN 93 N.E. (9660 3903 and 9663 3904). 'Stones' marked on O.S. 6-inch map 3rd edn. 1964. Two recumbent boulders of Old Red Sandstone, probably natural.

(RSS 31) SN 95 N.W. (9104 5517). Unmarked on O.S. maps, 455 m above O.D. Two large boulders lying upon glacial moraine.

O.S. Card SN 95 NW 6.

(RSS 32) SN 95 N.W. (9170 5572). Maen Cam, 463 m above O.D., is marked in Antiquity type on O.S. 6-inch 3rd edn. map (1964) and comprises two earthfast glacial erratics. Now lost.

O.S. Card SN 95 NW 1; James 1978–9, p. 25, 11/26; Lloyd MSS.

(RSS 33) SN 95 N.W. (9173 5574). Four earthfast recumbent stones, formerly erect, lie 40 m N.E. of Maen Cam.

O.S. Card SN 95 NW 10.

(RSS 34) SN 95 N.W. (9112 5658). Two stones 30 m N. of cairn O.S. Card SN 95 NW 8 (RC 155).

O.S. Card SN 95 NW 7.

(RSS 35) SN 96 S.W. (9310 6332 and 9301 6331). Two recumbent monoliths here are probably erratic boulders.

(RSS 36) SO 12 S.E. (1508 2149). N. of Llygadwy (in Llanfihangel Cwm Du), 160 m above O.D., between a hollow farm-way and a disused linear quarry, is a monolith 1.5 m high and 0.96 m by 0.3 m in section. It is now used as a rubbing post but was probably a boundary stone.

O.S. Card SO 12 SE 20; James 1970, Pls. 19a–b [these are misplaced and represent stones at 1804 2192]; Morgan 1982.

(RSS 37) SO 12 S.E. (1588 2256 and 1589 2253). 295 m above O.D. 'Two Stones' on O.S. 6-inch map (1964). Natural boulders. 9 iii 77

(RSS 38) SO 12 S.E. (1591 2411). 375 m above O.D. is a slab set on edge 1.01 m long E.–W. by 0.3 m wide by 0.58 m high. Probably natural.

9 iii 77

(RSS 39) SO 12 S.E. (1901 2099). 90 m above O.D.. Stone in hedge; one of a number of cleared field boulders.

(RSS 40) SO 12 S.E. (162 233). At Penlan built into a wall and 213 m above O.D. is a stone 0.94 m high, 0.81 m broad and 0.3 m thick. Possibly another one nearby.

James 1978–9, 29, 11/56.

(RSS 41) SO 13 S.W. (1278 3191). The King's Stone is in Llanywern Parish on the hill S. of Penyrallt Farm. A natural boulder, formerly a rocking stone.

Crawford, *L.B.C.*, p. 185; Jones, *Hist. Brecks.* II, ii (1809), p. 561; *Brecon County Times*, 22nd September 1921; O.S. MS 2-inch map 1814.

(RSS 42) SO 21 N.W. (2399 1781). 90 m above O.D. On W. side of Grwyne Fawr. Natural.

Marked and Memorial Stones

SO 01 S.E. (0731 1321), Ystrad Stone, see ECM 22

(RSS 43) SO 11 N.E. (1866 1985). In Penmyarth Park, formerly at 1882 1992, now removed to churchyard where it serves as an epitaph to Joseph Henry Russell, 2nd Baron of Glanusk, who died 11th January 1928. A weatherworn stone of squat shape 0.8 m long by 0.7 m wide at base and 1.8 m high tapering to a squarish top. There is a defaced and indecipherable inscription cut vertically on the W. face with Glanusk's epitaph on the other side (ECM 34).

Llanfihangel Cwm Du

(RSS 44; also listed as RECM 3) In a field on the E. side of Bwlch village at 200 m above O.D. is a monolith, the Llygadwy stone, of Old Red Sandstone

1.8 m high and 0.5 m square in section. Much weathered, it tapers to a point at the top. It has been suggested that both Ogam (on the N.W. edge) and Latin (on the S. face) could be read into this weathering, and the letters ANE were at one time thought to have been discernible. However, no inscriptions are now to be seen and scratches recorded during field visits seems more likely the result of wire-chafing. there is also a socket central to the S.W. face 1.3 m above ground which seems modern. There is a large irregular depression in the field to its N.W., probably an old pond.

O.S. Card SO 12 SE 8; James 1970; 1978–9, p. 25, 11/21; Macalister (1922), p. 219, *C.I.I.C.*, no. 324; G. Morgan in *Brycheiniog* 20 (1982–3), pp. 41–7.

Llanfihangel Cwm Du
SO 12 S.E. (1503 2195)   26 iv 76

Others:

(RSS 45) SN 84 N.E. (886 457). Incorrect grid reference (James 1978–9, pp. 13, 24). For site location, see SN 885 475.

(RSS 46) SN 85 S.E. (probably 851 591). Recumbent triangular stone on summit of Craig Irfon (Mrs R. Bidgood *in lit.*, 3 iv 78).

SN 91 N.E. (9626 1604). Bedd Llywarch (two supposed standing stones SN 9626 1604); see RSC 6.

(RSS 47) SN 91 S.E. (9783 1480). Carreg Saith Troedfedd is a small patch of stones which includes one over 1.25 m long which might have fallen from an upright position.

(RSS 48) SN 92 N.W. (923 269). Stone 1.6 m high (P. M. Jones, *Arch. in Wales* 16 (1976), p. 18, no. 30). Not found. Perhaps this is the stone in the hedge at SN 9241 2705.

(RSS 49) SN 92 N.E. (953 256). Two stones in hedge on N. side of road leading from Mynydd Illtud (just after bend by first farm off common). P. M. Jones, *in. lit.*   19 vi 81

(RSS 50) SN 92 S.W. (9020 2250). Two stones, one lying flat, near Pen y Waun Dwr (James 1978–9, p. 28, 11/46).   Not located

(RSS 51) SN 93 S.E. (9795 3248) 'Stone' at 350 m above O.D. Two upright stones of modern appearance. The shorter has large 'T' carved on one face.

(RSS 52) SN 94 N.W. (938 499). Standing stone said to have stood 8 ft (2.1 m) from the inscribed stone (ECM 14) within Llanlleonfel churchyard.

O.S. Card SN 94 NW 11; *C.I.I.C.* (2), p. 138, no. 986.

(RSS 53) SN 94 S.W. (9063 4068). 'Stone' marked on O.S. 6-inch 3rd edn. (1964).   Not visited

(RSS 54) SN 94 S.E. (9894 4317). 'Stone' marked on O.S. 6-inch 3rd edn. (1964).   Not visited

(RSS 55) SN 94 S.E. (9746 4115). 'Stone' marked on O.S. 6-inch 3rd edn. (1964).   Not visited

(RSS 56) SN 96 S.E. (956 607). At Pen Rhos 405 m above O.D. is a standing stone 0.71 m high, 0.61 m broad and 0.25 m thick.

O.S. Card SN 95 SE 6; James 1978–9, p. 28, 11/45.

(RSS 57) SO 02 S.E. (0684 2268). 'Stone' at 520 m above O.D. Not found.   24 v 78

(RSS 58) SO 02 S.E. (0705 2303). 'Stones' at 520 m above O.D. Not found.   24 v 78

(RSS 59) SO 02 S.W. (0495 2088). 'Stone' at 200 m above O.D. 0.84 m long 0.4 m wide and 0.23 m thick.
                    26 iv 76

(RSS 60) SO 02 S.E. (097 202). Three large (1 m high) stones incorporated into wall. Also one large stone in sunken, stone-lined enclosure built near wall.

(RSS 61) SO 11 N.E. (157 202). At Coed yr Ynys, 98 m above O.D., is a second stone on the S. bank of the River Usk 200 m N.W. of the example below. It is 1.3 m high and 1.6 m broad by 0.25 m thick.

(RSS 62) SO 12 N.W. (1143 2840). Inside Llanfihangel Tal y Llyn church porch, 174 m above O.D., is a stone which formerly stood in the graveyard. It is 1.47 m high, 0.41 m broad and 0.41 m thick with a basin-like hole hollowed in the top. This is probably medieval.

James 1970, Photo Pl. 31; 1978–9, p. 27, 11/27.

(RSS 63) SO 12 N.E. (159 252). Just N. of cairns (RC 269–71) 0.75 m high. P. M. Jones, *in lit.*, 17 ix 76.
Not found

(RSS 64) SO 12 N.E. (1572 2608). 506 m above O.D. 'Stones (O.S. 6-inch 1964) on Mynydd Llangorse. Not ancient.

(RSS 65) (v) SO 12 N.E. (169 221). Big stone in hedge. P. M. Jones, *in lit.*, 26 ii 85. Not visited.

(RSS 66) SO 12 N.E. (1572 2608). 'Stones' (O.S. 6-inch 1964) 506 m above O.D. O.S. pillar. Not ancient.

(RSS 67) SO 12 S.W. (146 223). 205 m above O.D. (no source given). Not found.

(RSS 68) SO 12 S.W. (1448 2342). At Pendre, 186 m above O.D., alongside the Bwlch–Llangorse road is a stone 0.94 m high, 0.56 m broad and 0.41 m thick. (O.S. Card SO 12 SW 27; James 1970; 1978–9, p. 26, 11/32.)

(RSS 69) SO 12 S.E. (166 247). Stone 1.5 m high near Clwyd y Graig farm. (*Arch. in Wales* 17 (1977), p. 12.)
Not located

(RSS 70) SO 12 S.E. (1789 2247). 115 m above O.D. (O.S. 6-inch map 1964). Drain cover.

(RSS 71) SO 12 S.E. (1789 2292), 125 m above O.D. 'Stone' (O.S. 6-inch map 1964). Lost

(RSS 72) SO 12 S.E. (181 219) At Tretower, 93 m above O.D., is a stone 2.26 m high, 1.12 m broad and 0.74 m thick. It lies in a hedge close to the Crickhowell–Talgarth Road. (James 1978–9, p. 24, 11/13.)

(RSS 73) SO 13 S.E./23 S.W. '2 Piles of Stones' (1994 3276) and 'Stone' (2000 3278). O.S. 6-inch 1964. Modern.

(RSS 74) SO 23 N.W. (2395 3735). Stone on Hay Bluff, 475 m above O.D., mentioned by James (1978–9, p. 26, 11/30), is part of the stone circle (SC 10).

Field and Other Place Names

In the following list TA = Tithe Award. The placename information is taken from parochial Tithe Award Maps in the Department of Maps and Prints at the N.L.W. All sites listed in this abbreviated account have been examined by Commission staff, and a record of visits is kept at the R.C.A.M.

(RSS 75) SN 92 N.W. (9155 2683 and 9153 2700). Cae Carreg Fawr (TA 1219) and Graig y Carney (TA 1220). Fields cleared of stone.

(RSS 76) SN 92 N.W. (9475 2740). Maescar, Cae Main Gwyn Maen (TA 710). Large natural stone of sandstone weathered white in western field boundary.

(RSS 77) SN 92 N.W. (9435 2860). Cae Garreg Wen (TA 914). Natural white stones at base of field.

(RSS 78) SN 92 S.W. (9042 2489). Pant Maen Llwyd (TA 691). Field bulldozed.

(RSS 79) SN 93 S.E. (9580 3257). Cae Maen Hir (TA 52). No trace of stone.

(RSS 80) SN 93 S.E. (9910 3975). Cae Maen (TA 124). No trace of stone.

(RSS 81) SN 94 N.W. (9325 4970) Maes Llech. Farm name. Not visited

(RSS 82) SO 03 N.W. Cae Garn (TA 741) (0250 3730) 260 m above O.D. A large stone slab 1.83 m long by 0.76 m wide and 0.35 m thick is set in the hedge (at 0245 3727). 14 ix 73

(RSS 83) SO 03 N.W. Cae Maen Gwyn (TA 611a) (0510 3635), 335 m above O.D. A stone marked on O.S. map at SO 0509 3613 next to the field boundary has been removed and an erratic boulder roughly 1 m in diameter lies in the hedge at SO 0520 3616. 16 x 73

(RSS 84) SO 03 N.W. Cae Maen Hir (TA 338) (0710 3525), 305 m above O.D. 16 x 73

(RSS 85) SO 03 N.W. Cae Maen (TA 78) (0220 3207). 1 xi 73

(RSS 86) SO 12 N.W. (1249 2757). Maen Llwyd (TA 79). Natural boulder or bedrock. 11 vi 74

(RSS 87) SO 12 N.W. (1425 2990). Cae y Garreg Fawr (TA 723). 10 vi 74

Mounds of Burned Stone

'Burnt mounds', 'boiling mounds' or 'prehistoric hearths' usually comprise collections of discoloured and broken, burned stone interdigitated with charcoal, sometimes in the form of a crescentic or circular mound, usually 10–20 m across and rarely more than 1 m high. They are being discovered and described in increasing numbers throughout Britain and Ireland.[1]

Some have been associated with troughs or pits. In Ireland, since experiments demonstrated the practicability of cooking upon similar sites by dropping heated stones into water-filled vessels containing meat (following practices referred to by a sixteenth-century historian), they became known as 'cooking mounds'.[2] It should be stressed that a broad range of features is encompassed by the definition of 'burned' or 'burnt mounds'. Some, (for e.g. BM 19) were probably hearths, though for what purpose, domestic or industrial, is quite unclear. However, for the most part, throughout Wales, sites follow a similar general pattern of shape, size and location. Before the First World War some 300 mounds were listed in south-west Wales[3] (an area which remains a focal point upon the distribution map).[4] More sites have since been discovered throughout Wales, and they are known in some numbers from Caernarfonshire[5] and Glamorgan.[6]

The number in Brecknockshire – twenty-two – is not great considering the size of the county, and taking into account the high rate of preservation for other types of settlement feature, particularly in the uplands. In Brecknockshire they occupy ground between 215 m and 500 m above O.D.; none are known from the lower-lying river valleys, where, if they did exist, they were no doubt either silted over, or have been removed in agricultural activity. Two-thirds of the Brecknockshire sample is associated with streams, a topographical setting most commonly associated with this type of monument. Of recorded sites, eleven survive fairly complete (though two are damaged either by stream erosion or access routes), six have been lost through afforestation, four more have been ploughed away, and 1 could not be relocated.

Where it has been possible to ascertain, the Brecknockshire mounds are crescent-shaped or occasionally circular. Some are similar in appearance to burial cairns. These circular mounds may be dished with hollowed-out crests. They range in size from less than 4 m to almost 16 m in diameter (or length). Most form only low earthen-stony spreads, though some rise to 1 m or higher.

Besides those already noted above, several theories have been advanced to explain their original functions. A few might result from smelting debris for surface gathered ores.[7] Another interpretation supposes them to have been sweat-houses.[8] Examples of other uses are to be found in ethnographic parallels both from antiquity and from recent practice.[9]

Excavation has brought to light surprisingly few artefacts or analysable organic material securely stratified in datable contexts, and radiocarbon dating has produced a broad range of dates, though the majority of these have fallen within the Bronze Age. Some dates have been Dark Age.[10] In three instances there is close topographical association between three Brecknockshire sites and early field systems or multi-period settlement, for example in Cwm Haffes (BM 1; US 6), on Cefn Esgair Carnau (BM 18; US 79), in Cwm Moel (BM 21; US 96) and upon Cefn Sychpant (BM 15), where there are also excavated structured cairns ascribable to the Bronze Age. Although these associations may signal Bronze Age uses for some, without excavation and palynological investigation, both their function and dating remain largely enigmatic.

[1] V. Buckley, (ed.), *Burnt Offerings: International Contributions to Burnt Mound Archaeology*, (Dublin: Wordwell, 1990); M. A. Hodder and L. H. Barfield, (eds.), *Burnt Mounds and Hot Stone Technology*, (Sandwell: Met. Borough Council, 1991).

[2] M. J. O'Kelly, *Jnl. Roy. Soc. Antiqs Ireland* 84 (1954), pp. 105–55.

[3] T. C. Cantrill and O. T. Jones, *Arch. Camb.* 61 (1905), pp. 17–34; *Arch. Camb.* 66 (1911), pp. 253–86.

[4] G. Williams, 'Burnt Mounds in south-west Wales', pp. 129–40 in Hodder and Barfield, *loc. cit.* n. 1; H. J. James, *B.B.C.S.* 33 (1986), pp. 245–65, 262–5 and Fig. 8, p. 263.

[5] *Inv. Caerns.* III, pp. lxii–lxiv, Fig. 14; 44 examples were known in 1964. R. S. Kelly suggests there may be many more; see 'Recent work in north-west Wales: the excavation of a burnt mound at Graeanog, Clynnog, Gwynedd, in 1983', pp. 117–28 in Hodder and Barfield, (eds.), *loc. cit.* n. 1.

[6] *Inv. Glam.* I (I), pp. 125–7.

[7] C. S. Briggs, (pp. 267–82) in C. B. Burgess and R. Miket, (eds.), *Settlement and Economy in the Third and Second Millennia B.C.*, (Oxford: B.A.R. 33, 1976), p. 278.

[8] L. H. Barfield and M. Hodder, *Antiquity* 61 (1987), pp. 370–9; *Current Archaeol.* 78 (August 1981), pp. 199–200.

[9] See monographs cited n. 1.

[10] James, *op. cit.* n. 4, pp. 264–5; besides James's work, Bronze Age radiocarbon determinations from Wales include: A. E. Caseldine and K. Murphy, *Arch. in Wales* 29 (1989), pp. 1–5; G. Williams, *B.B.C.S.* 24 (1987), pp. 228–43; the Dark Age dating is from G. H. Williams, *Ceredigion* 9 (1985), pp. 181–8.

Burned Mounds (BM 1–22)

(BM 1) Associated with hut-circles, clearances and a stony bank (US 6) on the moderately steep S.-facing slope of Allt Fach, about 435 m above O.D., is a turf-covered, crescent-shaped cooking mound, open to the W., measuring 7.5 m N.–S. by 6 m, and up to 1.5 m high.

Ystradgynlais (E), Ystradgynlais Lr (C)
SN 81 N.W. (8401 1771)   13 viii 87

(BM 2) In 1906 a prehistoric hearth was located on the S. side of a stream 80 yards (73 m) from the main road on the E. side of the Tawe Valley, 1¼ miles (2 km) N. of Capel Callwen and 370 m above O.D. Although this feature cannot now be re-identified with confidence, a tiny mound 3.4 m by 2.1 m and 0.3 m high survives on the tip of a stream ravine in ground falling to the W. Its apparent crescentic shape facing the stream is probably due to former scraping by sheep to form a shelter.

    O.S. Card SN 81 NE 2; T. C. Cantrill and O. T. Jones, *Arch. Camb.* 61 (1906), pp. 17–34; p. 24, no. 3.

Llywel (E), Traean-glas (C)
SN 81 N.E. (8526 1977)   16 ix 87

(BM 3–4) About 270 m N.E. of Cefn Cul farm, about 370 m above O.D., two small mounds, probably prehistoric hearths, were noted in 1906.[1] They lay upon the bank of a small stream forming a shallow ravine in ground falling steeply to the S.E. These were re-located in 1969,[2] though could not be found later due to the depth of bracken cover.[3]

    (BM 3) One was about 6.1 m in diameter with a dished centre, not more than 0.3 m high on the uphill side, but about 1.5 m high on the downhill. The S. side has been eroded away, revealing the mound to be composed of small stones and charcoal dust.

    (BM 4) The more northwesterly mound is about 9 m away, about 4.5 m long N.W.–S.E., by 3.7 m wide and 0.9 m high. There is a vague suggestion of concavity towards the stream.

[1] Cantrill and Jones, *op. cit.* (BM 2), p. 24, nos. 1–2.
[2] W. E. Griffiths, MSS fieldnotes, R.C.A.M.
[3] O.S. Card SN 81 NE 1 (1976).

Llywel (E), Traean-glas (C)
SN 81 N.E. (BM 3) (8620 1879); (BM 4) (8619 1880)
         15 v 87

(BM 5–6) Two cooking hearths, in 1906 said to be located one each on opposite sides of the stream 400 yards (365 m) about 250 m above O.D., S.S.E. of Bwysfa Fawr Farm,[1] have not been re-located, and are probably ploughed out.[2]

[1] Cantrill and Jones *op. cit.* (BM 1 above), pp. 26–7, nos. 88–9.
[2] O.S. Card SN 82 NE 3.

Llywel/Defynnog (E), Traean-glas/Crai (C)
SN 82 N.E. (886 279)   Not visited

(BM 7–8) Two undisturbed prehistoric hearths were found when levelling ground in front of the Congregational Chapel Manse in Llanwrtyd Wells, 215 m above O.D. in 1923. They were in a dry place, 1½ feet (0.45 m) below the surface, well below the ploughsoil, on the highest point between the building and the road. About 1½ yards (1.25 m) from each was a quantity of ashes and stones showing the action of fire, or 'pot boilers'. These are lost.

    O.S. Card SN 84 NE 5; Anon., *Arch. Camb.* 78 (1923), p. 175, quoting from the *Brecon and Radnor Express*, 24th May 1923; see also J. Lloyd MSS. 1/1/10, 49.

Llanwrtyd
SN 84 N.E. (8800 4675)   22 vii 77

(BM 9–10) On a S.-facing slope of Y Glas mountain over 300 m above O.D., by a streamlet at Ddu Fannog

Farm were two cooking mounds. The first, kidney-shaped and placed horizontally across the slope, was 15 yards by 5 yards (13.5 m by 4 m). The other, higher up the slope, was circular and 14 yards (12.5 m) in circumference. There was an associated abundance of ashes and cracked stones at both sites.[1]

The entire area is now changed through afforestation and the construction of the Llyn Brianne Dam.[2]

[1] E. Jones, *Arch. Camb.* 78 (1923), p. 154.
[2] O.S. Card SN 85 SW 2; 10 vii 80.

Llanddewi Abergwesyn
SN 85 S.W. (808 512) [Ddu Fannog Farm]
                                                    Not visited

(BM 11) A cooking mound was noted in 1923[1] 300 m above O.D. on Esgair Bustach in a narrow valley to the N. of Nant yr Ych on Pant y Clwydau farm. The area is now under dense forest cover.[2]

[1] E. Jones *op. cit.* (BM 10), p. 154.
[2] O.S. Card SN 85 SW 3; 10 vii 80.

Llanddewi Abergwesyn
SN 85 S.W. (804 531)
[Pant y Clwydau farm]   Not visited

(BM 12–13) Two cooking hearths were noted in 1923 on Llethr Cefn y Gwair., S. of Y Glas,[1] over 300 m above O.D.

(BM 12) One was a submerged mound a foot or more (over 0.3 m) below the adjoining surface and 10 yards (about 9 m) in circumference on the W. side of a small brook flowing into the Groesnant.

(BM 13) The other site was higher up the valley on the same slope and resembled a horseshoe 17 yards (about 15 m) long, 5 yards (about 4.5 m) wide and around 2 feet (0.6 m) high with a 6 foot (1.6 m) gap adjoining the water. There was an abundance of charcoal and chipped stone.

Both sites are apparently lost, largely owing to afforestation and the construction of the Llyn Brianne Dam.[2]

[1] E. Jones, *loc. cit.* (BM 10), p. 154.
[2] O.S. Card SN 85 SW 4; 10 vii 80.

Llanddewi Abergwesyn
SN 85 S.W. (81 50)   Not visited

(BM 14) On the S. side of, and adjacent to a stream flowing down the S.E.-facing slope into Nant Crew about 500 m above O.D., is a mound 8.5 m in diameter and 0.4 m high. Its edge seems to mark a change in vegetation and the mound itself supports short-cropped turf in contrast to longer grasses which surround it. On the stream side of the mound there is a slight, though perceptible indentation suggestive of the 'kidney' shape common to some larger examples of burned mounds.

Cantref
SN 91 N.E. (9968 1766)   5 iii 85

(BM 15) Low on the W. end of Cefn Sychpant, 340 m above O.D., in marshy ground on a level shelf sloping gently to N.W., is a horseshoe-shaped cooking mound, open to the S.W. and approximately circular. It is 17 m E.–W. and 1.2 m high with a central hollow about 4.5 m deep. The distance between the horns of the mound is about 8.2 m. It is surrounded on the N., E. and S. by watercourses, the southern one of which is *c.* 14 m from the mound, probably following its original course.

Penderyn
SN 91 S.E. (9717 1017)   x 85

(BM 16) Below and W. of Cefn Esgair Carnau, about 355 m above O.D., is a cooking mound lying within a sharp band of the small stream which feeds the Afon y Waun. It is situated in the same general area as a large number of clearances and enclosures (US 78–9).

Cantref
SN 91 S.E. (9773 1432)   8 iii 84

(BM 17) Overlooking Nant Cadlan from the S.W. slope of Cefn Sychpant, on open moorland 365 m above O.D., is a grass-grown horseshoe-shaped cooking mound, open to the marshy area on its E. It is 14.5 m long (N.–S.) by 13 m (E.–W.) and 0.5 m high on N., 1.2 m high on S. with a central hollow about 4 m across and a detached area on N.E., apparently narrowing the gap between the horns.

Penderyn
SN 91 S.E. (9800 1010)   xi 85

(BM 18) To the E. of the N. end of Cefn Esgair Carnau, lying adjacent to, and upon the E. bank of a small stream at a height of about 365 m above O.D., is a probable burned mound. It is horseshoe-shaped,

12.5 m (N.–S.) by 10 m, the central area is 8.3 m across, and stands up to 0.8 m high. The mound is basically grass-grown, and is defined by dense rush growth. The S.W. terminal abuts onto a large boulder.

Penderyn
SN 91 S.E. (9860 1406)   11 xi 83

(BM 19) A cooking hearth was located when digging a drain to Pen y Banc from a spring known as Ffynnon Ysgolheigion,[1] about 215 m above O.D. A layer of black earth 1 foot (0.3 m thick), with traces of burnt wood and fire-coloured stone was followed for 7 yards (6.4 m). Neither the spring nor the hearth can now be identified.[2]

[1] E. Jones, *loc. cit.* (BM 10), pp. 153–4.
[2] O.S. Card SN 95 SE 6; 14 vii 80.

Llanafan Fawr
SN 95 S.E. (953 516) [farm]   Not visited

(BM 20) Adjacent to Ffynnon Mary, some 425 m above O.D., is a horseshoe-shaped, grass-grown mound 11 m in diameter (N.–S.) by 9.1 m E.–W. and 0.9 m high. Its central feature is a gully about 2.7 m wide, which opens to the stream on the E. The stony nature of the mound was ascertained through probing.

O.S. Card SN 96 SE 23; 15 ix 78.

Llanafan Fawr (E), Llysdinam (C)
SN 96 S.E. (9822 6019)   15 ix 78

(BM 21) In Cwm Moel about 340 m above O.D., on the marshy W. bank of a stream is a crescentic mound, open to the stream on the S.E. It is about 14 m long (N.E.–S.W.) by 10.7 m wide. It is about 11 m across the 'horn' tips, and the raised bank is only about 1.8 m deep. The N.E. half has been flattened by the track to Cwm Moel, but the S.W. half remains upstanding to a height of about 1 m.

Vaynor
SO 01 S.W. (0382 1155)   ix 88

(BM 22) On Cefn Moel, 385 m above O.D. in a slight hollow on moorland immediately above the confluence of two rivulets, is a grass- and gorse-grown mound. It is crescentic and open to the E., 14 m long N.–S., 10.4 m wide and 1 m high. The hollow is 6.4 m wide between the horns and extends 4.3 m into the body of the mound.

O.S. Card SO 12 SE 51; 5 viii 81.

Llanfihangel Cwm Du
SO 12 S.E. (1610 2430)   xi 76

Later Prehistoric and Protohistoric Settlement

Introduction

Until about 1980, prehistoric Britain was commonly regarded as having supported a mixed agricultural economy during the Neolithic which was replaced during the early Bronze Age, at least in the uplands, by a more pastoral regime.[1] This pastoralism was thought to be demonstrated by the survival of fields,[2] huts and smaller enclosures in Wessex and some parts of upland Britain.[3] Pastoral practices were believed to have dominated farming well into Iron Age times, when hillforts formed settlement components central to the organisation of this economy.[4] However, more intensive upland reconnaissance,[5] palaeoecological investigation,[6] and hillfort studies[7] have led to continued re-evaluation of the prehistoric agricultural economy. This has resulted in an awareness of more widespread early exploitation of greater land resources than was appreciated hitherto. The indications seem to be of recurrent exploitation through both mixed farming and pastoralism of terrain today considered climatically or economically marginal to successful farming.

Early Accounts

Field observations of early clearance features, including some illustrations, are known from the antiquarian literature since the seventeenth century.[8] Curiously, the school of early nineteenth-century Welsh county historians made no significant contribution to this branch of archaeology, although Theophilus Jones did mention Cwm Cadlan, Penderyn (US 83–4) 'studded with Carneddau, [with] . . . at least 40 or 50 smaller heaps of stones in the fields adjoining the hill'.[9] There is also a contemporary sighting of a possibly sub-peat wall, by Archdeacon Henry Thomas Payne, at Dan y Graig, Llangattock (LS 9). These apart, the earliest known description (and graphic depiction) of non-funereal features in Brecknockshire was made by Gilbert Gilpin (LS 1) in 1801 (Fig. 168). The landscape he described, of clearances interdigitated with platform houses or scooped huts, is comparable to others swept away by improvement and enclosure in eighteenth- and nineteenth-century Britain,[10] Ireland,[11] Holland[12] and in Germany.[13]

In the main, antiquaries and archaeologists were unable to interpret montane stone clearances and enclosures as indicators of early permanent settlement owing to the widely held belief that upland environments had always been hostile to animal and plant husbandry. T. C. Cantrill was an exception whose observations in the closing years of the nineteenth century represented a more critical approach. In 1897, describing 'Old Sheepfolds or Goosefolds' along the River Dringarth and its tributaries Nant y gwain and Nant-y-gaseg, Cantrill saw a fold by the Dringarth which 'showed in one of its walls those cupboard-like recesses that [are] presumably nest-boxes'; another example of the Nant y gaseg had a 'floor-space of 7 ft' [3.1 m] square. There were others 'Along the sides of the Taf-fechan, Nant-Crew [US 65], and their tributary brooks', marked 'Old Sheepfolds' or 'Sheepfolds' on the 1891 O.S. 6-inch maps.

> The few larger ones (many of which contain half a dozen or more compartments) are certainly sheepfolds. But the majority are so small that it is not likely that these were used for folding sheep. In some cases, they occur in groups of four or more within a space of 100 yds. [*c*. 91 m] as for example, in the Taf Fechan (Lat. 51° 52[ft] 22[in], long 3° 25[ft] 30[in]) 9 1/2 furlongs above the dam of the Upper Neuadd Reservoir, which are so small as scarcely to be distinguished on the map from the conventional marks used for blocks of stones, except by their rectangular plan. They are small rectangular enclosures with rough walls built of unhewn stone blocks [MS illeg.] on the spot. The walls were probably not more than 3 ft. high [*c*. 1.0 m], but in many cases they have fallen. Some of the enclosures are divided into two by a cross-wall.

Folklore assisted his interpretation:

> In 1897 there still survives a local tradition that these structures are goose-folds; that in the summer months geese were brought up

from Dowlais, Merthyr, Hirwaun and other industrial centres, where presumably their owners were short of grazing-ground, and pastured along the mountain streams. At night the goose-herds would probably share the folds with their flocks.

Cantrill knew that the custom had 'long died out' and attributed it to the 'eighteenth or early nineteenth century'.[15] This is very useful in that it chronicles the context of building or re-using stone-built structures in remote, montane locations. Around the same time, Cantrill also noted a circular embanked feature he believed to be a hut-circle in Ystradfellte (RC 97), and another similar site, now lost, near Sink-y-Giedd (LS 2).

Although the early O.S. records which accompanied the maps Cantrill had found so valuable were lost during enemy action in 1940, a card index annotating place-names and archaeological features was built up and maintained by the Archaeology Division after the War. These Ordnance Survey Antiquity Cards often provided the only record of many non-funereal sites in the uplands; for the most part these features were overlooked as of only peripheral interest by mainstream archaeologists. However, the O.S. records formed a basis for the upland investigation undertaken by the Commission after 1980. During the 1970s some sites had been noted from aerial reconnaissance (for example in Nant Car US 95), by Prof. J. K. St. Joseph,[16] and the same features were observed by independent fieldworkers.[17]

At the outset of this study, few upland features other than burial cairns had been recorded in detail when fieldwork began, around 1970.[18] It was still then believed that hut-groups and early field systems hardly existed in Wales outside Snowdonia.[19] Mapping outside Wales (on Dartmoor, in Northumberland, Western Scotland and Ireland)[20] and aerial photography along the Marches helped alter attitudes to facilitate interpretation of the more enigmatic settlement types in upland Wales.[21] Under closer scrutiny, the South Welsh uplands yielded huts and field systems of comparable types to these and with the intensification and refinement of fieldwork and reconnaissance techniques, discovery and recognition of early landholding and settlement continues.

Owing to the largely indeterminate dating of the unenclosed sites and because the sheer scale of the task was so great, all undated unenclosed sites were omitted from the Inventory of Iron Age and Roman sites.[22] In 1983 an intensive field survey of O.S. 10 km grid square SN 91 was initiated as a pilot study. This covers an area comprising mainly upland common with some enclosed pasture on the south side of the Brecon Beacons. Resources permitting, it was hoped the area would extend to include not only the Brecon Beacons, but also the Carmarthenshire Black Mountain on the west and Monmouthshire Black Mountains on the east. This work ran in tandem with other Commission and O.S. mapwork revision. Surveys of O.S. grid squares 71, 81 and 91 were completed, with some mapwork revision (for the 1:50,000 Landranger series) of SO 00, 01 and 11. Landscapes were at first chain surveyed, but after 1984 an EDM (Electronic Distance Measurer, later fitted with a digital plotter) dramatically altered the pace of work. During the survey period, changing resource priorities resulted in differential coverage of the county. Consequently some landscape descriptions are more detailed than others. The south-central, more montane, part of the county, was generally more comprehensively fieldworked than the Black Mountains, Mynydd Epynt and the N.W. Plateau. Although some sites have been recognised from the air, in general, unenclosed settlement in Brecknockshire has not so far shown itself to be easily captured through aerial reconnaissance.

Originally, an important selection criterion for survey was the presumption that at least some features which lay close to Bronze Age burial mounds were likely to have been of contemporary date. Although initially most house platforms were ascribed to medieval or later times (since these were believed to have accommodated long-houses or *hafotai*), much less reliance is now vested in such a chronological and functional interpretation.[23] Consequently, whereas the sites described and planned here include all settlement features arguably pre-Norman, the surveys cover a broad spectrum of morphological features, some of which might in future be demonstrated to be dated much later than this. Conversely, in some instances, historic settlement may conceal earlier occupation.
Establishing a chronology and typologies for hut or homestead types, or for field wall construction or settlement pattern, remains a near-impossible task on the basis of fieldwork alone. Furthermore, few unenclosed settlements of any period have been tested by excavation in upland Wales. These problems have important implications for planning future palaeoenvironmental exploration strategies. Until more archaeological and palaeoecological data have been scrutinised, it remains difficult to undertake anything more than the most basic analysis of these settlement features.

[1] E.g., R. Bradley, *Prehistoric Settlement of Britain*, (London, 1978).

[2] H. C. Bowen, *Prehistoric Fields*, (London: Brit. Assoc. Advmnt Sci., 1961).

[3] For e.g., R.C.A.M. *Caerns* I, 1956.

[4] D. W. Harding, *Hillforts: Later Prehistoric Earthworks in Britain and Ireland*, (Edinburgh: U.P., 1976).

[5] D. A. Spratt and C. B. Burgess, *Upland Settlement in Britain: the second millennium B.C. and after*, (Oxford: B.A.R. 143, 1985).

[6] I. G. Simmons and M. J. Tooley, *The Environment in British Prehistory*, (London, 1981); A. Caseldine, *Environmental Archaeology in Wales*, (Lampeter: St David's University Coll., 1990).

[7] E.g., C. R. Musson, *The Breiddin Hillfort. A Late Prehistoric Settlement in the Welsh Marches*, C.B.A. Res. Rep. no. 76.

[8] C. S. Briggs, 'Early Observations on Early Fields', p. 145 in H. C. Bowen and P. Fowler, (eds.), *Early Land Allotment in the British Isles: A Survey of Recent Work*, (Oxford: B.A.R. 48, 1978).

[9] Jones, *Hist. Brecks.* II, ii (1809), p. 478.

[10] G. Gilpin, 'Mounds of earth near Pontneddfychan', *Gentleman's Mag.* (1802), part II, p. 985; G. L. Gomme, *Archaeology: A Classified Collection of the Chief Contents of 'The Gentlemans Magazine' from 1731–1868*, (London: Elliot Stock, 1886), pp. 289–90 (without illustrations).

[11] Briggs, *loc. cit.* n. 8.

[12] C. S. Briggs, 'Early Field Enclosures in Mid-Ulster: Records of stone walls from the Ordnance Survey Memoirs, 1835–7', (forthcoming); for more recent fields in Ireland, see: S. Caulfield, 'Neolithic Fields, the Irish Evidence', pp. 137–43, in H. C. Bowen and P. J. Fowler, (eds.), (1978), and 'The Prehistoric Settlement of North Connaught', pp. 195–216, in T. Reeves Smyth and F. Hamond, (eds.), *Landscape Archaeology in Ireland*, (Oxford: B.A.R. 116, 1983).

[13] J. A. Brongers, *1833: Reuvens in Drenthe, a contribution to the history of Dutch Archaeology in the First Half of the nineteenth century*, (Rijksdienst voor het oudheidkundig Bodemonderziek Fibula-van Dishoeck, 1973).

[14] C. von Estorff, *Heidnische Alterhümer der Gegend von Ülzen*, (Zelle, 1846).

[15] N.M.W., Cantrill MSS, foolscap MS List of Ancient Monuments in Wales, fos. 16–17, no. 41.

[16] A.P.s, C.U.A.P. CEQ, nos. 60–6.

[17] For example by members of The Merthyr Naturalists' Trust and Mr P. M. Jones of Tredegar.

[18] Though see Richard Kay's MSS notebooks (of observations collected c. 1960–1972) which cover all periods and contain sketch plans of some hut sites (N.M.R.). See also *History of Merthyr*, p. 36.

[19] A. H. A. Hogg, 'Some Unfortified Hut-Groups in Wales', *Celticum VI: Actes du Troisième Colloque International d'Etudes Gauloises, Celtiques et Protoceltiques: Supplement à OGAM, Tradition Celtique*, no. 86, pp. 245–56, (Rennes, 1963); espec. Fig. on p. 246; *cf. idem.* 'Native Settlement in Wales', pp. 23–38 in C. Thomas, (ed.), *Rural Settlement in Roman Britain*, (C.B.A., 1966); P. J. Fowler, 'Later Prehistory', pp. 63–300 in S. Piggott, (ed.), *The Agrarian History of England and Wales, I.i, Prehistory*, (Cambridge: U.P., 1981), pp. 176–7, 188.

[20] Piggott, *loc. cit. supra*, p. 188.

[21] Summarised in C. B. Burgess and D. A. Spratt, (eds.), *Upland Settlement*.

[22] R.C.A.M., *Brecks. Inv.* I, (ii).

[23] The problems of seasonal function, *hafotai* and upland settlement features are discussed by A. H. Ward, 'Transhumant or Permanent Settlement?', pp. 1–22 in H. James, (ed.), *Sir Gar: Studies in Carmarthenshire History, Essays in memory of W. H. Morris and M. C. G. Evans*, (Carmarthen: Antiquarian Soc. Monographs, vol. 4, 1991).

Problems of Study

Earth Processes

(i) *Valley Alluviation*

There are marked contrasts between elevated farmland and moorland and valley bottom site distributions of both settlement and burial sites. Few stone-built cairns survive in valley bottom locations (Fig. 53). The larger standing stones are more heavily concentrated in river valleys than upon moorland and may have been medieval, rather than prehistoric, in origin (p. 164). On this terrain reconnaissance may provide the only traces of earlier settlement. In Brecknockshire a few such sites have been detected in a limited compass of the middle Wye Valley between Llyswen and Hay (LS 7–8). These probably herald future discoveries of settlement elsewhere in the Wye and Usk valleys.

It seems probable that alluviation may account for some relict distributions.[1] Continuous agricultural practice through Roman and medieval times has also taken its toll in helping eradicate or modify traces of earlier valley settlement. Nevertheless, stray finds of artefacts from as early as the Mesolithic, the presence of megalithic tombs on fertile, low-lying land[2] and the discovery of unmarked Bronze Age burials (for example LBS 4–10) attest to continuous lowland settlement from the earliest times. These lowland burial sites appear most often to have been entirely earthen, or of stone and earth. Because they are particularly vulnerable to plough damage and stone scavenging, burial monuments are in consequence nowadays rarer in lowland than in upland locations. Only in a limited number of cases have prehistoric barrows survived on river floodplains in this part of Wales. Tested by the spade, the one at Y Dderw, Llyswen (RCS 5), yielded little information. In common with several other enigmatic lowland mounds (for e.g. RCS 6–8), this seems most likely to have been a medieval estate or garden viewing platform.[3] The excavation of a stone-built mound at Darren Fawr upon a terrace of the River Taf (RCS 4) demonstrated its more likely origin in recent field clearance practice than as an early burial site.

It is a commonplace that widespread deforestation at any period causes flooding and consequent erosion. In this connection Crampton propounded that Carn Goch (CT 10) had probably been built at a time when mountain streams were capable of flash floods which brought vast tonnages of boulders down from the hills onto the Usk river terrace where the mound is sited.[4] The validity of this theory depends partly on the supposed induction of devastating erosion through Iron Age deforestation. But whilst some forest indubitably existed from the earliest times, flooding seems an unlikely explanation for the site's original existence and subsequent preservation.

Stable mature river terraces tend to preserve cropmark settlement features which can be recognised through aerial photography. However, many early settlement complexes have certainly been eroded away or silted over. The degree of this erosion obviously depends on the stage of floodplain development. Although a variety of later prehistoric single-finds were made in river valleys (Fig. 123), few upstanding lowland earthwork sites are demonstrably earlier than the Iron Age. Most earthen Bronze Age burial mounds seem to have been ploughed beyond recognition, though a few may have been re-used in later periods.

[1] As suggested in *Brecks. Inv.* I (ii), p. 5.

[2] The Gwernvale megalith excavation, with finds from Mesolithic to Iron Age, provides a good illustration of this point.

[3] C. S. Briggs, 'Garden Archaeology in Wales', in A. E. Brown, (ed.), *Garden Archaeology*, C.B.A. Res. Rep. 78, (London, 1991), pp. 138–59.

[4] C. B. Crampton, 'A Proposed Re-interpretation of Carn Goch, near Crickhowell, Brecknock', *Arch. Camb.* 105 (1966), pp. 166–8.

(ii) *Limestone Solution*

Some of the most interesting karstic features in Britain are to be found in South Wales.[1] A significant part of Brecknockshire lies upon the Carboniferous Limestone separating the Glamorgan Coal Measures on the south from the Old Red Sandstones of the Brecon Beacons on the north (Fig. 121).[2] Karstic processes are not confined to the limestone; they also affect the Millstone Grit and adjacent Carboniferous sandstones.[3] Bare limestone is sporadically exposed in a number of places extending eastward from the Carmarthenshire Black Mountain, along the south of the Fans.[4]

Throughout this area bedrock is heavily overlain by glacial and fluvio-glacial deposits, often many metres in depth.[5] This overburden is sporadically punctuated by 'sink holes' or 'dolines', many of which are depicted upon the O.S. 1:10,000 and 1:25,000 maps. Some are sufficiently large to appear at a scale of 1:50,000.[6] Dolines were observed to open or to widen considerably during the period of investigation.[7]

Solution hollows may have affected the location or nature of early settlement, which appears almost ubiquitous in these limestone uplands. At present it is unclear how far these solution processes may be connected to global climatic factors (including, for example, acid rain), and whether or not accelerated shake-hole growth could relate directly to local vegetational change brought about by gazing practices.[8]

The dissolution process in the neighbourhood of monuments is illustrated, for example, upon Cefn Esgair Carnau (US 79; Fig. 144). One of the best examples is the wall traversing the western part of Llangynidr Common (US 105; Pl. 7). Whilst its course illustrates the several stages of shake-hole development, however, in some places the wall has now completely disappeared into trenches to become a 'negative' feature. It can therefore be deduced that the wall was built at a time prior to, or in the infancy of, shake-hole development in this area. Erosion features visible today therefore may not have seriously affected the way in which land was chosen for early settlement.

Solution processes may not have been so destructive within tree-covered environments as in open landscapes, owing to reduced run-off. After the first land-taking, deforestation and agricultural activity probably upset the balance of environmental stability in afforested terrain. Nature now appears to have taken over; much of the karstic land surface, and that of the adjacent strata, is slowly collapsing into cave systems. Through solution and soil-loss, man-made and natural surface features are left stranded upon limestone pavements.

A model of this process can be constructed, explaining man's probable causal role (Fig. 120).[9] On limestone areas and upon drift-strewn terrain covering limestone, field clearances and burial cairns invariably included a limestone boulder component. Limestone is still visible in some cairns (like Carn Caws RC 254), though only where the limestone was not later scavenged for agricultural purposes.

Blanket peat initiation followed abandonment of the

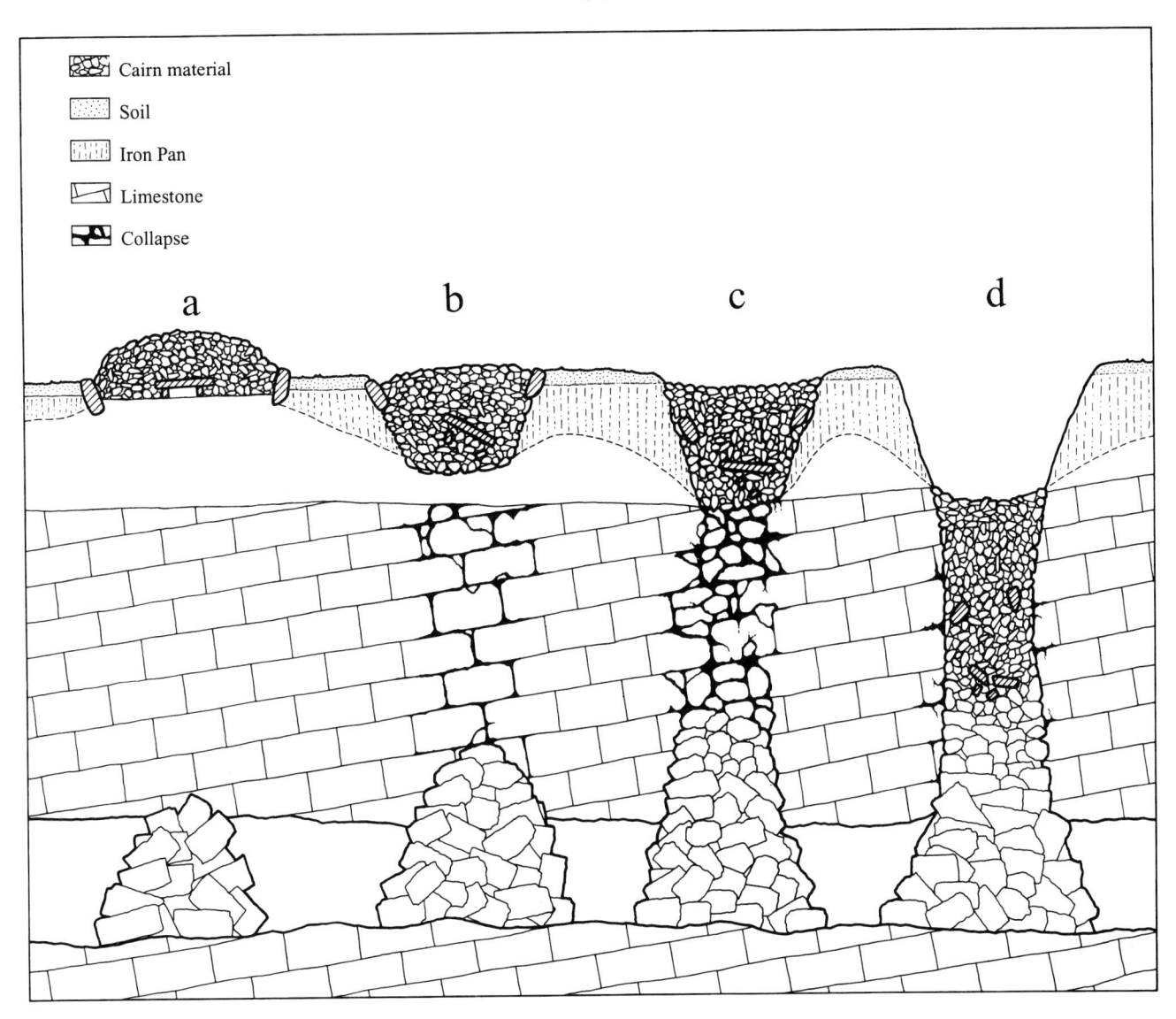

Key:
- Cairn material
- Soil
- Iron Pan
- Limestone
- Collapse

a b c d

120 Limestone erosion processes showing sink-hole formation

early agricultural landscape at a date between about 1500 and 1000 B.C. (pp. 6–7). Peat growth then overtook some upstanding monuments, impeding drainage and creating extensive hardpans. The edges of the monuments would be coterminous with hardpan formation. Beneath the structure there would be no hardpan because the presence of the monument protects it from the rain. In consequence, perimeter water would feed out of the hardpan beneath the site, percolating slowly through underlying drift to bedrock.

The speed of this process clearly depends on the depth of drift and proportions of limestone it contained. Rates of speleogenesis within the underlying solid limestone are now thought to be assisted by the role of micro-organisms which attack the more sulphide and hydrocarbon-rich strata.[10] Thus water carrying peat or other vegetational fragments could be expected to be a particularly effective limestone dissolution agent creating subterranean waterways and caverns.[11] In a number of cases the dolines resulting from this process would be negative replicas of the monuments. Accordingly, stone ponds would eventually replace cairns upon *mor*. Similarly, walls can become linear boulder trenches, often appearing indistinguishable from small englacial or periglacial boulder or debris flows.[12]

Knowledge of the speed and causes of this process may provide a key to dating the monuments it has affected. Excavations in shake-holes may produce results of limited interest to pedology and vegetational history, since organic material is unlikely to survive constant percolation. Water-filled shake-holes might more usefully repay sedimentological and pollen analytical study, and some clues are likely to be found stratified in deposits sealed within underlying cave systems. Although several extensive solution systems have been mapped in Brecknockshire, thorough sediment studies seem to be rare. Indeed, it seems likely that few cavers can be fully aware of the archaeological and palaeoecological potential to be realised from investigation of the underground deposits which are so often blasted away in the name of exploration and discovery.

Karren analysis, a technique developed to quantify dissolution rates of buried and exposed limestone boulders within early monuments,[13] is probably unsuited to this kind of terrain and its application may prove to be restricted to smaller boulder monuments. Controlled excavation in a variety of milieux around these monuments is clearly desirable.

The dissolution process of monuments has far-ranging implications for limestone landscape and settlement studies. In southern Brecknockshire the numerous 'negative' stone piles filling solution hollows are unlikely to have been created by recent intentional stone dumping. 'Boulder trains' or 'boulder lines' are common upon the same terrain. Many of these now appear more likely to be man-made rather than natural in origin. Conventional ground survey is probably inadequate for these fossil landscapes and future field investigation will need to be complemented by large-scale vertical aerial photography. Co-operative archaeological, geomorphological, speleological and palaeo-environmental approaches are clearly necessary to study and understand this process, which is slowly and imperceptibly infusing the works of nature with those of man.

[1] H. P. Chapman, *Caves and Cave Life*, (New Naturalist, 1993, pp. 89–92); D. J. Crowther, 'Karst geomorphology of South Wales', pp. 19–39, in *Limestones and Caves*; see also *Limestone and Caves*, passim.

[2] F. J. North, *The river scenery at the head of the Vale of Neath*, (4th edn., Cardiff: N.M.W., 1962); R. O. Jones, 'The evolution of the Neath-Tawe drainage', *Proc. Geol. Assoc.* 50 (1939), pp. 530–66; T. R. Owen, 'The Headwaters of the River Neath', pp. 74–84 in D. A. Bassett and M. G. Bassett, (eds.), *Geological Excursions in South Wales and the Forest of Dean*, (Cardiff: The Geologists' Association, South Wales Group, 1971); T. R. Owen and R. H. T. Rhodes, *Geology around the University Towns: Swansea, South Wales*, Geol. Assoc. Guide 17 (2nd edn., 1969).

[3] T. M. Thomas, 'Solution subsidence outliers of Millstone Grit on the Carboniferous Limestone of the North Crop of the South Wales coalfield', *Geol. Mag.* 91 (1954), pp. 220–6; 'Swallow Holes on the Millstone Grit and Carboniferous Limestone of the South Wales Coalfield', *Geograph. Jnl* 120 (1954), pp. 468–75; 'Solution subsidence in south-east Carmarthenshire and south-east Breconshire', *Trans Inst. Brit. Geogr.* 33 (1963), pp. 45–60; 'The Geology and Geomorphology of the Upper Swansea Valley Area with Particular Reference to Karstic Landforms', pp. 96–105, in D. A. Bassett and M. G. Bassett, (eds.), *loc. cit.* n. 2.

[4] T. M. Thomas, 'The limestone pavements of the North Crop of the South Wales coalfield with special reference to solution rates and processes', *Trans Inst. Brit. Geogr.* 50 (1970), pp. 97–105.

[5] T. M. Thomas, 'The Geomorphology of Brecknock', *Brycheiniog* 5 (1959), pp. 55–156.

[6] Thomas in *Geol. Mag., loc. cit.* n. 3.

[7] Particularly US 77–80; in the Mynydd y Garn Maun-Tincer area.

[8] J. N. Jennings, *Karst Geomorphology*, (1985).

[9] This erosion model was propounded by C. S. Briggs, *Problems and Processes*, pp. 60–5.

[10] T. K. Ball and J. C. Jones, 'Speleogenesis in the Limestone Outcrop North of the South Wales Coalfield: the Role of Micro-organisms in the Oxidation of Sulphides and Hydrocarbons', *Cave Science* 17 (1990), pp. 1–8.

[11] L.W. Price, *The Periglacial Environment, Permafrost, and Man*, (Washington: Assoc. Amer. Geogr., 1972); espec. Fig. 26, p. 33.

[12] O. C. Lloyd, 'The Hepste River Caves and Study of the Hepste-Mellte Area', *Proc. Univ. Bristol Speleol. Soc.* 15 (1979), pp. 107–27; G. J. Mullan, 'The Little Neath River Cave', *Proc. Univ. Bristol Speleol. Soc.* 18 (1988), pp. 314–16; P. A. Standing and O. C. Lloyd, 'Porth yr Ogof, Powys', *Proc. Univ. Bristol Speleol. Soc.* 12 (1970), pp. 213–29; 15 (1980), p. 259; P. A. Standing, M.D. Newson and A. G. Wilkins, 'The Little Neath River Cave', *Proc. Univ. Bristol Speleol. Soc.* 12 (1971), pp. 303–25.

[13] E. Plunkett-Dillon, 'Karren analysis as an archaeological technique', pp. 81–94 in T. Reeves-Smyth and F. Hamond, (eds.), *Landscape Archaeology in Ireland*, (Oxford: B.A.R. 116, 1983).

(iii) *Boulder Trains and Debris Flows and Features Resulting from Frost Action*

Boulder trains probably developed during glacial retreat and under later tundra climate conditions. Debris flows form upon steep slopes and are probably caused by sudden changes in environmental balance.[1] Flows today active in the Black Mountain area have been estimated to be no more than 700 years old.[2] This estimate may have important implications for dating settlement sites in the Upper Tawe Valley (US 30–38).

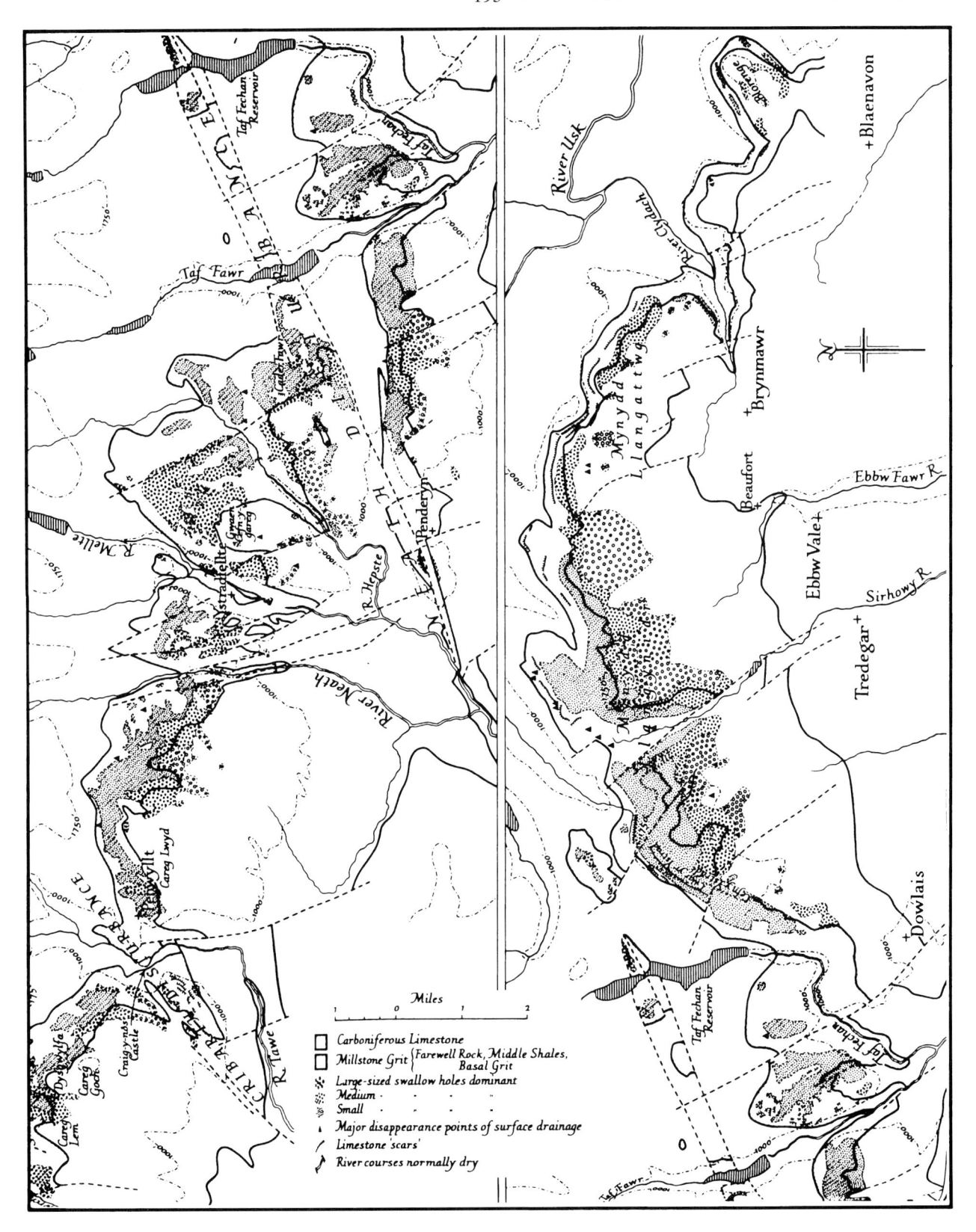

121 Limestone and boulder drift (from Thomas, *Geogr. Jnl* 1954)

On occasion, Holocene erosion has re-sorted and re-graded flows and boulder trains, merging their varied facies into stable landscape features. Some quite spectacular examples of trains survive on the break of slope beneath the Darren to the north of Crickhowell (for example, US 112).[3] Interdigitated with these are slightly terraced features and small stone groups which may be indications of early field clearances.[4] The possibility arises that some field walls or linear clearance piles actually enhance natural features, such as stone-lobed banks, gelifluction terraces, sorted stripes, earth hummocks and other features resulting from frost action.[5] Under sub-glacial and tundra conditions, both graded and ungraded boulders can form naturally in parallel lines, which, interspersed with stable, mature, post-glacial soils, could easily be converted to primitive plant or animal enclosures difficult to distinguish from natural features or from more certainly man-made boundaries.

[1] L. W. Price, *The Periglacial Environment, Permafrost, and Man*, (Washington: Assoc. Amer. Geogr., 1972), espec. p. 33, Fig. 26; recent research on debris flows and associated processes is summarised by C. K. Ballantyne in 'Present-day Periglaciation of Upland Britain', pp. 113–126 in J. Boardman, (ed.), *Periglacial processes and landforms in Britain and Ireland*, (Cambridge, 1987); espec. pp. 119–20.
[2] I. Statham, 'Debris Flows on Vegetated Screes in the Black Mountain, Carmarthenshire', *Earth Surface Processes* I (1976), pp. 173–80.
[3] P. M. Jones, *Arch. in Wales* 19 (1979), p. 9.
[4] Not surveyed for this volume.
[5] D. F. Ball and R. Goodier, 'Morphology and Distribution of features resulting from frost-action in Snowdonia', *Fld Stud.* 3 (1970), 193–218.

(iv) *Boulder Scavenging*

A major problem affecting all stone-built monuments is domestic and industrial stone collection. In common with many other areas, demands for building, roadstone and paths have indubitably affected many prehistoric monuments in Brecknockshire over several millennia. Roman and later economic pressures were probably responsible for removing many of the earlier monuments from much low-lying ground, now apparently stone-free. Erosion of the remoter upland monuments is now greatest from visitor pressure; many stone-built features are being slowly carried off or dramatically altered by hill-walkers.

Limestone collection, at one time a necessary agricultural activity, well documented from medieval times, would have been a selective process in cairn destruction. Although it seems likely that many monuments may have been entirely ransacked for their limestone content in areas some distance removed from limestone exposures, it is impossible to assess the degree to which this happened, or indeed to distinguish between deliberate limestone extraction and its natural disappearance in solution. Combined natural and human agencies are responsible for the complete destruction or partial survival of most surviving settlement and burial features.

F. J. North, *Limestones: Their origins, distribution and uses*, (1930), pp. 385–422; S. R. Hughes, *The Brecon Forest Tramroad*, R.C.A.M. (Wales), (1991).

(v) *Problems of Vegetation (including peat growth)*

It was not always possible to assess vegetational growth during archaeological field reconnaissance. Indeed, in some areas mapping field systems was hampered by peat overgrowth, or through more superficial vegetational invasion. The field systems on Waun Tincer (US 77–8), Cefn Esgair Carnau (US 79–80), and in Cwm Cadlan (US 83) are all partially masked, the former by vigorous heather growth. The Cwm Cadlan field system is still partially peat-covered. Peat also masks the more northerly extremes of the field system at Cwm Moel (US 96), whereas the fugitive field walls on Cefn Cilsanws (US 92) lie beneath thin grass (*Festuca*) cover, which when parched made the features more easily recognisable from the air.

Available studies mapping rates of moorland intake[1] demonstrate appreciable encroachment from farming during the period 1885–1975 (some 11 per cent), within the Brecon Beacons National Park. Although in the 1980s and 1990s overgrazing is believed to be a major problem on roughland and moorland, no data are yet available quantifying its effects upon either vegetational growth or peat erosion. There exists a general consensus of opinion among some graziers and hill-walkers in south Brecknockshire that recent recognition of such a quantity of fugitive settlement features upon areas of traditional commonage is due to great increases in sheep numbers since Commons Registration in 1976. This best explains the dramatic discovery rate of early field clearances in areas like Cwm Cadlan, already familiar to archaeologists for their stone burial cairns since the 1950s and '60s. Although local folk-memory maintains that parts of

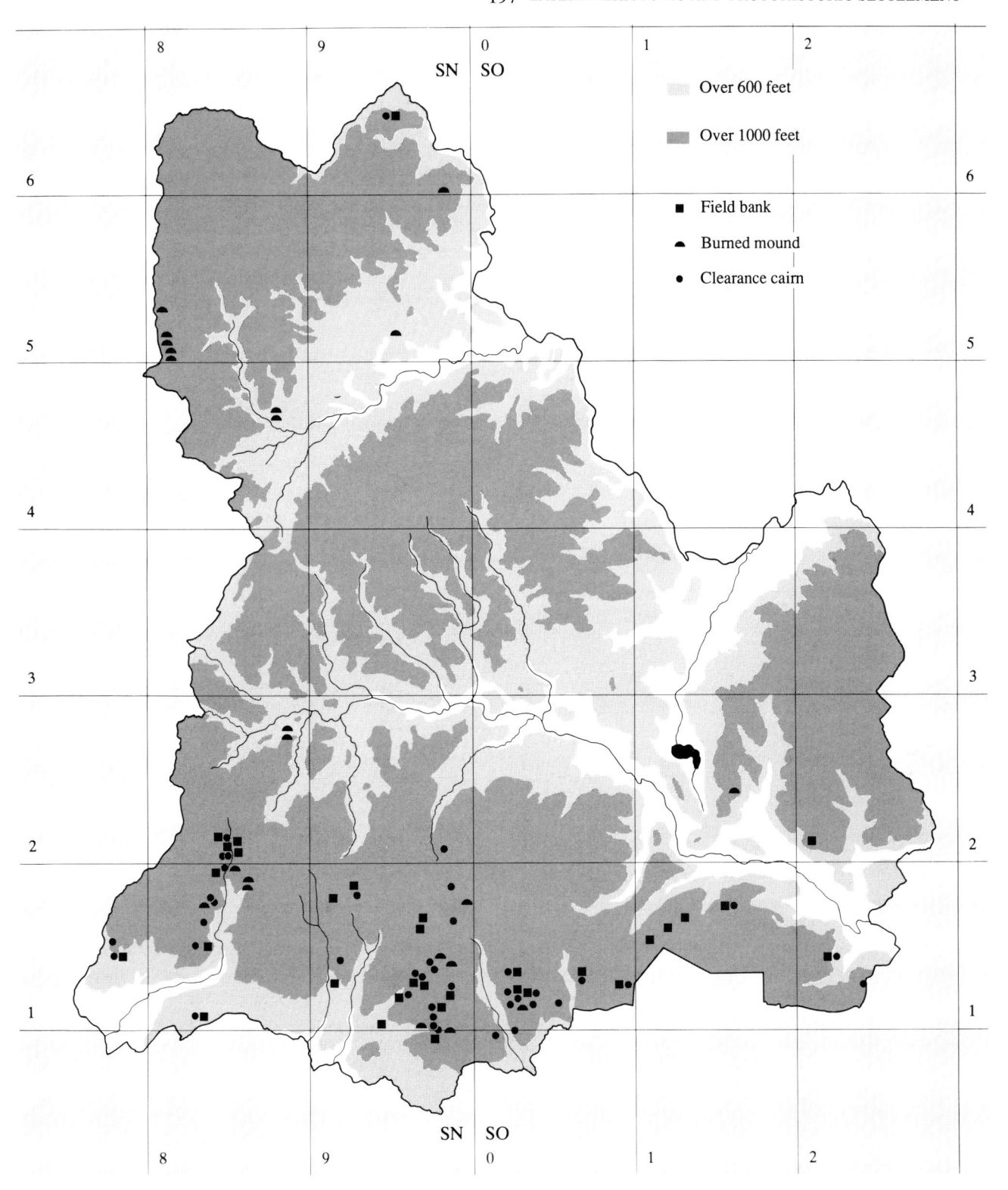

197 LATER PREHISTORIC AND PROTOHISTORIC SETTLEMENT

122 Early agricultural clearances and burned mounds

Cwm Cadlan remained waist-high in heather until the 1950s, there are no known photographs to confirm this potentially crucial assertion.

[1] C. E. Harkness, *Mapping Changes in the Extent of Woodland in Upland Areas (1885–1975)*, Surveys of moorland and roughland change, no. 12, Moorland Change Project, (Birmingham University, Dept of Geography, 1982); M. L. Parry, A. Bruce, and C. E. Harkness, *Changes in the extent of Moorland and Roughland in the Brecon Beacons National Park*, Surveys of moorland and roughland change, no. 7, Moorland Change Project, (Birmingham University, Dept of Geography, 1982).

Early Settlement and Agricultural Economy

Distribution and Chronology of Settlement

Delimiting the geographical extent of past settlement and farming practice is an exercise heavily governed by environmental and historical factors. It includes the major problem of differential site survival and recognition at the present day.

Those areas densest in known pre-industrial settlement sites are centred upon the headwaters of the Tawe, Nedd and Taf, with sporadic scatters east–west along the Carboniferous Limestone and Millstone Grit outcrops, mainly lying to the south of the Brecon Beacons. Brief accounts of factors affecting site preservation and discovery are given above.

Early settlement is relatively fugitive in the Black Mountains to the north of Abergavenny, probably due to destructive, post-medieval industrial development, which included quarrying, mining and intensive agriculture. Heavy clay soils upon the Old Red Sandstone do not as easily lend themselves to site recognition as do the lighter ones covering the better-drained Carboniferous rocks further south. Mynydd Epynt, also upon Old Red Sandstone, preserves few known prehistoric settlement sites, its landscape betraying the heavier erosive hand of medieval farming, here testified by widespread rig and furrow, now partially hidden beneath advancing bracken and heath. Large-scale farming on some of these fertile upland tracts may antedate the medieval plough; indeed, mention of a Dark Age estate at Llandeilo'r Fan (p. 278) betrays earlier origins. Only excavation and palaeoecology seem likely to elucidate this history further.

The north-western dissected plateaux of the county adjoining Cardiganshire and Radnorshire were also well settled in medieval and later times, much of the area having comprised monastic grange land (see US 87 for discussion). It is unclear how far pre-medieval clearances and settlement features survive in this area, though the presence of prehistoric cairns and the testimony of palaeoecology indicate human presence as early as the Mesolithic.

The northern part of the Afon Tawe with Cwm Haffes valleys, the Cribarth and Dan yr Ogof Plateaux lie at heights of between 400 and 440 m above O.D. and are mainly unenclosed. This landscape, which might usefully be divided between eroding limestone upland and aggrading river valleys, is punctuated by rock exposures and boulder scatters; these in turn are often interdigitated with, and indistinguishable from, field clearances and burial cairns. Early settlement has also left well-preserved, mainly rectangular huts, sheep pens and sharply incised moorland tracks. Few of these features are datable. Some are probably multi-period; many are described here more on account of their primitive appearance than due to any certainty of antiquity.

The erosive effects of agricultural practice can on occasion be detected in stream sections. In this respect, interest attaches to the section exposed in the east bank of the Afon Tawe (at around O.S. SN 8512 2163). In this, *c.* 0.1–0.15 m of turf overlies a layer of peat up to 0.1 m deep, onto a stony (possibly agricultural) soil up to 0.2 m above a red clayey coarser soil, lying in turn upon what may be an original early, possibly prehistoric, ploughsoil flecked with charcoal. The entire deposit is stratified above a surface of boulder clay. A similar exposure was noted in the west bank of the Nant Tarw, about 200 m north of the enclosure (US 29) near the eponymous stone circles (SC 2).

Recent changes in the karstic landscape are discussed above (pp. 192–4). Glaciation has left thick swathes of superficial deposit in some places (Fig. 121), which steep down-cutting has exposed where deposits lay adjacent to stream or river courses. Post-glacial vegetational history is obviously crucial to an understanding of man–land relationships and landscape development.

The headwaters of the Afonydd Nedd (Neath), Mellte, Llia, Hepste, and Taf,[1] which drain a significant part of the Beacons area, preserve one of the most interesting settlement palimpsest landscapes in Wales which has attracted interest for more than half a century.[2] The solid geology gives rise to a wide diversity of topography, ranging from karstic features, with innumerable swallow or sink holes and some limestone pavement on the east, around Ystradfellte.

[1] R. O. Jones, 'The evolution of the Neath-Tawe drainage', *Proc. Geol. Assoc.* 50 (1939), pp. 530–66; F. J. North, *The river scenery at the head of the Vale of Neath*, 4th edn., (Cardiff: Nat. Mus. Wales, 1962); T. R. Owen, 'The Headwaters of the River Neath', pp. 74–84 in D. A. and M. G. Bassett, (eds.), *Geological Excursions in South Wales and the Forest of Dean*, (Cardiff: The Geologists' Association, South Wales Group, 1971); T. R. Owen and R. H. T. Rhodes, *Geology around the University Towns: Swansea, South Wales*, (2nd edn.), (Geol. Assoc. Guide 17, 1969).

[2] C. Fox, 'A Croft in the Upper Nedd Valley, Ystradfellte, Brecknockshire', *Antiquity* 14 (1940), pp. 363–76.

Classification of Sites

(i) *Larger Enclosures*

Although hillforts (*Inv. Br.* I (ii), pp. 21–123) are the best-known form of large settlement site current in later prehistoric times, less spectacular enclosures are also known, some possibly contemporary with, or earlier than, the Iron Age.

In Brecknockshire a number of enclosures have been recognised with associated indications of early occupation. Some may have been intended as animal pens, or equally could have been designed for crop protection. Such sites may have continued in use into Dark Age times, or later. Some enclosures apparently without associated features, now appear to be entirely devoid of occupation. However, it should be borne in mind that wooden features do not easily survive; similarly, slight drystone footings are vulnerable to stone-robbing and would not easily be recognised after prolonged agricultural use. Examples of empty enclosures include (US 36) on Pant Sychpant and one on Gader Fawr (US 111 ii).

Some extensive enclosures interesting for their location and associations are situated upon the hillslopes of Mynydd y Garn, north of the Afon Hepste (Fig. 143). The largest complete example lies among swallow holes and encompasses several field clearance cairns and some short lengths of wall (US 75 i). A smaller enclosing wall to its south (US 75 ii) includes two hut-circles and several stone piles. Both enclosures seem to point to agricultural settlement, if, indeed, walls and hut-circles were contemporary. This area assumes greater interest when the groups of settlement features lying beyond these field boundaries to the north (US 77) and to the southeast (US 78) are taken into consideration.

One enclosure in Cwm Haffes (US 5 i) is ditched around the outer wall and includes small rectangular building platforms (Fig. 127). Further, irregularly-shaped boundary features on Allt Fach include a free-standing enclosure surrounding a variety of habitation structures (US 7 i–v) (Fig. 127), possibly indicative of multi-period occupancy.

Some slighter boundary banks (for e.g. at US 12) appear intended merely to isolate or protect discrete huts, homesteads or compounds. Some sites encompassing areas of ground less than about 10 m square were probably built as animal pens (US 13 i). The motive for isolating a plot high in the Upper Tawe Valley with a chord-shaped boulder wall (US 30) was probably also to protect animals, or to safeguard human or stock access to a small dam or running water. The reasons behind throwing a circular structure around a spring-head on flatter ground further up the valley (US 31 i) may have been similarly motivated. In Nant Crew the streamside embanked enclosure was probably intended for stock (US 64), but the purpose of a circular enclosure apparently without entrance on Carnon Gwinion (US 67) is quite enigmatic, as is the one associated with field walls at Dyffryn Nedd (US 68 i).

The embanked enclosure capping a streamside knoll in Nant Tarw (US 29) is included in this survey because of its proximity to, and possible association with, the eponymous stone circles (SC 2). However, its form is reminiscent of some small gardens[1] associated with peasant steadings, and it may be of much more recent origin than the prehistoric circles.

A growing body of information deriving from excavation is beginning to demonstrate the importance of wood in the construction of early dwellings and enclosures. This clearly has important implications for the future recognition and discovery of prehistoric and protohistoric non-earthwork sites, though those implications are already to some degree appreciated through the results of aerial photographic reconnaissance on lowland terrain.[2]

[1] C. S. Briggs, in *Jnl. Garden Hist.* 11 (1991), pp. 201–2.

[2] R. P. Whimster, *The Emerging Past: air photography and the buried landscape*, R.C.A.H.M. (E).

(ii) *Enclosed and Unenclosed Hut-groups*

Although early stone-built huts have been planned and studied in Wales for over a century,[1] their detailed evaluation through fieldwork did not begin until the Second World War.[2] Outside Brecknockshire, hut-groups are known from Anglesey,[3] Caernarfonshire,[4] Cardiganshire,[5] Denbighshire,[6] Glamorgan,[7] Merioneth,[8] and Pembrokeshire.[9] Their overall distribution has not been altered a great deal since Hogg reviewed unenclosed settlements in 1963.[10]

In Wales it was for long a convention to ascribe hut-groups a restricted floruit from the pre-Roman Iron Age to the later Roman period,[11] or to the Dark Ages. Although in 1951 Griffiths argued a Bronze Age origin for some Snowdonian sites,[12] this was not found acceptable[13] and the later datings continued.[14] Only more recent publication has vindicated Griffiths's view and it is now accepted that in Wales some may be as early as the Bronze Age.

Few huts have been excavated in recent years. Pre-construction activity at only one site, on Holyhead Mountain, Anglesey, has been radiocarbon dated to the early Bronze Age.[15] Neolithic pre-construction activity was in evidence at Moel y Gerddi, whilst there may have been late Bronze Age occupation (lasting well into the Iron Age) at Erw Wen in Merioneth.[16] Though poor in artefacts and organic finds,[17] Moel y Gerddi produced palaeoecological evidence hinting at occupancy during the later Bronze Age.[18] Generally, however, dating evidence is scant, and virtually none is known from Brecknockshire. Apparently in 1932 hut-circles survived near Tabor Chapel, Cefn Coed y Cymer (LS 5), in which a broken quern had been discovered. The later disappearance of this artefact makes it impossible to evaluate the site's cultural milieu. A further (rotary) quernstone was reported from the vicinity of enclosures and huts among the scree at Cwm-Gu (US 112). Here again the quernstone is lost. Neither quern was precisely associated with a hut site, and since rotary quernstones remained in use until recent historic times, these artefactual discoveries may have been unrelated to the earliest occupation of the sites.

In evaluations of huts and hut-groups, distinctions are usually drawn between groups completely enclosed and those without a visible or surviving curtilage, and those single, free-standing hut-circles.[19] These distinctions are rather more difficult to apply in South Wales than in Snowdonia. Built of softer sedimentary stone, habitation structures in Brecknockshire are generally not so well preserved as their northern counterparts; natural and human erosion has consequently taken a greater toll of their fabric. This makes them less capable of recognition, mensuration, or classification.

Round huts of varying sizes are recorded from some uncultivated parts of the county, though the best-known and best-preserved sites survive in the southwest, and in the Cwm Tawe–Cwm Taf area. These are variously associated with or include clearance cairns (for example at Dorwen, US 1 i), enclosed within or lying adjacent to extensive field systems (US 74), or lying within enclosure curtilages (US 75 ii). Their diameters range from about 3 m, 6 m (US 1 i) to 20 m (95 v); some too large to have accommodated a superstructure may have been animal pens. A handful of quite complex unenclosed hut-groups can also be recognised. Among linear banks and enclosures of indeterminate age and function lying alongside the Nant Llywarch are a handful of huts all less than 10 m in diameter, three appearing to lack entrances (US 58; Fig. 138). Not far to the east, at TonTeg, are a further five or more huts associated with two homestead platforms. Three of these are very closely grouped (US 59; Fig. 139). Round huts associated with features suggestive of multi-period occupancy include (US 7). Examples of single huts bounded by enclosing wall are located above the Nant Mawr stream at Nant Ganol (US 45). The conjoined structure lying between Nant Ganol and Nant Mawr (US 56; Fig. 137) might also have been enclosed.

The difficulties of distinguishing between ring cairns, or circular embanked burial monuments, and settlement huts are well illustrated by Cantrill's description of what he believed to be a hut-circle at Carnon Gwynion (RC 97). Later fieldworkers ascribed this a more certain sepulchral function. The structural resemblance between some ring cairns[20] and hut foundations clearly requires further investigation in this and possibly in other instances.[21]

The most comprehensive collection of hut-groups lies on the north side of Nant Car (US 95), where three distinct juxtaposed groups may have been occupied coevally, or may represent a succession of habitations on the same site. Site (95 vi), housing five huts, is the only enclosed hut-group in the county bearing an obvious resemblance to the Snowdonian examples, a resemblance also shared by the plan of Carn Canienydd (US 60), even though badly damaged through the more recent building of a sheepfold (Fig. 140).

In general, the softer lithologies of the South Wales uplands might not be expected to preserve upstanding structures of great antiquity quite as do the older, harder rocks of the North, but this example may signal otherwise unforeseen similarities in settlement type between the two regions.

[1] E. Owen, 'Arvona Antiqua', *Arch. Camb.* 21 (1866), pp. 215–28.

[2] W. J. Hemp and C. A. Gresham, 'Hut-circles in North-west Wales', *Antiquity* 18 (1944), pp. 183–96.

[3] *Inv. Anglesey*, pp. lxxiii–vi, (Walled Enclosures), pp. lxxvii–lxxix (Hut Types); B. J. O'Neil, 'Excavations at Porth Dafarch, Holyhead Island, Anglesey, 1936', *Arch. Camb.* 95 (1940), pp. 65–74; C. W. Phillips, 'The Excavation of a hut-group at Pant y Saer in the Parish of Llanfair Mathafarn Eithaf, Anglesey', *Arch. Camb.* 89 (1934), pp. 1–36.

[4] *Inv. Caerns.* II, pp. lxxxvii–cvii; C. A. Gresham, 'Dr Gerhard Bersu's Excavations in Cwm Ystradllyn', *Arch. Camb.* 121 (1972), pp. 51–60.

[5] W. Smith in D. R. Thomas, 'Prehistoric and other remains in Cynwil Gaio', *Arch. Camb.* 34 (1879); J. G. Evans, *Prehistoric Farmers of Skomer Island; an archaeological Guide*, West Wales Trust for Nature Preservation, (Cardiff, 1986); 'An Archaeological Survey of Skomer, Dyfed', *P.P.S.* 56 (1990), pp. 247–68.

[6] J. Manley, 'Fields, Cairns and Enclosures on Ffridd Brynhelen, Clwyd', pp. 317–50 in *Upland Settlement*; 'Fields, Farms and Funerary Monuments on Mynydd Poeth, Clwyd', *B.B.C.S.* 33 (1986), pp. 384–413; 'A Late Bronze Age landscape on the Denbigh Moors, northeast Wales', *Antiquity* 64 (1990), pp. 514–26.

[7] R.C.A.M., *Inv. Glamorgan* I (ii), pp. 72–9.

[8] C. A. Gresham, in *Hist. Merioneth*, pp. 176–224; R. S. Kelly, 'The Ardudwy Survey', *Jnl. Merioneth Archaeol. Hist. Soc.* 90 (1982), pp. 121–62; J. Latham, 'An Archaeological Field Survey of the Dolmelynllyn Estate, Merioneth', National Trust, unpubl. typescript, (Aberystwyth, 1983).

[9] H. James and G. H. Williams, 'Rural Settlement in Roman Dyfed', pp. 289–311 in D. Miles, (ed.), *The Romano-British Countryside*, (Oxford: B.A.R. 103, 1982), at p. 291; P. Drewett, 'An Interim Report on fieldwork on Mynydd Preseli', unpubl. typescript (London: Institute of Archaeology, 1983).

[10] A. H. A. Hogg, 'Some unfortified Hut-groups in Wales', pp. 244–56 in *Celticum VI; Actes du Troisième Colloque International D'Etudes Gauloises, Celtiques et Protoceltiques 1962*, (Supplément à Ogam Tradition Celtique, no. 86, 1963, (Rennes, 1963)); C. A. Smith, 'The excavation at Cefn Graenanog and the study of enclosed homesteads', in R. B. White, (ed.), *The Excavations at Cefn Graenanog*, Cambrian Archaeol. Assoc. Monographs, (forthcoming).

[11] The dating evidence is most succinctly summarised by R. S. Kelly in 'Recent Research on the Hut Group Settlements of North-west Wales', pp. 102–11, and G. Williams in 'Recent work on Rural Settlement in South-west Wales', pp. 112–22, in B. C. Burnham and J. L. Davies, (eds.), *Conquest, Co-Existence and Change: Recent work in Roman Wales, Trivium* 25, (Lampeter: S.D.U.C., 1990).

[12] W. E. Griffiths, 'Early settlements in Caernarvonshire', *Arch. Camb.* 101 (1950), pp. 38–71.

[13] *Caerns. Inv.* III, p. lvii; A. H. A. Hogg and R. G. Livens, 'Unfortified hut-groups in Wales: a consultative document', *Arch. in Wales* 16 (1976), pp. 8–12; the point is usefully discussed by C. A. Smith, 'Some Evidence of Early Upland Settlement from Wales', pp. 273–84, in *Upland Settlement*, at p. 275.

[14] B. E. Vyner, 'Romano-British Fields and Farms in the Vale of Glamorgan', *Britannia* 16 (1985), pp. 245–246; R. B. White, 'Cefn Graeanog', *Britannia* 9 (1976), p. 406; C. A. Smith, 'A Morphological analysis of late prehistoric and Romano-British settlements in north-west Wales', *Proc. Prehist. Soc.* 40 (1974), pp. 157–69; 'Late prehistoric and Romano-British enclosed homesteads in north-west Wales; an interpretation of their morphology', *Arch. Camb.* 126 (1974), pp. 38–52.

[15] C. A. Smith, 'Excavations at the Ty Mawr Hut-circles, Holyhead, Anglesey', *Arch. Camb.* 136 (1987), pp. 20–38.

[16] R. S. Kelly, 'Moel y Gerddi and Erw-wen: two late prehistoric circular enclosures near Harlech, Gwynedd', *P.P.S.* 54 (1988), pp. 101–51.

[17] *Ibid.*

[18] F. M. Chambers and S.-M. Price, 'The Environmental Setting of Erw-wen and Moel y Gerddi: Prehistoric Enclosures in Upland Ardudwy, North Wales', *P.P.S.* 54 (1988), pp. 93–100.

[19] *Caerns Inv.* III.

[20] A. H. Ward, 'Survey and Excavation of Ring Cairns in SE Dyfed, and on Gower, West Glamorgan', *P.P.S.* 54 (1988), pp. 153–72.

[21] C. S. Briggs, *Problems and Processes*.

(iii–iv) *Scoop and Platform Settlements*

(iii) *Scoop Settlements*

Scoop settlements are the sites of early huts, now manifest as slight, occasionally moon-shaped, excavated hillslope scars. Initially recognised and excavated in Scotland and in the Borders,[1] where a Bronze Age origin has been demonstrated by excavation, scoop sites are now found elsewhere. They are usually difficult to recognise and the slightest vegetation cover may obscure their presence. A few are noted in this survey, though without excavation cultural analogy with northern Britain should be treated with caution. Examples include Allt Fach (US 7 ii–iii), Rhyd Uchaf (US 44), Garn Ddu (US 71) and a group of features like a cross between platform houses and hut-scoops on Waun Tincer (US 78).

Their distributional ranges from the Carmarthenshire Vans, and through the Cwm-Haffes area, the Tawe Techan and Tawe Fawr, to form important components of the settlement areas in Cwm Cadlan, Pant y Gadair, and Waun Tincer. Whereas without excavation their dating is enigmatic, comparison with settlements excavated outside Wales suggest origins as early as the early Bronze Age.

(iv) *Homestead platforms*

Homestead platforms are a common feature throughout upland Wales.[2] Typologically diverse, they range from flat, slightly elongated featureless square or rectangular slope-excavated plots, and include slope-oriented and other substantial structures supporting the building footings or upstanding walls of long-houses. The longer, slope-excavated plots probably evolved from prehistoric scoop settlements. Some may be of Dark Age origin (p. 278)[3] or may even have been occupied continuously since prehistoric times. The architecture of these buildings encompassed a wide range of forms and functions, exhaustive discussion of which is beyond the present brief.[4]

Until recently there persisted a general view that higher altitude homestead sites had been almost exclusively associated with the practice of upland summer stock pasturing, or transhumance[5] an economic activity of uncertain antiquity. This gives rise to the traditional historic nomenclature *hafotai*. These have been described in some numbers on the Carmarthen Fans,[6] on Mynydd Epynt,[7] the Beacons[8] and in north Glamorgan.[9] Analysis of documentary source material, of excavated evidence, and field observations demonstrating ploughing and field enclosure apparently for crop husbandry at high altitude has brought this interpretation into question.[10]

Close inspection of a long hut at Nant y Moch, Dyffryn Nedd in 1940, confirmed its origins in the historic period.[11] Excavation upon comparable sites in Glamorgan yielded similar dating evidence.[12] Although a full study of distribution and type in Brecknockshire awaits future survey and publication, it will be useful to provide outline details of these homestead sites.

Some, perhaps the more recent examples, seem to be more closely grouped (for example in Cwm Tawe (US 32)). One quite extensive settlement comprises a series of platforms occupying the southern valley side of Nant Crew (US 65), which may be associated with medieval landholding, though in the cases of both US 32 and US 65 much greater longevity of occupancy may be suspected. On open moorlands, particularly in the southern part of the county, many stream meander cores preserve vestiges of early occupation in the form of huts or platforms. Although their state of preservation often suggests a date in the historic period, some are probably earlier. A fairly typical example with associated fieldbanks lies beside the Afon Taf gorge (US 63).

The footings of some meander-core buildings are probably lost through riverbank erosion and, originally, the Nant Tarw enclosure, for example (US 29), may have been appended to a hut long since swept from the adjacent stream bank. The Afon Tarw and its tributaries are generally well endowed with meander-core settlement sites, a feature common to many mountain streams in the Beacons.

The geographically widespread distribution of this location type is demonstrated by an example lying on the east bank of the Afon Irfon at about 470 m above O.D. (SN 8306 5976) in Llanfihangel Abergwesyn. Homestead sites are associated with hut-scoops of more primitive appearance on the Ystradfellte Reservoir (US 53).

One site at the west end of Cwm Cadlan (US 71) preserves a handful of scoop or platform-homestead features. The two-fold internal division of one long hut (US 71 iii) may indicate a relatively recent origin.

A number of platform or long hut sites are enclosed by walls, most insufficiently extensive to be considered defensive, except in a sense of safe-guarding animals or crops. The close proximity of a surviving enclosure wall to the sites of two long huts at Carn y Goetre (US 72) gives rise to the possibility of earlier, rather than later, occupation. In this case, it is possibly as early as the Iron Age or Romano-British period.

[1] D. Coggins and K. J. Fairless, 'The Bronze Age Settlement Site of Bracken Rigg, Upper Teesdale, Co. Durham', *Durham Archaeol. Jnl* 1 (1984), pp. 5–21; G. Jobey, 'Excavation of an unenclosed settlement on Standrop Rigg, Northumberland and some problems related to similar settlements between Tyne and Forth', *Archaeologia Aeliana* 5 (ser. 11) (1983), pp. 1–21.

[2] For a comprehensive review of the more recent evidence for platform houses, see D. M. Robinson, 'Medieval vernacular buildings below the ground: a review and corpus for south-east Wales', *Glamorgan-Gwent Archaeological Trust Annual Report* (1981–2), pp. 94–123.

[3] L. A. S. Butler, 'Continuity of Settlement in Wales in the Central Middle ages', pp. 61–65 in L. Laing, *Studies in Celtic Survival*, (Oxford: B.A.R. 87, 1977); suggestions that square or rectangular platform huts may have been of Roman or Dark Age origin were made by A. and C. Fox in 'Forts and Farms on Margam Mountain', *Antiquity* 8 (1934), pp. 395–413.

[4] But for full review of this aspect, see D. M. Robinson, loc. cit. h. 2.

[5] E. Davies, 'Hendre and Hafod in Denbighshire', *Trans Denbighs Hist. Soc.* 26 (1977), pp. 49–72; 'Hendre and Hafod in Caernarvonshire', *Trans Caerns Hist. Soc.* 40 (1979), pp. 17–46; 'Hafod and Lluest', *Folklife* 23 (1984–5), pp. 76–96; 'Hendre, Hafoty, and Lluest; their distribution, features and purpose', *Ceredigion* 9 (1980), pp. 1–41.

[6] C. B. Crampton, 'Hafotai Platforms on the North Front of the Carmarthen Fans', *Arch. Camb.* 117 (1968), pp. 121–6.

[7] C. S. Briggs, 'Sites on Mynydd Epynt', *Arch. in Wales* 30 (1990), p. 40.

⁸ C. B. Crampton, 'Hafotai platforms on the North Front of the Brecon Beacons', *Arch. Camb.* 115 (1966), pp. 99–107.
⁹ P. Davis, 'Long-huts and Hafotai in Upland Glamorgan', *Arch. in Wales* 29 (1989), pp. 66–7.
¹⁰ Archaeological questions were first asked by R. S. Kelly in 'The Excavation of a Medieval Farmstead at Cefn Graeanog, Clynnog, Gwynedd', *B.B.C.S.* 29 (1982), pp. 859–908; see also C. S. Briggs in *Upland Settlement* (1985), and the most recent and comprehensive summary by A. H. Ward, 'Transhumant or Permanent Settlement', pp. 1–22 in H. James, (ed.), *Sir Gâr: Studies in Carmarthenshire History: Essays in memory of W. H. Morris and M. C. G. Evans*, (Carmarthen: Antiquarian Soc. Monograph no. 4, 1991).
¹¹ C. Fox, 'A Croft in the Upper Nedd Valley, Ystradfellte, Brecknockshire', *Antiquity* 14 (1940), pp. 363–76.
¹² A. Fox, 'Dinas Noddfa, Gelligaer Common, Glamorgan: Excavations in 1936', *Arch. Camb.* 92 (1937), pp. 247–268; 'Early Welsh Homesteads on Gelligaer Common, Glamorgan: Excavations in 1938', *Arch. Camb.* 94 (1939), pp. 163–99.

Indications of Early Farmland and Fields Systems

(i) *Field Systems*

Besides embanked and walled enclosures, strong indicators of early farming may be preserved in various forms of ploughmark and lynchets. Although some lynchets are known from Brecknockshire, these seem more likely of medieval than of prehistoric origin, and appear to be gardens associated with larger farms or manor houses.

Whereas at present most early boundaries in Brecknockshire seem so fugitive or incomplete as to scarcely merit distinction as 'field systems', nevertheless some vestigial patterns can be recognised. One early attempt at recognition of a complex 'celtic' field system associated with a hillfort (Twyn y Gaer, Llandefalle)¹ must now be discounted as an unfortunate misinterpretation of aerial photographs (RS 1).² Because of their apparent attachment to one another, a more certain association of field boundaries possibly contemporary with a hillfort (or at least a D-shaped enclosure) is noted at Cilnsanws (US 92, visible in the foreground of AP CUAP ARG 28), whilst the relationship between broken-down walls (US 107) and Crug y Gaer hillfort is less convincing.

Vestigial field walls are associated with circular huts and larger enclosures at Dyffryn Nedd (US 68) (Fig. 141).

The two most outstanding areas of field systems are Cadair Fawr with Waun Tincer, and Cwm Cadlan.³ In Cwm Cadlan (US 83) a major axis can be recognised, along which the fields may have been planned, a feature reminiscent of the Dartmoor Reaves of Bronze Age origin.⁴ Similar co-axial fields are widely dispersed throughout upland Britain, and have been plotted in the lowlands from aerial photographs.⁵ It is remotely possible that the field system underlying a nineteenth-century enclosure at Ffynnon yr Oerfa (Mynydd Epynt see p. 205) belongs to a similar cultural milieu, though more probably it is much later.

The field system covering Waun Tincer and Cadair Fawr (US 77, 78–82) does not share the regularity or planning discernible in Cwm Cadlan. However, the enclosure walls overlooking the River Hepste and incorporated huts and larger enclosures, may have been built sinuously in order to accommodate or avoid topographical or landscape features like solution hollows. Lack of uniformity in layout may not therefore always offer a clear indication of age.

Nevertheless, the condition of some man-made features affected by limestone solution processes may eventually offer a key to the longevity of settlement in this area. A field pattern morphologically similar to that on the Hepste has been described from the Denbigh hills, where radiocarbon dates suggest a late Bronze Age milieu,⁶ and field patterns discernible at sites near Trawsfynydd in Merioneth⁷ in an area where Iron Age settlement is now well documented⁸ also bear some resemblance to these Brecknockshire enclosure patterns.

The configuration of walls lying to the east of Cefn Cilnsanws at Cwm Moel (US 96) could be taken to indicate a small, well-planned farm (to judge from the extent of surrounding stone-heaped field clearances). However, the nearby survival of an abandoned nineteenth-century farmstead might hint at later, post-medieval use of this cleared adjacent hillside as 'outfields'. Maintenance of low vegetation by grazing the part of the field system lying closest to the later holding might help explain why, with increasing distance from it, older wall lines become encroached upon by impeded drainage before eventually disappearing into bog.

Although 2 km outside the Brecknockshire county boundary in Glamorgan, the field system on land adjacent to Morlais Castle is clearly of interest to this discussion.⁹ This undated field system and huts occupy similar limestone terrain to the unenclosed settlement of Penderyn, Vaynor and Ystradfellte.

¹ Presented by C. B. Crampton, *Arch. in Wales* 6 (1966), p. 5, and *Arch. Camb.* 116 (1967), pp. 63–5; O.S. Card SO 03 NE 4.

[2] Discounted in *Inv. Br.* I (ii), p. 73.

[3] D. K. Leighton and D. J. Percival, 'Cwm Cadlan, Waun Tincer, Cadair Fawr and Mynydd y Garn', *Archaeol. in Wales* 26 (1986), pp. 25–6.

[4] A. Fleming, 'Coaxial field systems: some questions of time and space', *Antiquity* 67 (1988), pp. 188–202.

[5] *Upland Settlement*, passim.

[6] J. Manley, 'Fields, Cairns and Enclosures on Ffridd Brynhelen, Clwyd', pp. 317–350, in *Upland Settlement*; 'Fields, Farms and Funerary Monuments on Mynydd Poeth, Clwyd', *B.B.C.S.* 33 (1986), pp. 384–413; 'A late Bronze Age landscape on the Denbigh Moors, northeast Wales', *Antiquity* 64 (1990), pp. 514–526.

[7] P. Crew, 'Cyfanydd Fawr, Arthog', *Arch. in Wales* 18 (1978), p. 51; 19 (1979), pp. 18–19; 'Cracwellt West, Trawsfynydd', *Arch. in Wales* 26 (1986), p. 36; 27 (1987), p. 41; P. Crew and M. Griffith, 'Cracwellt South, Trawsfynydd', *Arch. in Wales* 26 (1986), p. 36.

[8] P. Crew, 'Excavations at Cracwellt, Merioneth 1986–9. A late prehistoric upland iron-working settlement', *Arch. in Wales* 29 (1989), pp. 11–16.

[9] D. Robinson, 'An aerial Survey of Morlais Castle, Merthyr Tydfil, Mid-Glamorgan', *B.B.C.S.* 30 (1981–3), pp. 431–9; Pl. VIII.

(ii) *Clearance Cairns*

Cairns created in land clearance rather than with the more specific intention of burial are commonplace throughout upland Britain.[1] In Wales examples have been described from the counties of Caernarfon,[2] Cardigan,[3] Carmarthen,[4] Denbigh,[5] Flint,[6] Glamorgan,[7] Merioneth,[8] Monmouthshire,[9] and Pembroke.[10] In Brecknockshire, as already noted, these cairns have been observed since the early nineteenth century (for e.g. LS 1), and in more recent times, they have formed an important focus of interest both in field survey,[11] and for excavation.[12] It is now generally agreed that cairnfields are unlikely to have been created to assist exclusively pastoral activities,[13] and that many, if not most, burial cairns were also probably of stone cleared from arable fields.[14] In the uplands, littered with glacial debris, stone clearance must have been a major activity in agriculture for some time after colonisation of virgin forest. This clearance problem probably did not generally arise to the same degree upon more low-lying, alluvial soils, where an absence of stone accounts for turf, not stone, burial mounds. There remain some uncleared upland areas in Brecknockshire, though these are quite uncommon. Indeed, it is difficult to ascertain to what degree any landscape in southern Britain has not been subjected to stone-drawing activities during the medieval period. Although wooden fences seem unlikely predecessors to stone in areas where there was no shortage,[15] stone margins were on occasion enhanced by stake fences,[16] and could have been structurally important with particular fieldstone lithologies.

The importance of stone removal upon soil cultivability has only recently been recognised.[17] Fieldstone acts as a store for daytime sun, releasing it at night and thus helping maintain a higher mean field temperature which assists spring germination.[18] Some of the S.-facing slopes investigated during this survey may account for up to 15 per cent of the available ground surface. Nant Car (US 95 i) is a case in point, where the cairnfield is surrounded by unmapped debris flows which (assuming that in antiquity they were not covered by soil or vegetation) could have been part of the intended field design. These stone mats and margins would have acted as night storage heaters, creating in effect a local microclimate facilitating both germination and ripening.[19] Hence, though these may look unconvincing fields for modern yields, they were probably very efficient as small cropping plots during prehistory.

Clearance cairns should probably be regarded as evidence for long-term agricultural practice. Some landscapes in which cairnfields occur are probably multi-period. Why collected stone should not more often have been incorporated into the boundaries of regular field enclosures is unclear. Current distributions of clearance cairns are obviously governed by the process of continuous removal of stone in recent historic times (see above, p. 196). As stone-picking and stone-piling remain vernacular practices in some areas, it is clear that even cairns surviving upon abandoned agricultural land need not be of any great antiquity. Greater confidence in interpretation of their function will emerge through more widespread palaeoenvironmental research.

Spreads of surface-collected stone taking virtually any shape are relatively common throughout the county. In some places they occur near huts, singly or in groups (for example, US 1, 8, 81, and 95). These might be considered to be of early, perhaps prehistoric, date. Some are clearly associated with incomplete linear banks, presumably all that now remains of field boundaries (for example, US 6, 20, 28, 31, 33, 74–5, 77, 83, 87, 93–7, 99–100, and 106–7). A few are associated with hut scoops (US 7, 74 and 78) and others with more elongated, even elaborate, linear platforms (US 7, 20, 31–2, 35, 43, 77 and 82) presumed to be of more developed, and therefore of later, type. A number of clearance cairns, single or grouped, are apparently unassociated with other settlement features (US 4, 10, 34, 43, 61–2, 69, 79, 81, 84–5, 89, and 90). These may be areas from which huts or easily recognisable walls and buildings have been scavenged for building materials.

[1] R. W. Feachem, 'Ancient agriculture in the highland of Britain', *P.P.S.* 39 (1973), pp. 332–53.

[2] W. E. Griffiths in *Arch. Camb.* 103 (1954), pp. 66–84.

[3] C. S. Briggs, 'Hafod Ithel', *Arch. in Wales* 14 (1974), pp. 9–10; K. Ray, 'An upland Archaeological survey at Carnau, Llanddewi Brefi', Unpubl. typescript: Ceredigion Archaeological Survey, (Lampeter: St. David's University College, 1988); 'Bryn Rhudd South, Llanddewi Brefi', *Arch. in Wales* 28 (1988), pp. 48–9.

[4] A. H. Ward, 'An Archaeological field survey project in south-east Carmarthenshire', *Carmarthen Antiq.* 10 (1974), pp. 17–36; 'The Cairns on Mynydd Llangyndeyrn: A focal point in the Early Bronze Age in South-East Dyfed', *Carms Antiq.* 12 (1976), pp. 3–21; 'Land Allotment of possibly prehistoric date on Mynydd Llangyndeyrn, South-East Dyfed', *Arch. Camb.* 138 (1989) pp. 46–58.

[5] J. Manley, 'Fields, Cairns and Enclosures on Ffridd Brynhelen, Clwyd', pp. 317–350 in *Upland Settlement*; 'Fields, Farms and Funerary Monuments on Mynydd Poeth', *B.B.C.S.* 33 (1986), pp. 384–413.

[6] M. Bevan-Evans and P. Hayes, 'Excavation of two stone heaps near Moel Fammau', *Trans Flints Hist. Soc.* 15 (1954–5), p. 140.

[7] A. Fox, 'Cairn Cemeteries', *B.B.C.S.* 8 (1936), pp. 274–5; A. Fox and L. Murray-Threipland, 'The excavation of two cairn cemeteries near Hirwaun, Glamorgan', *Arch. Camb.* 97 (1942), pp. 77–87; C. Fox and A. Fox, 'Field survey of Glamorgan', *B.B.C.S.* 7 (1935), pp. 418–420; C. Fox and A. Fox, 'Cairn Cemeteries', *B.B.C.S.* 8 (1938), pp. 92–3; H. G. Owen-John, 'A Group of Small Cairns Near Penrhiw Cradoc, Mountain Ash, Mid-Glamorgan (ST 0283 9938)', *B.B.C.S.* 33 (1986), pp. 266–82; A. H. Ward, 'Recent agricultural exploitation of a degraded landscape as an indicator of earlier landuse potential: the example of Cefn Bryn, Gower, West Glamorgan', *B.B.C.S.* 32 (1985), pp. 411–16; 'Evidence for Early Agriculture on Rhosili Down, Gower', *B.B.C.S.* 34 (1987), pp. 220–7; 'Survey and Excavation of Ring Cairns in SE Dyfed, and on Gower, West Glamorgan', *P.P.S.* 54 (1988), pp. 153–72.

[8] M. Freeman, 'A Group of Small Cairns at Ffridd Winog Fawr, Cors-y-Gedol, Merioneth', (Bangor: U.C.N.W. unpubl. dissertation, 1987).

[9] K. L. Dallimore, 'An archaeological survey of the Machen Ridge, Monmouthshire', *B.B.C.S.* 28 (1980), pp. 471–503.

[10] J. Fenton, 'Breseleu Hill', *Arch. Camb.* 8 (1853), pp. 81–9.

[11] D. P. Webley, 'Cairn Cemeteries in South Breconshire', *B.B.C.S.* 17 (1956), pp. 117–18.

[12] D. P. Webley, 'A cairn cemetery and secondary Neolithic dwelling on Cefn Cilsanws, Vaynor (Breckn.)', *B.B.C.S.* 19 (1958), pp. 79–88; J. Parkhouse, 'Darren Fawr round cairn, Vaynor', *Glamorgan-Gwent Archaeological Trust Ann. Report*, (1981), p. 32.

[13] *pace* A. W. R. Whittle, 'Climate, Grazing and Man', pp. 192–203 in A. F. Harding, (ed.), *Climate Change in Later Prehistory*, (Edinburgh: U.P., 1982).

[14] M. J. Yates, 'Field clearance and field survey: some observations and an illustration from SW Scotland', pp. 341–386, in F. Hamond and T. Reeves-Smith, (eds.), *Landscape Archaeology in Ireland*, (Oxford: B.A.R. 116, 1983); at pp. 342–3.

[15] *pace* Yates *loc. cit.*, p. 353.

[16] S. Caulfield, 'Neolithic Fields; the Irish Evidence', pp. 137–43, in H. C. Bowen and P. J. Fowler, (eds.), *Early Land Allotment*, (Oxford: B.A.R. 48, 1978).

[17] A. Fleming, 'Early settlement and the landscape in West Yorkshire', pp. 359–73, in G. Sieveking, I. H. Longworth and K. E. Wilson, (eds.), *Problems in Economic and Social Archaeology*, (London, 1976); see also Yates *loc. cit.* n. 14, pp. 341–2; see also C. S. Briggs in *Upland Settlement*, pp. 299–300.

[18] Yates, *op. cit.* n. 14, p. 342.

[19] Fleming, *op. cit.* n. 17.

(iii) *Plough-marks*

Narrow rig ploughing is at present not well known in the Brecknockshire landscape, although its distribution used to be widespread.[1] On Mynydd Epynt several hectares of narrow rig are associated with an unenclosed homestead, presumed to be of medieval date, at Ffynnon yr Oerfa.[2] Cultivation ridges, probably of 'cord-rig' type up to 2 m wide and 0.3 m high, were noted on the northeast side of Twyn y Gaer hillfort (Llandefalle),[3] though these were not necessarily contemporary with the fort. Further west, extensive hillsides of narrow rig can be seen climbing the hill of Mwmffri (Carms., 302 m above O.D.) to the north from the A40 about two miles on the Brecon side of Llandovery (centred upon O.S. SN 804 361). These marks extend to the summits of the steep pasture and partially abandoned slopes but appear only sporadically under suitable weather conditions.

Among Sir John Lloyd's papers in the Brecknocks Museum is a photograph of about 1930 on the reverse of which is written:[4]

> The photo of the other side is one of a small carn between Pen-Maen-Llwyd [SN 86 45] and Allt y Clych [SN 97 56]. These hills are worth visiting as they have been ploughed once upon a time and the ridges are as plain as if they had been ploughed within recent years.

It is unclear to which cairn this refers, and ploughmarks have not otherwise been observed in this area.

However, Sir John Lloyd's comment is not unexpected, since narrow rig, or cord-rig, ploughmarks were long regarded as a commonplace in South Wales.[5] Although there exists a tacit belief that these rigs were of medieval ploughlands, in Wales their origins and distribution have never been studied. One problem is of drawing a distinction between cord-rig, considered to be a product of spade cultivation,[6] and other forms of narrow rig which result from ploughing.[7] In recent years, the fruits of aerial reconnaissance and of excavation in Scotland and the Borders have underlined the possibility that cord-rig may have pre-medieval origins.[8] The earlier form displays an unmistakable regularity and its widespread distribution has been plotted throughout the southern uplands, where numerous upstanding examples survive.[9] Excavation long ago demonstrated these rigs to be at least as old as the Roman occupation.[10] However, the features recognised beneath a Bronze Age cairn at North Mains, Strathallan, where there were only three upstanding rigs, need not certainly represent spade cultivation.[11] On a small scale, stone stripes formed upon frozen ground under post-glacial tundra conditions are as regular as man-made rigs.[12] This dating evidence would be more convincing had it been corroborated by palaeoecological investigation. The study of early ploughlands is in its infancy, and the sparse dating evidence therefore needs to be treated with caution.

Ploughmarks have been noticed by antiquaries in upland Wales for almost two centuries.[13] None has so far been excavated, and the apparent association of narrow rig with an enclosed hut-group at Ffridd Bod y Fuddau near Trawsfynydd in Merioneth is therefore noteworthy.[14]

[1] M. Davies, 'Field systems of south Wales', pp. 480–529, in A. R. H. Baker and R. A. Butlin, (eds.), *Studies of Field Systems in the British Isles*, (London, 1973).

[2] O.S. Card SN 83 SE 1 (SN 8464 3325); C. S. Briggs, unpubl. typescript report on early settlement on Mynydd Epynt (R.C.A.M.) *Arch. in Wales* 30 (1990) p. 40; more recently supplemented through map and aerial photographic G15 transcription by T. G. Driver at RCAHMW, (1996).

[3] *Br. Inv.* I, ii, (HF 35), p. 73; these ploughmarks were ploughed up in 1981.

[4] Brecks Mus. MS 1/1/10 no. 62.

[5] Davies *op. cit.* n. 1.

[6] Rig-types are defined by S. P. Halliday, 'Cord Rig and Early Cultivation in the Borders', *Proc. Soc. Antiqs. Scotl.* 116 (1986), pp. 584–5.

[7] The earliest form of primitive plough described from a historical context in Wales is mentioned by Lewis Morris in the mid-eighteenth century; see R. J. Colyer, 'Crop husbandry in Wales before the onset of mechanisation', *Folklife* 21 (1983), pp. 59–70.

[8] S. P. Halliday, P. J. Hill, and J. B. Stevenson, 'Early Agriculture in Scotland', pp. 55-65 in R. Mercer, (ed.), *Prehistoric Agriculture in Britain*, (Edinburgh: U.P., 1981); P. Topping, 'The Prehistoric Field System of College Valley, North Northumberland', *Northern Archaeology* 2 (i) (1981), pp. 14–33; 'The Linhope Burn Excavations, Northumberland, 1989; Interim Report', *Northern Archaeology* 8 (1987) [1990], pp. 29–34; 'The context of Cord Rig Cultivation in Later Prehistoric Northumberland', pp. 145–57, in M. Bowden, D. Mackay, and P. Topping, (eds.), *From Cornwall to Caithness: Some Aspects of British Field Archaeology: Papers presented to Norman V. Quinnell*, (Oxford: B.A.R. 209, 1989).

[9] P. Topping, 'Early cultivation in Northumberland and the Borders', *Proc. Prehist. Soc* 55 (1989), pp. 161–79.

[10] J. P. Gillham, R. M. Harrison, and T. G. Newman, 'Interim report on excavations at the Roman fort of Rudchester, 1972', *Arch. Aeliana* 10 (5th ser.) (1982), pp. 81–6.

[11] G. J. Barclay, 'The cultivation remains beneath the North Main, Strathallon barrow', *Proc. Soc. Antiqs. Scotl.* 118 (1989), pp. 59–61.

[12] Examples of stone stripes are illustrated in J. Warburton, 'Characteristic ratios of width to depth-of-sorting for sorted stripes in the English Lake District', pp. 163–71, in J. Boardman, (ed.), *Periglacial processes and landforms in Britain and Ireland*, (Cambridge: U.P., 1987).

[13] J. C. Dyke, 'Early hill-ploughing', *Arch. Camb.* 36 (1881), pp. 344-5; G. Edwards, 'History of the parishes of Garthbeibio and Llangadfan', *Mont. Collns* 6 (1869), p. 17.

[14] P. Crew, 'Ffridd Bod y Ffuddau', *Arch. in Wales* 28 (1988), pp. 79–80.

Prehistoric Settlement and Land-Use in Brecknockshire *c.* 8,000 B.C. – 1000 A.D.

Consideration might now be given to the continuum of early settlement and any economic and social significance suggested by the features encountered in this survey.

The Chronological Framework

Whereas evidence is as yet only partial, a Mesolithic presence is attested in both upland and lowland areas by *c.* 8,000 –3,700 B.C., though this remains difficult to detect on or beneath lowland agricultural soils. From hunter-gatherers whose known activities affected mainly vegetational landscape elements probably under an improving climate, the land was slowly colonised by Neolithic farmers, the evidence for whom is attested by an unusually localised concentration of surviving megalithic tombs. The presence of one tomb (CT 2) on a coll beneath Mynydd Troed in the Black Mountains, complemented by stray-find artefact distributions (Fig. 123), suggests that agricultural land may have been taken into use at higher altitudes, though in detail the nature of contemporary land-holding in Wales is poorly understood. In Britain Neolithic fields are generally rare, and testimony as to their age can be ambivalent. It is assumed that in Brecknockshire evidence for such an early land apportionment has not survived (if it were present), and that most features like clearance cairns and coaxial field boundaries are later and of the Bronze Age, at earliest.

Even though direct dating evidence for Bronze Age land clearance and the development of organised field

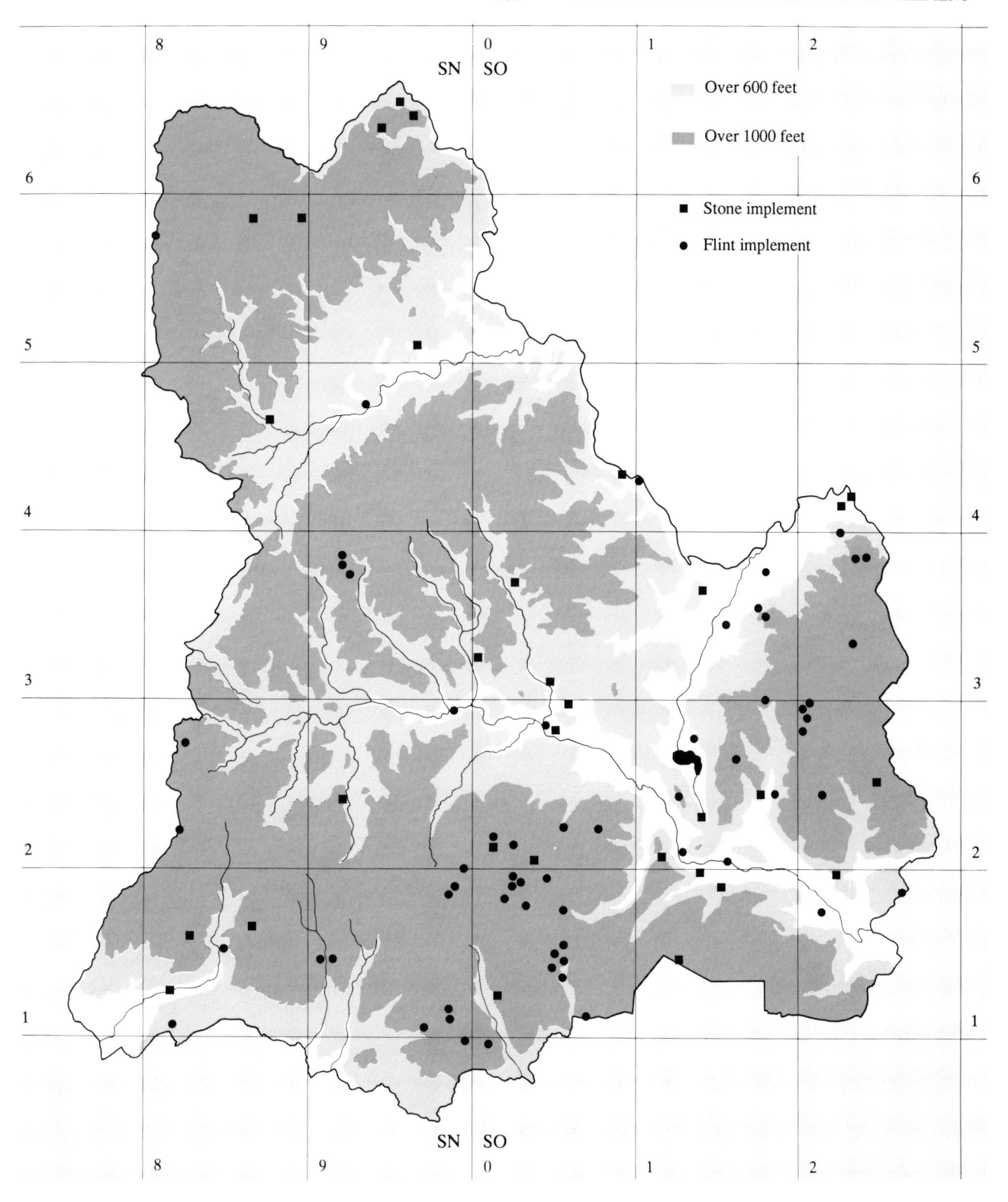

207 LATER PREHISTORIC AND PROTOHISTORIC SETTLEMENT

123 Distribution of prehistoric stone artefacts

systems or territorial markers is virtually absent from Brecknockshire, indirect evidence taken from vegetational studies (pp. 6–7), and high altitude cairn distributions strongly suggest that agricultural settlement was ubiquitous at this period. Indeed, these burial sites survive in locations which are at the present day considered climatically hostile to farming. For subsistence farming to have been successful during later prehistory, quite different weather regimes from those obtaining at the present day must be conjectured. Such climes would have been associated with, or dependent upon, the former presence of widespread vegetational cover preserving microclimates favourable to high altitude domesticated plant and animal husbandry.

It is possible that some hut structures recorded here date from the Bronze Age; others may be ascribable to the Iron Age. The paucity of hillforts or associated enclosures at higher altitudes (*Br. Inv.* I ii) has been taken to indicate the general abandonment of upland fields during Late Bronze Age – Iron Age times, due to decreasing soil fertility and deteriorating climate, though withdrawal from the uplands may have had other causes. Studies of early fields outside Wales demonstrate that they were invaded by peat subsequent to the Bronze Age. Because Bronze Age settlement patterns appear to contrast so fundamentally with those of the Iron Age, early upland depopulation has implications for both an understanding of contemporary farming practices and an appreciation of social organisation.

Little has survived to demonstrate native occupation in the South Wales uplands at the time Roman practice camps were being constructed in areas today remote from settlement. Although there is documentary evidence for the establishment of estates during the early medieval period, the nature of any accompanying settlements is unclear. Some field clearance features described here may relate to land-holding at that period.

Without a sound framework of dating and cultural association based upon extensive excavation and more detailed palaeoecological investigations, it is impossible to more than notionally place most unenclosed settlement features within broad chronological parameters encompassing the Bronze Age to the post-medieval period.

It is clear, however, that whilst most known upstanding man-made features are best-preserved in the uplands, their absence from lower altitudes or from apparently heavier soils need not imply an absence of early settlement. Aerial photography and artefact distributions are complementary indicators of a widespread lowland presence throughout later prehistory. Because field-scavenged building stone had a limited lowland availability, its scarcity and the need to re-cycle materials would govern the endurance of stone-built features. Reconnaissance for abandoned lowland sites is difficult under conditions where they may lie buried beneath ploughsoil or hillwash. Site reconnaissance is also currently hampered by a lack of fieldwalking. These difficulties of site recognition and discovery are common to an understanding of settlement distribution in Brecknockshire throughout the period encompassed by this volume.

Evidence for Early Agricultural Practice and its Interpretation

Besides dating problems both of ill-defined as well as the more readily classifiable settlements, the nature of early farming practices and their effects upon the environmental record are also important.

Traditions of herding and seasonality long occupying an important place in the interpretation of the historic Welsh upland landscape are still dominated by a widespread belief in the roles played by *hafotai* and *lluestau* as upland summer headquarters for successive generations of herdsmen. It has been suggested that these practices may have originated in later prehistoric times.[1] Present-day lowland settlement distributions and the knowledge that there had been a depopulation movement in the eighteenth and nineteenth centuries[2] are factors which have contributed to a view which disparages the agricultural potential of the Welsh uplands at earlier periods. It has long been a commonplace among archaeologists, folklorists and historians that 'the Welsh have always been primarily shepherds and herdsmen',[3] and furthermore, that this age-old tradition involved a form of peripatetic land-use or transhumance, an activity involving the summer migration of flocks to upland pastures with wintering at lower altitudes.[4] Some also hold the view that current land-use systems probably 'represent extremely ancient settlement patterns'.[5] How far does the surviving archaeological evidence from Brecknockshire fit these perceptions of early land use? An answer may only be reached through a joint approach interrelating the inquiries of climatology and palaeoecology, by constantly re-evaluating the nature and definition of archaeological evidence, and through the interpretation of historical documentation. Though not by any means conclusive, a critical review of some evidence[6] has already proposed the existence of quite considerable agriculturally-dependent land-holdings in upland Wales during historic times. Some areas appear to have been capable of supporting all-year-round subsistence agriculture.

The persistence into historic times of primitive land-clearing traditions and the continual re-use or adaption of earlier built structures to more recent herding and folding practices often make it difficult to draw distinctions between historic and prehistoric settlement features based only upon survey. Thus, great care will be required in the future interpretation of individual clearance cairns, plough-marks, enclosures and patterns of field and land use.

[1] R. Bradley, *The Prehistoric Settlement of Britain*, (London, 1978)

[2] D. Thomas, *Agriculture in Wales during the Napoleonic Wars*, (Cardiff: U.P., 1963), pp. 105-6, Figs 32-3.

[3] I.C. Peate, *The Welsh House*, (Liverpool: The Brython Press, 1944), p. 126.

[4] One view suggests that upland settlement in Caernarfonshire may have served summer use only, practices of arable farming being precluded by high altitude; see A. H. A. Hogg and R. G. Livens, *Arch. in Wales* 16 (1976), pp. 8-10; p. 10.

[5] D. Sylvester, *The Rural Landscape of the Welsh Borderland: a Study in Historical Geography*, (London: Macmillan, 1969), pp. 423-4.

[6] Briggs, in *Upland Settlement, passim.*

Unenclosed Settlements (US 1–113)

(US 1) To the W. of the Afon Twrch on the crest of a ridge at about 360 m above O.D., to the N. of the holding named Dorwen, is a group of three clearance cairns, mainly of turf consolidated fieldstone. One (US 1 i) is triangular in plan, 3.5 m N.E.–S.W., 3 m E.–W., another (US 1 ii), oval, 3 m N.E.–S.W. by 2.5 m, and the third (US 1 iii) is a rubble ring 4 m in diameter infilled with loose fieldstones.

Ystradgynlais (E), Ystradgynlais Lr (C)
SN 71 S.E. (US 1 i) (7786 1531); (US 1 ii) (7786 1532); (US 2 iii) (7787 1534)   8 vii 87

(US 2) To the S. of the above site are a hut-circle and two small ill-defined enclosures (possibly eroded hut-circles), together with a number of stone piles. The hut-circle (US 2 ix) is well preserved and shows as a stony ring bank up to 2 m wide and 0.3 m high, measuring 6 m in overall diameter. It is likely there was an entrance on the E., where the bank is lowest. A more fugitive feature (US 2 i) is the stony bank 2 m wide and 0.2 m high, measuring about 6 m (E.–W.) by 5 m. The largest feature (US 2 ii), also probably an enclosure, is defined by an amorphous stony bank 0.3 m high and 8 m at greatest width. There is a boulder embedded in the S. side.

Some 20 m to the N.E. of (US 2 ii) is a stone pile (US 2 iii) 6 m N.–S. by 2 m and 0.5 m high at the N. end, and another, turf-consolidated example (US 2 iv) 3 m N.E–S.W. by 2 m. There are four rubble clearance heaps in the vicinity (US 2 v–viii), including oval-shaped (US 2 v), 4 m (N.–S.) by 3 m, rectangular (US 2 vi) 7.5 m (N.E.–S.W.) by 3 m, and almost shapeless (US 2 vii) 6 m (N.E.–S.W.) by 3 m. To the E. of (US 2 vi) and (US 2 vii) is a linear rubble spread (US 2 viii) about 30 m long by 6 m wide and facing downslope.

Some 800 m to the S. is a short length of rubble wall (US 2 x) aligned E.–W. weathering from beneath the peat.

'Archaeology', by Clwyd-Powys Archaeological Trust in *Brynhenllys revised: An environmental assessment of opencast coal extraction*, British Coal Opencast Executive, unpubl. rep.

Ystradgynlais (E), Ystradgynlais Lr (C)
SN 71 N.E. (US 2 i) (7788 1510); (US 2 ii) (7787 1512); (US 2 iii) (7789 1514); (US 2 iv) (7792 1517); (US 2 v) (7795 1516); (US 2 vi) (7795 1514); (US 2 vii) (7797 1517); (US 2 viii) (7796 1518)
SN 71 S.E. (US 2 ix) (7796 1494); (US 2 x) (7781 1411)   8 vii 87; vi 93 (US 2 x)

Cwm Tawe (South) (US 3–19)

The Cwm Tawe area is split, for ease of reference, into the Dan yr Ogof plateau, Cwm Haffes and the Nant Tawe Fechan, and the Upper Tawe.

Dan yr Ogof Plateau

(US 3) In a dry valley S.W. of Pentre Cribarth, about 340 m above O.D., and to the N.E. of the modern wall bounding it, which runs N.N.E.–S.S.W. at the higher end, is a boulder wall (US 3 i) about 2 m wide and some 60 m long, following the N.E.–S.W. running valley bottom. At its extreme S.W. termination in a hollow below a N.E.-facing slope, interdigitated with shake-holes, are the remains of two, possibly three, ill-defined platform huts (US 3 ii), bounded by poorly defined rubble walls.

(US 3 iii) To the N. of this valley is a quarry trench running uphill perhaps 200 m E.–W. Immediately S. of this is a square enclosure with rubble walls up to 0.3 m high and about 15 m square.

Ystradgynlais (E), Ystradgynlais Hr (C)
SN 81 N.W. (US 3 i) (8366 1505); (US 3 ii) (8361 1502); (US 3 iii) (8356 1512)   27 ii 91

(US 4) Along the exposed limestone pavement plateau which spans Twyn Du and Twyn Walter in a patchy, discontinuous line about 1 km in length and up to 150 m in width at a height of 400–440 m above O.D. are a series of clearance features comprising collections of erratic boulders, mostly of Millstone Grit and Old Red Sandstone. Some are easily recognisable as cairns, though more often these constitute ill-defined groups lying stranded upon bare rock, with occasional hints of alignment suggesting fugitive walls. Limestone solution processes have almost certainly denuded the plateau of its soil, leaving a complex pattern in which it is often quite impossible to distinguish between natural and man-made features. The seven cairns listed below are the most obvious. Precise description of the whole area must await future intensive survey; clearer interpretation will depend to a degree upon a thorough understanding of local geomorphology. It is probable that at some time in the past many of the structures were scavenged for their limestone content. Some cairns still having a limestone component were probably soil-covered at the time of this robbing. Soil is therefore probably still eroding from this land surface.

(US 4 i) On fairly level ground at 420 m above O.D. on a S.E.-facing slope is a round cairn of mixed grade limestone and sandstone rubble, the perimeter consolidated by vegetation. It is 7.0 m in diameter and 0.3 m high. Slightly W. of centre lies a sandstone slab, 1.6 m long by 0.6 m wide and at least 0.14 m thick. This has a long axis aligned roughly N.–S. and may originally have been the capstone to a cist.

(US 4 ii) Lying in a natural hollow at 425 m above O.D. is a cairn 6.3 m (N.E.–S.W.) by 5.5 m, 0.4 m high. Built upon the outcropping rock, it is of mixed grade rubble.

(US 4 iii) About 405 m above O.D. are the remains of a cairn, the centre of which appears to be entirely robbed, giving it the appearance of a ring cairn. This is now defined by a low stony bank averaging 2 m wide and 0.2 m high with an overall diameter of 8.4 m. There is a slab 1 m long, 0.7 m wide and 0.12 m thick embedded within the bank on the S. side.

(US 4 iv) About 410 m above O.D. lies a cairn 9.5 m in diameter and 0.4 m high composed of unsorted rubble consolidated with light vegetation.

(US 4 v) In a slight valley to the W. of Twyn Du about 440 m above O.D. is a rubble cairn 7 m N.W.–S.E. by 5 m and 0.4 m high.

(US 4 vi) On an eminence about 440 m above O.D. is a cairn 8 m in diameter and 0.7 m high, composed of turf-consolidated boulders. A particularly large boulder lies towards its N.W. edge.

(US 4 vii) Lying some 20 m to the S.E. of (US 4 vi) is a similar mound 7 m in diameter and 0.6 m high, with two larger boulders close to its S. edge.

Ystradgynlais (E), Ystradgynlais Lr (C)
SN 81 N.W. (US 4 i) (8337 1677); (US 4 ii) (8336 1692); (US 4 iii) (8356 1675); (US 4 iv) (8351 1680); (US 4 v) (8346 1698); (US 4 vi) (8327 1712); (US 4 vii) (8327 1709)   22 v 87 (US 4 i–v); 15 vi 88 (US 4 vi–vii)

Cwm Haffes and the Nant Tawe Fechan

(US 5; Fig. 124) On the N.E.-facing slope on the S.W. side of Cwm Haffes between 350 and 390 m above O.D. are the remains of a small settlement which include a building platform and three small rubble-walled structures, set within an enclosure (US 5 i), the N.E., N.W., S.W. and S.E. sides of which consist of a rubble bank, the N.E. forming part of the edge of the gorge itself. The enclosed area is 155 m N.N.W.–S.S.E. by 120 m, the surrounding bank, more or less complete except on the N. corner, averages 2 m wide by 0.5 m high. Along its S. boundary there is an external ditch 2 m wide and 0.5 m deep.

(US 5 ii) A rectangular structure 7.3 m N.E.–S.W. by 5 m, is bounded by rubble banks 1.5 m wide and 0.3 m high, and lies within the enclosure, its N.W. side forming part of the enclosing bank. There is a turf-consolidated boulder platform extending some 2 m beyond the structure. From its appearance, the whole feature may have been rebuilt as a shelter in recent times.

(US 5 iii) A large platform 13 m W.–E. by 7 m, the level area only 7 m W.–E. by 5 m, its long axis at right angles to the line of slope, built up at the E. end to 2.5 m and scooped out at the W. to a depth of 1.5 m. There is a hint of stone revetting to the built-out part of the work, and it is possible that some slumping has occurred at the W. end.

(US 5 iv) Close to the edge of the gorge is a small rectangular structure 5 m E.–W. by 4.5 m, bounded by rubble walls 1.5 m wide and 0.3 m high. There is some evidence of a (W.) ditch but with no obvious entrance.

(US 5 v) A further small rectangular structure 7 m E.–W. by 5 m overall, lies on a slight platform within the enclosure, close to a spring. It is open on the E., but bounded on the N.W. and S. by a rubble wall up to 1.5 m wide and 0.3 m high.

Ystradgynlais (E), Ystradgynlais Lr (C)
SN 81 N.W. (US 5 i) (centred upon 8311 1692); (US 5 ii) (8375 1697); (US 5 iii) (8382 1697); (US 5 iv) (8387 1691); (US 5 v) (8379 1689)   i 88

(US 6) A settlement comprising hut-circles and banks (together with a cooking mound (BM 1)) is situated on the moderately steep S.-facing slope of Allt Fach between about 390 m and 460 m above O.D.

(US 6 i) A hut-circle (apparently without entrance), built on a slight platform and consisting of a stony bank varying between 1.3 m and 1.7 m wide and 0.3 m high. It encloses an oval grassy area 4.8 m N.–S. by 4.3 m.

(US 6 ii) A similar, though more poorly-defined circle, also without entrance, possibly having been robbed in recent times. It measures 6 m in diameter overall, with a well-spread bank 0.3 m high.

(US 6 iii) A cairn (presumably from ground clearance) of turf-consolidated rubble 2 m in diameter and 0.1 m high.

(US 6 iv) Lying to the E. of the above (US 6 i–iii) is a turf-covered stony bank 1.5 m wide, 0.3 m high running S.–N. for some 290 m.

(US 6 v) A second bank runs W.–E.

Ystradgynlais (E), Ystradgynlais Lr (C)
SN 81 N.W. (US 6 i) (8400 1777); (US 6 ii) (8400 1781); (US 6 iii) (8399 1784); (US 6 iv) (8402 1774 to 8399 1802); (US 6 v) (8403 1762 to 8411 1763)   13 viii 87

(US 7) On Allt Fach between about 300 m and 350 m above O.D. above the Tawe Valley are a series of field banks and other settlement features occupying a slight terrace which, dropping steeply from N.W. to S., has created a break in the otherwise sheer E.-facing slope.

(US 7 i) A large irregularly-shaped enclosure, 80 m N.–S. by 51 m E.–W. across the N. half, narrowing to about 28 m across the S. It is bounded by a rubble-boulder bank up to 2 m wide and 0.4 m high, with a gap some 6 m wide in the N.W. corner. It is bisected by a later N.–S. running drainage channel bounded on its E. side by a rubble bank. The interior is rock-strewn and contains evidence of several internal structures, all within the uphill, W. half. These are:

(US 7 ii) A semi-circular feature about 5 m N.–S. by 4 m, probably a platform, built against the enclosure wall, raised above the contour on the E. to about 1.2 m.

(US 7 iii) A similar platform 5 m N.S. by 3 m, scooped out on the inside 1 m deep, and lying above the contour 1.2 m on the E.

(US 7 iv) A more fugitive platform 4.5 m N.E.–S.W. by 3 m, built against the enclosing bank. There are hints of a rubble wall around the N.E, S.E. and S.W.

(US 7 v) A small oval enclosure, 6 m N.E.–S.W. by 4.5 m, possibly a hut-circle, incorporated into the enclosure bank (on its N.W.), and slightly built into the hillslope, raised above the contour on the S.E. to 0.8 m. The wall footings comprise a boulder wall 1 m wide and 0.4 m high, without obvious entrance.

To the S. of the large enclosure are the remains of two platforms and a further two possible hut-circles.

(US 7 vi) A large rectangular platform possibly originally built at two or more floor levels. The level area 8 m N.W.–S.E. by 5 m is built out above the contour to a height of 1.5 m scooped out on the N.W. to a depth of 0.8 m. There are traces of walling along the N.E.

(US 7 vii) A putative hut-circle 4 m N.E.–S.W. by 3 m, bounded by boulder walls 0.8 m wide and 0.3 m high. It is slightly platformed, built up on the S.E. to 0.8 m and scooped out to a similar depth on the N.W. The hut wall is revetted against the slope, and here again there is no obvious entrance.

(US 7 viii) A rectangular platform 8 m N.W.–S.E. by 7 m, built up and rubble-revetted on the S.E. to a height of 1 m, scooped out and revetted on the N.W. to a depth of 1 m. A boulder bank can be distinguished along the N.E. and S.E. sides, some 0.8 m wide and 0.4 m high.

(US 7 ix) Immediately S.W. of US 7 viii is a circular structure, probably a hut-circle, 4 m in overall diameter, bounded by boulder walls spread to about 1 m wide and 0.4 m high. It is possible that the entrance was on the S.E.

(US 7 x) Lying to the E. of the large enclosure and separated from it by an area of natural boulder scree, bounded on the S.E. by a steep-sided gully, is a series of banks forming a further though more fugitive, enclosure, open on the N.W. side. It measures 37 m S.W.–N.E. internally by about 50 m, and is bounded by a bank similar in size and construction to that of the larger site. There is some suggestion of an internal N.E.–S.W. internal dividing bank.

(US 7 xi) In the S. corner of US 7 x is a small irregularly-shaped sub-enclosure 10 m N.–S. by 4.5 m, bounded by banks about 1.2 m wide and 0.4 m high.

(US 7 xii) Close to the S. corner is a possible platform 6 m N.W.–S.E. by 4 m. The S.E. edge is built up to a height of 1.5 m, and appears to form part of a S.W.–N.E. running bank coming from the main enclosure. The N.W. side is scooped out to a depth of 1 m.

(US 7 xiii) To the N. of the enclosure is a rubble-filled circular feature, probably a hut-circle, 4.5 m in diameter. It is bounded by rubble walls 1 m wide, 0.4 m high, without obvious entrance.

There is a further group of enclosures lying at the head of a shallow, boulder-filled valley.

(US 7 xiv) The largest is 13.5 m N.–S. by 6.5 m, generally rectangular, though the N. end is distinctly rounded. It is bounded by boulder walls up to 1 m wide and 0.8 m high, with possibly an entrance midway along the western wall. Two fugitive E.–W. walls, respectively 6 m and 10 m from the N. end, divide the interior into three parts. A further, N.–S. wall, dividing the southernmost compartment, may be a later addition, forming a shelter in the S.W. corner.

(US 7 xv) To the S. is a smaller, rectangular, enclosure, 6 m N.–S. by 2.5 m (internally), bounded by a boulder wall up to 1 m wide and 0.4 m high, except on the S. where it is 2 m wide, probably forming a buttress at the downhill end of the structure.

(US 7 xvi) To the W. of (US 7 xiv–xv) is an oval structure 4.5 m N.W.–S.E. by 3 m internally, enclosed by boulder walls up to 12 m wide and 0.4 m high. There is some suggestion of an entrance at the S. end. From the S. corner, a wall runs 9 m towards the S.E.

(US 7 xvii) There is a substantial ditch 1.5 m wide and 0.6 m deep bounded on the E. by a boulder bank up to 2 m wide and 1 m high in a northerly, then a northwesterly direction.

(US 7 xviii) An oval enclosure 9 m E.–W. by 6 m, bounded by boulder walls 1 m wide and 0.8 m high. The N.W. half is sub-divided into two smaller compartments by similar walls.

Some 8 m S.E. is a rectangular structure 7.5 m N.–S. by 6 m, bounded by boulder walls up to 1.5 m wide, 0.5 m high, occupying a slight platform built up on the E. to 0.5 m high, scooped out on the W. to a similar depth.

(US 7 xix) Some 60 m to the N.E. is a large, edge-set stone on the lip of the valley, which may have been deliberately placed there. It is 3.5 m N.E.–S.E. by 1.5 m and stands 3 m high, buttressed against the hillslope on the N.W.

Glyntawe
SN 81 N.W. (US 7 i) (8454 1745); (US 7 ii) (8452 1473); (US 7 iii) (8452 1746); (US 7 iv) (8452 1747); (US 7 v) (8453 1748); (US 7 vi) (8453 1739); (US 7 vii) (8452 1738); (US 7 viii) (8453 1736); (US 7 ix) (8452 1735); (US 7 x) (8456 1754); (US 7 xi) (8457 1751); (US 7 xii) (8455 1755); (US 7 xiii) (8457 1757); (US 7 xiv) (8451 1959); (US 7 xv) (8451 1758); (US 7 xvi) (8449 1759); (US 7 xvii) (from 8449 1763 to 8441 1770); (US 7 xviii) (8450 1765); (US 7 xix) (8455 1770)   9 iii 88

(US 8; Figs. 124, 125–6) To the S. of Pwll y Wythen Fach on the Cribarth plateau about 370 m above O.D. and some 50 m N. of a nineteenth-century quarry tramroad, lying upon the flat, consolidated floor of a shake-hole about 40 m in diameter and 7 m deep,[1] is a hut-circle some 3.2 m (N.–S.) by 2.8 m, bounded by a low stone wall of roughly coursed slabs and blocks which survives 0.6 m thick, and 0.6 m high above the rubble-strewn interior (US 8 i). Accumulated fallen scree obscures the outer wall on the W. and N. On the W. is a well-marked boulder-flanked entrance adjacent to which is a particularly large boulder about 1.5 m in diameter. The entrance stones are 1.1 m and 1.3 m long, separated by a distance of 0.45 m. Within the boulder clay sides of the shake-hole outcropping Old Red Sandstone is visible, and although there is some erosion of boulder clay and stones into the shake-hole, its profiles appear stable.

(US 8 ii) Lying between this shake-hole and one 20 m to the S. is a clearance cairn 10 m in diameter and 0.5 m high, composed of fieldstones up to 0.2 m long. There is a large slab on the N.W. and an ill-defined central hollow about 0.3 m deep.

[1] The shake-hole is marked upon the O.S. 1:56,360 (1964) and later editions greater than this scale.

Ystradgynlais (E), Ystradgynlais Hr (C)
SN 81 N.W. (US 8 i) (8289 1510); (US 8 ii) (8292 1508)   26 ii 91

(US 9) On the S.W. bank of the Nant Tawe Fechan, at the base of the rock-strewn E. slope of Allt Fach, about 280 m above O.D., are the remains of two enclosures, one with a building attached. The larger enclosure (US 9 i) is trapezoidally shaped, 14.5 m N.W.–S.E., 14 m N.E.–S.W., 9 m S.E.–N.W. and 11.5 N.E.–S.W., lying within a boulder wall 2 m wide and 1 m high. The building is adjacent to its S.W. wall on the W. corner. It is 7.8 m S.W.–N.E. by 4.5 m, has an entrance in the S.W. end, and from the way its walls are coursed, may have succeeded the enclosure in date.

The second enclosure (US 9 ii), rectangular in plan with rounded corners, 11.5 m W.N.W.–E.S.E. by 8 m, lies to the S.E. It is subtended from the larger enclosure by a fugitive rubble wall.

Llywel (E), Traean-glas (C)
SN 81 N.W. (US 9 i) (8462 1790); (US 9 ii) (8465 1789)   22 iii 88

(US 10) On the S. slope of Allt Fach at about 450 m above O.D. is a group of at least eight small cairns, presumably resulting from field clearance. These are not described individually, but range in size from 2.5 m to 5 m in diameter and survive to heights of about 0.6 m.

Glyntawe
SN 81 N.W. (US 10) (8409 1762); (8406 1760); (8411 1753); (centred upon 8413 1753: four examples); (8408 1751); (8410 1751); (8412 1752); (8409 1747)
   i 88

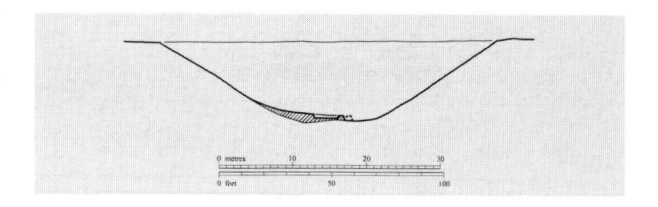

125   Pwll y wythen Fach hut circle in sink hole (US 8i)

(US 11) To the N.E. of Nant Tawe Fechan there is a discontinuous rubble-built bank, 2 m wide and 0.3 m high running across open moorland, first, S.S.E. (US 11 i), then after a break of 25 m, in a more S.W. direction a further 193 m before petering out (US 11 ii). There is a break when it reaches the stream (US 11 iii).

Llywel (E), Traean-glas (C)
SN 81 N.W. (US 11 i) (8408 1928); (US 11 ii) (8426 1905); (US 11 iii) (at 8413 1918)   vi 88

(US 12; Fig. 127) On the S.E. side of Cwm Haffes on the lip of a steep gorge, about 380 m above O.D., is an enclosure 18 m S.W.–N.E. by 17 m. It is bounded on the S.W. and N.W. by a rubble bank 2 m wide, 0.2 m high, and on the N.E. by the edge of the gorge, and adjacent to the natural scree. Upon it is a house platform (11.5 m S.W.–N.E. by 4 m) bounded by rubble walls 0.4 m high, uniformly 1.2 m wide except on the N.E. where it is up to 4.5 m wide, forming a buttress at the downslope end of the structure. From the E. corner there runs a rubble wall 2.5 m wide, in a S.E. direction some 5.5 m, then S.W. some 3 m. This forms an annex or yard to the main structure.

Glyntawe
SN 81 N.W. (US 12) (8460 1724)   i 88

(US 13; Fig. 86) On the S.-facing slope of Cwm Haffes 380 m above O.D. just beyond the limit of enclosed land are two small enclosures.

The first (US 13 i) is a stony, rush-grown oval feature built upon a platform 7 m N.E.–S.W. by 8.5 m and bounded by a wall 1.5 m wide and 0.4 m high. The wall is of coursed slabs on the S.W., and an entrance gap survives on the W., flanked by a projecting bank or wall about 3 m long.

126 Pwll y wythen Fach hut circle in sink hole (US 8 i) showing 'entrance'

The second site (US 13 ii), about 30 m S., is poorly defined, and measures 3 m overall. This is walled by a bank 0.9 m wide and 0.4 m high. There is a marked scarp behind the settlement suggesting deliberate landscaping of the site. Although the nature of walling on the larger site seems to indicate recent occupation, this may well indicate re-use of a hut-circle originally connected with further settlement remains a short distance to the N.

Glyntawe
SN 81 N.W. (US 13 i) (8410 1737); (US 13 ii) (8410 1733)   6 ix 88

(US 14; Fig. 127) On the E. slope of Allt Fach about 390 m above O.D. is a group of enclosures (US 14 i), recently used as sheepfolds, though almost certainly incorporating earlier features. The largest is irregular in plan, 14 m E.–W. by 11 m internally. A smaller one adjoins it on the E., this being divided by an E.–W. wall. The boundary walls of the larger enclosure are 2 m wide and 0.6 m high, those of the smaller, about 1 m wide and 0.5 m high. There are traces of a further enclosure about 4 m square internally, adjacent on the E.

From midway along the S. side of the largest enclosure there is a wall 2 m wide, 0.3 m high, running

S. about 8 m, before dividing, one branch running N.W. a further 30 m, the other continuing S. as a dispersed line to the N.E. corner of a poorly defined enclosure some 12 m N.–S. by 12 m. To the N.W. of the enclosure group, are shallow hillside scoops (US 14 ii), 5 m long, 3 m wide and up to 1 m deep. Rather than represent habitation sites, these may result from quarrying.

Glyntawe
SN 81 N.W. (US 14 i) (8446 1778); (US 14 ii) (8444 1780)   v 88

(US 15; Fig. 127) There is a rush-grown platformed structure (US 15 i) adjacent to the current enclosure boundary in Nant Tawe Fechan about 320 m above O.D. It is 6 m N.–S. by 3.7 m internally, bounded on the N.W. and S. by a boulder-built wall and ditch, the wall measuring 0.9 m wide by 1 m high. The N. wall includes on its inner face a large upright slab, 1.5 m long and 0.8 m high, by 0.3 m thick. The front, E. side of the platform is built out over the contour 1.54 m, upon a rubble-revetted wall 2 m wide.

About 75 m upstream on the E. bank is an oval structure (US 15 ii) 4.8 m N.–S. by 3.5 m, built on a natural S.-facing platform. It is bounded by boulder walls 1 m wide and 1 m high, having an entrance at the S. end of the W. side.

A further 70 m upstream on the W. bank is a rectangular enclosure (US 15 iii), the N. portion of which is eroded away by the stream. Only the W., S. and E., corners remain. Its surviving rubble and boulder enclosure walls are about 2 m wide, 0.9 m high, and measure 8.8 m (S.W.), 5.2 m (S.E.) and 4.5 m (N.E.).

Llywel (E), Traean-glas (C)
SN 81 N.W. (US 15 i) (8432 1851); (US 15 ii) (8431 1858); (US 15 iii) (8430 1865)   7 vi 88

(US 16) On the N.E. bank of the Nant Tawe Fechan about 430 m above O.D. are the remains of a structure in the form of a boulder wall spread to about 1.5 m wide, 0.5 m high, running N.W.–S.E. some 12 m, then N.E.–S.W. 4 m. These probably formed the N.E. and S.E. sides of a rectangular enclosure, the other two sides of which have been destroyed by stream action. A recent shelter has been incorporated into part of the wall towards the N.W. end of the longer side.

Llywel (E), Traean-glas (C)
SN 81 N.W. (8395 1891)   vi 88

(US 17) There are two small enclosures lying to the N.E. of a rock exposure near the S.E. end of the Fan Hir escarpment edge, about 610 m above O.D.

The northernmost (US 17 i) is kidney-shaped in plan, 6.5 m N.–S. by 5 m at the S. end, 4 m on the N. and bounded by boulder-built walls 0.8 m thick, 1 m high with a large natural boulder utilised at the S.E. corner. The structure is in good condition and has probably been most recently used as a sheepfold.

About 12 m S.S.E. is a smaller, rectangular enclosure (US 17 ii), 4 m N.–S. by 3 m, possibly the remains of an associated shelter. This has an entrance in the W. side. Its boulder walls are 0.5 m wide and 1 m high.

Llywel (E), Traean-glas (C)
SN 81 N.W. (US 17 i) (8393 1853); (US 17 ii) (8394 1852)   vi 88

(US 18) On a level shelf at the base of the steep N.E.-facing escarpment of Fan Hir, about 430 m above O.D. are the remains of two small enclosure complexes.

One, (US 18 i), is revetted by boulder walls 0.9 m wide by 0.9 m high. Adjacent on the E. is a small annex, measuring 3.5 m N.–S. by 2 m, possibly including the remains of a further, more easterly annex, 3.5 m N.–S. by 1 m which is open to the S. Both annexes have walls 0.4 m wide and 0.3 m high.

The second complex (US 18 ii) is about 15 m N.W. of the first and comprises a level platform 4.5 m E.–W. by 4 m. This has been built out from the base of the escarpment. The N. and E. sides are boulder-revetted and the E. side forms the S.W. of a quadrilateral enclosure, the floor level of which is about 1 m below that of the platform. The enclosure sides are 4 m S.E.–N.W.; 2.5 m W.–E.; 3.5 m N.W.–S.E.; and 3.5 m N.E.–S.W., and are about 1 m wide, and 0.5 m high. There is probably an entrance in the E. corner, and to the N. of the platform another annex, 6 m E.–W. by 4 m. The floor level is again 1 m below that of the platform. It is bounded on the W., N. and E. by a boulder wall 1 m wide, 0.5 m high, that on the E. joining the N. wall of the quadrilateral enclosure about midway along its length.

Llywel (E), Traean-glas (C)
SN 81 N.W. (US 18 i) (8401 1867); (US 18 ii) (8398 1868)   vi 88

(US 19) On the S.E.-facing slope to the S.W. of the Nant Tawe Fechan, about 400 m above O.D., are grouped the remains of several building structures. The main building, of roughly coursed walls some 0.8 m wide and up to 0.9 m high, extends 6–9 m N.–S. by 5.4 m. It is entered on the W. by a narrow opening 0.7 m wide. There is an annex of much cruder construction, 9 m N.E.–S.W. by 6 m, the walls 2m wide by 0.4 m high with an entrance on the E. corner and vestigial interior dividing walls aligned S.E.–N.W. The structures are separated by a levelled farmyard area, partially excavated from the hillside behind. Although most of this building looks relatively modern, the more southwesterly part appears much more ancient.

Llywel (E), Traean-glas (C)
SN 81 N.W. (US 19) (8425 1857)   vi 88

Upper Tawe

(US 20; Fig. 128) On the S.E.-facing slope on the W. side of Cwm Tawe, immediately N. of Nant y Coetgae between 340 and 370 m above O.D., lies a group of platforms, either side of a steeply incised stream flowing N.W.–S.E. into the Tawe. The site is bisected by two tracks which form the older drovers' route over the pass over the Upper Tawe.

The following sites (US 20 i–v) lie S.E. of the stream:

(US 20 i) A platform 7.5 m W.–E. by 4.5 m. The W. end is scooped out of the hillside to a depth of 1 m, the E. end built up to the same height.

(US 20 ii) A possible platform, 6 m N.E.–S.W. by 3.5 m, built upon the S.E. to about 1.2 m in height, putatively scooped on the N.W. side.

(US 20 iii) A rubble cairn about 2 m in diameter and 0.2 m high.

(US 20 iv) A platform 5 m W.N.W.–E.S.E. by 3.5 m. This has been scooped out of the slope on the W.S.W. side to about 1 m and built on the E.S.E. to 1.2 m. Towards the rear end are the remains of a rubble-walled structure measuring 3 m S.E.–N.E. by 2.5 m internally, the walls 1.5 m wide and 0.3 m high, except on the W. where they are revetted into the slope to 1 m high. There is a spread of loose rubble adjacent on the N.E. which may derive from this structure.

(US 20 v) A platform 9.5 m W.N.W.–E.S.E. by 6.5 m, scooped out on the W.N.W. end to some 2 m, the E.S.E. end built out 1.2 m. About 10 m N.W. is a rubble-built cairn about 3 m in diameter, 0.6 m high, of loose stones on a turf-consolidated base.

N.E. of the stream, four platforms (US 20 vi–ix) lie with their S.W. edges set to the edge of the gorge.

(US 20 vi) A platform 10 m W.N.W.–E.S.E. by 7.5 m scooped out at the W.N.W. to 1.5 m and built out on the E.S.E. to 1 m. The platform area is occupied by an enclosure, presumably a sheepfold, which fills the levelled area. Its walls are up to 1.2 m wide and 0.6 m high, with evidence of N.N.E.–S.S.W. division.

(US 20 vii) A platform 10.5 m W.N.W.–E.S.E. by 4.5 m. The W.N.W. end is scooped to 1.75 m, the scarp continuing round the W. half of the W.N.W. side, where there is an outer, counterscarp. There is some suggestion of a N.N.W.–S.S.E. mid-division. The W. half of the S.S.W. side is bounded by a rubble bank about 1 m wide, and 0.2 m high, lying on the very lip of the gorge.

(US 20 viii) A platform 9 m W.N.W.–E.S.E. by 5 m, scooped out 1.5 m at the W.N.W. end, the scarp being continued along the W. half of the N.N.E. side by a bank 1.8 m wide, 0.3 m high. The S.S.E. side is bounded by the gorge, but there is a slight inward facing counterscarp before the natural drop. The E.S.E. end is built up to 1.5 m and conjoined with the base of the bank is a structure 3.5 m N.N.E.–S.S.E. by 2.5 m overall, bounded by turf-consolidated rubble walls 0.3 m high.

(US 20 ix) There are indications of a platform 6 m N.N.W.–S.S.E. by 3 m. Only the rubble-built S.S.E. end is clearly defined, 1.5 m high. Built into the base of the bank there is a small structure 2 m square bounded by rubble walls up to 0.5 m high.

The remaining features are randomly distributed across the hillside to the N.W. of the stream.

(US 20 x) A short length of revetment bank composed of turf-consolidated rubble about 14 m N.E.–S.W., 1.2 m wide and 0.8 m high.

(US 20 xi) A large 'two-storey' platform, or two adjacent platforms. The upper, oval in plan, is 7.5 m W.–E. by 6 m, and the W. half is bounded by a turf-

UNENCLOSED SETTLEMENTS

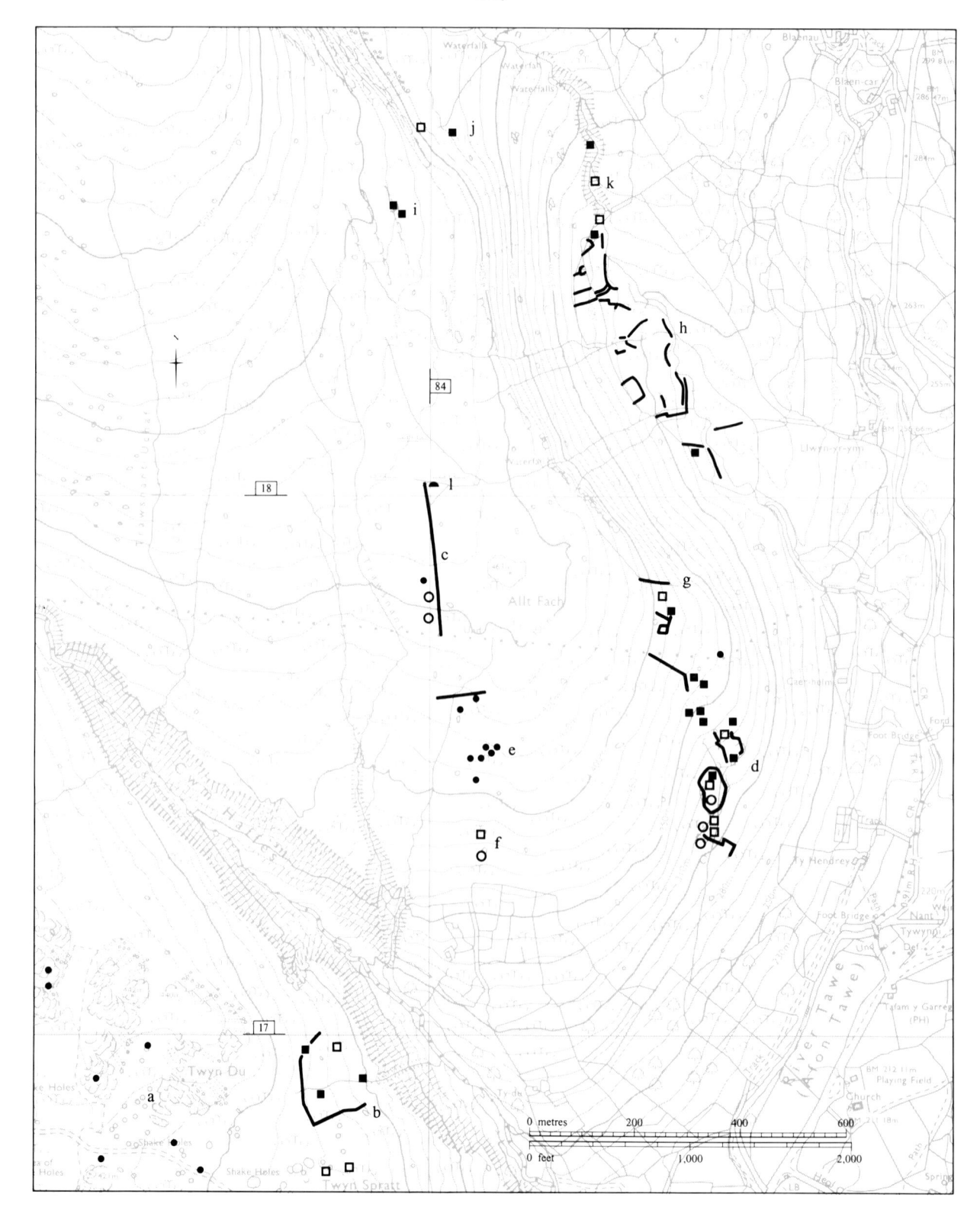

127 The Cwm Haffes-Allt Fach Tawe Fechan area: a. clearances around Twyn Du and Twyn Walter (US 4); b. Cwm Haffes enclosure (US 5); c. Field bank (US 11); d. (US 14); Nant Tawe Fechan showing field banks (US 12); e. Clearance cairns (US 10); f. (US 13); g. (US 7); h. (US 15); i. (US 16); j. (US 18); k. (US 19)

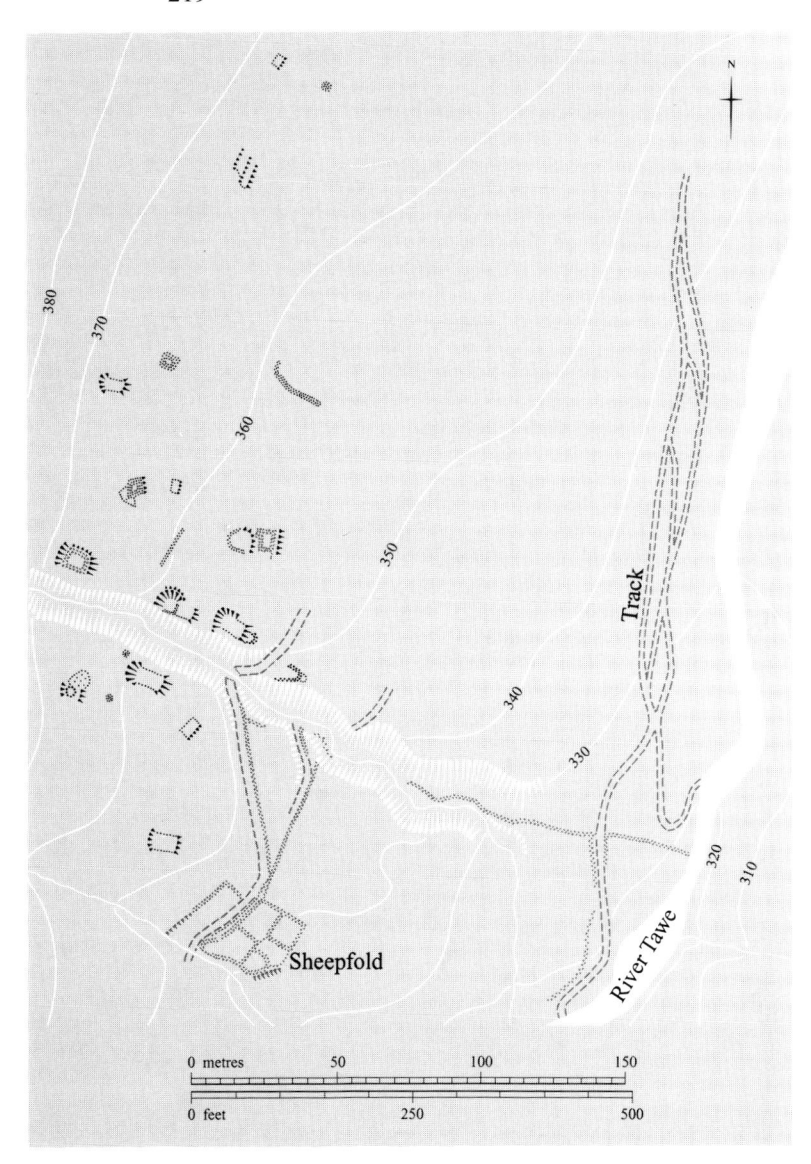

128 Huts, house-platforms and tracks at Nant y Coetgae (US 20)

consolidated rubble bank up to 1.5 m wide and 0.8 m high, with indications of an external ditch. The E. end is built up to about 1.5 m above the lower feature. This lower level is 6 m W.–E. by 7.5 m, built up on the E. to 0.6 m. It is occupied by an enclosure, more or less rectangular, with a distinct alcove at the E. end of the W. side. Overall (excluding the alcove 3 m N.–S. by 2 m) it measures 7.5 m N.–W. by 4.5 m. The whole is enclosed by rubble walls 1.5 m wide and 0.6 m high, the W. wall being revetted against the bank of the higher level.

(US 20 xii) A structure set upon a platform, the outer (E.) edge of which is raised some 1 m above contour level. The structure is rectangular 5.5 m N.–S. by 5 m, bounded by rubble-built walls 1.5 m wide and 0.3 m high. Adjacent to the S.W. corner there are indications of connecting banks hinting that this feature was originally more extensive.

(US 20 xiii) A platform 5 m N.N.E.–S.S.W. by 2.5 m, elevated upon rubble on the E.S.E. to 1 m. There is slight evidence of scooping out 1.5 m deep on the W.S.W.

(US 20 xiv) A platform 7 m W.N.W.–E.S.E. by 4 m scooped out 1.5 m on the W.N.W. and built out to a similar height.

(US 20 xv) A platform 5 m W.N.W.–E.S.E. by 4.5 m, scooped out on the W.N.W. to 1 m, built up similarly on the E.S.E. The levelled area is occupied by an enclosure with walls 1.5 m wide and 0.4 m high.

(US 20 xvi) A short, isolated length of rubble bank 2 m wide and 0.4 m high, running 4 m N.E.–S.W., then 18 m S.E.

(US 20 xvii) A 'two-storey' platform, the upper about 8 m N.E.–S.W. by 3 m, bounded on the N.W. and S.W. by a rubble-faced scarp up to 0.6 m high. The lower level is offset to the S.W., and measures 8 m N.E.–S.W. by 1.5 m. It lies about 0.7 m below the upper, and is separated from it by a rubble bank 1.5 m wide. The S.E. side is rubble-built to a height of 0.4 m.

(US 20 xviii) A loose rubble clearance cairn 4 m N.–S. by 3 m, and 0.2 m high.

(US 20 xix) Fugitive remains of a platform lying immediately S.E. of a natural outcrop, 4 m N.E.–S.W. by 2.5 m.

(US 20 xx) A turf-consolidated clearance cairn 5 m in diameter, 0.2 m high.

(US 20 xxi) A similar feature 4 m in diameter and 0.3 m high.

Llywel (E), Traean-glas (C)
SN 81 N.W. (US 20 i) (8482 1967); (US 20 ii) (8483 1971); (US 20 iii) (8480 1971); (US 20 iv) (8479 1972); (US 20 v) (8482 1972); (US 20 vi) (8479 1976); (US 20 vii) (8483 1974); (US 20 viii) (8485 1974); (US 20 ix) (8486 1972); (US 20 x) (8483 1977); (US 20 xi) (8485 1977); (US 20 xii) (8481 1978); (US 20 xiii) (8483 1978); (US 20 xiv) (8481 1982); (US 20 xv) (8482 1982); (US 20 xvi) (8487 1982); (US 20 xvii) (8485 1989); (US 20 xviii) (8488 1991); (US 20 xix) (8486 1992); (US 20 xx) (8488 1998); (US 20 xxi) (8488 1999) 16 vi 91

SN 81 N.E.

(US 21) To the N. of Carreg Lwyd about 450 m above O.D. is an enclosure with attached hut, of unknown date. The limestone rubble walls are crudely constructed, and measure 13 m N.–S. by 17 m E.–W. standing up to 0.4 m high. Integral with the N.E. corner is a small hut-like structure 4 m by 3 m. There are no signs of an obvious entrance in either enclosure or hut.

O.S. Card SN 81 NE 1.

Ystradgynlais (E), Ystradgynlais Hr (C)
SN 81 N.E. (US 21) (8622 1560) 23 ix 82

(US 22) On the S.-facing slope overlooking Pwll Byfre 500 m above O.D. are two possible hut-circles beside a modern track. The better preserved (US 22 i), apparently lacking an entrance, is about 7 m in overall diameter and 2.5 m internally, consisting of a stony bank up to 0.3 m high. About 35 m to the W. are the poorly preserved remains of the second circle (US 22 ii), about 5 m in diameter. This one is marked by a perimeter of stones protruding through the turf up to 0.3 m high, embanked slightly on the N.W.

Ystradgynlais (E), Ystradgynlais Hr (C)
SN 81 N.E. (US 22 i) (8750 1711); (US 22 ii)
(8747 1711) 14 viii 87

(US 23) In Blaen Crai on the N. bank of a minor stream within the Crai Rabbit Farm, 350 m above O.D., is a rectangular hut platform hollowed out of the stream bank to a maximum depth of 0.9 m and measuring about 4.3 m E.–W. by 1.8 m. It is bounded along the S. side by a bank up to 0.4 m high. Stones 0.8 m long are visible on the N. end. Although this may pre-date the rabbit farm, lack of clear definition upon the ground make it possible that this belongs to a much earlier period.

Defynnog (E), Crai (C)
SN 81 N.E. (US 23) (8718 1989) 15 ii 88

(US 24) Close to a tributary of the Gihirych at a height of 460 m above O.D. on ground falling steeply to the N. are the remains of a building platform, 9 m E.–W. by 4.5 m cut back into the hillside to 0.5 m.

Defynnog (E), Crai (C)
SN 81 N.E. (US 24) (8902 1987) vi 85

(US 25) Between tributaries of the Nant Gihirych at a height of 465 m above O.D. is a hut-circle, the entrance lying on the S.W. It is on the very edge of a recently ploughed and planted forestry plot.

O.S. Card SN 91 NE 9. Visible on A.P.s, R.A.F. F22/58/3618/0226–7; 21 vi 60.

Defynnog (E), Crai (C)
SN 81 N.E. (US 25) (8916 1972) vi 85

(US 26) On level ground on the W. bank of the Afon Tawe, just above its confluence with the Nant yr Wysg

340 m above O.D., are the remains of three man-made features, of which two are certainly huts.

(US 26 i) The more southerly site has ill-defined walls aligned N.N.W.–S.S.E. and stands about 5 m square. Its site abuts onto a face of the N.–S. outcropping rock.

(US 26 ii) About 15 m to the W. there is a similar enclosure built against the S.-facing rock outcrop. This one is a fairly well-defined rectangular structure about 8 m by 5 m, with walls of large boulders and slabs up to 1.5 m wide and 0.75 m high.

(US 26 iii) The third feature, about 10 m from the river bank, is roughly circular, some 5 m in diameter. It appears to have been joined to the rectangular hut (US 26 ii) by a poorly-defined wall.

Llywel (E), Traean-glas (C)
SN 81 N.E. (US 26 i) (8514 1996); (US 26 ii–iii) (8512 1996)   14 iii 91

(US 27) On the steep N.W.-facing slope overlooking the Nant Tywynni 310 m above O.D. is a building platform 5.5 m (N.W.–S.E.) by 4 m. It is cut back to a depth of 0.4 m, the stony lip built out to about 1 m above the contour. There are indications of some remaining stones among the rushes, and on its N. edge there is an upright block 0.5 m high.

Glyntawe
SN 81 N.E. (US 27) (8638 1838)   26 x 88

(US 28) Fieldwork in 1983 prior to opencast mining operations undertaken by the Clwyd-Powys Archaeological Trust on Mynydd y Drum, an upland ridge about 280 m above O.D. in the S.W. corner of Fforest Fawr, brought to light a series of clearance features of indeterminate age associated with two burial cairns (RC 16 and RC 17).[1] These comprised the following:

(US 28 i) A trapezoidally-shaped grass-grown stony outer 'ring' aligned roughly N.N.W. by S.S.E., 12.3 m by 15.75 m and enclosing a lower central area 5.52 m by 6 m,[2] possibly a hut site.

(US 28 ii) An oval spread of stone aligned roughly N.–S., about 13 m by 17.25 m. The S. part encloses an area about 5.1 m by 6.15 m and there is a relatively shapeless appendage on the N. enclosing a central lower area about 3 m in diameter. Excavation demonstrated there to have been larger stones in the bank, but suggested no dating.[3]

(US 28 iii) A level platform excavated into sloping ground adjacent to a stream, measuring 4 m by 6 m, was flanked by banks about 0.4 m high.[4]

(US 28 iv) On the eastern end of the hill was a cluster of eight clearance cairns, ranging in size from 2 m to 6 m in diameter, and between 0.2 and 0.4 m high. Total excavation of two of these features produced neither cultural nor environmental evidence.[5]

Two lengths of boundary bank were recognised:

(US 28 v) One with a shallow quarry scoop on the N. side passed W.–E. along the contour, (about 270 m above O.D.), through the area of clearance cairns (US 28 iv) about 600 m in total length. Although excavation produced two flints – a scraper and a flake – the wall, some 1.5 m wide by 0.25 m high, had clearly been laid over peat, and as it was constructed of clay mixed with peat,[6] this seems unlikely to have been prehistoric.

(US 28 vi–vii) The second boundary comprised two disjointed pieces of bank each 200 m and 50 m long lying to the S. of the longer stretch and apparently of similar construction.[7]

[1] P. Dorling and F. M. Chambers, *B.B.C.S.* 37 (1990), pp. 215–46.
[2] *ibid.* p. 217, site 11, Fig. 2; Pl. 1a.
[3] *idem.* site 13.
[4] *ibid.* p. 219, site 14.
[5] *idem.* sites 5–10, 17–18; Fig. 2, Pl. 1b.
[6] *idem.* site 4, section Fig. 2.
[7] *idem.* site 12.

Ystradgynlais (E), Ystradgynlais Hr (C)
SN 81 S.W. (US 28 i) (8285 1080); (US 28 ii) (8292 1116); (US 28 iii) (8196 1071); (US 28 iv) (centred upon 8290 1085); (US 28 v–vii) (unspecified)   viii 83

(US 29; Fig. 94) Occupying the knoll on the W. side of Nant Tarw, 345 m above O.D. and lying slightly to the N. of a line drawn between the more westerly stone circle and the denuded cairn (see SC 2), is a pentagonal enclosure overlooking the stream.[1] Its outline is ill-defined on the N., where the stream has eroded its enclosing bank, and where there might have been a hut, now eroded away or irreparably damaged by the track passing S.–N. downhill to the stream along the E. enclosure side.[2] Its banks are about 2 m wide and up to 0.3 m high, with a diameter of about 16 m. It is possible the E. track occupies the site of an outer ditch, but its former existence is not certain.

[1] Noted during field survey in January 1989.
[2] R.C.A.M., A.P.s, 88 MB 183–5.

Defynnog (E), Traean-glas (C)
SN 82 N.W. (US 29) (8193 2593)   viii 89

Upper Tawe (US 30–38 Fig. 129, 131)

(US 30) Above the plateau base of the Tawe floor at a height of 435 m above O.D., on the steep slope adjacent to a stream, is a chord-shaped enclosure, aligned E.–W. Its boundary bank comprises a stone swathe up to 3 m wide of boulders up to 8 m in diameter. From its E. end the wall runs E.–W. in a direct line for about 16 m. Downslope, a further 25 m curves towards the stream, and upslope a stretch of only about 15 m remains, leaving a gap of 30 m to the stream. A spring head rises immediately beneath this northern wall terminus, but otherwise the interior of the enclosure is boulder-strewn and lies upon a steep bank. More interior construction may have existed, though this would easily be carried away in flood by the cascading stream. At the furthest downslope limit of the site where the stream curves N., deflected from harder rock at this point, there is a flat area internally, which might have been a temporary damming.

Defynnog (E), Traean-glas (C)
SN 82 S.W. (US 30) (8478 2024)   14 iii 91

(US 31) Features lying to N. of Cerrig Duon.

(US 31 i) In an elongated reed-bottomed hollow about 420 m above O.D., on a slightly raised part of the valley side, invisible from all angles but above, lies a penannular enclosure. From upslope, N.–S., its diameter is 15 m; from E.–W., between the unjoined wall termini on the S., the distance is 11–12 m. It is cut on the E. by a stream at a point alongside the entrance, and the watercourse has been channelled alongside a piece of boggy ground on the S. of the feature, which widens E.–W. to about 125 m and extends about 20 m N.–S. It is possible that the original structure was built alongside a spring, or even that it was intended partly to enclose a pond, now silted up. The embanking wall is 2 m wide and rises to 0.75 m high enclosing a stone-strewn interior devoid of convincing structures.

(US 31 ii) Behind, to the S.W. of enclosure (US 31 i) at the foot of the hillslope immediately below the boulder train and apparently not part of it, is a field clearance cairn of rounded fieldstones and large boulders.

(US 31 iii) About midway between the penannular enclosure (US 31 i above) and the hut-group (US 32), are the remains of a subcircular hut about 5 m in diameter, with stones upstanding 0.3 m, the centre full of stones. This lies adjacent to a small stone scatter (US 31 iv) running N.N.W. along the base of the slope and forming the notional boundary to a cleared area, which, against the more heathy nature of the valley in general, is relatively green (on the E.). This may indicate its former fertility, and the immediate area seems to form a field roughly 39 m square adjacent to the hut.

(US 31 v) On ground raised very slightly above the marsh and rush, about 30 m to S. of the enclosure (US 31 i), is a slight platform, 0.45 m high, upon which is an amorphous cairn or an inwardly-collapsed circular or square corbelled hut about 5 m square.

(US 31 vi) About 30 m N.W. and uphill of the penannular enclosure (US 31 i), is a rectangular slope-scooped platform occupied by a rubble-built structure, probably a hut. Few stones have survived on the W., uphill side, but the N. and S. walls survive as rubble scatters about 2 m wide. It is about 7 m wide overall (E.–W.), by 12 m long (N.–S.), and lies along the contour, the rubble of the longer outer wall forming a 3 m wide swathe downslope.

(US 31 vii) A slope-built square hut platform 7 m E.–W. (upslope), and 6 m wide along the contour. This is embanked by a rubble wall 1.5–2 m wide at the rear, and terminating in a massive ground-set boulder on the S.W. corner, where it is overlain by loose material. There is possibly a further platform downslope.

(US 31 viii) Lying along the contour is a small hill-scooped hut about 8 m long (N.–S.). There is a crescent-shaped scatter downhill of the scoop, which runs the length of the feature and is about 4 m wide. There is a large stone 2+ m long and over 1 m wide on the N.E. corner.

(US 31 ix) The most northerly feature of the group is a small collection of large fieldstones thrown onto an outcropping rock about 4 m square and up to 1 m high.

(US 31 x) A roughly circular cairn 5 m in diameter, 0.5 m high of boulders and fieldstones of all sizes. There are two smaller cairns, or stone groups, lying on the hillside below.

(US 31 xi) Lying within an area of very large

UNENCLOSED SETTLEMENTS

boulders is a cairn lying upon the slope immediately below the sheep path. This is 3 m N.–S. by 2 m wide, backed (on the W.) by slope-set stones 0.75 m high and downslope by a rubble spread 4 m long. There is grass-grown rubble on the N. Close and S. of this is a cairn 7 m N.–S. and 5 m E.–W., 0.3 m high, of large fieldstones.

(US 31 xii) In the area of relatively stone-free ground lying to the E. of the above features is a wall running N.–S. about 30 m long, possibly associated with similar clearances in the same area.

(US 31 xiii) About 30 m S. of wall (US 31 xii), is a cairn which overlooks the river from a point immediately S. of an abandoned river meander. Standing 0.2 m high and 5 m in diameter, it is composed of a loose spread of boulders though with a couple of larger ones protruding centrally.

(US 31 xiv) About 25 m to the S.W. of the wall (US 31 xii) is a further, short stretch running W.N.W.–E.S.E. and about 15 m long.

(US 31 xv) A small clearance cairn about 3 m in diameter and 0.3 m high.

(US 31 xvi) Between wall (US 31 xii) and (US 31 xiii) is a small clearance cairn.

(US 31 xvii) Upslope and about 25 m W., above the penannular enclosure (US 31 i), lies another platform feature about 9 m long by 5 m wide.

(US 31 xviii) Some distance to the S.E. of the group described above about 385 m above O.D. and lying on the slightly raised central core of a river meander, are the remains of a house or enclosure wall. This feature is traceable for about 15 m, is of double-built walling, 0.6 m wide and eroded on the E., river, side. Piled stones, cairns and enclosure walls recorded near this spot (at SN 8518 2081) in 1968 were rejected as flood-deposited debris by the O.S. in 1976.

Defynnog (E), Traean-glas (C)
SN 82 S.E. (US 31 i) (8495 2147); (US 31 ii) (8484 2143); (US 31 iii) (8497 2142); (US 31 iv) (8496 2133–8496 2136); (US 31 v) (8497 2142); (US 31 vi) (8495 2150); (US 31 vii) (8500 2157); (US 31 viii) (8498 2164); (US 31 ix) (8500 2164); (US 31 x) (8501 2163); (US 31 xi) (8502 2149); (US 31 xii) (8509 2137); (US 31 xiii) (8511 2131); (US 31 xiv) (8507 2133–8509 2135); (US 31 xv) (8488 2143); (US 31 xvi) (8508 2132); (US 31 xvii) (8470 2150 approx.); (US 31 xviii) (8521 2080)

19 vi 91

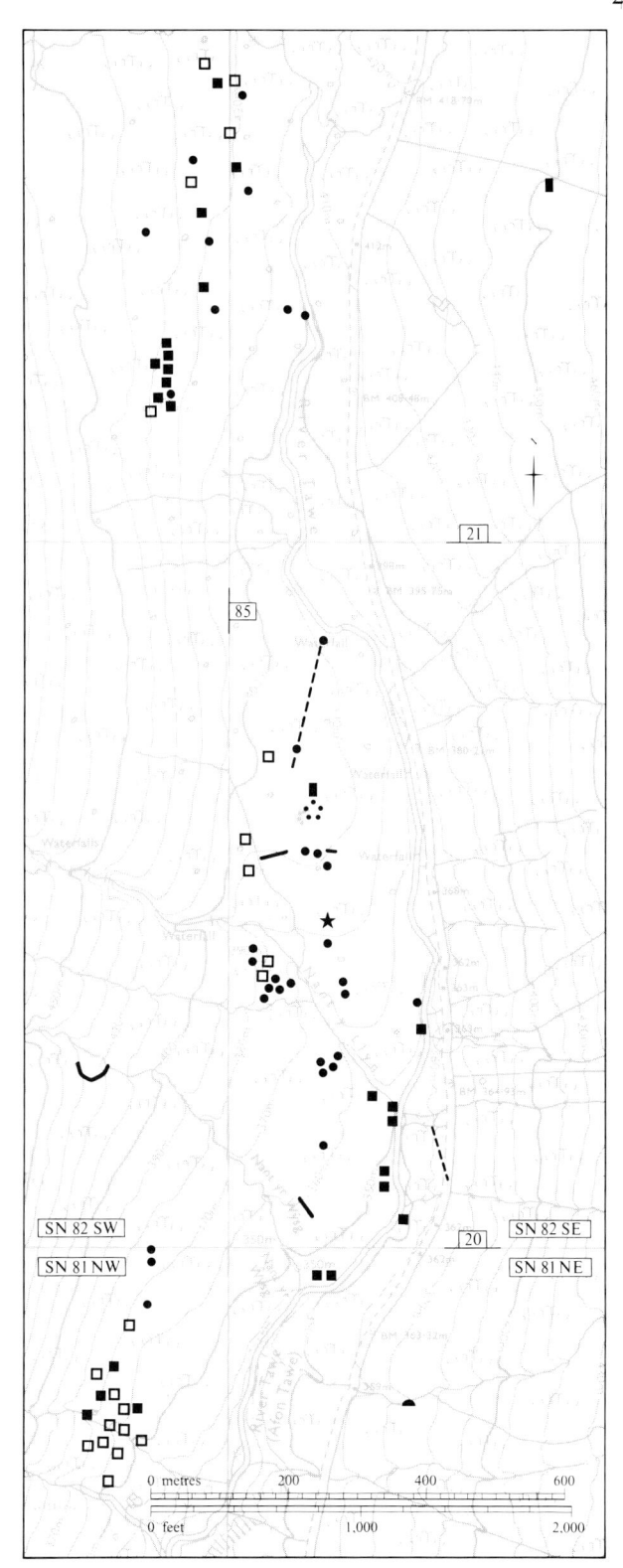

129 The Upper Cwm Tawe area centring upon Cerrig Duon (SC 3) and Maen Mawr (SS 3) including: Platforms at Nant y Coetgae (US 19–20) enclosures at Nant y Wysg (US 26) and a variety of sites in Cwm Tawe (US 33–4)

(US 32) Several long-huts survive in the watershed of the Upper Tawe, some, to the N. of the area described in detail here, are well-coursed with walls standing to a height of 1 m. Although of uncertain age, the group described below appears older and possibly of considerable antiquity, though of this there can be no certainty, and only excavation will determine this.

Lying immediately S. of the (US 31) area and about 410 m above O.D. is a group of huts also on the E.-facing W. valley side of Nant Tawe. No obvious signs of settlement could be seen between these and the Afon Tawe, and it is therefore possible that these represent a later occupation phase replacing earlier clearances similar to those lying both N. and S.

The huts are situated on a slight, E.-facing platform of natural origin, about 100 m long by about 50 m wide. It slopes gently towards the river at a depth of some 7–10 m below. There is a sharper break of slope immediately behind the structures. The locality is well watered with springs, though some stony features in the vicinity are at least partly rush-grown.

(US 32 i) The first hut is a double- or possibly even triple-storey platform with the remains of a hut on the lower part. Overall, the platform is 7 m long with an ill-defined width. The hut, subcircular in shape, is about 6 m in diameter, the interior space about 3.5 m (N.–S.) by 2 m, the entrance site facing downslope.

(US 32 ii) Hut 2 is about 5 m square with rubble walls rising to 0.4 m in height, and spread to 2 m wide, enclosing a central area 3 m wide and about 1.5 m wide.

(US 32 iii) Hut 3 is a rectangular structure 10 m long (E.–W.) by 6 m wide, enclosed by thick boulder walls. On the N.E. side is an annex of indeterminate shape about 1.5 m in diameter.

(US 32 iv) Hut 4 is oval-shaped to round and about 4 m long (E.–W.) by 3 m wide (N.–S.) in diameter. It is walled by large boulders.

(US 32 v) Hut 5 is almost adjacent to Hut 4, occupying a site some 5 m to its N.W. It is oblong, 4 m wide (N.–S.) by 5 m, and comprises a massive rubble and boulder enclosing wall which has collapsed into the interior, which it obscures.

(US 32 vi) Hut 6 is separated from 5 by a similar distance and comprises a wall 4 m square enclosing a small space now cluttered by the collapse of its walls.

Defynnog (E), Traean-glas (C)
SN 82 S.E. (US 32 i) (8491 2119); (US 32 ii) (8490 2120); (US 32 iii) (8491 2122); (US 32 iv) (8490 2124); (US 32 v) (8489 2125); (US 32 vi) (8491 2127)
14 iii 91

(US 33) The plateau area which forms the elevation upon which Cerrig Duon and Maen Mawr stand, some 390 m above O.D., is bisected by two hollow ways, running roughly N.–S., deflecting to E. and W. around the two major monuments some 120 m apart in a traverse of about 250 m. The plateau appears to have been drained, possibly during medieval times or in the industrial period, by diverting an E.–W.-flowing stream which descends onto a silting cone immediately W. of the circle area S., to the flow of the Nant yr Wysg. Under suitable weather conditions, a number of clearance features are evident on this plateau. Some may have been contemporary to the use of the monument, others are probably more recent in origin; in their present forms some are likely to relate to the period during which drovers' roads were in use.

Two sites lie to the N. of Maen Mawr:
(US 33 i) The more northerly is a small amorphous boulder cairn close to the bifurcation of the tracks some 200 m to the N. of the stone circle.

(US 33 ii) A further small cairn lies close to the track about 90 m N.N.W. of the circle. This was possibly intended to mark the route.

To the S. of Maen Mawr are:
(US 33 iii) Boundary bank
S. of Maen Mawr is a discontinuous linear feature comprising small field clearance cairns climbing ground rising from about 370 to 400 m above O.D. (E.–W.). There are three distinct disjointed stretches. The first lies due S. of the circle and comprises an elongated cairn 7 m (W.–E.) by 3 m (US 33 iiia) built against a larger stone about 1 m long and 0.2 m thick, and standing 0.35 m above the ground. Some 15 m further E. is a collection of about a dozen stones 1.5 m in diameter, and 2 m further E. again, a grass-grown cairn (US 33 iiib). A second bank runs N.–S. close to the terminus of these clearances. This short feature, at right angles to the first, about 6 m long and less than 1 m wide, is separated from the E.–W. bank by a gap 3 m wide through which a small bog drains (US 33 iiic).

This E.–W. linear feature re-appears further W. as a

length of bank, traceable through differential vegetation and occasional large fieldstones as it heads for the steeper slope. About 25 m along its course this is cut by a stream occupying an artificial channel up to 1.5 m deep and 2–2.5 m wide, cut to drain away spring water from the W. valley slopes, preventing erosion to the drovers' track on the N. side of the stone circle. Beyond the drain, it passes as a distinct collection of fieldstone (perhaps a debris flow enhanced by field clearance), climbing steeply along the slope for a distance of about 100 m, at least as far as the exposed rock strata which form a cascade on the stream (US 33 iiid).

A further stretch of wall traverses the plateau in a westerly direction, heading towards the Afon Tawe. This appears to be a continuation of the line already described. It can be seen descending the steep Tawe valley side as a fugitive rubble scatter sometimes defined by varying vegetational colour highlighting two discontinuous bands of stone which are only visible from the roadside (US 33 iiie).

As this feature appears not to be cut by medieval or later drovers' roads, a pre-medieval origin may be argued for it. If prehistoric, its relationship to the circle and standing stone makes this an important enclosure bank meriting more detailed investigation.

(US 33 iv) About 30 m S. of the discontinuous wall, and lying downslope from Cerrig Duon circle (SC 3), is a small collection of stones on the steeper slope overlooking a discrete plateau area about 560 m long by 15–20 m wide, and growing peat around two stagnant pools. It is amorphous, about 3 m in diameter and of large boulders up to 0.6 m in diameter.

(US 33 iv) At a point about 25 m beyond the spot where the old drovers' track rises from fording the stream to the plateau on the S. side of Cwm Tawe, and equidistant between two old hollow drovers' ways, at a height of about 370 m above O.D., is a prominent grass-covered stone cairn standing proud of the sloping ground to a height of 1 m. It is 10 m in diameter, and comprises both angular and rounded fieldstone up to 0.4 m in length; the centre has been much robbed, to leave a gaping hollow.

(US 33 vi–vii) There are two small grass-grown cairns adjacent to the more easterly of the two drovers' tracks, some 100 m S.W. of site (US 33 v). One (US 33 vi), of large slabs, is 6 m N.N.W.–S.S.E. by 4 m with further outlying stone. The other (vii) is moss-covered, 5–6 m N.–S. by 2 m wide and 0.2 m high. It is possible that both originally formed part of a discontinuous wall, or alternatively, they may comprise material excavated from wet weather excavation of the adjacent routeway. Such a process would have involved removing mud and clay as well as stone components to deepen or widen the track, but bare stone cairns would be left after the clay had eroded away.

Defynnog (R), Traean-glas (C)
SN 82 S.E. (US 33 i) (8513 2086); (US 33 ii) (8510 2070); (US 33 iiia) (8512 2056–8511 2056); (US 33 iiib) (8514 2055); (US 33 iiic) (8508 2056); (US 33 iiid) (8500 2046); (US 33 iiie) (8518 2971–8525 2071); (US 33 iv) (8514 2054); (US 33 v) (8514 2043); (US 33 vi) (8517 2036); (US 33 vii) (8516 2037)   14 iii 91

(US 34) Further clearances and settlements lie S. of the tributary stream which bounds the S. end of the Cerrig Duon plateau, about 370–395 m above O.D.

(US 34 i) Occupying the interfluve between two streams cutting the W. side of Cwm Tawe at a height of 375 m above O.D. several stone swathes are exposed. Although its origin was almost certainly natural (this was probably a debris flow), the whole interfluve appears to have been enhanced into slight terraces for cultivation or habitation. Its most definite feature is a terrace 15 m across (roughly N.–S.) and 8 m (W.–E.). This is bounded on the W. and S. by a scooped boundary, the other sides comprising stone swathes up to 2 m wide. Lying adjacent is a fugitive terraced habitation or cultivation scoop, about 8 m wide by 30 m long (N.N.W.–S.S.E.).

(US 34 ii) On the same interfluve and immediately downslope of the landscaped terrace is a series of at least seven low stone cairns, in an area roughly parallel to the terrace. They are mainly formless and small (1–2 m in diameter and up to 0.3 m high). There is a further circular outlier. It is moss-covered, about 2 m in diameter and lies on cleared ground about 3 m from the steep descent to the river on the N.

(US 34 iii) To the S. of the two W.–E.-flowing tributary streams described above, is an interfluve of well-cleared gently-sloping grassland heath strip roughly 250 m between streams and from 350 m to 380 m above O.D. On the steep valley side adjacent to the upper part of this stream is a massive boulder enclosure (US 30). On the flatter plateau area below, and closer to the more N. of the two streams is a group of 12 small clearance cairns. They occupy part of the triangular area between the junction of two old drovers' tracks, which meet about 100 m to their S. These cairns, closely spaced no more than about 7 m apart, are of both rounded fieldstones and boulders, and range from 1.5–3 m in diameter and up to 0.3 m high.

(US 34 iv) Between the junction of the Afon Tawe and its tributary at a height of 350 m above O.D. is a series of rubble banks representing two, possibly three huts, much obscured by rushes on the W. The features comprise a coursed boulder and ashlar stone wall about 10 m long, possibly representing the remaining (southern) longer axis of a hut, most of which has eroded into the river alongside (US 34 iva). On the E. this wall meets an indistinct rectangular rubble-strewn area about 7 m W.–E. by 4 m (externally), with a well coursed wall on the W. Some 5 m to the S. of this lies a scooped area about 6.5 m in diameter, cut back towards the E. side, protecting the interior from the river. Its W. wall is more recognisably linear and comprises a rubble bank.

(US 34 v) On the W. bank of the Afon Tawe at a height of 345 m above O.D. is a circular feature of large fieldstones and about 5 m in diameter. It rests on a slight slope and has a hollowed-out interior. Some 12 m to the S. is an ill-defined feature 5 m square, probably all that remains of a substantial hut. These features occupy the low shelf of an abandoned river terrace, the outside of which is strewn with fieldstone, suggesting that the plateau area on this W. river bank has at some time been cleared, if not cultivated.

(US 34 vi) Running to the N.N.W. of the area occupied by the huts (US 34 v) is a slight natural hollow (possibly created by running water or perhaps representing a periglacial feature). A swathe of rounded fieldstones up to 2 m wide, which appear as a series of discontinuous field clearance cairns, is oriented along the base for a distance of 45 m and seems to have been a primitive boundary or wall.

(US 34 vii) To the N. of the terminus of this wall are a pair of angular flat upright stones, separated at their base by about 1.3 m, and standing about 1 m high. They appear to have comprised part of a boulder, now split and broken, and may either have related to the clearance features in this locality, or could have been intended to offer some indication of the drovers' route which passes immediately to the N.

(US 34 viii–ix) Sitting on the river bank about 7 m above the stream at a height of 350 m above O.D. is an ill-defined pile of large slab-like boulders about 6 m N.–S. by 5 m W.–E. This resembles a much damaged hut, possibly associated with the area of sheltered, cleared ground occupying a slight hollow to its S.

Defynnog (E), Traean-glas (C)
SN 82 S.E. (US 34 i) (8506 2370–8506 2041); (US 34 iia) (8505 2036); (US 34 iib) (8506 2037); (US 34 iic–e) (8507 2037); (US 34 iif) (8508 2037); (US 34 iig) (8509 2038); (US 34 iii) (8513 2026; 8513 2025; 8514 2025; 8514 2026; 8515 2026; 8505 2027); (US 34 iv) (8522 2020; 8523 2018); (US 34 v) (8523 2009); (US 34 vi) wall (8512 2004–8510 2007); (US 34 vii) (8511 2008); (US 34 viii) (8519 2021 to 8521 2020); (US 34 ix) (8520 2021)   19 vi 91

(US 35) Although almost 700 m apart, for convenience of access three sites on the E. side of the N.–S. Abercraf–Trecastle road are described in this entry.

(US 35 i) The most northerly is an earthwork 370 m above O.D., emphasised by longer grass and reeds, lying at a point where the road and Afon Tawe are separated by a distance of no more than 20 m. At a point about 20 m S. of where a stream enters the river is a curving bank about 12 m long, 1.5–2 m wide and 0.3 m high, running N.–S. The northern terminal is 5 m above the river.

This feature lies on the opposite river bank from the fugitive wall (US 33 iiie).

(US 35 ii) Nestling above the Afon Tawe at a height of 345 m above O.D., on a N.-facing hollow, is an irregular flat area roughly 25 m around. This is separated from the river, 3 m below, by the remnant of a rubble bank, which survives 12 m long and 0.6 m high. About 5 m behind (E.) of this bank are possibly the remains of an upstanding turf-covered wall, about 6 m long and 0.8 m wide.

(US 35 iii) Some 200 m E. of (US 35 ii), on enclosed land sloping uphill to the E., at a height of 390 m above O.D. is a circular stone enclosure 10.4 m in diameter externally, 6.7 m internally. It is enclosed by a ruined drystone wall 0.6–0.9 m thick and up to 0.9 m high. It is approached through an entrance on the S. 0.9 m wide and partly blocked by a fallen stone. This was probably an animal pen.

Defynnog (E), Traean-glas (C)
SN 82 S.E. (US 35 i) (8527 2071); (US 35 ii) (8525 2004); (US 35 iii) (8536 2024)   19 vi 91

Cwm Cadlan and Pant Sychpant

(US 36; Fig. 130) In Pant Sychpant some 335 m above O.D. mostly lying within a forestry firebreak is a large sub-circular enclosure 23 m in diameter overall, with rubble banks marked by the selective growth of heather averaging 2.2 m wide and 0.3 m high with a grass-grown interior. Its form suggests the structure of a large hut. The enclosing bank appears indistinct on the S., and when visited by the Commission it was truncated on the N. by forestry plantation. The bank's course was discernible among the trees and drainage furrows. An entrance is suggested by a gap on the S.W.

O.S. Card SN 90 NE (10); visible on A.P.s, R.A.F. CPE/UK 2079/1091–2; 19 v 47. First noted by T. W. Burke, *B.B.C.S.* 19 (1961), p. 65.

Penderyn
SN 90 N.E. (US 36) (9960 0983)   15 vii 81

(US 37) On the W. bank of the Afon Nedd 335 m above O.D. is a low discontinuous grass-grown rubble bank up to 2 m wide and 0.25 m in height, incorporating a number of larger blocks and slabs no more than 0.4 m high. These appear densest on the S. and E. The tallest is about 0.4 m high. Stone piles deriving from recent field clearances are to be seen on the perimeter. This is possibly the site suggested to have been a stone circle (though referred to at SN 9082 1535) (RSC 5).

Ystradfellte
SN 91 N.W. (US 37) (9091 1518)   10 vii 85

(US 38) S. of Fan Nedd at 640 m above O.D. is a linear pile of unconsolidated stones measuring 8.5 m (E.–W.) by 1 m and 0.3 m high. It is difficult to establish whether or not this results from field clearance or more recent hill-walking activity.

Defynnog (E), Senni (C)
SN 91 N.W. (US 38) (9139 1794)   21 xii 84

(US 39) To the W. of Fan Llia, on a steep S.W.-facing slope about 330 m above O.D. is a settlement platform 7.6 m (N.E.–S.W.) by 6.5 m cut into the hillside. Although ill-defined, the platform appears to have been built out to a height of about 0.5 m. Some 50 m to the N.E., just beyond the modern field boundary, lies a small clearance pile, 3.5 m in diameter.

Visible on A.P.s, R.A.F. CPE/UK/2079/4109–10.

Ystradfellte
SN 91 N.W. (US 39) (9299 1547)   xii 84

(US 40) On the extreme S.W. end of Fan Llia, 465 m above O.D., on the steep, S.W.-facing valley side is a verdant, well-drained, settlement platform comprising a levelled area 8 m (N.–S.) by 6.5 m, cut into the hillside to a depth of about 1.2 m, the outer, downhill scarp having a height of about 0.8 m.

Ystradfellte
SN 91 N.W. (US 40) (9290 1757)   21 ii 84

(US 41) On the N. side of a steep gully 130 m N.W. of (US 54) is a lozenge-shaped platform, scarped on the S., S.W. and N. sides, though without evidence of back-cutting into the hillside, measuring 9 m

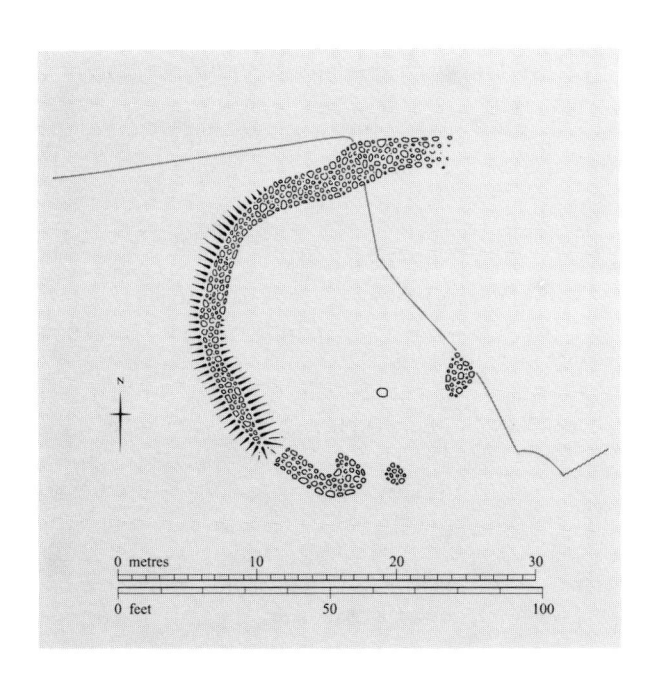

130   Pant Sychpant enclosure (US 36)

131 Upper Tawe area rubble-walled enclosure in Upper Tawe settlement area (US 31)

N.W.–S.E. by 6 m, about 1.5 m high. It consists of boulders and lies across the line of the gully.

Ystradfellte
SN 91 N.W. (US 41) (9268 1854) 26 xi 84

(US 42; Fig. 132) On a W.-facing slope above the Afon Llia about 420 m above O.D. are several rectangular enclosures with three or more associated building platforms and linear features. The southernmost of these measures 36 m N.–S. by 18 m E.–W. with a small sub-enclosure at the S. end on the W. side 11 m by 11 m. The enclosing banks are of boulder consolidated with turf, varying from 0.3 to 0.6 m in height. There is a small platform 5 m N.–S. by 3.5 m E.–W. and rising to 0.8 m high on the W., between the main and subsidiary enclosures. In the S.E. corner of the main site, intruding into the outer bank, is a further platform, this one oval, 5 m N.–S. by 3 m E.–W. Several entrances would have been possible through the E. bank of the larger enclosure or the N.W. corner of the sub-enclosure. In the corner formed between the main and sub-enclosures is a third platform 6 m N.–S. by 4 m E.–W., about 0.8 m high on the W.

Coterminous with the N. boundary of the S.

comprising five platforms and associated clearance piles at a point close to the spring-line. The most prominent and best-defined platform (US 43 i) comprises an overgrown level area 14.5 m (N.–S.) by 10 m, its long axis aligned along the contour. The platform cuts the hillside to a depth of about 1 m, and its outer limit is embanked to the same height. At the foot of the scarp lies a low bank of consolidated rubble, 1 m wide following the scarp toe. Another, less well-defined, but well-drained platform (US 43 ii) some 10 m N.–S. by 7 m lies 20 m downslope and rises to about 1.2 m from the contour. About 30 m N.E. of the first example lies a third (US 43 iii), badly-drained, overgrown platform, enclosing about 9 m square, and built out from the contour to 0.8 m. A fourth, ill-defined, site lies adjacent to the latter on its S. measuring 9 m (N.–S.) by 5 m (US 43 iv). Twenty-five metres to the S. of the first site is another (US 43 v), 7 m (N.–S.) by 6 m and rising to 1 m from the contour. There are a number of small stone piles, probably deriving from field clearance, lying to the S. of these platforms.

Visible on A.P.s, R.A.F. F22/58/3618/0127–8; 21 vi 60.

Ystradfellte
SN 91 N.W. (US 43 i) (9283 1805); (US 43 ii) (9282 1802); (US 43 iii) (9280 1805); (US 43 iv) (9285 1805); (US 43 v) (9285 1807)   16 xi 84

(US 44) On S.-facing ground to the N. of Rhyd Uchaf, about 400 m above O.D., on a gentle E.-facing slope is a U-shaped enclosure. It is sub-rectangular to oval 8 m N.–S. by 6 m internally, bounded on the W. by a simple inward-facing scarp 2.5 m wide and 0.5 m high, owing to interior levelling. On the N. and E. is a turf-covered stone and earthen bank 3 m wide and 0.2 m high. Nothing remains of any enclosure on the S.

Visible on A.P.s, R.A.F. 106G/UK1471/3471–2; 4 v 46.

Defynnog (E), Senni (C)
SN 91 N.W. (US 44) (9244 1905)   13 xi 84

(US 45; Fig. 134) On a small shelf above Nant Ganol 360 m above O.D. are the fragmentary remains of a roughly circular enclosure about 24.4 m in diameter, bounded by a scatter of stone wall footings about 1 m wide, but with no clear indication of entrance. At the upper end of the

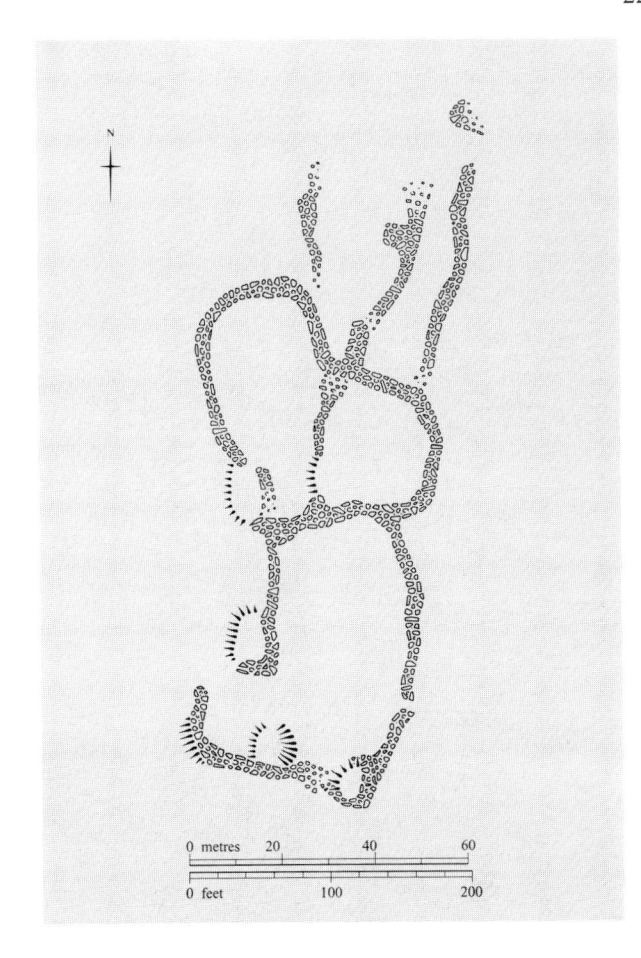

132   Complex enclosure above the Afon Llia (US 42)

enclosure are two further enclosures, the more westerly some 30 m N.–S. by 15 m E.–W., the more easterly 15 m by 15 m. The western enclosure is poorly defined on the S.W. corner, as is the common feature between the two enclosures. The other enclosing walls are boulder and turf banks 0.5–0.8 m high. To the N. of the enclosures three roughly parallel, ill-defined banks extend for about 30 m.

O.S. Card SN 91 NW 12; visible on A.P.s, R.A.F. F22/58/3618/0127–8.

Ystradfellte
SN 91 N.W. (US 42) (9275 1842)   26 xi 84

(US 43; Fig. 133) On the lower slopes of Fan Llia, on the steep E. side of the Afon Llia about 460 m above O.D. are the remains of a settlement

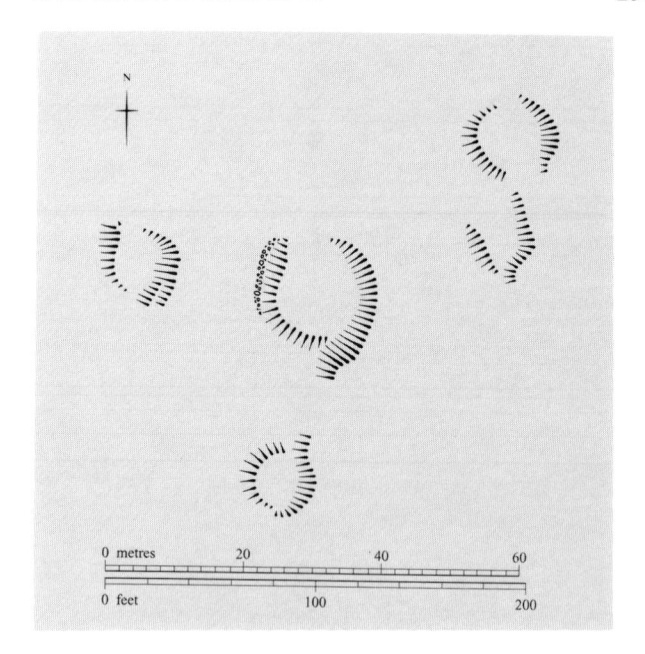

133 Lower slopes of Fan Llia, hut platforms (US 43)

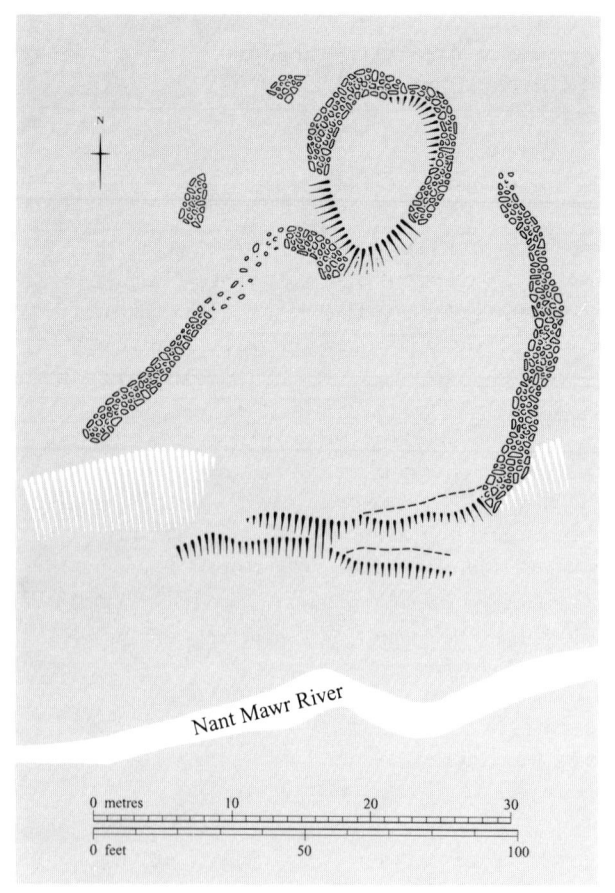

134 Enclosure at Nant Ganol (US 45)

enclosure is a settlement platform (10 m N.E.–S.W. by 7 m). The lower end of the platform is poorly defined, though discontinuous lengths of earthen and stone wall 1.2–1.5 m wide define its other three sides, and at the upper end, the bank stands to almost 1 m in height.

Ystradfellte
SN 91 N.W. (US 45) (9491 1567)   18 xii 84

(US 46) There is a small rectangular rubble-banked structure on a small platform cut into the steep E.-facing slope overlooking Afon Dringarth about 400 m above O.D. measuring 5.8 m square.

Ystradfellte
SN 91 N.W. (US 46) (9414 1694)   29 xi 84

(US 47) Cut into the same valley side as the above site (US 46), 350 m above O.D., is a small building platform 9.5 m (E.–W.) by 7.1 m bounded by rubble walls on the E., N.W. and S.

Ystradfellte
SN 91 N.W. (US 47) (9429 1688)   29 xi 84

(US 48) On the spur between the Afon Dringarth and the Nant yr Esgyrn, about 430 m above O.D., is a U-shaped enclosure recognisable on aerial photographs which could not be located in field survey.

A.P.s, R.A.F. CPE/UK 2079/4103–4; 19 v 47.

Ystradfellte
SN 91 N.W. (US 48) (9464 1623)   xi 85

(US 49) In Cwm Dringarth overlooking the river about 440 m above O.D. is a small rectangular structure resting on an overgrown building platform cut into the steep E.-facing slope. It lies adjacent to a stream on its E., and measures 8 m (E.–W.) by 6 m, embanked by rubble.

Ystradfellte
SN 91 N.W. (US 49) (9411 1736)   29 xi 84

(US 50) Cut into the same slope as the above (US 49) about 490 m above O.D. and adjacent to a springhead is a further platform site 10.3 m (N.–S.) by 6.8 m.

Ystradfellte
SN 91 N.W. (US 50) (9434 1855)   29 xi 84

(US 51; Fig. 135) On the same hillside as sites US 41 and 42, overlooking the Ystradfellte Reservoir about 390 m above O.D. is a rectangular platform on which are the remains of a rectangular building bounded on three sides by low rubble banks. The building measures 18 m (N.–S.) by 8.5 m. On the uphill side is another, smaller platform comprising a level grass-grown area measuring, overall, 7.3 m (E.–W.) by 6.2 m. Some 30 m S.E. of the main platform and on the edge of the gully is an oval area of consolidated, though probably eroded, rubble, measuring 5 m (N.W.–S.E.) by 3 m. This is probably a multi-period site, culminating in medieval occupation.

Ystradfellte
SN 91 N.W. (US 51) (9458 1807)   29 xi 84

(US 52; Fig. 136) Above the rivulet on the S.E.-facing steep N. slope of Nant Garlen Fawr overlooking the Ystradfellte Reservoir about 430 m above O.D., is a rectangular enclosure 33 m (N.E.–S.W.) by 20 m, bounded by a turf-covered rubble bank some 2 m wide and 0.2 m high. About mid-way along the S. bank and 4 m into its N. is a stony platform about 2 m in diameter and 0.2 m high and there is possibly an entrance about 8 m from the S.E. corner of the same bank. This may have been a settlement or stock enclosure.

O.S. Card SN 91 NW 15; visible on A.P.s, R.A.F. 1060/UK/1471/1467–8.

Ystradfellte
SN 91 N.W. (US 52) (9468 1858)   26 xi 84

(US 53) On the N.W. shore of the Ystradfellte Reservoir and occupying the N.E. bank of a stream 390 m above O.D., is a platform divided into three levels, descending N.W.–S.E. and measuring, overall, 24 m by 8 m. The highest level is bounded on the N.W. by a crescent-shaped turf bank about 1 m high. The platform is occupied by a rectangular structure 6 m (N.W.–S.E.) by 3 m consisting of rubble walls,

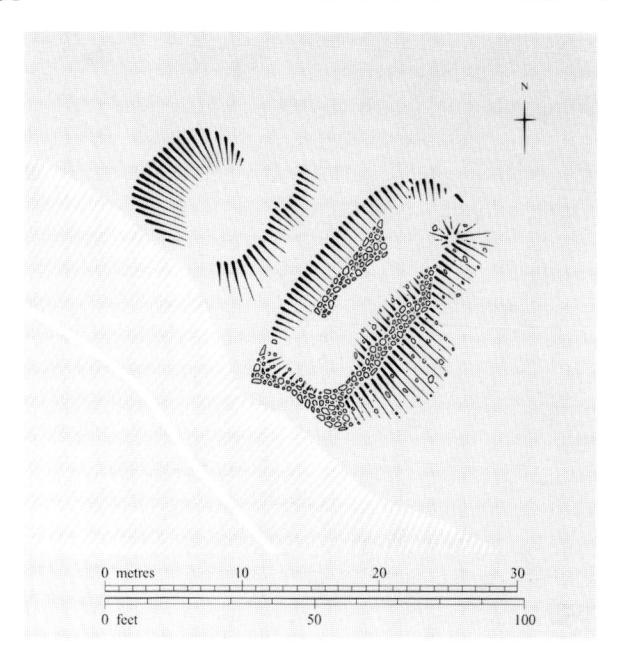

135   Hut platforms above Ystradfellte Reservoir (US 51)

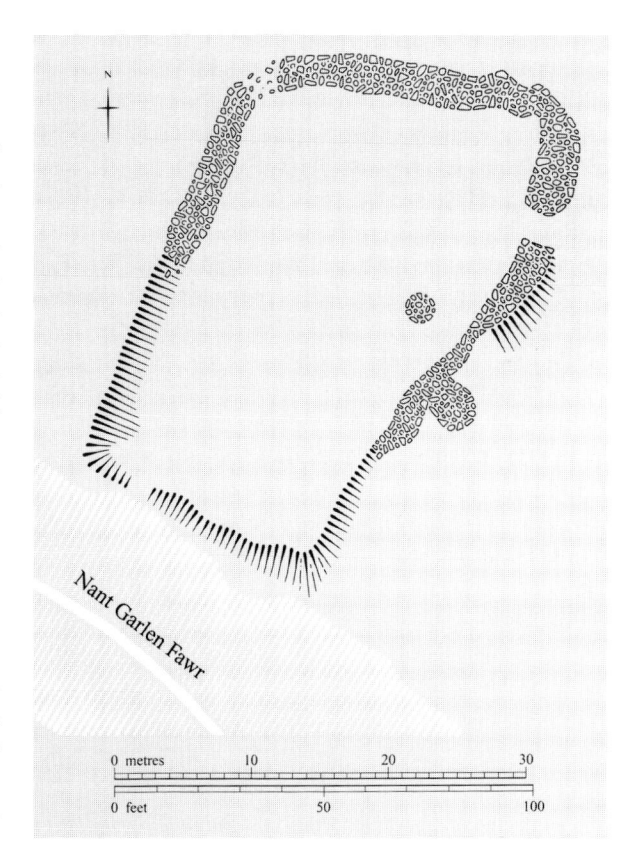

136   Enclosure above Nant Garlen Fawr (US 52): plan

about 0.6 m high. The interior is also rubble filled, with no sign of an entrance. The intermediate level is 0.8 m lower than the upper, 7 m square, bounded on the E. by a turf bank 0.4 m high. A structure is set central to this level, similar, though smaller, than the one above it, measuring 4.5 m by 2 m, and oriented N.E.–S.W. Discerning details of the lower level is made difficult by the reservoir boundary railing which cuts the site at right angles. However, this level is 0.5 m lower than the intermediate one and it is built out from the contour to a height of about 1.5 m on the S.W. and S.E. Although otherwise structureless, there is a slight central hollow.

Ystradfellte
SN 91 N.W. (US 53) (9473 1822) 31 i 85

(US 54) On the N.E. bank of Nant Garlen Fawr and 20 m above its inflow to the Ystradfellte Reservoir, about 390 m above O.D., is a platform with traces of a building 12 m (N.–S.) by 5 m E.–W. defined by rubble walls about 0.5 m high. At the N. end there are traces of possible further enclosure or room, 3.5 m N.–S. by 5 m E.–W. On the S. the platform is 2 m high, and it has been damaged in this area, probably at the time of reservoir construction. Built into the W. side of the platform is another structure, 2.5 m square enclosed by rubble walls 0.5 m high and open to the W.

There is a further platform on the opposite stream bank, some 20 m to N.W., measuring 4 m square. These sites appear to have been robbed for the construction of a sheepfold depicted on O.S. 1904 1:2500 map.

Ystradfellte
SN 91 N.W. (US 54) (9483 1839) 29 xi 84

(US 55) N.W. of Talcen y Garn on a N.-facing slope overlooking the Nant Mawr at a height of 395 m above O.D. is a circular enclosure with an internal diameter of 20.7 m surrounded by a low grass-grown bank 0.3 m high on the E. and W. and forming a scarp or terrace 0.6 m high on the N. and S. The entrance may have been on the W. The former existence of internal structures is suggested by the presence of large buried stones within the southern half of the enclosure.

Ystradfellte
SN 91 N.E. (US 55) (9512 1558) ii 85

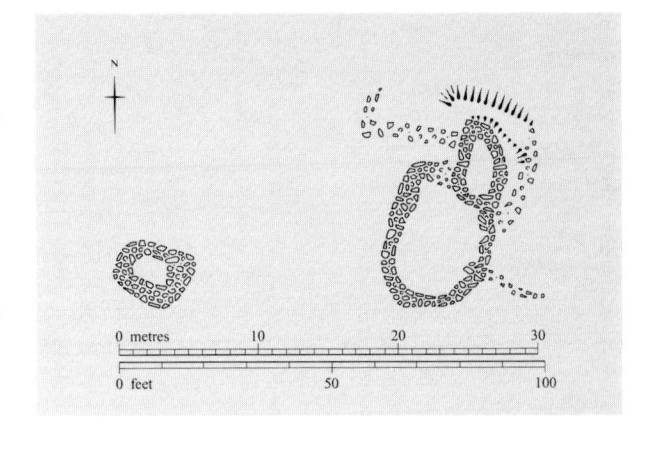

137 Hut and enclosure between Nant Mawr and Nant Ganol (US 56): plan

(US 56; Fig. 137) Facing S.W. on a level ledge among natural depressions on the spur between Nant Ganol and Nant Mawr at a height of 425 m above O.D. are the remains of a small, crudely-constructed hut and attached enclosure. The hut measures 6.0 m (N.–S.) by 4 m, and consists of rubble walls about 1 m wide and 0.8 m high. The enclosure, lying S.W. of the hut, is 8 m (N.–S.) by 6 m internally and is bounded by turf-consolidated rubble banks. There are further traces of a bank 0.6 m high and 1–2 m wide on the N. and E. sides of the hut, possibly the remains of an earlier structure. Fugitive traces of rubble banks 0.2 m high running W. from the hut for about 7 m and N. 3 m, and E. from the enclosure for 5 m, may also indicate an earlier phase of occupation.

The remains of a further structure lie in a shallow dry valley, about 60 m S.W. of this site measuring 5 m (E.–W.) by 4 m. It is bounded by turf-consolidated rubble walls 0.4 m high and 1–1.5 m wide.

Ystradfellte
SN 91 N.E. (US 56) (9556 1615) 31 i 85

(US 57) In Nant Mawr, about 430 m above O.D., lying upon a slight elevation above the surrounding marsh, is a small rectangular structure measuring 4 m square, with boulder walls about 0.3 m high.

Ystradfellte
SN 91 N.E. (US 57) (9596 1604) 31 i 85

(US 58; Fig. 138) In Nant Llywarch, about 450 m above O.D., is a series of fugitive low rubble banks and enclosures, generally no higher than 0.1 m above the vegetation. As some features are better defined than others, this probably represents a multi-period settlement. The site occupies an area of about 180 m (E.–W.) by 40 m, upon a terrace adjacent to and overlooking the stream.

To the W. end of the site are traces of a rectangular enclosure, internally 10 m (E.–W.) by 6 m (US 58 i). This is bounded by a rubble spread 1–2 m wide. It was probably entered at the E. of the S. wall.

Thirty metres E. are the remains of at least two ill-defined hut-circles (US 58 ii), each about 6 m in diameter. Immediately N. is what appears to be a low platform of rubble measuring 7 m across, and ill-defined on the W. Adjacent spreads of stone may conceal a further hut-circle. About 25 m S.E. of this lies a sub-rectangular enclosure 17 m (N.W.–S.E.) by 10 m overall, bounded for most of its perimeter by a low stony bank and on its S. by the stream scarp (US 58 iii). There is a wall on the E. meandering N.E. for a distance of about 15 m. S. of these features, below the terrace and beside the stream, is a small rectangular building 9 m (N.–S.) by 5 m, its rubble walls surviving to a height of 0.4 m, and probably of relatively recent date (US 58 iv). This may have been related to the small triangular embanked enclosure about 14 m (N.W.–S.E.) by 7 m internally, the wall standing to 0.3 m, and bounded to the S. by the eroding stream bank (US 58 v). There are traces of further serpentine walls to the E. and about 50 m away lies a further, though irregular, and poorly-defined enclosure 30 m (E.–W.) by 20 m. It is open to the E. and a curious circular stone feature about 0.5 m in diameter occupies the S.E. terminal of its bank. There is another, possibly related feature, about 1.5–2 m in diameter, overlying the enclosure on its N.W. perimeter (US 58 vi). Further fugitive stone spreads lying to the N. of this complex were insufficiently well defined to permit of useful recognition.

Ystradfellte
SN 91 N.E. (US 58 i) (9662 1625); (US 58 ii) (9665 1624); (US 58 iii) (9668 1623); (US 58 iv) (9669 1622); (US 58 v) (9671 1621); (US 58 vi) (9677 1624)
5 iii 85

(US 59; Fig. 139) Lying upon a level plateau between the Afon y Waun and Nant Llywarch about

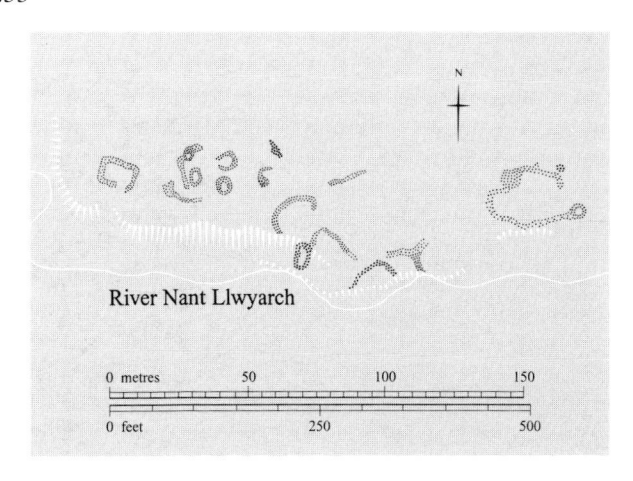

138 Nant Llywarch, Ton Teg (S) huts and enclosures (US 58)

440 m above O.D. is a complex of settlement structures which includes four, possibly five, huts, an enclosure, two or three platforms and several stone piles, covering an area of 2 ha. The walls are invariably of rubble, some 1–2 m wide and 0.2–3 m high.

At the S. end is a hut-group comprising one roughly circular hut about 5 m in internal diameter with a penannular annex on the N.W. (US 59 i) roughly forming a figure of eight. The annex measures 5 m (E.–W.) by 2.5 m internally. About 20 m S.W. is another sub-circular structure internally 4 m in diameter, probably difficult to recognise owing to wall-spread. Between these two huts, and slightly to E. is a smaller circle 5 m in overall diameter, enclosed by turf-consolidated walls. About 20 m E. of this group is a linear stone feature 23 m long (N.–S.) (US 59 ii).

On the W. of the settlement area is a linear stone pile some 32 m long (N.–S.), and to its W., close to the N. end, is a possible platform roughly triangular in form, measuring 6 m (E.–W.) by 5 m along the E. side and on the W it is built up to about 1 m in height (US 59 iii). A further, more fugitive turf-consolidated wall is traceable on the platform site.

Roughly central to the group is an oval enclosure, internally about 11 m (E.–W.) by 8 m, possibly entered through the gap on the S.E. (US 59 iv). Thirty metres to the E. of this site is a well-defined, turf-consolidated hut-circle 9.5 m in external diameter (US 59 v).

At the N. end of the site are two platforms cut into

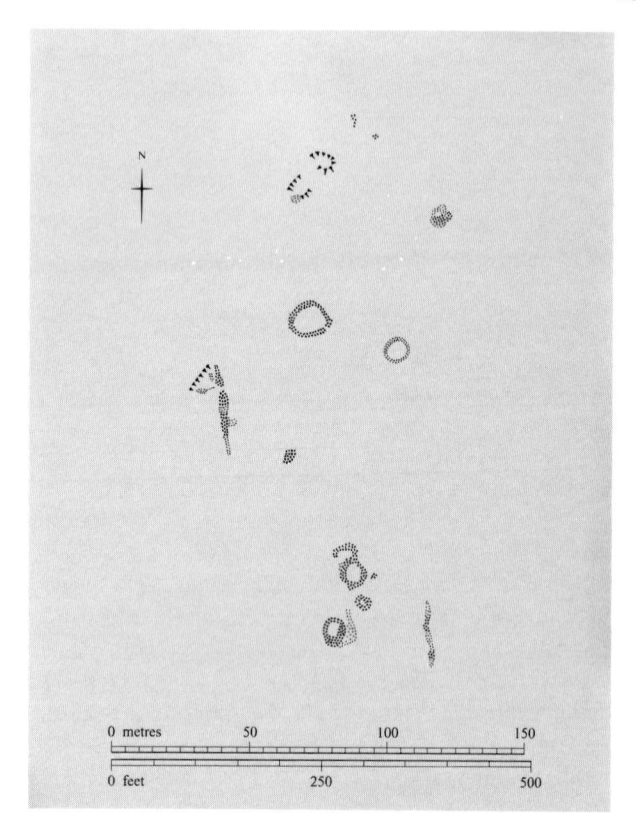

139 Nant Llywarch, Ton Teg (N.) hut platforms and clearances (US 59)

the rising slope. The more S.W. is 5 m square, and the other is 5 m (N.W.–S.E.) by 4 m. Both are built out from the contour to a height of about 1 m on their S.E. sides (US 59 vi).

At the N.E. of the group is a stone pile which may mark the site of a former hut-circle. It is turf-consolidated and measures 7 m in external diameter and consists of a circular bank with stone rather more tightly packed than the stony interior (US 59 vii). The site is littered with stony piles of varying shapes and sizes up to 6 m in diameter.

Close to, and possibly associated with the above, is a small enclosure or shelter on the opposite (E.) bank of the Waun, measuring 3 m square and at 0.4 m high, with walls standing slightly higher than those of the other group (US 59 viii).

Visible on A.P.s, R.A.F. F22/58/3618/0016–7.

Ystradfellte
SN 91 N.E. (US 59 i) (9684 1647); (US 59 ii) (9687 1645); (US 59 iii) (9680 1653); (US 59 iv) (9683 1656); (US 59 v) (9686 1655); (US 59 vi) (9683 1661); (US 59 vii) (9687 1660); (US 59 viii) (9707 1637)   25 ii 85

(US 60; Fig. 140) Carn Canienydd is a citadel-like complex of huts and enclosures, occupying a slight natural stony eminence and partly surrounded by boggy ground, lying to the E. of Nant y Cwrier at 405 m above O.D. The site is actively being eroded by visitor or farming practices, no doubt responsible for attempts to build or re-build shelters upon the site. It comprises four major elements:

(US 60 i) On the N.E. is a large enclosure bank, 1.5–3 m wide and 0.2 m high, capping the hill. This is the surviving part of a larger enclosure originally about 13 m in internal diameter. The S. part has been badly damaged by the erection of sheep shelters or overnight bivouac sites.

(US 60 ii) The W. part of the group comprises two turf-consolidated hut-circles linked by a spread rubble bank about 11 m long. The more westerly measures 4 m (N.–S.) by 3 m, and its neighbour 10 m (N.–S.) by 78 m internally; their banks are up to 2 m wide by 0.4 m high.

(US 60 iii) On the S.E., about 18 m S. of the main enclosure (US 60 i), is a third enclosure, partly cut into the slope, with rubble walls 3 m wide.

(US 60 iv) A fourth circle lies immediately S. of the main enclosure and consists of a depression bounded by a turf-consolidated rubble bank up to 1.5 m wide and 0.7 m high, with an internal diameter of 3 m.

(US 60 v) Not far distant from the 'citadel', and S.S.W. of it, is a stone clearance pile comprising a 10 m square scatter of stone and small boulders consolidated with light vegetation.

(US 60 vi) About 70 m beyond (US 60 v) is a small enclosure measuring 5 m square, with boulder walls about 0.2 m high and 1 m wide, lying upon an artificial platform, and with associated field clearance heaps.

It is possible that this is a multi-period site in which modern sheep-pens have been built over a prehistoric hut-group.

Cantref
SN 91 N.E. (US 60 i) (9804 1534); (US 60 ii) (9801 1533); (US 60 iii) (9805 1533); (US 60 iv) (9803 1532); (US 60 v) (9800 1521); (US 60 vi) (9805 1526)
                                                          30 i 85

UNENCLOSED SETTLEMENTS

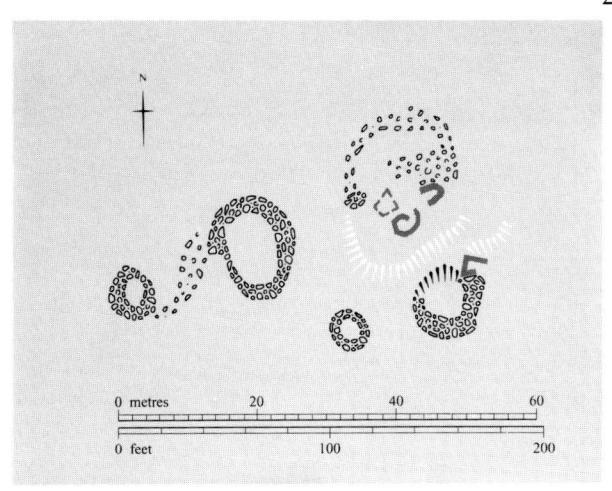

140 Carn Canienydd huts (US 60)

(US 61) On the E.-facing slope of Pant y Waun about 430 m above O.D. is a rectangular stony mound measuring 7 m (E.–W.) by 5.2 m and about 0.3 m high. It seems most likely that this was a field clearance mound.

A.P.s, R.A.F. F22/58 3618/0016–7.

Cantref
SN 91 N.E. (US 61) (9878 1652)   14 xi 83

(US 62) A number of settlement features were recognised during maintenance work in the Brecon Beacons Reservoir on the Taf Fawr, about 400 m above O.D. These included three longhouses, probably of medieval date, a small undated bowl furnace, walls and clearance cairns.

(US 62 i) There were four cairns, each up to about 2 m in diameter, grouped in close compass on a plateau upon the bluff adjoining the river, just over halfway down the W. side of the reservoir.

(US 62 ii) A N.–S. running field wall of widely-spaced boulders was located on the E. river floodplain.

(US 62 iii) A further wall skirts the steeper slope of the W. bank, but as this is probably heading N. towards one of the buildings, it is probably medieval.

No recent historical documentation could be found showing any of the settlement features discovered within this stripped reservoir landscape, and field observations provided a rare insight into clearance activity within an upland enclosed valley floodplain.

C. S. Briggs, *Arch. in Wales* 26 (1986), pp. 60–1.

Cantref
SN 91 N.E. (US 61 i) (9860 1857); (US 61 ii) (9883 1985); (US 61 iii) (9863 1864–9862 1869)   ix 86

(US 63) Lying parallel to the stream on a narrow floodplain on the W. side of the Taf Fawr gorge about 340 m above O.D., are the remains of a small rectangular building, presumably a house, and associated enclosures. It is 9 m N.–S. by 2.5 m internally, with rubble walls up to 0.6 m high and 1.5–2.0 m wide. The structure has traces of internal division about a third of the distance from the N. end, and there is an entrance midway along the W. side. Its N.W. corner is marked by a large boulder, and the entrance appears to have been along the N. wall. A smaller enclosure adjoins on the W., its S. boundary in line with the S. house wall. Bounded by a boulder and turf wall 1 m wide and 0.8 m high, this measures 20 m E.–W. by 17 m internally. The wall is revetted on the W. to accommodate the cliff and its W. bank appears to continue northwards for 18 m, though is poorly defined. There are further indications of a bank 0.2 m high and 1 m wide, running N.N.W. some 14 m from the N.E. house corner, before turning W. Both walls appear to form part of the E. edge of a terrace about 22 m (N.–S.) by 18 m raised above the floodplain.

O.S. Card SN 91 NE 5.

Cantref
SN 91 N.E. (US 63) (9910 1683)   12 ii 85

(US 64) On the floodplain of Nant Crew, about 360 m above O.D., on enclosed pasture, is a semicircular earthwork about 20 m N.N.E.–S.S.E. by 10 m wide, occupying a low-lying position on the stream bluff.

Cantref
SN 91 N.E. (US 64) (9967 1667)   17 viii 91

(US 65) On the N.-facing southern valley side of Nant Crew, 360–380 m above O.D, is a series of at least three platform houses and round huts (US 65 i–iii), which might represent continuous or sporadic occupation from prehistoric until medieval times. Further up the valley (in SN 01 N.E.) over 450 m above O.D., the limits of ancient agricultural or pastoral activity are defined by ragged margins of the cleared scree.

Cantrill MSS, N.M.W.; not surveyed by R.C.A.M.

Cantref
SN 91 N.E. (US 65 i) (9975 1678); (US 65 ii) (9886 1710); (US 65 iii) (9992 1712)   17 viii 91

(US 66) On the N.W.-facing slope of Cefn Crew (Tyle Brith) 640 m above O.D. lies a small rectangular enclosure measuring 9 m (N.E.–S.W.) by 3 m, bounded on two sides (N. and S.) by a rubble bank 0.8 m wide and 0.25 m high. On the N.E. the enclosure abuts onto what may be either the downhill spread of a building platform or a natural feature.

Cantref
SN 91 N.E. (US 66) (9940 1908)   4 xii 84

(US 67) Lying within the area of shake-holes upon the Pant Mawr (nineteenth-century) rabbit farm on Carnau Gwynion, about 370 m above O.D., is an enclosure, apparently much older than the other settlement features thereabouts. It is basically circular, about 30 m in internal diameter, appears to lack an entrance, and is bounded by well-robbed limestone boulder walls, 1–3 m wide and 0.2–0.7 m high.

Ystradfellte
SN 91 S.W. (US 67) (9028 1427)   viii 85

(US 68; Fig. 141) On the level summit of a poorly-drained slight ridge 290 m above O.D. to the N.E. of Dyffryn Nedd farmhouse and on the E. of the Afon Nedd, lies an oval enclosure (US 68 i) associated with a series of fugitive field walls of presumed agricultural origin. The enclosure measures 23 m (N.–S.) by 21 m internally and it is bounded by a boulder-based wall up to 2.5 m wide and 0.5 m high. Some boulders are up to 1 m in diameter. For part of its course on the W., the wall appears to take advantage of a natural rock outcrop, and on its northern boundary, the earlier enclosure is incorporated into a later field wall, where it can be distinguished by the presence of boulder orthostats and a turf with rubble infill.

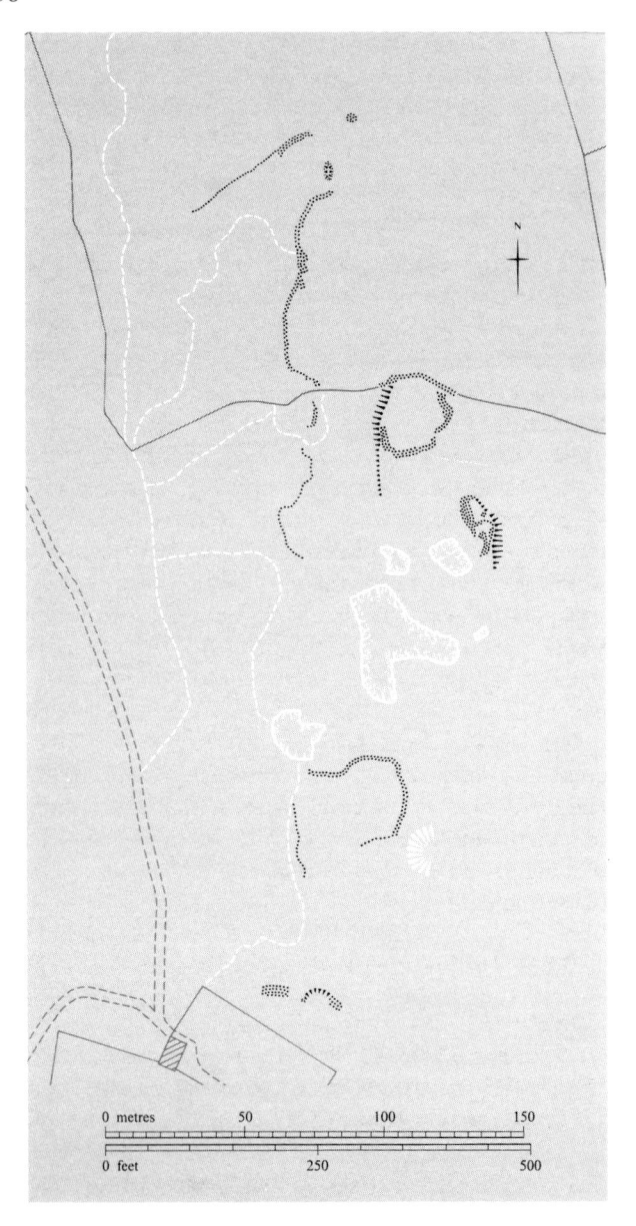

141 Walls and enclosures at Dyffryn Nedd (US 68): plan

(US 68 ii) There is a N.–S. discontinuous serpentine rubble wall some 35–40 m W. of this enclosure, and N. of that runs a 65 m length of straighter, roughly N.N.E.–S.S.W.-oriented wall, terminating in a field clearance mound, lying upon enclosed pasture, where their presence begs the question of how far the existing field system utilises a more ancient pattern.

(US 68 iii) Some 40 m S.E. of this enclosure and in

an area of irregular ground with outcropping limestone, is a putative building platform about 7 m N.–S. by 3.5 m, bounded on the W. by a possibly natural stony bank up to 3.5 m wide, and on the S. by the remains of a stone wall about 1 m wide and up to 0.3 m high.

(US 68 iv) There is a further, less distinct, rectangular enclosure, situated about 120 m to the S. of the ridge on which the first enclosure lies. This is 38 m (E.–W.) by 27 m internally, and is bounded on the N. by a boulder bank about 2 m wide and up to 0.7 m high. This is discontinuous, there being significant gaps on the N.W. corner (where a plethora of field boulders makes it impossible to discern) and along about half of the W. part of the S. side. About 50 m S. of this second enclosure is a crescent-shaped stony bank, 1.5 m wide and 0.3 m high, increasing on the E. (in a feature more certainly of field clearance) to some 3 m wide and 0.6 m high. There is also a rectangular pile of cleared boulders to the W. about 9 m (E.–W.) by 3.5 m and 0.3 m high.

(US 68 v) About 50 m S. of (US 68 iv) lies a crescentic stony bank some 17 m in length, 1.5 m wide and 0.5 m high, terminating on the E. in loose rubble 3 m across and 0.6 m high. Immediately to the W. is a rectangular pile of small boulders, 9 m (E.–W.) by 3.5 m and 0.3 m high.

O.S. Card SN 91 SW 18; R. E. Kay *in. lit.* to R.C.A.M., 17 vi 71.

Ystradfellte
SN 91 S.W. (US 68 i) (9137 1278); (US 68 ii) (9140 1278); (US 68 iii) (9139 1276); (US 68 iv) (9135 1266); (US 68 v) (9133 1259)   6 vi 85

(US 69) In an area of shake-holes to the W. of Blaen Nedd Isaf about 375 m above O.D. and within a depression falling N. to a sink-hole, is a stone mound 6 m in diameter and about 1 m high, probably a clearance cairn.

Ystradfellte
SN 91 S.W. (US 69) (9189 1421)   1 v 85

(US 70) Just W. of Pont Cwm Pwll y Rhyd at a height of about 380 m above O.D. is a building platform 8 m (N.–S.) by 6 m, built out 1.2 m above the contour.

Ystradfellte
SN 91 S.W. (US 70) (9204 1406)   1 v 85

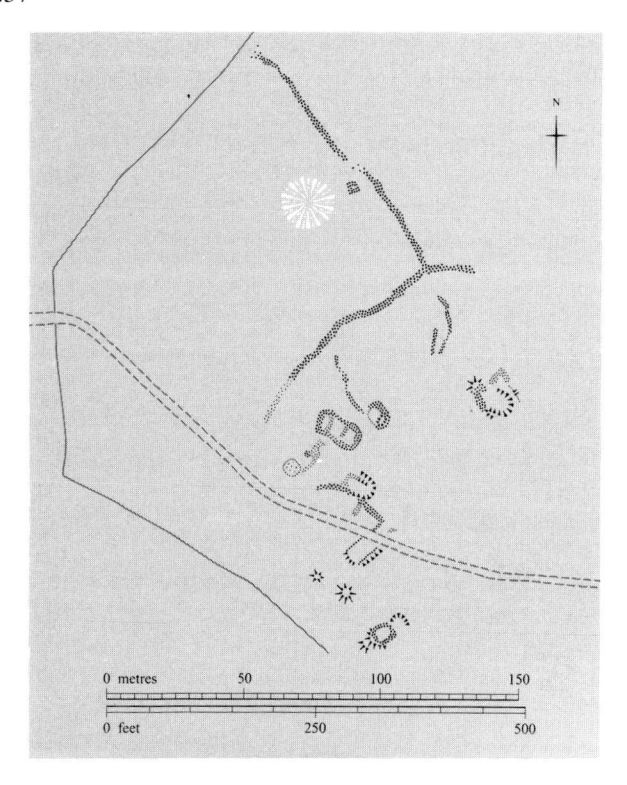

142 Garn Ddu hut group showing sink hole (US 71)

(US 71; Fig. 142) On the extreme S.W. end of Garn Ddu, on the N.W.-facing slope about 260 m above O.D., in a dry shallow tributary valley of the River Mellte, are a group of five building platforms, a rectangular building with associated field walls and stone piles. The two more southerly are oriented N.E.–S.W., the others, N.W.–S.E. Most are slope-excavated and levelled out using rubble infill.

(US 71 i) The southernmost site (14 m by 6 m), is dug out to about 0.3 m, built up about 1.5 m, though showing signs of slumping. Its S.W. part is occupied by a small enclosure 7 m square, outlined by banks 2 m wide and 0.4 m high. To the N.W. are two turf and rubble mounds, the larger 8 m (N.W.–S.E.) by 6 m, and 1.1 m high, the smaller, 4 m in diameter and 0.8 m high.

(US 71 ii) N. of (US 71 i) lies a second platform (10 m by 6 m), bisected by a modern farm track. This one is built up about 0.4 m on the N.W. and S.W. This is adjoined on the N.E. by a rubble bank running about 25 m N.W. There is a further platform (US 71 iii) (9.5 m by 4.5 m) aligned along the N. side of this wall, which is approached through an entrance about 1.2 m wide along its N. side.

(US 71 iv) About 20 m N. is a well-defined structure (13 m by 5 m) with internal divisions, resembling a medieval longhouse, and to its N.E. is a smaller, scooped site, dug out and built up 0.3 m above and below the level. This adjoins a boulder bank roughly at right angles, extending in a N.W. direction some 20 m and terminating in a circular setting of large boulders 6 m in diameter and set 0.4 m high with traces of rubble infill.

(US 71 v) Lying further up the hillslope than the others is another platform occupying a well-defined grassy area. This measures 11 m by 5 m, narrowing on the N.W., where it is built out with rubble to a height of about 0.8 m. On the S.E. it is bounded by a hood-shaped earthen bank up to 3 m wide built up to height of 1.2 m.

(US 71 vi) The remains of a field wall 80 m long are to be traced at the foot of the hillslope on the N.W., travelling in a S.W.–N.E. direction. This is joined at the more N. end by a further wall, travelling more directly N. a good 80 m before disappearing into an area of boulders and bracken. About 40 m from the junction is a structure 4 m square, the walls about 1 m wide and 0.5 m thick.

This is probably a multi-period site incorporating earlier field boundaries and platform-scoops into a later, medieval or post-medieval croft.

SN 91 SW, NAR 23; 'Farmstead'.

Penderyn/Cantref
SN 91 S.W. centred upon (9435 1035); (US 71 i) (9437 1030); (US 71 ii) (9436 1033); (US 71 iii) (9436 1035); (US 71 iv) (9435 1037); (US 71 v) (9437 1038); (US 71 vi) (9441 1039)   1 v 85

(US 72) Within and on the S. side of the craggy limestone exposures known as Carn y Goetre, on a S.W.-facing slope about 440 m above O.D. and immediately W. of a small rock outcrop, are a roughly triangular enclosure and two hut foundations. The enclosure measures 18 m N.W.–S.E. internally by 14 m N.E.–S.W. Its rubble stone enclosure bank averages 2 m in width and about 0.7 m high. Within the enclosure, and against the inner face of the S.E. side, is a rubble platform about 3 m across and 0.3 m high. The S.W. enclosure wall is produced to meet the outcrop and the area between enclosure and rock is occupied by two hut foundations, each roughly 6 m by 3 m, with walls 0.3 m high.

The form of this site suggests it may have been Iron Age or Romano-British in origin, though a later date is also possible.

O.S. Card SN 91 S.W. 12.

Ystradfellte
SN 91 S.W. (9464 1420)   3 iv 85

(US 73) Between Nant Garreg Fawr and Pont y Felin, on land which has recently been improved some 250 m above O.D., are the remains of a small split-level structure, terraced into the hillside with an adjacent yard or appended building platform.[1] The main structure is slope-orientated E.–W. and originally measured about 19 m long by 11 m wide. The adjoining platform was roughly 12 m by 6 m. This pasture seems to have been 'improved' through ploughing between 1975[2] and 1985, and the features as described above are now less perceptible, the third level (on the S.W.) having entirely disappeared. The main platform appears to be excavated into the hillside on its S.E., and to a depth of about 0.8 m, but is now only 11 m by 5 m. It is still built up on the S.W. and N.W. sides to about 0.3 m. The second platform, about 0.6 m below the first, is 7 m S.E.–N.W. by 6 m. It is built up to a height of 7 m on the N.W. side. Some indication of rubble is visible within these structures, beneath a verdant cover. Between March and June 1985, deep ploughing reduced the remains described here to a series of slight undulations.[3]

[1] Visible on A.P.s, R.A.F. CPE/UK 2079/2108–10; 19 v 47.
[2] O.S. Card SN 19 SW 17; 30 v 75.
[3] MSS. field notes, R.C.A.M.

Ystradfellte
SN 91 S.W. (US 73) (9368 1415)   iii 85–19 vi 85

(US 74) For ease of presentation, the landscape of SN 91 S.E. is dealt with under its four component topographical areas viz: Mynydd y Garn-Waun Tincer, Cefn Esgair Carnau, Nant y Gadair, and Cwm Cadlan-Cefn Sychpant.

Mynydd y Garn – Waun Tincer

(US 74 i) S.W. of Tir Mawr, on a N.W.-facing slope 335 m above O.D., is an oval stone-embanked enclosure about 36 m (N.–S.) by 28 m. The bank stands about 2 m wide and about 0.6 m high. There is an entrance on the N.W. 3.5 m wide, and about halfway along the S.E. side an ancillary bank projects internally, suggesting the original existence of a divisional arrangement. Immediately outside its N. corner are traces of a rectangular structure about 5 m (N.E.–S.W.) by 3 m, bounded by fugitive rubble banks. Further small enclosures, probably sheep shelters, adjoin the outside of the N.E. bank. These measure about 9 m (N.W.–S.E.) by 4.5 m. From their E. corner, a rubble bank runs upslope, S.E. a distance of 45 m. On the S. corner of the main enclosure there is a similar bank also running upslope, S.S.E. about 60 m before turning N.E. to parallel the later field wall.

(US 74 ii) About 80 m S.W. is a slope-cut hut platform measuring 11 m (N.E.–S.W.) by 6 m, excavated to a depth of about 0.8 m on the S.E. and built out to a height of 0.3 m on the N.W.

(US 74 iii) Some 90 m W. of the main enclosure are three clearance cairns aligned roughly E.–W. The most central, and largest, is disturbed centrally, and measures 5 m (E.–W.) by 2.5 m and 0.3 m high. About 10 m to the E. is a cairn 4 m (E.–W.) by 2 m and 0.2 m high. The third cairn lies about 11 m W. and measures 4 m (E.–W.) by 2.5 m and 0.5 m high.

(US 74 iv–v) Towards the S.W. end of the present day field enclosures, about 200 m S.W. of enclosure (US 74 i) is a complex of fugitive banks lying at the foot of a stone-strewn slope. They comprise two principal components: (US 74 iv) a rectangular structure 14 m (N.E.–S.W.) by 11 m, lacking any bank on the N., and apparently entered at the S.W. end of the N.W. side through a gap 3 m wide. It is enclosed by a stony bank 1.5 m wide and 0.3 m high. (US 74 v) The second structure is built similarly, 9.5 m (N.W.–S.E.) by 6 m with banks up to 0.5 m high and an entrance 1.5 m wide on the S.W. A rubble bank runs generally N. towards the cairns from close to the larger structure, and to the S.W. of the field are further, but incomprehensible earthwork features.

Towards the N. end of the field stands a limekiln with associated structures, the use of which may have been responsible for the robbing out parts of the site.

Ystradfellte

SN 91 S.E. (US 74 i) (9606 1217); (US 74 ii) (9600 1211); (US 74 iii) (9596 1214); (US 74 iv) (9588 1210); (US 74 v) (9587 1208)   iv 86

(US 75–8) There are four main settlement areas upon Mynydd y Garn:

(Fig. 143) On Mynydd y Garn (O.S. SN 95 13), partly under an eroding peat cover, are widespread indications of settlement and field systems. These are emerging more clearly as overgrazing eats back into the heather cover, baring the ground, at first yellow with decayed grass, then to the brown colour of the underlying peat. As noted elsewhere (pp. 3, 193–6), shake-holes form an important landscape component. On this hillside field boundaries occasionally skirt the holes, and some early features have fallen into their depressions, suggesting that whilst the process of shake-hole formation antedates some clearance activity, limestone solution also remains an active erosive agent.

(US 75) Between 320 m and 380 m above O.D. on the S. to S.E.-facing slope overlooking the River Hepste are about 60 ha of settlement and field systems, including enclosures, isolated lengths of bank or wall, hut-circles, and cairns which are presumed to date from later prehistoric times. The hillside is bisected by a shallow N.–S. running dry valley.

The enclosures are mainly irregularly-shaped and bounded by heather-covered rubble and boulder banks up to 0.4 m high and about 2 m wide. The largest, on the E. (US 75 i), is of about 3.5 ha, and to its S.W. is one of about 1.25 ha (US 75 ii). There are several smaller enclosures, some clearly more recent in date, though possibly reconstructed over earlier foundations (for example, US 75 iii–iv). One of these (US 75 iii), 21 m (N.–S.) by 16 m, with walls up to 1 m high and 1.2 m wide, though of coursed stone and having seen use as a sheepfold in recent times, is not unlike some Romano-British homesteads in appearance.

Disjointed wall sections are also to be found both within and outside the enclosures, suggesting an original pattern of considerable complexity.

Within the smaller of the two main enclosures (US 75 ii) are two small poorly-defined hut-circles (US 75 v–vi), each 4.5 m in overall diameter, and defined by rubble banks up to 0.3 m high. Close to them are stone piles which may obscure further habitation sites. There is another, larger, hut (US 75 vii) 9 m N.–S. enclosed

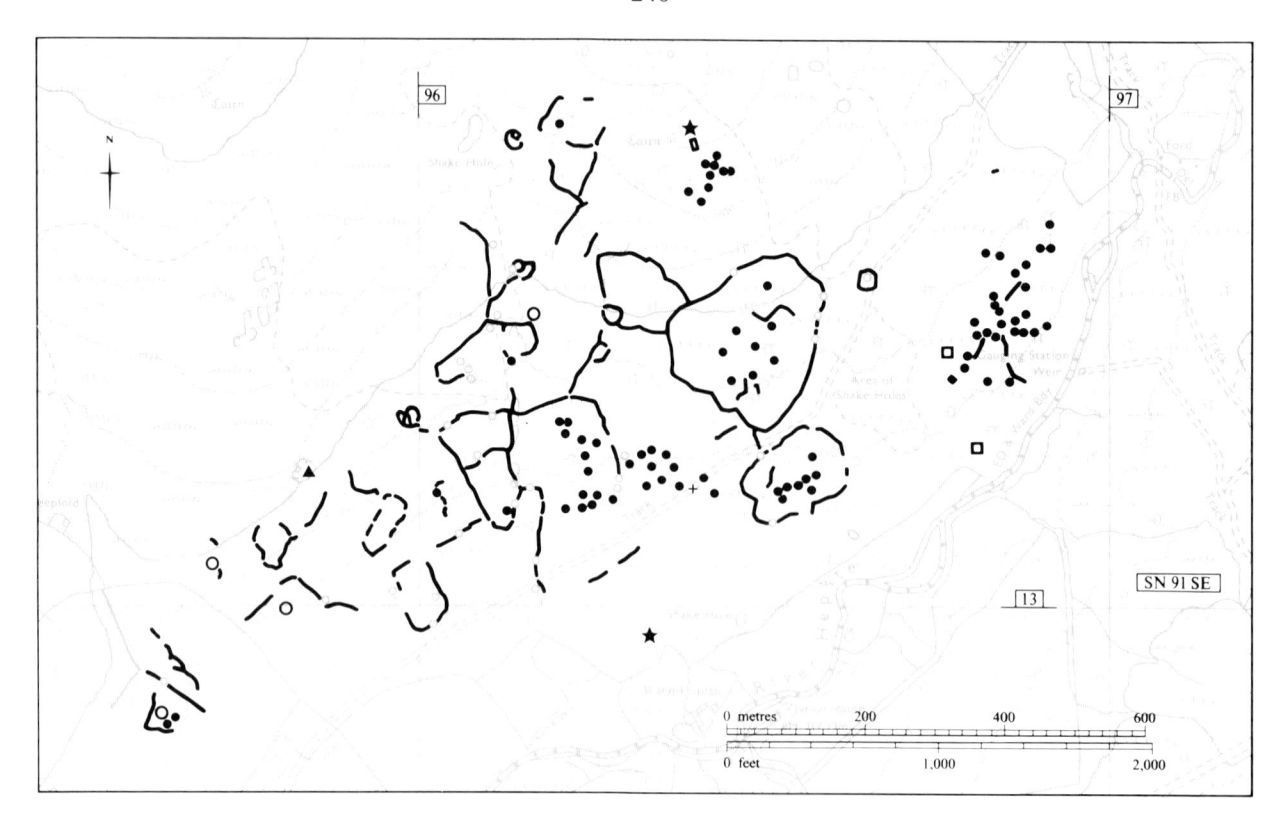

143 Mynydd y Garn: clearances, walls and settlements (US 75–77)

by banks 1.5 m wide and 0.2 m high and a further example with no entrance, (7 m (N.–S.) by 6 m), adjoining a field bank forming its S.W. wall (US 75 viii). On enclosed land further to the W. are two others (US 75 ix–x), 4.5 and 4 m in diameter, respectively.

Clearance cairns seem to be restricted to the eastern half of the site, and are particularly concentrated around the 330 m contour (US 75 xi). The majority are of rubble and boulders, generally circular or oval, ranging in size from 2 m to 10 m in diameter and up to 0.3 m high, though rectangular, triangular and linear clearances are also represented. A further three cairns are sufficiently large and regular to be considered as having been funereal. Two lie above the 330 m contour (US 75 xii–xiii) and both are about 7 m in diameter and 0.4 m high, with a slight central hollow. A further example (US 75 xv) and the hengiform earthwork (US 75 xiv) are described separately elsewhere (RC 109 and RC 107).

These features cannot be seen upon A.P.s, R.A.F. F21/58/3618/0012–3; 21 vi 60.

Ystradfellte
SN 91 S.E. (US 75 i) (9647 1336); (US 75 ii) (9564 1317); (US 75 iii) (9599 1326); (US 75 iv) (9613 1364); (US 75 v) (9652 1315); (US 75 vi) (9655 1316); (US 75 vii) (9580 1299); (US 75 viii) (9616 1329); (US 75 ix) (9562 1284); (US 75 x) (9565 1289); (US 75 xi) (9641 1359); (US 75 xii) (9621 1324); (US 75 xiii) (9623 1333); (US 75 xiv) (9633 1296); (US 75 xv) (9639 1366)   xii 85

(US 76) There is a small oval enclosure upon a broad spur of exposed, partly-vegetated rock on the middle part of the S.-facing slope of Mynydd y Garn, about 395 m above O.D. It measures 27 m (N.W.–N.E.) externally and its bank is slightly turfed over, though the enclosure is bounded for about 12 m by outcropping rock. The site has opposed entrances, a N. gap 3 m wide and a S. one 2 m wide.

O.S. Card SN 91 SE 10 (42, revised numeration).

Ystradfellte
SN 91 S.E. (US 76) (9550 1405)   xii 85

(US 77) Roughly E. and central to the fields and clearance features on this E.-facing hillside at the extreme S. end of Waun Tincer, beyond Mynydd y Garn, overlooking the River Hepste between about 330 and 340 m above O.D., is a group of small cairns associated with linear features, two platforms, and a small ruined rectangular building.

The platforms lie on the S.W. edge of the site, the largest (US 77 i), about 50 m from the river measuring 11 m (N.W.–S.E.) by 5 m, excavated into the hillside on the N.W. to a depth of about 1 m. A slightly smaller example (US 77 ii) lies just above it and measures 9 m (E.–W.) by 5 m, the W. end being cut about 1 m into the hillside. There is a rather better defined building platform (US 77 iii) 4 m (N.W.–S.E.) by 2 m enclosed by banks 1 m wide by 0.3 m high.

The clearance cairns are mainly circular, only slightly overgrown and varying in diameter from 2.5 m to 7 m, with heights up to 0.4 m. One (US 77 iv), rests upon a platform and may represent a habitation site.

There is no evident pattern to the four discontinuous banks which are promiscuously disposed among the cairns and which nowhere measure more than 40 m in length. One linear feature disappears beneath a peat bank (US 77 v), both demonstrating the partial nature of the site record and suggesting its potential antiquity.

Ystradfellte
SN 91 S.E. (US 77 i) (9680 1322); (US 77 ii) (9676 1336); (US 77 iii) (9677 1332); (US 77 iv) (9690 1361); (US 77 v) (9683 1361)   iii 86

(US 78; Figs. 144) On the S.-facing hillslope of Waun Tincer and in the valley bottom, straddling the River Hepste between 350 and 380 m above O.D., are about a dozen groups of settlement and clearance features, ranging in date possibly from prehistoric times to as late as the industrial period.

(US 78 i) On the river terrace overlooking the S. bank of the River Hepste is a small sub-oval enclosure (25 m N.–S. by 20 m E.–W.) within a low turfed-over perimeter wall about 2 m wide and 0.2 m high. The entrance lay on the E. uphill side and a small hut-circle is located inside the N.

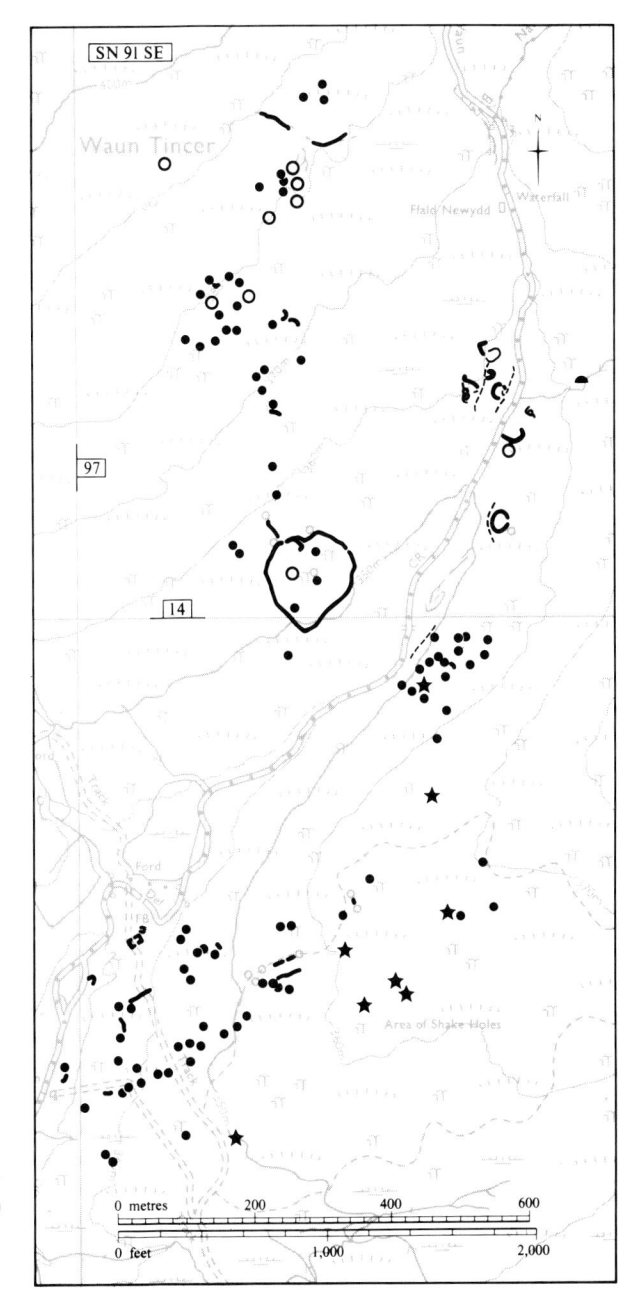

144   Cefn Esgair Carnau and Waun Tincer: clearances, huts and field walls (US 78–9)

wall. About 6 m E. of the N. side of the entrance is a small stone pile about 3 m by 2 m and adjacent to the S. side is a shake-hole 4 m N.–S. by 2 m E.–W. and 2 m deep. A further shake-hole some 5 m in diameter and 3 m deep appeared about 10 m to the N.N.E. between 1985 and 1987.

On the N. bank of the Hepste, straddling both the river terrace and the post-glacial flood plain on a southern aspect, are a group of three huts and a series of field enclosures. The first (US 78 ii) (15 m (N.–S.) by 13 m (E.–W.)) consists of a western stony bank 1.5 m wide by 0.3 m high protected from the river on the S. by what may be a man-made flood bank. It probably had an entrance on the N.E. Set above the flood plain is another small enclosure (US 78 iii) (20 m (N.E.–S.W.) by 13 m (N.W.–S.E.)) scarped into the natural slope on the W., with low orthostatic walling around the N.E. and E. and a slighter enclosure (US 78 iv) nestles against the western natural scarp with low walling 0.3 m high around the E. The largest (US 78 iii) houses a rectangular platform, but otherwise there are no further indications of huts. Further along the floodplain, and to the N.W., below the river bluff, is a cairn 6 m in diameter and 0.3 m high, surrounded by a more ill-defined area of stone, indications of clearance under the shelter of extreme N.W. and S.E. parts of the flood plain.

Immediately above the scarp on level ground is a hut-like structure (US 78 v) consisting of three interlocking stony circles averaging 5 m in diameter with rubble walls up to 0.3 m high. Adjacent disjointed linear walls were probably originally integrated into the field system on the hillside to the W.

On the lower S.E.-facing slope of Waun Tincer is a large enclosure (US 78 vi), associated with several large cairns. The main feature is heart-shaped, 135 m (N.–S.) by 120 m, with a perimeter bank of consolidated rubble, though fragmented on the N.W. Originally it must have achieved a considerable height, as the collapse is 4 m in width, though the picture is a little confused owing to the situation of a later wall to the E. of the N. entrance, about 1.5 m wide and 0.8 m high. There are entrance gaps on the N. and E., and both are 1.5 m wide. Within, there are three cairns and a possible hut-circle and outside it there is an ill-defined bank aligned to a large shake-hole and five clearance cairns, three of considerable size (greater than 10 m in diameter).

On the gentle S.E.-facing slope of Waun Tincer at elevations between 370 and 390 m above O.D. is a series of clearance cairns, hut-circles and a linear bank making over 30 features in all. There are two well-defined hut-circles interdigitated with more than a handful of half-circles and numerous clearance cairns. The features fall into two main groups, in the westernmost of which is the most complete circle (US 78 vii) (8.5 m in internal diameter and a S.E. entrance). To the N. of both groups is a discontinuous E.–W. bank, which appears to separate the huts from a further group of clearance cairns to the N. It seems possible that some of the circles may have been infilled by subsequent agricultural clearance. There is a full circle (6 m in diameter without entrance) upslope due N. of the W. part of the more S. group (US 78 viii).

Opposite the settlement complex on the N. side of the river bank are two well-defined sub-rectangular enclosures with adjacent hut-circles. The first (US 78 ix) an oval-shaped enclosure bounded by a bank on the S.E. and N.E., and on the N.W. by the river, is 30 m (E.–W.) by 16 m. There is a hut-circle on the S. outside and incorporated into the bank, but some damage has been done here by converting it to a shooting box. About 40 m to the N.E. (US 78 x) is another small enigmatic enclosure, basically comprising a hut-circle only 2 m in diameter set against (though separated from) the S.W. bank of a dog-leg wall enclosing an area to the E. about 8 m square.

To the E. and beyond the quarrying features and later settlement (see below), on the N.W.-facing slope of Cefn Esgair Carnau and S.E. of the River Hepste, between 350 m and 360 m above O.D. is a group of stone piles making up a cairn field which lies on a gently-sloping terrace above a river cliff (US 78 xi). The cairns are mainly circular or oval in plan, varying between 1.5 m and 8 m in diameter. Two are discontinuous banks, others are more shapeless. A nearby burnt mound is described elsewhere (BM 16).

During the industrial period, the ancient settlement area was joined by a stone bridge, which was probably utilised by the occupants of the coursed homestead structure adjacent to the river. Around them, a series of quarries (US 78 xii) attest to considerable mineral extraction during this period.

D. K. Leighton and D. J. Percival, *Arch. in Wales* 26 (1986), p. 25.

S.A.M. B 134a–g (US 78 xi)

(US 78 i), (US 78 xi–xii) Cantref; (US 78 ii–x) Ystradfellte
SN 91 S.E. (US 78 i) (9761 1413); (US 78 ii) (9759 1434); (US 78 iii) (9761 1431); (US 78 iv) (9760 1434); (US 78 v) (9756 1431); (US 78 vi) (9733 1405); (US 78 vii) (9731 1462); (US 78 viii) (9712 1463); (US 78 ix) (9763 1425); (US 78 x) (9765 1428); (US 78 xi) (9763 1389); (US 78 xii) (975 140)
1985–87

Cefn Esgair Carnau

(US 79; Fig. 144) On the more southerly aspect of Cefn Esgair Carnau overlooking the River Hepste is a spread of cairnfield features up to about 800 m long by 150–200 m wide comprising some 50 or more stone piles or amorphous cairns, and a handful of short, linear features lying between 330 m and 375 m above O.D. The majority of the cairns are circular, varying in diameter from 2 to 6 m, and averaging about 0.3 m in height. All are composed of mixed grade rubble limestone and Old Red Sandstone, and many are consolidated with vegetation. There is a particular concentration on part of the hill along a terrace aligned N.E.–S.W., below, and to the N.W. of the ridge. The following is a selection giving some idea of the variety of types which occur here.

(US 79 i–ii) Are respectively a small amorphous cairn some 4.9 by 3.4 m and 0.15 m high and a stony patch 3.7 by 2.8 m and about the same height, lying on the eastern aspect of the hill.

On the higher, featureless plateau are a number of larger examples. (Sites US 79 iii–x) are described in detail below.) Overall, these are sited along a line about 650 m long from N.E. to S.W. by 240 m wide. Six lie in slight depressions roughly 0.3 m deep. They vary in size between 13.2 m in diameter by 1.1 m high and 9.1 m in diameter by 0.5 m high, and are generally well preserved though centrally mutilated. An important feature at the N.E. end of this area is the apparent use of shake-holes as stone dumps. This dumping may be illusory, and these are probably what are elsewhere termed 'negative cairn features' or 'stone ponds' (p. 193 ff).

The linear features are fugitive and fragmentary, generally about 2 m wide, but hardly rising to more than 0.2 m. The recognition of two banks (US 79 xi) at right angles close to the river, and similarly, the parallel N.E.–S.W. banks (US 79 xii) closer to the N. of the grouping suggest partial field or enclosure boundaries.

Lying below the river bluff upon the recent floodplain of the Hepste, are two (presumably recent) longhouses, and also, occupying an abandoned meander core, an indeterminate structure, which, to judge from its form and position (US 79 xiii), may be of much greater antiquity.

(US 79 iii) The most southwesterly of the group is 15 m N.–S. by 13 m with a maximum height of 0.8 m. Shake-holes are appearing both on the N. margin, and to the S.E.[1]

(US 79 iv) A slightly oval mound 12 m (N.–S.) by 11 m in diameter and 0.6 m high. The cairn has been trenched E.–W., and the material left to add height to the site.[2]

(US 79 v) In a slight declivity on the spine of a low ridge is a cairn 11.6 m in diameter and 0.6 m high with a slight central depression.[3]

(US 79 vi) N.E. of the last is a very disturbed cairn 10.5 m in diameter and about 0.4 m high. Shake-holes appear to be developing on the S.E.[4]

(US 79 vii) There is a structure similar to the above situated in a slight depression 9.3 m in diameter and 0.5 m high, added to on the S. margin by a recent stone pile.[5]

(US 79 viii) A cairn 17.1 m in diameter and 1.2 m high. The centre is badly damaged by robber craters and a small cairn of stones built into a small shelter, to the N. It is impinged upon by two shake-holes.[6]

(US 79 ix) A much disturbed cairn base 11 m by 9.5 m.

(US 79 x) On the N. end of Cefn Esgair Carnau, upon a S.-facing slope is a much-disturbed round cairn 8.8 m N.E.–S.W. by 8 m with a maximum height of 0.25 m.

There are two ruined longhouses and a third, indeterminate structure, all probably of medieval or later date, towards the S. end of this area.[7]

[1] O.S. Card SN 91 SE 1; Roese, *Thesis*, no. 86.
[2] Roese, *Thesis*, no. 88.
[3] Roese, *Thesis*, no. 89.
[4] Roese, *Thesis*, no. 90.
[5] Roese, *Thesis*, no. 91.
[6] O.S. Card SN 91 SE 2; Roese, *Thesis*, no. 92.
[7] Centred upon 9703 1353; NAR 109.

Cantref
SN 91 S.E. (US 79 i) (9759 1365); (US 79 ii) (9760 1359); (US 79 iii) (9722 1327); (US 79 iv) (9738 1353); (US 79 v) (9741 1346); (US 79 vi) (9745 1349); (US 79 vii) (9747 1347); (US 79 viii) (9752 1375); (US 79 ix) (9753 1358); (US 79 x) (9714 1359); (US 79 xi) (9706 1343); (US 79 xii) (9730 1351); (US 79 xiii) (9702 1349)   15 xii 85

(US 80) Towards the N. end of Cefn Esgair Carnau on the edge of a gently sloping terrace before the ground falls away more steeply to the S.W., about 375 m above O.D., lies a roughly rectangular spread of stone, representing the remains of either a rubble cairn or a ruined building. It measures 27.5 m (E.–W.) by 14 m and stands about 0.5 m high.

Penderyn
SN 91 S.E. (US 80) (9804 1452)   x 85

UNENCLOSED SETTLEMENTS 244

Pant y Gadair

(US 81; Fig. 145) On the E.-facing slope of Pant y Gadair between 370 and 410 m above O.D. is a cairnfield which includes two (possibly three) hut-circles. It comprises 19 stone piles, mainly circular and oval, ranging from 2 to 8 m in diameter and up to 0.7 m high, some of which may have been for burial.

The first hut (US 81 i), 5.5 m in overall diameter, comprises a stony bank 1.5 m wide and 0.2 m high, but lacks an obvious entrance. The second (US 81 ii), 6 m in diameter, appears slightly scooped into the hillside. The third (US 81 iii) is a slightly oval enclosure (6 m (E.–W.) by 5.6 m) entered on the E., and with an extremely low bank, 1.2 m wide.

Penderyn
SN 91 S.E. (US 81 i) (9862 1262); (US 81 ii) (9851 1284); (US 81 iii) (9869 1265) xii 85

(US 82; Fig. 145) Covering the N.E.-facing slope of Pant y Gadair, below Cadair Fawr between 380 m and 420 m above O.D., are two enclosures, one unfinished, 11 hut platforms (not all listed below) and a field bank.

The main enclosure (US 82 i) (50 m (E.–W.) by 45 m) with a low perimeter bank about 2 m wide and 0.2 m high, broken midway along the N. (downslope) side by an entrance 3 m wide. To the E. and further downslope are three rectangular huts of similar size and construction, the best preserved (6 m (E.-W.) by 3 m internally) excavated into the slope at the W. end and built up at the E. (US 82 ii) with rubble walls 1 m wide and 0.5 m high and an entrance midway along the N. side. The other two huts differ from (US 82 ii) only in their entrances, one (US 82 iii) being on the S., whilst the other (US 82 iv) has no obvious entrance, though does have some indication of internal division. Running in a northeasterly direction from this group is a long field bank, making up three sides of an enormous enclosure. The bank encompasses much of the upper reaches of a small W.–E.-flowing stream which rises as a spring immediately outside the enclosure. The enclosure bank runs 120 m N.W., then turns almost through a right angle before travelling a further 140 m N.E., before disappearing into deeper vegetation downslope (US 82 v).

Clustered to the N. of this latter stretch are several more hut platforms similar to the first three, two (US 82 vi–vii) having rubble walls, and three, including (US 82 vi), possessing N.-facing entrances.

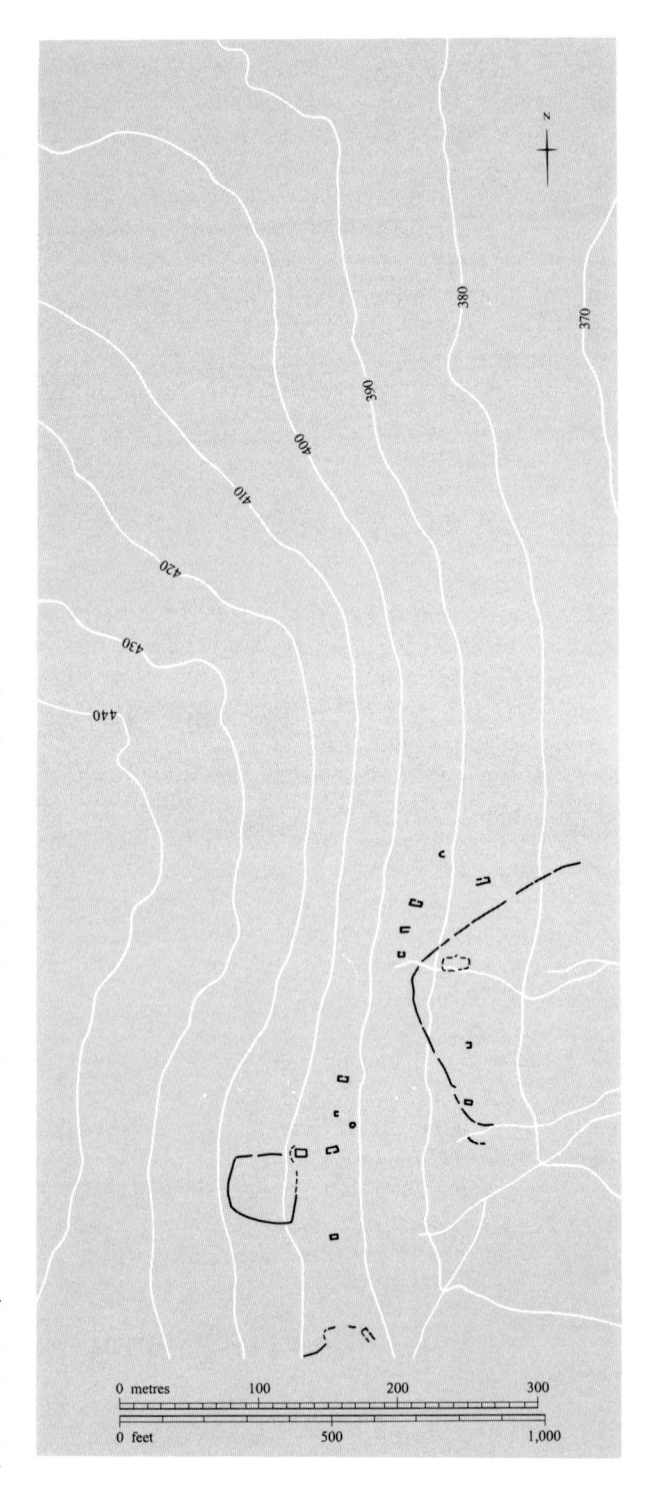

145 Pant y Gadair enclosures (US 82)

There are a number of features enclosed by the bank, including a further building platform (US 82 viii), considerably larger than the others, some 17 m E.–W. by 9 m, though completely without traces of structure upon it.

To the S. of the enclosure (US 82 i), is a further, slope-oriented platform 21 m long by 4 m wide. Heaped against the downhill, N.E. face, is a substantial rubble pile, triangular in shape (US 82 ix). Walling upon the platform hints at the former existence of a building. A bank is discernible running from the N.W. end of the platform S.W. up the hill for some 50 m.

The group is possibly later prehistoric in origin, though may be Romano-British or even medieval.

D. K. Leighton and D. J. Percival, *Arch. in Wales* 26 (1986), p. 25.

Penderyn
SN 91 S.E. (US 82 i) (9852 1229); (US 82 ii) (9858 1236); (US 82 iii) (9857 1232); (US 82 iv) (9855 1231); (US 82 v) (from 9868 1233 to 9874 1251); (US 82 vi) (9862 1245); (US 82 vii) (9868 1250); (US 82 viii) (9863 1247); (US 82 ix) (9860 1218)　　　　i 86

Cwm Cadlan–Cefn Sychpant

(US 83; Fig. 146) Immediately outside the area of enclosed, historically cultivated land on the Penderyn side of Cwm Cadlan, adjacent to Nant Maden farm is a boulder-strewn landscape on the northern valley slope between elevations of 360 and 420 m above O.D. It is covered by a system of linear banks, cairns and hut-circles, emerging from a heavily overgrazed sward from beneath which bare peat is beginning to emerge and dominate the ground colour. These features stretch across virtually the whole length of the common on the W., to close upon the forestry intakes on the E. The more westerly section covers some 36 ha,[1] and that on the E., about 20 ha.

Land clearance seems to have preceded peat growth and followed axial lines, the general trend of which was N.W.–S.E. and is mainly represented by low-spread fugitive stone banks, though in some places it is possible that field enclosure is represented by aligned clearance cairns, rather than by continuous banks. The system is bounded on the N. and N.W. by a discontinuous bank running N.E., curving round to the E. for some 750 m (US 83 i). There are three fugitive banks lines running along the same basic axis. On the W. is a discontinuous feature almost parallel to the first bank section (US 83 ii). This has a short but distinct S.-running 'tail', perhaps a relict part of the coaxial grid. Another 100 m further S. there seems to be a concordance between the alignment of this with clearance cairns and associated discontinuous low banks. The third main element is of 180 m, also along the N.E. axis and with only minor interruptions (US 83 iii). This might be aligned upon the S. boundary of the sub-rectangular enclosure (US 83 iv), or even upon a short stretch of fugitive clearance S. of its S.W. corner, running for about 15 m N.N.E.–S.S.W. There are three main coaxial features. The first is aligned with the W. boundary of enclosure (US 83 iv) and is discontinuous for almost 60 m northwards, with two low banks about 40 m long taking the feature as far as the Penderyn–Cwm Taf road. Boundary (US 83 iii) subtends a dog-leg S.-running stretch of walling about 45 m long, and there a further line is dependent upon the curving N.E. boundary, running S. a similar distance. The banks are up to 3 m wide and few rise above 0.3 m, and in fact some are actually exposed by erosion from below soil or peat level. The presence of some slight lynchetting is suggested from field observation.

To the E. of the enclosure (US 83 iv) is a flat triangular area, limited on the E. by a slight terrace, now being damaged by overgrazing, and on the W. it is bounded by the enclosure and the appended N.-running wall. This triangular area seems likely to have been intended as a field.

The enclosure (US 83 iv) lies N.W. of a small stream, which cuts it on the E. corner, and measures internally about 50 m N.W.–S.E. by 45 m. An interesting feature is the E. bank, part of which comprises a double wall, the centre robbed out. Perhaps it was originally of soil or even turf, as there is a suggestion of outer stone-facing.

There are two, possibly three hut-circles in the area. The first (US 83 v) is 6 m N.–S. by 5 m in internal diameter with a bank 1–1.6 m in width and 0.4 m high. The entrance is 0.5 m wide on the S. The second hut-circle (US 83 vi) is 6 m (N.E.–S.W.) by 5 m

UNENCLOSED SETTLEMENTS

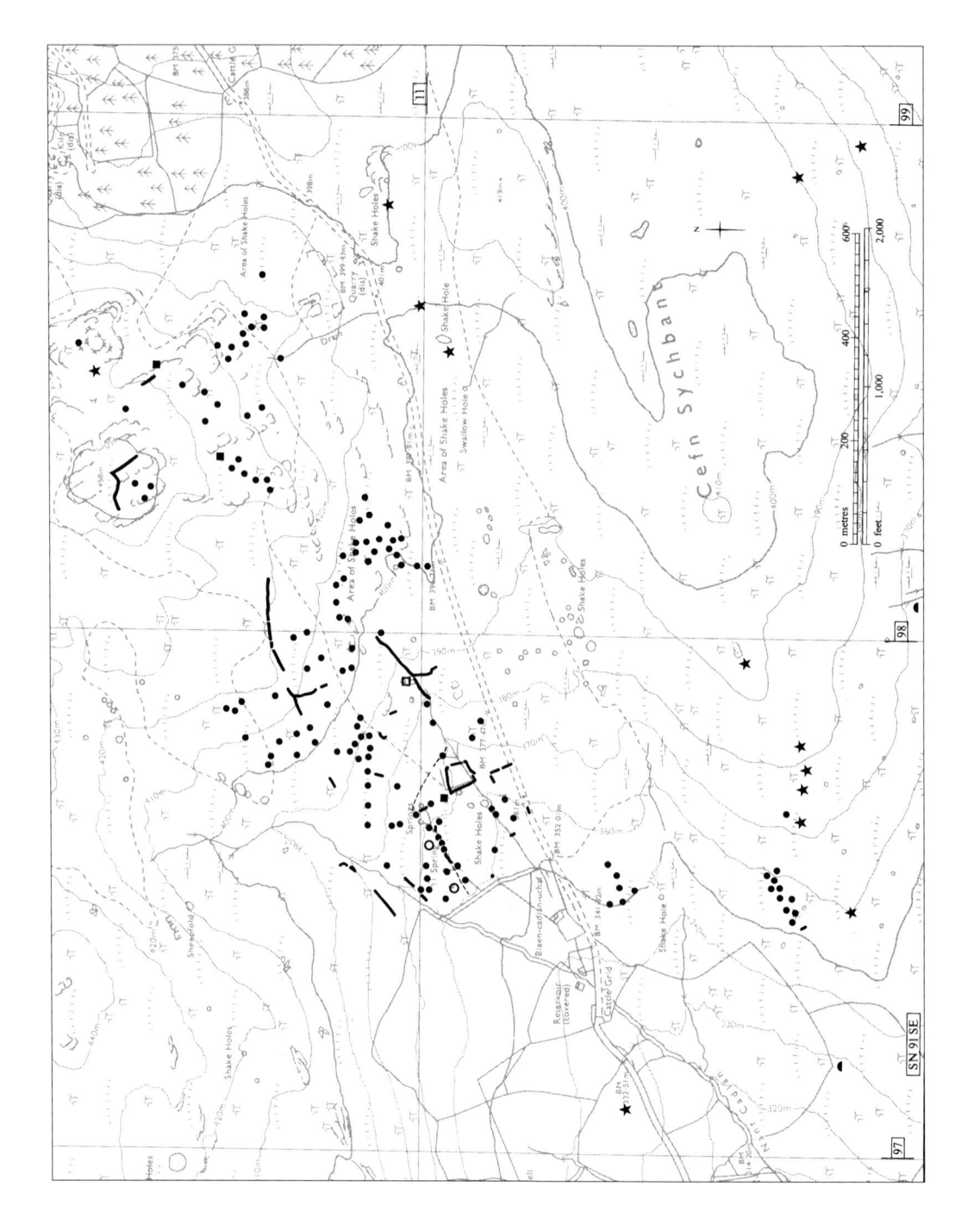

246

146 Cwm Cadlan and Cefn Sychpant: enclosures, field walls, clearance and ritual cairns (US 83–4: RC 111, 112–16, 117–18, 121–7)

internally, and is bounded by a stony bank 1 m wide and 0.2 m high, but apparently lacks an entrance. There is, on the W. of the enclosure (US 83 iv), a third putative hut, overlain by a field clearance cairn (US 83 vii).

The area is peppered with at least 75 field clearance cairns of varied stone composition mainly on the N., E. and W.

Further E. are two small outlying clearance cairns (US 83 ix–x), lying some 400 m W. of Coed Taf Fawr, 425 m above O.D., one 4.3 m in diameter and 0.5 m high, the other, 33 m to the S.W., 3.4 m in diameter and 0.3 m high.[2]

[1] MS in R.C.A.M. files; D. K. Leighton and D. J. Percival, *Arch. in Wales* 26 (1986), p. 25.
[2] Roese, *Thesis*, no. 242.

Penderyn
SN 91 S.E. (US 83 i) (from 9746 1130 to 9810 1130); (US 83 ii) (from 9748 1099 to 9753 1104); (US 83 iii) (from 9787 1098 to 9793 1109); (US 83 iv) (9772 1093); (US 83 v) (9750 1099); (US 83 vi) (9759 1098); (US 83 vii) (9762 1092); (US 83 ix) (9857 1132); (US 83 x) (9859 1135)   1990

(US 84; Fig 146) On the N.W. slope of Cefn Sychpant at elevations ranging from 350 to 385 m above O.D. are two groups of clearance, and possibly one, of burial, cairns. The two more westerly sites are felt to be 'cairn fields'.

(US 84 i) Eleven piles forming a linear group aligned roughly S.W.–N.E., with an outlier some distance to the S.E. These are generally irregularly shaped and of various sizes. The largest is 8 m by 4 m and 0.4 m high. The S.W. end of the group is marked by a short linear feature running roughly N.–S.

Four or five small cairns lying between this clearance feature and the cairn which caps Pant Sychpant are listed elsewhere (RC 112–16).

(US 84 ii) On the N. side of the W.-flowing stream just outside the limit of cultivation in Nant Cadlan about 350 m N. of (US 84 i) is a group of six small stone piles, the smallest 2.5 m in diameter, the largest 6 m long by 2 m wide, rising to about 0.3 m in height.

(US 84 iii) Well beyond this group and immediately W. of and outside the stone enclosed forestry plantation is a small circular enclosure lying on a slight W.-facing slope 390 m above O.D. It is 11 m in overall diameter with an enclosing bank about 1.5 m wide and 0.3 m high. There appears to be no entrance. It may have formed part of a larger settlement group robbed out during wall building.

Penderyn
SN 91 S.E. (US 84 i) (9750 1028); (US 84 ii) (9752 1061); (US 84 iii) (9906 1121)   ii 86

SN 92

(US 85) On the S. slope of Y Gyrn about 500 m above O.D. is a dished, possibly natural, hollow about 50 m by 20 m, in which there lies a collection of stones about 3 m in diameter and 0.2 m high, representing a small clearance area.

Defynnog (E), Senni (C)
SN 92 N.E. (981 208) (approx.)   iv 88

(US 86; Fig. 147) The cliffs of Craig Cerrig Gleisiad lying beneath Fan Frynach, appear to have offered natural protection to early settlement.[1] Land clearance, including medieval settlement and field boundaries,[2] is focused around a classic embanked, peat-filled late-glacial cwm or corrie,[3] between about 375 and 475 m above O.D. The cwm is drained from a point on its N.E. lip by a small stream, which passes through the settlement; there is a second, more northerly watercourse, running from behind the cwm, draining the N.-facing S. cliff, possibly having been a focus for settlement features which have been more vulnerable to human and natural erosion. There appear to be two or three phases of settlement here: the earliest characterised by boulder-wall enclosures, a second represented by the associated enclosure, longhouse hut-circle, which may be contemporary or overlap with more certain medieval or post-medieval occupation, evidenced by the rubble walls of two[4] buildings and a longhouse[5] enclosure and field banks.

(US 86 i) The most westerly site[6] lies at about 520 m above O.D., beside a dry gully beneath a slight break in the E.-sloping side of the cwm wall. It comprises an irregular tumbled rubble wall up to 2 m wide, some 35 m across the slope and between about 30 and 45 m transversely. Uphill from this are: a rectangular hut

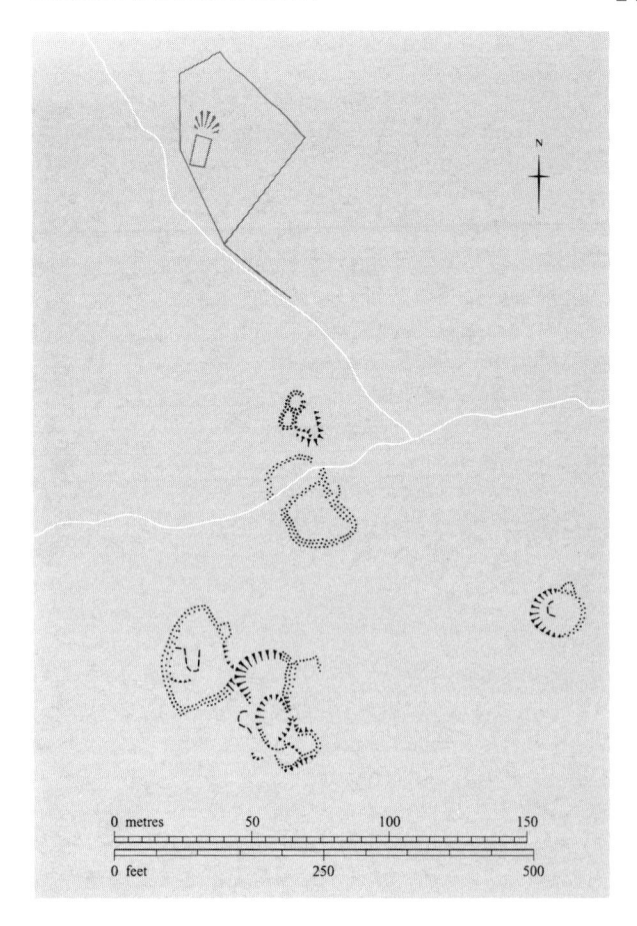

147 Craig Cerrig Gleisiad: enclosures and huts (US 86)

platform some 6 m by 3 m, a hut-circle with a low rubble wall, some 3 m in internal diameter; and within the bottom on the gully, the footings of a stone building some 3 m by 2 m.

(US 86 ii–vi) The earlier settlement complex occupies the E.-facing outer slope of the cwm between 402 and 442 m above O.D., and measures 160 m (E.–W.) by 140 m (N.–S.). It comprises a group of hillslope-set scooped enclosures including hut-circles and associated embankments.

(US 86 ii) The most northwesterly is a pair of roughly circular hut platforms set upon a natural, boulder-strewn semi-circular rush-grown terrace to the N. of the stream which now drains the cwm. The hut embankments recognised here by the O.S. in 1976 were difficult to distinguish with confidence in 1981 and 1991. This hut-group lies immediately outside (US 86 iii), which is a sub-rectangular enclosure embanked by rubble walls up to 3 m wide and 0.4 m high, the longer axis aligned N.N.W.–S.S.E. (of *c.* 35 m by 23 m). This is bisected unequally by the stream, leaving a smaller, more incomplete enclosed area on the N. bank, whilst an internal E.–W. dividing bank makes a full enclosure of the steeply-sloping southern part, which is entered through a gap about 2 m wide about halfway down the E. side. Protruding from the S. terminal is a linear outwork curving away a few metres to the N.

(US 86 iv) The main settlement feature is a large uneven sub-triangular, grass-grown enclosure set into the eastern cwm bank, measuring 38 m (N.–S.) by 26 m, with rubble banks of variable width, but up to. 3.5 m wide on the W., uphill side, where it attains a maximum 1.2 m height. Elsewhere the bank is between 0.4 m and 1 m high (on the E. and N. respectively). There are signs of subdivision on the steeper, western side.

(US 86 v) Adjoining this enclosure on the S.E. is a further complex scooped enclosure and hut-group. It is bounded on N. and W. by its own escarpment, and on the E., partly enclosed by a low rubble bank up to 5 m wide. Its level interior lies some 2.5 m below that of the adjacent site, and measures 18 m (N.E.–S.W.) by 13 m. It was possibly entered on the N.E. where there is slight evidence for an annex about 8 m by 5 m.

Three further, though smaller enclosures adjoin this larger platform on the S. The first and largest is oval, 12 m (N.–S.) by 8 m internally. It rises to a maximum 1 m high on the N., uphill side. On the E. is a well-defined entrance 1.5 m wide, flanked by low rubble banks up to 2.5 m wide. Immediately to the W. of this enclosure is a poorly-defined oval platform.

The two smaller enclosures, which again are scooped, lie immediately to the S. These are separated by an indistinct bank. Both are oval, the more easterly measuring 10 m E.–W. by 6 m (internally); the other 8 m E.–W. by 7 m. The more northeasterly example is the better-defined of the two, and this is bounded on the E. by a low rubble bank about 3 m wide.

(US 86 vi) Some distance to the E., and scooped from the S.-facing break of slope of the naturally embanked interfluve between the two streams draining the cwm area, is an oval rubble-scattered platform 15 m N.N.W.–S.S.E. by 13 m internally. This is bounded on the W. by its own escarpment (up to 1.3 m high), and on the E. by a low rubble bank over 2 m wide. It may have been entered through a gap on the E. Along the N. circumference there is a small triangular annex.

(US 86 vii) On the N.-facing S. bank of the more southerly stream lies a slightly embanked enclosure, some 50–60 m E.–W. by about 25 m N.–S. This was observed under heavy frost, and its re-location under the normal weather conditions later proved impossible.

(US 86 viii) Rig and furrow ploughmarks are recognisable to the N. of the settlement area, covering an area of several acres N.E. and beyond the more northerly stream. The rigs are particularly well-pronounced in marshy, rush-grown ground immediately N.N.E. of feature (US 86 ii). Although most likely medieval in their present form (they are probably focused upon the longhouse),[5] the existence of three earlier settlement foci could provide an earlier date for their origins.

[1] O.S. Card SN 92 SE 3; first detected on A.P.s, R.A.F. F21/58/3638/0083–4, 21 vi 60, in 1974, later from field examination in 1976; P. M. Jones, *Arch. in Wales* 19 (1979), p. 10, no. 13.
[2] Besides the features described in this account, at least three foci of medieval or post-medieval settlement and agriculture were noted during fieldwork.
[3] M. J. C. Walker, *Nature* 287 (1980), pp. 133–5.
[4] O.S. Card SN 92 SE 5.
[5] O.S. Card SN 92 SE 2.
[6] O.S. Card SN 92 SE 4.

Defynnog (E), Glyn (C)
SN 92 S.E. (US 86 i) (9615 2231); (US 86 ii) (9653 2233); (US 86 iii) (9650 2230); (US 86 iv) (9642 2222); (US 86 v) (centred upon 9644 2222); (US 86 vi) (9659 2224); (US 86 vii) (9688 2205); (US 86 viii) (9643 2245 [longhouse])   iii 91

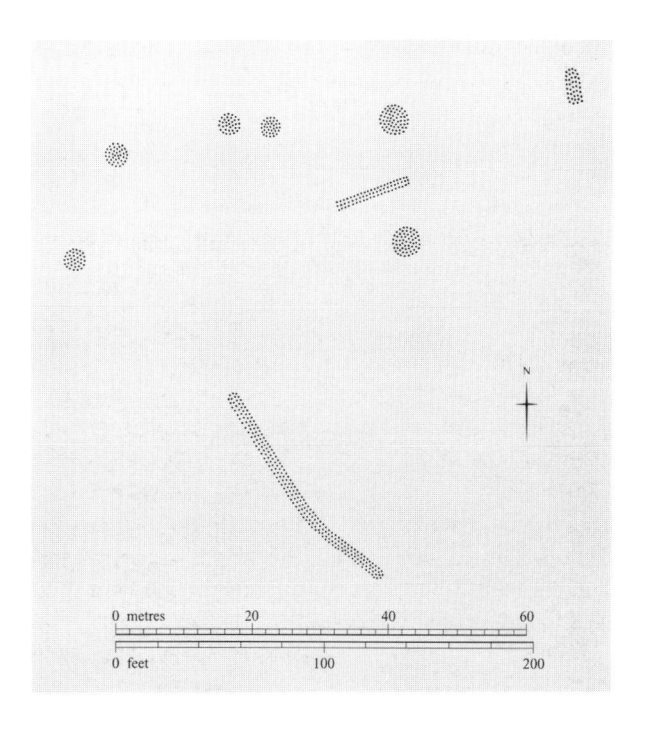

SN 96

(US 87; Fig. 148) Carn Gafallt, comprising part of Llanwrthwl Commons, is a ridge of heather-clad uncultivated ground about 3.5 km long (E.–W.) and averaging about 1 km wide. It rises to 475 m on the W. at Clap Round with several high spots above 400 m further E. Formerly in the ownership of the Glanusk Estate, it was sold to the Royal Society for the Protection of Birds in 1983, and is now managed as a nature reserve. Searches[1] of aerial photographs[2] reveal at least four separate areas of rig and furrow ploughing (US 87 i–iv). These ploughrigs, up to 2.5 m wide, could indicate medieval land-taking associated with monastic agriculture undertaken from the Grange of Cwm Ddeuddwr.[3]

Immediately N.W. of (US 87 i), is a group of at least seven clearance cairns (US 87 v) composed of rubble collected in turf-consolidated mounds averaging 3–4 m in diameter and 0.3–0.6 m high. There are also three lengths of turf-grown rubble bank between 1.3 m and 2 m wide and 0.3 to 0.5 m high, their profiles enhanced at the time of observation by extremely low, dead, heather occasioned by ravages of the heather beetle (*Lochmaea suturalis*). These clearances occupy a slight N.–S. running col between 420 and 430 m above O.D. about 600 m N.N.E. of burial cairns RCs 172–6. The clearance cairns comprise small rounded boulders and more angular fragmenting pieces of the locally outcropping Ordovician volcanic mudstones and grits, together with some metamorphic erratics of more distant origin, visible in boulder clay sections beside the farm track cut along the entire length of the hill in 1982.

148   Carn Gafallt clearance cairns and boundaries (US 87)

Several small enclosures and long-huts have also been located upon the Common,[4] which also has abandoned access tracks, massive (2–3 m wide) field boundaries, and small-scale quarrying features. These were not surveyed in detail by Commission staff as their surviving pattern is considered most likely to be medieval. The presence nearby of three large, supposedly Bronze Age cairns (RC 172–6) poses the problem of recognising earlier agricultural clearances now obscured by abandoned medieval agricultural lands. Such a succession of farming settlement appears to be corroborated from pollen analytical investigation.[5]

[1] By Mr R. Knight, R.S.P.B. Warden, Cwm, Llanwrthwl.
[2] Visible on A.P.s, O.S. 76 042 030–33, 39–42; 78 006 143–5, 178–80, 197–9.
[3] D. Williams, *An Atlas of Cistercian Lands in Wales*, (Cardiff: Wales U.P., 1990).
[4] By the O.S. (O.S. Card SN 96 SW 29), by Mr R. Knight, and by Commission staff.
[5] Information kindly made available by Mrs P. Wiltshire, Ashtead, Surrey, from unpublished investigation.

Llanwrthwl
SN 96 S.W. (US 87 i) (9475 6469)
SN 96 S.E. (US 87 ii) (951 645); (US 87 iii) (953 643); (US 87 iv) (961 649); (US 87 v) (centred upon 9475 6479)   21 ii 91

SO 00 NW

(US 88) On a gentle N.E.-facing slope on the edge of the cairnfield (US 89), is a house platform, 7.8 m N.N.E.–S.S.W. by 3 m, cut back to a depth of 0.4 m and built out 0.2 m above the contour. The top of the hood is slightly embanked, and interpretation of other features is to some degree hampered by tree growth. There is also an old field bank lying close to the platform on the S.E.

Penderyn
SO 00 N.W. (US 88) (0115 0975)   i v 90

(US 89) Within a forestry plantation 380 m above O.D. on Penmoelallt, nine small clearance cairns visible from fire-breaks were noted by the Commission. All were overgrown with moss, grass or rushes. Some had been planted, though none of these examples were ploughed.

(US 89 i) 6 m N.W.–S.E. by 5.5 m and 0.4 m high on N.E. side.

(US 89 ii) On the edge of a fire-break, 5 m N.N.E.–S.S.W. by 4 m and 0.4 m high.

(US 89 iii) Just within the plantation, 4.5 m in diameter and 0.2 m high.

(US 89 iv) Just within the plantation, tree-grown, 7 m in diameter and 0.5 m high.

(US 89 v) Within the plantation, 6.5 m (E.–W.) by 5 m and 0.75 m high.

(US 89 vi) Within a fire-break, 6.5 m in diameter and 0.3 m high.

(US 89 vii) Just within plantation, 5.5 m (N.E.–S.W.) by 4.5 m and 0.3 m high.

(US 89 viii) Tree-grown, 11.5 m in diameter and 0.5 m high.

(US 89 ix) In a clearing, 5 m (N.W.–S.E.) by 4 m and 0.4 m high.

Penderyn
SO 00 N.W. (US 89 i) (0135 0958); (US 89 ii) (0130 0961); (US 89 iii) (0132 0961); (US 89 iv) (0128 0964); (US 89 v) (0126 0966); (US 89 vi) (0122 0970); (US 89 vii) (0121 0970); (US 89 viii) (0119 0974); (US 89 ix) (0126 0970 [approx.])   1 v 90

(US 90) On Cefn Cilsanws on a plateau, 420 m above O.D., in addition to the funereal cairn felt the most likely to have produced the riveted dagger (RC 201) is a group of fifteen low mounds, probably field clearance cairns. They are built largely of limestone blocks. One (US 90 i) has been excavated and was found to overlie the site of a Neolithic structure (see p. 24).[1] The cairns fall into two basic groups, a western and an eastern. The more easterly group[2] scattered around the summit of the limestone plateau, comprises:

(US 90 i) The 'Cairn' marked on the O.S. map[3] is 4.9 m in diameter and 0.3–0.45 m high. It displays signs of having been trenched into on the N. and W. and of its centre being dug out in recent times (1978).

(US 90 ii) About 30 m S.W. from (US 90 i) is a cairn 29.3 m in diameter and 0.3–0.45 m high into which are incorporated some large blocks.

(US 90 iii) Only 5.5 m W. of S. from (US 90 i) is a cairn 3.4 m in diameter and 0.2 m high.

(US 90 iv) About 25 m almost due S. of (US 90 i) is a cairn 4.6 m in diameter and 0.45 m high, the centre dug out to form a deep crater.

(US 90 v) Some 32 m due W. from (US 90 iv), is a cairn 3.7 m in diameter and 0.2 m high with a central crater.

(US 90 vi) About 20 m S.S.E. from (US 90 v), is a

149 Cairns and early boundary on Coedcae'r Gwartheg (US 91) (CUAP ARG 92)

cairn 4.3 m in diameter and 0.25 m high with a central crater.

(US 90 vii) Some 12 m S.S.E. from (US 90 vi), is a cairn 4 m in diameter and 0.2 m high which appears undisturbed.

(US 90 viii) About 14 m W. by S. from (US 90 vii), is a slight mound 2.3 m in diameter and 0.15 m high.

(US 90 ix) 20 m to the E. of (US 90 i) is a small low oval mound of consolidated stones 3.5 m by 2.3 m and 0.25 m high.

The more westerly group of larger cairns includes:

(US 90 x) An oval mound of consolidated stones and small boulders 5 m (E.–W.) by 3 m and 0.25 m high.

(US 90 xi) To the N.W. of (US 90 x) is a mound 3.3 m in diameter of consolidated stones and boulders 0.3 m high, to which material has been added on the S.E. creating an oval effect.

(US 90 xii) A mound of consolidated stones and boulders 4 m in diameter and 0.3 m high.

(US 90 xiii) N. of W. from this feature is an oval mound of consolidated stones and boulders 6 m (N.W.–S.E.) by 3.0 m and 0.3 m high.

(US 90 xiv) Lying outside and to the S.E. of this

main grouping is a further, oval, cairn some 75 m N.N.E. of (RC 201). It is 6 m (E.–W.) by 5 m and 0.5 m high and is composed of consolidated stones and small boulders with some loose material around a central depression about 2 m in diameter. About midway between the two cairns is a smaller stone scatter.

[1] D. P. Webley, *B.B.C.S.* 17 (1958), pp. 117–18; pp. 195–6; *P.P.S.* 23 (1957), pp. 228; 24 (1958), pp. 219–20.
[2] O.S. Card SO 00 NW 3.
[3] O.S. 6-inch map (1964 Edition).

Vaynor
SO 00 N.W. (US 90 i) (0248 0995); (US 90 ii) (0245 0995); (US 90 iii) (0247 0996); (US 90 iv) (0248 0992); (US 90 v) (0245 0992); (US 90 vi) (0246 0991); (US 90 vii) (0248 0990); (US 90 viii) (0251 0987); (US 90 ix) (0251 0997); (US 90 x) (0238 0984); (US 90 xi) (0236 0986); (US 90 xii) (0234 0987); (US 90 xiii) (0228 0988); (US 90 xiv) (0253 0988)   12 viii 90

SO 01

(US 91; Fig. 149) On the summit of Coedcae'r Gwartheg 410 m above O.D. are five cairns:

(US 91 i) A stone-built cairn 26 m in diameter and 1.6 m high.

(US 91 ii) A similar cairn 15 m in diameter and 1.3 m high.

(US 91 iii) A cairn 16 m in diameter and 1.2 m high.

(US 91 iv) A cairn 11 m in diameter and 0.4 m high.

(US 91 v) A cairn 16 m in diameter and 0.8 m high.

Vaynor
SO 01 S.W. (US 91 i) (0223 1148); (US 91 ii) (0224 1155); (US 91 iii) (0222 1158); (US 91 iv) (0230 1141); (US 91 v) (0229 1142)

(US 92; Fig. 150) On the N. end of Cefn Cilnsanws, about 400–410 m above O.D., is a series of fugitive linear field banks associated with a D-shaped enclosure Coedcae'r Ychain, described elsewhere as a hillfort.[1]

The main southern axis of field bank (US 92 i) is about 200 m in length and aligns roughly S.–N. along the hilltop from cairns lying to the S. (RC 210–12). Its connection to the S. side of the enclosure is unclear, if indeed one existed. The western side of the enclosure itself includes a W.-running offset, about 60 m long (US 92 ii).

This is one of four E.–W. offsets discernible, running in discontinuous lengths from the main S.–N. axis. The next two (US 92 iii–iv) each project a good 100 m W. from the axis. A further line (US 92 v) projects N. from (US 92 iii) for a distance of 25 m, hinting at the existence of a lost grid-pattern. The only indications of any eastern offset projection are at the extreme S. end of the axial spine, where the surviving E.–W. length apparently anchors the other recognisable features (US 92 vi). There is also some indication of further alignment in a field adjacent to the enclosure, where it is visible upon another aerial photograph.[2]

The S.–N. main axis line appears to continue, running roughly N.N.E. along the plateau edge after climbing the slight incline N. of the enclosure (US 92 vii).

[1] Designated hillfort in *Br. Inv.* I (ii) (1986), (HF 19), pp. 47–8; the field walls are clearly visible upon Fig. 52, p. 48.
[2] *ibid.*, C.U.A.P., ARG 28.

Vaynor
SN 01 S.W. (US 92 i) (from 0239 1100 to 0240 1118); (US 92 ii) (from 0230 1125 to 0236 1127); (US 92 iii) (from 0227 1115 to 0240 1118); (US 92 iv) (from 0232 1111 to 0240 1112); (US 92 v) (from 0232 1118 to 0233 1121); (US 92 vi) (from 0232 1100 to 0247 1100); (US 92 vii) (from 0235 1132 to 0228 1146)

ii 90

(US 93) About 450 m S.W. of the summit of Garn Ddu, about 395–410 m above O.D., extending over a scree-covered terrace into the saddle of open marshy moorland, are ten cairns (most likely the result of land clearance); two, possibly three, enclosures (which may have been huts); and a stretch of ancient field wall.

(US 93 i) On level ground at the foot of Garn Ddu is a small enclosure 15 m in diameter, consisting of a circular bank up to 0.25 m high, of consolidated stones and boulders varying in width between 3 m wide on the N.E. and 12 m on the S. It is very indistinct for about 3 m of the circumference on the S.W., and this apparent gap may have been an entrance. Within the rubble-strewn interior it is possible to faintly distinguish a linear N.W.–S.E. scatter, possibly representing an original subdivision.

(US 93 ii) To the N.N.E. of (US 93 i) lies a small, well-defined oval enclosure 12.4 m E.–W. by 11.5 m. It is embanked to about 0.3 m high by

UNENCLOSED SETTLEMENTS

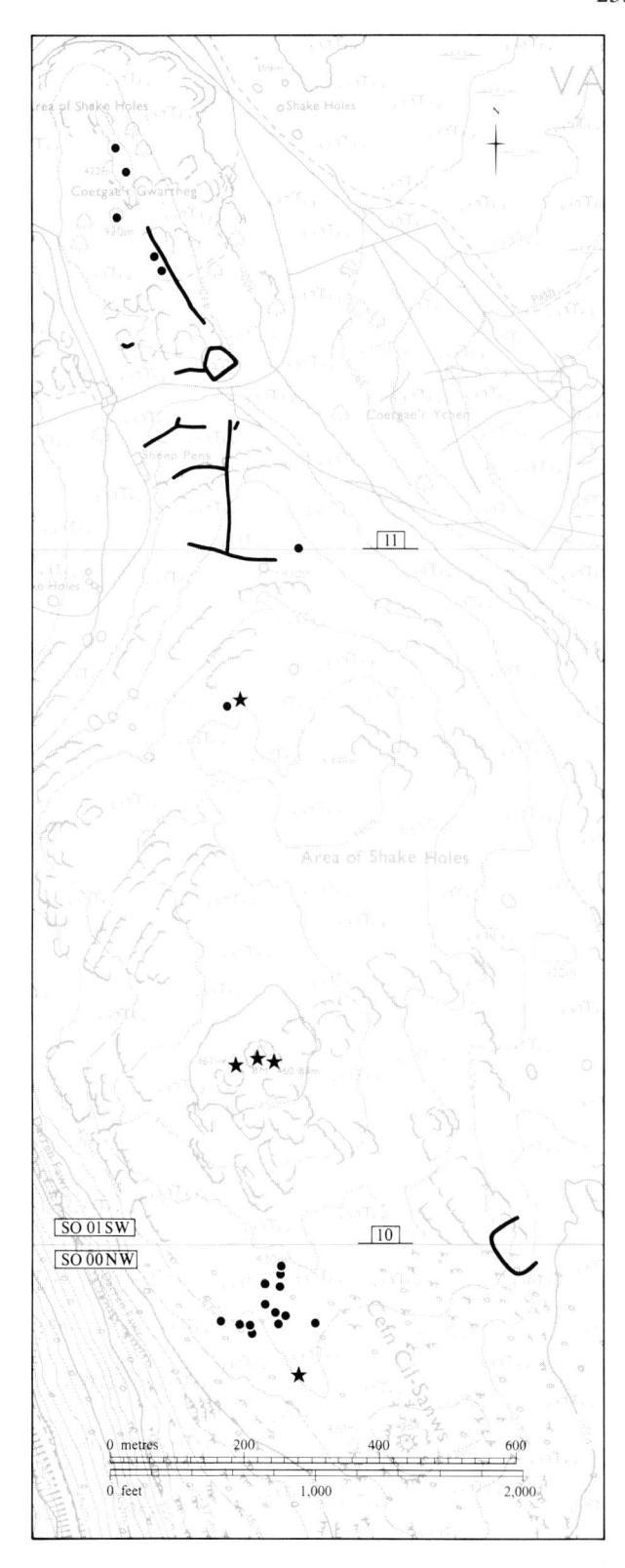

consolidated stones and boulders. A trench has been dug into the centre of the site from the outer edge, and there is a small rubble heap beside it on the W. This may have been either a cairn or a small hut-circle.

(US 93 iii) A round cairn 8 m in diameter and 0.5 m high, on the S. slope of Garn Ddu.

(US 93 iv) A cairn 3 m in diameter, 0.3 m high (on uphill side) and 0.9 m high (downhill side) lying on a steep scree slope, if not upon an extensive clearance area. This might be a relatively recent cairn.

(US 93 v) A pile of consolidated stones and earth 4 m by 3 m in diameter, and up to 0.3 m high.

(US 93 vi) An oval cairn of loose material over consolidated rubble 6 m E.–W. by 5 m, up to 0.4 m high.

(US 93 vii) On a terrace on the S.E.-facing slopes of Garn Ddu is a disturbed round cairn 7.7 m in diameter and 0.4 m high. There is a central shallow depression 1.5 m in diameter. The site is of grass consolidating stones and boulders, except where disturbed about 10 m to the N.W. of the cairn, where a length of bank can be seen in the form of rubble piled against the hillscarp. This is 2 m to 5 m wide and 8 m long, the inner chord 6 m wide. It is 0.4 m high, and is terminated by two boulders at the W. end.[1]

(US 93 viii) A stony mound 2.5 m long, 1 m wide and 0.2 m high with a large block set up at the N. end in the manner of a headstone.

(US 93 ix) A stony mound 3 m in diameter 0.3 m high.

(US 93 x) A stony mound 3 m in diameter 0.3 m high.

(US 93 xi) An oval stony mound 2.2 m by 1.6 m in diameter and 0.2 m high.

(US 93 xii) An L-shaped mound 3 m by 1 m and 0.2 m high.

(US 93 xiii) An oval mound 6.7 m (S.E.–N.W.) by 4.2 m and 0.4 m high.[2]

(US 93 xiv) A sinuous wall 77 m long, comprising a stone clearance pile 1.6 m wide and 0.3 m high, extending downslope along the terrace, terminating in marshy ground. Further stones protruding from the soil in this vicinity hint at its potential as an early field system, since the ground in this locality appears to be otherwise quite stone-free.

---

[1] Although the entire site has been described as 'a sub-circular enclosure, 21 m N.E.–S.W. by 18 m', (O.S. Card SO 01 SW 33) difficulty was experienced in confirming that suggestion.

[2] There seemed to be no evidence that it was 'half-constructed' (*cf.* O.S. Card SO 01 SW 33).

150 Cefn Cilnsanws cairns, enclosures and boundaries (US 92)

Vaynor
SO 01 S.W. (US 93 i) (0262 1188); (US 93 ii) (0261 1189); (US 93 iii) (0262 1196); (US 93 iv) (0257 1210); (US 93 v) (0257 1202); (US 93 vi) (0268 1201); (US 93 vii) (0278 1203); (US 93 viii) (0265 1200); (US 93 ix) (0266 1193); (US 93 x) (0268 1193); (US 93 xi) (0269 1194); (US 93 xii) (0270 1195); (US 93 xiii) (0264 1191); (US 93 xiv) (from 0269 1203 to 0273 1197)   31 viii 82

(US 94) On the W. slope of Garn Ddu, on moderately sloping ground some 410 m above O.D. between two small streams, are two lengths of bank.

(US 94 i) A penannular bank, open on the S. and enclosing an area of consolidated rubble, overlain by more obviously loose material against the N.E. bank. It has an overall diameter of 8.5 m, the bank 0.35 m high, 1 m wide on the E., and 1.7 m on the W.

(US 94 ii) About 25 m N.E. of (US 94 i) is a gently curving stone and boulder bank capped with some loose rubble. It is about 25 m long, 3 m wide and 0.3 m high, forming an arc, the chord of which is 23 m.

(US 94 iii) A horseshoe-shaped rush-grown enclosure, open on the S. and lying on the side of a hollow on the W. slope of Garn Ddu. It is composed of consolidated rubble about 2.5 m to 3 m wide and 0.3 m high, with a narrow gap on the N.E. corner and measures 12.6 m N.–S. by 10 m. About 30 m to the E., on the other side of the hollow, is a ruined building with substantial upstanding drystone walls.

(US 94 iv) Occupying a slight eminence on the W. slope of Garn Ddu are the vestiges of a cairn, now 2.5 m in diameter, though surrounded by a scatter of consolidated rubble. Whether originally sepulchral or agricultural, this feature has probably been robbed out to build the upstanding structure mentioned above (US 94 iii).

(US 94 v) On the N.W. slope of Garn Ddu, before its steep dip into Nant Car, is a stone pile 7 m E.–W. by 5 m, about 0.2 m high. There are other similar piles in the vicinity.

Vaynor
SO 01 S.W. (US 94 i) (0206 1227); (US 94 ii) (0208 1229); (US 94 iii) (0211 1230); (US 94 iv) (0214 1232); (US 94 v) (0217 1238)   11 vii 82

(US 95; Figs 151–60) On the spur between two tributaries of the Afon Taf, the Nant Gwineu and Nant Car, lying between 375 and 430 m above O.D. is a series of clearances, huts and enclosures, some closely grouped, others more dispersed.[1]

(US 95 i) On a gentle slope, 375 m above O.D., about 200 m to the S.W. of (US 95 iv) is a cairn field[8] comprising 19 clearance mounds from 3 m to 8.5 m in diameter, and from 0.3 m to 0.75 m high, of irregular size and shape. The group lies on a slight plateau sloping S., the upper part surrounded by outcropping rock and scree, difficult to distinguish from deliberately gathered stone. Indeed, the stone comprising natural features here tends to be of a similar grade to that of field clearance.

(US 95 ii) About 600 m N.N.E. of (US 95 i) lies a group of three, possibly four, hut-circles (Fig. 153),[2] ranging from 6 to 11 m in diameter. Adjacent to them are three or four heaps of fieldstone, grouped together upon a broad shelf towards the E. end of Cefn Car. To their W. and apparently comprising a part of this group, lies a putative 'platform' house, 3 m by 3 m. The huts appear to lack entrances.

(US 95 iii; Figs 154–5) Some 200 m to the E. of the clearance cairns (US 95 i) lies a fallen, collapsed, semi-annular enclosure wall about 2 m wide and 0.3 m high, the N. part runs from the N.N.E. for about 30 m, then it turns downslope N.–S. 30 m, then S.S.E. c. 20 m. Its southern termination takes the form of a roughly triangular paddock. Incorporated into the wall about halfway down the slope are two smaller enclosures, one each side of the wall, together with a field clearance cairn, inside, on the E. Apparently incorporated into this settlement are two nearby excavations reminiscent of platform houses, one oblong, the other circular with a further nearby field clearance cairn.

(US 95 iv–vii; Fig. 151) The most extensive group of enclosures occupies the arc of a S.-facing spur to the S.E. of (US 95 ii).[3] This comprises the remains of seven structures, which may have been dwelling huts or animal pens. The most westerly (US 95 iv) is circular and 7.5 m in diameter, open on the E., with two conjoined, roughly circular features c. 20 m in diameter (US 95 v; Fig. 156), with walls up to 3 m thick immediately to the N. Protruding from the N. wall joining the two sites is a small penannular structure reminiscent of a hut-circle. The original entrance to the more southerly enclosure appears to have been on the E., or possibly on the N.E.

The next site (US 95 vi) is morphologically the most interesting. Described as a 'probable courtyard house with walls up to 4 m thick, roughly triangular in plan and measuring 26 m along the S. side and 28 m from

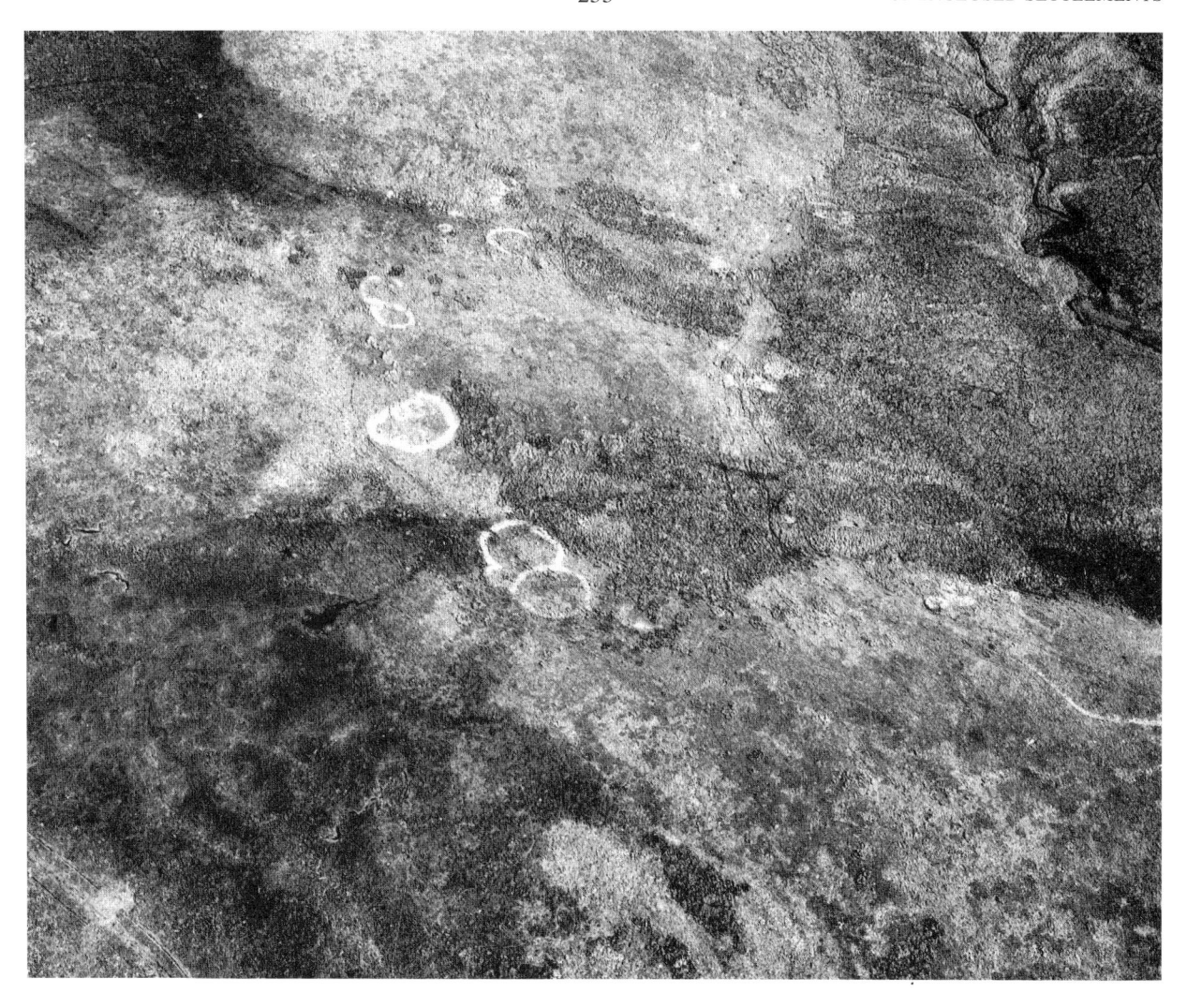

151 Cefn Car: hut circles and enclosures (US 95 iv–x) (CUAP CEQ 60)

base to apex',[4] it houses five oval or circular huts of the thick-walled oval homestead type,[5] or of class IVb.[6]

Further E. lies a tadpole-shaped enclosure[7] (US 95 vii; Figs 157–8) aligned roughly body W., tail to E., with a detached stretch of wall to the S. The detached circle or 'body' is 10 m in diameter and the incomplete circle or 'tail', 12 m in diameter, with walls up to 3 m thick.

About 80 m S.S.E. is an outlying sub-group (US 95 viii–x; Fig. 159) comprising three further huts,[8] the most northerly (US 95 viii), a small oval measuring 4.5 m by 3 m. Downslope and S. of it lies an oval enclosure (US 95 ix) 16 m N.–S. by 14.3 m transversely (internal).

Adjacent, along the S. of the site is a quarry feature, probably a platform hut site, which is enclosed by a further wall, roughly 12 m long. The group is completed by a small hut-circle (US 95 x) on the E., of roughly 7.5 m in overall diameter, the walls roughly 2.5 m wide, and about 0.4 m high. Immediately to the N. is a short trace of a linear band about 1 m wide.

The most northwesterly site comprises two enclosures, one D-shaped (US 95 xi),[9] some 30–32 m in diameter, the entrance at the narrow, eastern end, a western 'tail' or wall up to 0.3 m high and 24 m long, suggestive of further, continuous field or garden

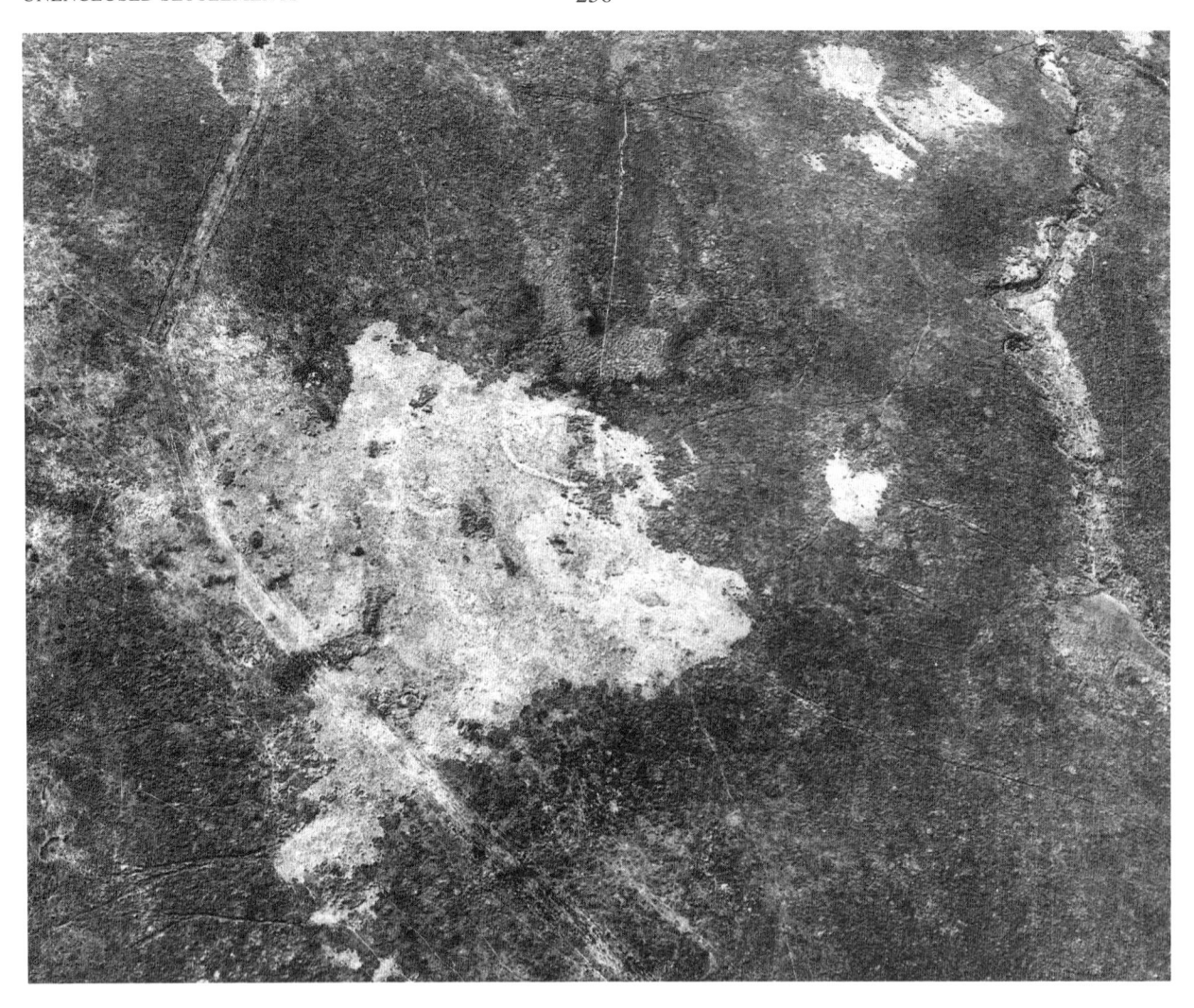

152   Cefn Car: early enclosures (US 95) (CUAP CEQ 63)

enclosure. Immediately to its S. there are two further features, the more easterly, a smaller enclosure about 11 m in diameter with walls up to 0.5 m high, which resembles a hut (US 95 xii; Fig. 160). This appears to lack an entrance, but it is possible to suggest there may be a collapsed inturned entrance on the N.W., and possibly a fireplace site on the N.E., distinguishable within the irregular rubble interior. The remaining feature of this group is an 'S'-shaped sinuous wall, lying between the enclosure and the hut.

There are two 'longhouse' sites with remains of a fugitive enclosure wall, presumed to be of medieval origin, lying to the S. of (US 95 x).[10]

[1] These sites were independently noted from field walking by the Merthyr Naturalists' Society (from about 1970); by the Ordnance Survey Antiquities Division (initially from aerial photographs A.P.s, R.A.F. F21 58/3609/0243–4 in 1973 (O.S. Card SO 01 SW 10); and also by Prof. J. K. St. Joseph, who overflew the area during the mid-1970s (C.U.A.P., A.P.s, CEQ 60–66). The site is discussed by C.S. Briggs in *Upland Settlement*, pp. 287–9, 308–9, Figs. 15.2–3.
[2] O.S. Card SO 01 SW 24.
[3] O.S. Card SO 01 SW 10; visible on A.P.s, R.A.F. F21 58/3609/0243–4; 20 vi 60.
[4] By Mr D. R. Bark on O.S. Card SO 01 SW 10; 28 vii 76.
[5] *Inv. Caerns.* III, (1964), p. xcix.
[6] N. Johnson, *B.B.C.S.* 29 (1981), pp. 381–417; p. 391.
[7] Found by Mr D. R. Bark; O.S. Card SO 01 SW 23.
[8] O.S. Card SO 01 SW 9; visible on A.P.s, R.A.F.,

CPE/UK/2075/1077–8; 19 v 47; D. P. Webley, *B.B.C.S.* 17 (1957), pp. 117–18; p. 117; see also H. E. Roese, *Thesis*.

[9] O.S. Card SO 01 SW 11.
[10] O.S. Card SO 01 SW 25; at SO 0239 1317.

Vaynor

SO 01 S.W. (US 95 i) (0195 1293–0217 1307); (US 95 ii) (0208 1350); (US 95 iii) (0215 1306); (US 95 iv) (0215 1322); (US 95 v) (0217 1325); (US 95 vi) (0224 1329); (US 95 vii) (0209 1330); (US 95 viii) (0234 1328); (US 95 ix) (0234 1326); (US 95 x) (0237 1326); (US 95 xi) (0236 1366); (US 95 xii) (0239 1362)

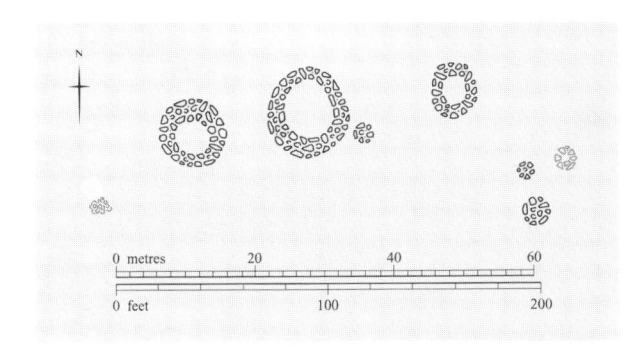

153 Cefn Car: hut-circles or cairns and clearances (US 95 ii)   18 v 87

154 Cefn Car: early wall and enclosures (US 95 iii) (CUAP CEQ 66)

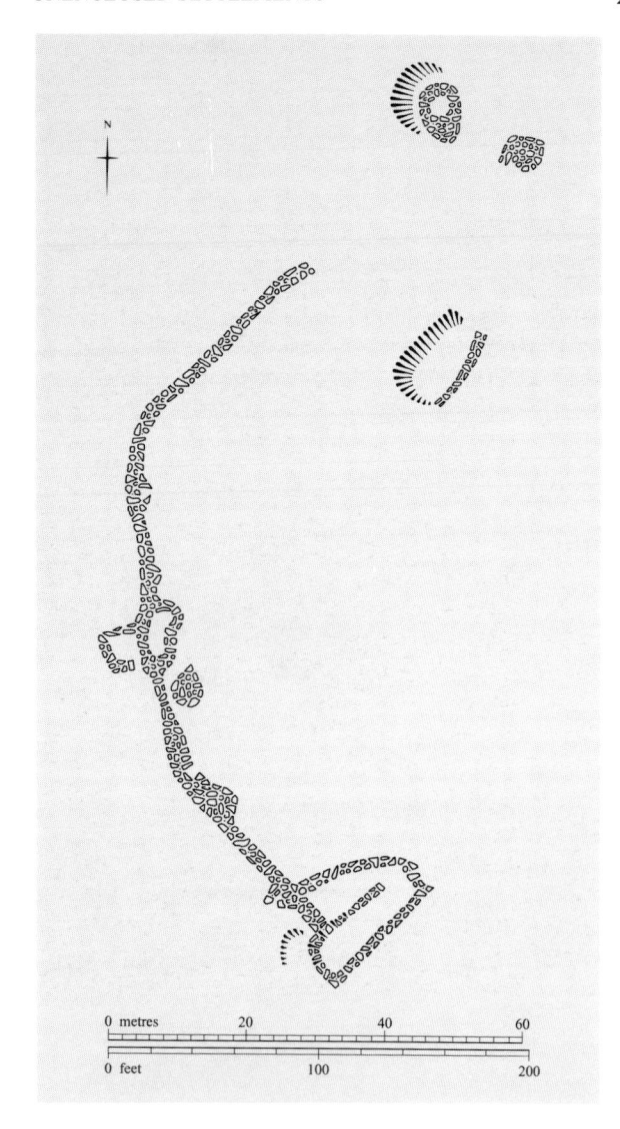

UNENCLOSED SETTLEMENTS

155 Cefn Car: wall and enclosures (US 95 iii)

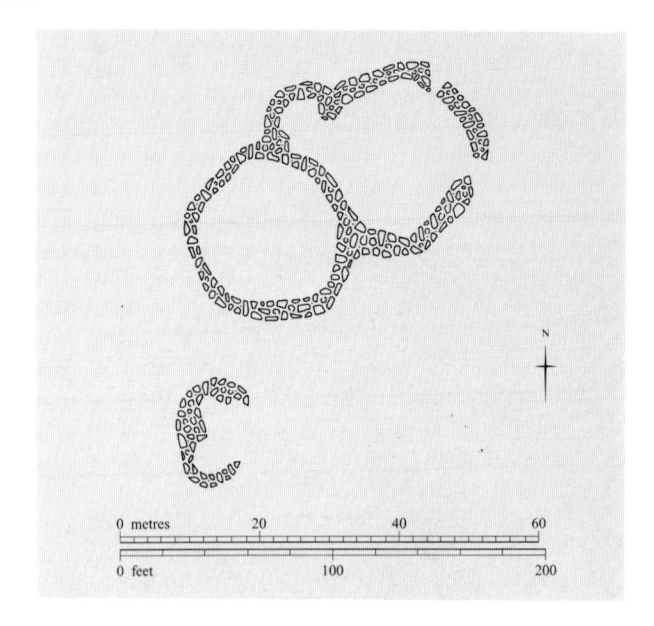

156 Cefn Car: enclosures (US 95 iv–v)

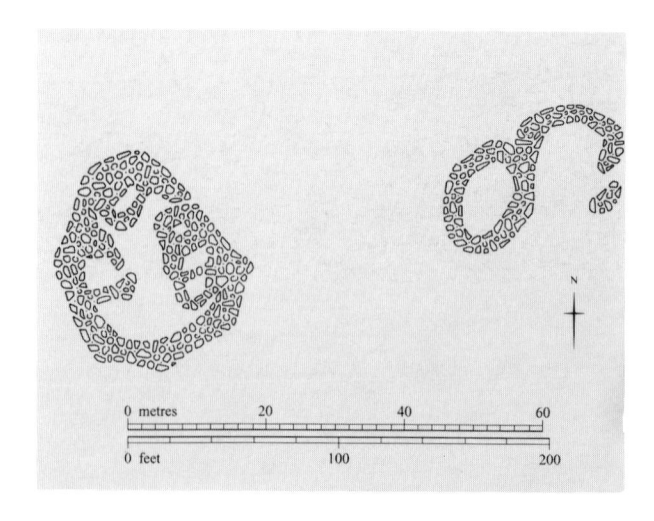

157 Cefn Car: complex hut and tadpole-shaped enclosure (US 95 vi–vii)

(US 96; Fig. 161) Close to the source of the Glais Brook, lying around 370–380 m above O.D., is a series of clearance cairns, platforms and stony banks, making up a fugitive field system.[1] These features occupy the S.-W.-facing slope of a spur on the W. bank of a stream, on the opposite, E. side of which is the ruined farmhouse of Cwm Moel.

It seems unlikely that these clearances are nineteenth century,[2] although a historic date is possible for its currency. The field system is not depicted upon the Tithe Award Map for Vaynor of c. 1845[3] and probing at the N. end of the site demonstrates that the walls disappear beneath a peat cover, though this need not be of any great antiquity.

(US 96 i) The main enclosure is roughly rectangular, 75 m N.W.–S.E. by 35 m, and is bounded by a discontinuous wall up to 4 m wide and 0.5 m high. Beyond its N.W. end a number of short lengths of bank hint at the presence of an annex which could have measured up to 65 m by 50 m.

158 Cefn Car: looking S.W. into 'tadpole-shaped enclosure' (US 95: vii)

(US 96 ii) Lying close to the site are some 39 cairns, mainly stony clearance mounds of variable shape and size, between 2.5 m and 11 m across and standing up to 0.3 m high. Some actually lie within the enclosure, though most are concentrated in two groups to its N.W. and S.E, upon the plateau or terrace lying alongside the stream.

A short distance to the W. of the enclosure and cairns are two platforms cut into the E.-facing slope above Nant Moel.

(US 96 iii) One platform is 9 m N.–S. by 4.5 m, scooped out 0.6 m and built up on the outside to 0.2 m.

(US 96 iv) The other, which lies 22 m W. of (US 96 iii), is better defined and measures 10 m N.E.–S.W. by 7 m, cut back to a depth of 0.75 m and built out to 0.4 m high. There is a third possible platform between the two, though this is very poorly defined.

[1] First mentioned in *The Story of Merthyr Tydfil*, (Cardiff, 1932), p. 38; visible on A.P.s, R.A.F./CPE/UK/2079/1077–8; 19 v 47; D. P. Webley, *B.B.C.S.* 17 (1957), pp. 117–118; Roese, *Thesis*, no. 117.

[2] As suggested on O.S. Card SO 01 SW 9.

[3] in N.L.W., Dept. of Maps and Prints.

Vaynor
SO 01 S.W. (US 96 i) (centred upon 0365 1149); (US 96 ii) (centred upon 0366 1144); (US 96 iii) (0370 1156); (US 96 iv) (0367 1156)   20 v 87

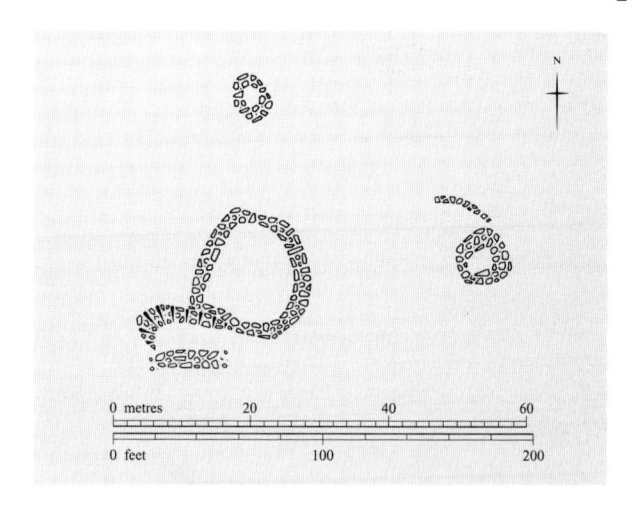

159 Cefn Car: huts and enclosure (US 95 viii–x)

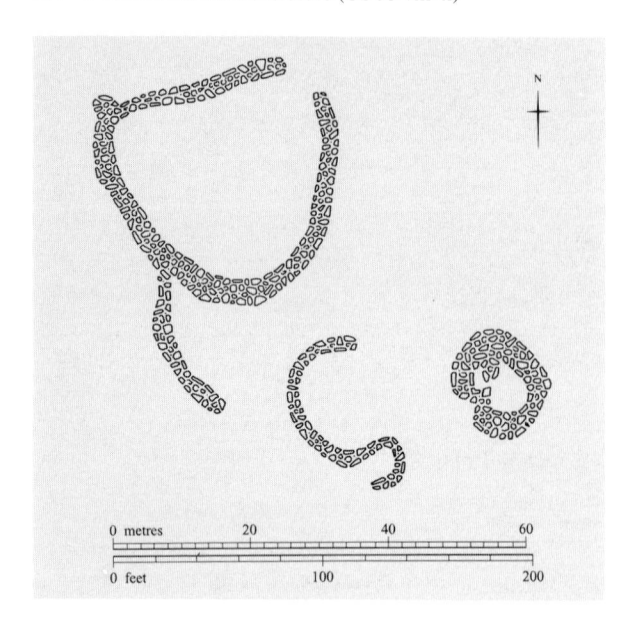

160 Cefn Car: enclosures and hut (US 95 xii)

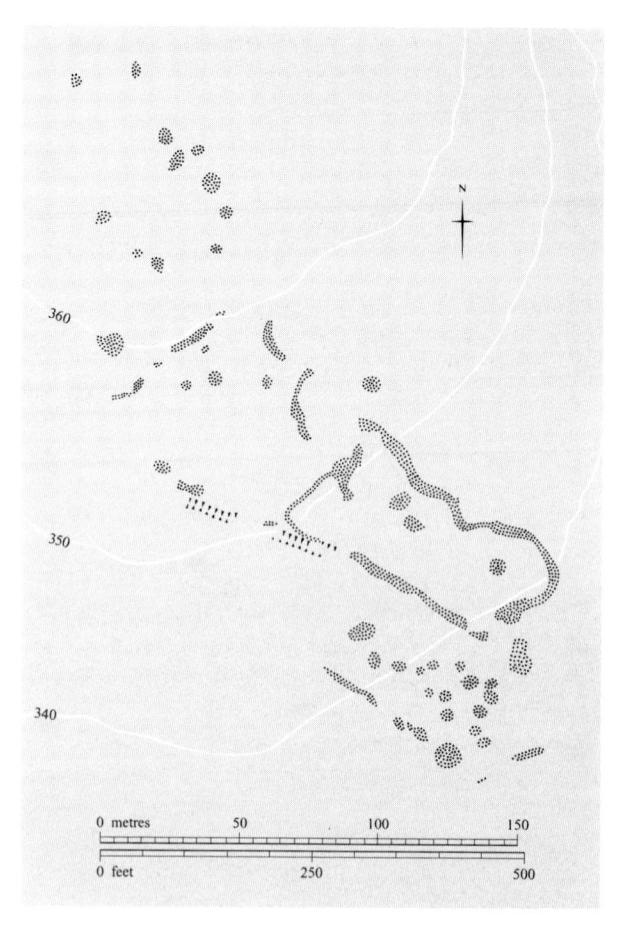

161 Cwm Moel field system and agricultural clearances (US 96)

(US 97) About 500 m S.E. of Garn Ddu on level ground about 380 m above O.D. is an irregular stone pile and a short length of walling. The stone pile has a basically 'figure of eight' configuration and measures 14 m (E.–W.) by 5 m. It is composed of mixed grade stones with some large boulders and stands about 0.25 m high. Immediately to the E. is some walling 5 m long (E.–W.), 1.5 m wide and 0.4 m high. This is of stone blocks and small boulders.

Vaynor
SO 01 S.W. (US 97) (0380 1216)   29 vii 82

(US 98) North of Garn Pontsticill, 380 m above O.D., are five cairns and three dubious smaller mounds. With the exception of (US 98 i) they are aligned (N.–S.) about 130 m long on the broad crest of a slight swelling of the moor. (US 98 i) lies on slightly higher ground some 80 m to the S.W.

(US 98 i) A roughly circular cairn some 5.8 m in diameter and 0.45 m high at the centre.

(US 98 ii) Another roughly circular cairn 6.1 m in diameter and 0.3 m high.

(US 98 iii) An oval cairn 5.8 m long (N.E.–S.W.) by 4.6 m wide and 0.3 m high.

(US 98 iv) A circular cairn 3.4 m in diameter and 0.3 m high.

(US 98 v) A ring cairn, externally 16.2 m in diameter, the stony surrounding bank 1–1.5 m wide and 0.3 m high.

Close to (US 98 v) and (US 98 vi) are three tiny stone mounds of unknown significance.

O.S. SO 01 NE 17; P. M. Jones, *Arch. in Wales* 18 (1978), p. 32, no. 11.

Vaynor
SO 01 S.E. (US 98 i) (0520 1160); (US 98 ii) (0527 1165); (US 98 iii) (0526 1168); (US 98 iv) (0528 1176); (US 98 v) (0527 1177)   9 iv 80

(US 99; Fig. 162) On the W. of Craig y Llwyni, overlooked by an old discontinuous boundary wall on the N. side of the stream and occupying ground between the Old Limekilns and Old Sheepfolds marked on the O.S. 1:50,000 map, but closer to the former than the latter, are a number of cairns, fugitive walls and clearances. These are variously shaped and sited, some more regular and circular, others ill-defined. The group is bifurcated by the E.–W. track of a nineteenth-century mineral railway (presumably for lime), and to the E., the site is overlain by a quarry tip, presumably of overburden removed during limestone extraction.

(US 99 i) Within the natural scree-lain escarpment overlooking the stream to its N., is a circular hut, 3 m in diameter, lying on a slight shelf within the slope, open on the N.E.

(US 99 ii) Close to (US 99 i) and lying at right angles to the hill is a U-shaped structure about 5 m long, and 3.5–4 m wide internally, a little like a reversed shooting butt, barely discernible among the scree. Its walls, of stones up to 1 m long, are 1 m thick and almost 1 m high.

(US 99 iii) The northern, downslope margin of the cleared ground, overlooking the stream to its N., is covered in swathes of small grade stones among larger boulders for a distance of about 110 m. This line continues to the S.W. as a quarry face about 4 m deep. On the N.E. the clearance feature peters away beyond the hut sites (US 99 i) and (US 99 ii).

(US 99 iiia) One is possibly a clearance cairn, about 6 m in diameter, 0.5 m high, all of small grade stone.

(US 99 iv) An ill-defined stony eminence about 4 m in diameter.

(US 99 v) On a slight platform, adjacent to the tramway embankment, and separated from it by only 3 m, is a penannular grouping of 6–8 stones open on the N. and about 4 m from N.–S. The stones stand no more than 0.3 m long and the more westerly are buried edgewise in the ground. It seems most likely to have been a hut, though might be a kerb cairn.

(US 99 vi) A fugitive grass-grown vaccinium covered wall, travelling E. by S. uphill for about 30 m.

(US 99 vii) A boulder clearance cairn 6 m long by 5 m wide.

(US 99 viii) A boulder clearance cairn 7 m long (E.–W.) and varying from 3 to 6 m wide.

(US 99 ix) An overgrown cairn, 4–5 m in diameter, the hollow centre exposed, possibly robbed for its limestone content.

(US 99 x) A small cairn, elongated E.–W., 6 m by 5 m.

(US 99 xi) A partly overgrown boulder cairn about 7 m in diameter and 0.25 m high.

(US 99 xii) A handful of boulders, possibly having been a cairn, but truncated by the tramway.

(US 99 xiii) A cairn of bilberry-covered fieldstones with a few boulders 9 m long E.–W. by 5 m wide. The centre appears to be robbed.

(US 99 xiv) A large area of boulders and fieldstones about 30 m across (E.–W.) by 25 m (N.–S.), possibly all that remains of a settlement site. There is a swathe of stone, possibly a wall, about 10 m long (N.N.E.–S.S.W.) appointed to this clearance mass, and parallel to it.

(US 99 xv) A loose scatter of stone giving the impression, possibly illusory, of a wall.

(US 99 xvi) and (US 99 xvii) are boulder scatters up to 3 m in diameter.

(US 99 xviii) A scatter of large stones, about 8 m E.–W. and 3.5 m N.–S. This appears to be part of a linear feature travelling downhill on the W.

(US 99 xix) A narrow swathe of fieldstones, probably a wall, about 23 m long, accentuated by summer vegetational growth.

(US 99 xx) A linear, wall-like clearance feature.

(US 99 xxi) Two small scatters of limestone boulder, possibly associated with quarrying.

(US 99 xxii) A small cairn elongated N.–S., 2.5 m long, 1 m wide and 0.2 m high.

(US 99 xxiii) A triangular-shaped clearance cairn, 5 m by 9 m by 7 m, though rather dispersed and ill-defined.

(US 99 xxiv) An elongated cairn of fieldstones 5.6 m E.–W. by 9 m long (N.–S.), overlooking the stream to N.

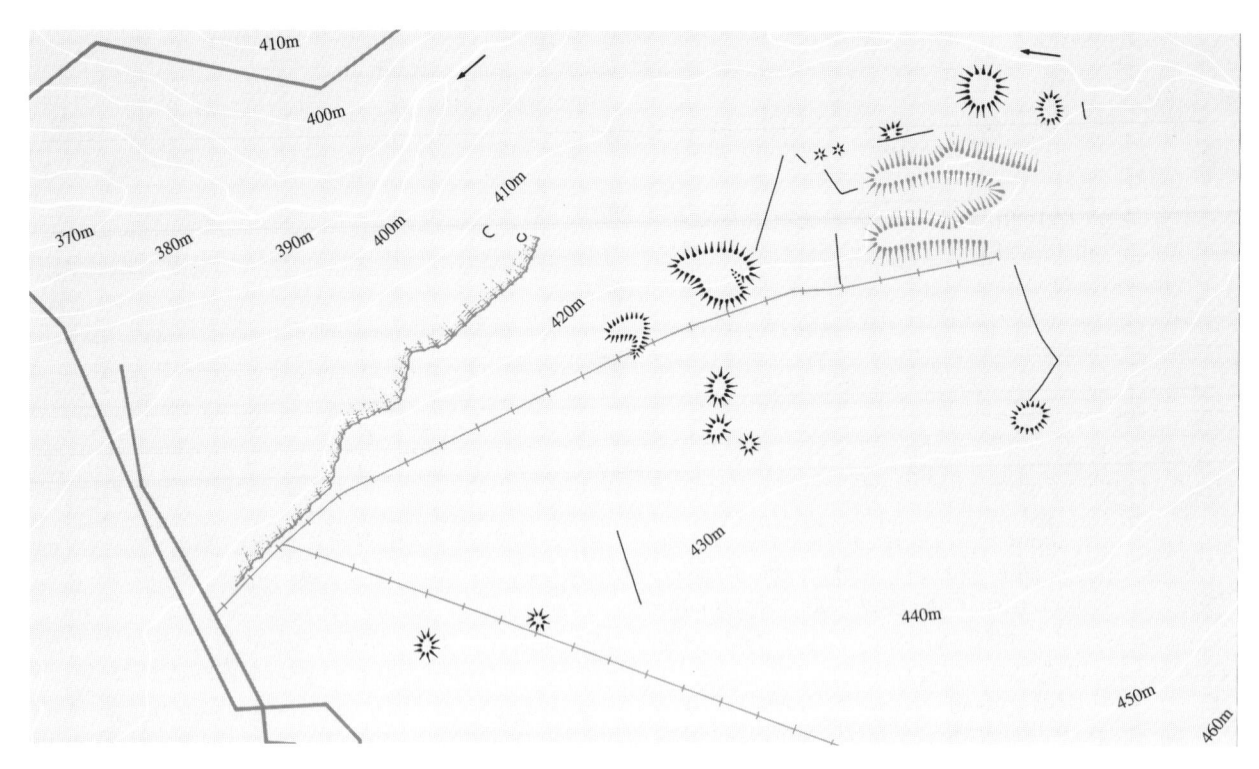

162 Craig y Llwyni clearances, showing early mineral railway (US 99)

(US 99 xxv) A similar clearance cairn 5 m long by 2 m wide, which may pass beneath tipped overburden from the limestone quarrying.

(US 99 xxvi) A fugitive dogleg length of wall some 60 m long (N. stretch running W. by N.–E. by S.; S. stretch E. by N.–W. by S.).

(US 99 xxvii) At the S. end is a limestone boulder spread on an axis of about 12 m N.N.E. by 10 m N.N.W.–S.S.E.

First noted by B. O'Hanlan of Merthyr Tydfil; C. S. Briggs, *Arch. in Wales* 26 (1986), p. 61.

Llanddeti

SO 01 S.E. (US 99 i) (0663 1290); (US 99 ii) (0665 1289); (US 99 iii) (from 0659 1283 to 0666 1289); (US 99 iv) (0662 1275); (US 99 v) (US 99 vi) (0669 1279 to 0669 1276); (US 99 vii) (0668 1282); (US 99 viii) (0669 1283); (US 99 ix) (0674 1282); (US 99 x) (0673 1283); (US 99 xi) (0673 1284); (US 99 xii) (0669 1286); (US 99 xiii) (0669 1286); (US 99 xiv) (0672 1288); (US 99 xv) (0675 1293 to 0675 1292); (US 99 xvi) (0676 1292); (US 99 xvii) (0677 1292); (US 99 xviii) (0676 1291 to 0677 1291); (US 99 xix) (0677 1289 to 0676 1287); (US 99 xx) (0678 1292 to 0680 1293); (US 99 xxi) (0680 1289); (US 99 xxii) (0677 1291); (US 99 xxiii) (0682 1294); (US 99 xxiv) (0684 1293); (US 99 xxv) (0685 1294 to 0686 1293); (US 99 xxvi) (0683 1288 to 0685 1285 to 0683 1283); (US 99 xxvii) (0684 1283)   iii 1990

(US 100) There are two small enclosures lying along the Cwar yr Hendre ridge 565 m above O.D. on the northern S.-facing slope of a dry valley.

(US 100 i) The first is a square enclosure of large limestone boulders about 30 m by 12 m with walls upstanding to *c*. 1 m. It appears to incorporate a hut-circle in the N.W. corner. Some 30 m to the E. of the eastern enclosure wall is a cave entrance from which it is said bovid remains were recovered, which are now at the N.M.W.

(US 100 ii) About 300 m S.E. of the above, on sloping ground under the shelter of a scarp, lies a similar, smaller embanked enclosure, elliptical in form and *c*. 8 m by 10 m. There appears to be an internal hut platform, rectangular (*c*. 3 m by 2 m), built against the upper (scarp-edge) wall.

Noted by P. M. Jones of Tredegar

Llanddeti
SO 01 S.E. (US 100 i) (0890 1385); (US 100 ii) (0905 1376) (100 i only) 88

(US 101; Fig. 163) Straddling the county boundary with Monmouthshire along Cefnpyllauduon at a height of 550 m above O.D. is a handful of limestone boulder features of forms suggesting field clearance and settlement. These are:

(US 101 i) A circular stony mound 4.3 m in diameter and 0.6 m high.

(US 101 ii) About 75 m S.E. is a circular mound 5 m in diameter and 0.3 m high, in the form of two concentric arcs.

(US 101 iii) About 55 m N.W. of (US 101 ii) is a roughly oval enclosure 7.5 m (N.–S.) by 7.3 m, open on the E. side. It consists of a stony bank consolidated by vegetation, 0.3 m high and 1–1.5 m wide. The nature of gaps in the bank is unclear.

(US 101 iv) Between cairns (US 101 i) and (US 101 v) is an irregularly-shaped stone pile which may be incorporated into the bank of a small enclosure network.

(US 101 v) On Twyn Ceiliog is a disturbed cairn about 2.7 m in diameter and 0.45 m high. This may have been built as a modern boundary cairn.

(US 101 vi) Between (US 101 v) and (US 101 vii) is a short length of consolidated stony bank about 7 m (E.–W.) by 2 m and 0.3 m high.

(US 101 vii) A much disturbed cairn about 7.6 m in diameter and 0.9 m high, with an irregularly-shaped central robber trench. It appears to have formed the western part of a larger cairn about 11 m in diameter and 1.2 m high (on the N.E.), though it is largely obscured by heather.

(US 101 viii) A low, circular cairn about 5.2 m in diameter and 0.45 m high with traces of central disturbance.

(US 101 ix) On the edge of a slight declivity on the

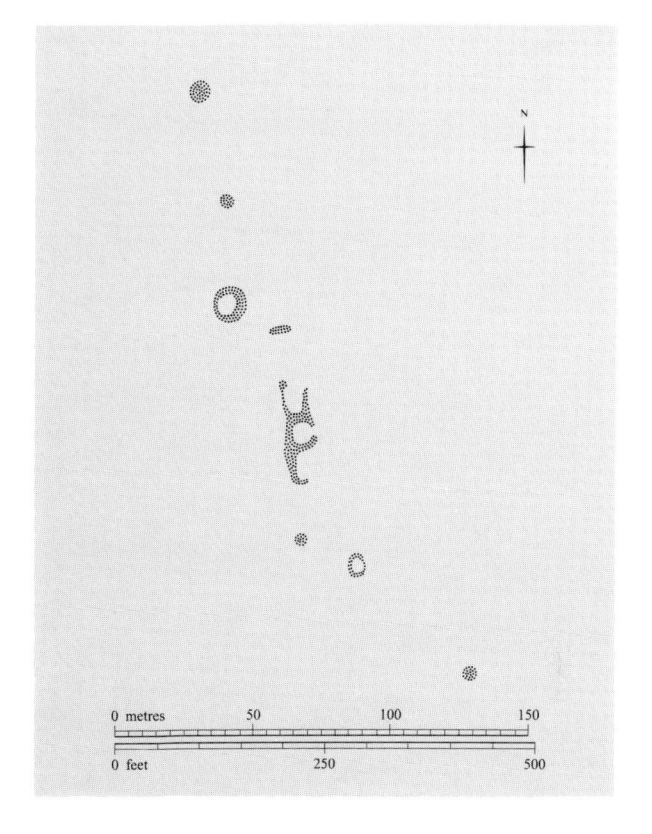

163   Cefnpyllauduon cairns and clearances (US 101)

N. is a further possible cairn, about 7.3 m in diameter. It is occupied centrally by a large robber crater, around the edge of which stones are piled to a height of 0.6 m.

Twyn Ceiliog is noted by Roese, *Thesis*, no. 134.

Llangynidr
SO 01 S.E. (US 101 i) (0988 1269); (US 101 v) (0988 1275); (US 101 vi); (US 101 vii) (0988 1279); (US 101 viii) (0988 1282); (US 101 ix)
(0988 1287)   22 ix 82

SO 11

(US 102; Fig. 164) Close to the junction of the old track climbing from Llangynidr to Trefil at Cwm Pyrgad is a series of clearances and enclosures lying upon a heath- and reed-grown plateau.

On a projecting spur of moorland between the upper reaches of Nant Pyrgad and a minor stream are settlement remains comprising three stretches of walling, a platform, embanked enclosures and a hut-circle within an area 170 m square. The settlement lies between 420 m and 460 m above O.D. on land sloping away towards the west.

(US 102 i) Bounding the N. edge of the area, overlooking the steep fall to Nant Pyrgad, is a collapsed wall 165 m in length, spread to 2 m wide and 0.3 m high.

(US 102 ii) Bounding the E. end of the site is a

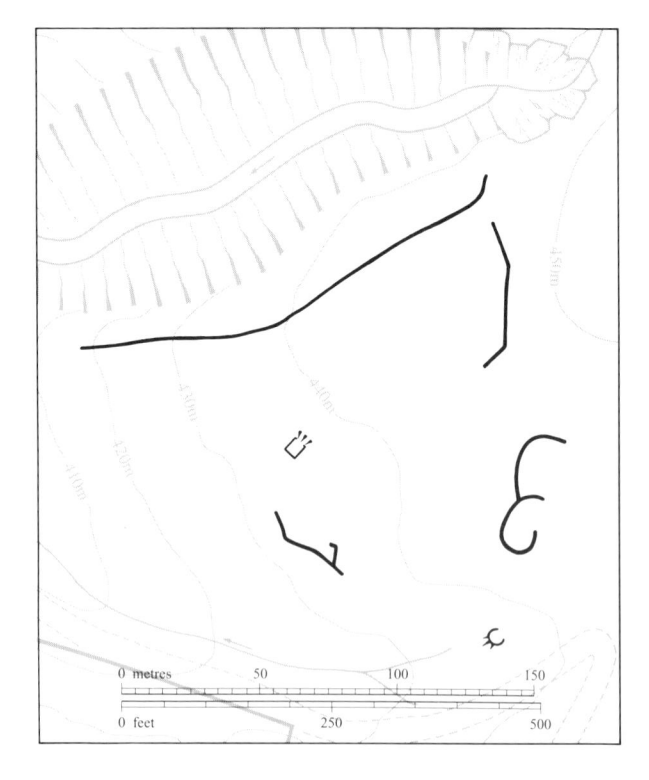

164 Cwm Pyrgad settlement features (US 102): plan

length of stony bank, oriented N.–S., 55 m long and spread to 2 m wide and 0.3 m high.

(US 102 iii) To the S. of this are two conjoined C-shaped banks, open to the E., the more northerly measuring 21 m N.–S. by 14 m overall and the other 21 m N.–S. by 12 m. The banks are stony, between 1.3 and 2.0 m wide and up to 0.3 m high.

(US 102 iv) To the S. of these, immediately E. of a spring, is a hut-circle terraced into the W.-facing slope. It measures 8.0 m E.–W. by 5.5 m overall; the internal area is 5.0 m E.–W. by 3.0 m and the enclosing bank, incorporating stones up to 0.6 m long, rises to 0.3 m above floor level.

(US 102 v) To the N.W. is a stony bank 35 m long, oriented N.W.–S.E. It is spread to 2 m wide in parts and stands to 0.3 m high; remains of an L-shaped wall 7.0 m N.–S. by 3.0 m adjoin the N. side.

(US 102 vi) To the N. is a stone-edged platform measuring 5.1 m N.W.–S.E. by 5.4 m. It is terraced into the slope 0.9 m deep on the N.E. and built up to 0.6 m high on the S.W.

Llangynidr
SO 11 N.W. (US 102 i) (1080 1547–1095 1553); (US 102 ii) (1095 1546–1095 1551); (US 102 iii) (1097 1542); (US 102 iv) (1096 1537); (US 102 v) (1089 1540); (US 102 vi) (1088 1543)   11 xii 91

(US 103) Lying on a slight declivity in a depression on the well-quarried S. side of Clo Cadno at about 500 m above O.D. is an almost square, low stony bank, of limestone and sandstone boulders 20 m from N. to S. (the W. bank quite rounded), 26.2 m along the N. and 27.2 m along the S. It encloses a heath-covered area with a small hut-like enclosure 6.5 m by 4 m midway along the E. side. A similar, though more fugitive enclosure, 4.6 m long by 3 m wide lies midway along the S. side. The site's antiquity appears to pre-date lime-workings scarring the ground immediately to its W., and the presence of excavated boulders on the S.W. hint that in their industry the lime-workers ignored surface limestone boulders and used only quarried material.

Found in 1988 by P. M. Jones, Tredegar.

Llangynidr
SO 11 N.W. (1175 1625) approx.   7 vi 89

(US 104) On the S. slope of Clo Cadno falling towards the dry valley and set just below the exposed limestone outcrop at about 486 m above O.D. is an enclosure almost exactly 12.3 m square externally, set within a boulder stone bank about 2 m wide and up to 0.75 m high. Some 2 m to the W. but aligned with and adjacent to it is a house site some 8 m long (N.–S.) by 5 m wide (E.–W.) apparently of both quarried stone and fieldstone.

Noted by P. M. Jones of Tredegar.

Llangynidr
SO 11 N.W. (1186 1690)   7 vi 89

(US 105; Pl. 7) A low stone bank crosses Llangynidr Common, covering a distance of about 1 km in a roughly S.S.E.–N.N.W. direction crossing land lying between about 490 and 515 m above O.D.

The size and lithology of component boulders varies throughout its length; in general they appear to reflect the material of outcropping rock and contents of local boulder clay. In some places it resembles a wall and stands up to 0.8 m high, and may be widespread over 2.5 m of ground. A remarkable, though by no means unique aspect of this feature is its behaviour in relation to superficial geology and soil. Whereas there are considerable stretches of apparently undisturbed linear rubble, in places the wall seems to occupy low troughs,

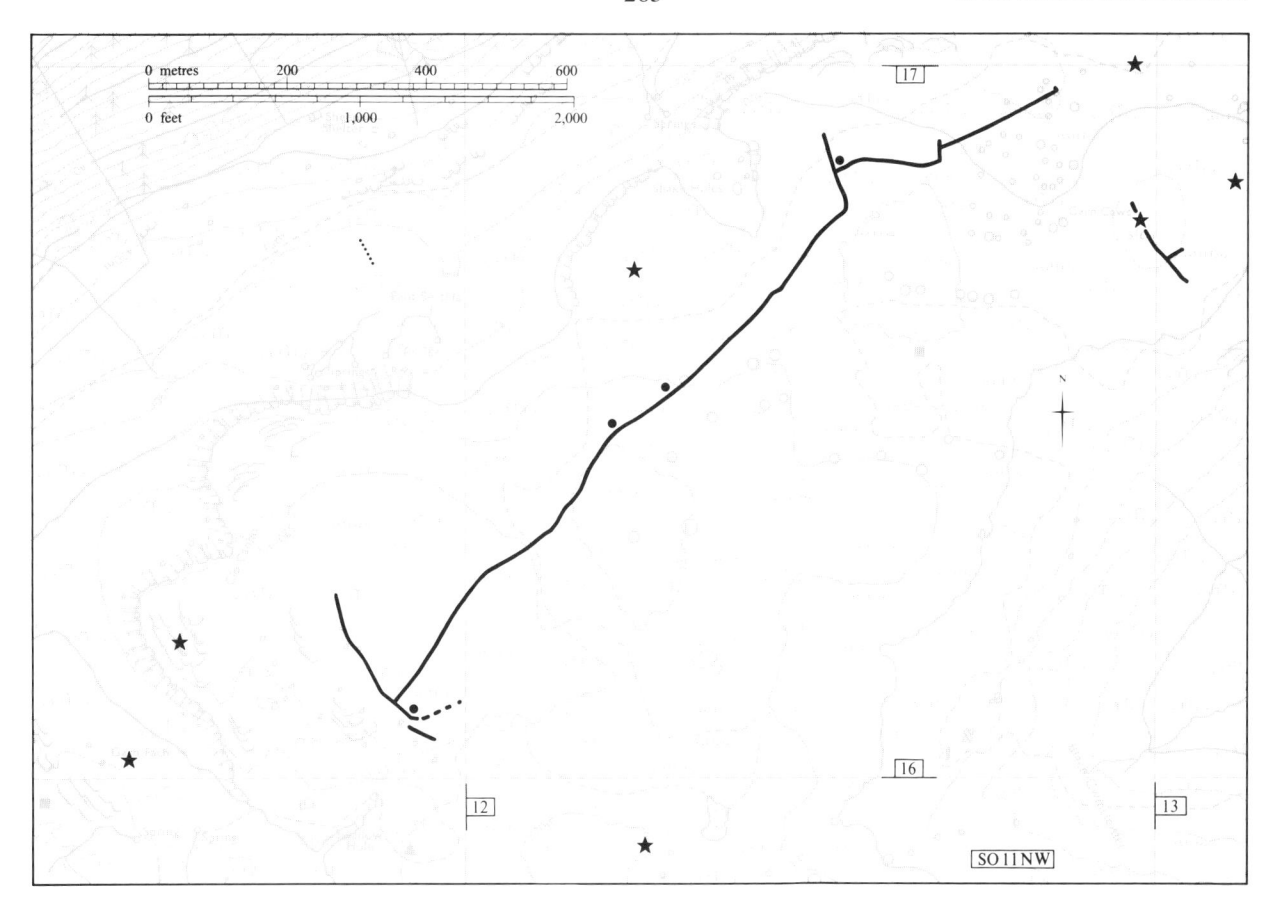

165 Trefil Area: wall or boundary (US 105) running over limestone solution features to Carn Caws with several enclosures

almost as if excavated into the earth. In some cases these troughs might better be defined as sink-holes. The wall leads an ambivalent course in relation to these natural features; in certain instances the linear bank disappears at the sink-hole edge whilst in others it may be traced across the collapsed ground. At a point not far from the wall's more southern terminal, its line crosses a sink-hole almost supported upon a bridge 2 m below ground level.

Assuming few changes in local geography, its builders appear to have no topographical preferences for its course, though in two places the wall skirts escarpment edges.

At the more southerly terminal there is a staggered T-junction followed by a brief intermittent continuation of the wall's main axis. From the first main junction (the more northerly) an appendage travels at right angles almost 200 m in a nornorwesterly direction. Before it becomes indistinct, this line crosses one large sink-hole about 10 m in diameter and 4 m deep, into which the wall has clearly fallen.

The two shorter southern terminal adjuncts are less than 50 m long. Neither appears to travel far.

About 850 m towards the N.N.E. there is a further T-junction, the original wall line having turned N., then slightly W. of N., it becomes aligned along a further axis, travelling nearly W.–E. and the original line peters out about 60 m to the N. of the junction. Beyond this there are three short N.-running adjuncts of no more than 25 m each, the final one of which marks the wall's ascertainable terminus.

Although no direct connection exists between them, there is fugitive evidence for a further line at right angles to the main axis which runs N.N.W.–S.S.E. This would have had a gap of about 150 m between projections of the two lines. This second line, about 150 m long, runs alongside Carn Caws, with a further

(US 106; Fig. 166) The north-central part of Mynydd Llangattock (Llangatwg) below Blaen Onneu comprises a N.-facing plateau some 400–440 m above O.D., centred upon an outcrop running N.W.–S.E., which overlooks Waun Llech with its prehistoric monolith or early boundary stone (SS 27). This is an area with complex Commonage Rights administered by the Duke of Beaufort as Lord of the Manor. Whereas the nature of farming practice during medieval times is unclear, since the eighteenth century the area has been extensively grazed. It was clearly also subjected to stone-drawing and extensive quarrying, mainly for lime-burning. Today some of the older settlement features (particularly US 106 ii), together with some more recent sites), are under threat from promiscuous trench digging by the Army, an activity permitted by the Duchy.

(US 106 i) Lying on uncultivated common land at Blaen Onneu a height of about 430 m above O.D. is a series of field clearance cairns intensively covering an area of about 1 ha (50 m (N.W.–S.E.) by 200 m), and perhaps as much again if the less densely populated area to the S.W. is included. The group comprises at least 40 small amorphous cairns, some quite overgrown, and two or three lengths of short stony bank. These mounds vary greatly in shape and size but average 5 m in diameter and 0.4 m high. The banks are short and discontinuous. Together they appear to form no coherent pattern.

(US 106 ii) To the S. of (US 106 i), lying on the S.W.-facing slope on the plateau edge lie three extensive, amorphous collections of fieldstone. These may enhance existing natural hollows. The most westerly is about 10 m N.S. by about 12 m. Around it the fieldstone and boulders appear to have been disturbed, though whether by natural or human agency is unclear. About halfway along the N. edge a wall line emerges for about 2 m, travelling due N.

To the E. of this is a moon-shaped clearance heap with an irregular inner (S.W.) profile, about 15 m (N.W.–S.E.) long overall, by some 4 m at greatest width.

About 13 m to the N.E. is a further collection of stone. This one is in the outline profile of a hog's head, up to 15 m long (W.–E.) by 9 m N.–S.

On the lower, flatter ground to the E. of this and to the N. of an area used for slaking lime, are two small cairns, both about 3 m in diameter and no more than

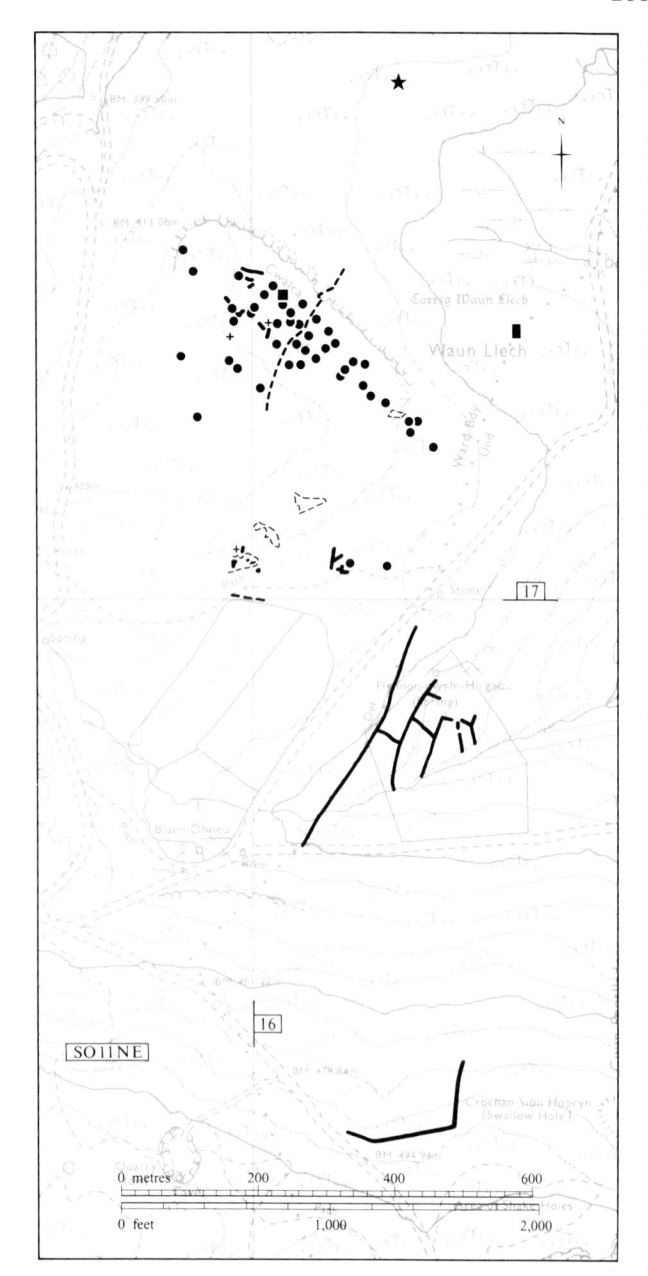

166   Blaen Onneu-Waun Llech area clearances and fields (US 106)

minor adjunct about 30 m long turning back to the E., roughly parallel to the major axis. The age of this bank and the processes which formed it remain enigmatic.

Llangynidr
SO 11 N.W. (1191 1609–1304 1670)   13 xi 91

0.25 m high. Between them and the larger clearances two small groups of wall termini are visible; the more westerly length runs 10 m E. by N. to W. by S. with a short tangent of 5 m striking out at 2 o'clock from about halfway up. The other terminal, only 4 m E., comprises three conjoined lengths, each about 1.5 m long.

(US 106 iii) Within the steeply-sloping N. side of a narrow valley between 360 and 380 m above O.D. is a series of fugitive field banks, only perceptible under snow, or in low light at certain times of the year. The longest line (which may represent a fundamental for an original grid layout) lies outside a large square nineteenth-century enclosure (itself probably originally a Commoners' sheep pound). It travels roughly N.N.E.–S.S.W., along the line of the parish boundary between Llangynidr and Llangatwg. Within the modern enclosure are two further fugitive banks, coming from the S.E. These meet a further line parallel to the more westerly, about halfway down the enclosure. A further piece of bank is subtended beyond, running almost due E. The near-parallel N.E.-running lines are a W.N.W.–E.S.E. line which joins the more easterly, all run roughly along the contour.

(US 106 iv) On the E. side of the Llangynidr–Beaufort road is a boulder wall up to about 3 m wide and 0.5 m high, which travels along the contour (about 473 m above O.D.) for about 150 m then turns sharply downslope almost at right angles, running 70 m N. towards the minor road to Llangatwg before disappearing among shallow limestone trenches and shake-holes. Although at one time this wall may have been respected as the parish boundary between Llangynidr and Llangatwg, it seems likely that this wall may have formed part of an earlier enclosure, or could have been the component part of an otherwise lost field system.

(US 106 v) On the W. side of the same road there are indications of 'solution features' including discontinuous walls, infilling trenches, and reportedly also hut-circles.

Llangynidr
SO 11 S.E. (US 106 i) (centred upon 1604 1738); (US 106 ii) (centred upon 1610 1707); (US 106 iii) (the longer axis from 1606 1665 to 1637 1706; the lower axis terminating at 1641 1670); (US 106 iv) (from 1613 1612 to 1629 1635); (US 106 v) (centred upon 1625 1600) ix 91

SO 12 N.E. (1986 2911) for hut circle see RC 275

SO 21

(US 107) Immediately N.W. of the hillslope enclosure Crug y Gaer[1] at a height of about 290 m above O.D. are several small stone cairns which may represent remnant field walls. Some ruined field walls also appear in this vicinity, testifying to the existence of a lost field system.

[1] *Inv. Br.* I (ii), pp. 116–18 (HF 68).

Llanelli
SO 21 N.W. (2243 1438) 11 xi 76

(US 108) To the S.E. of Twr Pen Cyrn on Mynydd Pen Cyrn at about 525 m above O.D. lying among the scree of the limestone escarpment are the remains of two huts or hut-groups discovered by R. E. Kay.[1]

(US 108 i) The more northerly building appears to have been a platform house built at right angles to the slope and probably until recently used as a sheepfold.

(US 108 ii) The more southerly feature (which was not located by the Commission) appears to have comprised two roughly square huts set into a rectangular enclosure.

[1] Kay MSS, vol. III, ser. III, p. 225.

Llangatwg
SO 21 S.W. (US 108 i) (2038 1442); (US 108 ii) (2028 1433) 17 vi 70

(US 109) On a N.-facing plateau running roughly N.N.E.–S.S.W. and about 420–445 m above O.D., on unenclosed land which straddles the boundary between the old counties of Brecknockshire and Monmouthshire, across Gilwern Hill, lies a series of settlement or clearance features, set along the trend of

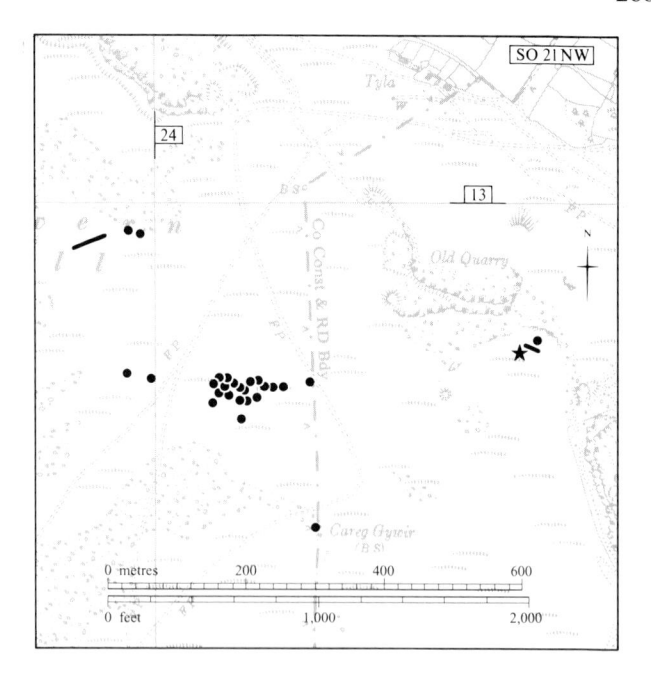

167 Gilwern Hill clearance cairns (US 109)

the plateau.¹ The ground from which they are cleared is bounded to the S. by Millstone Grit or Gannister Rock exposed in low cliffs strewn with boulders over bare crag. These cliffs fall up to 10 m in altitude, sheltering the cleared ground from southwesterly winds. The cleared plateau rises towards the N., where it is broken up by boulder trains which form a natural boundary. Beyond these are extensive quarrying features and limekilns of post-medieval date. This clearance area extends roughly from the quarry lip at SO 2460 1255, on the E., to the road at SO 2370 1250 on the W.

The cairns vary in size and form from regular circles to amorphous masses impossible to distinguish from neighbouring, more certainly natural, boulder trains. Whereas some comprise small, rounded fieldstone, others are amalgams of much larger, more angular boulders, and some stone groups were clearly deliberately piled up around detached Grit masses too large to move. Excepting these detached blocks, few of the features rise perceptibly above the present land surface, and those not entirely free of vegetation are to be distinguished by greener growth, usually of bilberry. Some cairns are obviously overgrown and partly soil-covered. The following features were observed:

(US 109 i) To the S. of the cliff, on a higher plateau than the main cairn group lies a cairn (probably modern) about 5 m in diameter and up to 1.5 m high, covering craggy outcropping rock, situated at the N. end of a partly infilled tramroad track running N.–S.

(US 109 ii) A cairn c. 1.5 m in diameter.

(US 109 iii) A cairn 2 m in diameter and 2 m to the E., a further cairn (US 109 iv) 1 m in diameter.

(US 109 v–viii) Cairns 2.5 m in diameter, (US 109 vii) incorporating a large angular boulder. (US 109 ix) is an overgrown clearance feature measuring 4 m N.–S. by about 2 m E.–W.

(US 109 x) A cairn 2 m in diameter.

(US 109 xi) An amorphous cairn 1.5 m N.–S. by 4 m E.–W.

(US 109 xii) A cairn 2 m in diameter.

(US 109 xiii) A cairn about 4 m in diameter and about 5 m N.E. of it; another cairn (US 109 xiv) 2.5 m in diameter composed almost entirely of large angular stone blocks.

(US 109 xv) A cairn about 3 m N.–S. by 4 m E.–W.

(US 109 xvi–xvii) Two cairns about 2 m in diameter, (US 109 xvi) built around a large angular block.

(US 109 xviii) A clearance feature about 3 m N.–S. by 4 m E.–W.

(US 109 xix) A cairn 2 m in diameter.

(US 109 xx, xxii, xxiii) Three cairns each 4 m in diameter.

(US 109 xxi) is a clearance feature 2 m N.–S. by 3 m E.–W.

(US 109 xxiv) A linear E.–W. stone-embanked feature, grass-covered on the W, becoming barer as it travels E., where it marked out or surrounded by cairns; one (US 109 xxv) is 2 m in diameter.

(US 109 xxvi–xxvii) Two cairn-like features roughly aligned along the wall. Both measure roughly 6 m E.–W. by 2 m N.–S.

(US 109 xxviii) An elongated cairn 3 m N.–S. by 7 m E.–W.

(US 109 xxix) Over the county boundary in Monmouthshire is a cairn 1.5 m in diameter, revetted by an outer ring of 11 carefully-laid stones, possibly the base of a kerb cairn.

(US 109 xxx) Immediately N. of cairn (US 109 xxix) in a bracken-covered area are the remains of a low wall. This is probably part of the perimeter of a field cleared close to the edge of the rock outcrop.

¹ First noted by Mr P. M. Jones of Tredegar.

Llanelli/Llanfoist Fawr (Monmouthshire)
SO 21 S.W. (US 109 i) (2423 1255); (US 109 ii) (2412 1270); (US 109 iii–iv) (2413 1273); (US 109 v) (2414 1273); (US 109 vi) (2417 1275); (US 109 vii) (2417 1275); (US 109 viii) (2416 1274); (US 109 ix) (2415 1274); (US 109 x) (2415 1275); (US 109 xi) (2414 1275); (US 109 xii) (2414 1274); (US 109 xiii–xiv) (2411 2475); (US 109 xv) (2410 1276); (US 109 xvi) (2410 1275); (US 109 xvii) (2665 1292); (US 109 xviii) (2409 1275); (US 109 xix) (2409 1274); (US 109 xx) (2410 1274); (US 109 xxi) (2408 1272); (US 109 xxii) (2399 1276); (US 109 xxiii) (2396 1276); (US 109 xxiv–v) (2388 1293 to SO 2392 1295); (US 109 xxvi–vii) (from 2393 1296 to 2396 1296); (US 109 xxviii) (2398 1296); (US 109 xxix) (2456 1281); (US 109 xxx) (from 2454 1280 to 2456 1281)   vii 90

SO 22

(US 110) On Twyn Du about 420 m above O.D. is a roughly pentagonal enclosure situated on a moderately sloping ledge on the W.-facing slope. It measures 30 m across and is bounded by a low bank up to 0.3 m high on the uphill side. There is no obvious entrance and recognisable breaks in the bank are probably due to modern paths.

O.S. Card SO 22 NW 5; visible on A.P., R.A.F. 106 G/UK 1; 11 vii 46.

Llanbedr Ystrad Wy
SO 22 N.E. (2239 2722)

(US 111 i; Fig. 167) On ground rising steeply eastward to the W. of Pen y Gader Fawr at a height of about 650 m above O.D. lies a sub-circular enclosure of spread rubble bank about 3–4 m wide and 40 m in overall diameter.[1] The bank is of large grass- and heather-consolidated boulders with a maximum height of 1 m above the exterior on the W., downhill side, and 0.9 m above the interior on the E. side, where there is an entrance.

(US 111 ii) Lying about 200 m S.E. is a linear bank up to 4 m wide and over 1 km long, falling from a height of about 730 to 450 m O.D. It traverses in a curving path from a point roughly N.E., about 300 m E. of Pen y Gader Fawr cairn (RC 301), running downhill from N. to W., ending at the stream cutting immediately N. of Ffald y Nant.

[1] P. M. Jones, *Arch. in Wales* 18 (1978), p. 60.

Talgarth
SO 22 N.W. (US 111 i) (2215 2855 [approx.]); (US 111 ii) (from 222 285 to 226 288 [approx.])   7 v 82

(US 112) The upper slopes of Cwm-Gu, at heights of 425–610 m above O.D., are seamed in vestiges of ruined walls, enclosures, drystone sheepfolds, and possibly platform house sites. These features occupy a great arc of sloping mountainside running roughly N.N.E.–S.S.W. It is very difficult to distinguish between scree-runs and ruined stone walls, or to tell patches of outcrop and ruined cairns or round huts apart. Some platforms may be natural, or might equally be artificial, or they may be natural positions adapted to occupation.

Features so far recognised here include:

(US 112 i) An oval enclosure, 425 m above O.D., which includes a small, modern, circular sheep shelter, all lying upon the contour, following a long, ragged scree-like line of stones. Possibly the enclosure noted by P. M. Jones.[1]

(US 112 ii) A hut or fold, 455 m above O.D. upon a patch of scree.

(US 112 iii) A long-hut or fold, possibly on an earlier site, 565 m above O.D. upon a patch of scree.

(US 112 iv) Several small shapeless enclosures, possibly sheep shelters, within the scree. Some larger ones appear further downslope to the W. The discovery of a rotary quern in a dry streambed at SO 2025 2294 or 2017 2303 is noteworthy.[2]

(US 112 v) An enclosure and huts 505 m above O.D., upon a patch of scree.

(US 112 vi) Enclosures and huts upon a patch of scree 535 m above O.D.

(US 112 vii) A low linear rubble spread associated with other stone structures, small circles and walling runs along the end of a spur, possibly forming part of a larger structure.[3]

[1] P. M. Jones, *Arch. in Wales* 19 (1979), p. 9, no. 1; O.S. Card SO 22 SW 20.
[2] O.S. Card SO 22 SW 3.
[3] P. M. Jones, *loc. cit.* n. 1.

Llanfihangel Cwm Du
SO 22 S.W. (US 112 i) (2087 2133); (US 112 ii) (2092 2180); (US 112 iii) (2090 2252); (US 112 iv) (2030 2294; 2027 2299; 2021 2300; 2021 2317); (US 112 v) (2112 2185); (US 112 vi) (2107 2207); (US 112 vii) (212 212)   7 vi 73

(US 113) Roughly halfway between Pen Allt Mawr and a small stream draining into the Grwyne Fawr, on a shelf about 505 m above O.D., are the remains of a large ring of piled stones, the surrounding wall of which is very ruined, with only the footings remaining. The interior, which forms an overgrown hollow, and the encircling wall, except on the W., occupy level ground, but the W. portion of the wall climbs over the base of steeply rising ground and is about 2.4 m higher than the interior. The ring is oval in plan and measures internally 47.6 m long N.–S., by 38.4 m wide. The encircling wall appears to have been about 2.4 m wide, but reached 6.1 m in places, due to scattering. There is no clear sign of an entrance.

Llanfihangel Cwm Du
SO 22 S.W. (2106 2451)   7 v 80

Lost Settlement Sites (LS 1–9)

(LS 1; Fig. 168) In 1801 the Nedd Valley appears to have been full of clearance features noted by Gilbert Gilpin. He wrote:

The banks of the Neath River, above . . . [Pontneathfechan] . . ., for near a mile in length, and about half a one in width, on each side, contain a great number of mounds of earth and stones, of about 2 or 3 yards [2–3 m] long, 1 wide and 12 high: and some few of about 4 or 5 yards long, 1 or 2 wide, and 1 high. They all appear of great antiquity. They lie pretty nearly in straight lines up to the ascents of the ground, with their sides opposite thereto and to each other [Plate II]. Their distances from each other are various: in some cases only 3 or 4, and in others more than 20 yards. Their numbers on each side of the river must have been several hundreds; but of late years they have been greatly diminished by levelling them for the purposes of facilitating the ploughing of the land. These mounds are evidently artificial, an excavation on the upper side of each, from whence the matter was got to form them, is still visible. It is not likely that they have been the effect of quarrying, or even trying for stones, because they are situated in the most earthy parts, and in the midst of grounds whose surface is in many places almost covered with stones that are detached from the rocks, and, of course, might have been removed at a less expense, and with greater facility, than in the opening of new quarries. Several stones are also contained in the mounds themselves, which would not have been the case if quarrying had been their only object. It is not probable that they have been the effect of any mining adventure, because the rock itself is not a mineral measure . . .

A large stone, of a rude oblong square form, 8 feet [c. 2.6 m] long and about 2½ feet [c. 0.6 m] square, lies upon the ground near the mounds on the Glamorganshire side, and may at some time probably have been erect . . .
Are these mounds (for it is evident they have been erected for defence), therefore, Roman or British?[1]

Although now under hill pasture, much of the area alluded to has since been ploughed, and a great deal is afforested. None of the features have yet been re-located and at this distance in time from Gilpin, interpretation is difficult. It remains possible that such regular lines of mounds (Fig. 168), containing only small quantities of

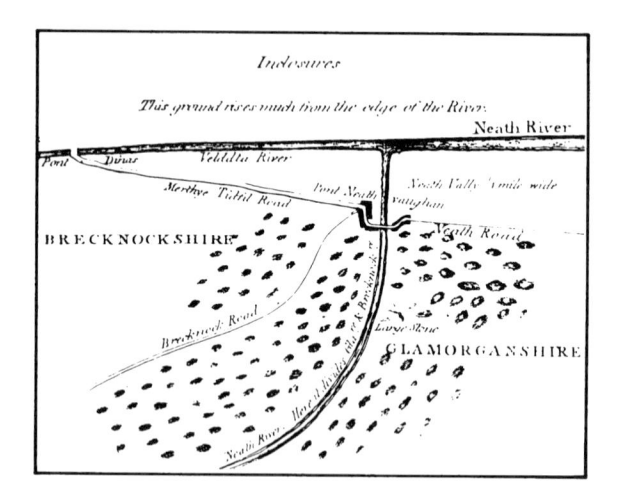

168   Clearances near Pontneathfechan (LS 1) (from *Gentleman's Magazine* 1801)

stone, could have been of natural (glacial or periglacial), rather than of human, origin. Gilpin (about whose reliability we know nothing) had examined the mounds at first hand and gave cogent reasons for stating his belief that they were artificial. Interestingly, the description he provides, of mounds created from the downcast from slight hillslope quarrying, suggests he was possibly looking at platform houses or hut scoops of types that are still common in South Wales (see p. 201). Such an explanation cannot entirely account for the 'straight lines', and with hindsight it could be suggested that he was looking at platform scoops interdigitated with field clearance mounds and cairns, some possibly making up regular field divisions not then clearly evident because of topographical irregularities.

[1] G. Gilpin, 'Mounds of earth near Pontneddfychan', *Gentleman's Mag.* (1801), part II, p. 985; and G. L. Gomme, *Archaeology: A Classified Collection of the Chief Contents of "The Gentleman's Magazine" from 1731–1868*, (London: Elliot Stock, 1886), pp. 289–90.

Ystradfellte/Neath Hr, Rhigos, Glamorgan
SN 80 N.E./SN 90 N.W. (approx. 895 075–905 080 to 895 095–910 095)

(LS 2) According to T. C. Cantrill 'On Brecon [Old O.S. 6-inch map] 37, Lat. 51°50[ft]43[in], long. 3°44[ft]41[in], on the moorland, 480 yds W. 10°S. Of Sink-y-Giedd, 40 yds north-east of a swallow-hole into which a small stream drains from the peat on the south' was a hut-circle 'About 21 ft. in diameter, entrance facing east, flanked on each side with a stone'. This indication places the site on Carreg Lem. It has not since been re-located. Cantrill thought it comparable to one now considered to be a cairn, situated upon Carnon Gwynion (RC 97).

T. C. Cantrill, *List of Sites of Archaeological Significance in Wales*, unpubl. MSS in N.M.W.

Ystradgynlais (E), Ystradgynlais Lr (C)
SN 81 N.W. (8020 1730)

(LS 3) Within 'an extensive natural hollow' below the peat in a bog at Cefn Blaen y Nant, Trallwm,[1] at a height of 500 m above O.D. in the Abergwesyn area, peat-cutters found sharpened wooden piles of oak and birch during the 1920s and earlier.[2] Some of the piles were apparently arranged in more or less parallel lines, buried about 1 m below the surface, some with their points driven through to the underlying clay. No other artefacts were found and some of the wood was given to the National Museum.[3] It has been suggested that the piles may represent enclosures used in stock-raising during the later Bronze Age[4] and a date of *c.* 1000 B.C. was at one time suggested.[5]
Peat is no longer won from this area which is today overgrown.

[1] O.S. Card SN 85 NE.
[2] H. N. Jerman, *B.B.C.S.* 3 (1922), p. 282.
[3] Grimes, *Prehist. Wales*, (2nd ed.), p. 232.
[4] H. N. Savory, *Prehist. Brecks.* (I), p. 114
[5] H. N. Jerman, *Antiq. Jnl* 15 (1935), pp. 68–9, (illus.).

Llanfihangel Abergwesyn
SN 85 N.E. (8657 5552)   Not located 1988

(LS 4) To the E. of Pen y Garn Goch some 470 m above O.D. a 'collapsed hut-circle internally 6 paces by 5 paces' is recorded by the National Museum of Wales at an unknown date. The site now lies in a densely afforested area and could not be located at the time of investigation.

O.S. Card SN 85 SE 8; N.M.W. Record O.S. 6-inch sheet x N.W.

Llangamarch (E), Treflys (C)
SN 85 S.E. (8858 5031)   20 v 81

(LS 5) Behind the residence of Penbryn, Cefn Coed y Cymer, about 240 m above O.D., 'Celtic' hut-circles were reported in 1932. A quern said to have been found there was in the Cyfarthfa Castle Museum.[1] Nothing can now be ascertained of either the quern or the huts. Penbryn was demolished to make way for the Heads of the Valleys Road *c.* 1950.[2]

[1] *Merthyr*, p. 36.
[2] O.S. Card SO 00 NW 5.

Vaynor
SO 00 N.W. (0298 0804) (former site of Penbryn)

(LS 6) In 1961, on the extreme E. end of Pant Sychpant at a height of 340 m above O.D., T. W. Burke[1] noted a circular enclosure some 30 feet (about 10 m) in diameter, probably a hut-circle. Although its existence in 1947 is attested from aerial photographs,[2] the site is now under forestry plantation.

[1] O.S. Card SO 01 SW 16; T. W. Burke, *B.B.C.S.* 19 (1961), pp. 165–6; p. 165.
[2] A.P.s, R.A.F./CPE/UK/2079/1084–5; 19 v 47.

Penderyn
SO 01 S.W. (0066 1029)

(LS 7; Fig. 169) Crop or parchmark features visible on aerial photographs of land adjacent to the River Wye near Llyswen some 95 m above O.D. indicate a field system of unknown antiquity, though possibly as early as the Romano-British period. These may be described as follows:

(LS 7 i) Two separate ditch or boundary lines appearing as dark marks up to 40 m long and about 30 m apart (on C.U.A.P. CJT 77) S. of the old railway embankment.

(LS 7 ii) One of the above ditches re-appears on the N. side of the same embankment, running in the direction of the river (on C.U.A.P. CJT 78).

C.U.A.P., CJT (76), 77, 78.

Llys-wen, Glasbury (E), Pipton (C)
SO 13 N.W. (LS 7 i) (1421 3819); (LS 7 ii) (1420 3822)

169 Llyswen parchmarks (LS 7) (CUAP CJJ 77)

(LS 8; Fig. 170) About 200 m E. of Pipton farmhouse on the S. side of the road to Llyswen, about 90 m above O.D. is a series of three distinct parchmark features. Two main elements seem to be represented: angular land divisions distinguished by both narrow ditches and embanked lines which may be prehistoric, Roman or medieval in origin, and circular ring ditches, more likely later prehistoric in date. If later rather than earlier, these land divisions may relate to a medieval settlement of Pipton today represented by the farmhouse, its surrounding earthworks and motte on the N. side of the road.

(LS 8 i) The most westerly feature is of discontinuous parallel lines about 5 m wide and some 200 m long, running roughly N.N.E.–S.S.W. and crossing the road (on C.U.A.P. CDQ 8), running towards the River Wye.

(LS 8 ii) Bifurcated by the road is a parchmark circle, some 20–25 m in diameter, one of between six and ten similar circles, most of which appear to be about 4–5 m in diameter. These are possibly the circles of huts or barrows.

(LS 8 iii) In the eastern part of the same field, approaching the circle group from the eastern field boundary travelling for about 100 m parallel with the road, is a further pair of parallel lines, about 8 m wide.

C.U.A.P., CDQ 5–13.

Glasbury (E), Pipton (C)
SO 13 N.E. (LS 8 i) (from 1621 3800 to 1627 3782); (LS 8 ii) (centred upon 1635 3792); (LS 8 iii) (from 1638 3790 to 1646 3793)

170 Pipton parchmarks (LS 8) (CUAP CDQ 5)

(LS 9) During land-taking at Dan y Graig, about 300 m above O.D., the Rev. Archdeacon Henry Thomas Payne recorded 'Meini Hirion' appearing from beneath the valley peat. These could have been part of a buried field wall or might have been a stone row (RSC 7).

H. T. Payne, *Conjectural Remarks on the early Celtic Inhabitants of Britain*, (c. 1806), N.L.W. MS 184A.

Llanelli
SO 21 N.W. (235 155; approx. site of bog)

Rejected Settlements and Field Systems

(RS 1) In 1967 C. B. Crampton presented a study[1] suggesting the existence of an extensive system of small fields around the hillfort Twyn y Gaer[2] on Mynydd Illtud. These were felt to have been Celtic fields aasociated with the Iron Age hillfort. During subsequent field visits by R.C.A.M. it was felt that whereas a few of the lines appeared to correspond to sheep tracks and some were in fact pillow mounds, it was not possible to trace most of the suggested boundaries, which were being propounded in areas where narrow or cord rig was discernible.[3]

[1] *Br. Inv.* I (ii), p. 73
[2] C. B. Crampton, *Arch. Camb.* 116 (1967), pp. 60–3.
[3] A. H. A. Hogg and W. E. Griffiths, *Arch. in Wales* 9 (1969), p. 7, no. 3.

Llanfihangel Fechan SO 03 N.E. (054 352) (centred on)

Dyke (D 1)

Only one defensive earthwork resembling a dyke has so far been reported from the county.

(D 1) According to H. N. Jerman[1] there existed an earthwork dyke connecting Maen Gam with Fannog Farm, some 8 miles (*c.* 13 km) to the S.W. This was first noticed between the bifurcated Afon Commarch near Fedw and at Hen Clawdd. Only alignments formerly bearing a fence were published on the O.S. 6-inch map. The dyke is supposed to have continued in a southwesterly direction at least as far as Cwrt y Cadno.

Although possible fragments of the dyke are said to be visible along the indicated route[2] all traces of the bank have proved elusive in recent years.

[1] H. N. Jerman, *B.B.C.S.* 7 (1933–5), pp. 82–4.
[2] O.S. SN 85 SE 6.

Llanafan Fawr and others
SN 85/95 Maen Gam (SN 917 557); Fannog (SN 819 516 now submerged under Llyn Brianne); Fedw (SN 894 543); Hen Clawdd (SN 913 552); Cwrt y Cadno (SN 691 441)

HILLFORTS

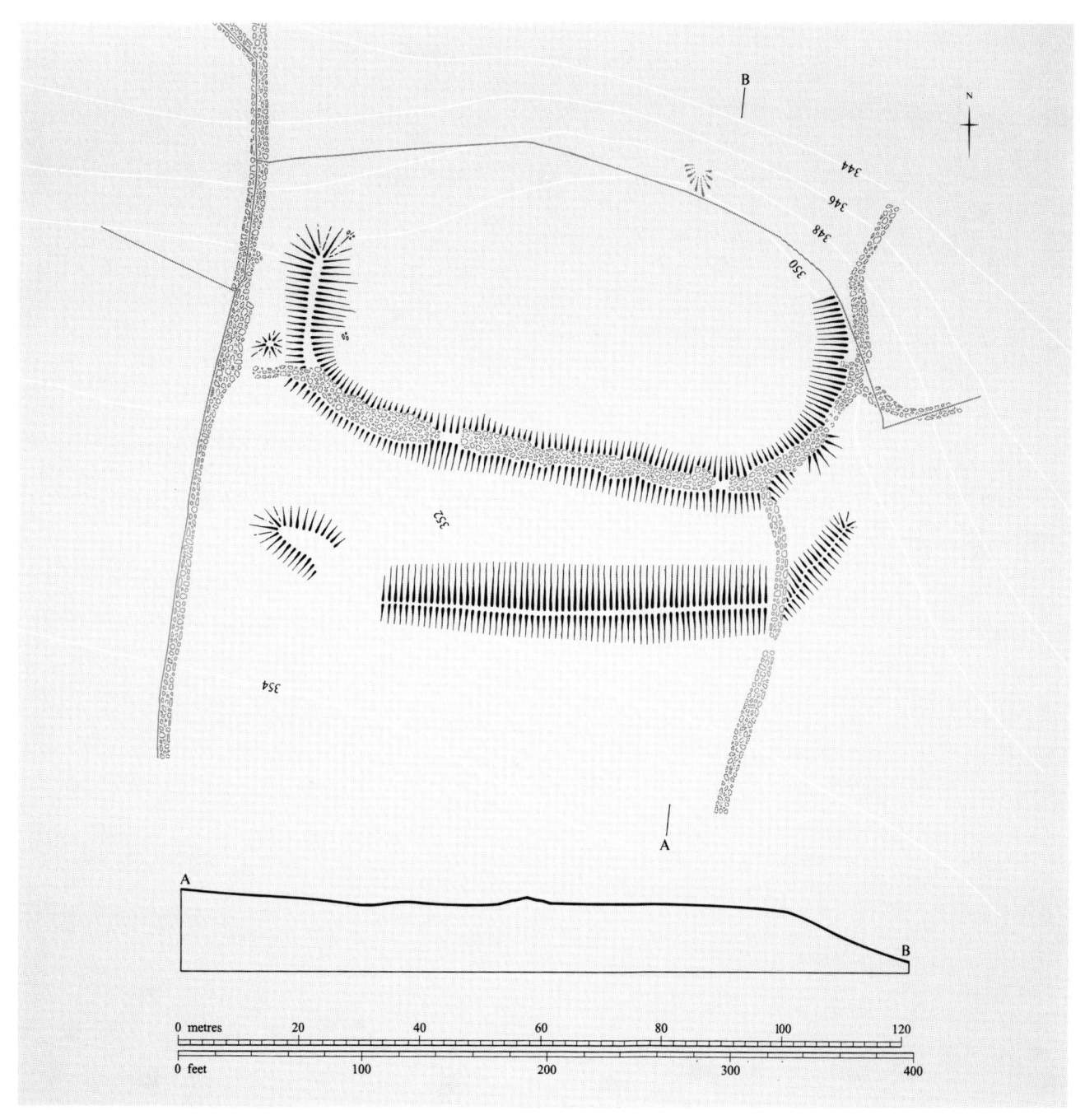

171 Lan Fawr, Llangynidr hillfort (HF 65)

Hillforts (Addendum to vol I (ii))

(HF 65; Fig. 171) On a spur bordering the pastures of Lan Fawr at a height of 350 m above O.D. is an enclosure comprising an annular inner bank and probably a partly concentric outer bank and ditch. Overlying or immediately adjacent is a sequence of later boundaries, the latest of which are modern wire fences. A stone, partly ruined commons enclosure wall, lies to the S.W., standing up to 1.8 m high and constructed in a mixed build of coursed sandstone slabs and roughly coursed sub-angular boulders, with a 'soldiered' crown. Where there are gaps these have been closed by iron hurdles and post and wire fencing.

There is an even earlier field system comprising ruined, structureless walls constructed of small sub-angular sandstone boulders, the best part of which runs along the crest of the inner bank. At the W. end of this wall there is an entrance through the gap created between it and a further wall running N.–S. There are two further gaps on the E. which may also have been entrances, and a more modern opening has been created by farm traffic on the S.E. The wall is extensively robbed, creating hollows, and elsewhere, the wall is merely a low bank of grassed rubble.

A small undated horseshoe-shaped quarry is cut into the upper part of the N. scarp slope of this spur. In the field to the E. of the site, close to and roughly parallel with the field wall shown on the plan, are two scarps which may be artificial and probably mark the limits of ploughing.

The inner bank of the older earthwork consists of a broad, low, bank, of grass-grown rubble, up to about 0.5 m high, in places covered with bracken. The bank, indistinct from vehicular erosion, is punctuated by occasional small hollows caused by stone robbing. Mutilation is particularly pronounced on the W. The bank terminates on the N.E. and N.W., coinciding with a sharp steepening in the natural slope of the spur. The only possible entrance site is at the S.E. corner, where there appears to be a re-entrant in the bank's outer line. Downslope of the N.W. terminal is an accumulation of grass- and bracken-covered rubble talus. There is a low, grass-covered rubble mound protruding from the bank near the S.W. corner, though its origin is unclear. Alongside the inner toe of the bank, on the S.W., is a very shallow hollow, possibly the last remaining indication of a quarry ditch. There is no sign of an outer ditch associated with the bank.

A low linear swelling of the ground up to 0.45 m high, and an associated hollow to the S.W. between 8 m and 15 m in front of the latter bank are probably the remains of an outer defensive system.

No interior features are visible.

The dating and cultural affiliations of the site are uncertain, but there is a general similarity in plan between later prehistoric, multivallate enclosures with concentric, wide-spaced ramparts.

D. M. Browne and D. J. Percival, *Arch. in Wales* 28 (1988), p. 45.

SO 11 N.E. (1707 1838) 5 ix 94

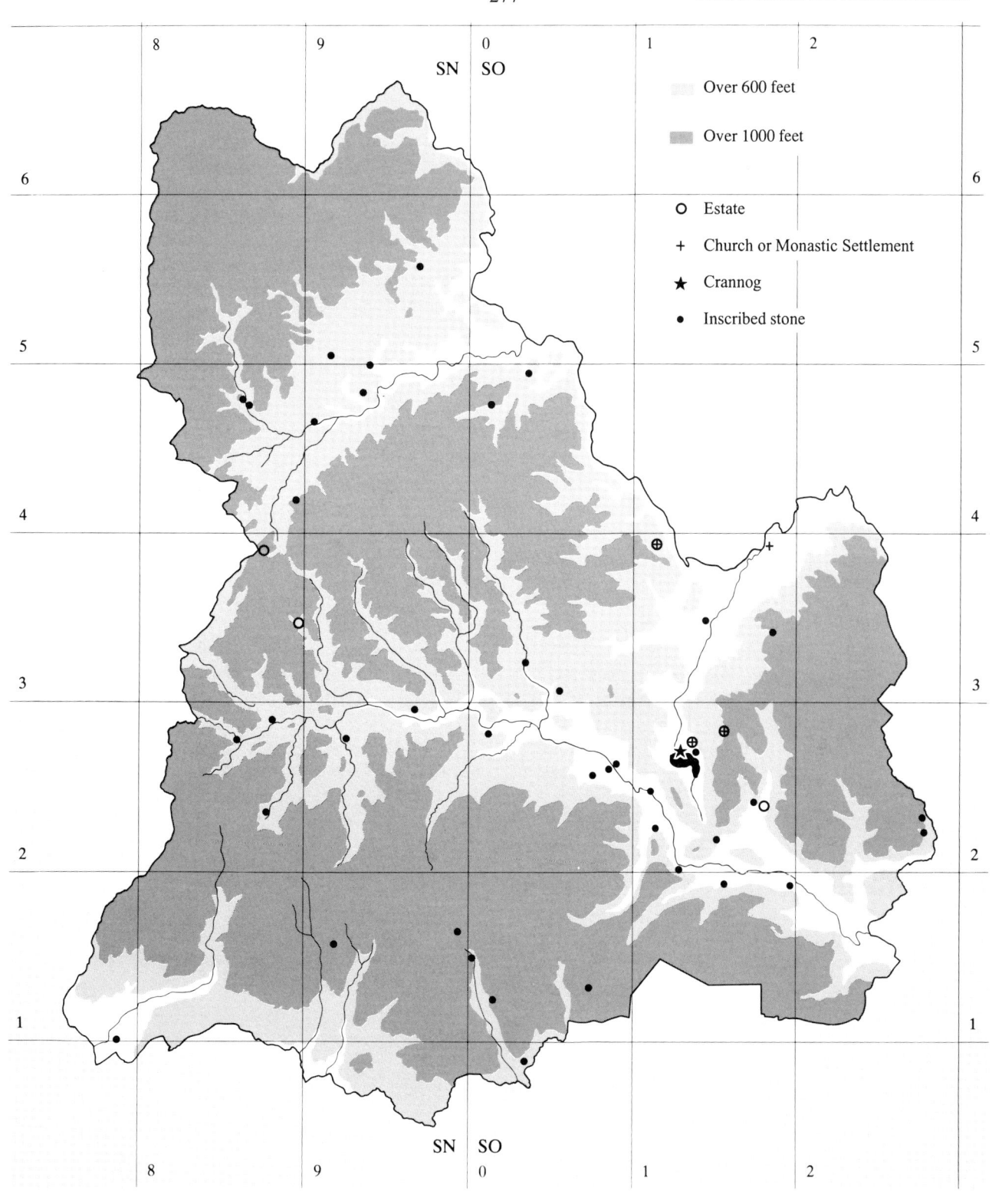

172 Brecknockshire during the Early Medieval Period

Early Medieval Land-holding, Estates and Ecclesiastical Centres

Post-Roman Settlement Sites

It is difficult to assess to what degree Dark Age settlement patterns followed those which existed at the end of the Roman occupation. Although Brecknockshire has produced several Roman forts and fortlets, only one villa site is known,[1] so an appreciation of contemporary Romano-British settlement patterns is extremely restricted. Furthermore, whereas it is likely that some hut-groups are of Romano-British origin (and morphological analogy from Caernarfonshire suggests this is likely), no undefended Roman sites have so far been properly investigated in southern Powys. Pollen analytical evidence does, however, attest to agricultural activity during this period (see above, p. 7).

Early medieval settlement sites are also elusive, though pertinently recent attention has focused upon the possibility, if not the likelihood, that some of the rectilinear huts and undefended enclosures mapped in Snowdonia might have been occupied during this period.[2] Attention has been drawn to the importance of investigating earlier, proto-historic hut-groups in order to appreciate both chronological and typological domestic developments of later longhouses.[3] In this respect the excavations by Sir Cyril and Lady Fox of medieval platform houses on Gelligaer Common, Margam Mountain (Glamorgan), are noteworthy.[4] Whilst yielding only thirteenth-century artefacts, it has been suggested[5] that these could have originated in habitations associated with the nearby seventh-century memorial stone. The question of Dark Age continuity of settlement into what has been termed the 'central Middle Ages' is, however, fraught with many imponderables.[6]

Sporadic new hillfort settlement is likely at this period, and as re-settlement within existing hillforts is known throughout the Roman period[7] and it is likely that some of these[8] continued in use or were re-occupied during the Dark Ages.[9] It is ironic that the only Dark Age settlement site in the county proved by excavation, a crannog (see below, pp. 281–3), should be of such an unusual type.

Estates, monasteries and 'Clasau'

Little is known of settlement activity upon the Dark Age estates mentioned in the *Liber Landavensis*.[10] This is a collection of earlier charters compiled in A.D. 1120, though in an altered form. Attempts to correlate these with modern place-names have met with limited success.[11] It must be noted in parentheses that the absolute reliability of this document is undemonstrated, and its critical use in the location or definition of early estates needs to be complemented by archaeological field survey.

Four Brecknockshire estates are specifically named in this source; these are Llandeilo'r Fan (*c.* A.D. 720),[12] Llanfihangel Cwm Du (A.D. 750),[13] Llangoed (*c.* A.D. 595),[14] and Llangorse (*c.* A.D. 720).[15] The Llandielo'r Fan estate, of some 3,500 acres (*c.* 1,400 ha), lay not far off the line of the Roman road and included land between 1,300 and 1,500 ft (400–460 m) above O.D.[16] Davies presumes such high land as this to be unsuitable for predominantly agricultural use,[17] but aerial photographs show considerable parts of this parish clothed in rig and furrow cultivation,[18] indicating widespread tracts given over to the plough. The late A. H. A. Hogg tentatively pinpointed one feature of this boundary, an enclosure (Castell Ceir Tut), upon the Epynt moorland (at SN 8711 3908).[19]

Llangorse appears to have been a territory of about 1,000 acres (*c.* 400 ha) under monastic administration covering at least the period *c.* A.D. 724–925.[20] Because charters record that Awst the King of Brycheiniog donated his sons' and grandsons' bodies to the church for burial, it has been suggested that Llangorse church could have been a royal burial site.[21] The O.S. considers that this early church may be equated with the present site of the parish church (St. Paulinus), which lies within a probable D-shaped enclosure.[22] The place-names Cwrt y Prior and Capel[23] sited further east in Llanbeilin are probably indicate a later, possibly monastic or ecclesiastical connection.[24] 'Clas' is a place-name element generally considered the equivalent of 'monastery'. Because it incorporates this element, Glasbury-on-Wye, on the county border with Radnorshire, may have been an early medieval or Dark Age ecclesiastical settlement.[25]

The Distribution of Early Christian Inscribed Stones (Fig. 172)

Over fifty inscribed stones are known from the period c. A.D. 450–1000 in Brecknockshire, though about a fifth of the sample is now lost.[26] Of these, seventeen bore simple inscriptions of the fifth to seventh century; nineteen are cross-decorated stones of the seventh to ninth century; and five are sculptured crosses and cross slabs of the ninth to the eleventh century.[27]

Although interpreting distribution patterns of Early Christian stones is the subject of considerable discussion and speculation, present-day findspots are to an unknown degree obviously determined by their host churches to which some stones have been brought in comparatively recent times. The current location of inscribed stones need not therefore accurately reflect their original findspots. It has been noted that the earliest stones appear to lie in close proximity to Roman roads,[28] and that at least eighteen stones occur close to Roman roads has been felt worthy of comment.[29]

Church Dedications

Attempts have been made to determine settlement areas with reference to early Celtic saints' dedications of churches.[30] This proves to be an exercise of limited value because so many dedications date from medieval times, or later.[31] The cultural connections between the churches in Wales and Ireland which are generally felt to have been strong during this period[32] are also thought to have affected historic Brycheiniog. Connections are shown by finds of inscribed bilingual Ogam stones, and in the belief that Llangorse crannog has Irish affinities (see below, p. 281). The adoption of Latin name forms is considered to reflect Gallic or Mediterranean connections, although there appear to be no specific examples of those from historic Brycheiniog.[33]

Curvilinear Churchyards

In the popular study of early churches circular or curvilinear shapes have long been considered indicative of great antiquity. In a recent study of curvilinear sites, attention has been directed to a small concentration of circular examples in north Brecknockshire,[34] some of which combine suggestibility of shape with the actual presence of Early Christian monuments, such as Defynnog, Llanafan Fawr[35] and Llaneleu.[36] Clearly the recent histories of these enclosures require close scrutiny before sweeping conclusions are drawn from curvilinearity as observed at the present time, since even sites with apparently secure pedigrees can on occasion be shown upon methodical investigation to owe their forms to recent factors of land-holding or churchyard building policies.[37]

Whilst extensive and well-studied documentary sources do exist for the study of the Dark Ages,[38] archaeological knowledge of settlement and habitation sites during the period A.D. 500–1000 in Wales remains poor and difficult to reconcile with the written word.

---

[1] The chronology, distribution and morphology of Roman sites is discussed in *Inv. Br.* I (ii), pp. 125–86.

[2] P. Crew, 'Rectilinear Settlements in Gwynedd', *B.B.C.S.* 31 (1984), pp. 320–1.

[3] *idem.*, p. 320.

[4] C. Fox and A. Fox, 'Forts and Farms on Margam Mountain', *Ant. J.* (1934), pp. 395–413.

[5] By J. K. Knight, 'Glamorgan A.D. 400–1000: Archaeology and History', in H. N. Savory, (ed.), *Glamorgan County History: Vol. II, Early Glamorgan, Prehistory and Early History* pp. 315–64, (espec. pp. 320–4).

[6] This problem is considered, albeit inconclusively, by L. A. S. Butler in 'Continuity of settlement in Wales in the central Middle Ages', in L. Laing, (ed.), *Studies in Celtic Survival*, (Oxford: B.A.R. 37, 1977), pp. 61–6.

[7] Discussed briefly by M. A. Avery, 'Hillforts in the British Isles: A Student's Introduction', in D. M. Harding, (ed.), *Hillforts: Later Prehistoric Earthworks in Britain and Ireland*, (London, 1976), pp. 1–58; pp. 44–5.

[8] R.C.A.M., *Inv. Br.* I (ii), pp. 9–123.

[9] cf. the evidence for Glamorgan in J. K. Knight, 'Sources for the Early History of Morgannwg', pp. 365–409, p. 401, in H. N. Savory, (ed.), *Glamorgan County History: Vol II, Early Glamorgan, Prehistory and Early History*, pp. 365–410, (espec. pp. 399–402); briefly discussed by M. L. Jones in *Society and Settlement in Wales and the Marches: 500 B.C. to A.D. 1100*, (Oxford: B.A.R. 121, 1984), pp. 65, 77–8; I. Burrows, *Hillfort and Hill-top Settlement in Somerset in the First to Eighth Centuries A.D.*, (Oxford: B.A.R. 91, 1981).

[10] J. G. Evans and J. Rhys, (eds.), *The Text of the Book of Llan Dav*, (Oxford, 1893); W. Davies, *The Llandaff Charters*, (Aberystwyth: Nat. Lib. Wales, 1979). Problems posed by the document are noted in P. Simms-Williams, *Jnl. Ecclesiastical Hist.* (1982), 124–129.

[11] W. Davies, 'Roman Settlements and Post-Roman Estates in South-east Wales', pp. 153–173 in P. J. Casey, (ed.), *The End of Roman Britain*, (Oxford: B.A.R. 71, 1979).

[12] LL 154, Lannguruaet (SN 896 347).

[13] LL 167, (47) E., Lann Mihacel Tref Ceriau (SO 180 239). This estate is also mentioned in charter 237b (133) H, a dispute of c. A.D. 925. There is some confusion as to how authentic the earlier charter may be, and whether or not the two documents relate to the same property and whether or not Llangorse may also be involved in the earlier document (Davies, *loc. cit.* n. 10, pp. 138, 171, 184).

[14] LL 166, Lanncoit (SO 113 394); Davies's ascription to Llangoed is only tentative.

[15] LL 146, Lann Cors (SO 135 276); J. E. Lloyd, *History of Wales* i, (1939), p. 272; W. Rees, *Historical Atlas of Wales*; Davies, *loc. cit.* n. 10, p. 71; the dating is discussed by E. Campbell and A. Lane in 'Llangorse: a 10th century royal crannog in Wales', *Antiquity* 63 (1989), pp. 675–81; p. 679.

[16] W. Davies, *An Early Welsh Microcosm: Studies in the Llandaff Charters*, (London: Roy. Hist. Soc., 1978), pp. 27–8, 30.

[17] *ibid.*, p. 35.

[18] References to rig and furrow and to several enclosures and house platforms within this parish are noted by C. S. Briggs, in 'Sites on Sennybridge Training Area', *Arch. in Wales* 30 (1990), p. 40. Similar features and clearance cairns have been noted by D. K. Leighton during R.C.A.M. survey for O.S. map revision in Glamorgan at Llandeilo Talybont (SM 60 04), a parish also occupying ground apparently hostile to agriculture at the present day. See also p. 206 fn. 2.

[19] MS note on R.C.A.M. field map. Nothing was found here during ground survey by Commission staff in February 1974.

[20] W. Davies, *loc. cit.* n. 10, pp. 35, 122, 124, 136, 172, 188; Campbell and Lane, *op. cit.*

[21] Campbell and Lane, *idem.*

[22] *Britain in the Dark Ages*, O.S. Map, (Southampton, 1966), revised 1973), index, p. 53, where the site is advanced as a *Clas*.

[23] T. Roberts, 'Welsh Ecclesiastical Place-Names and Archaeology', pp. 41–44, in N. Edwards and A. Lane, (eds.), *The Early Church in Wales and the West*, (Oxford: Oxbow Monograph 16, 1992), p. 43; Redknap, 'The Llangorse Landscape Project', *Arch. in Wales* 33 (1993), pp. 36–7.

[24] Traces of banks in fields close to Llanbeilin (SO 1549 2835) may be significant in this respect.

[25] J. E. Lloyd, *History Wales* i, (1939), p. 272; W. Rees, *Historical Atlas of Wales*; D. Knowles and R. M. Hadcock, *Medieval Religious Houses, England and Wales*, (1953), p. 356.

[26] Since the death of W. G. Thomas in 1994, plans to revise the corpus *E.C.M.W.* have been taken over by the Board of Celtic Studies; see also *Kingdom of Brycheiniog* and C. Thomas's book *And Shall These Mute Stones Speak?: post-Roman Inscriptions in Western Britain*, (Cardiff: U.P., 1994) for some rather speculative interpretations of the scant evidence.

[27] It is not the purpose of this volume to offer critical assessment of the dating, typology or hagiography of these stones. The most comprehensive list is in *E.C.M.W.*, where the types of stone are explained and listed in detail.

[28] R. E. M. Wheeler, 'Excavations at Brecon Gaer', *Y Cymmrodor* 37 (1926).

[29] *Kingdom of Brycheiniog*, p. 7.

[30] See W. N. Yates, 'The distribution and proportion of Celtic and non-Celtic church dedications in Wales', *Jnl Hist. Soc. Church in Wales* 28 (1973), pp. 1–17; the idea is more popularly presented in E. G. Bowen, *The Settlement of the Celtic Saints in Wales*, (Cardiff: U.P., 1954).

[31] M. L. Jones, *loc. cit.* n. 9, pp. 68–70.

[32] *idem.*, pp. 273–5.

[33] J. K. Knight, 'The Early Christian Latin inscriptions of Britain and Gaul: chronology and context', pp. 45–50, in Edwards and Lane, (eds.), *loc. cit.* n. 23.

[34] D. Brook, 'The Early Christian Church East and West of Offa's Dyke', pp. 77–89 in Edwards and Lane, (eds.), *idem.*

[35] J. K. Knight in 'New finds of Early Christian Monuments', *Arch. Camb.* 126 (1977), pp. 61–4, at p. 60 notes this churchyard as 'only part of a once larger enclosure which has been recorded from the air by Professor J. K. St. Joseph'. Although showing an old field bank parallel to the churchyard bank, for part of its circumference, close examination of A.P.s, C.U.A.P. AUF 47, 48 and CPAT 92-NB-0179–80 (by C. R. Musson) does not inspire confidence in the certain existence of any former curvilinear enclosure.

[36] Brook, *op. cit.* n. 34, p. 85.

[37] See for example C. S. Briggs, 'Ysbyty Cynfyn Churchyard Wall', in *Arch. Camb.* 128 (1979), pp. 138–46.

[38] N. Edwards and A. Lane, *Early Medieval Settlements in Wales AD 400–1100*, (Cardiff and Bangor: Early Medieval Wales Archaeology Research Group, 1988).

Crannog

Introduction

A crannog is an artificial island. Its occurrence as a habitation type-site within the British Isles is almost exclusively Irish and Scottish. Crannogs have been built and occupied at most periods from as early as Neolithic times until as late as the seventeenth century. Although claims have been made for the existence of crannogs situated in Welsh bogs,[1] the only one known certainly from Wales is situated in Llangorse Lake.[2]

(CR 1; Fig. 173) Ynys Bwlc is a crannog lying about 40 m offshore on the N. side of Llangorse Lake at a height of 155 m above O.D. It comprises a small overgrown island which, though often submerged in winter, at times protrudes 0.8–1 m above the water, forming an area 40 m E.–W. and 30 m N.–S. Now known to have been connected to the shore by a plank-driven causeway up to 3 m wide,[3] the site was first described and excavated during the 1860s.[4] The structure then revealed was stake-supported, oak piles having been driven through an amalgam of clay and stones. Beneath this is a layer of peat which overlies Mesolithic flints (MS 14). Recognition of its potential interest to Dark Age settlement is recent[5] and has resulted in a long-term excavation programme, ongoing at the time of writing. Re-planning of the submerged features reveals two concentric lines of timber piles (marked upon the plan, Fig. 173) forming three independent runs of planks and revetting lumps of sandstone dumped upon a brushwood mattress under a lacework of timber, within a complex which included a thick layer of peat. Wattle and protruding softwood timber were also noted.

Finds have so far included a log boat (the second from the lake, radiocarbon dated to the ninth century A.D.), part of an antler comb, fragments of carbonised textile tentatively dated between the fifth and tenth centuries A.D., carbonised grain and animal bone.[6] Sapwood dates have been precisely given as 890/893 A.D. It is possible that the structure was prefabricated. A historical explanation has been advanced for the site as the seat of the kings of Brycheiniog[7] and attention has also been drawn to the nearby presence of Llangorse monastery in c. 925 A.D. (mentioned above, p. 278), and to the destruction of a site on Brecenanmere in 916.[8]

How far such a structure (which differs fundamentally in design from the Irish and Scottish sites which give their name to the habitation type) might have been copied from them remains a matter of speculation.[9] As recent limnology has demonstrated quite dramatic increases in lake sedimentation during the second–third centuries A.D.,[10] it is possible that an earlier habitation site on the low-lying lakeside was slowly inundated when outlet silting impeded drainage during the Dark Ages.

---

[1] E. Jones, 'Remains of lake dwellings,' *Arch. Camb.* 128 (1923), pp. 154–5; I. Peate, 'A reported lake dwelling site near Tregaron', *B.B.C.S.* 4 (1927), pp. 283–284; *Antiquity* 2 (1928), p. 473; H. N. Jerman, 'Oak piles from the Peat in North Breconshire', *Antiq. Jnl* 15 (1935), pp. 68–69; W. F. Grimes, *The Prehistory of Wales*, (Cardiff, 1951), p. 232.

[2] J. G. Roberts and R. Peterson, 'Crannog Sites in Wales and the Marches,' *Arch. in Wales* 29 (1989), p. 40.

[3] Where not based upon visits by R.C.A.M. staff, the above description derives from the excavators' accounts, *viz*: E. Campbell and A. Lane, 'The Llangorse Crannog, Investigations in 1987 and 1988: an interim statement', *Arch. in Wales* 28 (1988), pp. 67–8; E. Campbell and A. Lane, 'Llangorse: a 10th century royal crannog in Wales', *Antiquity* 63 (1989), pp. 675–81; M. Redknap, 'Crossing the Divide: Investigating Crannogs', pp. 16–22 in J. M. Coles and D. M. Goodburn, (eds.), *Wet Site Excavation and Survey: Proceedings of a Conference at the Museum of London, October 1990*, (Museum of London, 1990); 'New Patterns from the Past', *Amgueddfa* Winter 1990, p. 5; Excavation reports appear in *Med. Archaeol.* 33 (1989), p. 241; 34 (1990), pp. 250–1; 35 (1991), pp. 235–6.

[4] E. N. Dumbleton, 'On a crannog, or stockaded island, in Llangorse Lake, near Brecon', *Arch. Camb.* 25 (1870), pp. 192–8. Although the original plan is now in the collections of the Royal Institution, Swansea, efforts by Commission staff during the mid-1970s failed to locate either Dumbleton's finds or any further archive documentation.

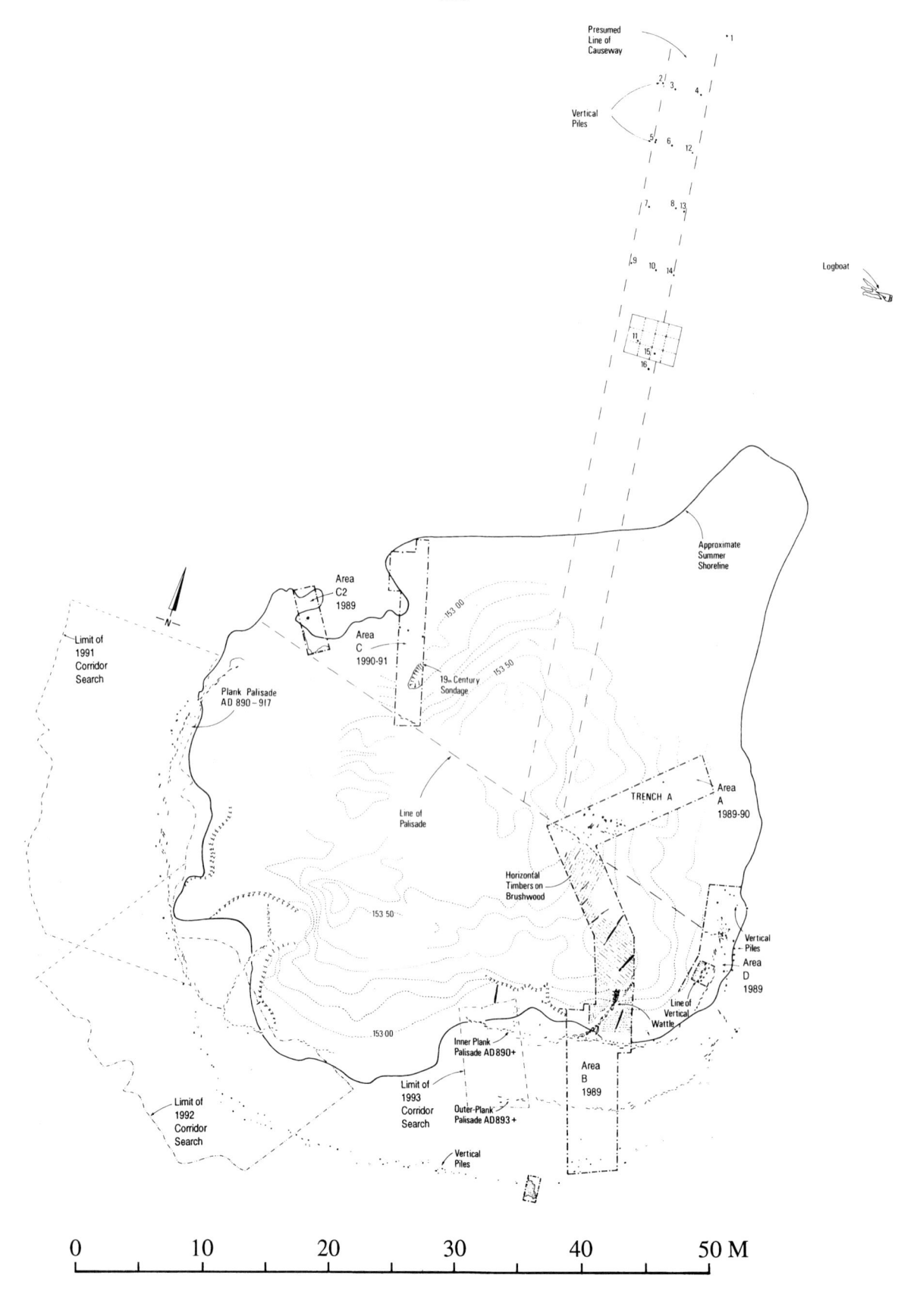

173 Bwlc Crannog: plan, following excavations (by courtesy of the National Museum of Wales)

[5] A. Lane, pp. 121–3 in N. Edwards and A. Lane (eds.), *Early Medieval Settlements in Wales AD 400–1100*, (Cardiff and Bangor: Early Medieval Wales Archaeology Research Group, 1988).

[6] Redknap, *loc. cit.* n. 3 and in *Arch. in Wales* 33 (1993), pp. 36–7.

[7] By E. Campbell and A. Lane, 'Llangorse: a 10th-century royal crannog in Wales', *Antiquity* 63 (1989), pp. 675–81, following W. Davies, *An Early Welsh Microcosm*, (London, 1978), p. 184; *Wales in the Early Middle Ages*, (Leicester, 1982), p. 97.

[8] S. Taylor, (ed.), *The Anglo-Saxon Chronicle; a collaborative edition, Volume 4, Manuscript B*, (Cambridge: U.P., 1983), p. 64.

[9] Campbell and Lane, *loc. cit.* n. 7.

[10] F. M. Chambers, 'Flandrian environmental history of the Llynfi catchment, South Wales', *Ecologia Mediterranea*, Tome XI (Fascicle 1), pp. 73–80; R. Jones, K. Benson-Evans, F. M. Chambers, B. Abell Seddon and Y. C. Tai, 'Biological and chemical studies of sediments from Llangorse Lake, Wales', *Verh. Internat. Verein. Limnol.* 29 (1978), pp. 642–8; R. Jones, K. Benson-Evans and F. M. Chambers, 'Human impact upon sedimentation at Llangorse Lake, Wales', *Earth Surface Processes and Landforms* 10 (1985), pp. 227–35.

Llangorse
SO 12 N.W. (1289 2690)   19 ix 91

A Handlist of Early Christian Stones (ECM 1–46; LECM 1–9, RECM 1–3)

Note: Detail provided in this handlist is meant for the purposes of indicating areas which may have been settled during the Dark Ages and as an introduction to the cultural and historical significance of inscribed stones. Original provenances are justified with reference to earliest sightings; otherwise, only basic bibliographical references are provided. Dating and interpretation of the stones is corroborated from *E.C.M.W.* II (kindly made available by the editors prior to its publication), in which the epigraphy will be discussed in detail. Unless otherwise indicated the grid references refer to findspots.

(ECM 1) Ystradgynlais Parish Church. Latin inscribed pillar stone fifth–sixth century.

O.S. SN 71 SE 1; *C.I.I.C.* pp. 332–3, no. 346; Dawson, *Churches of Brecon*, pp. 238–9; *E.C.M.W.*, p. 82, no. 75, Pl. vii, Fig. 60.

(ECM 2) Ystradgynlais Parish Church. Latin inscribed pillar stone (part), sixth century.

Arch. Camb. 10 (1855), p. 7; *C.I.I.C.* pp. 332–3, no. 347; Dawson, *Churches of Brecon*, pp. 238–9; *E.C.M.W.*, p. 82, no. 76, Pl. vii, Fig. 61.

SN 71 S.E.. (7870 1007)

(ECM 3) Traeanglas, Llywel. From a hedge bank at Aberhydfer (1954). Ogam inscribed stone fifth century. Latin inscription scored across by Ogam. In Llywel Church.

O.S. SN 82 NE 9; R. S. O. Tomlin in *Arch. Camb.* 124 (1975), pp. 68–72.

SN 82 N.E. (859 278)

(ECM 4) Trecastle, Llywel. In a cairn on Pentre Poeth Farm, *c.* 1878. Ogam and Latin inscribed two-phase pillar of fifth–sixth centuries and seventh–tenth centuries. In the British Museum.

SN 82 NE 2; *Arch. Camb.* 33 (1878), pp. 221–224, 236; *C.I.I.C.* i, pp. 325–7, no. 341 and illus.; *E.C.M.W.* pp. 81–2, no. 71, Fig. 57.

SN 82 N.E.. (8829 2645)

(ECM 5) Llanwrtyd, Llawrdref Farm (1897). From the remains of Ystafell Fach cottage. Cross-inscribed pillar, seventh–ninth century, bearing incised penannular ring device divided transversely into two halves. Now at Llanwrtyd (St. David's) Parish Church (8589 4517).

O.S. SN 84 NE 3; *Arch. Camb.* 57 (1903), pp. 293–7; *E.C.M.W.*, p. 77, no. 64, Pl. xxviii; Dawson, *Churches of Brecon*, p. 150.

SN 84 N.E. (8636 4779) [findspot]

(ECM 6) Llandulas, Penlan Wen, Tirabad. Sandstone pillar bearing linear ring-cross with dots and cruciform panel of ninth–tenth century.

O.S. SN 84 NE 3; *E.C.M.W.*, p. 73, no. 48, Pl. xv, Fig. 5, 25.

SN 84 S.E. (894 419)

(ECM 7) Ystradfellte, Pen y Mynydd (eighteenth-century find). Pillar stone of fifth–sixth centuries with incomplete Ogam inscription and incised Latin wheel-cross of possibly seventh–ninth centuries. In Cyfarthfa Castle Museum, Merthyr Tydfil.

O.S. SN 91 NW 5; *C.I.I.C.* i, pp. 331–2, no. 348; *Arch. Camb.* 49 (1894), pp. 329–30; C. J. O. Evans, *Glamorgan*, (1938), pp. 191–2; *Lapidarium Walliae* (1876), pp. 70–1; Gough's *Camden*, II, Pl. 14, Fig. 4; *Archaeologia* 4 (1777), p. 8, Pl. 1, Fig. 5; *E.C.M.W.*, p. 82, no. 74, illus.

SN 91 N.W. (91 50)

Maen Llia (SN 91 N.W. 9242 1918). See SS 12

(ECM 8; Fig. 174) Ystradfellte, Maen Madoc Stone (1777). Latin inscribed pillar, fifth–sixth century. (Excavation discussed above, p. 162).

   O.S. SN 91 NW 2; *Archaeologia* 4 (1777), p. 8 and Pl. 1, Fig. 3; *C.I.I.C.* i, p. 381, no. 344; *Arch. Camb.* 94 (1939), pp. 31–2, Pl. 1a; 95 (1940), pp. 210–16, Pls. 1, 2, Figs. 1, 2, 3; *E.C.M.W.*, p. 82, no. 73, Pl. vii, Fig. 58.

SN 91 N.W. (9183 1577)

(ECM 9) Nant Crew farm, Cantref (1957). Now at Cefn Coed Parish Church. Latin inscribed sandstone pillar of the sixth century.

   Arch. Camb. (1958), pp. 123–4.

SN 91 N.E. (993 165)

(ECM 10) Defynnog Parish Church. Latin inscribed pillar stone of fifth–sixth centuries re-used as cross-inscribed sandstone pillar in the tenth or eleventh century.

   O.S. SN 92 NW 4; *C.I.I.C.* 1, no. 317–18; *E.C.M.W.*, pp. 69–70, Pl. 1, Fig. 42, no. 44. II, 87.

(ECM 11) Defynnog Parish Church (1955). Part of slab with ring-cross, possibly of 10th century, now forming doorway lintel into ringing chamber on first floor of W. tower.

   Kingdom of Brycheiniog, p. 5; W. G. Thomas, in *Arch. Camb.* 133 (1984), pp. 152–3, illus. B6–7.

SN 92 N.W. (9252 2794)

(ECM 12) Trallwng Parish Church (*c.* 1860). Ogam and Latin cross-inscribed pillar stone, first inscribed in the early sixth century, then re-used as a cross in the seventh–ninth centuries.

   Arch. Camb. 17 (1862), pp. 52–6; *C.I.I.C.*, pp. 328–9, no. 1342; 24 (1869), pp. 161–4; Dawson, *Churches of Brecon*, pp. 230–1; *E.C.M.W.*, p. 81, no. 70, Pl. 1, Fig. 56.

SN 92 N.E. (9667 2962)

(ECM 13) Llanwrtyd, Treflys, Cildu Farm. Pillar stone with linear cross of seventh–ninth centuries. In Brecknock Museum.

174   Maen Madoc inscribed standing stone (ECM 8)

   O.S. SN 94 NW 4; *E.C.M.W.*, p. 76, no. 58, Pl. XVI.

SN 94 N.W. (9052 4659)

(ECM 14) Llanlleonfel Churchyard. Inscribed pillar with three crosses and inscription of seventh–ninth centuries.

   O.S. SN 94 NW 5, 11; *C.I.I.C.* 2, p. 138, no. 986; *E.C.M.W.*, p. 62, no. 62, PL. xxi.

SN 94 N.W. (9387 4993)

(ECM 15) Llangammarch Parish Church porch. Part of slab bearing incised outline ring-cross and other devices. Of seventh–ninth centuries.

   Arch. Camb. 8 (1853), p. 334; *E.C.M.W.*, p. 76, no. 57, Pl. xvi, Fig. 5:10.

SN 94 S.W. (9346 4832)

(ECM 16) Llanafan Fawr Parish Church. Sandstone pillar with ring-cross, of ninth–tenth centuries.

E.C.M.W., p. 71, no. 45, Fig. 5:10, Pl. xv.

(ECM 17–19) Three slabs of local gritstone bearing roughly pecked crosses. Where datable, seventh–eighth centuries.

J. K. Knight in *Arch. Camb.* 126 (1977), pp. 60–4.

SN 95 N.E. (9690 5578)

(ECM 20) Vaynor, Abercar. Formerly lintel to a farmhouse on W. side of Brecon to Merthyr road. Provenance discussed in *E.C.M.W.* II. Latin inscribed sandstone slab, of 6th century. In Merthyr Tydfil Parish Church.

O.S. SO 01 SW 1; *C.I.I.C.* 1, pp. 319–321, no. 331; *E.C.M.W.*, p. 69, no. 41, Pl. vii.

(ECM 21) Vaynor, Abercar. Found as above. Latin inscribed quadrangular pillar. Formerly in Merthyr Tydfil Parish Church, but now lost.

C.I.I.C. i, pp. 322, no. 331; *Arch. Camb.* 13 (1858), pp. 162–3 and illus.; *E.C.M.W.*, p. 69, no. 40, Pl. VII, Fig. 39.

SO 01 S.W. (01 12)

(ECM 22) Llanddeti: Pontsticill, Cwm Criban or Ystrad Ogam pillar stone. Fifth–sixth centuries.

NLW Llanstephan MS 186, fol. 5; *Parochialia* II, p. 90; *Arch. Camb.* 27 (1872), p. 386; *Arch. Camb.* 106 (1957), pp. 118–21, Pl. xvi, Fig. 7; James 1978–9, 22, 11/43; *E.C.M.W.*, p. 79, no. 67a.

SO 01 S.E. (0731 1321)

(ECM 23) Llanspyddid Parish Church (found *c*. 1700). Pillar stone with cross and ring-crosses, probably of ninth–tenth centuries.

O.S. SO 02 NW 5, 6; Jones, *Notebook*, fo. 32; Dawson, *Churches of Brecon*, pp. 190–1; *Arch. Camb.* 8 (1853), pp. 311, 334; *E.C.M.W.*, no. 63, p. 79, Pl. xvi.

SN 02 N.W. (0118 2819)

(ECM 24) Llanfrynach Parish Church (found *c*. 1855). Tall slab incised with linear cross of tenth–eleventh centuries.

Arch. Camb. 11 (1856), pp. 51, 140; *E.C.M.W.*, pp. 75–6, no. 56, Pl. liii.

SO 02 N.E. (0752 2579)

(ECM 25) Llanfigan. Ty Newydd Farm (*c*. 1935). Sandstone slab incised ring-cross of seventh to ninth centuries. Now in N.M.W.

O.S. SO 02 NE 4; *Arch Camb.* 111 (1936), pp. 134–7; *E.C.M.W.*, p. 74, no. 53, Fig. 5, Pl. xv.

SO 02 N.E. (0850 2617)

(ECM 26) Llanhamlach Parish Church (found pre-1850). Rectangular sandstone slab decorated with inscription, figures, and plaitwork of tenth–eleventh centuries.

Arch. Camb. 6 (1852), pp. 273–5; *E.C.M.W.* I, no. 61, pp. 76–7, Pl. liii.

(ECM 27) Llanhamlach. Edge of broken sandstone slab decorated with three-strand plait. Built into outside W. face of church tower.

E.C.M.W. II, *forthcoming*.

SO 02 N.E. (0895 2645)

(ECM 28) Llandefaelog Fach. In churchyard *c*. 1700. Panelled late-tenth century decorated and incised rectangular sandstone slab.

Stowe MS 1023, fo. 166; Jones, *Notebook*, fo. 8, 'copied Camden'; *Arch. Camb.* 27 (1872), pp. 383–4; 13 (1858), p. 306; *Britain in Dark Ages Map*, (O.S., 1966), Index, p. 50; *E.C.M.W.*, p. 73, no. 49, Pl. liii.

(ECM 29) Llandefaelog. Built into tower arch. Catvc inscribed stone. Known only from antiquarian sources.

Lhuyd, *Parochialia* ii; *C.I.I.C.* i, p. 321, no. 333; Jones, *Hist. Brecks.* II, p. 174; Dawson, *Churches of Brecon*, p. 101; *Britain in Dark Ages Map*, (O.S., 1966), Index, p. 50; *E.C.M.W.*, p. 74, no. 50.

SO 03 N.W. (0339 3239)

(ECM 30–1) Llanddew Parish Church. Rectangular slab inscribed and cross-decorated stone. Date uncertain, possibly both eighth and twelfth centuries.

Two fragments of sculptured sandstone, possibly of a pillar cross, eleventh–twelfth centuries.

O.S. SO 03 SE 5; *Arch. Camb.* 40 (1885), 147–8; *C.I.I.C.* 2, no. 980 (illus.); *E.C.M.W.*, p. 73, 46a, Fig. 44, Pl. xvii.

SO 03 S.E. (0549 3074)

(ECM 32) Llanynys, Maesmynys, from Neuadd Siarman (pre-1809). Moulded pillar cross of Anglian type, late ninth–tenth centuries. In Brecknock Museum.

O.S. SO 04 NW 1; Jones, *Hist. Brecks.* II (1809), p. 280; *Arch. Camb.* 2 (1847), p. 27; 8 (1853), p. 334; *E.C.M.W.*, pp. 31, 34, 35, 78, Fig. 52, Pl. xl (no. 65).

SO 04 N.W. (0123 4760)

(ECM 33) Llanddewi'r Cwm, Erwhelm Cross. Tenth-century moulded pillar stone. In Brecknock Museum.

Ant. J. 19 (1939), p. 149 and photos; *E.C.M.W.*, p. 73, no. 47, Pl. xlii.

SO 04 N.W. (035 494)

(ECM 34) Llanfihangel Cwm Du (Crickhowell), Glanusk Park. Sandstone pillar with defaced Latin inscription. Formerly between gate lodge and chapel, now set in private graveyard in Penmyarth Park. One face re-cut with epitaph to Joseph Henry Russell, 2nd Baron Glanusk, 11th January 1928.

O.S. Card SO 11 NE 4; *C.I.I.C.*, no. 974, pp. 131–2.

SO 11 N.E. (1881 1992) original site; present site (1866 1985)

(ECM 35) Llansantffraid, 'Pentre Yskythrog' (probably Scethrog). 'Victorinus' inscribed pillar stone of sixth century. Now in Brecknock Museum.

O.S. SO 00 NW 11 and O.S. 02 SE 13; Stowe MS 1023, fo. 163; Gough's *Camden*; Jones, Notebook, fo. 16; Jones, *Hist. Brecks.* II ii, Pl. vi, iii; *Lapidarium Walliae* (1879), p. 59; *Arch. Camb.* 6 (1851), p. 226; 7 (1852), pp. 274–5; 57 (1922), pp. 198–9; Dawson, *Churches of Brecon*, p. 135; *B.B.C.S.* 7 (1935–6), p. 70; *C.I.I.C.* i, p. 324, no. 339; *E.C.M.W.*, p. 79, nos. 68 and 72, Pl. vii, Fig. 54; *E.C.M.W.* II.

SO 12 N.W. (106 252 or 112 248) original area; possible alternative, SO 12 S.W. (1105 2485)

(ECM 36) Llangorse Parish Church (found pre-1874). Sandstone burial slab. Inscribed and with outline cross and decoration, possibly of *c.* 1000 A.D.

O.S. SO 12 NW 4; Dawson, *Churches of Brecon*, p. 121; *E.C.M.W.*, p. 76, no. 59, Fig. 48, Pl. xvi.

(ECM 37) Llangorse Parish Church (1881). Sandstone pillar inscribed with eleventh–twelfth inscription.

O.S. SO 12 NW 5; *Arch. Camb.* 45 (1890), pp. 224–5; *C.I.I.C.* 1, pp. 323–4, no. 337; *E.C.M.W.*, p. 76, no. 60, Pl. lx, Fig. 49.

(ECM 38) Llangorse Parish Church. Fragment of sandstone slab with zoomorphic decoration of ninth–twelfth centuries.

C.I.I.C. I, no. 337, p. 324.

SO 12 N.W. (1350 2764)

(ECM 39) Llanddeti Parish Church. Sandstone pillar, decorated and incised with three faces inscribed in Latin.

E.C.M.W., p. 71, no. 46, p. 28, Fig. 43.

SO 12 S.W. (1280 2024)

(ECM 40) Llanfihangel Cwm Du: Penygaer (the Gaer) (found *c.* 1700); later from a field called Tir Gwenlli. Catacus inscribed sandstone pillar of seventh century. Built into Cwmdu Church in 1830.

O.S. SO 12 SE 11; MS letter E. Lhuyd 1698/9 (N.L.W. MS Penrhos V, No. 237); MS Proc. Soc. Ants, Nov. 1773, (Meeting of Society; Daines Barrington, communicated by Maskelyne); Gough, *Camden* III, p. 103; Jones, *Notebook*, fo. 59; *Hist. Brecks.* II, Pl. lxiii, Fig. 1; *C.I.I.C.* 1, p. 322, no. 324 (I); Dawson, *Churches of Brecon*, p. 193; *Arch. Camb.* 26 (1871), p. 261, no. 5; 8 (1853), p. 311; 27 (1872), p. 162; *Lapidarium Walliae* (1871), p. 55, Pl. 32, no. 4; *Y Cymmrod*, (1905), p. 49; *Gents Magazine* (1861), p. 39; *E.C.M.W.*, p. 74, no. 54, Pl. vii, Fig. 46; E. Gwynne Jones in *B.B.C.S.* 17 (1956–7), p. 110.

SO 12 S.E. (173 215) original site

(ECM 41) Llanfihangel Cwm Du Church. Pillar slab with incised cross of seventh–ninth centuries. Another face with Lombardic style inscription of twelfth–thirteenth centuries.

Arch. Camb. 7 (1852), p. 272; *E.C.M.W.*, p. 74, no. 54a; Pl. lxiii, Fig. 47.

(ECM 42) Llanfihangel Cwm Du. Slab fragment bearing incised linear Latin cross of seventh–ninth century.

E.C.M.W. II.

SO 12 S.E. (1805 2385)

(ECM 43–4) Llaneleu Parish Church. Two cross-inscribed stones, one a pillar, the other a slab, both of seventh–ninth centuries.

Dawson, *Churches of Brecon*, p. 115; *E.C.M.W.*, p. 74, no. 51, 52, Pls. xv, xvi, Figs. 5:40, 5:4.

SO 13 S.E. (1850 3419)

(ECM 45) Crickhowell: Ty yn y Wlad farm (1777). Turpilli stone. Sandstone conglomerate pillar in Ogam and Latin. Formerly in Glanusk Park and now in Brecknock Museum.

O.S. SO 11 NE 15; *Archaeologia* 4 (1777), pp. 18–19, Fig. 2; T. Jones, *Hist. Brecks.* 3 (1911), pp. 142–3; *Arch. Camb.* 8 (1853), pp. 324, 332; 17 (1862), p. 234; 24 (1869), pp. 153–5; 26 (1871), pp. 158–162; *E.C.M.W.*, p. 69, no. 43, Fig. 41, Pl. I.

SO 21 N.W. (225 193) The O.S. gives the Glanusk site which is SO 11 N.E. (1965 1930)

(ECM 46) Patrishow Parish Church, font. 'Menhir me fecit'. Eleventh–twelfth centuries.

E.C.M.W., p. 79, no. 67, Pl. lxiii, Fig. 53.

SO 22 S.E. (2783 2243)

Lost Monuments (LECM 1–9)

(LECM 1–2) Found at Mynachty, and removed to Merthyr Cynog Church (found pre-1809). Two cross-decorated stones. Now lost.

Jones, *Hist. Brecks.* II (1809), p. 183.

SN 93 N.E. (984 374)

(LECM 3) Vaynor or Cantref: possibly from Nant Ddu 'from Cornal y Bedde' (found early nineteenth century). Inscribed pillar stone of fifth–sixth centuries.

Jones, *Hist. Brecks.* II (1809), Pl. 6, Fig. 5; *E.C.M.W.*, p. 79, no. 66; *C.I.I.C.* i, pp. 368–9, no. 330.

SO 01 N.W. (0025 1500)

(LECM 4–5) Llanfrynach Parish Church (found c. 1855). Large inscribed stone and fragment of stone with outline cross with vertical inscription. Discovered during demolition of the old parish church and buried in foundations of new building.

O.S. SO 02 NE 5; *E.C.M.W.*, p. 74, no. 55; *Arch. Camb.* 11 (1856), p. 51, and illus. opp. p. 51; 82 (1927), p. 207; *Arch. Camb.* 11 (1856), p. 52.

SO 02 N.E. (075 258)

(LECM 6) Llangynidr Parish Church (near). Formerly inscribed.

O.S. SO 11 NE 3; Jones, *Hist. Brecks.* II, ii (1809), p. 516.

SO 11 N.E. (1560 1935)

(LECM 7) Talybont. 'By the highway side from Talybont to Llangattwg, within a mile of ye former'. sixth-century inscription overlain by seventh–ninth century cross (lost).

E.C.M.W., p. 81, no. 69; NLW Llanstephan MS 185, fo. 53; *Parochialia* II, p. 91.

SO 12 S.W. (12 21) (findspot)

(LECM 8) Patrishow Parish Church from a field near. Stone with two incised crosses. Now lost.

Jones, *Hist. Brecks.* II (1809), p. 417; *Arch. Camb.* 69 (1904), pp. 62–3.

SO 22 S.E. (2777 2339)

(LECM 9) Llanigon, c. 1690. 'Pitch'd in a hedge by ye way side call'd hewl y groes within 3 qrs of a mile of Llaneigon Church – qr of a yard broad, 5 inches thick, an ell high above ground. As the centre is not placed.' (Cross rudely shaped.)

Llanstephan MS 185, fol. 56; *Parochialia* II, p. 91.

SO 24

Rejected Early Christian Monuments (RECM 1–3)

(RECM 1) Defynnog: monument known as Capel y Fynwent, and mentioned by Edward Lhuyd in the late seventeenth century. This early account of a fifth–sixth century Latin inscribed stone is considered more likely to be attributable to the Pentre Poeth stone now in the British Museum (see ECM 4) above.

Parochialia II, p. 85; *C.I.I.C.* 1, p. 318, no. 329 (4); *Britain in the Dark Ages Map*, (O.S., 1966), Index, p. 50; *E.C.M.W.*, p. 69, no. 42, Fig. 40; *E.C.M.W.* II (Rejected monument).

SN 82 S.E. (877 235)

(RECM 2) Defynnog Parish Church font. Although it has been suggested that the circumferential rim inscription is Roman and Runic, compelling arguments have been presented to suggest that the present font is a composite of post-medieval origin.

C.I.I.C. no. 975, p. 132; *cf. E.C.M.W.* II (Rejected monument).

SN 92 N.W. (9252 2794)

(RECM 3) Llanfihangel Cwm Du Llygadwy: Bwlch. A standing stone considered to have been Ogam, inscribed by Macalister in 1922, is considered recent, the marks resulting from grooving by barbed wire. (See also RSS 44).

O.S. 12 SE 8; *Arch. Camb.* 77 (1922), p. 210; *C.I.I.C.*, 1, no. 338.

SO 12 S.E. (1510 2196)

Later Prehistoric Lithic Finds (SF 1–92)

Key

A.B.: Audrey Bird, Aberdare; A.W.F.: Alan W. Foxall, 107 Malvern Road, Redditch, Worcs, B97 5DR; P.M.J.: Peter M. Jones, 15 Harford St, Tredegar, Gwent; K.P.: Ken Palmer, Monmouth Cap Farmhouse, Llangua, Abergavenny, NP7 8HD.

Br 1–15: Implements numbered according to C.B.A. List of Petrographic Identifications (Wales: Breconshire, C. H. Houlder); p. 247 in *Stone Axe Studies*, (eds.) T. H. McK. Clough and W. A. Cummins, (London: C.B.A. Res. Rep. 79, 1988).

All finds are of flint unless otherwise stated. When the period of the find is uncertain (as it is in the case of most flakes), it appears under the Bronze Age section.

For Mesolithic, see MS 1–18; RMS 1–3

Neolithic

(SF 1) Mynydd y Drum. Flint axehead. N.M.W. Br 6.

Arch. Camb. 87 (1932), pp. 406–8; p. 407.

SN 80 N.W. (825 097)

(SF 2) Llanwrtyd School (Llanwrtyd). Axe. Brecknocks Mus. Br 7.

SN 84 N.E. (87 48)

SN 85 N.W. Nant y Stalwen. Undiagnostic flints, see MS 4.

(SF 3) Wernlas Farm, Penderyn. Lozenge-shaped flint arrowhead.

SN 90 N.E. (965 099)

(SF 4) Large convex flint scraper.

Arch. in Wales 15 (1975), p. 26, no. 7.

SN 90 N.E. (969 098)

(SF 5) Possibly Ystradfellte. Plano-convex knife (found 1978). C.P.A.T.

SN 91 S.W. (92 13)

(SF 6) Cilgwyn Farm (1976). Flint axe. N.M.W.

SN 93 S.E. (9823 3308)

(SF 7) Wern Figyn Farm. Trallong (1969). Leaf-shaped arrowhead. Brecknocks Mus.

Savory, *Prehist. Brecks.* II, p. 8.

SN 93 S.W. (94 30)

(SF 8) 'Near Brecon'. Axe; Private. Br 9.

SO 02 N.W. (04 28)

(SF 9) Bwlch Duwynt (Modrydd). Worked flint.

K. Palmer, *Arch. in Wales* 18 (1978), p. 31, no. 7.

SO 02 S.W. (000 205)

(SF 10) Waun Gunllwch (Crickadarn). Flint scraper, triangular arrowhead, two scrapers and both worked and unworked flakes.

SO 04 S.E. (063 415 and 063 416)

(SF 11) Erwood, Crickadarn. Stone hammer head. Brecknocks Mus. Br 8.

SO 04 S.E. (09 42)

(SF 12) Pendre Housing site, Builth Wells. Polished stone axe. N.M.W. Br 10.

Brycheiniog 4 (1958), p. 128; 6 (1960), p. 120; *B.B.C.S.* (1961), p. 167.

SO 05 S.W. (034 512)

(SF 13) River Bridge, Builth. Stone axe. Brecknocks Mus. Br 24.

SO 05 S.W. (043 512)

(SF 14) Nant y Ffin, Crickhowell. Polished flint axe. N.M.W. Br 25.

Savory, 1947, pp. 286–8; *B.B.C.S.*, p. 125; Grimes, 1951, p. 147, no. 120.

SO 11 N.E. (199 197)

(SF 15) Talgarth area. Three leaf-shaped arrowheads. Brecknocks Mus.

SO 11 S.E. (15 14)

(SF 16) Ty Isaf (Talgarth). Ploughed field S. of Castell Dinas. Flint flakes and ?scraper. Private.

SO 12 N.E. (181 293)

(SF 17) Ty Isaf long barrow. Axes, arrowheads, sandstone disc, scraper (CT 3).

SO 12 N.E. (182 291)

(SF 18) Trebinshun Farm, Llangasty-Talyllyn. Partly polished axe. N.M.W. Br 4.

Grimes, *Prehist. Wales*, p. 147, no. 118.

SO 12 S.W. (137 242).

(SF 19) River Llynfi, Aberllynfi, pre-1971. Stone axe. Private. Br 17.

Savory, *Prehist. Brecks.* II, p. 10.

SO 13 N.E. (15 35)

(SF 20) Ffostyll (Llaneleu). Implements and flakes from fields in area of barrow sites, 1920s and 1980 (CT 5–6).

Vulliamy, *Arch. Camb.* 76 (1921), pp. 300–305; *Arch. Camb.* 78 (1923), pp. 320–4.

SO 13 S.E. (179 349)

(SF 21) Glasbury area. Fragment of Neolithic polished flint axe and eight leaf-shaped arrowheads. Brecknocks Museum.

SO 13 S.E. (17 39)

(SF 22) Upper Paper Mill, Glangrwyne, Llangenny (1860). Four polished axes, one of flint. Private. Br 1–3; 23.

Arch. Camb. 31 (1876), p. 348; A. H. Williams, *Arch. Camb.* 96 (1941), p. 19; W. B. Dawkins, 'On a find of Neolithic Celts near Crickhowell, Breconshire', *Arch. Camb.* 73 (1918), pp. 1–5.

SO 21 N.W. (2410 1780)

(SF 23) Gwernvale megalith (CT 11). Polished axe. C.P.A.T. Br 19.

SO 21 N.W. (211 192)

(SF 24) Llanelli. Chert axe. N.M.W. Br 5.

SO 21 S.W. (23 14)

(SF 25) Gilwern, Llanelli. Axe. Private. Br 18.

SO 21 S.W. (24 14)

(SF 26) Gader Fawr, Mynydd Du, Llaneleu. Polished chert axe. Brecknocks Mus. Br 22.

SO 22 N.W. (2324 2851)

(SF 27) Chwarel y Fan, Llaneleu. N.M.W. Br 20.

SO 22 N.E. (253 293)

Bronze Age

(SF 28) Waun Fignen Felen. Tanged and barbed arrowhead. See (MS 2).

SN 81 N.W. (824 184)

(SF 29) Garn Goch, Mynydd y Drum. Five worked flints, several flakes. See (RC 16–17).

SN 81 S.W. (8178 1077) Garn Goch; (8188 1073) ring cairn.

(SF 30) Ogof Ffynnon Ddu, Penwyllt. Flint knife. See (PCS 2).

SN 81 S.W. (848 152)

(SF 31) Mynydd Wysg, Llywel. Two arrowheads, one barbed and tanged; one straight-sided with hollow base. N.M.W.

> Savory 1948–50, pp. 110, 162.

SN 82 N.W. (82 27)

(SF 32) Fan Foel round cairn. Flint flakes only. See (RC 26)

SN 82 S.W. (8213 2234)

(SF 33) Pant Sychpant, Penderyn. Implements including three barbed and tanged arrowheads and plano-convex knife. See (MS 7).

SO 90 N.E. (995 098)

(SF 34) Beacons Reservoir. See also (MS 9). Flint scraper. [(9884 1840) Natural Flint Nodule]

SN 91 N.E. (9886 1889).

(SF 35) Two flint knives.

> *Arch. in Wales* 26 (1986), p. 61, 11–13 (C. S. Briggs); 31 (1991) (P. Dorling).

SN 91 N.E. (9858 1855)

(SF 36) Hepste, Ystradfellte. Flake ?chert. A.B.

SN 91 S.W.

(SF 37) Nr Coed y Garreg, Ystradfellte. Many flints with Beaker burial. (See RC 90, BB5.)

> K. Holloway, *Arch. in Wales* 5 (1965), p. 6, no. 5.

SN 91 S.W. (9075 1466)

(SF 38) Cairn, Plas y gors, Ystradfellte, flint dagger, knives, scrapers. See (RC 91).

SN 91 S.W. (9156 1466)

(SF 39) Nant Maden Cairn. Worked flint. See (RC 111).

SN 91 S.E. (9709 1059)

(SF 40) Twyn Bryn Glas, Cwm Cadlan, Penderyn. Worked flint. See (RC 127).

SN 91 S.E. (9850 1166)

(SF 41) Stone disc, Cefn Sychpant. See (RC 126).

SN 91 S.E. (9864 1101)

(SF 42) Aberbrân Mill. Convex flint scraper. Brecknocks Mus.

SN 92 N.E. (988 294)

(SF 43) Pont ar Daf-Corn Du path. Flints in excavated cairn.

> A. M. Gibson, *Arch. in Wales* 29 (1989), p. 42. See (LBS 3).

SN 92 S.E. (9945 2005)

(SF 44) Dixie's Corner, Llanfihangel Nant Brân. Tanged and barbed arrowhead. N.M.W.

> Savory, *Guide*, p. 97, no. 79. illus.

SN 93 N.W. (92 37)

(SF 45) Ynys-hir round cairn excavation. Flint knife and flakes. See (RC 138).

SN 93 N.W. (9207 3825)

(SF 46) Three flint flakes from stone circle adjacent. See (SC 5).

SN 93 N.W. (9211 3826)

(SF 47) Llangammarch. Tanged and barbed arrowhead. Brecknocks Mus. R.777.

> Savory, *Prehist. Brecks.* I, p. 25, no. 72.

SN 94 N.W. (93 47)

(SF 48) Pen Moel Allt Plantation. Flint scatter and slug knife.

Arch. in Wales 15 (1975), p. 20, no. 6.

SO 00 N.E. (009 095)

See SF 56

(SF 49) Upper Neuadd, Llanfrynach. Flakes and implements probably Neolithic and Bronze Age. Private.

See 'Prehistory', pp. 147–60, in Merthyr Teachers' Centre Group, (eds.), *Merthyr Tydfil: A Valley Community*, (Cowbridge, 1981), p. 147; illustrated in *Taf* 1982, p. 88.
See (MS 10).

SO 01 N.W. (0265 1938 and 0305 1905).

(SF 50) Craig Fan Ddu. Flint flakes. K.P.

K. Palmer, *Arch. in Wales* 20 (1980), p. 20, 5.

SO 01 N.W. (019 182)

(SF 51) Nr. Upper Neuadd. Tanged and barbed arrowhead. A.B.

SO 01 N.W. (0266 1916)

(SF 52) S. of Cwm Oergwm. Plano-convex flint knife. Brecknocks Mus.

SO 01 N.W. (04 19)

(SF 53) Lower Neuadd, Llanfrynach. Flakes.

P. M. Jones, *Arch. in Wales* 14 (1974), p. 7, no. 2.

SO 01 N.W. (0325 1780)

(SF 54) In 1897, 21 worked flints were picked up on the N.E. shore of the reservoir. Cantrill nos. 871–91 (N.M.W.).

SO 01 N.E. (05 15)

(SF 55) Coetgae Llwyn (carpark area). Flint artefacts (including scraper) and flakes. P.M.J.

Arch. in Wales 12 (1972), p. 11, no. 2; *Arch. in Wales* 14 (1974), p. 7, no. 2.

SO 01 N.E. (055 175)

(SF 56) Blaencar, Llanddeti; scraper and flakes. N.M.W. (See MS 12.)

Savory 1971, p. 5.

SO 01 S.W. (048 141)

(SF 57) Cwm Car cist burial. Barbed and tanged arrowhead. See (LBS 5).

SO 01 S.E. (054 135)

(SF 58) Dolygaer Reservoir. Large flakes struck from nodular flint. P.M.J.

SO 01 S.E. (055 145)

(SF 59) Twynau Gwynion, Pontsticill (Glam). Tanged and barbed arrowhead.

SO 01 S.E. (068 106)

(SF 60) Near Brecon. Hammer. N.M.W. Br 21.

SO 02 N.W. (04 28)

(SF 61) Cribyn. Fragment of serrated blade.

K. Palmer, *Arch. in Wales* 20 (1980), p. 20, 5.

SO 02 S.W. (024 214)

(SF 62) Pen y Fan. Flint knife/re-worked arrowhead. K.P., P.M.J.

Arch. in Wales 23 (1983), p. 6, 5.

SO 02 S.W. (012 216)

(SF 63) Bryn (Llanfigan). Thumb scraper.

SO 02 S.E. (0760 2240)

(SF 64) Cwm Oergwm, Llanfrynach. Flint knife. Brecknocks Mus.

Savory, *Prehist. Brecks.* I, p. 101.

SO 02 S.E. (05 22)

(SF 65) Mynydd Llangorse. Flint knife and flakes. P.M.J.

O.S. Card SO 12 NE 2; P. M. J. *Arch. in Wales* 18 (1978), p. 32, 13.

SO 12 N.E. (161 265)

(SF 66) Mynydd Troed. Flint spall. P. Dorling.

SO 12 N.E. (165 291)

(SF 67) Destroyed tumulus behind Vicarage, Llangorse. Three flint arrowheads. (LBS 8).

R.C.A.M., *Mins of Evidence*, 1912, no. 1466.

SO 12 S.W. (135 277)

(SF 68) Buckland Old Mill, Llansantffraid. Mace head. Private. Br 14.

Savory, *Arch. in Wales* 1 (1961), p. 3, no. 1; *B.B.C.S.* 19 (1960–62), p. 252.

SO 12 S.W. (128 210)

(SF 69) Allt-y-Gaer [?for Allt yr Esgair], Llangorse. Flint point. Brecknocks Mus.

SO 12 S.W. (125 243)

(SF 70) Llwyn y Fedwen, Llanfihangel Cwmdu. Flint flakes in field.

SO 12 S.E. (1561 2046)

(SF 71) Myarth Hill. Retouched flint flake fragment on Myarth Hillfort. P. Dorling.

SO 12 S.E. (174 207)

(SF 72) Llanfihangel Cwmdu. Axe hammer. Brecknocks Mus. Br 11.

SO 12 S.E. (18 24)

(SF 73) Gaer in Gwernyfed Park. A flint scraper, a knife tip and unworked flakes were found during excavation of the hillfort (HF 57).

Inv. Br. I (ii), pp. 111–112; Savory, *Brycheiniog* 4 (1958), pp. 33–71.

SO 13 N.E. (1750 3759)

(SF 74) Tŷ Du (?Ffostyll). Beaker flint dagger and knife. See (LBS 9).

SO 13 N.E. (179 349)

(SF 75) Ffostyll round barrow excavation. Pygmy cup and triangular worked flakes. See (LBS 10).

SO 13 N.E. (1795 3501)

(SF 76) Talgarth. Barbed and tanged arrowhead. Brecknocks Mus. R.159.

SO 13 S.E. (15 34)

(SF 77) Castell Dinas, flint flakes. Found on the second rampart at S.E. corner of the hillfort (HF 50).

Inv. Br. I (ii), p. 99.

SO 13 S.E. (1797 3006)

(SF 78) The Gaer, Aberllynfi. Chert scraper and tip of flint plano-convex knife.

H. N. Savory, 'Excavations at Aberllynfi', *B.B.C.S.* 14 (1951), 251–?

SO 14 N.E. (175 376)

(SF 79) Erwood. Axe hammer of grit. Brecknocks Mus.

Savory, *Prehist. Brecks.* I, p. 26.

SO 14 S.W. (10 43)

(SF 80) Mynydd Llisiau, N. of. Flint scraper.

Arch. in Wales 23 (1983), p. 6, no. 4.

SO 20 N.W. (202 282)

(SF 81) Hendre Forwydd, Llangattock. Tanged and barbed arrowhead. Brecknocks Mus.

SO 21 N.W. (21 07)

(SF 82) Tanged and barbed arrowhead. A.B.

SO 21 N.W. (0266 1916)

(SF 83) Sugar Loaf (Mm). Unworked flint. K.P.

SO 21 N.E. (27 19)

(SF 84) Pen Trumau. Two flint flakes.

Arch. in Wales 16 (1976), p. 18, 9. P.M.J.

SO 22 N.W. (204 296)

(SF 85) Flint flakes.

Arch. in Wales 21 (1981), p. 6 (6).

SO 22 N.W. (205 290)

(SF 86) Clyro area. Plano-convex knife. Brecknocks Mus.

SO 22 S.W. (21 24)

(SF 87) Scraper from Pen Trumau. P.M.J.

SO 22 S.E. (297 205)

(SF 88) Penywrlod chambered tomb, Llanigan. Flint flakes.
See (CT 12).

SO 23 N.W. (2248 3986)

(SF 89) Twyn y beddau cairn. Flint flakes, possibly lanceolate blade.
See (RC 311)

SO 23 N.W. (2416 3860)

(SF 90) Flint core. A.B.

SO 23 S.W. (233 334)

(SF 91) Bottom half of barbed and tanged flint arrowhead on eroded length of Offa's Dyke path. P. Dorling.

SO 23 S.E. (254 352)

(SF 92) Chwarel Ddu and Waun Capel area, to W. of Twyn y Beddau (RC 311), Llanigon. Flint cores of large size on the plateau. Some used as gunflints.

Poole, *Hist. Brecks.*, (1886), p. 215.

SO 24 N.W. (23 38)

Handlist of Bronze Age Bronze Artefacts (BR 1–35)

(Note: where references are to Inventory entries, no further bibliographical detail is provided. Otherwise reference is made to a recent publication or other most relevant source.)

(BR 1) SN 81 N.W. (8276 1601) Ogof yr Esgyrn. Razor, gold bead, dirk, etc.
See (PCS 1)

(BR 2) SN 81 N.E. (86 16) Penwyllt. Blade of dagger, six socketed axes, two gouges (one with wooden haft), trunnion axe, three casting jets.

Savory, *Guide*, pp. 49, 55, 65, 122, illus. 191.

(BR 3) SN 81 S.W. (815 127) Hen Neuadd, Abercrave, (1955), Socketed axe.

Savory, *Arch. Camb.* 107 (1958), p. 37; p. 45, Fig. 2, 4.

(BR 4) SN 84 N.E. (87 46) Llanwrtyd, (1746). Socketed chisel.

Albert Way MSS (Soc. Ants Lond.), Unpubl.

(BR 5) SN 85 N.E. (86 58) Drygarn, Abergwesyn. Rapier.

Savory, *Guide*, pp. 54, 113, illus. 175.

(BR 6) SN 85 N.E. (895 585) Bwlch y Ddaufaen, (1883). Dagger.

Grimes, *Prehist. Wales*, p. 183, no. 512; Fig. 62, 8; Savory, *Prehist. Brecks.* I, p. 101, Pl. V, 3.

(BR 7) SO 92 S.W. (920 241) Fan Bwlch Chwyth, Brychgoed, Sennybridge, (1955). Loopless central rib palstave.

Savory, *Prehist. Brecks.* I, p. 102, n. 78.

(BR 8) SN 95 S.E. (965 509) Rhos y Gilwern, Garth, (1965). Loopless central rib palstave.

Savory, *Prehist. Brecks.* II, p. 17.

(BR 9) SN 96 N.E. (955 654) Coppa, Llanwrthwl, (1903). Socketed axe.

C. B. Burgess, *Trans Radnor Soc.* 32 (1962), p. 21; p. 13; Fig. 5b.

(BR 10) SN 96 S.W. (943 639) Talwrn, Dulas Valley. Penannular gold ring.

Savory, *Guide*, p. 126.

(BR 11) SN 96 S.E. (963 646) Cefn, Llanwrthwl. Four gold torcs.

Savory, *Guide*, pp. 67–8; 125–6, illus. p. 195, Pl. VI.

(BR 12) SO 01 S.W. (01 12) Llwyn Onn, Cwm Taf, (1923). Trident pattern palstave.

Savory, *Guide*, p. 46, 105, illus. p. 170.

(BR 13) SO 02 N.W. (049 282) Watton, Brecon. Socketed axe.

Savory, *Prehist. Brecks.* I, p. 111.

(BR 14) SO 02 N.E. (057 298) Ffynnonau, Bishop's Meadow, Brecon. Hoard: dirk, knife, ferrules, palstaves.

C. B. Burgess, *Arch. Jnl* 125 (1968), p. 4, no. 21; p. 5, Fig. 2.1; Savory, *Guide*, pp. 54, 57.

(BR 15) SO 02 S.W. (0121 2158) Pen y Fan, Llansbyddyd, (1991). Hoard in cairn.
See (RC 226).

(BR 16) SO 02 S.W. (0371 2057) Fan y Big, (1982). Razor in excavated urn.
See (LBS 6).

(BR 17) SO 03 N.W. (024 369) Castell Madoc, Upper Chapel. Looped trident pattern palstave.

Savory, *Guide*, pp. 89, 153.

(BR 18) SO 03 S.W. (002 325) Canvas, Battle Fawr, Battle. Socketed axe.

Savory, *Prehist. Brecks.* I, p. 111.

(BR 19) SO 03 S.W. (046 311) N. of Pytin Du, W. of Llanddew. Socketed axe.

Savory, *Guide*, pp. 49, 110, illus. p. 173.

(BR 20) SO 04 S.E. (092 435) Crickadarn School/Lesser Clettwr Stream. Socketed axe.

Savory, *Prehist. Brecks.* I, p. 111.

(BR 21) SO 11 N.W. (1388 1985) Dan y Graig, Llanddeti, (1797). Sword.

H. T. Payne, N.L.W. MS 184A, fos. 149, 157.

(BR 22) SO 11 N.E. (152 189) Claister Stream, Llangynidr. Socketed axe.

Savory, *Prehist. Brecks.* II, p. 17, Fig. 4.1.

(BR 23) SO 11 S.W. (12 13) Trefil Las, Llangynidr. Palstave.

Lewis, *Top. Dict. s.v.* Dyfryn and Llangynider.

(BR 24) SO 12 S.W. (115 207) Pant y Wenallt, Llanddeti. Socketed axe.

Savory, *Guide*, pp. 49, 110, illus. p. 174.

(BR 25) SO 12 S.E. (1405 2315) Middlewood Farm, Cathedine, (1982). Two bronze socketed axes.

Briggs, *Arch. in Wales* 26 (1986), p. 25.

(BR 26) SO 12 S.E. (176 244) Pen Tir, Cwm Du, Crickhowell. Sword.

Savory, *Guide*, pp. 55, 114; illus. p. 176.

(BR 27) SO 13 N.W. (1402 3650) Pentre Sollars Farm, (1982). Socketed axe.

Briggs, *Arch. in Wales* 26 (1986), p. 25.

(BR 28) SO 21 N.W. (223 197) Wern, Crickhowell, (1838 or 1839). Loopless central rib palstave.

Savory, *Guide*, p. 105, illus. p. 169.

(BR 29) SO 22 N.W. (247 252) Cwm Ddaunant (1960s). Haft-flanged axe.

Savory, *B.B.C.S.* 15 (1971), pp. 205–206; Savory, *Prehist. Brecks.* II, p. 17, Pl. IIIB, 3.

(BR 30) SO 24 S.W. (23 42) Hay (pre-1881). Shield-pattern palstave.

Savory, *Prehist. Brecks.* I, p. 102.

(BR 31) SO 24 S.E. (23 42) River Wye, near Hay, (before 1847). Socketed spearhead.

Savory, *Guide*, pp. 51, 112; illus. p. 175.

(BR 32) 'north Breconshire' (1910), (unplotted).

Savory, *Prehist. Brecks.*, p. 102.

(BR 33) Probably Brecknocks (unplotted). Spearhead, Ashmolean Museum. Cast in Brecknocks Museum (R. 789).

(BR 34) Probably Brecknocks (unplotted). Unnumbered in Brecknocks Museum. Looped trident pattern palstave. Possibly one of those formerly in the possession of Rev. H. T. Payne.

(BR 35) Brecknocks, 'found under a Druid Altar', (unplotted).

Anon., *Arch. Camb.* 11 (1856), p. 123; quoting *Archaeologia* 4, p. 24.

Index of National Grid References

Caves

SN 8276 1601 PCS 1
SN 8449 1580 OCS 1
SN 8498 1533 OCS 2
SN 8476 1514 and
SN 8645 1589 PCS 2
SN 983 126 PCS 3
SO 1273 1519 PCS 4
SO 1926 1566 OCS 3

Upper Palaeolithic and Mesolithic Sites and Findspots

SN 8178 1077 RMS 1
SN 8199 1263 MS 1
SN 824 184 MS 2
SN 8535 1589 RMS 2
SN 871 360 MS 3
SN 805 575 MS 4
SN 840 550 MS 5
SN 85 52 MS 6
SN 994 098 MS 7
SN 925 157 MS 8
SN 9865 1889 MS 9
SO 0265 1938 MS 10 i
SO 0292 1910 MS 10 ii
SO 0300 1915 MS 10 iii
SO 0305 1905–0305 1892 MS 10 iv
SN 028 192 MS 10
SO 0315 1780 MS 11
SO 048 141 MS 12
SO 000 205 RMS 3
SO 049 335 MS 13
SO 1289 2690 MS 14
SO 211 192 MS 15
SO 228 293 MS 16
SO 230 287 MS 17
SO 243 342 MS 18

Neolithic Chambered Tombs

SO 0877 3037 RCT 2
SO 072 395 RCT 3
SO 0984 2638 CT 1
SO 1130 2140 RCT 4
SO 150 282 RCT 5
SO 1615 2843 CT 2
SO 1819 2906 CT 3
SO 1833 2944 RCT 6
SO 1505 3156 CT 4
SO 1833 3365 RCT 7
SO 1789 3489 CT 5
SO 1791 3495 CT 6
SO 1672 3626 CT 7
SO 1604 3727 CT 8
SO 1822 3806 CT 9
SO 2123 1771 CT 10
SO 219 180 RCT 8
SO 2110 1920 CT 11
SO 2248 3986 CT 12
SO 2357 3797 RCT 9 and
SO 239 373
SO 212 431 CT 13

Bronze Age Burial Structures and Sites

SN 7790 1519 RC 1
SN 7882 1835 RC 2
SN 773 141 RC 3
SN 7833 1267 RC 4–5
SN 7873 1379 RC 6
SN 785 149 RC 7
SN 7886 1400 RC 8
SN 8110 1838 LBS 1
SN 8558 1871 RC 9
SN 8684 1958 RC 10
SN 8805 1915 RC 11

INDEX OF NATIONAL GRID REFERENCES

SN 8949 1573 RC 12
SN 8909 1507 RC 13
SN 8987 1571 RC 14
SN 8152 1035 RC 15
SN 8178 1077 RC 16
SN 8188 1073 RC 17
SN 8290 1443 RC 18
SN 8290 1443 RC 19
SN 8178 2585 RC 20
SN 8198 2586 RC 21
SN 8654 2920 RC 22
SN 8808 2506 RC 23
SN 8852 2553 RC 24
SN 8934 2918 RC 25
SN 8213 2234 RC 26
SN 8243 2206 RC 27
SN 8278 2476 RC 28
SN 8287 2499 RC 29
SN 8453 2235 RC 30
SN 8514 2046 RC 31
SN 8812 2486 RC 32
SN 8772 3677 RC 33
SN 8885 3687 RC 34
SN 8314 3098 RC 35
SN 8305 3118 RC 36
SN 8305 3101 RC 37
SN 8462 3002 RC 38
SN 8600 3185 RC 39
SN 8604 3170 RC 40
SN 8764 3060 RC 41
SN 8885 3364 RC 42
SN 8942 3005 RC 43
SN 8941 3251 RC 44
SN 8949 3256 RC 45
SN 8215 4515 RC 46
SN 8321 4708 RC 47
SN 8308 4983 RC 48
SN 8451 4597 RC 49
SN 8475 4660 RC 50
SN 8706 4775 RC 51
SN 8712 4809 RC 52
SN 8715 4820 RC 53
SN 8119 5688 RC 54
SN 8628 5841 RC 55
SN 8675 5857 RC 56
SN 8897 5775 RC 57
SN 8939 5657 RC 58
SN 8970 5790 RC 59
SN 8464 5463 RC 60
SN 8757 5248 RC 61
SN 8848 5028 RC 62

SN 8960 5213 RC 63
SN 9681 0981 RC 64
SN 9742 0899 RC 65
SN 9749 0884 RC 66
SN 9735 0890 RC 67
SN 9759 0827 RC 68
SN 9766 0871 RC 69
SN 9790 0853 RC 70
SN 9710 0909 RC 71
SN 9812 0818 RC 72
SN 9818 0886 RC 73
SN 9947 0979 RC 74
SN 9184 1507 RC 75
SN 9140 1790 RC 76
SN 9182 1887 RC 77
SN 9233 1896 RC 78
SN 9264 1896 RC 79
SN 9353 1816 RC 80
SN 9385 1540 RC 81
SN 9496 1401 RC 82
SN 9602 1564 RC 83
SN 9713 1508 RC 84
SN 9845 1679 RC 85
SN 9800 1712 RC 86
SN 9013 1151 RC 87
SN 9014 1160 RC 88
SN 9016 1161 RC 89
SN 9075 1466 RC 90
SN 9156 1466 RC 91
SN 9207 1437 RC 92
SN 9217 1458 RC 93
SN 9219 1437 RC 94
SN 9220 1440 RC 95
SN 9239 1447 RC 96
SN 9240 1445 RC 97
SN 9390 1252 RC 98
SN 9325 1387 RC 99
SN 9332 1432 RC 100
SN 9333 1425 RC 101
SN 9338 1413 RC 102
SN 9435 1169 RC 103
SN 9533 1120 RC 104
SN 9569 1372 RC 105
SN 9597 1436 RC 106
SN 9633 1296 RC 107
SN 9615 1384 RC 108
SN 9639 1366 RC 109
SN 9605 1439 RC 110
SN 9709 1059 RC 111
SN 9750 1014 RC 112
SN 9766 1026 RC 113

INDEX OF NATIONAL GRID REFERENCES

SN 9775 1025 RC 114
SN 9779 1027 RC 115
SN 9795 1932 RC 116
SN 9769 1197 RC 117
SN 9776 1188 RC 118
SN 9757 1271 RC 119
SN 9774 1221 RC 120
SN 9890 1026 RC 121
SN 9895 1014 RC 122
SN 9833 1088 RC 123
SN 9855 1095 RC 124
SN 9864 1101 RC 125
SN 9885 1108 RC 126
SN 9850 1166 RC 127
SN 9814 1459 RC 128
SN 9815 1464 RC 129
SN 9820 1482 RC 130
SN 9865 1459 LBS 2
SN 9916 1092 RC 131
SN 9944 1088 RC 132
SN 9959 1081 RC 133
SN 9965 1040 RC 134
SN 9739 2639 RC 135
SN 9696 2237 RC 136
SN 9631 2320 RC 137
SN 9955 2005 LBS 3
SN 9207 3825 RC 138
SN 9497 3788 RC 139
SN 9480 3856 RC 140
SN 972 389 RC 141
SN 9252 3475 RC 142
SN 9454 3195 RC 143
SN 9888 3057 RC 144
SN 9838 3140 RC 145
SN 9612 4642 RC 146
SN 9604 4635 RC 147
SN 9248 4307 RC 148
SN 9274 4336 RC 149
SN 9341 4076 RC 150
SN 9314 4365 RC 151
SN 9321 4373 RC 152
SN 9328 4380 RC 153
SN 9113 5655 RC 154
SN 9120 5663 RC 155
SN 9160 5883 RC 156
SN 9180 5905 RC 157
SN 9567 5895 RC 158
SN 9852 5773 RC 159
SN 9033 5320 RC 160
SN 9110 5457 RC 161
SN 9117 5463 RC 162

SN 9978 5176 RC 163
SN 9195 6182 RC 164
SN 9285 6336 RC 165
SN 9303 6332 RC 166
SN 9314 6307 RC 167
SN 9317 6320 RC 168
SN 9439 6142 RC 169
SN 9437 6141 RC 170
SN 9441 6122 RC 171
SN 9422 6442 RC 172–3
SN 9431 6440 RC 174
SN 9434 6437 RC 175–6
SN 9561 6068 RC 177
SN 9567 6064 RC 178
SN 9570 6044 RC 179–80
SN 9571 6060 RC 181
SN 9572 6052 RC 182
SN 9578 6053 RC 183
SN 9548 6057 RC 184
SN 9532 6171 RC 185
SN 9586 6204 RC 186
SN 9599 6256 RC 187
SN 9712 6043 RC 188
SN 9784 6007 RC 189
SN 9796 6147 RC 190
SN 9813 6150 RC 191
SN 9816 6153 RC 192
SN 9823 6157 RC 193
SN 9767 6226 RC 194
SN 9788 6268 RC 195
SN 9810 6047 RC 196
SN 9822 6016 RC 197
SN 9855 6033 RC 198
SN 9873 6030 RC 199
SN 9975 6110 RC 200
SO 0250 0981 RC 201
SO 0278 1924 RC 202
SO 0281 1923 RC 203
SO 1088 1948 RC 204
SO 0289 1914 RC 205
SO 0289 1916 RC 206
SO 0290 1918 RC 207
SO 0012 1055 RC 208
SO 008 125 LBS 4
SO 0241 1081 RC 209
SO 0240 1027 RC 210
SO 0243 1028 RC 211
SO 0246 1027 RC 212
SO 0310 1211 RC 213
SO 0358 1259 RC 214
SO 0385 1230 RC 215

INDEX OF NATIONAL GRID REFERENCES

SO 054 135 LBS 5
SO 0662 1208 RC 216
SO 0665 1196 RC 217
SO 0162 1198 RC 218
SO 0769 1228 RC 219
SO 0734 1328 RC 220
SO 0735 1331 RC 221
SO 0880 1361 RC 222
SO 0884 1370 RC 223
SO 0875 1537 RC 312
SO 0993 1311 RC 224
SO 0075 2133 RC 225
SO 0121 2158 RC 226 and LBB1
SO 0237 2132 RC 227
SO 0371 2057 LBS 6
SO 052 296 UCB 1
[SO 059 249] UCB 2
[SO 069 262] UCB 3
SO 0315 3988 RC 228
SO 0084 3328 RC 229
SO 0086 3331 RC 230
SO 0106 3376 RC 231
SO 0463 4648 RC 232
SO 018 405 BB 19
SO 0255 4057 RC 233
SO 0280 4090 RC 234
SO 0281 4089 RC 235
SO 0282 4087 RC 236
SO 0289 4077 RC 237
SO 0296 4026 RC 238
SO 0247 4164 RC 239
SO 0264 4128 RC 240
SO 0321 4053 RC 241
SO 0321 4122 RC 242
SO 0322 4110 RC 243
SO 0432 4032 RC 244
SO 0615 4113 RC 245
SO 0085 5676 RC 246
[SO 11] UCB 4
SO 1103 1585 RC 247
SO 1127 1234 RC 248
SO 1159 1619 RC 249
SO 1225 1589 RC 250
SO 1233 1511 RC 251
SO 1219 1668 RC 252
SO 1296 1699 RC 253
SO 1297 1678 RC 254
SO 1340 1520 RC 255
SO 1313 1682 RC 256
SO 1306 1750 RC 257
SO 136 189 LBS 7

SO 1526 1563 RC 258
SO 1538 1583 RC 259
SO 1541 1566 RC 260
SO 1568 1560 RC 261
SO 1579 1560 RC 262
SO 1623 1772 RC 263
SO 1946 1540 RC 264
SO 1289 1431 RC 265
SO 1872 1477 RC 266
SO 1968 1453 RC 267
SO 135 277 LBS 8
SO 1579 2550 RC 268
SO 1594 2501 RC 269
SO 1595 2500 RC 270
SO 1595 2502 RC 271
SO 1658 2612 RC 272
SO 1678 2622 RC 273
SO 1963 2924 RC 274
SO 1986 2911 RC 275
SO 1076 2304 RC 276
SO 1546 2291 RC 277
SO 1570 2270 RC 278
SO 1561 2342 RC 279
SO 1561 2371 RC 280
SO 1591 2398 RC 281
SO 1593 2422 RC 282
SO 1597 2430 RC 283
SO 1658 2387 RC 284
SO 1654 2388 RC 285
SO 1610 2441 RC 286
SO 1621 2475 RC 287
SO 1643 2406 RC 288
SO 1758 2440 RC 289
LBB 2 and UCB 5
SO 142 326 UCB 6
SO 179 349 LBS 9
SO 1795 3501 LBS 10
SO 1808 3832 RC 290
SO 1945 3315 RC 291
[SO 2123 7171 CT 10]
SO 2587 1896 RC 292
SO 2600 1895 RC 293
SO 2027 1445 RC 294
SO 2030 1447 RC 295
SO 2031 1441 RC 296
SO 2032 1445 RC 297
SO 2101 1452 RC 298
SO 2130 1403 RC 299
[SO 24 17] RB 1
[SO 22] UCB 7
SO 2026 2607 RC 300

SO 2294 2877 RC 301
SO 2019 2319 RC 302
SO 2028 2331 RC 303
SO 2062 2386 RC 304
SO 2069 2433 RC 305
SO 2166 2241 RC 306
SO 2175 2223 RC 307
SO 2278 2316 RC 308
SO 2596 2344 RC 309
SO 234 379 UCB 8
SO 2442 3676 RC 310
SO 2416 3860 RC 311

Stone Circles and Stone Rows

SN 773 142 RSC 1
SN 8177 2585 SC 2 iv
SN 8187 2583 SC 2 i
SN 8193 2593 SC 2 vi
SN 8197 2578 SC 2 ii
SN 8199 2589 SC 2 iii
SN 8208 2505 SC 2 v
SN 8331 1539 SC 1
SN 8314 3098 SC 4 iv
SN 8319 3118 SC 4 i
SN 8331 3106 SC 4 ii
SN 8335 3109 SC 4 iii
SN 8511 2060 SC 3 ii
SN 8512 2062 SC 3 i
SN 8514 2064 SC 3 iii
SN 8339 3107 SC 4 vi
SN 8608 1458 RSC 2
SN 8636 4779 RSC 3
SN 8942 5830 RSC 4
SN 9082 1535 RSC 5
SN 9626 1604 RSC 6
SN 9211 3826 SC 5
SN 9492 6030 SC 6
[SO 09 26] RSC 7
SO 0500 4635 SC 7
SO 1186 1673 SC 8
SO 1325 1758 SC 9
[SO 22 28] RSC 8
SO 2395 3735 SC 10

Standing Stones (SS 1–41)

SN 8488 1709 RSS 20
SN 8535 1962 RSS 21
SN 8608 1458 RSS 22
SN 8852 1326 RSS 1
SN 8360 2567 SS 1
SN 8407 2732 RSS 23
SN 8425 2611 RSS 24
SN 8599 2456 RSS 25
SN 8744 2337 RSS 26
SN 8333 2835 SS 2
SN 8512 2062 SS 3
SN 8546 2150 SS 4
SN 8339 3107 SS 5
SN 8860 3310 RSS 2
SN 8922 3242 RSS 3
SN 856 498 RSS 27
SN 8584 4984 SS 6
SN 8849 4744 SS 7
SN 885 475 RSS 45
SN 8343 5960 SS 8
SN [851 591] RSS 46
SN 8692 5425 RSS 28
SN 888 547 LSS 1
SN 8210 6247 SS 9
SN 8644 6201 SS 10
SN 8813 6136 SS 11
SN 9242 1918 SS 12
SN 9783 1480 RSS 47
SN 9722 1848 SS 13
SN 9020 2250 RSS 50
SN 9042 2489 RSS 78
SN 953 256 RSS 49
SN 9638 2538 RSS 4
SN 9640 2599 RSS 5
SN 9762 2650 RSS 6
SN 9155 2683 and
SN 9153 2700 RSS 75
SN 9475 2740 RSS 76
SN 9435 2860 RSS 77
SN 923 269 RSS 48
SN 9387 2595 SS 14
SN 9498 3720 SS 15
SN 9450 3729 SS 16
SN 9580 3257 RSS 79
SN 9675 3468 SS 17
SN 9910 3975 RSS 80
SN 9795 3248 RSS 51
SN 9645 3864 RSS 29
SN 9660 3903 and
9663 3904 RSS 30
SN 9063 4068 RSS 53
SN 9129 4044 and
SN 9132 4122 RSS 7

INDEX OF NATIONAL GRID REFERENCES

SN 9325 4970 RSS 81
SN 938 499 RSS 52
SN 9746 4115 RSS 55
SN 9894 4317 RSS 54
SN 9104 5517 RSS 31
SN 9170 5572 RSS 32
SN 9173 5574 RSS 33
SN 9112 5658 RSS 34
SN 9160 5878 SS 18
SN 9486 5584 SS 19
SN 9766 5503 SS 20
SN 9900 5698 SS 21
SN 9319 6246 RSS 8
SN 9333 6259,
SN 9326 6243,
SN 9310 6332 and
SN 9301 6331 RSS 35
SN 9545 6061 LSS 2
SN 956 607 RSS 56
SN 9757 6372 SS 22
SO 074 132 RSS 43
SO 0495 2088 RSS 59
SO 0684 2268 RS 57
SO 0705 2303 RSS 58
SO 0836 2447 SS 23
SO 097 202 RSS 60
SO 0894 2675 SS 24
SO 097 262 LSS 3
SO 0063 3063 SS 25
SO 0173 3017,
SO 0147 3465 and
SO 0120 3384 RSS 9
SO 0220 3207 RSS 85
SO 0510 3635,
SO 0509 3613 and
SO 0520 3616 RSS 83
SO 0710 3525 RSS 84
SO 0697 3738,
SO 0754 3696,
SO 0766 3695,
SO 0707 3703,
SO 0709 3752,
SO 0850 3895,
SO 0806 4342 and
SO 0862 3845 RSS 10
SO 0900 3840 RSS 11
SO 0250 3730 and
SO 0245 3727 RSS 82
SO 0028 4029 RSS 12
SO 0280 4103 RSS 13
SO 0809 4348 RSS 14

SO 022 497 LSS 4
SO 0131 5804 SS 26
SO 1638 1738 SS 27
SO 1586 1995 SS 28
SO 1828 1985 SS 29
SO 1866 1985 RSS 43
SO 1579 2540 SS 30
SO 1168 2375 SS 31
SO 146 223 RSS 67
SO 1143 2840 RSS 62
SO 1249 2757 RSS 86
SO 1425 2990 RSS 87
SO 1448 2342 RSS 68
SO 1562 2038 SS 32
SO 157 202 RSS 61
SO 1579 2020 RSS 15
SO 159 252 RSS 63
SO 1572 2608 RSS 64
SO 1572 2608 RSS 66
SO 1503 2195 RSS 44
SO 1508 2149 RSS 36
SO 1588 2256 and
SO 1589 2253 RSS 37
SO 1590 2309 and
SO 1594 2304 RSS 16
SO 159 243 LSS 5
SO 1591 2411 RSS 38
SO 159 244 LSS 6
SO 169 221 RSS 65
SO 162 233 RSS 40
SO 166 247 RSS 69
SO 1789 2247 RSS 70
SO 1789 2292 RSS 71
SO 181 219 RSS 72
SO 1804 2192 SS 33
SO 1901 2099 RSS 39
SO 1000 3887 RSS 17
SO 1229 3958 SS 34
SO 1278 3191 RSS 41
SO 1278 3191 LSS 34
SO 1820 3475 LSS 8
SO 1994 3276 RSS 75
SO 1212 3897 LSS 7
SO 2125 1686 SS 36
SO 2218 1846 SS 37
SO 2399 1781 RSS 42
SO 2398 1781 and 2396 1784 SS 38–9
SO 2382 1133 RSS 18
SO 2423 1253 RSS 19
SO 2405 1787 SS 40
SO 2260 2762 SS 41

SO 2395 3735 RSS 74
SO 2000 3278 RSS 73

Burned Mounds (BM 1–22)

SN 8401 1771 BM 1
SN 8526 1977 BM 2
SN 8620 1879 BM 3
SN 8619 1880 BM 4
SN [886 279] BM 5–6
SN 8800 4675 BM 7–8
SN [808 512] BM 9–10
SN 804 531 BM 11
SN [81 50] BM 12–13
SN 9968 1766 BM 14
SN 9717 1017 BM 15
SN 9773 1432 BM 16
SN 9800 1010 BM 17
SN 9860 1406 BM 18
SN [953 516] BM 19
SN 9822 6019 BM 20
SO 0382 1155 BM 21
SO 1610 2430 BM 22

Unenclosed Settlement (US 1–113)

SN 7786 1531 US 1 i
SN 7786 1532 US 1 ii
SN 7787 1534 US 1 iii
SN 7787 1512 US 2 ii
SN 7788 1510 US 2 i
SN 7789 1514 US 2 iii
SN 7792 1517 US 2 iv
SN 7795 1516 US 2 v
SN 7795 1514 US 2 vi
SN 7796 1518 US 2 viii
SN 7797 1517 US 2 vii
SN 7781 1411 US 2 x
SN 7796 1494 US 2 ix
SN 8356 1512 US 3 iii
SN 8361 1502 US 3 ii
SN 8366 1505 US 3 i
SN 8336 1692 US 4 ii
SN 8337 1677 US 4 i
SN 8346 1698 US 4 v
SN 8351 1680 US 4 iv
SN 8356 1675 US 4 iii

SN 8327 1709 US 4 viii
SN 8327 1712 US 4 vii
SN 8311 1692 US 5 i
SN 8375 1697 US 5 ii
SN 8379 1689 US 5 vi
SN 8382 1697 US 5 iv
SN 8387 1691 US 5 v
SN 8399 1784 US 6 iii
SN 8400 1777 US 6 i
SN 8400 1781 US 6 ii
SN 8402 1774–8399 1802 US 6 iv
SN 8403 1762–8411 1763 US 6 v
SN 8449 1759 US 7 xvi
SN 8449 1763–8441 1770 US 7 xvii
SN 8450 1765 US 7 xviii
SN 8451 1759 US 7 xiv
SN 8451 1758 US 7 xv
SN 8452 1735 US 7 ix
SN 8452 1738 US 7 vii
SN 8452 1743 US 7 ii
SN 8452 1746 US 7 iii
SN 8452 1747 US 7 iv
SN 8453 1736 US 7 viii
SN 8453 1748 US 7 v
SN 8453 1739 US 7 vi
SN 8454 1745 US 7 i
SN 8455 1755 US 7 xii
SN 8455 1770 US 7 xix
SN 8456 1754 US 7 x
SN 8457 1751 US 7 xi
SN 8457 1757 US 7 xiii
SN 8289 1510 US 8 i
SN 8292 1508 US 8 ii
SN 8462 1790 US 9 i
SN 8465 1789 US 9 ii
SN 8406 1760,
SN 8408 1751,
SN 8409 1747,
SN 8409 1762,
SN 8410 1751,
SN 8411 1753,
SN 8412 1752 and
SN 8413 1753 US 10
SN 8408 1928 US 11 i
SN 8413 1918 US 11 iii
SN 8426 1905 US 11 ii
SN 8460 1724 US 12
SN 8410 1733 US 13 ii
SN 8410 1737 US 13 i
SN 8444 1780 US 14 ii
SN 8446 1778 US 14 i

INDEX OF NATIONAL GRID REFERENCES

SN 8430 1865 US 15 iii
SN 8431 1858 US 15 ii
SN 8432 1851 US 15 i
SN 8395 1891 US 16
SN 8393 1853 US 17 i
SN 8394 1852 US 17 ii
SN 8398 1868 US 18 ii
SN 8401 1867 US 18 i
SN 8425 1857 US 19
SN 8479 1972 US 20 iv
SN 8479 1976 US 20 vi
SN 8479 1976 US 20 vi
SN 8480 1971 US 20 iii
SN 8481 1978 US 20 xii
SN 8481 1982 US 20 xiv
SN 8482 1967 US 20 i
SN 8482 1972 US 20 v
SN 8482 1982 US 20 xv
SN 8483 1971 US 20 ii
SN 8483 1974 US 20 vii
SN 8483 1977 US 20 x
SN 8483 1978 US 20 xiii
SN 8485 1974 US 20 viii
SN 8485 1989 US 20 xvii
SN 8486 1972 US 20 ix
SN 8485 1977 US 20 xi
SN 8486 1992 US 20 xix
SN 8487 1982 US 20 xvi
SN 8488 1991 US 20 xviii
SN 8488 1998 US 20 xx
SN 8488 1999 US 20 xxi
SN 8622 1560 US 21
SN 8747 1711 US 22 ii
SN 8750 1711 US 22 i
SN 8718 1989 US 23
SN 8902 1987 US 24
SN 8916 1972 US 25
SN 8512 1996 US 26 ii–iii
SN 8514 1996 US 26 i
SN 8638 1838 US 27
SN 8196 1071 US 28 iii
SN 8285 1080 US 28 i
SN 8290 1085 US 28 iv
SN 8292 1116 US 28 ii
SN 8193 2593 US 29
SN 8478 2024 US 30
SN 8470 2150 US 31 xvii
SN 8488 2143 US 31 xv
SN 8494 2143 US 31 ii
SN 8495 2147 US 31 i
SN 8495 2150 US 31 vi

SN 8496 2133–8496 2136 US 31 iv
SN 8497 2142 US 31 iii
SN 8497 2142 US 31 v
SN 8498 2164 US 31 viii
SN 8500 2157 US 31 vii
SN 8500 2164 US 31 ix
SN 8501 2163 US 31 x
SN 8502 2149 US 31 xi
SN 8507 2133–8509 2135 US 31 xiv
SN 8508 2132 US 31 xvi
SN 8509 2137 US 31 xii
SN 8511 2131 US 31 xiii
SN 8521 2080 US 31 xviii
SN 8489 2125 US 31 v
SN 8490 2120 US 32 ii
SN 8490 2124 US 32 iv
SN 8491 2119 US 32 i
SN 8491 2122 US 32 iii
SN 8491 2127 US 32 vi
SN 8500 2046 US 33 iiid
SN 8508 2056 US 33 iiic
SN 8510 2070 US 33 ii
SN 8513 2086 US 33 i
SN 8512 2056–8511 2056 US 33 iiia
SN 8514 2055 US 33 iiib
SN 8514 2054 US 33 iv
SN 8514 2043 US 33 v
SN 8516 2037 US 33 vii
SN 8517 2036 US 33 vi
SN 8518 2971–8525 2071 US 33 iiie
SN 8505 2027 US 34 iii
SN 8505 2036 US 34 iia
SN 8506 2037 US 34 iib
SN 8506 2370–8506 2041 US 34 i
SN 8507 2037 US 34 iic–e
SN 8508 2037 US 34 iif
SN 8509 2038 US 34 iig
SN 8513 2026,
SN 8513 2025,
SN 8514 2025,
SN 8514 2026,
SN 8515 2026,
SN 8522 2020 and
SN 8523 2018 US 34 iv
SN 8523 2009 US 34 v
SN 8511 2008 US 34 vii
SN 8512 2004–8510 2007 US 34 vi
SN 8519 2021–8521 2020 US 34 viii
SN 8520 2021 US 34 ix
SN 8525 2004 US 35 ii
SN 8527 2071 US 35 i

INDEX OF NATIONAL GRID REFERENCES

SN 8536 2024 US 35 iii
SN 9960 0983 US 36
SN 9091 1518 US 37
SN 9139 1794 US 38
SN 9299 1547 US 39
SN 9290 1757 US 40
SN 9268 1854 US 41
SN 9275 1842 US 42
SN 9280 1805 US 43 iii
SN 9282 1802 US 43 ii
SN 9283 1805 US 43 i
SN 9285 1805 US 43 iv
SN 9285 1807 US 43 v
SN 9244 1905 US 44
SN 9491 1567 US 45
SN 9414 1694 US 46
SN 9429 1688 US 47
SN 9464 1623 US 48
SN 9411 1736 US 49
SN 9434 1855 US 50
SN 9458 1807 US 51
SN 9468 1858 US 52
SN 9473 1822 US 53
SN 9483 1839 US 54
SN 9512 1558 US 55
SN 9556 1615 US 56
SN 9596 1604 US 57
SN 9662 1625 US 58 i
SN 9665 1624 US 58 ii
SN 9668 1623 US 58 iii
SN 9669 1622 US 58 iv
SN 9671 1621 US 58 v
SN 9677 1624 US 58 vi
SN 9680 1653 US 59 iii
SN 9683 1656 US 59 iv
SN 9683 1661 US 59 vi
SN 9684 1647 US 59 i
SN 9687 1645 US 59 ii
SN 9686 1655 US 59 v
SN 9687 1660 US 59 vii
SN 9707 1637 US 59 viii
SN 9800 1521 US 60 v
SN 9801 1533 US 60 ii
SN 9803 1532 US 60 iv
SN 9804 1534 US 60 i
SN 9805 1526 US 60 vi
SN 9805 1533 US 60 iii
SN 9878 1652 US 61
SN 9860 1857 US 62 i
SN 9863 1864–9862 1869 US 62 iii
SN 9883 1985 US 62 ii

SN 9910 1683 US 63
SN 9967 1667 US 64
SN 9886 1710 US 65 ii
SN 9975 1678 US 65 i
SN 9992 1712 US 65 iii
SN 9940 1908 US 66
SN 9928 1427 US 67
SN 9137 1278 US 68 i
SN 9139 1276 US 68 iii
SN 9135 1266 US 68 iv
SN 9133 1259 US 68 v
SN 9140 1278 US 68 ii
SN 9189 1421 US 69
SN 9204 1406 US 70
SN 9435 1035 US 71 i
SN 9435 1037 US 71 v
SN 9436 1033 US 71 iii
SN 9436 1035 US 71 iv
SN 9437 1030 US 71 ii
SN 9437 1038 US 71 vi
SN 9441 1039 US 71 vii
SN 9464 1420 US 72
SN 9368 1415 US 73
SN 9587 1208 US 74 v
SN 9588 1210 US 74 iv
SN 9596 1214 US 74 iii
SN 9600 1211 US 74 ii
SN 9606 1217 US 74 i
SN 9562 1284 US 75 ix
SN 9565 1289 US 75 x
SN 9580 1299 US 75 vii
SN 9564 1317 US 75 ii
SN 9599 1326 US 75 iii
SN 9613 1364 US 75 iv
SN 9616 1329 US 75 viii
SN 9621 1324 US 75 xii
SN 9623 1333 US 75 xiii
SN 9633 1296 US 75 xiv
SN 9639 1366 US 75 xv
SN 9641 1359 US 75 xi
SN 9647 1336 US 75 i
SN 9652 1315 US 75 v
SN 9655 1316 US 75 vi
SN 9550 1405 US 76
SN 9676 1336 US 77 ii
SN 9677 1332 US 77 iii
SN 9680 1322 US 77 i
SN 9683 1361 US 77 v
SN 9690 1361 US 77 iv
SN 9712 1463 US 78 viii
SN 9731 1462 US 78 vii

INDEX OF NATIONAL GRID REFERENCES

SN 9733 1405 US 78 vi
SN 975 140 US 78 xii
SN 9756 1431 US 78 v
SN 9759 1434 US 78 ii
SN 9760 1434 US 78 iv
SN 9761 1413 US 78 i
SN 9761 1431 US 78 iii
SN 9763 1389 US 78 xi
SN 9763 1425 US 78 ix
SN 9765 1428 US 78 x
SN 9702 1349 US 79 xiii
SN 9706 1343 US 79 xi
SN 9714 1459 US 79 x
SN 9722 1327 US 79 iii
SN 9730 1351 US 79 xii
SN 9738 1353 US 79 iv
SN 9741 1346 US 79 v
SN 9745 1349 US 79 vi
SN 9747 1347 US 79 vii
SN 9752 1375 US 79 viii
SN 9753 1358 US 79 ix
SN 9759 1365 US 79 i
SN 9760 1359 US 79 ii
SN 9804 1452 US 80
SN 9851 1284 US 81 ii
SN 9862 1262 US 81 i
SN 9869 1265 US 81 iii
SN 9852 1229 US 82 i
SN 9855 1231 US 82 iv
SN 9857 1232 US 82 iii
SN 9858 1236 US 82 ii
SN 9862 1245 US 82 vi
SN 9863 1247 US 82 viii
SN 9868 1233–9874 1251 US 82 v
SN 9868 1250 US 82 vii
SN 9860 1218 US 82 ix
SN 9746 1130–9810 1130 US 83 i
SN 9748 1099–9753 1104 US 83 ii
SN 9750 1099 US 83 v
SN 9759 1098 US 83 vi
SN 9762 1092 US 83 vii
SN 9772 1093 US 83 iv
SN 9787 1098–9793 1109 US 83 iii
SN 9750 1028 US 84 i
SN 9752 1061 US 84 ii
SN 9906 1121 US 84 iii
SN 981 208 US 85
SN 9615 2231 US 86 i
SN 9642 2222 US 86 iv
SN 9643 2245 US 86 viii
SN 9644 2222 US 86 v

SN 9650 2230 US 86 iii
SN 9653 2233 US 86 ii
SN 9659 2224 US 86 vi
SN 9688 2295 US 86 vii
SN 9475 6479 US 87 vi
SN 948 647 US 87 i
SN 951 645 US 87 ii
SN 953 643 US 87 iii
SN 961 649 US 87 iv
SO 0115 0975 US 88
SO 0119 0974 US 89 viii
SO 0121 0970 US 89 vii
SO 0122 0970 US 89 vi
SO 0126 0966 US 89 v
SO 0126 0970 US 89 ix
SO 0128 0964 US 89 iv
SO 0130 0961 US 89 ii
SO 0132 0961 US 89 iii
SO 0135 0958 US 89 i
SO 0228 0988 US 90 xiii
SO 0234 0987 US 90 xii
SO 0236 0986 US 90 xi
SO 0238 0984 US 90 x
SO 0245 0995 US 90 ii
SO 0245 0992 US 90 v
SO 0246 0991 US 90 vi
SO 0247 0996 US 90 iii
SO 0248 0990 US 90 vii
SO 0248 0992 US 90 iv
SO 0248 0995 US 90 i
SO 0251 0987 US 90 viii
SO 0251 0997 US 90 ix
SO 0253 0988 US 90 xiv
SO 0222 1158 US 91 iii
SO 0223 1148 US 91 i
SO 0224 1155 US 91 ii
SO 0229 1142 US 91 v
SO 0230 1141 US 91 iv
SO 0227 1115–0240 1118 US 92 iii
SO 0230 1125–0236 1127 US 92 ii
SO 0232 1100–0247 1100 US 92 vi
SO 0232 1111–0240 1112 US 92 iv
SO 0232 1118–0233 1121 US 92 v
SO 0235 1132–0228 1146 US 92 vii
SO 0239 1100–0240 1118 US 92 i
SO 0257 1210 US 93 iv
SO 0257 1202 US 93 v
SO 0261 1189 US 93 ii
SO 0262 1188 US 93 i
SO 0262 1196 US 93 iii
SO 0264 1191 US 93 xiii

INDEX OF NATIONAL GRID REFERENCES

SO 0265 1200 US 93 viii
SO 0266 1193 US 93 ix
SO 0268 1193 US 93 vi
SO 0269 1194 US 93 xi
SO 0269 1203–0273 1197 US 93 xiv
SO 0270 1195 US 93 xii
SO 0278 1203 US 93 vii
SO 0206 1227 US 94 i
SO 0208 1229 US 94 ii
SO 0211 1230 US 94 iii
SO 0214 1232 US 94 iv
SO 0217 1238 US 94 v
SO 0195 1293–0217 1307 US 95 i
SO 0208 1350 US 95 ii
SO 0209 1330 US 95 vii
SO 0215 1306 US 95 iii
SO 0215 1322 US 95 iv
SO 0217 1325 US 95 v
SO 0224 1329 US 95 vi
SO 0234 1328 US 95 viii
SO 0234 1326 US 95 ix
SO 0236 1366 US 95 xi
SO 0237 1326 US 95 x
SO 0239 1362 US 95 xii
SO 0365 1149 US 96 i
SO 0366 1144 US 96 ii
SO 0367 1156 US 96 iv
SO 0370 1156 US 96 iii
SO 0380 1216 US 97
SO 0520 1160 US 98 i
SO 0526 1168 US 98 iii
SO 0527 1165 US 98 ii
SO 0527 1177 US 98 v
SO 0528 1176 US 98 iv
SO 0659 1283–0666 1289 US 99 iii
SO 0662 1275 US 99 iv
SO 0663 1290 US 99 i
SO 0665 1289 US 99 ii
SO 0668 1282 US 99 vii
SO 0669 1279–0669 1276 US 99 vi
SO 0669 1283 US 99 viii
SO 0669 1286 US 99 xii–xiii
SO 0672 1288 US 99 xiv
SO 0673 1283 US 99 x
SO 0673 1284 US 99 xi
SO 0674 1282 US 99 ix
SO 0675 1293–0675 1292 US 99 xv
SO 0676 1292 US 99 xvi
SO 0676 1291–0677 1291 US 99 xviii
SO 0677 1289–0676 1287 US 99 xix
SO 0677 1291 US 99 xxii

SO 0677 1292 US 99 xvii
SO 0678 1292–0680 1293 US 99 xx
SO 0680 1289 US 99 xxi
SO 0682 1294 US 99 xxiii
SO 0683 1288–0685 1285–0683 1283 US 99 xxvi
SO 0684 1283 US 99 xxvii
SO 0684 1293 US 99 xxiv
SO 0685 1294–0686 1293 US 99 xxv
SO 0890 1385 US 100 i
SO 0905 1376 US 100 ii
SO 0984 1274 US 101 iii
SO 0988 1269 US 101 i
SO 0988 1272 US 101 iv
SO 0988 1275 US 101 ii, v
SO 0988 1277 US 101 vi
SO 0988 1282 US 101 viii
SO 0988 1287 US 101 ix
SO 1080 1547–1095 1553 US 102 i
SO 1088 1543 US 102 vi
SO 1089 1540 US 102 v
SO 1095 1546–1095 1551 US 102 ii
SO 1096 1537 US 102 iv
SO 1097 1542 US 102 iii
SO 1175 1625 US 103
SO 1186 1690 US 104
SO 1191 1609–1304 1670 US 105
SO 1604 1738 US 106 i
SO 1606 1665–1637 1706; 1641 1670 US 106 iii
SO 1610 1707 US 106 ii
SO 1613 1612–1629 1635 US 106 iv
SO 1625 1600 US 106 v
SO 2243 1438 US 107
SO 2028 1433 US 108 ii
SO 2038 1442 US 108 i
SO 2388 1293–2392 1295 US 109 xxiv–v
SO 2393 1296–2396 1296 US 109 xxvi–xxvii
SO 2396 1276 US 109 xxiii
SO 2398 1296 US 109 xviii
SO 2399 1276 US 109 xxii
SO 2408 1272 US 109 xxi
SO 2409 1274 US 109 xix
SO 2409 1275 US 109 xviii
SO 2410 1274 US 109 xx
SO 2410 1275 US 109 xvi
SO 2410 1276 US 109 xv
SO 2411 1275 US 109 xiii–iv
SO 2412 1270 US 109 ii
SO 2412 1274 US 109 xii
SO 2413 1273 US 109 iii–iv
SO 2414 1273 US 109 v
SO 2414 1275 US 109 xi

SO 2415 1274 US 109 ix
SO 2415 1275 US 109 x
SO 2416 1274 US 109 viii
SO 2417 1275 US 109 vi–vii
SO 2423 1255 US 109 i
SO 2454 1280–2456 1281 US 109 xx
SO 2456 1281 US 109 xix
SO 2665 1292 US 109 xvii
SO 2239 2722 US 110
SO 2215 2855 US 111 i
SO 2170 2820–US 111 ii
SO 2260 2880
SO 2087 2133 US 112 i
SO 2092 2180 US 112 ii
SO 2090 2252 US 112 iii
SO 2021 2300,
SO 2021 2317,
SO 2027 2299 and
SO 2030 2294 US 112 iv
SO 2107 2207 US 112 vi
SO 2112 2185 US 112 v
SO 212 212 US 112 vii
SO 2106 2451 US 113

Lost Settlement Sites LS 1–10

SN 895 075–905 080–895 095–910 095 LS 1
SN 8220 1730 LS 2
SN 8657 5552 LS 3
SN 8858 5031 LS 4
SO 0298 0804 LS 5
SO 0066 1029 LS 6
SO 1421 3819 LS 7 i
SO 1420 3822 LS 7 ii
SO 1621 3800–1627 3782 LS 8 i
SO 1635 3792 LS 8 ii
SO 1638 3790–1646 3793 LS 8 iii
SO 235 155 LS 9

Dyke D 1

SN 691 441–SN 819 516–SN 894 543–SN 85/95–SN 913 552–SN 917 557

Hillfort

SO 1707 1838 HF 65

Crannog Site

SO 1289 2690 CR 1

A Handlist of Early Christian Stones

SN 7870 1007 ECM 1–2
SN 859 278 ECM 3
SN 8829 2645 ECM 4
SN 877 235 RECM 1
SN 8636 4779 [findspot] ECM 5
SN 894 419 ECM 6
SN 91 50 ECM 7
SN 9183 1577 ECM 8
MAEN LLIA see SS 12 SN 9242 1918
SN 993 165 ECM 9
SN 9252 2794 ECM 10–11; RECM 2
SN 9667 2962 ECM 12
SN 984 374 LECM 1–2
SN 9052 4659 ECM 13
SN 9387 4993 ECM 14
SN 9346 4832 ECM 15
SN 9690 5578 ECM 16–19
SO 0025 1500 LECM 3
SO 01 12 ECM 20–21
SO 0731 1321 ECM 22
SO 0118 2819 ECM 23
SO 0752 2579 ECM 24
SO 075 258 LECM 4–5
SO 0850 2617 ECM 25
SO 0895 2645 ECM 26–7
SO 0339 3239 ECM 28–29
SO 0549 3074 ECM 30–31
SO 0123 4760 ECM 32
SO 035 494 ECM 33
SO 1560 1935 LECM 6
SO 1881 1992 original site; present site 1866 1985 ECM 34
SO 106 252 or 112 248 original area; possible alternative, SO 1105 2485 ECM 35
SO 1350 2764 ECM 36–38
SO 1280 2024 ECM 39
SO 12 21 (findspot) LECM 7
SO 1510 2196 RECM 3
SO 173 215 original site ECM 40
SO 1805 2385 ECM 41–2
SO 1850 3419 ECM 43–4
SO 225 193 ECM 45
SO 2783 2243 ECM 46
SO 2777 2339 LECM 8
SO 24 LECM 9

Lithic Finds from Brecknocks (SF 1–92)

SN 825 097 SF 1
SN 87 48 SF 2
SN 965 099 SF 3
SN 969 098 SF 4
SN 92 13 SF 5
SN 9823 3308 SF 6
SN 94 30 SF 7
SO [04 28] SF 8
SO 000 205 SF 9
SO 063 415 and
063 416 SF 10
SO 09 42 SF 11
SO 034 512 SF 12
SO 043 512 SF 13
SO 199 197 SF 14
SO 15 14 SF 15
SO 181 293 SF 16
SO 182 291 SF 17
SO 137 242 SF 18
SO 15 35 SF 19
SO 179 349 SF 20
SO 17 39 SF 21
SO 2410 1780 SF 22
SO 211 192 SF 23
SO 23 14 SF 24
SO 24 14 SF 25
SO 2324 2851 SF 26
SO 253 293 SF 27
SN 824 184 SF 28
SN 8178 1077 and
8188 1073 SF 29
SN 848 152 SF 30
SN 82 27 SF 31
SN 8213 2234 SF 32
SN 995 098 SF 33
SN 9886 1889 SF 34
SN 9858 1855 SF 35
SN 91 S.W. SF 36
SN 9075 1466 SF 37
SN 9156 1466 SF 38
SN 9709 1059 SF 39
SN 9850 1166 SF 40
SN 9864 1101 SF 41
SN 988 294 SF 42
SN 9945 2005 SF 43
SN [92 37] SF 44

SN 9207 3825 SF 45
SN 9211 3826 SF 46
SN 93 47 SF 47
SO 009 095 SF 48
SO 0265 1938 and
SO 0305 1905 SF 49
SO 019 182 SF 50
SO 0266 1916 SF 51
SO 04 19 SF 52
SO 0325 1780 SF 53
SO 05 15 SF 54
SO 055 175 SF 55
SO 048 141 SF 56
SO 054 135 SF 57
SO 055 145 SF 58
SO 068 106 SF 59
SO [04 28] SF 60
SO 024 214 SF 61
SO 012 216 SF 62
SO 0760 2240 SF 63
SO 05 22 SF 64
SO 161 265 SF 65
SO 165 291 SF 66
SO 135 277 SF 67
SO 128 210 SF 68
SO 125 243 SF 69
SO 1561 2046 SF 70
SO 174 207 SF 71
SO 18 24 SF 72
SO 1750 3759 SF 73
SO 179 349 SF 74
SO 1795 3501 SF 75
SO 15 34 SF 76
SO 1797 3006 SF 77
SO 175 376 SF 78
SO 10 43 SF 79
SO 202 282 SF 80
SO 21 07 SF 81
SO 0266 1916 SF 82
SO 27 19 SF 83
SO 204 296 SF 84
SO 205 290 SF 85
SO 21 24 SF 86
SO 297 205 SF 87
SO 2248 3986 SF 88
SO 2416 3860 SF 89
SO 233 334 SF 90
SO 254 352 SF 91
SO 23 38 SF 92

Bronze Artefacts from Brecknocks (BR 1–35)*

SN 8276 1601 BR 1
SN 86 16 BR 2
SN 815 127 BR 3
SN 87 46 BR 4
SN 86 58 BR 5
SN 895 585 BR 6
SN 920 241 BR 7
SN 965 509 BR 8
SN 955 654 BR 9
SN 943 639 BR 10
SN 963 646 BR 11
SO 01 12 BR 12
SO 049 282 BR 13
SO 057 298 BR 14
SO 0121 2158 BR 15
SO 0371 2057 BR 16
SO 024 369 BR 17
SO 002 325 BR 18
SO 046 311 BR 19
SO 092 435 BR 20
SO 1388 1985 BR 21
SO 152 189 BR 22
SO 12 13 BR 23
SO 115 207 BR 24
SO 1405 2315 BR 25
SO 176 244 BR 26
SO 1402 3650 BR 27
SO 223 197 BR 28
SO 247 252 BR 29
SO 23 42 BR 30
SO 23 42 BR 31

[* four sites unplotted]

Glossary: General

Words adequately defined in the Shorter Oxford English Dictionary are not included unless they have been used in a more specialised sense than is given there. The list is further limited by the exclusion of proper names and terms of cultural significance, as well as typological definitions of artefacts, which can be ascertained from standard works. Definitions are only given in the list when reference to an appropriate section of the Inventory will not suffice. Welsh words are indicated by (W).

Barrow – an earthen mound built with the intention of housing the remains of the dead. See p. 71
Burned mound – see p. 184.
Cairn – see pp. 67–71.
Clas (W) – see p. 278.
Clearance cairn – see p. 204.
Cord-rig – see p. 206.
Cromlech (W) – To the dictionary definition it should be added that the 'large, flat stone resting on . . . stones set upright' often has a convex upper surface, as signified in the use of the element *crom*.

Doline – A hollow in limestone caused by the downward erosive percolation of acidic water.
Extra-revetment – see p. 29.
Iron pan – A hard layer formed in a soil profile by precipitation of dissolved iron.
Lynchet – A roughly levelled area formed by cultivation on sloping ground; the boundary between one field and the next on a slope.
Maenhir/[menhir, Anglicised version] (pl. Meini Hirion) (W).
Orthostat – An upright, earthfast stone.
Pillow mound – A ridged, artificial mound, thought to have served as a rabbit warren.
Platform house – A rectangular hut, sometimes of medieval date, with long axis roughly perpendicular to the contours, set on an artificially levelled platform.
Radiocarbon dating – A technique of age measurement involving the assessment of residual radioactivity in organic material.
Ring cairn – see p. 71.
Scoop-settlement – see p. 201.
Sink-hole – see Doline.
Standing stone – see p. 162 ff.

Glossary: Welsh Place-name Elements

Only the singular form is given.

Aber	Mouth of river; confluence	Garth	Enclosure
Afon	River	Glyn	Valley; glen
Allt, Gallt	Hillside; slope	Heol	Track; road
Bach (fach, fechan)	Small; minor	Llan	Sacred enclosure
Bedd	Grave	Llech, Llechfaen	Slab
Brenin	King	Llwyn	Bush
Bwlch	Gap; pass	Llys	Court
Cae	Field	Maen	Stone
Caer (Gaer)	Fort	Maes	Open field
Carreg (Garreg)	Stone	Mawr (fawr)	Big; great
Castell	Castle	Moel (foel)	Bare mountain
Cefn	Ridge; back	Mynydd	Mountain
Celli (Gelli)	Grove	Nant	Stream
Clawdd	Hedge; bank	Ogof	Cave
Coed	Wood	Pant	Hollow
Cors (Gors)	Bog; fen	Pen	Head; summit
Craig (Graig)	Rock	Pwll	Pool; pit
Crib	Narrow ridge	Rhiw	Ascent; slope
Crug	Rocky hillock	Rhyd	Ford
Cwm	Narrow valley	Sarn	Causeway
Dinas (Ddinas)	Settlement; fort	Tor	Rocky height
Esgair	Ridge	Twyn	Knoll; small hill
Ffos	Ditch	Tyle	Hill
		Tŷ	House
		Ystrad	Dale

General Index

Page numbers in *italics* refer to illustrations, maps and plans. Where there is textual reference to the subject on the same page as the illustration, italics have not been used. Welsh river or valley names may be preceded by *afon*, *cwm* or *nant*.

Aberbrân Mill: lithic finds (SF 42) 292
Abercamddwr (Ceredigion): round cairn 69
Abercar:
    burial site (LBS 4) 68, 72, 134
        artefacts recovered (BB 15) 133
    inscribed stones (ECM 20–1) 286
Abercrave: bronze socketed axe (BR 3) 296; Mesolithic chert implement (MS 1) 19, *see also* Dan yr Ogof
Abergavenny: Llangenny urn 72
Abergwesyn: bronze rapier (BR 5) 296; pebble mace head (MS 5) 20; sharpened oak piles (LS 3) 271
Aberllynfi: chambered tomb (CT 9) 25, 27, 28, 51–4, *53*; the Gaer: lithic finds (SF 78) 294; stone axe (SF 19) 291
Aberysgir: round cairns (RC 144–5) 103
aerial photography 69, 73, 81, 82, *87*, *89*, 138, 144, *148*, 150, 190, 192, 199, 203, 208, 230, 249, *251*, *255–7*, 271, 272, 273, 278
Afan: site of his murder 171
Afon Commarch: dyke (D 1) 274
Afon Dringarth 189; enclosure (US 48) 230; round cairn (RC 81) 90; settlement platforms (US 46–7) 230
Afon Llia: enclosures (US 42) 228–9; round cairns: (RC 79) 89
Afon Llynfell 11
Afon Llynfi 3, 38, 40, 48
Afon Mellte: round cairns (RC 100–2) 92–3
Afon Nedd: rubble bank (US 37) 227
Afon Rhiangoll: chambered tomb (CT 3) 36; corn-drying kiln 65
Afon Taf: hut platforms (US 63) 202, *see also* Cwm Taf
Afon Tawe *see* Tawe Valley
Afon Twrch 76; round cairn (RC 2) 76
Afon y Waun: hut groups: (US 59) 233–4; standing stone (SS 13) 170
Allt Fach: map of enclosures *218*;
    clearance cairns: (US 6) 212; (US 10) 214
    cooking mound (BM 1) 186, 212;
    enclosures: (US 9) 214; (US 14) 215–16
    hut circle (US 6) 212; hut groups (US 7) 199, 200, 201, 212–13
Allt y Gaer: lithic finds (SF 69) 294
alluviation of valleys 191–2
Anwyl, Edward: Llangenny urn (RB 1) 137
artefact assemblages *see* Bronze Age, artefacts; flint assemblages and artefacts
Ashmolean Museum: bronze spearhead (BR 33) 297
astro-archaeology 143, 145, 153
Aubrey, John 24, 31
awls: bone 11; bronze 11, 73, 133

Awst, king of Brycheiniog 278–9
axes:
    bronze 296, 297
        see also palstaves
    chert 22, 291; flint 21, 22, 290, 291; grit 294; stone 37, 291

Banc Paderau: round cairn (RC 61) 85
Banc y Celyn: round cairn (RC 232) 120; stone circle (SC 7) 144, 158
Banc y Cwm: round cairns: (RC 146–7) 103
Bancystradwen: round cairns: (RC 190–3) 109
Banks, *Sir* Joseph: cairn excavation 67
Bannau Sir Gaer: stone circle 144
barley 7
barrows: round 40, 55, 71, *see also* cairns; chambered tombs; long barrows; round cairns
Battle: boundary stones (RSS 9) 179; bronze axe (BR 18) 297; round cairns (RC 229–31) 120; standing stone (SS 25) *pl.3*, 172–3
beads: anthracite 72, 133; Bronze Age 102; burnt clay 79, 132, 133; gold (PCS 1) 11, *14*, 296; lignite 72; pottery 72; Romano-British 61; Tŷ Isaf 28
Beaker: Bell type 135; burial site (LBS 9) 25, 40, 68, 135–6; Dol-y-gaer grave (LBS 5) 68, 72, 133, 134; flint artefacts 13, 91; fragments 37, 72, 91, 99, 132, 133, 134; Handled A Beaker 100, 129, 133; long necked 134; Pant y Waun grave (LBS 2) 68, 72, 132–3, 134, *see also* Enlarged Food Vessel; pottery sherds; urns
Beaufort Estate: commons (US 106) 266–7
Bedd Illtud: round cairn (RC 135) 101
Bedd Llywarch: stone row (rejected) (RSC 6) 161, 182
Bedd y Forwyn: boundary stones (RSS 9) 179
Benson, D G: and Blaen Digedi stone circle (SC 10) 160
Berth Ivan: round cairn (RC 24) 79
Bird, A J: siting of standing stones 164
Black Mountains 1, 6, 7, 22; long barrows 25, 27–9, 38
Blaen Cadlan Uchaf: round cairns: (RC 117–18) 96
Blaen Cam Uchaf: round cairn (RC 268) 124
Blaen Clydach-Bach: round cairns: (RC 39–40) 80–1
Blaen Crai: hut platform (US 23) 220
Blaen Cwm Cleister: round cairn RC 250) 122
Blaen Digedi Fawr: mound (RCT 9) 65; stone circle (SC 10) 65, 159–60
Blaen Nedd Isaf: clearance cairn (US 69) 237
Blaen Nedd Uchaf: stone circle (rejected) (RSC 5) 161

Blaen Onneu: clearance cairns (US 106) 266; lost cairn (LC 8) 139
Blaen Tawe: round cairn (RC 30) 79
Blaen y Cwm Uchaf: standing stone (SS 30) 175
Blaenau Isaf: natural boulder (RSS 24) 180
Blaencar: chipping site (MS 12) 21; lithic finds (SF 56) 293
bone handle plate: Tŷ Isaf (CT 3) 133
bone pin: Tŷ Isaf (CT 3) 28, 37, 133
bone pipe: (CT 4) 28, 40
bones *see* skeletal remains
boulder scavenging: from ancient monuments 196, 208
boulder trains 194–6, 222
boundary banks 199
boundary stones 161, 162, 163–4, 174, 175, 177, 179–80, 181; (RSS 1–19) 179–80, *see also* marked and memorial stones; natural boulders; parish boundaries; standing stones
Bowen, E: standing stones recorded 162
bowls, Neolithic: Ffostyll South (CT 5) 42; Gwernvale (CT 11) 59; Tŷ Isaf (CT 3) 37
Bran/Cilieni interfluve: round cairn (RC 142) 103
Breanog Mountain: cairns 68
Brecenanmere: Dark Age site 281
Brecknock Museum: Bronze Age bronze artefacts 297;
 inscribed stones: (ECM 13) 285; (ECM 32–3) 287; (ECM 35) 287; (ECM 45) 288
 Neolithic and Bronze Age lithic finds 290, 291, 292, 293, 294, 295
Brecon 3; bronze artefacts (BR 13–14) 296; flint(?) hammer (SF 60) 293; St John the Evangelist: boundary stone (RSS 9) 179; burial site (UCB 1) 72, 136
Brecon Beacons 1, 3, 5, 7; burial sites map 116
Brecon Beacons Reservoir: flint arrowhead (MS 9) 20; lithic finds (SF 34) 292; settlement features (US 62) 235
Brecon Boys' Grammar School: burial site (UCB 1) 72, 136
Breuil, H: dating Tŷ Illtud 32
British Museum: inscribed stone (ECM 4) 284
Britnell, W J: artefacts and bones [at Gwernvale] 28; excavation at Gwernvale 56, 60; on the potential repetition of Gwernvale type discoveries 17, 22
Bronllys: chambered tomb (CT 7) 24, 27, 28, 47–8
Bronze Age: artefacts 11, *14*, 72, 73, 117, 133, 135, 137, *207*, 208, 296–7; burial practices 11, 163; burial sites and cairns: distribution *66*, *70*, 71, 73, 191; burial structures 67–141; burials correlated 132–3; cave burial 9, 11; population and cairn density 69; sites and find spots 291–5
bronzes (Bronze Age): Pen y Fan hoard (RC 226) 117, 133
Bryn (Llanfigan): lithic finds (SF 63) 293
Bryn Llechwen: round cairn (RC 15) 77
Bryn Tywarch: natural boulder (RSS 23) 180
Bryn y Garn: round cairn (RC 34) 80
Bryn y Groes (Croesllechau):
 chambered tomb (CT 7) 24, 27, 28, 47–8
 Lhuyd's sketches *47*; plan of *48*
Brynceinion: round cairn (RC 158) 105
Buarth y Caerau: round cairns: (RC 220–1) 115
Builth: stone axes (SF 12–13) 291
Builth-Llanwrtyd Depression 3
burial practices: Bronze Age 11, 72–3, 163; Neolithic 29, 56, *see also* cremation
burial sites: Brecon Beacons: map of 116; distribution of 26–7, *66*, *70*, 71, 73, 191, 208; royal 279; tithe award names 139–41
burials: Bronze Age *see* Bronze Age

Burke, T W: circular enclosure noted (LS 6) 271; discovery of flint chipping site 21; round cairn excavations 68
Burl: and stone circle sizes 145
burned mounds 184–8; map of distribution 197
Burrow Wood: standing stone (SS 35) 176
Bwlc Crannog *see* Ynys Bwlc
Bwlch: inscribed stone (RSS 44, RECM 3) 163, 181–2; standing stone alignments 163
Bwlch Bryn Rhudd: ring cairn (RC 10) 77
Bwlch Duwynt: worked flint find (SF 9) 290
Bwlch Owen 5
Bwlch y Ddau Faen: stone circle (rejected) (RSC 4) 161
Bwlch y Ddaufaen: bronze dagger (BR 6) 296
Bwlch y Groes: Mesolithic flint blade (MS 3) 19; round cairn (RC 33) 80
Bwysfa Fawr Farm: cooking hearths (BM 5–6) 186

Cader Fawr 13; round cairns: (RC 119–20) 97
Cadyr Arthur *see* Pen y Fan
Cae Carne Uchaf: lost cairns (LC 4) 138
Cae Dol Maen Isaf: flint manufactory (MS 6) 20
Cae Garn: ring cairns (RC 4–5) 76
Cae Garu: round cairn (RC 195) 109
Cae Gwin: burial site (UCB 2) 136
Cae Twmpyn: burial site (UCB 8) 137
 cairns 7, 20, 21, 22, 24, 27, 198; clearance cairns 88, 96, 101, 199, 204, see also settlement, unenclosed sites
 distribution of *66*, *70*, 71, 73, 191, 208; trapezoid 28, 46, *see also* barrows; chambered tombs; long barrows; round cairns
Cambrian Archaeological Association (anonymous contribution): standing stone (SS 6) 166–7
Cambrian Factory (Llanwrtyd): standing stone (SS 7) 167–8
Cantref: burial site (LBS 6) 135;
 clearance cairns: (US 78) 241–2; (US 79) 243
 cooking mound: (BM 14) 187; (BM 16) 187
 enclosures: (US 64) 199, 235; (US 66) 236
 field clearance mound (US 61) 235; flint and chert artefacts and flakes (MS 9 & 10) 20–1; hut and enclosure (US 63) 235;
 hut groups: (US 60) 200, 234, *235*; (US 65) 189, 202, 235–6; (US 78) 201, 241–2
 inscribed stone (lost) (LECM 3) 288; platforms and scoop settlements (US 71) 201, 237–8;
 round cairns: (RC 85–6) 90; (RC 119) 97; (RC 202–4) 110–12; (RC 227) 118
 settlement features: (US 62) 235; (US 79) 243
Cantrill, T C: Carnau Gwynion round cairns (RC 91, RC 96–7) 68; Cefn Sychpant round cairn (RC 123) 68; excavations near Ystradfellte and the Cribarth 68, 90, 91; Fan Foel round cairn (RC 26) 68, 79; 'hut circle' (RC 97) 71, 92, 190, 200; observations of clearance features 189–90; Pwll y Cig Beaker grave (LBS 1) 68, 134; Share y Wlad round cairns (RC 92–5) 68; Sink y Giedd hut circle, since lost (LS 2) 271; upper Afon Twrch round cairns: (RC 2) 76
Capel 279
Carcwm: round cairn (RC 62) 85–6
Careg Gywir: boundary stone (RSS 19) 180
Careg y Fedw: round cairn (RC 59) 84
Carlisle, Nicholas: account of excavations on Mynydd Llangynidr 67; notes of standing stones 163; reference to Glyn Collwyn cairn (UCB 7) 68
Carn: distribution of place names 74

Carn Cabal 106
Carn Canienydd: hut groups (US 60) 200, 234, 235
Carn Caws: fugitive wall (US 105) *pl.7*, 122, 192, 264–6; round cairn (RC 254) 122, 192
Carn Disgwylfa: round cairn (RC 309) 68, 130
Carn Gafallt: huts and clearance cairns (US 87) 249–50; round cairns (RC 172–6) 106–7
Carn Goch: chambered tomb (CT 10) 25, 27, 28, 54–6, *55*
Carn Paderau: round cairn (RC 61) 85
Carn Pantmaenllwyd: round cairn (RC 158) 105
Carn Pwll Mawr: round cairn (RC 104) 93
Carn Wen: round cairn (RC 196) 110
Carn y Bugail: round cairn (RC 222) 115–16, *115*
Carn y Geifr: round cairn (RC 188) 109
Carn y Goetre: hut groups (US 72) 202, 238
Carn yr Arian: round cairn (RC 98) 92
Carnau: round cairns: (RC 169–71) 106
Carnau Cefn y Ffordd: round cairns (RC 177–84) 107–8; standing stone (lost) (LSS 2) 178
Carnau (Carnon) Gwynion: enclosure (US 67) 199, 236; 'hut circle' (RC 97) 71, 92, 200, 271;
   round cairns: (RC 91) 68, 91; (RC 96–7) 68, 92
Carnau ridge: round cairn (RC 57) 84
Carnon Gwynion *see* Carnau (Carnon) Gwynion
Carreg Lem: hut circle (lost) (LS 2) 271
Carreg Lwyd: enclosure (US 21) 220
Carreg Maen Taro: boundary stone (RSS 18) 180
Carreg Saith Troedfedd: standing stone (rejected) (RSS 47) 182
Carreg Waun Llech *see* Waun Llech
Carreg Wen Fawr: standing stone (SS 9) 169
Carreg Wen Fawr y Rugos: round cairn (RC 257) 123; stone row (SC 9) 158–9
Careg y Fedw *see* Careg y Fedw
Castell Ceir Tut: enclosure 278
Castell Dinas, hillfort: chambered tomb (CT 3) 36; lithic finds (SF 77) 294
Castell Llysgoden: round cairn (RC 54) 82
Castell Madoc: bronze trident palstave (BR 17) 297
casting jets: bronze 296
Cathedin (Cathedine): bronze axes (BR 25) 297;
   round cairns: (RC 268) 124; (RC 280) 125
   standing stone (SS 30) 175
cave systems 3, 9–16; burial 9, 11–12; Dan yr Ogof stratigraphy *12*; map of distribution 16
Cefn Blaen y Nant: sharpened oak piles (LS 3) 271
Cefn Brynich: standing stone (SS 14) 170
Cefn Car: hut groups and clearance cairns (US 95) 254–7, *258*, *259*, 260
Cefn Cilsanws:
   field systems:
      (US 90) 6, 24, 110, 250–2
      artefacts recovered (BB 14) 133
      fugitive field walls (US 92) 196, 203, 252, *253*;
   round cairns:
      (RC 201) 68, 73, 110
      artefacts recovered (BB 13) 133
      (RC 211–12) 68, 73
      see also Cilsanws Mountain
Cefn Clawdd:
   round cairns: (RC 228) 118–20; (RC 237) 120; (RC 240–4) 121
Cefn Coed church: inscribed stone (ECM 9) 285

Cefn Coed y Cymer (Glam): hut circles (LS 5) 200, 271
Cefn Crew: enclosure (US 66) 236
Cefn Cul: natural boulder (RSS 21) 180; prehistoric hearths (BM 3–4) 186; round cairn (RC 9) 76
Cefn Esgair Carnau: burned mound (BM 18) 184, 187–8;
   clearance cairns: (US 78) 242; (US 79) 243
   cooking mound (BM 16) 187;
   field systems: (US 79–80) 196, 243; (US 79) 184, 192, 243
   and limestone dissolution 192;
   round cairns: (RC 128) 100; (RC 129) 100
Cefn Ffordd 7
Cefn Gardys: ring cairn (RC 63) 86
Cefn Gwernffrwd (Carms): Bronze Age complex 145
Cefn (Llanwrthwl): gold torcs (BR 11) 296
Cefn Merthyr Cynog: round cairn (RC 141) 103
Cefn Moel: burned mound (BM 22) 188;
   round cairns: (RC 269–71) 124; (RC 277–83) 125–6; (RC 286–7) 126
Cefn Onneu: round cairns (RC 258–62) 123
Cefn Sychpant: burned mound (BM 15) 184; clearance cairns (US 84) 247;
   cooking mounds: (BM 15) 187; (BM 17) 187
   round cairns: (RC 112–16) 96; (RC 121–6) 97–9, *98*, *99*; (RC 123) *pl.8*, 68, *97*;
      (RC 125) 68, 98–9; artefacts recovered (BB 9) 132
      (RC 132–4) 101; (RC 208) 113
   stone disc (SF 41) 292
Cefn Tŷ-Mawr: round cairn (RC 159) 105
Cefn yr Ystrad 3; round cairns: (RC 216–17) 114; (RC 220–3) 115–16
Cefnpyllauduon: cairns and clearances (US 101) 263; round cairn (RC 224) 116
Celtic fields (RS 1) 274
cereals 6, 7, 24
Cerrig Calch: round cairns: (RC 306–7) 68, *see also* Pen Cerrig-calch
Cerrig Duon: clearance cairns (US 31) 222–3, *228*;
   hut structures: (US 31) 222–3, *228*; (US 32) 224
   stone circle (SC 3) 143, 144, 150–3, *151*
chambered tombs 21–2, 24–65; distribution of 26–7, 191; history of study and excavation 24–5; 'information processing nodes' 30n; map of distribution 26; occurrence of lithic material 24, 28; ritual use 50; structure and structural types 27–8, *29*; use as hermit's cell 32, *see also* barrows; cairns; cists; long barrows; ossuaries; round cairns
Chambers, F M: Cefn Ffordd investigation 7
charcoal: fragments 90, 132, 133, 134, 136, 149; layers 5, 17, 19, 25, 41, 49, 55, 60, 72, 77, 102, 129, 130–1
Chartist's Cave: skeletal remains (PCS 4) 13
chert: adze (MS 17) 22;
   assemblages and artefacts 19, 20, 21, 22, 41, 78, 291, 292, 294;
   distribution *207*, 208
   see also flint assemblages and artefacts
chisel: bronze: socketed 296
churches: curvilinear churchyards 279; dedications 279
Chwar Mawr: round cairn (RC 264) 123
Chwarel y Fan (Llaneleu): lithic finds (SF 27) 291
Cil Haul: round cairn (RC 273) 124
Cil Rhudd: round cairns (RC 144–5) 103
Cildu Farm: inscribed stone (ECM 13) 285

Cilgwyn Farm: flint axe (SF 6) 290
Cilsanws Mountain:
  round cairns: (RC 209) 113–14; (RC 210–12) 114
  see also Cefn Cilsanws
cists see cairns; chambered tombs
Clap Round: huts and clearance cairns (US 87) 249–50
Clark, *Sir* George: ring cairn illustrated (RC 63) 71, *86*
Clarke, David: and Beaker sherds at Nant Maden 72
clas: place names 279
climate: change due to deforestation 7; history 5–7, 208
Clo Cadno: enclosures: (US 103–4) 264; round cairn (RC 249) 122
cloth fragments 72, 102, 133
Clwyd y Graig (farm): standing stone (RSS 69) 183
Clwyd-Powys Archaeological Trust 68–9, 77–8, 117, 158, 221
Clyro (Rads): piano convex knife (SF 86) 295
Clyro Court Farm (Rads): chambered tomb (CT 13) 27, 63–4
Cnapau Hafod Llewelyn: round (platform) cairn (RC 47) 81–2
coalfield fringe 1, 3
Coed Cefn: standing stone (SS 37) 177
Coed Taf 5, 7; round cairns (RC 131–2) 100–1
Coed y Garreg: lithic finds (SF 37) 292;
  round cairn (RC 90) 72, 90–1; artefacts recovered (BB 5) 132
Coed yr Ynys:
standing stones: (RSS 61) 182; (SS 28) 174
Coedcae'r Gwartheg: possible clearance cairns (US 91) *251*, 252
Coedcae'r Ychain, hillfort 252; possible ring cairn (RC 209) 113–14
Coetgae Llwyn: lithic finds (SF 55) 293
coins: Roman 55, 61–2
Coity Bach: round cairn (RC 276) 125
Colt Hoare, *Sir* Richard: Bryn y Groes (CT 7) noted 48; Gwernvale excavation 25, 56, 67
cooking mounds *see* burned mounds
Coppa: bronze axe (BR 9) 296
copper artefacts *see* Bronze Age, artefacts
Corcoran: on chambered tombs 28, 46, 62
cord rig *see* rig and furrow
Corn Du: deterioration of cairns 73, 116–17; flint flake/arrowhead (RMS 3, RC 225) 23; Pont ar Daf path: lithic finds (SF 43) 292; possible cairn (LBS 3) 134; research by P Crew (RC 225) 69; round cairn (RC 225) 23, 116–17, *117*
Cornelau Uchaf (BB 19) 133
Cotswold-Severn tombs 27–8, 29
Cradoc Station: boundary stone (RSS 9) 179
Crai: cooking hearths (BM 5–6) 186; Erw'r Garn (RCS 1) 137; hut circle (US 25) 220; hut platforms (US 23–4) 220;
  round cairns: (RC 11) 77; (RC 23–4) 79; (RC 32) 80
Craig Cerrig Gleisiad 5; settlement features (US 86) 247–9
Craig Fan Ddu: lithic finds (SF 50) 293
Craig Irfon: standing stone (rejected) (RSS 46) 182
Craig y Ciliau: nature reserve 15
Craig y Fro 5
Craig y Llwyni: clearance cairns (US 99) 261–2
Craig y Llyn (Glam): lithic assemblages 18
Craig y Nos 13; Saith Maen stone row (SC 1) *pl.1*, 143, 147
Craig y Rhiwarth 13
Crampton, C B: on Carn Goch (CT 10) and flash floods 192; field system around Twyn y Gaer suggested (RS 1) 273; round cairn excavations 68
crannog *see* Ynys Bwlc
Crawford, O G S: and authenticity of the King's Stone 63; dating Tŷ Illtud 32; discovery of Mynydd Troed cairn 35; discovery of Tŷ Isaf cairn 36; Ffostyll excavations 40; Twyn y Beddau cists 130–1
cremation 11, 37, 41, 72–3, 75, 91, 95, 100, 131, 133, 134, 135, *see also* burial practices
Crew, P: Corn Du research (RC 225) 69
Cribarth Plateau: caves 11; clearance cairns (US 3–4) 77; hut circle and clearance cairn (US 8) 213–14, *215*;
  kerb cairns: (RC 18) 78; (RC 19) 71, 78
  unenclosed land 198
Cribyn: lithic finds (SF 61) 293; round cairn (RC 227) 117, *118*
Crickadarn: bronze axe (BR 20) 297; flint finds (SF 10) 290; long mound (RCT 3) 64;
  round cairns: (RC 237) 120; (RC 241–5) 121
  stone hammer head (SF 11) 290
Crickhowell: Breanog Mountain cairns 68; bronze palstave (BR 28) 297; bronze sword (BR 26) 297; flint axe (SF 14)) 291; Glanyrafon (RCT 8) 65; inscribed stone (ECM 45) 288; long cairn *see* Gwernvale; round cairn (RC 308) 130; standing stone (SS 37) 177
Croesllechau (Bryn y Groes):
  chambered tomb (CT 7) 24, 27, 28, 47–8
  Lhuyd's sketches *47*; plan of *48*
cropmarks: settlement features 192, 271, *272*; and timber rings 144; unproven (LC 1–9) 138–9
Y Crug: round cairn (RC 139) 102
Crug Du: round cairn (RC 150) 104
Crug y Gaer hillfort: and contiguous field system (US 107) 203, 267
Crugiau Bach: round cairn (RC 167) 106
Crynfryn: round cairn (RC 194) 109
Cusop: round cairns (RC 144–5) 103
Cwar yr Hendre: enclosures (US 100) 262–3
Cwm Banw: round cairn (RC 308) 130
Cwm Betws: round cairn (RC 195) 109
Cwm Cadlan:
  field systems: (US 83–4) 189; (US 83) 196–8, 203, 245–7
  hut groups (US 71) 202; lithic finds (SF 40) 292; round cairns: (RC 123) *pl.8*, 97–8
Cwm Car (farm) burial site (LBS 5) 72, 134; artefacts recovered (BB 16) 133; flint arrowhead (SF 57) 293
Cwm Criban: round cairn: (RC 220) 115
Cwm Ddaunant: bronze axe (BR 29) 297
Cwm Ddeuddwr: grange land 249
Cwm Dringarth: settlement platforms: (US 49–50) 230–1
Cwm Du: bronze sword (BR 26) 297; round cairn (RC 302) 72
Cwm Fforch Wen: round cairn (RC 6, RC 8) 76
Cwm Fforest: corn-drying kiln (RCT 6) 65
Cwm Gors: natural boulder (RSS 23) 180
Cwm Gu: settlement features (US 112) 269–70
Cwm Haffes: map of enclosures 218; burned mound (BM 1) 184; field system (US 6) 184, 199;
  settlement structures: (US 5) 211–12; (US 12) 214; (US 13) 214–15
  unenclosed land 198
Cwm Irfon: natural boulder (RSS 27) 181; standing stone (SS 6) 162, 166–7, *see also* Irfon Valley
Cwm Moel: burned mound (BM 21) 184, 188; field system (US 96) 184, 196, 203; platforms and clearance cairns (US 96) 258–9, *260*
Cwm Nant: round cairn (RC 99) 92
Cwm Oergwm: lithic finds (SF 52, SF 64) 293
Cwm Pyrgad: enclosures and clearances (US 102) 263–4

Cwm Shenkin: round cairn (RC 268) 124; standing stone (SS 30) 175
Cwm Taf Reservoir: burial site (LBS 4) 134, *see also* Afon Taf
Cwm Tawe: huts and clearance cairns (US 34) 225–6; settlement sites 210–27, *see also* Tawe Valley
Cwm y Meirch (RCS 2) 137
Cwm-Gu: lost quernstone (US 112) 200
Cwrt y Cadno: dyke (D 1) 274
Cwrt y Gollen: standing stone (SS 36) *pl.5*, 163, 176–7
Cwrt y Prior 279; possible cromlech (RCT 5) 64
Cyfarthfa Castle Museum: inscribed stone (ECM 7) 284
Cynant Fach: round cairn (RC 46) 81

daggers: Beaker: flint 294; Bronze Age: bronze 68, 110, 114, 133, 136, 137, 296; flint 68, 72, 73, 91, 132, 133, 135, 292
Dan y Graig: bronze sword (BR 21) 297; standing stones (LS 9) 163; sub-peat wall (LS 9) 189, 273
Dan yr Eglwys: flint artefacts (MS 13) 21
Dan yr Ogof: cave system (PCS 1–4, OCS 1–3, RMS 1) 9–15, *see also* Abercrave
Dan yr Ogof Plateau: clearance cairns (US 3–4) 77, 210–11; unenclosed land 198
Daniel, G E: and Cotswold-Severn tombs 27; on Pen y Garn-goch round cairns 85–86
Daren Fach: possible ring cairn (RC 209) 113–14
Dark Age: estates 278; settlement 278, 281–3
Darren: boulder trains 196; field system (US 112) 196; natural boulders (RSS 34) 181; round cairns: (RC 154–5) 104
Darren Ciliau *see* Ogof Darren Ciliau
Darren Fawr: mound (RCS 4) 137, 192
Dartmoor Reaves 203
Davies, V E: Pen Gloch y Pibwr excavation (RC 302) 68, 129
Davies, M: Eglwys Faen excavation 15; survey of Dorwen stone circle (RSC 1) 160–1
Davies, Wendy: on the suitability of high ground for agriculture 278
Davies, William: Tŷ Du finds (LBS 9) 135
Y Dderw (farm): mounds (RCS 5–6) 138, 191
Ddu Fannog Farm: cooking mounds (BM 9–10) 186–7
Defynnog:
    clearance cairns: (US 31) 222–3, *228*; (US 33–4) 224–6
    clearance pile (US 38) 227; clearance stones (US 85) 247; cooking hearths (BM 5–6) 186; curvilinear churchyard 279;
    enclosures: (US 29) 199, 202, 221; (US 30) 222; (US 35) 226
    Erw'r Garn (RCS 1) 137; hut circle (US 25) 220; hut platforms (US 23–4) 220;
    hut structures: (US 31) 222–3, *228*; (US 32) 224; (US 34) 225–6
    inscribed stones: (ECM 10–11) 285; (rejected) (RECM 1–2) 289
    round cairns: (RC 11) 77; (RC 23–4) 79; (RC 32) 80; (RC 76–9) 88–9; (RC 136–7) 101
    scoop settlements (US 44) 201, 229; settlement features (US 86) 247–9; settlement sites: (US 35) 226;
    standing stones: (SS 12) 88, 143, 162, 170; (SS 14) 170
    stone circles 143
dendrochronological studies: Llangorse Crannog (CS 1) 7
Devil's Quoit (Stackpole) 163
disc: perforated shale 19; sandstone 68, 99, 132, 291; stone 28, 292
Dixie's Corner: flint arrowhead (SF 44) 292
Dol y Felin Dolmaen: standing stone (SS 20) 171, 173
Dol y Gaer: Cwm Car (LBS 5) 72, 134
Dol y Gaer Reservoir: lithic finds (SF 58) 293
dolines: and evidence for settlement 192–4, *see also* shake-holes; sink-holes

Dorwen: clearance cairns (US 1) 200, 210; hut circle (US 2) 210; round cairn (RC 3) 76; stone circle (rejected) (RSC 1) 160–1
drovers' markers 104, 144, 147, 150, 161, 163
Druid's Altar: bronze find (unplotted) (BR 35) 297
Druid's Altar Stone: standing stone (SS 40) 177
Drum Ddu 3; round cairns (RC 177–84) 107–8; round cairns (RC 188) 109
Drum Nant y Gorlan: mound 82; standing stone (SS 8) 163, 168–9
Drygarn Fawr 3; round (kerb) cairns: (RC 55–6) 75, 82–3; (RC 55) *84*; (RC 56) *85*
drystone walling: of chambered tombs 25, 31, 37, 38; of round cairns 71, 78
Dulas Valley: gold ring (BR 10) 296
Dunn, C J: Mesolithic graver found 22
Dunning, G C: and drovers' markers 144; Ynys-hir excavation (RC 138) 68
Dwr Llwydan: standing stone (SS 2) 166
Dyfed: standing stones 163
Dyffren Crawhen: stone alignment (SC 9) 158–9
Dyffryn Nedd (farm): enclosures (US 68) 199, 203, 236–7
dyke (D 1) 274

Earnshaw, Carole: stone circle discovery 158
earthwork *see* dyke
ecclesiastical estates 278–9, *see also* monasteries, grange land
Eglwys Caradog: cave site (OCS 1) 13
Eglwys Faen: cave site (OCS 3) 15
Ellwood, John: plan of a cave at Darren Ciliau 15
emmer wheat 6, 7, 135
enclosures: site classification 199–202; (timber), used in stock raising 271
Enlarged Food Vessel 72, 91, 95, 132, 133, *see also* Beaker; urns
environmental data 6
Epynt Plateau 1, 3, *see also* Mynydd Epynt
erosion: Holocene 196; its effect on settlement features 191–4
Erw Wen (Merioneth): hut groups 200
Erwhelm Cross: inscribed stone (ECM 33) 287
Erwood: grit axe hammer (SF 79) 294; stone hammer head (SF 11) 290
Erw'r Garn (RCS 1) 137
Esgair Bustach: cooking mound (BM 11) 187
Esgair Dafydd: round cairn (RC 46) 81
Esgair Fraith: round cairn (RC 58) 84
Esgair Garn: round cairn (RC 48) 82
Esgair Irfon: round cairn (RC 60) 85
Evans, Evan: Gwernvale noted 25

Fan Bwlch Chwyth: bronze palstave (BR 7) 296; lost cairn (LC 6) 138
Fan Foel:
    round cairn (RC 26) 68, 79
    artefacts recovered (BB 1) 132; lithic finds (SF 32) 292
    see also Twr y Fan Foel
Fan Frynach (Fan Frynych): round cairns: (RC 136–7) 101; settlement features (US 86) 247
Fan Gihirych: round cairn (RC 11) 77
Fan Hir 5; enclosures (US 17–18) 216
Fan Llia: round cairn (RC 80) 89; settlement platforms: (US 39–41) 227–8; (US 43) 229, *230*
Fan Nedd: clearance pile (US 38) 227; mound (RCS 3) 137; round cairns: (RC 76–7) 88
Fan y Big:
    burial site (LBS 6) 7, 69, 72, 73, 117, 135
    artefacts recovered (BB 17) 133; bronze razor (BR 16) 296

Fannog (farm): dyke (D 1) 274
Fedw: dyke (D 1) 274
Felindre: mound (RCS 8) 138, 191
Fenni-fach: boundary stone (RSS 9) 179; round cairn (RC 290) 126–7
Fenton, Richard: Bryn y Groes (CT 7) noted 48; flint dagger at Llaneleu noted 68, 135
Fforest Fawr 1, 3, 150, 221
Ffosfaehog: round cairns (RC 185–7) 108–9
Ffostyll:
    Beaker burial site (Tŷ Du) (LBS 9) 40, 72, 135–6
    lithic finds (SF 74) 294
        chambered tombs (CT 5 & 6) 25, 27, 28, 40–6; Ffostyll North (CT 6) 43–6, *44*; artefacts recovered (BB 23) 133; skeletal remains 46
        Ffostyll South (CT 5) 41–3, *41*; skeletal remains 41–2
    lithic finds (SF 20) 291; plan of sites *40*;
    round barrow (LBS 10) 40, 72; artefacts recovered (BB 24) 133; lithic finds (SF 75) 294
    standing stone (lost) (LSS 8) 178
Ffridd Bod y Fuddau (Merioneth): plough-marks 206
Ffynnon Dafydd Bevan: round cairns (RC 149–9) 103–4
Ffynnon Mary: mound (BM 20) 188; round cairn (RC 197) 109, 110
Ffynnon y Gwyddau: natural boulder (RSS 25) 180
Ffynnon yr Oerfa: field system 203, 205
Ffynnon Ysgolheigion: cooking hearth (BM 19) 188
field clearance 79, 81, 93, 101, 112, 189, 192, 196, 198, 199, 204, 208; map of *197*, *see also* cairns, clearance cairns; settlement, unenclosed sites
field survey 190
field systems 190, 196–8, 203–4, 206–8; and hut groups 200
field walls *pl.7*, 122, 189, 190, 192, 194, 196, 199, 210–11, 252, 253, 260, 264–6
Fish Stone: standing stone (SS 29) 174–5, *175*
flint: arrowheads 19, 20, 21, 23, 24, 37, 60, 72, 73, 111, 133, 134, 135, 290, 291, 292, 293, 294, 295;
    assemblages and artefacts 5, 6, 9, 12–13, 17, 19–23, 24, 35, 41, 46, 50, 60, 61, 64, 68, 72, 78, 79, 90, 91, 92, 102, 111, 131, 132, 133, 134, 136, 221, 290, 291, 292, 293, 294, 295; distribution *207*, 208, *see also* chert
    axes 21, 22, 290, 291, 294; blades 19, 20, 21, 22, 91, 131, 132, 293; daggers 68, 72, 73, 91, 132, 133, 135; graver 22; knives 20, 21, 40, 72, 78, 91, 132, 133, 290, 292, 293, 294, 295; scrapers 19, 20, 21, 22, 61, 78, 91, 132, 221, 290, 291, 292, 293, 294, 295; strike-a-lights 20
flooding: seasonal 3
flute: bone (CT 4) 28, 40
forest: clearance and deforestation 5–7, 17, 78, 149, 192; vegetation 5–7
Fox, *Lady* Aileen: excavations on Gelligaer Common (Glam) 278; excavations (RC 65, RC 98) 87, 92
Fox, *Sir* Cyril: excavations on Gelligaer Common (Glam) 278; and the Tump Wood Site (RCT 4) 64
Freshwater East (Pembs): flint finds 19
frost action: and boulder trains 194–6

Y Gader:
    lithic finds: (MS 16–17) 22; (SF 26) 291
    stone circle (lost) (RSC 8) 143, 161, *see also* Pen y Gader Fawr
Gamrhiw:
    round cairns: (RC 168) 106; (RC 169–70) 106; (RC 171) 75, 106, *107*, *108*; (RC 185–7) 108–9

Gareg Las: round cairn (RC 2) 76
Garn Ddu (Penderyn): lost cairn (LC 5) 138; platforms and scoop settlements (US 71) 201, 237–8
Garn Ddu (Vaynor): round cairns (RC 213–15) 114; settlement features (US 93–4) 252–4; wall and stone pile (US 97) 260
Garn Dwad: round cairns: (RC 51–3) 82, *83*
Garn Fawr: round cairn (RC 251) 122
Garn Felen: round cairn (RC 223) *115*, 116
Garn Goch: Bronze Age cairn (RMS 1, RC 16) 22, 77; lithic finds (SF 29) 291
Garn Las: round cairns: (RC 28–9) 79
Garn Lwyd: round cairn (RC 164) 105–6
Garn Pontsticill: cairns (US 98) 260–1
Garn Wen (Llandeilo'r Fan): round cairns: (RC 33–4) 80
Garn Wen (Llanfihangel Abergwesyn): round cairn (RC 160) 105
Garn Wen (Llanfihangel Nant Brân): round cairn (RC 150) 104
Garn Wen (Llanwrtyd): round cairns: (RC 49) 82
Garn Wen (Pant Brwynog): round cairn (RC 86) 90
Garreg Fawr: standing stones (SS 15–16) 170, *171*
Garth: bronze palstave (BR 8) 296; round cairns (RC 196–9) 109–10
Y Garth: standing stone (SS 19) 171
Garthbrengi *see* Dan yr Eglwys
gelifluction terraces 196
Geological Survey 68
geology: map 4; in the physical background 1–5
Gibson, A M: Pen y Fan cairn plan 117
Gileston (farm): standing stone (SS 31) 164, 175, *176*
Gilpin, Gilbert: observation of clearance features (LS 1) 189, 270–1
Gilwern: flint axe (SF 25) 291
Gilwern Hill: cairns and clearance features (US 109) 267–9
glaciation 3, 5; effect on Palaeolithic occupation debris 9, *see also* periglacial features
Glais Brook: platforms and clearance cairns (US 96) 258–9
Glanusk, *Lord*: cited 101, *see also* Russell, Joseph H, 2nd Baron Glanusk
Glanusk Estate 249
Glanyrafon (Crickhowell) (RCT 8) 65
Y Glas: cooking mounds (BM 9–10) 186–7
Glasbury 279; burial site (UCB 6) 137;
    cropmarks or parchmarks: (LS 7) 192, 271, *272*; (LS 8) 272, *273*
    lithic finds (SF 21) 291; long barrow (CT 8) 6, 25, 27, 28, 29, 48–51; mound (RCS 8) 138
Glasbury Church: round cairn (RC 290) 126–7
Glog Las:
    round cairns: (RC 106) 93; (RC 110) 93–4
Glyn: boundary stones (RSS 4–5) 179; round cairns: (RC 136–7) 101; settlement features (US 86) 247–9
Glyn Collwn: burial site (UCB 7) 137
Glyn Fach (Gospel Pass): flint graver (MS 18) 22
Glyntawe: clearance cairns: (US 10) 214; enclosures: (US 14) 215–16; flint core (RMS 2) 23; hut groups (US 7) 199, 200, 201, 212–13; hut platform (US 27) 221; Ogof Ffynnon Ddu (PCS 2, RMS 2) 23; ring cairn (RC 10) 77;
    settlement structures: (US 12) 214; (US 13) 214–15
    Twll Carw Coch (PCS 3) 13
Gochcarreg: natural boulder (RSS 26) 180
Godre'r Garn-las: round cairn (RC 21) 78–9
Golden Valley (Herefords): Neolithic cairns 27
'Goosefolds' 189–90

Gors Wen (farm):
  round cairns: (RC 87–9) 90; (RC 87): artefacts recovered (BB 4) 132
Gospel Pass: flint graver found (MS 18) 22
graffiti: in chambered tombs 32
Grange of Cwm Ddeuddwr (US 87) 249
gravegoods 72
Green, Francis: Mynydd Bach Trecastell excavation 80
Green, H S *see* Healey, E & Green
Griffiths, W E: and Clyro Court tomb 63; on hut groups 200; and Pen y Fan cairn 117
Grimes, W F: on Cerrig Duon 150, 151; cited on (RC 300) excavation 129; Gwernvale planned 56; Mynydd Troed planned (CT 2) 35; on Nant Tarw stone circles 150; on Pen y Garn-goch round cairns 86; Saith Maen (Llanwrthwl) planned 157; on the structure of Tŷ Illtud (CT 1) 31; on Trecastle Mountain stone circles (SC 4) 153n; Tŷ Isaf excavation (CT 3) 36, 37
Grinsell, L V: on Tŷ Illtud graffiti 32
grit stone: axe hammer 294
Grwyne Fawr: enclosure (US 113) 270; natural boulder (RSS 42) 181; standing stone (SS 40) 177
Guest, *Lady* Charlotte 106
Gunless (Gunleus), prince of Glewissig 13
Gwaen Hepste: round cairn (RC 98) 92
Gwarafog: round cairns: (RC 146–7) 103
Gwaun Dan y Daren: round cairns: (RC 312) 131
Gwaun Nelly: round barrow (RC 163) 105
Gwaunydd Hepste: round cairn (RC 103) 93
Gwenddwr: round cairn (RC 232) 120; stone circle (SC 7) 144, 158
Gwern Wyddog: standing stone (SS 2) 166
Gwern y Figyn Uchaf: round cairn (RC 143) 103
Gwernvale:
  chambered tomb (CT 11) 6, 21–2, 24, 25, 27, 28, 29, 56–60, *57*, 73
  structure 56–9
  exploitation of ungulates 18, 22; flint assemblage (MS 15) 5, 6, 17, 21–2, 24; flint axe (SF 23) 291; radiocarbon dating (CAR–113) 29, 60
Gwernyfed Park:
  hillfort 25
  lithic finds (SF 73) 294
Gwynne, A F: excavations at Ffostyll 40
Gwys Fawr: round cairn (RC 2) 76
Y Gyrn: clearance stones (US 85) 247

hafotai 190, 202, 208
hammers: flint(?) 293, 294; stone 290
Hay: artefacts found (BB 29) 133; bronze palstave (BR 30) 297; bronze spearhead (BR 31) 297; round cairns: (RC 310–11) 130–1
Hay Bluff: standing stone (RSS 74) 183; stone circle (SC 10) 65, 144, 159–60
Hazleton Long Barrow (Glos) 25, 29
Healey, E & Green, H S: exploitation of ungulates at Gwernvale 18
hearths: Ogof yr Esgyrn (PCS 1) 11; 'prehistoric' 184
Hen Clawdd: dyke (D 1) 274
Hendre Forwydd: flint arrowhead (SF 81) 294
Heol Ddu: standing stone 163
Hepste: lithic finds (SF 36) 292
Hepste Fechan: round cairn (RC 109) 93

hillforts 25, 199, 203, 205, 208, 252, 273, 274, 275, 276, 278
Historia Britonum 106
hoards:
  Bronze Age: bronzes, Pen y Fan (RC 226) 117, 133; from Bishops' Meadow (Brecon) (BR 14) 296; Llansbyddyd (BR 15) 296
Hoare, R Colt *see* Colt Hoare: R
Hogg, A H A: and unenclosed settlements 200, 278
Holford, John: Mynydd Bach Trecastell excavation 80
Holloway, K: Coed y Garreg cairn excavation 91
Holocene erosion 196
Holyhead Mountain: hut groups 200
Howell, George: Llangattock mound (UCB 4) 137
hut groups and circles 71, 92, 190, 200–1, 208
hut platforms 149, 150, 189, 190, 201–2
hypocaust (Roman): Maesderwen (UCB 3) 136

inscribed stones 181–3; Early Christian: distribution of 279; sites of 284–9
Irfon Valley 3, 20, *see also* Cwm Irfon

Jacobi, R M: on seasonal movement in the Mesolithic 18
James, D J: Battle tumulus 173; Ffostyll 'track' stone 178; standing stone alignments 163
javelin points: flint: at Pant Sychpant 20
Jerman, H N: earthwork reported (D 1) 274
Jones, John Rhys: Trecastle mountain stone circles (SC 4) 153
Jones, Nigel: Banc y Celyn site surveyed 158
Jones, Peter M: enclosure noted in Cwm Gu 269; field observation 69; and Pen y Fan cairn 117
Jones, Theophilus: Bedd Illtud described 101; on clearance features 189; Eglwys Faen cave noted 15; excavations on Mynydd Llangynidr 67; Garn Du round cairns mentioned 114; Gwernvale excavation 25; King's Stone (RCT 2) noted 64; Llandefalle Hill boundary stone (RSS 10(g)) 180; Llaneleu flint dagger noted 68, 135; reference to Croesllechau (CT 7) 48; and standing stones 162, 164; and stone circles 143–4, 147, 155, 157, 161; Twyn y Beddau, noted (RC 311) 69, 130
Jones, Thomas: discovery of animal tooth 91

karren analysis 194
karstic process and features 192–4, 198–9, 264–7
Kay, R E: hut group discovery (US 108) 267
Keith, *Sir* Arthur: human remains at Ffostyll 42, 46
kerb cairns 68, 69–71, 82–3, *84*, 85, 87, 88, 91, 93, 97, 100, 101–2, 104, 110, 116, 122, 127, 130, 143, 145, *see also* round cairns
Kilvert, Francis: and the Twyn y Beddau excavations 68, 130
King's Stone: disputed cromlech (RCT 2, RSS 41) 64, 181
Knight, Bernard: evidence to the inquest concerning Chartist's Cave bones 13
knives: bronze 68, 114, 133, 296; flint 20, 21, 40, 72, 78, 91, 132, 133, 290, 292, 293, 294, 295

Lan Fawr: hillfort (HF 65) *275*, 276; standing stone (lost) (LSS 1) 178
Lewis, Daniel: Cwrt y Prior (RCT 5) noted 64
Lewis, R G: excavation in Chartist's Cave 13
Lewis, Samuel: cited 123, 143, 163
ley-lines 164, 165
Lhuyd, Edward 24, 31; accounts of standing stones 162, 166, 176, 178; annotated sketches of Bryn y Groes (Croesllechau) (CT 7) *47*

Liber Landavensis: Dark Age estates 278
lime workings 264, 266; limestone collection 196
limekilns 239, 261, 268
limestone solution *see* karstic process
lithic assemblages and artefacts: distribution 207, 208; Mesolithic 17–18
Little Lodge: chambered tomb (CT 9) 25, 27, 28, 51–3, *53, 54*
Llan-gors (Llangorse): artefacts found (BB 21) 133; burial site (LBS 8) 135;
  Crannog:
    post-Roman site (CS 1) 7, 279, 281–2
    see also Ynys Bwlc
  Cwrt y Prior (RCT 5) 64; round cairn (RC 272) 124; flint assemblage (MS 14) 21; inscribed stones (ECM 36–8) 287; lithic finds (SF 69) 294;
  Llangorse Lake 3; evidence from cores 6, 7; Mynydd Troed cairn (CT 2) 35, 206
  monastic lands 278–9, 281;
  Vicarage: burial site (LBS 8) 135; flint arrowheads (BB 21, SF 67) 133, 135, 294
Llan-y-wern: King's Stone (RCT 2) 64
Llanafan Fawr: cooking hearth (BM 19) 188; curvilinear churchyard 279; dyke (D 1) 274; inscribed stone (ECM 16) 286; mound (BM 20) 188;
  round cairns: (RC 154–7) 104–5; (RC 159) 105; (RC 161–2) 105; (RC 188–9) 109; (RC 246) 121
  standing stones: (SS 18–20) 104, 171; (SS 26) 173
Llanbadarn Fawr (Ceredigion) 164
Llanbedr Ystrad Yw: enclosure (US 110) 269; lithic finds (MS 17) 22; round cairn (RC 307) 129–30; standing stone (SS 41) 177; stone circle (lost) (RSC 8) 161
Llanbeilin 279
Llanddeti: bronze axe (BR 24) 297; bronze sword (BR 21) 297; clearance cairns (US 99) 261–2; enclosures (US 100) 262–3; flint chipping site (MS 12) 21;
  inscribed stones: (ECM 22) 286; (ECM 39) 287
  lithic finds (SF 56) 293; round cairns (RC 216–24) 114–16; Tump Wood (RCT 4) 64
Llanddew: bronze axe (BR 19) 297; inscribed stones (ECM 30–1) 286–7
Llanddewi Abergwesyn: cooking mounds (BM 9–13) 186–7; flint assemblage (MS 4) 20; round cairns (RC 48, RC 54) 82; standing stone (SS 9) 169
Llanddewi'r Cwm: inscribed stone (ECM 33) 287
Llandefaelog: inscribed stone (ECM 29) 286
Llandefaelog Fach: boundary stones (RSS 9) 179; inscribed stone (ECM 28) 286
Llandefalle:
  boundary stones: (RSS 11) 180; (RSS 17) 180
  standing stone (SS 34) *pl.6*, 175–6, 178
Llandefalle Hill: boundary stones (RSS 10) 179–80
Llandeilo'r Fan: boundary stones: (RSS 7) 179; Cwm y Meirch (RCS 2) 137; Dark Age estate 198, 278; flint blade (MS 3) 19;
  round cairns: (RC 33–4) 80; (RC 42) 81; (RC 44–5) 81
Llandulas: inscribed stone (ECM 6) 284
Llaneglwys: long mound (RCT 3) 64
Llaneleu: artefacts found (BB 23–5) 133; burial sites (LBS 9–10) 40, 68, 72, 73, 133, 135–6; chambered tombs (CT 5 & 6) 25, 27, 28, 40–6; curvilinear churchyard 279; flint dagger burial (LBS 9) 68, 73, 133, 135–6; inscribed stones (ECM 43–4) 288;
  lithic finds: (MS 16–17) 22; (SF 26–7) 291
  Rhos Fach (or Fawr) (RCT 7) 65; round cairn (RC 291) 127; standing stone (lost) (LSS 8) 178; stone circle (lost) (RSC 8) 161, *see also* Ffostyll
Llanelieu *see* Llaneleu
Llanelli (Brecknocks): axe finds (SF 24–5) 291; cairns and clearance features (US 109) 267–9; cairns and field walls (US 107) 203, 267; sub-peat wall (LS 9) 189, 273
Llanelwedd (Rads) 6
Llanfigan: burial site (UCB 7) 137; inscribed stone (ECM 25) 286; lithic finds (SF 63) 293; round cairn (RC 276) 125;
  standing stones: (SS 23) 172, *174*; (SS 31) 164, 175, *176*
Llanfihangel Abergwesyn: flint manufactory (MS 6) 20;
  round cairns: (RC 55–8) 82–4, *84, 85*; (RC 60–1) 85; (RC 63) 86; (RC 160) 105
  sharpened oak piles (LS 3) 271; standing stone (SS 8) 163, 168–9; standing stone (lost) (LSS 1) 178
Llanfihangel Brynpabuan:
  round cairns: (RC 158) 105; (RC 188) 109
  standing stone (SS 21) 171; stone row (SC 6) 157–8
Llanfihangel Crucorney (Monm): flint arrowhead (MS 9) 20; pebble flint deposits 18
Llanfihangel Cwm Du: artefacts found (BB 26–7, LBB 2) 133; burial site (UCB 5) 137; burned mound (BM 22) 188; Dark Age estate 278; enclosure (US 113) 270;
  inscribed stones: (ECM 40–2) 287; (RSS 43, ECM 34) 181, 287; (RSS 44, RECM 3) 163, 181–2, 289
  lithic finds: (SF 70) 294; (SF 72) 294
  monastic boundary stones 163–4, 175, *177*; natural boulder/boundary stone (RSS 36) 181;
  round cairns: (RC 269–73) 124; (RC 277–9) 125; (RC 281–9) 125–6; (RC 300) 128–9; (RC 302–6) 129
  settlement features (US 112) 269–70;
  standing stones: (SS 29) 174–5; (SS 32) 163, 164, 175, *177*; (SS 33) 175
  standing stones (lost) (LSS 5–6) 178
Llanfihangel Fechan: field system discounted (RS 1) 203, 274
Llanfihangel Nant Brân: artefacts found (BB 12) 133; boundary stone (RSS 7) 179; flint arrowhead (SF 44) 292;
  round cairns: (RC 138–40) 101–2; (RC 142) 103; (RC 150) 104
  standing stones (SS 15–17) 170–1; stone circle (SC 5) 144, 145, 155–7
Llanfihangel Tal y Llyn: standing stone (RSS 62) 182
Llanfoist Fawr (Monmouths): cairns and clearance features (US 109) 267–9
Llanfrynach: artefacts found (BB 18) 133;
  burial sites: (UCB 2) 136; (UCB 3) 133, 136–7
  flint assemblage (MS 11) 21; inscribed stone (ECM 24) 286; inscribed stones (lost) (LECM 4–5) 288;
  lithic finds: (SF 49) 293; (SF 53) 293; (SF 64) 293
  round cairn (RC 203–7) 111–13
Llangammarch: collapsed hut circle (LS 4) 271; flint arrowhead (SF 47) 292; inscribed stone (ECM 15) 285;
  round cairns: (RC 62) 85–6; (RC 146) 103; (RC 148–9) 103–4; (RC 151–3) 104
Llanganten: round cairn (RC 163) 105
Llangasty-Talyllyn: polished axe (SF 18) 291
Llangatwg (Llangattock): boulder wall and clearance features (US 106) 164, 266–7; burial site (UCB 4) 137; chambered tomb (CT 10) 54–6; excavations by H T Payne 67–8; flint

arrowhead (SF 81) 294; hut groups (US 108) 267; lost cairn (LC 7) 138;
  round cairns: (RC 264) 123; (RC 266–7) 123–4; (RC 294–9) 127–8
  standing stone (SS 27) *pl.4*, 162, 164, 174; sub-peat wall (LS 9) 189
Llangenni (Llangenny): polished axes (SF 22) 291; round cairns (RC 292–3) 127;
  standing stones: (SS 36) *pl.5*, 176–7; (SS 37–40) 177
  urn (RB 1) 72, 137
Llangoed: Dark Age estate 278; standing stone (SS 34) *see* Llangoed Castle
Llangoed Castle: standing stone (SS 34) *pl.6*, 162, 175–6
Llangoed Wood: standing stone (lost) (LSS 7) 178
Llangorse *see* Llan-gors
Llangynidr 5; artefacts found (BB 20) 133; bronze axe (BR 22) 297; bronze palstave (BR 23) 297; burial site (LBS 7) 72, 135; cairns and clearances (US 101) 263; cave site 13, 15;
  clearances: (US 102) 263–4; (US 106) 266–7
  enclosures: (US 102–4) 263–4; (US 106) 266–7
  fugitive wall (US 105) *pl.7*, 122, 192, 264–6; hillfort (HF 65) 275, 276; inscribed stone (lost) (LECM 6) 288; lost cairn (LC 8) 139;
  round cairns: (RC 247–63) 121–3; (RC 265) 123; (RC 312) 131
  standing stones: (SS 27) *pl.4*, 162, 164, 174; (SS 28) 174
  stone rows (SC 8–9) 158–9, *see also* Mynydd Llangynidr
Llangynidr Common: and the limestone dissolution process (US 105) *pl.7*, 192, 264–6
Llanhamlach: cairn (CT 1) 31–4; inscribed stones (ECM 26–7) 286; standing stone (SS 24) 164, 172; standing stone (lost) (LSS 3) 178; stone circle or row (lost) (RSC 7) 144, 161, 273
Llanigon: artefacts found (BB 28–9) 133; burial site (UCB 8) 137; chambered tomb (CT 12) 25, 27, 28, 60–2, *61*, 72; inscribed stone (lost) (LECM 9) 288; lithic finds (MS 18) 222; round cairns (RC 310–11) 130–1; stone circle (SC 10) 65, 159–60
Llanllywenfel (Llanlleonfel): inscribed stone (ECM 14) 285; round cairns: (RC 146–7) 103; standing stone (RSS 52) 182
Llansantffraid: cairn (CT 1) 31–4; inscribed stone (ECM 35) 287; mace head (SF 68) 294
Llansbyddyd (Llanspyddyd): artefacts found (BB 17, LBB 1) 133; bronze hoard (BR 15) 296; inscribed stone (ECM 23) 286; lithic finds (RMS 3) 23; possible cairn (LBS 3) 134; round cairn (RC 135) 101; round cairns (RC 225–6) 116–17
Llanthony Mountain: round cairns 68
Llanwrthwl: bronze axe (BR 9) 296; gold torcs (BR 11) 296; huts and clearance cairns (US 87) 249–50;
  round cairns: (RC 55–6) 82–3, *84*, *85*; (RC 59) 84; (RC 157) 105; (RC 164–88) 105–9; (RC 190–200) 109–10
  standing stones: (SS 9–11) 169; (SS 22) 171; (lost) (LSS 2) 178
  stone circle (rejected) (RSC 4) 161
Llanwrtyd 3; bronze socketed chisel (BR4) 296; flint axe (SF 2) 290;
  inscribed stones: (ECM 5) 284; (ECM 13) 285
  round cairns: (RC 46–7, RC 49–51) 81–2, *83*; standing stone (SS 6–7) 162, 166–8; stone circle (lost) (RSC 3) 161
Llanwrtyd Wells: prehistoric hearths (BM 7–8) 186
Llanynys: inscribed stone (ECM 32) 287
Llanywern: King's Stone: (RCT 2, RSS 41) 64, 181
Llethr Cefn y Gwair: cooking hearths (BM 12–13) 187
Llethyr Melyn: round cairns: (RC 161–2) 105
Llethyr Waun Lwyd: round cairns (RC 189) 109

Llorfa ridge: round cairn (RC 7) 76
Lloyd, *Sir* John C: Mynydd Epynt excavation (RC 151–3) 68, 104, 129; plough-mark photograph 205; standing stone photographs 178, 180n
lluestau 208
Llwyn Llwyd: round cairns: (RC 145) 103
Llwyn Onn: bronze trident palstave (BR 12) 296
Llwyn y Fedwen: lithic finds (SF 70) 294; standing stone (SS 32) 163, 164, 175, *177*
Llwyncwmstabl: round cairn (RC 1, RC 3) 76
Llygadwy: inscribed stone (RSS 44, RECM 3) 163, 181–2; natural boulder/boundary stone (RSS 36) 181
Llyn Brianne Dam 187, 274
Llyn Mire (Rads) 6
Llyn Nant Llys: round cairn (RC 42) 81
Llyn-y-Fan: Fawr and Fach 5, 76
Llynfi, river *see* Afon Llynfi
Llys-wen: cropmarks or parchmarks (LS 7) 192, 271, *272*; mounds (RCS 5–6) 138, 191; standing stone (lost) (LSS 7) 178
Llysdinam: mound (BM 20) 188;
  round cairns: (RC 159) 105; (RC 188–9) 109; (RC 246) 121
  standing stone (SS 26) 173
Llywel: artefacts found (BB 1–3) 132; cooking hearths (BM 5–6) 186;
  enclosures: (US 9) 214; (US 17–18) 216
  field systems (US 33) 150; flint arrowheads (SF 31) 292; inscribed stones (ECM 3–4) 284; platforms (US 20) 217–20;
  prehistoric hearths: (BM 2) 186; (BM 3–4) 186
  round cairns: (RC 9) 76; (RC 20–2) 78–9; (RC 25–31) 79–80; (RC 35–41) 80–1; (RC 43–5) 81
  rubble bank (US 11) 214;
  settlement structures: (US 15–16) 216; (US 19) 217; (US 26) 220–1;
  standing stones (SS 1–4) 166;
  stone circles: (SC 2) 144; (SC 2–4) 144, 147–55
Lombardic inscriptions 287
long barrows 6, 25, 35, 40–6, 48–54, *see also* barrows; cairns; chambered tombs
longhouses 243, 247, 249, 256, 278
Longueville Jones, H 31, 33
Lower Neuadd Reservoir: lithic finds (SF 53) 293
Lynch, F M: 'clinker like' Neolithic pottery 28; kerb cairns 71
lynchets 203; suggested 245

Mabinogion 106
Macalister: Maen Llia inscriptions 170
mace head 20, 294
Maen Cam: dyke (D 1) 274; natural boulders (RSS 32–3) 181
Maen Gweddiau: boundary stone (RSS 1) 179
Maen Illtud: standing stone (lost) (LSS 3) 178
Maen Llia: standing stone (SS 12) 88, 143, 162, 170
Maen Llwyd: standing stone (SS 41) 177
Maen Madoc: flint and chert assemblage (MS 8) 20; standing stone (ECM 8) 162, 163, 169, 285
Maen Mawr: clearance cairns (US 33) 224–5; round cairn (RC 31) 79–90; standing stone (SS 3) 143, 144, 150, 151, 163, 166
Maen Richard: standing stone (SS 17) 171, *172*
Maes Clytha Wood: standing stones (lost) (LSS 5–6) 178
Maes Coch: mound (RCT 9) 65
Maescar: boundary stones (RSS 4–6) 179; standing stone (SS 14) 170

Maesderwen:
    burial site (UCB 3) 136–7
    artefacts recovered (BB 18) 133
Maesmynys: inscribed stone (ECM 32) 287; standing stone (lost) (LSS 4) 163, 178
Manby, George: Gwernvale noted 25
Map of South Wales (E Bowen) 162
marked and memorial stones (RSS 43–4) 181–3, *see also* boundary stones; natural boulders; standing stones
Medieval: farming practice 266; settlement patterns 278
Megalithic tombs *see* chambered tombs
Meini'r peder Gawres 143
Mellte Castle 91
memorial stones 181–3
Merthyr Cynog: artefacts found (BB 19) 133; Deverel-Rimbury urn 72, 133; inscribed stones (lost) (LECM 1–2) 288;
    round cairns: (RC 141) 103; (RC 228) 118–20; (RC 233–6) 120; (RC 238–40) 120–1
    standing stone (SS 17) 171, *172*
Merthyr Tydfil (Tudful) (Glam) 3; inscribed stone (ECM 20) 286
Mesolithic sites and findspots (MS 1–18, RMS 1–3) 17–23
microliths: at Gwernvale (MS 15) 22; at Llanddeti (MS 12) 21; at Llaneleu (MS 16) 22; at Pant Sychpant (MS 7) 20; at Upper Neuadd Reservoir (MS 10) 21; at Waun Fignen Felen (MS 2) 19
Modrydd: artefacts found (BB 17, LBB 1) 133; boundary stone (RSS 6) 179; lithic finds (RMS 3) 23; possible cairn (LBS 3) 134; round cairns (RC 225–6) 116–17; worked flint (SF 9) 290
Moel Feity: round cairn (RC 30) 79
Moel y Gerddi (Merioneth): hut groups 200
monasteries 278–9; grange land 198, 249
Moore, George: Llangenny urn site (RB 1) 137
Moore, P D: on cereal pollen at Llyn Mire 6
moorland: encroachment of farming onto 196
Morgan, E E: Pen Gloch y Pibwr excavation (RC 302) 129
Morgan, G J: monastic boundary stones 163–4
Morgan, Llewellyn: on Nant Tarw stone circles 150; Ynyshir stone circle planned 155
Morlais Castle (Glam): field system 203
Murray-Threipland, P: mound excavation (RC 89) 90
music pipe: bone (CT 4) 28, 40
Mwmffri (Carms): plough-marks 205
Myarth Hillfort: lithic finds (SF 71) 294
Mynachty: inscribed stones (lost) (LECM 1–2) 288
Mynydd Bach Trecastell: round cairns: (RC 35–8) 68, 80
Mynydd Bwlch y Groes: round cairn (RC 33) 80
Mynydd Du: lithic finds: (SF 26, SF 28) 291
Mynydd Epynt 1, 3, 19, 68; round cairns: (RC 138) 101–2, 155; (RC 148–9) 103–4; (RC 150) 104; (RC 151–3) 68, 104
    stone circles: (SC 2) 144, 147–50; (SC 5) 102, 144, 155–7; (SC 7) 144
Mynydd Illtud: boundary stones (RSS 4–6) 179; round cairn (RC 135) 101; standing stone (RSS 49) 182, *see also* Twyn y Gaer, hillfort
Mynydd Llangattock (Llangatwg): enclosure and clearance features (US 106) 266–7
Mynydd Llangorse: chambered tomb (CT 2) 35; lithic finds: (SF 65) 293; round cairn (RC 272) 124; standing stones: (RSS 64) 183
Mynydd Llangynidr: excavations 67–8; round cairn (RC 248) 121–2, *see also* Llangynidr

Mynydd Llysiau: lithic finds (SF 80) 294
Mynydd Pen Cyrn: hut groups (US 108) 267; lost cairn (LC 7) 138; round cairns: (RC 266–7) 123–4; (RC 294–9) 127–8
Mynydd Pen y Fal:
    round cairns: (RC 292–3) 127; (RC 292) *127*, *128*
Mynydd Troed: chambered tomb (CT 2) 25, 27, 28, 35–6, 206; lithic finds: (SF 66) 294
Mynydd Wysg: flint arrowheads (SF 31) 292
Mynydd y Drum: flint axe (SF 1) 290; hut site and clearance cairns (US 28) 221; lithic finds (SF 29) 291; round cairns: (RC 15–17, US 28) 69, 77–8, *see also* Nant Helen
Mynydd y Garn: enclosures: (US 76) 240–1; field systems: (US 75–8) 71, 239–42; (US 78–81) 93
    hut groups and clearance cairns: (US 75) 199, 200, 239–40; (US 77) 199, 241
    ring cairns: (RC 105) 93; (RC 108) 93
Mynydd y Glog: round cairns: (RC 65–73) 86–8

Nab Head (Pembs): flint finds 19
Nant Brân: round cairn (RC 150) 104
Nant Cadlan: cooking mound (BM 17) 187;
    round cairns:
        (RC 74) 68, 88
        see also Pant Sychpant (MS 7)
        (RC 134) 101
Nant Calisfor: round cairn (RC 255) 122
Nant Car: hut groups (US 95) 190, 200, 204
Nant Cerdin: standing stone (SS 7) 167–8
Nant Crew: cooking mound (BM 14) 187; enclosure (US 64) 199, 235; hut platforms (US 65) 189, 202, 235–6; inscribed stone (ECM 9) 285
Nant Cymrun:
    round cairns: (RC 177–9) 108; (RC 194) 109
Nant Diged: *see* Hay Bluff stone circle
Nant Ddu: inscribed stone (lost) (LECM 3) 288
Nant Ffrancon (Caerns): evidence of early settlement 5
Nant Ganol: enclosed hut: (US 45) 200, 229–30; hut and enclosure: (US 56) 200, 232
Nant Garlen Fawr:
    settlement platforms: (US 52) 231; (US 54) 232
Nant Garreg Fawr: hut platforms (US 73) 238
Nant Gihirych: hut circle (US 25) 220; hut platforms (US 24) 220
Nant Gwys: ring cairns (RC 4–5) 76
Nant Helen: cairns: (RC 16–17) 7; pollen evidence 5, 6, 7, *see also* Mynydd y Drum
Nant Llywarch:
    hut groups: (US 58) 200, 233; (US 59) 233–4
Nant Maden: field systems: (US 83) 196–8, 203, 245–7; kerb cairn: (RC 111) 7, 68, 71, 72, 94–6, *95*
    artefacts recovered (BB 8) 132; lithic finds (SF 39) 292
Nant Mawr: enclosure (US 55) 232; hut and enclosure: (US 56) 232; hut structure (US 57) 232; round cairn (RC 83) 90
Nant Pyrgad: enclosures and clearances (US 102) 263–4
Nant Tarw: enclosure (US 29) 199, 202, 221; round cairns (RC 20–1) 78–9; soil section exposed 198; stone circles (SC 2) 144, 147–50
Nant Tawe Fechan: map of enclosures 218; enclosure (US 9) 214; rubble bank (US 11) 214;
    settlement structures: (US 5) 211–12; (US 15–16) 216; (US 19) 217
Nant Tywynni: hut platform (US 27) 221
Nant y Coetgae: platforms (US 20) 217–20

Nant y Cwrier: hut groups (US 60) 234
Nant y Ddalfa: round cairns: (RC 44–5) 81
Nant y Ffin: flint axe (SF 14)) 291
Nant y Gaseg 189
Nant y Gwain 189
Nant y Moch: long hut 202; ring cairn (RC 14) 77
Nant y Stalwen: flint assemblage 20, 290, 292; flint finds (MS 4) 19–20
Nant yr Esgyrn: enclosures: (US 48) 230
Nant yr Ych: cooking mound (BM 11) 187
narrow rig *see* rig and furrow
natural boulders (RSS 20–42) 180–1, *see also* boundary stones; marked and memorial stones; standing stones
Neolithic: economy 29, 189, 198–9; sites and find spots 290–1
Newchurch (Herefords): Neolithic cairn 27
Northern Plateau 1, 3

Offa's Dyke Path: flint arrowhead (SF 91) 295
Ogam inscriptions 284, 285, 286, 288; disputed 182, 289
Ogmore-on-Sea: lithic assemblages 18
Ogof Darren Ciliau 15
Ogof Fawr *see* Chartist's Cave
Ogof Ffynnon Ddu: flint assemblage (PCS 2, RMS 2) 9, 11–12, 17, 23; flint knife (SF 30) 292; skeletal remains (PCS 2) 11–12
Ogof yr Esgyrn: bronze artefacts (BR 1) 296; ossuary/inhumation (PCS 1) 9, 11, 72–3; plan of (PCS 1) *10*; sherds (PCS 1) 72
O'Hanlon, B: discovery of flint flakes (MS 11) 21
ossuaries 9, *see also* chambered tombs
Owen, D E: and Llanwrtyd stone circle (RSC 3) 161

palaeoecology: and settlement studies 190, 200, 206, 208
Palmer, K: flint arrowhead find 20
palstaves:
  bronze 296, 297
  see also axes, bronze
Pant Brwynog: round cairn (RC 86) 90
Pant Mawr: enclosure (US 67) 236; round cairn (RC 12–13) 77
Pant Serthfa: round cairn (RC 252) 122; stone row (SC 8) 158
Pant Sychpant: circular enclosure noted (LS 6) 271; enclosure (US 36) 199, 227; flint assemblage (MS 7, SF 33) 6, 17, 18, 20, 292, *see also* Nant Cadlan, round cairn (RC 74)
Pant y Clwydau (farm): cooking mound (BM 11) 187
Pant y Gadair: hut circles (US 81) 244; platforms and enclosures (US 82) 244–5
Pant y Waun:
  Beaker grave (LBS 2) 68, 72, 134
  artefacts recovered (BB 11) 132–3
  field clearance mound (US 61) 235; round cairn (RC 130) 100
Pant y Wenallt: bronze axe (BR 24) 297
parish boundaries 164, 174, 179–80, 267, *see also* boundary stones
Patrishow:
  inscribed stones: (ECM 46) 288; (lost) (LECM 8) 288
Payne, H T: on clearance features 189; Gwernvale excavation 25, 67; looped trident pattern palstave 297; 'Meini Hirion' in the peat (LS 9, RSC 7) 273; round cairn excavations 67–8; standing stones recorded 162, 164; and Tŷ Illtud circle (RSC 7) 161
peat: growth of 193, 196–8, 208
Pen Allt Mawr: enclosure (US 113) 270;
  round cairns:
    (RC 300) 72, 128–9

  artefacts recovered (BB 26) 133
  (RC 304–5) 129
Pen Cerrig Calch 1; round cairns: (RC 306–7) 129–30, *see also* Cerrig Calch
Pen Father Uchaf: round cairn (RC 82) 90
Pen Gloch y Pibwr:
  round cairns:
    (RC 302) 68, 72, 129
    artefacts recovered (BB 27) 133
    (RC 303–4) 129
Pen Maen Wern: standing stone (SS 10) 163, 169
Pen Moel Allt Plantation: lithic finds (SF 48) 292
Pen Rhiw-wen (Carms) 6
Pen Rhos: standing stone (RSS 56) 182
Pen Trumau: lithic finds (SF 84, SF 87) 295; round cairn (RC 275) 125
Pen Twr: ring cairn (RC 63) 71, 86
Pen y Beacon: round cairn (RC 310) 130
Pen y Bont (Newbridge): standing stone (SS 26) 173
Pen y Carn-goch: round cairn (RC 62) 85–6
Pen y Fan 1; lithic finds (SF 62) 293;
  round cairn:
    (RC 226) 73, 117, *118*, *119*
    artefacts recovered (LBB 1) 133; deterioration 73, 117; excavation 69
Pen y Gader Fawr 7, 22; enclosure (US 111) 199, 269; round cairn (RC 301) 129; standing stone (SS 41) 177, *see also* Y Gader
Pen y Garn Goch: collapsed hut circle (LS 4) 271
Pen y Gorllwyn: round cairns: (RC 156–7) 104–5; standing stone (SS 18) 104, 171
Pen y Gorof: round cairns: (RC 100–2) 92–3
Pen y Lan: round cairn (RC 239) 121
Pen y Mynydd: inscribed stone (ECM 7) 284
Pen y Waun Dwr: standing stone (RSS 50) 182
Pen y wrlod Talgarth: chambered tomb (CT 4) 6, 25, 27, 28, 29, 38–40; radiocarbon dating (HAR-674) 29
Pen yr Heol:
  round cairns: (RC 284–5) 126; (RC 288) 126
Pen-pont: round cairn (RC 135) 101
Pen-y-Garn Goch (RCT 1) 64
Penbuallt:
  round cairns: (RC 146) 103; (RC 148–9) 103–4; (RC 151–3) 104
Pencelli: standing stone (SS 23) 172, *174*
Penderyn: artefacts found (BB 8–11) 132–3; Beaker grave (LBS 2) 134; burned mound (BM 18) 184, 187–8; Chartist's Cave (PCS 4) 13; circular enclosure noted (LS 6) 271;
  clearance cairns: (US 83) 196–8, 203, 245–7; (US 84) 247; (US 89) 250
  cooking mounds: (BM 15) 187; (BM 17) 187
  enclosure (US 36) 199, 227;
  field systems: (US 80) 243; (US 83–4) 189
  house platform (US 88) 250;
  hut circles: (US 81) 244; (US 83) 196–8, 203, 245–7
  lithic finds: (SF 3) 290; (SF 33) 292; (SF 40) 292
  lost cairn (LC 5) 138; microliths and flint assemblage (MS 7) 20; platforms and enclosures (US 82) 244–5; platforms and scoop settlements (US 71) 201, 237–8;
  round cairns: (RC 64–74) 86–8; (RC 104) 94; (RC 111–18) 94–6; (RC 120–34) *pl.8*, 97–101; (RC 127) 68, 71, 72, 99–100; (RC 208) 113
  unenclosed settlement 203

Pendre: standing stone (RSS 68) 183
Penfai: lost cairns: (LC 3) 138; round cairns: (RC 25) 79; (RC 43) 81
Penlan: natural boulder (RSS 40) 181
Penlan Wen: inscribed stone (ECM 6) 284
Penlan Wood: round cairn (RC 200) 110
Penmoelallt: clearance cairns (US 89) 250; house platform (US 88) 250
Penmyarth Park: inscribed stone (RSS 43, ECM 34) 181, 287; standing stone (SS 29) 174–5, *175*
Pennant T: Gwernvale noted 25
Penpont: boundary stone (RSS 5) 179
Pentir: bronze sword (BR 26) 297;
    round cairn (RC 289) 126; artefacts recovered (LBB 2) 133
Pentre Cribarth: boulder wall and platform huts (US 3) 210–11
Pentre Poeth: inscribed stone (ECM 4) 284
Pentre Sollars Farm: bronze axe (BR 27) 297
Penwyllt: bronze artefacts (BR 2) 296; flint knife (SF 30) 292
Penwyllt Cave: skeletal remains (animal) (OCS 2) 15
Penywrlod Llanigon:
    chambered tomb (CT 12) 25, 27, 28, 60–2, *61*, 72
        artefacts recovered (BB 28) 133; Enlarged Food Vessel 72; lithic finds (SF 88) 295
periglacial features 196n, 206, *see also* glaciation
peristaliths *see* kerb cairns
Perthi Duon: boundary stone (RSS 17) 180
Peterstone: standing stone (SS 24) 164, 172
Pipton: burial site (UCB 6) 137;
    cropmarks or parchmarks: (LS 7) 192, 271, *272*; (LS 8) 272, *273*
    long barrow (CT 8) 6, 25, 27, 28, 29, 48–51; structure 49–51
    mound (RCS 7) 138, 191
Plas y gors: Roman site 7;
    round cairns: (RC 75) 88;
        (RC 91) 72, 91; artefacts recovered (BB 6) 132; lithic finds (SF 38) 292
    platform settlements 201–2
plough-marks 202, 203, 205–6, 249, 274, 278, *see also* rig and furrow
pollen analysis 5–7, 17, 24, 29, 73, 78, 95–6, 145, 194, 250, 278
Pont ar Daf-Corn Du path: lithic finds (SF 43) 292
Pont Cwm Pwll y Rhyd: building platform (US 70) 237
Pont Nedd Fychan (Pontneathfechan): settlement features (lost) (LS 1) 270–1
Pont y Felin: hut platforms (US 73) 238
Pontsticill (Glam): flint arrowhead (SF 59) 293
Pontsticill Junction (Glam): round cairns (RC 216–17) 114
Poole, Edwin: Glanyrafon (RCT 8) noted 65; on Gwernvale excavations 56, 60n; and Hay Bluff stone circle (SC 10) 159
Post-Dy (farm): round cairn (RC 32) 80
post-holes: Gwernvale 24, 56; Nant Tarw 149; Ynys-hir 156
pottery sherds: Bronze Age 11, 72, 78, 91, 117;
    Neolithic 20, 24, 28, 35, 37, 41–2, 46, 49, 61, 68; Abingdon ware 40, 59; Peterborough tradition 60
    see also Beaker
Powell's Cave: skeletal remains (animal) (OCS 2) 15
Price, Charles: Maesmynys 'Druid Altar' (LSS 4) 178
Price, Thomas: Ffostyll barrows noted 40, 43
Pumlumon 3
Pwll Byfre: hut circle (US 22) 220
Pwll y Cig: lost burial site (LBS 1) 134
Pwll y Wythen Fach: hut circle and clearance cairn (US 8) 213–14, *215*

pygmy cups 72, 80, 81, 100, 102, 129, 132, 133, 134, 135, 136, 294
Pytin Du: bronze axe (BR 19) 297

quernstone: Cefn Coed y Cymer discovery (LS 5) 200, 271; Cwm-Gu discovery (US 112) 200, 269

radiocarbon dating 6, 11, 13, 17, 22, 28, 29, 60, 77, 78, 134, 200, 203, 281
radiometric dating 96
rapiers: bronze 9, 11, *14*, 296
razor: bronze (PCS 1) 11, *14*, 296
Rees, William: excavation on Mynydd Bach Trecastell 68, 80
Rhigos (Glam): settlement features (lost) (LS 1) 270–1
Rhiw Cwmstab: round cairn (RC 291) 127
Rhiw Trumau: round cairn (RC 274) 124–5
Rhiwiau Brook 64
Rhos Fach (or Fawr) (RCT 7) 65
Rhos y Beddau: round cairn (RC 200) 110
Rhos y Gilwern: bronze palstave (BR 8) 296
Rhos y Saith Maen: round cairns (RC 177–84) 107–8; stone row (SC 6) 157–8
Rhyd Uchaf: ring cairns: (RC 78–9) 71, 88–9; scoop settlements (US 44) 201, 229
rig and furrow 198, 249, 272, *see also* plough-marks
ring cairns 71; and ritual 71, 131, *see also* round cairns
rings: gold 296
ritual: and ring cairns 71, 131; and standing stones 163; and stone circles 153; use of chambered tombs 50
Roese, H E: on cairn distribution and siting 69, 71, 73; cited 80; on shelter building 88; siting of standing stones 165; upper Afon Twrch round cairns (RC 2) 76
Roman: coins 55, 61–2; hypocaust at Maesderwen (UCB 3) 136; practice camps 144, 153, 208; roads 278, 279; settlement 7
Roman Camp: Mynydd Bach Trecastell 80, 153
Roman site: Plas y gors 7
Roman villa: Maesderwen (UCB 3) 136–7
Romano-British: beads 61; field system 271; possible cave burial 9, 11; possible settlement sites 238, 239; settlement patterns 278
round cairns 66–131; structure and forms 69–71, 73–5, *see also* barrows; cairns; chambered tombs; kerb cairns; ring cairns
Rowlands, J: survey of Dorwen stone circle (RSC 1) 160–1
Royal Society for the Protection of Birds 249
Runic inscription: disputed (RECM 2) 289
Russell, Joseph H, 2nd Baron Glanusk: epitaph stone (RSS 43, ECM 34) 181, 287, *see also* Glanusk *Lord*
rye (*Secale*): pollen evidence 7

Saith Maen (Craig y Nos): stone row (SC 1) *pl.1*, 143, 147
Saith Maen (Llanwrthwl): stone row (SC 6) 157–8
Saith Maen Penwyllt (RSC 2, RSS 22) 161, 180
Sand Hill: round cairn (RC 12–13) 77
Sandeman, R G: excavation on Pen Allt Mawr (RC 300) 128–9
Savory, H N: flint chipping site reported (MS 12) 21; and the Ogof Ffynnon Ddu flint core 23; on Pen y Garn-goch round cairns 86; Pipton (CT 8) excavation 48–50
scoop settlements 201, 202
sediment analysis 194
Senni: clearance pile (US 38) 227; clearance stones (US 85) 247; round cairns: (RC 76–9) 88–9; scoop settlements (US 44) 201, 229; standing stone (SS 12) 88, 143, 162, 170

Sennybridge: bronze palstave (BR 7) 296
settlement: agricultural economy 198–209; Dark Age sites 278, 281–3; distribution and patterns of 198–206; evidence for 5–7, 24, 149, 150, 189–209; land use 206–9;
  medieval: patterns of 278; use of ancient sites 231, 238, 243, 247, 249, 250, 256
  population and cairn density 69;
  Romano-British: patterns of 278; possible sites 238, 239
  study problems 191–8; unenclosed sites 210–74; in valley bottoms 71, 73, 191
Severn Valley Caving Club 13
shake-holes 3, 76, 77, 90, 147, 192–4, 210, 213, 214n, 236, 237, 267, *see also* dolines; sink-holes
Share y Wlad:
  round cairns: (RC 92–5) 68, 91–2; (RC 95): artefacts recovered (BB 7) 132
sheep pound (possible) 267
'Sheepfolds' 189–90
Sink y Giedd: hut circle (lost) (LS 2) 190, 271
sink-holes 265, *see also* dolines; shake-holes
skeletal remains: loss and deterioration 29; radiocarbon dating 11, 13, 29; Abercar (LBS 4) 133, 134; Brecon (UCB 1) 136; Cae Gwin (UCB 2) 136; Carn Goch (CT 10) 28, 54–5; Cefn Cilsanws (RC 201) 110, 133; Chartist's Cave (PCS 4) 13; Coed y Garreg (RC 90) 91, 132; Cwm Car (LBS 5) 133, 134; Fan y Big (LBS 6) 135; Ffostyll North (CT 6) 46; Ffostyll round barrow (LBS 10) 133, 136; Ffostyll South (CT 5) 41–2; Gwernvale (CT 11) 25, 29, 56, 59; Little Lodge (CT 9) 28, 52; Maesderwen (UCB 3) 136; Ogof Ffynnon Ddu (PCS 2) 11–12; Ogof yr Esgyrn (PCS 1) 11; Pen Allt Mawr (RC 300) 129; Pen y wrlod Talgarth (CT 4) 29, 40; Penywrlod Llanigon (CT 12) 61; Pipton (CT 8) 50–1; Tredustan Court (UCB 6) 137; Twll Carw Coch (PCS 3) 13; Twyn Bryn Glas (RC 127) 100; Twyn y Beddau (RC 311) 130–1; Tŷ Isaf (CT 3) 29, 37; Ynys-hir (RC 138) 102
skeletal remains (animal): Coed y Garreg (RC 90) 91, 132; Ffostyll North (CT 6) 46; Ffostyll South (CT 5) 41; Little Lodge (CT 9) 52; Pen y wrlod Talgarth (CT 4) 40; Penwyllt Cave (OCS 2) 11, 12, 13, 15; Pipton (CT 8) 50; tooth at Share y Wlad (RC 95?) 91; Twyn Bryn Glas (RC 127) 100
skulls *see* skeletal remains
smelting sites 184
South Wales Caving Club 11
spearheads: bronze 297
speleogenesis 193–4
spindlewhorl: Pant y Waun find 133, 134
stake-holes: Cefn Cilsanws 24; Mynydd y Drum (RC 17) 78
standing stones 162–83; distribution of *142*; in Dyfed 163; and ritual 163; sitings 164–5, 191; tithe award names 183; uses 162, 163–4, *see also* boundary stones; marked and memorial stones; natural boulders
Star Carr (Yorks): flint finds 19
stone: artefacts: distribution of *207*, 208; axes: at Aberllynfi (SF 19) 291; at Builth (SF 12–13) 291; at Tŷ Isaf (CT 3, SF 17) 37, 291
  hammer head: at Erwood (SF 11) 290
stone circles and rows 143–61; Blaen Digedi Fawr (RCT 9, SC 10) 65; distribution of *142*, 144; noted by Edward Lhuyd 31; and ritual 153; use 145–6
stone stripes 196, 206n
Storrie, John: reconstruction of Cwm Car Beaker 134

Stowe [MS]: on Tŷ Illtud (Brit.Lib. MS 1023–4) 24
Strange, John: note of standing stones 162, 166
Sugar Loaf (Monm): lithic finds (SF 83) 295
sweat-houses 184
swords (bronze): Dan y Graig (BR 21) 297; Llangattock (UCB 4) 137; Pentir Hill find (RC 289, UCB 5) 133, 137

Taf Fawr: hut and enclosure (US 63) 235; settlement features (US 62) 235
Tafarn y Garreg Inn: natural boulder (RSS 20) 180
Talcen y Garn: enclosure (US 55) 232
Talgarth: artefacts found (BB 22) 133; Beaker burial (LBS 9) *see* Tŷ Du; chambered tomb (rejected) (RCT 6) 65;
  chambered tombs: (CT 2) 25, 27, 28, 35–6, 206; (CT 3) 6, 25, 27, 28, 29, 36–8, 72; (CT 4) 6, 25, 27, 28, 29, 38–40
  enclosure (US 111) 199, 269;
  lithic finds: (MS 17) 22; (SF 15–16) 291; (SF 76) 294
  mound (RCT 9) 65;
  round cairns: (RC 274–5) 124–5; (RC 301) 129; (RC 309) 130
  standing stones: (SS 35) 176; (SS 41) 177
Talwrn: gold ring (BR 10) 296
Talybont 3; inscribed stone (lost) (LECM 7) 288
Tawe Valley: panorama showing sites *Fig.124*; prehistoric hearth (BM 2) 186;
  settlement sites: (US 26) 220–1; (US 30–8) 194–6, 199, 222–7; (US 30) 222; (US 31) 222–3, *228*; (US 32) 202, 224; (US 35) 226
  see also Cwm Tawe
Thom, A & A S: astro-archaeological studies 145
Thomas, J: removal of bones from tombs 29
timber rings: and cropmarks 144
Tir Mawr: hut groups (US 74) 200, 239
Tir yr Onnen: field systems: (US 45–6) 71, *94*; ring cairn: (RC 107) 71, 93, *94*
Tirabad: inscribed stone (ECM 6) 284
tithe award names: burial sites 139–41; standing stones 183
Ton Teg:
  hut groups: (US 58) 200, 233; (US 59) 200, 233–4
  stone row (rejected) (RSC 6) 161
  tool assemblages: Mesolithic 17–18
topographic zones 1–5; map 2
Topographical Dictionary (1833) S Lewis: cited 123, 143, 163
Tor y Ffynnon: round cairns (RC 144–5) 103
torcs: gold 296
Tower Hill: round barrow (RC 163) 105
Traean-glas: artefacts found (BB 1–3) 132;
  clearance cairns: (US 31) 222–3, *228*; (US 33–4) 224–6
  cooking hearths (BM 5–6) 186;
  enclosures: (US 9) 214; (US 17–18) 216; (US 29) 199, 202, 221; (US 30) 222; (US 35) 226
  field systems (US 33) 150;
  hut structures: (US 31) 222–3, *228*; (US 32) 224; (US 34) 225–6
  inscribed stone (ECM 3) 284; platforms (US 20) 217–20;
  prehistoric hearths: (BM 2) 186; (BM 3–4) 186
  round cairns: (RC 9) 76; (RC 20–2) 78–9; (RC 26–31) 79–80; (RC 35–41) 80–1; (RC 43) 81
  rubble bank (US 11) 214;
  settlement structures: (US 15–16) 216; (US 19) 217; (US 26) 220–1
  standing stones (SS 1–4) 166; stone circles (SC 2–4) 144, 147–55

Traean-mawr: round cairn (RC 25) 79
Traeth Mawr 5
Trallwng (Trallong): inscribed stone (ECM 12) 285; leaf-shaped arrowhead (SF 7) 290; round cairn (RC 143) 103
Trawsfynydd (Merioneth): field patterns 203
Trawsnant: chipping site (MS 12) 21
Tre-Felin: standing stone (SS 21) 171
Trebinshun Farm: polished axe (SF 18) 291
Trecastle: inscribed stone (ECM 4) 284
Trecastle Mountain:
 round cairns:
  (RC 34–7) 72
  artefacts recovered (BB 2) 132
  standing stone (SS 5) 166; stone circles (SC 4) 144, 153–5
Tredustan Court: burial site (UCB 6) 137
Trefeurig (Ceredigion): round cairn 69
Trefil: fugitive wall (US 105) *pl.7*, 192, 264–6
Trefil Las: bronze palstave (BR 23) 297
Treflys: collapsed hut circle (LS 4) 271; inscribed stone (ECM 13) 285; round cairn (RC 62) 85–6
Tregoed (Tregoyd and Felindre): mound (RCS 8) 138; round cairn (RC 290) 126–7
Trembyd hill: round cairns: (RC 190–3) 109
Tretower:
 standing stones: (RSS 72) 183; (SS 33) 175
Trevil Glas Cairn: excavation 67
Tri Chrugiau: round cairns: (RC 151–3) 104
Troed Rhiw Wen: standing stone (SS 1) 166, *167*
troglodytic occupation 9
Tump Wood (RCT 4) 64
Twll Carw Coch: skeletal remains (PCS 3) 13
Two Stones: natural boulders (RSS 37) 181
Twr y Fan Foel: round cairn (RC 27) 79, *see also* Fan Foel
Twyn Bryn Glas:
 round cairn (RC 127) 68, 71, 72, 99–100
 artefacts recovered (BB 10) 132; lithic finds (SF 40) 292
Twyn Ceiliog: cairn (US 101) 263
Twyn Cerrig-Cadarn: round cairn (RC 140) 102
Twyn Disgwylfa: round cairn (RC 263) 123
Twyn Du: clearance cairns (US 4) 211; enclosure (US 110) 269
Twyn Garreg Wen: round cairn (RC 85) 90
Twyn Walter: clearance cairns (US 4) 211
Twyn y Beddau:
 round cairn (RC 311) 68, 69, 71, 130–1
 artefacts recovered (BB 29) 133; lithic finds (SF 89, SF 92) 295
 standing stones 163
Twyn y Big: round cairn (RC 232) 120
Twyn y Gaer, hillfort: cultivation ridges 205, 274; field system discounted (RS 1) 203, 274
Twyn y Garn: lost cairn (LC 2) 138; round cairn (RC 23) 79
Twyn y Llyn: round cairns (RC 247) 121
Twyn y Post: round cairns: (RC 233–8) 120
Twynau Gwynion: flint arrowhead (SF 59) 293; round cairn (RC 219) 114–15
Tŷ Aderyn: round cairn (RC 265) 123
Tŷ Du:
 burial site (LBS 9) 40, 72, 135–6
 artefacts recovered (BB 25) 133; lithic finds (SF 74) 294
Tŷ Illtud:
 chambered tomb (CT 1) 24, 27, 31–4, *34*

graffiti 32, *33*
 stone circle (lost) (RSC 7) 144, 161
Tŷ Isaf:
 chambered tomb (CT 3) 6, 25, 27, 28, 29, 36–8, 72
 artefacts recovered (BB 22) 133; structure of 36–7
 lithic finds (SF 16–17) 291
Tŷ yn y Llwyn: burial site (UCB 2) 136
Tyle Brith: enclosure (US 66) 236
Tyle Bychan: standing stone (SS 14) 170
Tyle Mawr: round cairn (RC 22) 79
Tŷ'n Coed: chipping site (MS 12) 21
Tŷ'n y Pant: round cairns: (RC 165–7) 106

Upper Neuadd Reservoir: animal enclosures near 189; flint and chert artefacts (MS 10) 21, 111; lithic finds: (SF 49, SF 51, SF 54) 293;
 round cairns: (RC 202–7) 110–13; (RC 202) *111*, *112*; (RC 205) *112*, *113*; (RC 206) *113*; (RC 207) *113*
Upper Palaeolithic sites and findspots (MS 1–18; RMS 1–3) 17–23
Upper Paper Mill (Glangrwyne): polished axes (SF 22) 291
urns: Bronze Age cinerary 37, 72, 80, 133, 134, 136; cordoned 7, 68, 69, 72, 73, 135; Deverel-Rimbury globular 72, 77, 133; Overhanging-Rim 72, 95, 99, 132, 133, 135, *see also* Beaker; Enlarged Food Vessel
Usk Llynfi Basin 3
Usk Valley 3, 5, 18, 31, 56; Upper Palaolithic presence see Gwernvale

Varlen:
 round cairn (RC 41) 72, 81
 artefacts recovered (BB 3) 132
Vaynor: artefacts found (BB 13–16) 133; burial sites (LBS 4–5) 68, 72, 134–5; burned mound (BM 21) 184, 188;
 cairns: (US 91) *251*, *252*; (US 98) 260–1
 clearance cairns: (US 90) 6, 24, 110, 250–2; (US 95) 254–7, *258*, *259*, *260*; (US 96) 258–9, *260*
 fugitive field walls (US 92) 196, 252, 253; house platforms (US 96) 258–9, *260*; hut circles (LS 5) 200, 271; hut groups (US 95) 254–7, *258*, *259*, *260*;
 inscribed stones: (ECM 20–1) 286; (lost) (LECM 3) 288
 mound (RCS 4) 137;
 round cairns: (RC 201) 110; (RC 209–15) 113–14
 settlement features (US 93–4) 252–4; unenclosed settlement 203; wall and stone pile (US 97) 260
vegetation: ground cover inhibits field reconnaissance 196–8; history 5–7, 144–5
Vulliamy, C E: excavation near Glasbury Church 127; excavations at Ffostyll 40, 41, 43, 45, 46, 135, 136; excavations at Little Lodge 51–3; round cairn excavation (LBS 10) 68; and skeletal remains at Little Lodge 28

Waen Lleuci: standing stone (SS 4) 166, *168*, *169*
Walters, Mark: and Banc y Celyn stone circle 158
Watton (Brecon): bronze axe (BR 13) 296
Waun Coll: round cairn (RC 50) 82
Waun Ddu:
 burial site (LBS 7) 72, 135
 artefacts recovered (BB 20) 133
Waun Dywarch: round cairn (RC 83) 90
Waun Fach South 7, 22

Waun Fignen Felen *pl.2*; assemblages and artefacts (MS 2, SF 28) 17, 19, 291; charcoal deposits (MS 2) *pl.2*, 6, 17

Waun Gunllwch: flint finds (SF 10) 290; round cairn (RC 245) 121

Waun Llech: standing stone (SS 27) *pl.4*, 162, 164, 174

Waun Lydan: standing stone (SS 11) 169

Waun Tincer:
   clearance cairns: (US 77) 241; (US 78) 241–2
   field systems: (US 77–82) 203; (US 77–8) 196
   hut groups: (US 77) 241; (US 78) 201, 241–2
   round cairn (RC 84) 90

Waun y Gwair: round cairn (RC 218) 114

weaving comb: Ogof yr Esgyrn (PCS 1) 11

Webley, D P: location of Maes Coch (RCT 9, SC 10) mound 65, 159–60; round cairn excavations 68, 95, 99; soil samples from tomb sites 27

Wern: bronze palstave (BR 28) 297

Wern Las: round cairn (RC 64) 86

wheat: impression of grain 135; pollen evidence 6, 7

whetstone: Twyn y Beddau find (RC 311) 131, 133

Williams, G H: standing stone inscriptions 163

Wilson, L A: Blaen Nedd Uchaf circle (RSC 5) 161

Wilson, J W: siting of standing stones in Anglesey 164–5

woodland *see* forest

Woolhope Club: Cadyr Arthur 117; excavation at Penywrlod Llanigon 60–1; excavation at Twyn y Beddau (RC 311) 68, 130

woven material *see* cloth

Wye valley 3, 5, 6, 18, 40, 48, 51, 63

Ynys Bwlc: Dark Age Settlement 281–3; flint assemblage (MS 14) 17, 21, 281; Mesolithic artefacts 29, *see also* Llan-gors (Llangorse), Crannog

Ynys-hir:
   round cairn (RC 138) 68, 71, 72, 101–2, 145, 155
   artefacts recovered (BB 12) 133; lithic finds (SF 45) 292
   stone circle (SC 5) 144, 145, 155–7; lithic finds (SF 46) 292

Ysclydach: round cairns: (RC 44–5) 81

Ystrad: round cairn (RC 246) 121

Ystradfellte 3; artefacts found (BB 4–7) 132;
   clearance cairns: (US 69) 237; (US 75) 239–40; (US 77) 199, 241; (US 78) 241–2
   enclosed hut: (US 45) 200, 229–30;
   enclosures: (US 42) 228–9; (US 48) 230; (US 55) 232; (US 67) 236; (US 68) 199, 203, 236–7; (US 76) 240–1
   flint and chert assemblage (MS 8) 20; hut and enclosure: (US 56) 232;
   hut groups: (US 59) 233–4; (US 72) 202, 238; (US 74) 200, 239; (US 75) 200, 239–40; (US 77) 199, 241; (US 78) 201, 241–2
   hut platforms (US 73) 238; hut scoops (US 53) 202, 231–2; hut structure (US 57) 232; huts and enclosures (US 58) 233;
   inscribed stones (ECM 7–8) 284–5; lithic finds (SF 36–8) 292; Maen Madoc (ECM 8) 162, 163, 285; mound (RCS 3) 137; plano-convex knife (SF 3) 290;
   round cairns: (RC 12–14) 77; (RC 75) 88; (RC 80–4) 89–90; (RC 87–103) 90–3; (RC 105–10) 93–4
   rubble bank (US 37) 227; settlement features (lost) (LS 1) 270–1;
   settlement platforms: (US 39–41) 227–8; (US 43) 229, 230; (US 46–7) 230; (US 49–52) 230–1; (US 54) 232; (US 70) 237
   standing stone (SS 13) 170; stone circle (rejected) (RSC 5) 161; stone row (rejected) (RSC 6) 161; unenclosed settlement 203

Ystradfellte Reservoir: hut scoops (US 53) 202, 231–2; settlement platforms: (US 51–2) 231; (US 54) 232

Ystradgynlais: boulder wall and platform huts (US 3) 210–11; cave systems 11–15;
   clearance cairns: (US 1) 200, 210; (US 4) 211; (US 6) 212; (US 8) 213–14
   cooking mound (BM 1) 186; enclosure (US 21) 220; flint finds 19, 22; hut circle (lost) (LS 2) 190, 271;
   hut circles: (US 2) 210; (US 6) 212; (US 8) 213–14, *215*; (US 22) 220
   hut site and clearance cairns (US 28) 221; inscribed stones (ECM 1–2) 284; lithic find (RMS 1) 22; lost burial site (LBS 1) 134;
   round cairns: (RC 1–8) 76; (RC 15–19) 77–8
   settlement structures (US 5) 211–12; stone circle (rejected) (RSC 1) 160–1; stone row (SC 1) 147

Ystradowen 76